PORTRAITS OF
AMERICAN POLITICS

PORTRAITS OF
AMERICAN POLITICS
A Reader

BRUCE ALLEN MURPHY
Pennsylvania State University

Houghton Mifflin Company   Boston

Dallas   Geneva, Illinois   Palo Alto   Princeton, New Jersey

Drawings by Vint Lawrence. Copyright © 1991 by Vint Lawrence.

Chapter 1: James Madison
Chapter 2: Bruce Babbitt
Chapter 3: George Bush
Chapter 4: Robert Dole and Thomas Foley
Chapter 5: Elizabeth Dole
Chapter 6: William Rehnquist
Chapter 7: Ron Brown
Chapter 8: Marian Wright Edelman
Chapter 9: Lesley Stahl

Printed in the U.S.A.

Library of Congress Catalog Card Number: 90-83008

ISBN: 0-395-55385-7

BCDEFGHIJ-CS-9987654321

For the best-read man I know,
Jim Milholland, and his wife, Pam

CONTENTS

PREFACE

The idea for this book began several years ago in a late-night conversation with two Penn State students. At the time, I was planning the reading list for my introductory American government course. I am constantly searching for materials that my students will enjoy reading, and over the years I have discovered that although an American government textbook is helpful, students really want, and benefit from, illustrations of how our government *truly* operates.

Indeed, in that late-night discussion, the two students, who prided themselves on not reading assigned texts, insisted that I add Anthony Lewis's *Gideon's Trumpet* to my class reading list. Like their classmates, these students wanted to read about real people and real events rather than about theories and maxims. Through descriptions of politics in action, students can come to understand the people and institutions that dominate American government. For example, Lewis's account of a poor man's fight for the right to counsel can teach students more about how the Supreme Court makes decisions than can volumes of legal theory.

The construction of this reader comes from the other side of my professional work. As a biographer with a political focus, I have a great love for biographical narrative and a belief that through this craft we can instruct nonspecialists in the art of politics. Over the years, I have collected a variety of compelling biographical accounts of American politics in action, many written by some of the finest authors of our time, which I have used in my classes to supplement the core materials. Some of these pieces are portraits of people; others are descriptions of institutions or events. All of them capture the rich human drama of American politics.

This volume contains many of these materials. The articles are drawn from some of the best political biographies and from accessible journals such as *American Heritage, The New York Times Magazine, The Atlantic,* and *The New Yorker.* These narratives describe the central players and events in American politics, particularly those of the last twenty years. For example, D. B. Hardeman and Donald Bacon profile legendary Speaker of the House Sam Rayburn. William Greider presents former Budget Director David Stockman and explains why many of Ronald Reagan's economic plans were doomed from the start. And Joseph Persico explores the Iran-contra scandal from the perspectives of two principals, William Casey and Oliver North.

Some selections focus on turning points in our political history and show how these historic events have shaped the context of events today. For instance, Charles Mee explains the hardball politics of the fight to ratify the Constitution. Theodore White describes how the 1960 campaign and election of John F. Kennedy changed presidential campaigning. And Ethan Bronner shows why Robert Bork's nomination for the Supreme Court may have changed the way the Senate confirms Supreme Court justices.

This book is designed primarily to be used with a core text in the introductory American government course. It can also be used as the main text for that course, or for a course such as "Film and Politics" that draws on political writings but does not use them exclusively. Recognizing the range of uses, I have employed a number of pedagogical tools so that each piece can stand on its own. First, each reading has a thorough introduction that places it in historical and political context and an epilogue that brings the issue up to date. Annotations throughout the reading explain unfamiliar events, terms, or people. A unique feature of this reader is the list at the beginning of each selection that identifies and explains the prominent people in that reading.

The *Instructor's Resource Manual with Test Items* that accompanies this book contains the following for each reading: a summary of the selection, multiple-choice and essay questions, suggestions for classroom use, and a list of suggested videos. I thank Kelly Keating for her assistance in preparing this manual.

I am very grateful to each of the reviewers for their valuable suggestions:

John F. Bibby, University of Wisconsin–Milwaukee
Paul Hain, Corpus Christi State University
Vivian Kallen, Northern Virginia Community College–Annandale
Thomas R. Marshall, University of Texas at Arlington
Keith Nicholls, University of South Alabama
Charles Prysby, University of North Carolina at Greensboro
Richard C. Rich, Virginia Polytechnic Institute and State University
Leonard Ritt, Northern Arizona University
Jonathan Webster, Walla Walla Community College
Kathryn Yates, Richland College

My thanks go also to my fellow biographer, and former teacher, Stephen B. Oates of the History Department at the University of Massachusetts at Amherst for suggesting that a political science version of his own history reader, *Portrait of America*, might work well. And thank you to Bob Holste and Phil Gutis, the two students who initially suggested that I use these kinds of readings. I would like to acknowledge the highly professional staff at Houghton Mifflin for their help at every stage of the book's creation. I would also like to thank my colleagues at Penn State's Institute for the Arts and Humanistic Studies and its current and former directors, George Mauner and Stanley Weintraub, for providing an oasis of fellowship and support for my work. Finally, it is always a pleasure to thank my wife, Carol, who makes life worthwhile, and my children, Emily and Geoffrey, who inspire me with their love and enthusiasm.

B.A.M.

PORTRAITS OF
AMERICAN POLITICS

CHAPTER 1

THE CONSTITUTION

Behind Closed Doors

Richard B. Morris

The U.S. Constitution is an extraordinary and visionary document. The difficulty of creating such a blueprint for governing should become evident again as countries throughout Eastern Europe attempt to write their own constitutions. Yet the brilliant men who wrote the Constitution were also practical politicians. Having thrown off the yoke of the British monarchy, they had tried a more democratic government under the Articles of Confederation, in which the thirteen states had virtually all the power. The failure of that system to govern the entire nation led to a call for the Constitutional Convention. The main question before that convention was how much power the states had to give up to create a successful central government.

The founders knew that their individual power, and the power of their peers, resided in the state governments, and they were fearful that their influence would be superseded by the new central government. They were also afraid that other states and other people would gain an unfair advantage. In describing the various battles, Richard Morris conveys the founders' fear of a truly democratic system in which they, the elite, might have less power. As Massachusetts delegate Elbridge Gerry put it, they had a prevailing fear of "the dangers of the leveling spirit." Hence the founders, as representatives of their individual states, were concerned with protecting their own positions. The result was a battle between large states and small states; delegates from large states wanted representation to be based on population, where they had the advantage, and those from small states fought for equal representation for all states.

The genius of the Constitution is found in the Connecticut Compromise, which reconciled the conflict between large and small states to create a unique governmental system. At the same time, however, the issue of slavery caused continuing conflict between the northern and southern states. Although the founders reached enough of a compromise over slavery to form the Constitution, the seeds were sown for the turmoil that culminated in the Civil War seventy years later.

The irony is that in spite of these personal issues, and the attendant political battles, a constitution was created that transcended the individual concerns of the framers and their states and became the model for democratic government around the world. Note that the Constitution has been amended only twenty-six times in over two hundred years, with ten of those amendments coming at the time of ratification. The brilliant vagueness of the Constitution has allowed the Supreme Court to interpret it over the years in various ways to keep pace with present-day demands.

Notice the title of the selection: "Behind Closed Doors." Could these very political men have done such work if their actions had been visible to their constituents? Could they have taken such extreme and unpopular positions for the purpose of achieving a useful compromise if they had feared that revelation of their words would end their careers? Ironically, the world's most open democratic system most likely could have been created only in total secrecy. Morris and others would not have been able to study the framers' actions had James Madison not published his notes of the Constitutional Convention, but that was done thirty years after the event. This is certainly not the kind of politics we know now, where information is leaked to the press almost the moment something happens, and battles are deliberately played out for all to see.

BENJAMIN FRANKLIN   The senior delegate at the Constitutional Convention.

ALEXANDER HAMILTON   New York delegate who favored a strong central government.

JAMES MADISON   Principal chronicler of the Constitutional Convention; pushed for the Virginia Plan.

GEORGE MASON   Antifederalist delegate from Virginia; one of three delegates *not* to sign the Constitution.

WILLIAM PATERSON   Delegate who proposed the New Jersey Plan.

EDMUND RANDOLPH   Virginia governor and delegate who proposed the Virginia Plan (Randolph Plan) to the Convention.

GEORGE WASHINGTON   Presiding officer of the Constitutional Convention.

JAMES WILSON   Federalist delegate from Pennsylvania; advocate of strong presidency.

▶ In the steaming hot summer of 1787, fifty-five delegates met in convention in the State House of Philadelphia and devised a new national government for the thirteen states and all those that were to enter the Union thereafter. The delegates sat almost daily for four months and argued out their ideas in long, heated sessions in secret and behind closed doors. On September 17 they gave to the people the final document, five pages of parchment setting forth a plan of union calculated "to secure the Blessings of Liberty to ourselves and our Posterity." This document is our Federal Constitution. It provided for a sovereign government with broad, if clearly defined, powers and responsibilities.

The spare, eloquent language, much of it attributed to the talented Gouverneur Morris, outlined a republican government that steered a course between the equal dangers of tyranny and ineffectualness by providing by implication for a separation of powers among the three coequal branches of the government: Congress, the President, and an independent judiciary, all curbed by a system of checks and balances.

It created a unique system called federalism, in which the central government was delegated authority in international and national affairs, including the power to tax and to regulate commerce, to provide for the common defense and the general welfare, and to make all laws necessary and proper for carrying into execution the powers vested in the Constitution. As its Preamble declares, it is a government of the people, not of the states, and lines of demarcation between the national government and the states were laid down. It guaranteed to the states a republican form of government and declared the Constitution and the laws and treaties of the national government to be the supreme laws of the land. Finally, it wisely provided for a method of amendment.

That delegates from so many regions of the country and with such widely diverse interests could unite in creating an entirely new governmental system was, for George Washington, who presided over the Convention, "little short of a miracle." It was also testimony to the fact that, with a few exceptions, the delegates who attended were committed to a more national frame of government than the Articles of Confederation had provided, and were in general agreement about the powers to be conferred on a central government. On much else there was a sharp disagreement and heated debate, but the spirit of compromise that prevailed attested to the common wisdom and common sense of the participants.

It is more than chance that both the Great Declaration and the Constitution were adopted at the Pennsylvania State House in Philadelphia, a shrine now called Independence Hall. Both documents enlisted the wisdom and statecraft of many of the same men. These men recognized that merely winning independence did not suffice. They knew the newly emerging nation would have to be soundly structured.

In London, John Adams declared the Convention "the greatest single effort of national deliberation that the world has ever seen." Thomas Jefferson was later to refer to the Convention as "an assembly of demigods," for, with a few notable exceptions, virtually of America's big names were found on the roster of delegates.* Indubitably, the Convention's greatest asset was the presiding officer, George Washington, the unanimous choice to chair its sessions, and one who could count on advice from a prestigious delegation from his own state. Pennsylvania's delegation claimed Benjamin Franklin, then eighty-one years old, as its senior member; he brought to the assemblage his wit, common sense, and unrivaled experience in the service of empire, colonies, state, and nation, as well as his international renown as diplomat, scientist, and humanitarian. Virginia's most erudite member was James Madison, an ardent nationalist with whom we are now familiar. And there were first-class legal minds like James Wilson of Pennsylvania, who never lost his Scottish burr, John Rutledge of South Carolina, and William Livingston, the learned and witty governor of New Jersey.

The only state to dispatch an Antifederalist delegation was New York, where an Antifederalist legislature, under prodding from Governor George Clinton, passed over John Jay, certainly one of the best qualified for the task at hand, but grudgingly included Alexander Hamilton, who, as the author of the Annapolis resolution, could not conceivably be left out, but curbed his independent authority by including two antinationalists in the delegation, John Lansing and Robert Yates, both upstate lawyers. Since the pair consistently outvoted Hamilton and then left the Convention in disgust, the state that Hamilton represented was, in effect, deprived of a vote. How well Hamilton could operate under these handicaps was, as we shall see, the special concern of his fellow nationalists and well-wishers of his hometown.

How wisely the delegates performed their task may be judged from the ability of their instrument of government to surmount the trials and crises of two hundred years. The prescience, innovative capability, drafting skills, and awareness of the need to compromise on the part of the Convention's delegates are attested to by the Constitution's durable qualities. Over a period of two centuries, dozens of constitutions adopted in other countries, whether in imitation of the American model or based on quite different plans, have gone into the scrap heap. The United States Constitution has outlived all its successors.

Fortunately for posterity, James Madison chose a seat up front. Not missing a single day, the diligent and meticulous Virginian took systematic notes, providing us with the principal record of the debates in the convention. The ordeal, he later said, "almost killed" him; but having undertaken the task, he was "determined to accomplish it." Some nine others also took notes, but none are as full, as impartial (despite some corrections that Madison, some forty years later, saw fit to make), or as accurate as Madison's. It is through James Madison chiefly that we are let in on the secret debates by which the most delicate and crucial

---

* At the time of the Constitutional Convention, John Adams was ambassador to Great Britain and Thomas Jefferson was ambassador to France.

issues were resolved and a constitution drafted and adopted between May 25 and September 17, 1787. . . .

[On] May 25 [1787], a quorum of seven state delegations were seated in the East Room of the State House. Here the Declaration of Independence had been signed, and here the old Congress had mostly sat until they were humiliatingly driven out by an insubordinate state militia wanting back pay. The East Room, forty by forty feet, with a twenty-foot-high plaster ceiling, proved adequate for the business at hand. The delegates seated themselves at tables covered with green baize, three or four delegates to a table. Before the session began, Washington talked informally to the delegates, urging them to create a plan of government of which they could be truly proud. As Gouverneur Morris later reminisced, Washington exhorted them, "Let us raise a standard to which the wise and honest can repair! The event is in the hands of God."

The first order of business was the election of a presiding officer. In the absence of the senior delegate, Benjamin Franklin, who was indisposed that day, Robert Morris moved that General Washington be the presiding officer, a motion seconded by John Rutledge. Unanimously elected, Washington was escorted to his chair by his two co-sponsors. In a brief speech he thanked his fellow delegates for the honor conferred upon him, and asked their indulgence for any errors he might commit in the execution of that post. Then the delegates picked as secretary William Jackson, a former army officer, and decided on the rules to be followed.

It was agreed that a majority of the states present could decide any question, each state to have an equal vote. This was an initial victory for the small states, and one that conformed to the voting rules of the Continental Congress. Then a rule of secrecy was adopted, the delegates feeling that they could talk more freely and be willing to modify their declared positions if word of what they said did not leak to their constituents back home. The rule, with strict injunctions laid down by Washington, was vigilantly respected. The wide, lofty windows ranging on both sides were nailed shut. Guards were posted outside the doors. Throughout a torrid summer the delegates sweated it out, but in the main what was happening inside never got outside. No one raised the issue of the public's "right to know," although Jefferson, from his post in Paris, protested privately to John Adams in England that the "precedent" of "tying up the tongues of the delegates was abominable." What came out of Philadelphia on September 17 has been called "an open covenant secretly arrived at." And years later Madison would insist that "no Constitution would ever have been adopted by the convention if the debates had been public."

The initial victory of the small states would quickly prove abortive. The Virginia delegation now seized the initiative. On May 29, Governor [Edmund] Randolph rose from his seat at a nod from General Washington and, with a degree of modesty concealing his own indecisiveness, declared:

"I regret that it should fall to me, rather than those of greater standing in life and longer experience, to open the great subject of this mission. But my colleagues from Virginia imposed this task on me.

"I need not comment on the crisis that confronts us, on the weakness of the Union under the Articles of Confederation, and on the dangers of our situation. But here is the remedy I am offering, which I am proposing in the form of a resolution."

Randolph, to reassure his listeners, began with the timid resolution proposing that the Articles be "corrected and enlarged." Ahead lay the real shockers, the fourteen following resolutions, which in essence proposed to demolish the Articles of Confederation and erect in their stead a strong national government on a popular foundation. The resolutions set up a bicameral legislature, the lower house chosen by popular election, the upper house picked by the lower from the candidates named by the state legislatures. Each house's representation was to be proportional to population. This Congress would have the authority to make laws "in all cases in which the separate states are incompetent" and to nullify any state laws contrary to the Federal Constitution.

The Virginia Plan provided for a President to be called the National Executive, who was to have all the executive powers granted Congress under the Articles. With the concurrence of a number of federal judges, the President would have veto power over the acts of Congress. He was to be chosen by Congress and would serve for a term of seven years. The plan also proposed to set up a system of federal courts.

This audacious plan transcended a mere revamping of the Articles, placing in its stead a different constitutional structure embracing a balanced government of three branches, supreme over the states.

The Convention now went into a committee of the whole. For a few moments the response to the Virginia Plan seemed auspicious. On the motion of Gouverneur Morris, the Convention voted six to one "that a *national* government ought to be established consisting of a *supreme* Legislative, Executive, and Judiciary." The dissenting state was Pennsylvania, whose delegation yielded to Benjamin Franklin's long predilection for a unicameral legislature, such as had been operative in Pennsylvania. Once taken and never reversed, the vote on the Morris resolution was perhaps the most significant made by the Convention, amounting as it did to a commitment to set up a supreme central government.

Other parts of the Randolph Plan provoked serious debate. The proposition that "the first branch of the legislature" should be elected by the people quickly raised two questions: First, how much democracy did the Founding Fathers really want? And second, how much power were the states ready to yield to the people? Perhaps to the surprise of most delegates, two old Patriots with long-established radical credentials quickly sought the floor to contest this proposition.

The first to do so was Roger Sherman, a delegate from Connecticut, signer of the Declaration of Independence, one-time shoemaker, and one of the few ex-artisans present at the Convention. The second was Elbridge Gerry, the fiery maverick from Marblehead, who stunned some of his colleagues with his uninhibited antidemocratic outpourings, among them:

> *The evils we experience flow from the excess of democracy. The people do not want virtue, but are the dupes of pretended patriots. Just look at Massachusetts. There it would seem to be a maxim of democracy to starve the public servants. There has been a perfect clamor to reduce salaries, and even the governor has had to cut his salary. I have been too republican, heretofore; I am still republican, but I have been taught by experience of the dangers of the leveling spirit.*

The nationalists who looked to the people, not to the states, for support of their program, could not let these remarks go unchallenged. George Mason, more democrat than nationalist, rejoined: "I am for an election of the larger branch of the legislature by the people. That is to be the grand depository of the democratic principle of government. We ought to attend to the rights of every class of the people. Perhaps we have been too democratic in the past, but let us not now run into the opposite extreme. However indifferent the affluent may be on this subject, let me remind you gentlemen: Every selfish motive, every family attachment, ought to recommend such a system as would provide no less carefully for the rights and happiness of the lowest than the highest orders of citizens."

Mason had brought the class issue out in the open. Two others, more enthusiastically nationalistic, now manifested their concern about attaching the people to the national government. James Wilson wanted to raise "the federal pyramid to a considerable altitude," and for that reason "to give it as broad a base as possible." He warned that "no government could long subsist without the confidence of the people." To put elections in the hands of the state legislatures would only increase their weight rather than reduce it.

Madison had impatiently waited his turn on an issue so vital to the nationalist cause. He contended that to have one branch of the national legislature elected by the people was "essential to every plan of free government." "The excessive flirtations" of indirect elections now being practiced in some of the states, was, in his opinion, being "pushed too far." He was prepared to have such indirect elections for the second branch of the legislature as well as for the president and the judiciary. But the great fabric to be raised would be more solid and durable "if it should rest on the solid foundation of the people themselves." . . .

How far the delegates were prepared to trust the judgment of the people was reflected in the stirring debate over the method of electing senators. Once the committee of the whole had approved by a vote of six states to two the election to the "first branch" (the House of Representatives) by the people, how was the "second branch" (the Senate) to be picked? Randolph, arguing in support of his original proposition that the Senate be elected by the House, maintained that the "second branch" should be small enough "to exempt it from the passionate proceedings to which numerous assemblies are liable."

This proposal was entirely unacceptable to James Wilson, who took his nationalistic notions of popular sovereignty seriously, and favored having both branches elected by the people. John Dickinson, a man of elitist inclinations, strongly disagreed. The senators, he insisted, would more accurately reflect the "sense of the states" if they were picked by their respective legislatures. Such a method, in his judgment, was better calculated than election by the people to attract "the most distinguished for their rank in life and their weight of property." The model that he had in mind for the Senate was the House of Lords, and he wanted the second branch to conform as closely as possible to that aristocratic chamber.

Over this issue the committee of the whole was deadlocked. Neither Wilson nor Madison, each supporting different proposals, was impressed by Dickinson's arguments. Neither saw the least danger that the states would be devoured by the national government if their senators were elected either by the people, as Wilson urged, or by the House of Representatives, as Madison preferred. Wilson flatly denied the applicability of the British model. "Our manners, our laws, the abolition of entails and of primogeniture, the whole genius of the people, are opposed to it," he contended. On this point Madison concurred, and thereupon he began a wrangle with Gerry over whether the people or the legislatures had been responsible for the paper-money experiments that Madison loathed.

With no agreement obtainable, the issue was put off for another week. Madison reaffirmed his support for the Virginia proposition. Arguing for a relatively small Senate, he asserted that the more the senators "partook of the infirmities of their constituents, the more liable they would come to be divided among themselves either from their own indiscretions or the artifices of the opposite faction." Contrariwise, when the weight of a set of men "depends on the degree of political authority lodged in them, the smaller the number, the greater the weight."

Dickinson entered a persuasive plea for his own proposition on the ground that "the preservation of the states in a certain degree of agency is indispensable." It would preserve a useful check on the popularly elected House. After further debate and over Madison's persistent objections, Dickinson's motion for the appointment of the senators by the state legislatures was adopted nine to two, only Pennsylvania and Virginia registering negative votes. . . .*

How long should the senators serve? Terms varying from nine years down to four were proposed, but in the end the Convention was persuaded by Randolph's plea for rotation, along with Madison's argument for a considerable du-

---

* U.S. senators were elected by state legislatures until 1913, when the Seventeenth Amendment provided for direct election by the people.

ration of term "in framing a system which will last for ages." It was finally agreed that senators would serve six-year terms, one-third to be up for election biennially.

The Convention, having resisted a renewed effort to have the state legislatures elect the House of Representatives, now had to deal with the ticklish issue of whether representation should be equal, as in the old Congress, or proportionate to population, and, if the latter, how the population was to be counted. George Mason pointed out that under the existing Confederation, Congress represented the *states* and *not* the people of the states, and that the acts of Congress operated on the states and not the people. The new plan he advocated of election to the House by the people would reverse this. While favoring having the people vote from large districts, he was silent on the issue of proportional representation. But since Virginia, Pennsylvania, and Massachusetts—the largest states in population—had the most at stake in pressing their demand for proportional representation, and the smaller states the least, the issue brought on a direct confrontation between the larger and smaller states.

For a time it seemed that the nationalist momentum would be stalled. New Jersey, in the person of William Paterson, insisted that the convention was acting *ultra vires,* as the delegates were expected to proceed under a commission to amend the Articles of Confederation. "We have no power to go beyond the federal scheme," he declared, "and if we had, the people are not ripe for any other. We must follow the people; the people will not follow us." Arguing that a confederacy "supposes sovereignty in the members composing it, and sovereignty supposes equality," he warned that his state would never part with her sovereignty.

Thus far the method of election to the legislative branch had been determined. The most troublesome issue remained to be resolved. How would representation in each house be apportioned? That issue, arraying the small states against the large, consumed a large portion of the Convention deliberations for a full month and was not to be settled until the middle of July. The debate it precipitated revolved around a major question: Would the government be a consolidated nation, with the national government holding its authority directly from the people, or would it be a federal union in which some degree of sovereignty would be recognized as proper to the states and some check be placed upon popular rule?

Initially, attention focused on the "first house" (the House of Representatives). Connecticut's Roger Sherman proposed that representation be proportionate to the numbers of free inhabitants; Rutledge, that it be according to the respective quotas of contributions. The issue seemed clearcut: people against wealth. In supporting his fellow South Carolinian, Pierce Butler reminded the delegates that "money was power and that the states ought to have weight in the government in proportion to their wealth." Rufus King rejoined that, if voting were made proportionate to revenue, nonimporting states like New Jersey and Connecticut would suffer serious discrimination.

At this point Benjamin Franklin, that unreconstructed democrat, in a paper read for him by James Wilson, urged that voting be proportional to population, citing the case of England and Scotland, whose union failed to bring about adverse actions in Parliament against minority Scottish interests. He even advanced a formula to equalize the contributions of the states, but his rather diffuse proposals seemed to perplex the delegates.

By a vote of seven to three the committee of the whole voted for proportional representation in the first house, without settling the most troublesome point, *who* would be represented? James Wilson's answer: representation and direct taxation should be based proportionate "to the whole number of white and other free citizens and inhabitants of every age, sex, and condition, including those bound to servitude for a term of years, and three-fifths of all other persons, except Indians not paying taxes."

When it was proposed, few realized that, after furious debate, Wilson's formula would be adopted, for he had unwittingly touched a sensitive chord among Northerners opposed to slavery and unprepared to grant the slave states the advantage in numbers that this proposal embodied. Gerry promptly voiced a vigorous dissent. "Are we to enter into a separate compact with slaves?" he asked, responding to his own query with a vigorous "No!" In his customary blunt style he amplified his question by raising a second one: "Why should the blacks, who were property in the South, be in the rule of representation more than the cattle or horses of the North?"

Ultimately Wilson's motion prevailed, thereby encouraging the nationalists to press their victory. Wilson and Hamilton now proposed that the right of suffrage for the second house (the Senate) be the same as for the first house. The vote was close—six states in favor, five against, a forecast of an ominous division ahead.

Meanwhile, the nationalists had pushed through agreements on the supremacy of the laws of Congress and national treaties, on giving necessary and proper powers to Congress, and even on allowing the national government a veto of state laws contravening the Constitution, the clause on treaties being added by Franklin.

The long-brewing confrontation between the large and small states began on June 14. Regardless of whether a final settlement would apportion seats in the national legislature according to taxes paid or according to the number of the state's free inhabitants plus three-fifths of the slaves, the small states saw themselves completely outvoted in a national legislature by a few large states.

On June 15 it was clear what form an alternative proposal would take. Its spokesman was William Paterson, New Jersey's former attorney general, a rather diminutive figure whose modest demeanor cloaked respectable learning and oratorical talents. Paterson now split the convention apart by proposing the Small-State or New Jersey Plan in the form of nine resolutions. These called for a one-house legislature elected by states regardless of population, with a plural executive elected by Congress and a Supreme Court chosen by the executive.

Paterson made one obeisance to the national system. He was prepared to declare the acts of Congress and all treaties "the supreme law of their respective states," binding "upon the State courts," regardless of state law to the contrary. Otherwise, save for granting Congress the right to tax and regulate commerce, the New Jersey Plan would have continued almost intact the old Articles of Confederation.

Franklin had always been congenial to a unicameral legislature such as his own state possessed, to the dismay of conservatives. The Old Doctor caused some gossip by reputedly letting slip to a friend his concern about a bicameral system. The latter he compared to a snake with two heads. "One head chose to go on the right side of the twig; the other on the left. So that time was spent in the contest; and before the decision was completed the poor snake died of thirst."

But even Franklin's metaphor could not save Paterson's unicameral proposal, which moved against the tide of delegate opinion. From the moment Randolph initiated his proposals, it had become evident that the delegates would not content themselves with an amended set of Articles. Paterson's proposal was too little and came too late. After three days of sharp debate, the New Jersey Plan was defeated seven to three, a decisive vote that amounted to a complete rejection of the Confederation frame of government and of any notion of returning the nation to where it had been before the Annapolis Convention. That point was driven home by New York's Lansing. "New York," he declared, "would never have concurred in sending deputies to the Convention if she had supposed the deliberations were to turn on a consolidation of the states and a national government."

Lansing's negativism was too much for Paterson, who now sought to strike a more constructive tone. He was not opposed to a national government, nor were the people, he conceded. What he did oppose was the inequality of the present plan, which, as in Great Britain, "has ever been a poison contaminating every branch of government." Without restraint on the legislative authority, he asked, is there not danger of "a legislative despotism"? Randolph responded with a spirited defense of the Virginia Plan.

Now it was Alexander Hamilton's turn. He had said very little over the first three weeks, but Paterson's proposals struck alarm bells in his ears. He foresaw a fatal compromise that would in effect seriously reduce the powers of the national government. Perhaps to bring the delegates back to their senses, perhaps because he was not noted for his discretion, on June 18, the day before the New Jersey Plan was rejected, Hamilton revealed his own plan in what was probably the most controversial speech he ever would make, and one that was as damaging as any to the people's perception of him as a republican leader.

Neither the Virginia nor the New Jersey Plan appealed to him, he confessed, but he found the latter more unpalatable. His own proposals amounted to reducing the states to mere subdivisions. An executive in each state would be appointed by the national government, while the Chief Executive would be elected for life by electors. Hamilton was brutally frank. Arguing that two sovereignties could not coexist within the same lines, he sought to mollify his shocked listeners by arguing that if the states were extinguished, great economies could be effected.

Piling one sledgehammer blow on top of another, Hamilton proposed a Senate chosen for life and invested the executive with an absolute veto. Beyond that, he denounced both the Virginia and the New Jersey plans as too democratic. Since Hamilton was a rational man, the extremist solutions that he offered, solutions that shocked even the ultranationalists, were proffered evidently to offset the Paterson proposals rather than with any expectation on his part that his own notions would prevail. As time would show, Hamilton, despite his indiscreet remarks of June 18, would in essence back the basic Virginia Plan as the best obtainable.

Could a republican government be established over so great an extent of territory? Hamilton asked. While he was not prepared to offer an alternative, he did hold up the British political system as "the best in the world." Hence there should be a life Senate, since no temporary Senate, he asserted, not even one of seven years, "will have firmness enough to answer the purpose. When a great object of government is pursued which seizes the popular passions, they spread like wildfire and become irresistible." A hereditary monarch, like the King of England, was, he declared, "above the dangers of being corrupted," and to guarantee such executive incorruptibility he called for a National Executive chosen for life.

Is this a republican government? Hamilton asked his now thoroughly aroused audience. His answer: "Yes, if all the magistrates are appointed and vacancies are filled by the people or a process of election originating with the people." Thus, to Hamilton, the Randolph Plan did not go far enough. Hamilton confessed that he was offering what was merely a sketch, not a set of formal propositions, but with the idea of further underpinning the Randolph Plan as it evolved in the Convention.

Hamilton consumed most of the day, and when he gathered up his papers, his auditors sat stunned and silent. Then the committee of the whole rose and the house adjourned.

Hamilton's audacious assault on the weaknesses of the constitutional proposals thus far submitted left their imprint. On the very next day the New Jersey Plan was defeated, but not before James Madison had torn it to shreds. He attacked it as too "federal," as fantasizing the idea of the large states combining against the small, and prophesied that if the New Jersey principle were admitted, it would "infuse mortality into a Constitution which we wished to last forever."

Debate on the Randolph Plan was resumed, but the small states were not content, insisting on an equal vote in the Senate. Some ten days elapsed before a compromise could be hammered out. Hamilton took the occasion of the last speech he was to make for a considerable time to characterize the issues as "a contest for power, not for liberty, but for *their* liberty," meaning the states'. "States," he pointed out, "are a collection of individual men. Which ought we respect most, the rights of the people composing them, or the artificial beings resulting from the composition? Nothing would be more preposterous or absurd than to sacrifice the former to the latter." Reminding his hearers that "this was a critical moment for forming a respectable government," he urged that the delegates "should run every risk in trusting to future amendments." If we do not act now, he warned, while we still have some sentiments of union, now when we are weak and sensible of our weakness, it may be too late when we are "feeble and the difficulties greater."

In one version of Hamilton's closing, he charged that "the people are gradually ripening in their opinion of government. They begin to be tired of an excess of *democracy*—and what even is the Virginia plan, but *pork still, with a little change of the sauce.*"

A stunned audience sat in silence. Hamilton had gone the furthest in advocating a centralist plan that would forever label him as undemocratic and pro-monarchical. Outvoted by the two other New York delegates who soon quit the Convention, thereby depriving him of a vote, and depressed by the depth of what he felt to be states'-rights sentiment, Hamilton left the Convention on June 29 and headed for New York on the pretext of private business.

Hamilton did not depart without administering one more shock. The day before he quit, the debate on the Convention floor over the suffrage in the lower house reached a state of such acrimony that Benjamin Franklin, never celebrated for his religious orthodoxy, called on the delegates to invite a clergyman to offer prayers at the beginning of each session. Hamilton, among others, contended that this action would spread word out of doors that dissensions within the Convention had suggested a measure that had not been initiated at its start. One later version, as had already been noted, had Hamilton express confidence that the convention could transact the business entrusted to its care without "the necessity of calling in foreign aid." He could not have timed his departure more opportunely.

The Great Compromise

Even before Hamilton temporarily quit the Convention, animated debate had begun over a compromise plan proposed by the Connecticut delegation and effectively argued by Roger Sherman, Oliver Ellsworth, and William Samuel Johnson. Dr. Johnson eloquently reminded his fellow delegates that the United States was for many purposes "one political society" composed of individuals, while for other purposes the states also constituted political societies with interests of their own. These notions, Johnson observed, were not contradictory. "They were halves of a unique whole," and as such "ought to be combined" to the end that "in *one branch* the *people* ought to be represented, in the *other* the states."

The Connecticut Compromise, providing for equality of the states in the Senate, elicited strong rejoinders from the nationalist camp, whose notable leaders now were James Madison and James Wilson, and the debate waxed fierce. On the critical motion for equal representation in the Senate the nationalists succeeded in obtaining a tie vote. The resolution of the issue was now assigned to a special committee made up of one member from each state, an arrangement favorable to the small-states group. On July 5, that committee reported in favor of the Connecticut Plan, and a week later the convention agreed that representation and direct taxes in the lower house should be based "in proportion to the whole number of white and other free citizens and inhabitants of every age, sex, and condition including those bound to service for a term of years and three-fifths of all other persons not comprehended in the foregoing description, except Indians not paying taxes." This proposal had been advanced by James Wilson some weeks before to gain Southern support for basing representation on population rather than property, that population to be determined by a census ordained by the Constitution. While in essence this adopted motion became Article 1, Section 2 of the final Constitution, the drafters avoiding spelling out distinctions of color, substituting the phrase "the whole number of free persons" for "white and other free citizens," but continuing to abstain from mentioning slavery by referring to the enslaved blacks as "all other Persons." In this form the rule of representation survived until the Civil War and the ratification in 1868 of the Fourteenth Amendment.

Eleven days later the Convention removed the last element in the controversy by accepting the principle of equal representation in the Senate. It should be noted that for proportioning representation no distinction of sex was made either in the free or slave population. Hence, for purposes of representation, women were to be counted, but since qualifications for voting were left to the state legislatures to determine, women gained no rights of suffrage—except in New Jersey by an accident of legislative drafting, and then for all too brief a time.

For James Madison, his defeat on the composition of the Senate, a proposal advantageous to his own state of Virginia but only to be scuttled by the Connecticut Compromise, convinced him of the need for executive independence and separation of powers, thus making it much easier for him to collaborate on *The Federalist* with the two other contributors who had long voiced these views.

The Slavery Concession: The Sections in Confrontation

Back in Philadelphia, earlier in August, the Convention agreed to give Congress the power to regulate commerce with foreign nations and among the several states, and added, on Madison's motion, "with the Indian tribes." Although all had agreed that conferring power over commerce on the national government was a prime motive for calling the Convention, Southern delegates were shocked by the notion that this clause would work out purely to the North's advantage. Charles Cotesworth Pinckney wanted to restrict commercial legislation to a two-thirds vote of each house rather than a simple majority, and George Mason, in support of the two-thirds vote, declared:

> *The southern states are the* minority *in both houses. Is it to be expected that they will deliver themselves bound hand and foot to the eastern states, and enable them to exclaim in the words of Cromwell, on a certain occasion— "The Lord hath delivered them into our hands"?*

James Madison, countering in one of his most effective speeches, pointed out that "as we are laying the foundation for a great empire, we ought to take a permanent view of the subject." The great object, he pointed out, was "the necessity of securing the West India trade to this country." Madison prevailed, and Congress won the power to regulate commerce.

Nonetheless, every regional concession brought its price and begot a compromise. Thus the great slavery issue, which hitherto had been swept under the rug, came to the fore when the delegates took up the matter of import and export duties. A fortnight after the commerce clause victory, the South proposed that Congress be forbidden from levying a tax on the importation of slaves, both into and between the states, and from prohibiting such importation altogether.

To the consternation of most Northerners, Roger Sherman favored the proposition. He disapproved of the slave trade, he explained, but felt it expedient to offer as few impediments to the proposed scheme as possible, especially when one realized, he remarked in an optimistic vein, that "the abolition of slavery seemed to be proceeding throughout the United States." If the Connecticut Yankee's support for leaving the slave trade unrestrained provided an agreeable surprise to the Southerners, their equanimity was short-lived. Virginia's elder statesman, George Mason, took the floor and shocked the delegates from the Lower South with his tirade against what one day the South would defend as its "peculiar institution." While attributing the blame for the original slave traffic to British merchants and to the refusal of the British government to allow the colonies to prohibit the traffic, Mason painted an ugly picture on a broad canvas, one that did not spare his fellow Southerners. Mason's blast stands out as one of the most stirring speeches of the Convention:

> *The present question concerns not the importing states alone, but the whole Union. The evil of having slaves was experienced during the late war. Had slaves been treated as they might have been by the enemy, they would have proved dangerous instruments in their hands. But instead they were as foolish in dealing with the slaves as they were with the Tories. Maryland, Virginia, and North Carolina have*

prohibited the importation of slaves. But all this would be in vain if South Carolina and Georgia remained at liberty to import them. The West is calling out for slaves, and will fill their country if the states in the Lower South remain at liberty to import. Slavery discourages arts and manufactures. The poor despise labor when performed by slaves. Slavery prevents whites from immigrating, and produces the most pernicious effect on manners.

Every master of slaves is born a petty tyrant. They bring the judgment of heaven on a country. As nations cannot be rewarded or punished in the next world they must be in this. By an inevitable chain of causes and effects providence punished national sins by national calamities. I hold it essential to every point of view that the General Government should have power to prevent the increase of slavery.

Rutledge, replying for the Lower South, was unimpressed by the moral and economic arguments Mason had marshaled. He warned that "the people of those states would never be such fools as to yield on so vital a point nor agree to the plan of union unless the right to import slaves were untouched." Charles Cotesworth Pinckney reaffirmed Rutledge's threat.

With the Northern delegates divided between those from Connecticut, who preferred not to meddle in the slave trade, and others, like John Dickinson and New Hampshire's John Langdon, who placed the issue on the high moral ground of honor and conscience as well as safety, the Convention was prepared, as Randolph suggested, to find "some middle ground." The signal contribution to such "middle ground" was the proposal now forthcoming from New Jersey's governor, William Livingston, Jay's father-in-law. No prohibition shall be permitted before the year 1800, he recommended. Mollified by this spirit of concession, Charles Cotesworth Pinckney substituted "the year 1808" for Livingston's 1800.

Despite Madison's objection that "twenty years will produce all the mischief that can be apprehended from the liberty to import slaves," and that a term of that length was "dishonorable to the American character," the "Father of the Constitution" was overruled once again. With minor modifications of phraseology, the Convention voted eight to four to bar prohibition of the slave trade before 1808. Even the North divided on this crucial vote, nor was there a solid South, as Virginia voted "nay."

The word "slavery," Abraham Lincoln would someday note, was "hid away in the Constitution, just as an afflicted man hides away a wen or cancer, which he dares not cut out at once, lest he bleed to death." Instead we find, "The migration or importation of such persons as any of the states now existing shall think proper to admit, shall not be prohibited by the Congress prior to the year one thousand eight hundred and eight; but a tax or duty may be imposed on such importation, not exceeding ten dollars for each person" (Article I, Section

9). Thus slavery was in effect validated by this and the two other compromises—the three-fifths rule for representation and direct taxes (Article I, Section 2), and the provision for the return to their owners of fugitive slaves ("persons held to Service or Labour" is the description used) crossing state lines (Article IV, Section 2). By these three compromises with Southern sensibilities, the Framers negated the Great Declaration's assertion that all men are created equal.

These concessions to the slave states allayed but failed to end the tensions between North and South, tensions that had earlier emerged during the Confederation years over the issue of the West and the Mississippi, and now would embrace slavery, the last a smoldering source of contention, which one day would erupt in a tragic conflagration.

In the meantime, since numerous issues had already been settled, the Convention adjourned on July 26 until August 6 to give the Committee of Detail an opportunity to "report a Constitution conformable to the resolutions passed by the Convention." The committee was composed of John Rutledge of South Carolina, Edmund Randolph of Virginia, James Wilson of Pennsylvania, Oliver Ellsworth of Connecticut, and Nathaniel Gorham of Massachusetts. Randolph wrote a preliminary draft and Wilson the revised draft that formed the final report. The committee did more than adopt the resolutions previously carried. It amplified them and provided innovations of its own. Thus, it took the very brief resolution on the "National Judiciary," and itemized in some detail the jurisdiction of the "Supreme Court" more or less in the form that it appears in the final Constitution. Again, it transformed the vague powers conferred on the national legislature into a series of specific powers, including the crucial "necessary and proper" clause that permitted the broad or "Hamiltonian" construction of the Constitution that was to govern the Supreme Court for many years to come. It adopted or paraphrased a number of clauses in the old Articles of Confederation, perhaps to convey the illusion that the Constitution was a mere revision of the Articles—a fiction that was transparent to everyone.

The Committee of Detail's report, submitted to the Convention on August 6, was debated until September 10, when the Convention adjourned to await the work of the Committee of Style, which had been named to prepare a new version of the Constitution. Since the Convention continued to make changes, such as in the mode of electing the President, and removing from the Senate the power to make treaties and appoint Supreme Court justices, the Constitution that emerged from the Committee of Style had to take these matters into consideration, but the Committee of Detail's report remained the core of the final version.

Numerous divisive issues continued to be resolved even after the Committee of Detail had completed its work. One of the most important was the manner of electing the President. Should he be elected by Congress, as the original Virginia Plan proposed, or should he be elected directly by the people rather than by the states? Those committed nationalists, James Wilson and Gouverneur Morris, eloquently pleaded the case for having the President elected by the people, while the aristocratic George Mason, although himself a foremost civil libertarian, considered Wilson's proposal to be as unnatural as asking a blind man to pick out colors. The final decision, after countless proposals, was to have the President elected by electors who would be chosen in each state "in such manner" as its legislature might "direct." The electors would vote by ballot for two persons, of whom one could not be an inhabitant of the same state. The person having the greatest number of votes would become President; the second highest Vice-President. It was Roger Sherman who proposed that if no one person gained a majority of the electors, the House of Representatives should choose the candidate from among the top five, each state's delegation casting one vote. The plan, perhaps conceived to propitiate the states, proved instead a victory for both nationalism and democracy, for very shortly after 1789 nearly all the state legislatures provided for the election of their states' presidential electors by popular vote.

How long should the President's term be, and should he be eligible for re-election? Hamilton, who, on his return to the Convention, took an active and constructive role, had originally indicated his preference for a life term, others for a seven-year term without eligibility to run again; toward the end, Hamilton opted for a mere three years. The Convention finally settled on a four-year term without placing a limitation on the President's right of reelection.

A vexing issue at the Convention was where to locate the power to declare state laws unconstitutional. Even ardent nationalists shied away from granting the power to Congress. In the end it was a bitter states'-rights man who hit upon a satisfactory solution. Drawing upon the phraseology of the now discarded New Jersey Plan, slovenly Luther Martin, whom one delegate castigated as "an insufferable bore and blustering obstructionist," inserted a clause making the Constitution and the laws and treaties of the United States "the supreme law of the land," binding upon the judiciary of each state. The supremacy clause, as it is called, which had its origins in a resolution drafted by John Jay for the old Congress, became the cornerstone of national sovereignty in 1789, when Congress passed a judiciary act providing for appeals from state courts to the federal judiciary. The Convention prudently abstained from spelling out just what body would have the right to declare acts of Congress unconstitutional, but from the sense of the debates it was implied that the federal judiciary would exercise the power.

A large number of dissenting Christian sects, along with the Jews, had a stake in the outcome at Philadelphia, but no way of knowing for sure whether religious tests for officeholding, such as still existed under some of the state constitutions, would be incorporated into the Federal Constitution still in the drafting stage. In Pennsylvania, for example, the state constitution required members of the assembly to subscribe to a declaration that ended in these words: "I do acknowledge the Scriptures of the Old and New Testament to be given by divine inspiration." Most states had removed, or were about to remove, such effective bars to officeholding, but the disqualification in the Maryland Constitution of 1776 barring Jews from public office was not removed until 1825. Rhode Island, once the home of religious liberty, did not secure equal rights for the Jews until the adoption of the state constitution in 1842, and North Carolina not until 1868. In the main, though, the religious minorities were beneficiaries of the movement in the original thirteen states to remove religious bars to public office holding.

It was the federal government rather than the states that provided the most vigorous impetus to the movement. The old Congress, on July 13, 1787, ordained in the very first article of the Northwest Ordinance that "no person, demeaning himself in a peaceable and orderly manner, shall ever be molested on account of his mode of worship, or religious sentiments in the said territory."

Would the Federal Convention meeting simultaneously in Philadelphia adopt so liberal a stance? The answer was soon forthcoming. On August 20, Charles Cotesworth Pinckney had submitted to the Convention, for reference to the Committee of Detail, a number of propositions. Among them was this: "No religious test or qualification shall ever be annexed to any oath of office under authority of the United States." This proposition was referred to the Committee of Detail without debate or further consideration. When the committee reported back on August 30, Charles Pinckney then moved to amend the article with the addition of these words: "but no religious test shall ever be required as a qualification to any office or public trust under the authority of the United States." Roger Sherman thought the clause unnecessary, "the prevailing liberality being a sufficient security against it." But Gouverneur Morris and Charles Cotesworth Pinckney approved the motion, which was agreed to unanimously. The entire article was adopted, with only North Carolina and Maryland divided.

Not knowing what had transpired, Jonas Phillips, a long-time patriot of New York of the Jewish faith, who had removed to Philadelphia before the start of hostilities and had served in the Philadelphia militia, memorialized the Convention on September 7 to omit from a test oath the phrase regarding the divine inspiration of the New Testament, so that "the Israelites will think themselves happy to live under a government where all religious societies are on an equal footing." Phillips, along with persons from other minority religious groups, appears to have been unduly concerned. In its final form, Article VI of the Federal Constitution requires all federal and state officials to take an oath or affirmation to support the Constitution, with the provision "but no religious Test shall ever be required as a qualification to any office or public trust under the United States."

Although Article VI was adopted with little debate, it was a particular target for that Antifederalist diehard, Luther Martin. At the Maryland ratifying Convention, Martin singled out the supporters of the article, contrasting them, in his customary vein of heavy sarcasm, with "some members *so unfashionable* as to think that a *belief of the existence of a Deity,* and of a *state of future rewards and punishments* would be some security for the good conduct of our rulers, and that, in a Christian country, it would be *at least decent* to hold out some distinction between the professors of Christianity and downright infidelity or paganism."

Martin's harangue did not deter proponents of religious freedom, nor did it keep James Madison from including as the first article of the Bill of Rights a prohibition of Congress from making any "law respecting an establishment of religion, or prohibiting the free exercise thereof." . . .

With the basic charter of government hammered out, the Constitution was entrusted to the skillful hands of the Committee of Style, to which some of the most talented writers among the delegates were named. William Samuel Johnson was the committee's chairman, with Gouverneur Morris, Madison, Hamilton, and Rufus King serving under him. It was Morris, however, who was largely responsible for the final phraseology of the Constitution, producing in a mere two days a document distinguished for its precision of language and clarity of style. Morris's most noteworthy contribution was in changing the wording of the Preamble. Since the new government would go into operation upon ratification of nine states, and no one could be certain which states would ratify, Morris very sensibly reworded the Preamble as drafted earlier by the Committee of Detail. Instead of "We the people of the States of New Hampshire, etc., . . . do ordain, declare, and establish the following Constitution for the government of ourselves and our posterity," Morris's Preamble designated the people as the source of authority, thereby elevating the sights of government and couching its purposes in eloquent language. As he reworded it, the Preamble read:

> *WE THE PEOPLE of the United States, In order to form a more perfect Union, establish Justice, insure domestic Tranquility, provide for the common defence, promote the general Welfare, and secure the Blessings of Liberty to ourselves and our Posterity, do ordain and establish this CONSTITUTION for the United States of America.*

One other point: While the attribution is not certain, it is most probable that Alexander Hamilton persuaded his colleagues on the Committee of Style to add a clause forbidding any state from passing any "law impairing the obligation of contracts." Property interests would not be neglected.

Just two days after the Committee of Style submitted its final draft to the Convention, it was approved, and on September 17 the Convention adjourned. On that closing day the engrossed Constitution was read and adopted, but not before a number of moving speeches were heard.

Hamilton conceded that no man's ideas were "more remote" from the final plan than his were known to be, but offered the delegates the choice "between anarchy and Convulsion on one side, and the chance of good to be expected on the other." Randolph surprised his fellow delegates by disclosing that he would not sign because he wanted to feel uncommitted as to what his final judgment would be about the Constitution—an odd admission from a man whose initial plan provided the basis of the charter finally adopted. The prolix Elbridge Gerry warned that the Constitution would promote dangerous divisiveness in his state. He could not sign the document because he would not pledge himself to abide by it.

Old Doctor Franklin expressed certain reservations, but admitted that if he lived long enough he might change his mind. "The older I grow," he remarked, "the more apt I am to doubt my own judgment and to pay more respect to the judgment of others." He did not consider himself infallible, and told of the French lady, who in a dispute with her sister, remarked, "I don't know how it happens, sister, but I meet with nobody but myself who is always in the right—*il n'y a que moi qui a toujours raison*." Franklin's enthusiasm for the Constitution burgeoned on reflection. About a month later he wrote to an old friend of America, Ferdinand Grand, the Paris banker, suggesting that if the Constitution succeeded in being ratified, "I do not see why you might not in Europe carry the project into execution by forming a federal union and one grand republic of all the different states and kingdoms; by means of a like Convention, for we had many interests to reconcile." . . .

Of the original fifty-five delegates who attended some or part of the sessions, thirty-nine signed. Washington's diary tells us that after that last session the delegates "adjourned to the City Tavern, dined together and took a cordial leave of each other."

They were no longer behind closed doors.

Epilogue

The battle for the Constitution was not over, however. The divisive issue of state versus national power continued to be debated in the individual states during the ratification process, as described in the next selection.

The Morris article suggests another important issue that has contemporary relevance. According to Article V of the Constitution, the document can be amended if two-thirds of both branches of Congress pass an amendment and then three-fourths of the state legislatures or state ratifying conventions ratify it. But it can also be amended if two-thirds of the states call for another constitutional convention for the purpose of considering an amendment. No one knows if such a convention could "run away" and rewrite the entire document, and few want to find out. When all but a handful of states had called for a convention for the purpose of having direct popular election of the Senate, Congress quickly proposed and the states just as quickly ratified the Seventeenth Amendment. Now we are just a few state resolutions away from a call for a constitutional convention for the Balanced Budget Amendment. If a constitutional convention were to take place today, would it be as successful as the first one? Would it be possible to work "behind closed doors" again? Or would there be a disastrous political free-for-all, played out in the media, as some people fear? This prospect seemingly ensures that there will not be another constitutional convention, and that any proposed amendments will have to come from Congress.

Ratification

Charles L. Mee, Jr.

Most people believe that the debates over the Constitution ended with the Constitutional Convention in 1787. In fact, those debates were just the beginning of the formation of a government. The new Constitution would be a meaningless exercise in semantics unless nine of the thirteen states ratified it—and, given the sharpness of the debates in the Constitutional Convention, ratification was not going to be easy. Was this a government of the people or of the states? What authority did the Constitution have? Who would have power under the new system, and who would ensure that these persons or groups exercised their power wisely? These and other questions remained to be resolved before the American people, who had paid a high price for their freedom, would agree to obey this new document.

Many imagine the creation of the Constitution to have been a very logical process, with rational men carefully considering the precepts that would govern the nation for centuries to come. Thanks to Charles Mee's vivid portrayal of the ratification process, however, we are able to see that the formation of our government was as much a matter of sometimes vicious hardball politics as it was of high-flown political philosophy. The battles that took place in various states tell us a great deal about the economic and sociological differences among regions and hint at the difficulties that would occur in applying the new constitutional mandates. We also see that the power of the new central government frightened people more than did the power of the states. The result was the first ten amendments, or the Bill of Rights—limitations on the new government that were necessary to secure ratification.

For years the state of Connecticut put "The Constitution State" on its license plates. Who can justifiably claim that they were finally responsible for the document's adoption? Furthermore, did this ratification process help rally the nation around the new Constitution, or did it help magnify the differences among people? And when some legal theorists argue that we must follow "the intent of the founders" in interpreting the Constitution, is this intent possible to determine?

SAM ADAMS   One of the leaders in the ratification fight in Massachusetts.

JOHN HANCOCK   An influential figure in the Massachusetts ratification debate.

PATRICK HENRY   Antifederalist leader in Virginia.

JAMES MADISON, ALEXANDER HAMILTON, JOHN JAY   Co-authors of *The Federalist;* led the fight for ratification.

EDMUND RANDOLPH   One of the leaders in the ratification fight in Virginia.

ROBERT WHITEHILL   Antifederalist leader in Pennsylvania.

JAMES WILSON   One of the principal proponents of the Constitution.

▶ The initial reaction to the constitution was one of surprise, even shock. It was one thing to write a constitution, and quite another to have it accepted. When the constitution was first broadcast across the country, it seems fair to say, the majority of the people were completely against it. "The greatness of the powers given" to this new government, declared the renowned Revolutionary hero Richard Henry Lee of Virginia, "and the multitude of places to be created, produce a coalition of monarchy men, military men, aristocrats and drones, whose noise, impudence, and zeal exceed all belief." To say, said Lee, "as many do, that a bad government must be established, for fear of anarchy, is really saying, that we must kill ourselves, for fear of dying."

Here was a central government far too strong, with a president sure to grow to royal proportions, a senate already constituted with the lineaments of aristocracy, and a house of representatives that was, as Colonel [George] Mason said, "not the substance, but the shadow only of representation," or as Lee declared, "a mere shred, or rag of representation." There was no bill of rights in this constitution; there was an unlimited power for the central government to levy taxes. What, many of the veterans of the American Revolution wondered, had they fought the war for?

Before the opposition could quite gather its forces, however, the plan was slipped dexterously past Congress. Madison, William Samuel Johnson of Connecticut, Rufus King, Nathaniel Gorham, Langdon and Gilman of New Hampshire, were all in New York to help push it through Congress and on to the special ratifying conventions that the plan called for. Only eight days after the new constitution was presented to Congress, a vote was called. Of those who were present to vote, nearly a third had been delegates to the Constitutional Convention, and the momentum they gave to its passage through Congress was irresistible. Richard Henry Lee objected to this unseemly haste, which seemed to smack of stampeding the Congress before its members had had a chance to digest the proposal.

The resolution that sent the constitution along to the state legislatures, calling on the states to summon special ratifying conventions, opened with the words "Resolved unanimously." This was a nasty piece of trickery, said Lee, giving the impression that the Congress had some sort of unanimously positive feeling for the new plan; there was nothing unanimous about Congress's reaction to the constitution except their agreement to pass it on to the states.

What was possibly even a nastier piece of trickery was that the defenders of the constitution had taken to calling themselves federalists. In truth, "federalists" were people who believed in the federal form of government provided by the Articles of Confederation. Partisans of the constitution, who believed in a strong national government, ought honestly to have called themselves nationalists. But the designation federalist had a long and familiar tradition, and Americans loved it; so the pro-constitution forces absconded with the word, insisting that they meant they favored a strong and efficient federal government; and the true federalists were reduced to calling themselves antifederalists.

Jefferson, in Paris, was showered with copies of the constitution by Madison, Washington, Franklin, and others of his friends and colleagues. Elbridge Gerry managed to rush the first copy to him, with a few prejudicing remarks about it. Jefferson looked over the plan dispassionately and concluded that its lack of a bill of rights was a deep fault. He hoped, Jefferson wrote to Madison, with the sensibility of an Olympian, that "the first 9 conventions may receive, and the last 4 reject [the constitution]. The former will secure it finally, while the latter will oblige them to offer a declaration of rights in order to complete the union. We shall thus have all its good, and cure its principal defects."

Those who had spent the summer in the caldron of Philadelphia were not as detached as Jefferson. Even before the text of the constitution had reached the Congress in New York, Franklin had appeared before the Pennsylvania state legislature, and prodded one of his colleagues to read the document aloud to the Assembly.

The Assembly, as it happened, was in its closing days, getting ready to adjourn and to have its members stand for a new election. The framers of the constitution wanted the Assembly, before it adjourned, to set up elections to a ratifying convention. One of the framers proposed a motion to that effect.

Robert Whitehill, a backcountry man, whose farm lay out beyond the Susquehanna River near Harrisburg, rose on the floor of the Assembly. Whitehill had been one of the authors of the Pennsylvania constitution of 1776, which had provided for a one-house legislature, annual elections, and election of the president of the Supreme Executive Council by the legislature—a model democratic system, now about to be buried under the new federal constitution. Whitehill opposed the motion, charging its defenders with a lack of candor in trying to jam the constitution through before the people had had a chance to become acquainted with it.

But the friends of the framers held a majority in the Pennsylvania Assembly, and they insisted, by a margin of forty-three to nineteen, on bringing the issue of ratification to a vote on the floor that very afternoon. Then, just after taking that vote, they adjourned until four o'clock.

During the recess, Whitehill and the gathering band of opponents of the constitution, most of them western Pennsylvanians, supporters of the old radical

Pennsylvania constitution of '76, agreed on a strategy to stop the framers. The Assembly consisted of sixty-nine members; a quorum of forty-six was required for the Assembly to conduct business. Whitehill's antifederalists, by staying away from the afternoon session, could keep a quorum from appearing in the Assembly hall and so force an adjournment.

When the Assembly resumed that afternoon, a roll call showed only forty-four members present, and so the following morning, the Assembly dispatched the sergeant at arms to round up missing members. The sergeant at arms returned soon enough with the news that the missing members refused to attend the session. The Assembly adjourned, with the partisans of the constitution angered by Whitehill's ruse.

The next day the Assembly gathered for yet another session. Again a quorum was missing. Again the sergeant at arms was sent out to gather up the missing members. By this time, the resolution of the Congress in New York (which called for state legislatures to summon ratifying conventions) had arrived in Philadelphia, and the sergeant at arms went out with this resolution authoritatively in hand. He was backed up by a group of the framers' supporters, who went along with him, raising a ruckus as they careened from tavern to tavern, stirring up partisans on both sides.

Eventually, the little self-appointed posse came upon two of Whitehill's men ensconced in their lodgings. The resolution of Congress was read to the recalcitrant members. Still the members refused to budge. And so the unofficial posse swarmed into the rooms, took hold of the two Assembly members, and dragged them, protesting, back through the streets of Philadelphia and into the Assembly hall. There a large group of local artisans, always dependably hostile to country men, and especially to westerners, crowded around—shouting and mocking the out-of-towners, following them into the Assembly hall, jamming the doors, and blocking any chance of escape. The two westerners were unceremoniously shoved forward, their clothes torn, their faces, it was said, "white with rage." One of the westerners, keeping his mind clearly focused on the Whitehill strategy, offered to pay a fine for his absence, but the crowd laughed him down. And when he turned to make his escape, the crowd shouted out, "Stop him!"—and he was turned back into the room. With their quorum assembled, the Pennsylvania legislature duly voted—with only two votes against the motion—to set the first Tuesday in November as election day for delegates to the Pennsylvania ratifying convention.

The strong-arm tactics of the federalists aroused terrific passion, and although the federalists controlled most of the newspapers, the editor of Philadelphia's *Independent Gazetteer* took up the cudgels against the federalists and published a series of attacks written under the byline Centinel. According to Centinel, Pennsylvanians had "the peculiar felicity of living under the most perfect system of local government in the world"—now about to be replaced by "the supremacy of the lordly and profligate few." These few were attempting to stampede the people into accepting their new scheme by saying there was

·"no alternative between adoption and absolute ruin." This, said Centinel, was "the argument of tyrants." These conniving aristocrats tried to dignify their cause by dressing it up with the presence of Washington and Franklin. "I would be far from insinuating that the two illustrious personages alluded to, have not the welfare of their country at heart; but that the unsuspecting goodness and zeal of the one has been imposed upon, in a subject of which he must be necessarily inexperienced . . . and that the weakness and indecision attendant on old age has been practiced on in the other."

Centinel was joined by some others in criticizing the constitution—most notably by one of the very framers, Colonel George Mason, who published his list of objections in the *Pennsylvania Packet*. The story circulated widely that Mason had declared that he would sooner cut off his right hand than put his signature to the constitution.

This defection, among other goads, brought James Wilson out of his study and into the garden on the south side of the State House to address a public meeting. Public speaking was not Wilson's strong suit. His manner, his "lordly carriage," was so naturally offensive to most people that one federalist newspaper writer labored to explain that Wilson *had* to hold his head as he did in order to keep his spectacles from falling off his nose. But he spoke with his customary close reasoning, and his audience evidently listened closely.

The greatest, and most commonly heard, charge against the constitution, said Wilson, was that it lacked a bill of rights. But in the constitution, every right that was not specifically granted to the central government was reserved to the states. To have drawn up a list of particular rights would only have duplicated what was already in the state constitutions. Strictly speaking, Wilson's arguments were true: All rights not specifically given the federal government were reserved to the states and the citizens. But Wilson's opponents knew that reasoning of this sort was too abstract for comfort.

As for the omission of a provision for trial by jury in civil cases, said Wilson, the usages of the various states so differed as to make a uniform law impossible. As for the issue of a standing army, the power of direct taxation, and other matters, Wilson explained the reasoning of the Constitutional Convention in each case. His speech was superb; it only lacked an attempt to deal with the central complaint of the antifederalists—that the new constitution set a federal government above a state government that was, in Pennsylvania's case at least, more democratic. He tried to get around that difficult issue simply by tarring his opponents. "It is the nature of man," said Wilson, "to pursue his own interests in preference to the public good." And so he was not surprised that so many men opposed this new constitution, since it threatened to eliminate lucrative state offices which they currently held and otherwise affected their "schemes of wealth and consequence."

For their part, the antifederalists struck back at Wilson with the locally familiar charge that he "has always been strongly tainted with the spirit of *high aris-*

tocracy; he has never been known to join in a truly popular measure, and his talents have ever been devoted to the patrician interest."

And to that a federalist writer replied with a recipe for an "Antifederal Essay." The correct ingredients were these: "*Well-born,* nine times—*Aristocracy,* eighteen times— . . . *Negro slavery,* once mentioned—*Trial by Jury,* seven times—*Great Men,* six times repeated—MR. WILSON, forty times—and lastly, GEORGE MASON'S *Right Hand in a Cutting-Box,* nineteen times—put them all together, and dish them up at pleasure."

If the antifederalists tended toward exaggeration and violence in their diatribes, the federalists tended toward condescension and contempt in theirs. But since Philadelphia was a cosmopolitan, commercial port city—and so a federalist one—the defenders of the constitution had the clearest advantage in mob action. Roving bands of supporters of the new constitution roamed the streets, banging on doors and lobbing rocks through windows. They did little real damage, though they tried to spread as much fear as they could. When the antifederalists demanded the arrest of the disorderly gang that attacked one lodging place of their fellows, the city administration—a federalist lot—failed to find any of the unruly mob.

When at last elections were held for the ratifying convention, the antifederalists had managed to elect some colorful old country politicians to represent their cause—among them two native Irishmen, John Smilie, a former house carpenter; and William Findley, a weaver. Findley, a big fellow with shaggy hair and a genial, disrespectful manner, affected his own form of patrician dress. He had a fondness in particular for white beaver hats. He and his colleagues were wily politicians of long experience, deeply dedicated to frontier liberties and individualism, men far better able to cajole a crowd than James Wilson was; but their talents did not count for much. The federalists had outpolled the antifederalists in the election by a margin of two to one; and when the convention gathered on November 21, the federalists had forty-six delegates to the antifederalists' twenty-three. Men of both sides would grapple heroically with each other in debate; but when it came to voting, they would split exactly along federalist/antifederalist lines.

Unable to affect the outcome by persuasion, Whitehill resorted to parliamentary maneuvers—trying to get the convention to rearrange itself as a committee of the whole, a ruse calculated to delay the convention, to give the antifederalists time to rally opposition to the constitution. But Whitehill's motion—like all the other maneuvers of the antifederalists—was brought quickly to a vote, and voted down by a margin of two to one. Gradually, in one vote after another, the antifederalists were brought around grudgingly to the final vote—whether or not to ratify the constitution as a whole—and the state of Pennsylvania declared itself in favor of the constitution, forty-six to twenty-three.

The vote placed the crucial state of Pennsylvania in the column of supporters of the constitution—but at an enormous price. Having won by virtue of sheer power—and even of brute force—the federalists did much to damage their own cause across the country. If these were to be their consistent tactics, they might well anticipate defeat. A couple of weeks after the Pennsylvania ratifying convention, at a bonfire celebration of the new constitution, a gang of antifederalists came out of the dark armed with clubs and attacked James Wilson. Wilson fought back and was knocked to the ground, and he might have been done in had not an old soldier who was present thrown himself on top of Wilson to shield the convention's staunchest defender of popular suffrage from the blows of the people.

Yet if ratification in Pennsylvania was a bitter experience, several other states came along without any great battle. Indeed, the little states fell into line with surprising ease. After all the trouble they had caused at the Constitutional Convention, they proved now the most eager to put themselves under the protection of this strong new government. Delaware, with the support of John Dickinson and George Read, had actually preceded Pennsylvania in approving the constitution—thus, in the words of one of the Pennsylvania antifederalists, having "reaped the honor of having first surrendered the liberties of the people"—by a unanimous thirty to zero vote of its delegates to the ratifying convention. New Jersey's ratifying convention debated for a full week before voting unanimously in favor of the constitution—with [William] Paterson leading the way. In Maryland, the elections to the ratifying convention gave such a large margin to the federalists that they did not even bother debating. They simply sat back, listened to Luther Martin and his colleagues rail at them for four days, and then called for a vote. The vote went sixty-three to eleven in favor of the constitution. Georgia voted unanimously in favor. Connecticut came along with somewhat more thoughtfulness and ambivalence, voting in favor of ratification by 128 to forty.

Even so, as these federalist victories piled up, several key states of the Union—Massachusetts, Virginia, and New York—all of them crucial to the success of the new plan, had yet to be heard from. And each, in its way, was to prove very difficult. To assist the federalist cause in the resistant political atmosphere of New York, a series of essays commenced to appear in the newspapers, signed with the pen name Publius, that argued in favor of adopting the new constitution—essays that would come to be known collectively as *The Federalist*. It had been Hamilton's idea to turn out these essays, with which he hoped to overwhelm the New York opposition. And overwhelm the opposition he did, publishing eighty-five essays in all, one every two or three days, for a period of six months, essays that considered the proposed constitution from every angle of dispute, answered its opponents' objections, and explained the principles on which the constitution rested.

To help him write some of the essays in this rhetorical tour de force, Hamilton recruited Madison—who had, of course, been at the convention every day that summer, and knew the plan inside out—and John Jay, who had not been in

Philadelphia, but was a learned lawyer (who would become the first chief justice of the Supreme Court), and a man who shared Hamilton's admiration for the established order, for aristocracy if not monarchy.

The Federalist is, perhaps, not the best of all possible guides to just what the constitution is and is meant to be, since it was intended—to be altogether candid—as the text for a sales campaign. Moreover, it was written by one man (Hamilton) who was so opposed to the basic ideas of the constitution that he did not attend most of the sessions of the convention, who spoke rarely in the convention, and when he did speak, spoke most eloquently on behalf of aristocracy; by another (Jay) who was not at the convention at all and whose Anglophilia would have predisposed him to a far more aristocratic scheme than the one the conventioneers finally framed; and by a third (Madison) who had a view of a necessarily unfettered supremacy of the national government that had not been accepted by the other delegates. Under the circumstances, it cannot be surprising that *The Federalist* promotes a conception of the constitution that is, among other things, more aristocratic than the consensus of those who actually wrote the document.

Hamilton opened the series with an outline of the whole project, promising that the series would cover the necessity of the Union, the deficiencies of the Confederation, the need for an energetic government, and the ways in which the proposed constitution corresponded to republican principles. Jay followed with four essays on the need for a union to cope with foreign dangers and sectional disputes—arguing, among other things, that the breadth of interests in the new government would be so great as to inhibit men's natural proclivities to go to war; that, in this sense as well as in others, the extended republic would actually give rise to public virtue.

The essays took up issues of the military, of the separation of powers, of the house and senate, of the means of election, of the presidency, and of the judiciary—all of them issues that had been debated in the convention in detail. Several of Madison's essays constituted a neatened-up version of the notes on ancient and modern confederacies that he had used throughout the convention debates. One of Madison's most famous essays, *Federalist* Number 10, spoke of the way in which factions are formed—along economic lines—which he had gone into at some length during the convention: of how the poor need to be protected from the rich as well as the rich from the poor, and how all the citizens need to be protected from the depredations of whatever factions are formed.

Nothing in *The Federalist* would have been unfamiliar to a delegate to the Constitutional Convention (except the absence of sharply conflicting views). Here were the arguments—and the references to history, to renowned political philosophers, to the examples of England and Germany and ancient Greece and Rome, to more recent and common American experience—that had been heard in Philadelphia, here expressed in classically balanced and elegant language, with perfectly honed phrases, and pruned into a coherent, if not entirely representative, vision.

The Federalist was not without its critics. The antifederalists were particularly incensed that Publius alleged that they wanted several separate confederacies, which was simply not true. And one friendly observer, even as he praised *The Federalist,* said he could not understand why Publius had taken such pains to argue what seemed so evident, that a strong, efficient government was better "than the States disunited into distinct, independent governments, or separate confederacies." But General Washington pronounced himself pleased with the essays, saying he thought no other public presentation of the arguments in favor of the constitution was "so well calculated . . . to produce conviction on an unbiased mind." And Jefferson thought *The Federalist* was "the best commentary on the principles of government which ever was written."

The essays were reprinted in newspapers and magazines around the country, though not very widely reprinted: Twenty-two publications printed at least one of the essays, but only six journals printed six or more of them. Although they received wide circulation in book form, what was crucial about the writings of Publius was not that they were a great popular success but that they circulated among those men who were taking part in ratifying conventions across the country, and gave partisans of the constitution the best arguments they could use in favor of the new plan.

Such arguments were essential—and proved crucial—in the state of Massachusetts, whose ratifying convention of 350 members gathered on January 8, 1788, in Boston's Brattle Church, with a narrow but distinct majority opposed to the constitution.

The Massachusetts convention had among its delegates some of the famous old figures of the Revolution, including the radical democrat Sam Adams, and John Hancock, who was enormously popular and enormously powerful. Because Hancock was so sensitive to the ways the political breezes were blowing, he was able to side with the rich Boston merchants and with Daniel Shays at the same time.* (Hancock stayed away from the early sessions, claiming that his gout was too severely painful to let him leave home—holding back on purpose, his critics said, waiting until the outcome of the convention was certain so that he would be sure to be on the winning side.)

Unlike Pennsylvania, the ratifying convention that was assembled in Boston was not stacked with federalists; among the members of the convention were not only a fair sampling of farmers from the western parts of Massachusetts but even twenty-nine men who had fought with Shays.

"Sir," said the plainspeaking Samuel Thompson to the chairman of the convention, "gentlemen have said a great deal about the history of old times" in

---

* In 1786 and 1787, Shays led a revolt of fifteen hundred farmers in western Massachusetts to protest farm foreclosures. Shays's Rebellion stirred fears of domestic unrest and demonstrated the weakness of the new central government, which could not come up with funds to fight the rebels.

proving the superiority of this new constitution over the old democratic ways of New England. "I confess, I am not acquainted with such history—but I am, sir, acquainted with the history of my own country." And from that acquaintance, said Thompson, "I suspect my own heart, and I shall suspect our rulers." Too much power was granted to the distant new government, and without adequate restraints built in. He wondered at the great rush to push this constitution through to acceptance. "There are some parts of this constitution which I cannot digest: and, sir, shall we swallow a large bone for the sake of a little meat? Some say swallow the whole now, and pick out the bone afterwards. But I say, let us pick off the meat, and throw the bone away."

Massachusetts was a state full of enthusiasts for the tradition of the democratic town meeting and deeply suspicious of any republican idea of the delegation of authority to elected representatives. And opponents of the constitution filled the newspapers with attacks on "the hideous daemon of aristocracy . . . the NOBLE order of Cincinnatus, holders of public securities, bankers and lawyers, who were for having the people gulp down the gilded pill blindfolded."

The idea that a single central government, said another of the delegates, could efficiently and justly rule in every small town of such a vast continent was absurd. "You might as well attempt to rule Hell by prayer."

That the new plan called for senators to be elected for terms of six years was outrageous in the eyes of men who believed annual elections to be the most basic requirement of democracy. The senate was an aristocratical bunch, said one delegate, and the house was nothing but an "assistant aristocratical branch."

"Had I a voice like Jove," thundered Samuel Nason, a saddler and storekeeper from Maine,* "I would proclaim it throughout the world—and had I an arm like Jove I would hurl from the world those villains that would attempt to establish in our country a standing army! I wish, sir, that gentlemen of Boston would bring to their minds the fatal evening of the 5th of March, 1770, when by standing troops they lost five of their fellow-townsmen."

"These lawyers," said Amos Singletary, a self-taught farmer from Worcester County who had sat in the state legislature for years, "and men of learning, and moneyed men that talk so finely, and gloss over matters so smoothly, to make us poor illiterate people swallow down the pill, expect to get into Congress themselves. They expect to be the managers of the Constitution, and get all the power and all the money into their own hands. And then they will swallow up us little fellows."

This remark by Singletary drew forth at last a reply from another fellow farmer, Jonathan Smith, a Berkshireman. "Mr. President," said Smith, "I am a plain man, and get my living by the plough. I am not used to speak in public, but I beg your leave to say a few words to my brother ploughjoggers in this house. I have lived in a part of the country where I have known the worth of

---

* Maine was part of Massachusetts until it became a separate state in 1820.

good government, by the want of it. There was a black cloud that rose in the east last winter [Smith did not need to mention Shays by name], and spread over the west."

At this, another delegate rose and challenged Smith to say what he meant by the east.

"I mean, sir, the county of Bristol," said Smith. "The cloud rose there and burst upon us, and produced a dreadful effect. It brought on a state of anarchy that led to tyranny. I say, it brought anarchy. People that used to live peaceably, and were before good neighbors, got distracted, and took up arms against government."

Here another delegate rose angrily and asked what this had to do with the constitution. Sam Adams intervened, and asked that the house let the gentleman "go on in his own way."

". . . People, I say, took up arms, and then, if you went to speak to them, you had the musket of death presented to your breast. They would rob you of your property, threaten to burn your houses; oblige you to be on your guard night and day; alarms spread from town to town; families were broke up; the tender mother would cry, O, my son is among them! . . . Then we should hear of an action, and the poor prisoners were set in the front, to be killed by their own friends. . . . Our distress was so great that we should have been glad to snatch at anything that looked like a government."

When Smith saw this new constitution, "I found that it was a cure for these disorders . . . I got a copy of it and read it over and over. I had been a member of the convention to form our own state constitution, and had learnt something of the checks and balances of power, and I found them all here. I did not go to any lawyer to ask his opinion—we have no lawyer in our town, and we do well enough without. I formed my own opinion, and was pleased with this constitution. My honorable old daddy there [gesturing to Amos Singletary] won't think that I expect to be a congressman and swallow up the liberties of the people. I never had any post, nor do I want one. But I don't think the worse of the constitution because lawyers and men of learning and monied men are fond of it."

While the debates went along in this way, freer than the debates had been in Pennsylvania, and more down-to-earth, the federalists worked behind the scenes to do all they could, short of the strong-arm tactics their colleagues had used in Pennsylvania, to influence the outcome. They were not having an easy time of it. Madison, who kept his eye on the progress of the constitution through each of the state ratifying conventions, wrote to Washington that the news from Massachusetts "begins to be very ominous."

The most crucial piece of politicking the federalists labored to bring off was to recruit John Hancock to their side, and they finally succeeded at this with the aid of Sam Adams. At first Adams had been opposed to the constitution. "I stumble at the threshold," he wrote to Richard Henry Lee. "I meet with a national government instead of a federal union of sovereign states." Adams was helped across the threshold by a shrewd plan for compromise. The constitution had been presented to Massachusetts, as to the other states, in a take-it-or-leave-it fashion. The states were not to be allowed to set any conditions to their acceptance of the constitution; they must ratify it exactly as it stood, or turn it down. But as it began to appear that the antifederalists might defeat the constitution altogether, a group of federalists got together with Adams and came up with what they called a Conciliatory Proposition—a plan to mollify the anxieties of the antifederalists, and of Adams and others. Their notion was that the constitution ought to be ratified, but with a number of "suggestions" for amendments attached to it. The suggestions would not be demands or conditions; they would simply be Massachusetts' first order of business for the new government to take up.

The Massachusetts men came up with a list of nine amendments, a list of fairly mundane concerns, including a limitation on the federal power of taxation, a limitation on federal power to govern elections, and a prohibition against Congress establishing a "company of merchants with exclusive advantages of commerce." The items were not matters of great political principle; they were not a bill of rights. They were reflections of local concerns. But they were, also, a precedent: an insistence that Massachusetts would not accept a take-it-or-leave-it demand on the constitution. Massachusetts would simply go ahead and begin the process of amending the constitution. Thus, Adams and his colleagues not only broke the resistance of the Massachusetts convention to the constitution, they also provided an example for the states that would come after Massachusetts to present similar lists of suggestions. It was this example that led quickly to the Bill of Rights (which was ratified by the requisite number of states by December 5, 1791).

The group had Theophilus Parsons, a prominent Boston attorney, draw up a speech to present the Conciliatory Proposition to the convention, and then a little delegation of them called on John Hancock at his commodious home on Beacon Hill. They found Hancock languishing, his legs propped up and wrapped in flannel. The delegation told Hancock that the convention had reached the moment of decision, and that he could turn it in favor of the constitution. They told him, too, that according to the gossip, if he did join their cause he could expect their support for the next gubernatorial election in Massachusetts. Even more, they told him that it looked as though Virginia might not ratify the constitution. And if Virginia did not ratify, then Hancock would be the "only fair candidate for President" of the new United States. With that, Hancock's gout began to improve. He was carried like a hero into the convention, his legs still wrapped in flannel, and he delivered Theophilus Parsons's speech as though he had written it himself. The effect was wonderful. The convention was transformed.

To be sure, some of the antifederalists pointed out that a list of suggestions for amendments would have no binding effect. Such a set of proposals might make the men of Massachusetts feel better, but the objectionable system would remain exactly as it was. The hopes of the antifederalists would be defeated, and there would be no chance in the future to revive them.

Yet, after a few days of debate, minds began gradually to change. The question turned, in effect, on whether the process for amending the constitution seemed fair and workable, or, at least, better than the process for amending the Articles; if it did, then there seemed much less reason to oppose the constitution. Finally, a young antifederalist lawyer from Andover named William Symmes announced his change of position. He felt in his own mind, he said, that what he was doing was right. He knew that his constituents did not agree with him, but he hoped they would forgive him for what he was about to do. (As it turned out, his constituents never did see things Symmes's way; in fact, when he got back home, his neighbors made life so unpleasant for him that he had to move out of Andover.) With Symmes's change of mind, others followed.

Adams almost lost the momentum the federalists had acquired when he proposed a series of amendments to guarantee freedom of the press and the rights of conscience, to prohibit standing armies and unreasonable search and seizure. The effect of Adams's proposals was to throw the convention into a panic: If Adams thought such guarantees were necessary, then perhaps the new government did threaten to deprive the citizens of the states of their basic rights. And so Adams withdrew his motion.

In the end, when the final vote was called, the constitution was approved by a slim margin of 19 votes, 187 to 168. But then a most remarkable thing occurred. In place of the bitterness that had marked the conclusion of the Pennsylvania ratifying convention, a good deal of warm feeling was expressed in Brattle Church. Abraham White of Bristol County declared that he had opposed the constitution with all his will; but now, since a majority had decided in its favor, he would return home and work to persuade his constituents to live happily under it. Where the Pennsylvania convention had left bitterness in its wake, the Massachusetts convention left a sense—and a model for others to follow—of an agreement reached by those unique guarantors of legitimacy, the free exercise of speech and the ballot.

By June 2, when the Virginia delegates assembled at last in Richmond for their ratifying convention, eight states had voted in favor of the constitution. Only one more was needed, and it appeared that the Virginia vote could well be that one. But the Virginia delegates felt their vote was more important than simply the clinching one: Whether it was strictly true or not, the Virginians believed that there would be no Union at all without their own state, which had taken the lead in so much of the history of America, not to mention the constitution itself.

To be sure, the Virginians assembled a ratifying convention of some of the most illustrious men in the Union. Among the defenders of the constitution were Madison; George Wythe (who had had to leave the Philadelphia convention to attend to his sick wife); John Marshall (who would be chief justice of the

Supreme Court, and was at the moment an intense young man of thirty-three)*;
George Nicholas (a famous orator at the time, a rotund man whom a local cari-
caturist immortalized as a plum pudding with little legs); Judge Edmund Pen-
dleton (chosen as the presiding officer of the convention, a commanding man
whose presence was made even more riveting by the fact that he got about on
crutches because he had injured a hip, and so rose to speak with elaborate,
slow dignity). To the annoyance of Richard Henry Lee, his cousin Light Horse
Harry Lee was to be found among the federalists too. And of course, the presence of General Washington, though he himself stayed carefully aloof at Mount
Vernon, was felt in the hall on the side of the federalists.

Among the antifederalists were Colonel Mason (dressed most severely in
black silk), James Monroe (at the moment an obscure young man of thirty),
Benjamin Harrison (the father of President William Henry Harrison), John Tyler
(the father of another president), and Richard Henry Lee. In the back of the hall
were fourteen gun-toting delegates from frontier Kentucky (a territory still in
the possession of Virginia).

The antifederalist forces were led by that extraordinary speechmaker Patrick
Henry. Tall and stoop-shouldered, the practiced old orator could get so wound
up in the heat of debate that he would take to twirling his ill-fitting brown wig
around on his head as he laid about him with rhetorical flourishes. No one was
his equal for sheer thespian dazzle. He had, it was said, the powers of Shakespeare and Garrick† combined—or as Madison complained, Henry could demolish, merely with a pause or a shake of the head, an hour's worth of carefully
constructed debate before he had even begun to speak. In Virginia, the antifederalists were called Henryites.

By contrast, Madison was his usual retiring self. So small he could barely be
seen by the spectators, so soft-spoken he could often not be heard, he fell ill
finally, in the midst of these exhausting debates, as he had in Philadelphia. It
is a wonder that he was able, after all these interminable months of struggle for
his cherished plan, to revive; but he did bounce back after several days, and
took up the debate again—and even showed some sly sense of theatrics of his
own. When he rose to speak, he would hold his hat in his hand (his painstakingly prepared notes were concealed inside his hat) and speak modestly, as
though some little thought had just occurred to him—which he would then
convey with his customary precise logic.

Patrick Henry opened the debate in Virginia by inquiring what right had the
men who wrote the constitution to begin with the words *We the people?* "My
political curiosity, exclusive of my anxious solicitude for the public welfare,
leads me to ask, who authorized them to speak the language of *We the people,*
instead of, *We the states?* States are the characteristics and the soul of a confederation. If the states be not the agents of this compact, it must be one great con-

---

* See Selections 2.1 and 6.1 on the significance of Marshall's tenure as chief justice.
† David Garrick was an eighteenth-century English actor.

solidated national government, of the people of all the states. . . . The people gave them no power to use their name. . . . You must, therefore, forgive the solicitation of one unworthy member, to know what danger could have arisen under the present confederation, and what are the causes of this proposal to change our government."

Men spoke of dreadful unrest and dangers in the future, but had there been a single instance of such unrest in Virginia? To Henry and his followers, the Madisonian cure far exceeded the disease. If some difficulties had arisen among the states, then the powers of Congress to regulate trade needed to be strengthened, and the state governments needed to be given new vigor; but surely there was no need to surrender vast powers of taxation to a central government, to organize a court system that would cause the state courts to be swallowed up by the federal courts, to establish a standing army, to create a chief executive who would enslave America, to destroy the states, which were the bastions of liberty.

The constitution, said Henry, was as "radical" a document as the resolution "which separated us from Great Britain. . . . The rights of conscience, trial by jury, liberty of the press, all your communities and franchises, all pretensions to human rights and privileges, are rendered insecure, if not lost, by this change. . . . Is this tame relinquishment of rights worthy of freemen? . . . It is said that eight states have adopted this plan. I declare that if twelve states and a half had adopted it, I would with manly firmness, and in spite of an erring world, reject it. . . . Liberty, greatest of all earthly blessings—give us that precious jewel, and you may take everything else! But I am fearful I have lived long enough to become an old fashioned fellow.

"Whither," asked Henry, "is the spirit of America gone? Whither is the genius of America fled? . . . We drew the spirit of liberty from our British ancestors. But now, Sir, the American spirit, assisted by the ropes and chains of consolidation, is about to convert this country into a powerful and mighty empire. . . . There can be no checks, no real balances, in this government. What can avail your specious, imaginary balances, your rope-dancing, chain-rattling, ridiculous ideal checks and contrivances?"

(Here, it was said—such was the power of Henry to conjure—a delegate "involuntarily felt his wrists to assure himself that the fetters were not already pressing his flesh.")

The Henryites did well in the debates; their arguments were moving and impressive as they returned again and again to the theme that liberty and democracy would, under this new constitution, be sacrificed to the juggernaut of nationalism and expansive imperialism. Whether they spoke of taxation or courts or the powers of the presidency, their theme was always the same: The government of Virginia was small, responsive, free, and good; and there was no need to sacrifice it to a vision of a powerful nationalism. "Look at the use which has been made in all parts of the world of that human thing called power. Look at the predominant threat of dominion which has invariably and uni-

formly prompted rulers to abuse their power. . . . I conjure you to remember
. . . that when you give power, you know not what you give. . . . The experience of the world teaches me the jeopardy of giving enormous power."

Yet from the very beginning, the Henryites were undermined by a position
that Edmund Randolph took in the debate. Randolph had switched his position
again since the convention. No longer opposed to the Madisonians, he favored
the constitution now—and the precise way in which he expressed his approval
was particularly damaging to the Henryites. He had, he said, from the very first,
liked the constitution drawn up by the Philadelphia convention, providing it
could be improved, by the adoption of certain amendments, before it was ratified. It seemed to him that it was essential to make these amendments before
the constitution was ratified. Now, however, he had come to realize that this
procedure would cause dangerous delay in adopting a new form of government, that the delay would be such that the very survival of the Union would
be jeopardized. That, said Randolph, was out of the question. He would rather,
he said (in a rhetorical threat that was becoming altogether common), "assent
to the lopping of [his right arm] before I assent to the dissolution of the union."
Now Massachusetts had come up with a different means of proceeding—to propose amendments to be adopted at a later date—and Randolph liked this idea.
It was a way of leaving the constitution open to improvement by way of a perfectly acceptable voting procedure. If one trusted the way the constitution was
to be thus subject to the collective will of the people, there was nothing left to
oppose. Given the choice between insisting on "previous amendments"—those
insisted upon before the states agreed to ratify—and risking the fate of the
Union, or settling for the Massachusetts example of "subsequent amendments"—those made in the future, after all the states had ratified—Randolph
did not hesitate in taking the Massachusetts example.

Thus, Randolph set the terms of the debate: Delegates were given the choice
not so much whether or not they would accept the constitution, but whether
or not they would insist on previous amendments or settle for subsequent
amendments. The antifederalists were forced to argue for previous amendments; the federalists opted for subsequent amendments—and as the debate
wore on from day to day, the antifederalists came more and more to seem like
mere obstructionists, who would not trust the democratic process of the future.
And so it was the vacillating Randolph who, perhaps more than anyone else,
finally tipped the balance toward ratification.

It can hardly be surprising that the Henryites were furious with Randolph.
Henry himself turned to Randolph at one point in the debate and said: "That
honorable member will not accuse me of want of candor when I cast in my
mind what he has given to the public"—this in reference to a letter Randolph
had written some time before to the Virginia legislature to explain why he had
not signed the constitution—"and compare it to what has happened since."
What was Henry about to do? Under the code of honor that held sway in the
eighteenth century, he could not accuse Randolph of dishonesty, of having

been bribed, of having been offered high office in the new government in trade for his support—at least not directly. "It seems to me very strange and unaccountable that that which was the object of his execration, should now receive his encomiums. Something extraordinary must have operated so great a change in his opinions."

Randolph had no doubt what Henry meant, and he rose with his temper flaring. "I disdain his aspersions," said Randolph to the convention, "and his insinuations. His asperity is warranted by no principle of parliamentary decency, nor compatible with the least shadow of friendship: and if our friendship must fall—let it fall, like Lucifer, never to rise again." Such words could not pass without consequences. That night Henry's second called on Randolph to arrange the particulars of a duel. But friends of the two men stepped in, mollified tempers, and the matter was settled, as it was said, "without a resort to the field."

Through all this, as the two sides counted and re-counted their delegate strength—and estimated that a change of four or five votes, or three votes, or eight votes, would decide the outcome—Madison rehearsed his familiar arguments: about the weakness of confederacies as seen in ancient examples, about the need for direct taxation in place of the old system of requisitions, about the need to treat with foreign nations as a united country.

And Henry spoke of how few votes had decided the issue in Massachusetts, how great was the opposition to the constitution in Pennsylvania, how uncertain the outcome might be in New York. Enormous numbers of people opposed this constitution; there was no reason to have it rushed through to adoption, without amendments, in the face of such clear and substantial opposition.

"He tells you," Henry said of Madison, "of important blessings which he imagines will result to us and mankind in general, from the adoption of this system. I see the awful immensity of the dangers with which it is pregnant. I see it. I feel it." As Henry went on speaking, conjuring up forebodings of the future, of the powerful government they were about to set above themselves, of the dangers to liberty and self-government that they had fought so hard to secure in the war of the revolution, of the momentousness of the decision about to be made in such haste, storm clouds gathered over the convention hall. Darkness fell, and, at last, a storm broke with terrific thunder and lightning—as though the heavens confirmed Henry's worst forebodings—and the convention had to adjourn for the day.

It was the next day that a final vote was called. To turn the vote in their favor, the federalists accepted every suggestion the Henryites put forth for subsequent amendments. The list that Henry and Mason and their colleagues prepared contained a full bill of rights and twenty other amendments calculated to trim the power of the new national government, to preserve the states, to diminish the powers of the executive and of the Congress and of the judiciary, and to preserve local rule against the tendencies of empire. The objections of the localists were, in large measure, answered.

The vote went in favor of the constitution, by a margin of eighty-nine to seventy-nine—a close vote, but a decisive victory for the federalists. The Virginians imagined that they had been the ninth, and therefore clinching, state to ratify. They found, in fact, when news arrived a few days later, that New Hampshire had beaten them to it by several days. Virginia was the tenth state to ratify.

Under the circumstances, reluctant New York had little choice but to join the Union. Hamilton had maneuvered to hold the vote in New York until after news of the Virginia vote arrived. Thus, faced with union or ostracism, New York chose union. That, far more than the arguments of *The Federalist,* decided the issue for New Yorkers, as it had, in some degree, for many of those who finally went along with the momentum of the new plan. New York was the eleventh state to ratify. North Carolina did not come along until November of 1789. Rhode Island, the thirteenth state, acquiesced to the inevitable, finally, in 1790, by a stubborn vote of thirty-four to thirty-two, and the United States were joined together in a common rule of law. . . .

Epilogue

One understands why the Civil War came a mere seventy years after ratification. The differences among the various states were too great, and the answers to central governmental questions too hazy, to avoid serious disputes. In the end, the unresolved matter of the power of the central government as opposed to the power of the state governments, combined with the vastly different economies and lifestyles of the urban northern and slaveholding southern states, was too much for the Constitution to handle peacefully.

This description of the ratification process helps explain why so few amendments have been added to the Constitution. Apparently the framers designed this difficult ratification process to prevent the Constitution from being amended so many times that it would have, in the words of Chief Justice Marshall, "the prolixity [wordiness] of a legal code."

The Hour of the Founders

Walter Karp

One of the unresolved concerns of the framers of the Constitution was the prospect that they would be replacing the hated king of England with a new king in the form of an American president. For this reason they created the system of "checks and balances," whereby the president's authority was limited by the separate powers of the legislative and judicial branches. Should that system fail, the Constitution provided for the possible removal of the chief executive through an impeachment process. A president would be impeached (indicted) by the House and tried in the Senate; the chief justice of the United States would preside over the trial. Still, there were those who feared that this removal process was too cumbersome to prevent an ambitious and unchecked president from warping and perhaps destroying the democratic system.

Walter Karp describes a time when the authority of the Constitution was tested. President Nixon was accused of violating his constitutional duties by helping to obstruct the investigation of the 1972 break-in of the Democratic National Committee headquarters in Washington's Watergate Hotel—a burglary whose plan was traced to members of the administration. Nixon's lawyers argued that his administration had not broken any laws, that in the public interest a president is allowed latitude in carrying out policy. Nixon's defenders contended that his staffers had done nothing that previous administrations had not done. Nixon's opponents argued that the Watergate break-in was just one aspect of a major effort to subvert the Constitution—including the use of the FBI, IRS, and CIA against opponents of the administration and the invasion of a neutral nation, Cambodia, in the course of the Vietnam War.

Karp shows not only why the nation was transfixed watching the Senate Watergate hearings on television in the summer of 1974, but also how the episode still arouses passion in people today. Perhaps we will never

From Walter Karp, "The Hour of the Founders," *American Heritage*, June/July 1984. Reprinted with permission from *American Heritage*, Volume 35, Number 4. Copyright 1984 by American Heritage, a Division of Forbes, Inc.

know, as Senator Howard Baker asked so pointedly, "What did the president know, and when did he know it?" but we do know that the system devised by the founders works, and that it can work again if necessary.

ARCHIBALD COX   Special prosecutor for the Watergate investigation.

JOHN DOAR, ALBERT JENNER   Counsel for the House Judiciary Committee.

SAM ERVIN   Chair of the Senate Watergate Committee.

RICHARD NIXON   President of the United States, 1969–1974.

PETER RODINO   Chair of the House Judiciary Committee.

▶ [In August 1974] the thirty-seventh President of the United States, facing imminent impeachment, resigned his high office and passed out of our lives. "The system worked," the nation exclaimed, heaving a sigh of relief. What had brought that relief was the happy extinction of the prolonged fear that the "system" might not work at all. But what was it that had inspired such fears? When I asked myself that question recently, I found I could scarcely remember. Although I had followed the Watergate crisis with minute attention, it had grown vague and formless in my mind, like a nightmare recollected in sunshine. It was not until I began working my way through back copies of the *New York Times* that I was able to remember clearly why I used to read my morning paper with forebodings for the country's future.

The Watergate crisis had begun in June 1972 as a "third-rate burglary" of the Democratic National Committee headquarters in Washington's Watergate building complex. By late March 1973 the burglary and subsequent efforts to obstruct its investigation had been laid at the door of the White House. By late June, Americans were asking themselves whether their President had or had not ordered the payment of "hush money" to silence a Watergate burglar. Investigated by a special Senate committee headed by Sam Ervin of North Carolina, the scandal continued to deepen and ramify during the summer of 1973. By March 1974 the third-rate burglary of 1972 had grown into an unprecedented constitutional crisis.

By then it was clear beyond doubt that President Richard M. Nixon stood at the center of a junto of henchmen without parallel in our history. One of Nixon's attorneys general, John Mitchell, was indicted for obstructing justice in Washington and for impeding a Securities and Exchange Commission investigation in New York. Another, Richard Kleindienst, had criminally misled the Senate Judiciary Committee in the President's interest. The acting director of the Federal Bureau of Investigation, L. Patrick Gray, had burned incriminating

White House documents at the behest of a presidential aide. Bob Haldeman, the President's chief of staff, John Ehrlichman, the President's chief domestic adviser, and Charles Colson, the President's special counsel, all had been indicted for obstructing justice in the investigation of the Watergate burglary. John Dean, the President's legal counsel and chief accuser, had already pleaded guilty to the same charge. Dwight Chapin, the President's appointments secretary, faced trial for lying to a grand jury about political sabotage carried out during the 1972 elections. Ehrlichman and two other White House aides were under indictment for conspiring to break into a psychiatrist's office and steal confidential information about one of his former patients, Daniel Ellsberg.* By March 1974 some twenty-eight presidential aides or election officials had been indicted for crimes carried out in the President's interest. Never before in American history had a President so signally failed to fulfill his constitutional duty to "take care that the laws be faithfully executed."

It also had been clear for many months that the thirty-seventh President of the United States did not feel bound by his constitutional duties. He insisted that the requirements of national security, as he and he alone saw fit to define it, released him from the most fundamental legal and constitutional constraints. In the name of "national security," the President had created a secret band of private detectives, paid with private funds, to carry out political espionage at the urging of the White House. In the name of "national security," the President had approved the warrantless wiretapping of news reporters. In the name of "national security," he had approved a secret plan for massive, illegal surveillance of American citizens. He had encouraged his aides' efforts to use the Internal Revenue Service to harass political "enemies"—prominent Americans who endangered "national security" by publicly criticizing the President's Vietnam War policies.

The framers of the Constitution had provided one and only one remedy for such lawless abuse of power: impeachment in the House of Representatives and trial in the Senate for "high Crimes and Misdemeanors." There was absolutely no alternative. If Congress had not held President Nixon accountable for lawless conduct of his office, then Congress would have condoned a lawless Presidency. If Congress had not struck from the President's hands the despot's cudgel of "national security," then Congress would have condoned a despotic Presidency.

Looking through the back issues of the *New York Times,* I recollected in a flood of ten-year-old memories what it was that had filled me with such foreboding. It was the reluctance of Congress to act. I felt anew my fury when mem-

---

* In 1971 Ellsberg, who worked in the Office of International Security Affairs in the Pentagon, gave classified documents intended to discredit the Vietnam War to the *New York Times* and the *Washington Post.* The Pentagon Papers became the subject of an intense freedom-of-the-press debate (in *New York Times* v. *United States,* the Supreme Court allowed the documents to be published), and Ellsberg became the target of CIA wiretapping and burglary.

bers of Congress pretended that nobody really cared about Watergate except the "media" and the "Nixon-haters." The real folks "back home," they said, cared only about inflation and the gasoline shortage. I remembered the exasperating actions of leading Democrats, such as a certain Senate leader who went around telling the country that President Nixon could not be impeached because in America a person was presumed innocent until proven guilty. Surely the senator knew that impeachment was not a verdict of guilt but a formal accusation made in the House leading to trial in the Senate. Why was he muddying the waters, I wondered, if not to protect the President?

It had taken one of the most outrageous episodes in the history of the Presidency to compel Congress to make even a pretense of action.

Back on July 16, 1973, a former White House aide named Alexander Butterfield had told the Ervin committee that President Nixon secretly tape-recorded his most intimate political conversations. On two solemn occasions that spring the President had sworn to the American people that he knew nothing of the Watergate cover-up until his counsel John Dean had told him about it on March 21, 1973. From that day forward, Nixon had said, "I began intensive new inquiries into this whole matter." Now we learned that the President had kept evidence secret that would exonerate him completely—if he were telling the truth. Worse yet, he wanted it kept secret. Before Butterfield had revealed the existence of the tapes, the President had grandly announced that "executive privilege will not be invoked as to any testimony [by my aides] concerning possible criminal conduct, in the matters under investigation. I want the public to learn the truth about Watergate. . . ." After the existence of the tapes was revealed, however, the President showed the most ferocious resistance to disclosing the "truth about Watergate." He now claimed that executive privilege—hitherto a somewhat shadowy presidential prerogative—gave a President "absolute power" to withhold any taped conversation he chose, even those urgently needed in the ongoing criminal investigation then being conducted by a special Watergate prosecutor. Nixon even claimed, through his lawyers, that the judicial branch of the federal government was "absolutely without power to reweigh that choice or to make a different resolution of it."

In the U.S. Court of Appeals the special prosecutor, a Harvard Law School professor named Archibald Cox, called the President's claim "intolerable." Millions of Americans found it infuriating. The court found it groundless. On October 12, 1973, it ordered the President to surrender nine taped conversations that Cox had been fighting to obtain for nearly three months.

Determined to evade the court order, the President on October 19 announced that he had devised a "compromise." Instead of handing over the recorded conversations to the court, he would submit only edited summaries. To verify their truthfulness, the President would allow Sen. John Stennis of Mississippi to listen to the tapes. As an independent verifier, the elderly senator was distinguished by his devotion to the President's own overblown conception of a "strong" Presidency. When Nixon had ordered the secret bombing of Cambodia, he had vouchsafed the fact to Senator Stennis, who thought that concealing the President's secret war from his fellow senators was a higher duty than preserving the Senate's constitutional role in the formation of United States foreign policy.

On Saturday afternoon, October 20, I and millions of other Americans sat by our television sets while the special prosecutor explained why he could not accept "what seems to me to be non-compliance with the court's order." Then the President flashed the dagger sheathed within his "compromise." At 8:31 P.M. television viewers across the country learned that he had fired the special prosecutor; that attorney general Elliot Richardson had resigned rather than issue that order to Cox; that the deputy attorney general, William Ruckelshaus, also had refused to do so and had been fired for refusing; that it was a third acting attorney general who had finally issued the order.* With trembling voices, television newscasters reported that the President had abolished the office of special prosecutor and that the FBI was standing guard over its files. Never before in our history had a President, setting law at defiance, made our government seem so tawdry and gimcrack. "It's like living in a banana republic," a friend of mine remarked.

Now the question before the country was clear. "Whether ours shall continue to be a government of laws and not of men," the ex-special prosecutor said that evening, "is now for the Congress and ultimately the American people to decide."

Within ten days of the "Saturday night massacre," one million letters and telegrams rained down on Congress, almost every one of them demanding the President's impeachment. But congressional leaders dragged their feet. The House Judiciary Committee would begin an inquiry into *whether* to begin an inquiry into possible grounds for recommending impeachment to the House. With the obvious intent, it seemed to me, of waiting until the impeachment fervor had abated, the Democratic-controlled committee would consider whether to consider making a recommendation about making an accusation.

Republicans hoped to avoid upholding the rule of law by persuading the President to resign. This attempt to supply a lawless remedy for lawless power earned Republicans a memorable rebuke from one of the most venerated members of their party: eighty-one-year-old Sen. George Aiken of Vermont. The demand for Nixon's resignation, he said, "suggests that many prominent Americans, who ought to know better, find the task of holding a President accountable as just too difficult. . . . To ask the President now to resign and thus relieve Congress of its clear congressional duty amounts to a declaration of incompetence on the part of Congress."

The system was manifestly not working. But neither was the President's defense. On national television Nixon bitterly assailed the press for its "outra-

---

* The acting attorney general who carried out the firing was Solicitor General Robert Bork, later a controversial Supreme Court nominee. (See Selection 8.3, "Battle for Justice.")

geous, vicious, distorted" reporting, but the popular outrage convinced him, nonetheless, to surrender the nine tapes to the court. Almost at once the White House tapes began their singular career of encompassing the President's ruin. On October 31 the White House disclosed that two of the taped conversations were missing, including one between the President and his campaign manager, John Mitchell, which had taken place the day after Nixon returned from a Florida vacation and three days after the Watergate break-in. Three weeks later the tapes dealt Nixon a more potent blow. There was an eighteen-and-a-half-minute gap, the White House announced, in a taped conversation between the President and Haldeman, which had also taken place the day after he returned from Florida. The White House suggested first that the President's secretary, Rose Mary Woods, had accidentally erased part of the tape while transcribing it. When the loyal Miss Woods could not demonstrate in court how she could have pressed the "erase" button unwittingly for eighteen straight minutes, the White House attributed the gap to "some sinister force." On January 15, 1974, court-appointed experts provided a more humdrum explanation. The gap had been produced by at least five manual erasures. Someone in the White House had deliberately destroyed evidence that might have proved that President Nixon knew of the Watergate cover-up from the start.

At this point the Judiciary Committee was in its third month of considering whether to consider. But by now there was scarcely an American who did not think the President guilty, and on February 6, 1974, the House voted 410 to 4 to authorize the Judiciary Committee to begin investigating possible grounds for impeaching the President of the United States. It had taken ten consecutive months of the most damning revelations of criminal misconduct, a titanic outburst of public indignation, and an unbroken record of presidential deceit, defiance, and evasion in order to compel Congress to take its first real step. That long record of immobility and feigned indifference boded ill for the future.

The White House knew how to exploit congressional reluctance. One tactic involved a highly technical but momentous question: What constituted an impeachable offense? On February 21 the staff of the Judiciary Committee had issued a report. Led by two distinguished attorneys, John Doar, a fifty-two-year-old Wisconsin Independent, and Albert Jenner, a sixty-seven-year-old Chicago Republican, the staff had taken the broad view of impeachment for which Hamilton and Madison had contended in the *Federalist* papers. Despite the constitutional phrase "high Crimes and Misdemeanors," the staff report had argued that an impeachable offense did not have to be a crime. "Some of the most grievous offenses against our Constitutional form of government may not entail violations of the criminal law."

The White House launched a powerful counterattack. At a news conference on February 25, the President contended that only proven criminal misconduct supplied grounds for impeachment. On February 28, the White House drove home his point with a tightly argued legal paper: If a President could be impeached for anything other than a crime of "a very serious nature," it would expose the Presidency to "political impeachments."

The argument was plausible. But if Congress accepted it, the Watergate crisis could only end in disaster. Men of great power do not commit crimes. They procure crimes without having to issue incriminating orders. A word to the servile suffices. "Who will free me from this turbulent priest," asked Henry II, and four of his barons bashed in the skull of Thomas à Becket. The ease with which the powerful can arrange "deniability," to use the Watergate catchword, was one reason the criminal standard was so dangerous to liberty. Instead of having to take care that the laws be faithfully executed, a President, under that standard, would only have to take care to insulate himself from the criminal activities of his agents. Moreover, the standard could not reach the most dangerous offenses. There is no crime in the statute books called "attempted tyranny."

Yet the White House campaign to narrow the definition of impeachment met with immediate success. In March one of the members of the House of Representatives said that before voting to impeach Nixon, he would "want to know beyond a reasonable doubt that he was directly involved in the commission of a crime." To impeach the President for the grave abuse of his powers, lawmakers said, would be politically impossible. On the Judiciary Committee itself the senior Republican, Edward Hutchinson of Michigan, disavowed the staff's view of impeachment and adopted the President's. Until the final days of the crisis, the criminal definition of impeachment was to hang over the country's fate like the sword of Damocles.

The criminal standard buttressed the President's larger thesis: In defending himself he was fighting to protect the "Presidency" from sinister forces trying to "weaken" it. On March 12 the President's lawyer, James D. St. Clair, sounded this theme when he declared that he did not represent the President "individually" but rather the "office of the Presidency." There was even a National Citizens Committee for Fairness to the Presidency. It was America's global leadership, Nixon insisted, that made a "strong" Presidency so essential. Regardless of the opinion of some members of the Judiciary Committee, Nixon told a joint session of Congress, he would do nothing that "impairs the ability of the Presidents of the future to make the great decisions that are so essential to this nation and the world." . . .

Fortunately for constitutional government, however, Nixon's conception of a strong Presidency included one prerogative whose exercise was in itself an impeachable offense. Throughout the month of March the President insisted that the need for "confidentiality" allowed him to withhold forty-two tapes that the Judiciary Committee had asked of him. Nixon was claiming the right to limit the constitutional power of Congress to inquire into his impeachment. This was more than Republicans on the committee could afford to tolerate.

"Ambition must be made to counteract ambition," Madison had written in *The Federalist*. On April 11 the Judiciary Committee voted 33 to 3 to subpoena the forty-two tapes, the first subpoena ever issued to a President by a committee of the House. Ambition, at last, was counteracting ambition. This set the stage for one of the most lurid moments in the entire Watergate crisis.

As the deadline for compliance drew near, tension began mounting in the country. Comply or defy? Which would the President do? Open defiance was plainly impeachable. Frank compliance was presumably ruinous. On Monday, April 29, the President went on television to give the American people his answer. Seated in the Oval Office with the American flag behind him, President Nixon calmly announced that he was going to make over to the Judiciary Committee—and the public—"edited transcripts" of the subpoenaed tapes. These transcripts "will tell it all," said the President; there was nothing more that would need to be known for an impeachment inquiry about his conduct. To sharpen the public impression of presidential candor, the transcripts had been distributed among forty-two thick, loose-leaf binders, which were stacked in two-foot-high piles by the President's desk. As if to warn the public not to trust what the newspapers would say about the transcripts, Nixon accused the media of concocting the Watergate crisis out of "rumor, gossip, innuendo," of creating a "vague, general impression of massive wrongdoing, implicating everybody, gaining credibility by its endless repetition."

The next day's *New York Times* pronounced the President's speech "his most powerful Watergate defense since the scandal broke." By May 1 James Reston, the newspaper's most eminent columnist, thought the President had "probably gained considerable support in the country." For a few days it seemed as though the President had pulled off a coup. Republicans on the Judiciary Committee acted accordingly. On the first of May, 16 of the 17 committee Republicans voted against sending the President a note advising him that self-edited transcripts punctured by hundreds upon hundreds of suspicious "inaudibles" and "unintelligibles" were not in compliance with the committee's subpoena. The President, it was said, had succeeded in making impeachment look "partisan" and consequently discreditable.

Not even bowdlerized transcripts, however, could nullify the destructive power of those tapes. They revealed a White House steeped in more sordid conniving than Nixon's worst enemies had imagined. They showed a President advising his aides on how to "stonewall" a grand jury without committing perjury: "You can say, 'I don't remember.' You can say, 'I can't recall. I can't give any answer to that, that I can recall.'" They showed a President urging his counsel to make a "complete report" about Watergate but to "make it very incomplete." They showed a President eager for vengeance against ordinary election opponents. "I want the most comprehensive notes on all those who tried to do us in. . . . They are asking for it and they are going to get it." It showed a President discussing how "national security grounds" might be invoked to justify the Ellsberg burglary should the secret ever come out. "I think we could get by on that," replies Nixon's counsel.

On May 7 Pennsylvania's Hugh Scott, Senate Republican Minority Leader, pronounced the revelations in the transcript "disgusting, shabby, immoral performances." Joseph Alsop, who had long been friendly toward the President in his column, compared the atmosphere in the Oval Office to the "back room of a second-rate advertising agency in a suburb of hell." A week after Nixon's seeming coup Republicans were once again vainly urging him to resign. On May 9 the House Judiciary Committee staff began presenting to the members its massive accumulation of Watergate material. Since the presentation was made behind closed doors, a suspenseful lull fell over the Watergate battle-ground.

Over the next two months it was obvious that the Judiciary Committee was growing increasingly impatient with the President, who continued to insist that, even in an impeachment proceeding, the "executive must remain the final arbiter of demands on its confidentiality." When Nixon refused to comply in any way with a second committee subpoena, the members voted 28 to 10 to warn him that "your refusals in and of themselves might constitute a ground for impeachment." The "partisanship" of May 1 had faded by May 30.

Undermining these signs of decisiveness was the continued insistence that only direct presidential involvement in a crime would be regarded as an impeachable offense in the House. Congressmen demanded to see the "smoking gun." They wanted to be shown the "hand in the cookie jar." Alexander Hamilton had called impeachment a "National Inquest." Congress seemed bent on restricting it to the purview of a local courthouse. Nobody spoke of the larger issues. As James Reston noted on May 26, one of the most disturbing aspects of Watergate was the silence of the prominent. Where, Reston asked, were the educators, the business leaders, and the elder statesmen to delineate and define the great constitutional issues at stake? When the White House began denouncing the Judiciary Committee as a "lynch mob," virtually nobody rose to the committee's defense.

On July 7 the Sunday edition of the *New York Times* made doleful reading. "The official investigations seem beset by semitropical torpor," the newspaper reported in its weekly news summary. White House attacks on the committee, said the *Times,* were proving effective in the country. In March, 60 percent of those polled by Gallup wanted the President tried in the Senate for his misdeeds. By June the figure had fallen to 50 percent. The movement for impeachment, said the *Times,* was losing its momentum. Nixon, it seemed, had worn out the public capacity for righteous indignation.

Then, on July 19, John Doar, the Democrats' counsel, did what nobody had done before with the enormous, confusing mass of interconnected misdeeds that we labeled "Watergate" for sheer convenience. At a meeting of the Judiciary Committee he compressed the endlessly ramified scandal into a grave and compelling case for impeaching the thirty-seventh President of the United States. He spoke of the President's "enormous crimes." He warned the committee that it dare not look indifferently upon the "terrible deed of subverting the

Constitution." He urged the members to consider with favor five broad articles of impeachment, "charges with a grave historic ring," as the *Times* said of them.

In a brief statement, Albert Jenner, the Republicans' counsel, strongly endorsed Doar's recommendations. The Founding Fathers, he reminded committee members, had established a free country and a free Constitution. It was now the committee's momentous duty to determine "whether that country and that Constitution are to be preserved."

How I had yearned for those words during the long, arid months of the "smoking gun" and the "hand in the cookie jar." Members of the committee must have felt the same way, too, for Jenner's words were to leave a profound mark on their final deliberations. That I did not know yet, but what I did know was heartening. The grave maxims of liberty, once invoked, instantly took the measure of meanness and effrontery. When the President's press spokesman, Ron Ziegler, denounced the committee's proceedings as a "kangaroo court," a wave of disgust coursed through Congress. The hour of the Founders had arrived.

The final deliberations of the House Judiciary Committee began on the evening of July 24, when Chairman Peter Rodino gaveled the committee to order before some forty-five million television viewers. The committee made a curious spectacle: thirty-eight strangers strung out on a two-tiered dais, a huge piece of furniture as unfamiliar as the faces of its occupants.

Chairman Rodino made the first opening remarks. His public career had been long, unblemished, and thoroughly undistinguished. Now the representative from Newark, New Jersey, linked hands with the Founding Fathers of our government. "For more than two years, there have been serious allegations, by people of good faith and sound intelligence, that the President, Richard M. Nixon, has committed grave and systematic violations of the Constitution." The framers of our Constitution, said Rodino, had provided an exact measure of a President's responsibilities. It was by the terms of the President's oath of office, prescribed in the Constitution, that the framers intended to hold Presidents "accountable and lawful."

That was to prove the keynote. That evening and over the following days, as each committee member delivered a statement, it became increasingly clear that the broad maxims of constitutional supremacy had taken command of the impeachment inquiry. "We will by this impeachment proceeding be establishing a standard of conduct for the President of the United States which will for all time be a matter of public record," Caldwell Butler, a conservative Virginia Republican, reminded his conservative constituents. "If we fail to impeach . . . we will have left condoned and unpunished an abuse of power totally without justification."

There were still White House loyalists of course; men who kept demanding to see a presidential directive ordering a crime and a documented "tie-in" between Nixon and his henchmen. Set against the great principle of constitutional supremacy, however, this common view was now exposed for what it was: reckless trifling with our ancient liberties. Can the United States permit a President "to escape accountability because he may choose to deal behind closed doors," asked James Mann, a South Carolina conservative. "Can anyone argue," asked George Danielson, a California liberal, "that if a President breaches his oath of office, he should not be removed?" In a voice of unforgettable power and richness, Barbara Jordan, a black legislator from Texas, sounded the grand theme of the committee with particular depth of feeling. Once, she said, the Constitution had excluded people of her race, but that evil had been remedied. "My faith in the Constitution is whole, it is complete, it is total and I am not going to sit here and be an idle spectator to the diminution, the subversion, the destruction of the Constitution."

On July 27 the Judiciary Committee voted 27 to 11 (six Republicans joining all twenty-one Democrats) to impeach Richard Nixon on the grounds that he and his agents had "prevented, obstructed, and impeded the administration of justice" in "violation of his constitutional oath faithfully to execute the office of President of the United States and, to the best of his ability, preserve, protect, and defend the Constitution of the United States, and in violation of his constitutional duty to take care that the laws be faithfully executed."

On July 29 the Judiciary Committee voted 28 to 10 to impeach Richard Nixon for "violating the constitutional rights of citizens, impairing the due and proper administration of justice and the conduct of lawful inquiries, or contravening the laws governing agencies of the executive branch. . . ." Thus, the illegal wiretaps, the sinister White House spies, the attempted use of the IRS to punish political opponents, the abuse of the CIA, and the break-in at Ellsberg's psychiatrist's office—misconduct hitherto deemed too "vague" for impeachment—now became part of a President's impeachable failure to abide by his constitutional oath to carry out his constitutional duty.

Lastly, on July 30 the Judiciary Committee, hoping to protect some future impeachment inquiry from a repetition of Nixon's defiance, voted 21 to 17 to impeach him for refusing to comply with the committee's subpoenas. "This concludes the work of the committee," Rodino announced at eleven o'clock that night. Armed with the wisdom of the Founders and the authority of America's republican principles, the committee had cut through the smoke screens, the lies, and the pettifogging that had muddled the Watergate crisis for so many months. It had subjected an imperious Presidency to the rule of fundamental law. It had demonstrated by resounding majorities that holding a President accountable is neither "liberal" nor "conservative," neither "Democratic" nor "Republican," but something far more basic to the American republic.

For months the forces of evasion had claimed that impeachment would "tear the country apart." But now the country was more united than it had been in years. The impeachment inquiry had sounded the chords of deepest patriotism, and Americans responded, it seemed to me, with quiet pride in their country and themselves. On Capitol Hill, congressional leaders reported that Nixon's impeachment would command three hundred votes at a minimum. The Senate began preparing for the President's trial. Then, as countless wits remarked, a funny thing happened on the way to the forum.

Back on July 24, the day the Judiciary Committee began its televised deliberations, the Supreme Court had ordered the President to surrender sixty-four taped conversations subpoenaed by the Watergate prosecutor. At the time I had regarded the decision chiefly as an auspicious omen for the evening's proceedings. Only Richard Nixon knew that the Court had signed his death warrant. On August 5 the President announced that he was making public three tapes that "may further damage my case." In fact they destroyed what little was left of it. Recorded six days after the Watergate break-in, they showed the President discussing detailed preparations for the cover-up with his chief of staff, Bob Haldeman. They showed the President and his henchman discussing how to use the CIA to block the FBI, which was coming dangerously close to the White House. "You call them in," says the President. "Good deal," says his aide. In short, the three tapes proved that the President had told nothing but lies about Watergate for twenty-six months. Every one of Nixon's ten Judiciary Committee defenders now announced that he favored Nixon's impeachment.

The President still had one last evasion: on the evening of August 8 he appeared on television to make his last important announcement. "I no longer have a strong enough political base in Congress," said Nixon, doing his best to imply that the resolution of a great constitutional crisis was mere maneuvering for political advantage. "Therefore, I shall resign the Presidency effective at noon tomorrow." He admitted to no wrongdoing. If he had made mistakes of judgment, "they were made in what I believed at the time to be in the best interests of the nation."

On the morning of August 9 the first President ever to resign from office boarded Air Force One and left town. The "system" had worked. But in the watches of the night, who has not asked himself now and then: How would it all have turned out had there been no White House tapes?

Epilogue

The House Judiciary Committee, including members of Nixon's own party, voted articles of impeachment, and only his resignation from office prevented impeachment by the whole House and certain conviction on at least some of the charges. His subsequent pardon by President Gerald Ford squelched a resolution of many of the issues. Even today Nixon writes of his innocence and blames his assistants for the transgressions. Some say that Nixon was guilty but that his resignation and pardon spared the nation more grief. The political fallout from Watergate has carried over even today to the Nixon Library, which has opened in California. The library contains Nixon's effects and personal papers, but the governmental documents from his administration are kept by the federal government in a warehouse in Alexandria, Virginia. Several years ago Congress passed a law removing these papers from Nixon's control because of fears they would not be preserved intact. The Supreme Court later upheld this act, making Nixon the only president not to retain control over his administration's papers.

For an account of a recent constitutional crisis concerning the presidency, the Iran-contra scandal, see Selection 5.2.

CHAPTER 2

V. Lawrence '90

FEDERALISM

A Nation of States: States' Rights vs. National Supremacy

Fred W. Friendly
and Martha J. H.
Elliott

In an attempt to correct the ineffectiveness of the Articles of Confederation, the new Constitution established a unique system of government called *federalism*. In federalism, powers are shared between a central government and regional (state) governments. In the decades following ratification, there was much debate over how governmental powers should be divided: Should the national government or the states have supremacy? Was the central government assumed to be derived from the powers of the states (so that the states would be supreme) or from the powers of the people (giving more power to the central government)? It is noteworthy that the framers chose to begin the Constitution with the words "We the people."

Friendly and Elliott explain the first efforts to determine the federal structure. When the nation began, there was no central system of roads or banking, no national taxation system, and no uniform commerce and tax system from state to state. In discussing whether the central government could do anything about these matters, political philosophers found conflicting instructions in the Constitution. Article I, Section 8 renders to Congress the power to do anything "necessary and proper" to put its powers into effect. Thomas Jefferson and Alexander Hamilton led the debate over the meaning of this phrase. Was it intended to be a broad grant of power by which Congress could do anything that might be convenient in the exercise of its many powers (according to Hamilton)? Or was it a narrower grant of authority, by which Congress could do only those things *absolutely* necessary to execute that authority? The interpretation of this phrase would determine the strength of the central government.

Moreover, there is ambiguity in the Tenth Amendment, which was added to the Constitution as part of the ratification fight. In seeking to establish the boundaries of the two levels of government, the amendment declares that "the powers not delegated to the United States by the Constitution . . . are reserved to the states respectively, or to the people." But what are the powers of the central government in the first place? Should the national government be allowed only those powers expressly delegated by the Constitution? Such an interpretation would give great authority to the states.

Resolving these considerations fell to the Supreme Court, under the guidance of Chief Justice John Marshall. As you will see in this article, he helped to create the strong central government we now have.

JOSEPH HOPKINSON   Attorney for the state of Maryland.

JAMES WILLIAM McCULLOCH   Cashier for the Baltimore branch of the Bank of the United States.

JOHN MARSHALL   Chief justice of the United States, 1801–1835.

DANIEL WEBSTER   Attorney for Dartmouth *(Dartmouth College* v. *Woodward)* and for the Bank of the United States *(McCulloch* v. *Maryland).*

JOHN WHEELOCK   President of Dartmouth College.

We must never forget that it is a constitution we are expounding . . . intended to endure for ages to come, and consequently, to be adapted to the various crises of human affairs.

John Marshall,
McCulloch v. *Maryland*

The question of the relation of the States to the federal government is the cardinal question of our constitutional system. At every turn of our national developments we have been brought face to face with it, and no definition either of statesmen or of judges has ever quieted or decided it. It cannot, indeed, be settled by one generation because it is a question of growth, and every successive stage of our political and economic development gives it a new aspect, makes it a new question.

Woodrow Wilson,
Constitutional Government in the United States

▶ When the delegates to the Constitutional Convention met in Philadelphia during the summer of 1787, they came as representatives of 12 sovereign states (Rhode Island refused to send delegates)—states that had developed as virtually independent entities and banded together in a loose confederation for the common goal of obtaining liberty from Great Britain. The hastily drafted Articles of Confederation had not been a sufficient framework to tie together those diverse sovereignties into a new nation. As Edmund Randolph of Virginia stated at the opening of the Constitutional Convention, "the confederation produced no security against foreign invasion." It "could not check the quarrels between states" or protect itself "against the encroachments from the states," nor was it "even paramount to the state constitutions." So the framers met for more than three months, with the formidable task of writing a constitution that would not only solve the problems of the day, but also, as James Madison put it, frame "a system which we wish to last for ages."

In the early days and weeks of the convention, it was not clear that the delegates would be able to accomplish their task. One problem was that some delegates came as firm representatives of their states. Others, such as Gouverneur Morris, felt they had come "as a representative of America . . . [and] to some degree as a representative of the whole human race." Benjamin Franklin commented on Thursday, June 28, "The small progress we have made after 4 or five weeks close attendance & continual reasonings with each other—our different sentiments on almost every question, several of the last producing so many noes as ays, is methinks a melancholy proof of the imperfection of the Human Understanding. We indeed seem to feel our own want of political wisdom, since we have been running about in search of it." The issue that seemed to crop up at every point in the debates was that of states' rights. Would states be represented as equal entities or by population? What powers would be taken away from the states in forming the government? How could a national, supreme government be formed without completely eviscerating the power of the states?

Those favoring a strong central government argued that encroachments by the states on the federal government were far more likely than encroachments by the federal government on the states. They contended that in all successful governments "there must be one supreme power, and one only." Those supporting states' rights accused the others of wanting to abolish the state governments altogether and questioned whether the convention had the power to change the nature of the confederation. Underlying all these issues was the basic question of whether the new government was to be a confederation of the states or a creation of the people themselves.

There was no area where the conflict appeared more sharply than in the question of how the states were to be represented in Congress. The Virginia Plan, put forth by Edmund Randolph, had called for election by the people and representation according to either contributions (i.e., the amount of tax paid) or population. In response, William Paterson of New Jersey had proposed a plan in which the Congress would be elected by the state legislatures and each state would be represented equally.

The oppressive Philadelphia summer heat was intensified by the passions of the debate over representation. For several months, advocates of the two plans rose to explain their respective positions, each side remaining unconverted.

Realizing that all might be lost, the delegates finally reached a compromise. The lower house of the Congress (House of Representatives) would be elected by the people, and each state would send representatives according to population (each slave being counted as three-fifths of a person and Indians not being counted at all). The upper house (Senate) would be elected by the state legislatures and each state would be equally represented by two senators.

The compromise helped resolve the deadlock in Philadelphia but did not resolve the basic issue of states' rights versus national sovereignty. Indeed, as soon as delegates met in state conventions to debate and ratify the Constitution, the issue emerged. Patrick Henry, who had declined to go to the convention, shouted, "The question turns, sir, on that poor little thing—the expression, We, the people, instead of the states of America. What right had they to say, *We the people?* Who authorized them to speak the language of *We the people,* instead of, *We the states?*"

At the ratifying conventions, many Antifederalists, concerned about encroachments by the federal government on personal liberties and on states' rights, called for a bill of rights. After the Constitution was ratified and the First Congress met in 1789, James Madison pushed for those guarantees, which included what was to become the Tenth Amendment: "The powers not delegated to the United States by the Constitution, nor prohibited by it to the States, are reserved to the States respectively, or to the people." In the discussion over the amendment, Representative Thomas Tudor Tucker of South Carolina moved to add the word "expressly" before the word "delegated," but Madison objected. It would be "impossible to confine a Government to the exercise of express powers; there must necessarily be admitted powers by implication unless the Constitution descended to recount every minutia." At Madison's insistence, the word was not included. The extent of the powers of the federal government thus remained ambiguous.

Even to the Antifederalists, the Tenth Amendment was a declaratory statement, a recitation of the obvious, not a special grant of power to the states. As Justice Potter Stewart recently stated, "The Tenth Amendment just confirms a truism that the federal government is a government of specific and limited powers."

The first organized states' rights movements came in 1798 in a protest over the Alien and Sedition Acts, which gave the government the right to expel aliens and to punish seditious libel. In a daring move, the Virginia and Kentucky legislatures (led by Madison and Jefferson, respectively) passed resolutions declaring the acts unconstitutional. The Kentucky resolves stated that any acts in which the federal government transcended its constitutional powers could be declared void by state legislatures. Virginia asserted that a state had the right to interpose its authority between its citizens and the federal government. The legislatures called for other states to join in the protest. Although this amounted to no more than a protest, it did help to rally the Republicans to a victory in 1800, with the election of Jefferson as president.

The issue of state versus national power eventually led the country into civil war and has continued to appear intermittently up to the present time. The doctrine of states' rights has been invoked as often by liberals as by conservatives. Although the question of the extent of national power has never been completely settled, the firmest foundation of such power lies in the opinions of Chief Justice John Marshall.

The Dartmouth College Case

On the morning of February 2, 1819, Chief Justice Marshall's first act was to read his opinion in *Dartmouth College* v. *Woodward,* a case that had been argued the previous March but left undecided. The announcement of that decision marked the beginning of what has been called "the greatest six weeks in the history of the court," a period that would be climaxed by Marshall's own treatise on states' rights versus national supremacy.

The facts of the Dartmouth case were complicated. John Wheelock, the son of Dartmouth College founder Eleazer Wheelock, had ascended to the presidency of the college in 1779. Under the charter from King George, Eleazer could name his own successor, who would serve indefinitely unless at some time his appointment was "disapproved by the trustees." Although some of the trustees had balked at the idea of naming John, who had virtually no qualifications for the office, they had gone along with Eleazer's wishes, probably because John was willing to serve without pay and the college lacked funds to hire a president.

Over the years, however, that marriage of convenience had fallen apart. Wheelock had become an increasingly stiff and rigid man, who, characteristically, "wore the old-fashioned outfit of dun-colored coat, knee breeches with buckles, white stockings, and three-cornered beaver hat." He had run the college on his own terms, making all appointments to the faculty and instituting strict rules. By 1809 a new set of trustees had come in, and they challenged Wheelock's authority by vetoing his appointments to the faculty and then, as a final slap, passing a resolution that released him from his teaching duties.

But Wheelock was not about to be outdone. Several years later, in 1815, he wrote a pamphlet entitled *Sketches of the History of Dartmouth College . . . with a Particular Account of Some Late Remarkable Proceedings of the Board of Trustees from the Year 1779 to the Year 1815,* in which he outlined the "abuses" of the trustees. Wheelock made sure that each member of the New Hampshire state legislature had a copy to read. The legislature, which was at this time Federalist by a slim majority, agreed to look into the matter and sent a committee to Hanover in August. Much to Wheelock's dismay, the committee's report was severely critical—not of the trustees, but of the president. With the report as ammunition, and using the disapproval provision of the college's charter, the board of trustees mustered enough courage to oust Wheelock.

But Wheelock had made some friends in Concord, the Jeffersonian Republicans. The plight of the college became a major issue in the 1816 elections, and the Republicans, crusading for the aging president, won their first majority in the legislature. They quickly passed legislation that dissolved the royal charter, returning to Wheelock control of a new institution, Dartmouth University, under a new charter. In order to get around the trustees, the legislature increased the number of board members from 12 to 21 and provided for a board of overseers, which could veto decisions of the trustees.

What resulted was a tragic farce. The college retained the students, yet the university had the buildings. The college scraped by with contributions from alumni and parents, and classes continued to meet wherever space could be found in the town of Hanover. The original board of trustees took its case to court, but, not surprisingly, lost in the New Hampshire courts.

The college was soon out of money; it couldn't even collect its meager endowment money, because the university held all the account books. In desperation, the trustees turned to a member of the class of 1801, Daniel Webster, who was at this point a congressman from Portsmouth. Ironically, Wheelock had been trying to get Webster's support all along, but Webster had been unwilling to get involved unless it were on a "professional" basis—that is, unless Wheelock was prepared to pay his fee. When the trustees asked for help, Webster issued the same ultimatum. His fee, for himself and Baltimore lawyer Joseph Hopkinson, would be $1,000. A gift to the college made the appeal to the Supreme Court possible.

By the time the case reached the high court, John Wheelock had died and his son-in-law had taken over as head of the university. Arguments were scheduled for March 10, 1818. The courtroom that day was crowded with representatives of private colleges, who realized that their fate also hung in the balance. Webster, the first to address the Court, gave the trustees their money's worth. He spoke for four hours, deftly bringing up every argument he could lay his hands on and driving home one important constitutional argument, that the contract clause of the Constitution forbade states from impairing the obligation of contracts. He reminded the Court that in 1810, in the case of the Georgia Yazoo land fraud, the justices had decided that "a grant is a contract." In that case the Supreme Court had overturned an act of the Georgia legislature whose effect was to repeal an act of a previous legislature selling land at ridiculously low prices. Marshall's reasoning had been that as the land subsequently had been sold to innocent third parties, those contracts could not be violated by the new legislature.

Making his debut as one of the most prominent attorneys in the United States, Webster struck a chord that he knew Marshall, the great defender of property rights, would hear:

This, sir, is my case. It is the case not merely of that humble institution, it is the case of every college in our land. . . . It is more. It is, in some sense, the case of every man who has property of which he may be stripped for the question is simply this: Shall our State legislature be allowed to take that which is not their own, to turn it from its original use, and apply it to such ends or purposes as they, in their discretion, shall see fit?

Then he continued, in the words that every Dartmouth alumnus can recite, "It is, sir, as I have said, a small college, and yet *there are those that love it.*" His voice quivered, his eyes filled with tears; the justices were transfixed, and Marshall was almost moved to tears. But despite this dramatic presentation, Marshall announced at the end of the oral arguments that some of the justices had not made up their minds and that the rest were divided. The next morning, he informed the parties that the case would be continued until 1819.

When the Court reconvened almost a year later, the Chief Justice "pulled an eighteen-page opinion from his sleeve" and declared that a charter was a contract within the meaning of the Constitution. The New Hampshire legislation was unconstitutional. Dartmouth College would regain its charter.

First, citing the framers' sensitivity to "giving permanence and security to contracts," Marshall concluded that "the acts of the legislature of New Hampshire . . . are repugnant to the constitution of the United States." He said that the New Hampshire legislature had converted "a literary institution, moulded according to the will of its founders, and placed under the control of private literary men, into a machine entirely subservient to the will of government. This may be for the advantage of this college in particular, and may be for the advantage of literature in general; but it is not according to the will of the donors, and is subversive of that contract, on the faith of which their property was given."[1] A contract could not be violated under the Constitution—not even by a state.

As Richard N. Current comments in his essay on the case, its repercussions were diverse and important: "The Dartmouth case enhanced the prestige of John Marshall and the Supreme Court. It extended the national power at the expense of state power. It confirmed the charter rights not only of Dartmouth College but of all private colleges. It protected and encouraged business corporations as well as nonprofit corporations. And, incidentally, it brought Daniel Webster to the top of the legal profession." Webster would play a role a few weeks later in Marshall's ultimate statement of national sovereignty.

The Bank Case: *McCulloch* v. *Maryland*

James William McCulloch was the cashier of the Baltimore branch of the Bank of the United States. It was his job to issue bank notes and take deposits. But, beginning in May 1818, each transaction he completed was illegal, because the state of Maryland had passed a law requiring banks not chartered by the state to either purchase special stamped paper or pay $15,000 a year. Neither McCulloch nor any of the bank officers had any intention of complying. They knew that the state tax was an attempt to force the Bank out of the state, and they were not about to back down without a fight. So when the state sent John James— a bounty hunter of sorts, who received half of the fines he collected—to the bank for the purpose of gathering evidence that the state law was being violated, it was the beginning of a case that would not only call into question the constitutionality of the Bank, but the powers of the federal government over the states.

The Baltimore branch was one of 18 offices of the second Bank of the United States. It had been chartered in 1816 by the Republican Congress to try to get the country out of a monetary crisis following the War of 1812. Its predecessor, Alexander Hamilton's progeny of 1791, had been allowed to expire in 1811. The idea of a national bank had been controversial from the beginning. It had created a schism in the Washington administration between Secretary of the Treasury Hamilton and Secretary of State Thomas Jefferson. Hamilton espoused the "loose construction" theory of the Constitution:

> *Every power vested in a government is in its nature sovereign, and includes by the force of the term, a right to employ all the means requisite . . . to the attainment of the ends of such power . . . If the end [i.e., purpose of the legislation] be clearly comprehended with any of the specified powers, and if the measure have an obvious relation to that end and is not forbidden by any particular provision of the Constitution, it may safely be deemed to come within the national authority.*

Jefferson espoused the "strict constructionist" view that the "necessary and proper clause" did not give Congress the power to pass laws for convenience. He said that the national Bank was not strictly necessary, because state banks could be used for government funds. Madison agreed, arguing that in passing the bill establishing the Bank Congress had gone beyond its constitutional authority. But President Washington had sided with Hamilton and had signed the bank legislation.

The second Bank was as controversial as the first. Jeffersonian Republicans— the agrarian interests—hated all banks. State bankers despised the Bank because it competed with their own and was capable of destroying them by expanding and contracting credit. Underlying the whole bank issue was the matter of states' rights. The states knew that the control of the purse strings was an important power and they were not about to surrender it. They felt that the Bank was unconstitutional because the Constitution did not explicitly give Congress the power to charter corporations. To the states' rights advocates, the nation was a confederation of sovereign states, whose power must not be usurped by a greedy or overzealous Congress.

The Bank's opponents derived further ammunition from the fact that the Bank failed to resolve the country's monetary problems. By 1818, as a result of land speculation, the dumping of British goods on the American market, and a drop in the price of American products, the country was well on the road to depression. The Bank became the scapegoat. Some members of Congress had even tried to kill it—but unsuccessfully.

At this point, Maryland was determined to make the Bank pay or get out and took it to court. McCulloch and the Bank lost in the Baltimore County court and, on appeal, in the Maryland Court of Appeals. The next step was the United States Supreme Court.

But before the case reached the high court, the bank issue became still more complicated. Word got around that many of the branches were being misman-aged and that funds were being misused. The Baltimore branch was no excep-tion. Although the charter had limited the number of shares any stockholder could vote, McCulloch and three other stockholders had devised a scheme whereby they would purchase the shares in other people's names and then vote the shares as the people's attorneys. So, rather than having only 30 votes each (for a total of 120), they were able to control 4,000 votes and appoint their own directors. To top this off, McCulloch as cashier had been able to loan himself and his partners the money to purchase the shares. In other words, they were using the Bank's own money to buy its shares, causing a great increase in the price of the stock. After Congress got wind of some of the problems in Balti-more and elsewhere, it ordered an investigation of the Bank, ousted its presi-dent, and tried to clean things up before the *McCulloch* case reached the Su-preme Court. (Eventually, McCulloch and his cohorts were charged with conspiracy but were acquitted.)

The Court Hears the Case

Arguments for *McCulloch* began on February 22, 1819, and lasted for nine days. In a rare move, the Court suspended its own rule that only two lawyers could argue for each side and allowed three each. For the Bank were Daniel Webster, William Pinkney, and United States Attorney General William Wirt. For the state of Maryland were Joseph Hopkinson (who had argued with Webster in the *Dartmouth* case),Walter Jones, and Luther Martin, Maryland's attorney general and an ardent states' rights advocate who had been a delegate to the Constitu-tional Convention.

Because the facts of the case were not disputed, there were only two major issues for the Court to decide: Was the Bank constitutional? Did Maryland have the power to tax the Bank?

Webster began the arguments by saying that the questions before the Court were "deeply interesting" and could "affect the value of a vast amount of private property." He reminded the justices that the bank had been legislatively ac-cepted for nearly 30 years and concluded that "it would seem almost too late to call it in question unless its repugnancy with the constitution were plain and manifest."[2]

Webster then went on to argue that the Bank was constitutional. He stressed that Congress was not limited to those powers that are enumerated, but could use all suitable means in raising and disbursing revenue. "It is not enough to say, that it does not appear that a bank was in the contemplation of the framers of the constitution. It was not their intention, in these cases, to enumerate particulars. The true view of the subject is, that if it be a fit instrument to an authorized purpose, it may be used, not being specially prohibited." He told the Court that the grant to the Congress to pass laws that were "necessary and proper" for carrying out its powers did not mean solely those laws that were *"absolutely indispensable,"* or otherwise the "government would hardly exist." Webster continued, "A bank is a proper and suitable instrument to assist the operations of the government, in the collection and disbursement of the revenue; . . . the only question is, whether a bank . . . is capable of being so connected with the finances and revenues of the government, as to be fairly within the discretion of Congress."

On the question of whether the state of Maryland could tax the bank, Webster pointed out that in ratifying the Constitution the people had seen fit to "divide sovereignty, and to establish a complex system." But he asserted that the Constitution itself and the laws passed by Congress were the *"supreme law of the land."* Reminding the Court that if the state could tax the Bank, it could tax other government operations, including judicial proceedings, Webster warned, "If the States may tax the bank, to what extent shall they tax it, and where shall they stop? An unlimited power to tax involves, necessarily, a power to destroy; because there is a limit beyond which no institution and no property can bear taxation."

Webster concluded by insisting that the operation of the Bank could not be impeded by state legislation. "To hold otherwise, would be to declare that Congress can only exercise its constitutional powers subject to the controlling discretion, and under the sufferance of the State governments."

The two sides took turns making their presentations, until all six lawyers had spoken. Attorney General Wirt and Pinkney refuted many of the specific points raised by the other side. Pinkney, who concluded the arguments for the Bank in a forceful three-day argument, asserted that the "constitution acts directly *on* the people, by means of powers communicated directly *from* the people." Because the people had ratified the Constitution, not the states, the federal government was just as sovereign as the state governments. On the issue of the Tenth Amendment, Pinkney stated: "All powers are given to the national government, as the people will. The reservation in the 10th Amendment to the constitution . . . is not confined to powers not *expressly* delegated. Such an amendment was indeed proposed but it was perceived, that it would strip the government of some of its most essential powers, and it was rejected."

Joseph Hopkinson, for the state of Maryland, began his argument by trying to show that the Bank was not constitutional. Even if the first Bank had been constitutional, he said, the circumstances had changed so that the Bank was no longer "necessary" and therefore not constitutional. His next point was that even if the Bank were found to be within the scope of the constitutional powers of Congress, it could not establish branches within the states without the permission of the states. He said that Congress had unconstitutionally delegated the power of establishing branches to the directors of the Bank. Thus, Hopkinson argued, the branches were "located at the will of the directors," who represented the stockholders. He continued, "If this is the case, can it be contended, that the State rights of territory and taxation are to yield for the gains of a money-trading corporation; to be prostrated at the will of a set of men who have no concern, and no duty, but to increase their profits? Is this the necessity required by the constitution for the creation of undefined powers?"

On the question of the tax, Hopkinson argued that the right to tax "is the highest attribute of sovereignty, the right to raise revenue; in fact, the right to exist; without which no other right can be held or enjoyed." He said that there was nothing in the Constitution which put limit on the states' right to tax, and he urged the Court to maintain this right so that the states and the federal government could remain on friendly terms.

Walter Jones argued that the Constitution had not been formed and adopted by the people at large, "but by the people of the respective States. To suppose that the mere proposition of this fundamental law threw the American people into one aggregate mass, would be to assume what the instrument itself does not profess to establish." He asserted that the Constitution was "a compact between the States, and all the powers which are not expressly relinquished by it are reserved to the States." He then argued that the Bank was an arbitrary exercise of power, not one that was "necessary and proper."

Maryland Attorney General Luther Martin made the argument that the Tenth Amendment was written to assure the people that the central government would not try to usurp power from the states. He said that if the people had been aware of what vast powers the Congress would claim, the Constitution would never have been adopted. "We insist, that the only safe rule is the plain letter of the constitution, the rule which the constitutional legislators themselves have prescribed, in the tenth amendment, . . . that the powers not delegated to the United States nor prohibited to the States, are reserved to the States respectively, or to the people." He insisted that the power to establish a corporation was one that was reserved to the states.

The Decision

On March 6, four days after the oral arguments had concluded, Marshall announced the decision of the Court in a ringing pronouncement of national supremacy and his own theories of federalism. Indeed, the decision was such an overwhelming victory for the Bank that parts of it sounded almost like recitations of the arguments of Webster, Wirt, and Pinkney.

On the question of the constitutionality of the Bank, Marshall began by referring to Webster's argument in the following way: "It has been truly said that this can scarcely be considered as an open question."[3] He then proceeded to answer it as if it were an open question, adding foundation to his belief that the Bank was constitutional. Accepting Pinkney's argument that the United States was a government of the people and rejecting Jones's argument that the government was a federation of states, Marshall described the process by which the Constitution was adopted by convention. "It is true, they assembled in their several States. . . . No political dreamer was ever wild enough to think of breaking down the lines which separate the states, and of compounding the American people into one common mass," he stated. "But the measures they adopt do not . . . cease to be measures of the people themselves, or become the measures of the State governments." He continued:

> *The government proceeds directly from the people; is "ordained and established" in the name of the people. . . . The assent of the States in their sovereign capacity, is implied in calling a Convention, and thus submitting that instrument to the people. But the people were at perfect liberty to accept or reject it; and their act was final. It required not the affirmance, and could not be negatived, by the State governments. The constitution, when thus adopted was of complete obligation, and bound the State sovereignties.*

Here Marshall was fortifying the argument made so many times by James Madison and James Wilson during the Constitutional Convention: the federal government must be a government that derives its power and purpose from the people as a whole and the only way to transcend state rivalries was to make the United States a nation of people, not of states.

The Chief Justice then moved to the question of the extent of the powers of the federal government, a question which he admitted "is perpetually arising, and will probably continue to arise, as long as our system shall exist." He said, "If any one proposition could command the universal assent of mankind, we might expect it would be this—that the government of the Union . . . is supreme within its sphere of action." He acknowledged that among the enumerated powers there was not one to establish a bank. However, he said, it would have been impossible for the framers to spell out all the powers; had they done so, the Constitution would have been more like "a legal code." Then, in the words most often quoted, Marshall asserted, "In considering this question . . . we must never forget that it is a *constitution* we are expounding." He said that the necessary and proper clause was made "in a constitution intended to endure for ages to come, and consequently, to be adapted to the various *crises* of human affairs."

The Bank was a "means" to an "end." It was up to Congress to determine if those means were necessary in carrying out the enumerated powers.

> *But we think the sound construction of the constitution must allow to the national legislature that discretion, with respect to the means by which the powers it confers are to be carried into execution, which will enable that body to perform the high duties assigned to it, in the manner most beneficial to the people. Let the end be legitimate, let it be within the scope of the constitution, and all means which are appropriate, which are plainly adapted to that end, which are not prohibited, but consist with the letter and spirit of the constitution, are constitutional.*

Marshall concluded his discussion of the constitutionality issue by declaring that the Court had ruled unanimously "that the act to incorporate the Bank of the United States is a law made in pursuance of the constitution, and is a part of the supreme law of the land."

The second issue to be determined was that of the tax. In his characteristic way, Marshall began by asserting the right of states to tax but then added the qualification that a state could only tax its own people and their property. The state governments had no power to tax people of other states. As the federal government was a government of all the people, the state of Maryland could not tax it. Echoing Webster's arguments, Marshall three times declared that "the power to tax involves the power to destroy." If the states could tax the Bank, they could also tax the mails or the judicial process or any other means of government. That power would change the character of the Constitution, he said. "We shall find it capable of arresting all the measures of government, and of prostrating it at the foot of the States. . . . this principle would transfer the supremacy, in fact, to the States."

In conclusion, Marshall said, "The Court has bestowed on this subject its most deliberate consideration. The result is a conviction that the States have no power, by taxation or otherwise, to retard, impede, burden, or in any manner control the operations of the constitutional laws enacted by Congress." Thus the law passed by the Maryland legislature was "unconstitutional and void."

Reaction to the Decision

Many states' rights advocates reacted to the opinion with a sense of outrage. The issue of states' rights as it pertained to slavery was being debated in Congress over the Missouri question . . . , and many believed that the Court had gone too far. Jefferson criticized the Court as a "subtle corps of sappers and miners constantly working underground to undermine the foundations of our constitutional fabric."

When Marshall returned to Virginia after the Court had adjourned, he met with a hostile reception. Many found the Court's reasoning "heretical" and "damnable." The Virginia legislature passed resolutions denouncing the decision and calling for a constitutional amendment to set up an independent tribunal to settle matters between states and the federal government.

A series of articles were printed in the *Richmond Enquirer* attacking the decision. In a rare move, Marshall himself, using the pseudonym "A Friend of the Constitution," countered with a series of letters in the *Philadelphia Union* and *Alexandria Gazette,* defending the decision.

Although Marshall's decision in *McCulloch* is considered the ultimate statement of national supremacy, some historians have concluded that it had little effect until after the Civil War. During the 30 years following the decision, the issue of states' rights flared repeatedly.

In 1828 in response to tariffs passed by Congress the legislature of South Carolina, with the help of Vice President John C. Calhoun, who remained a "silent partner" in the document, passed an exposition that resurrected the theories of the Virginia and Kentucky resolves of 1798. The federal government, this document declared, was a compact among sovereign states, and each state had a right to judge when its "agent," the federal government, had gone beyond its constitutional powers. Any congressional act that was judged to constitute such a usurpation of power could be nullified by the state.

Four years later in 1832, South Carolina formally acted on this theory by declaring that the tariffs imposed by Congress were "unauthorized by the constitution of the United States, null and void." South Carolina's Nullification Act forbade the collection of tariffs in South Carolina ports, and the state threatened secession if the government tried to blockade Charleston. President Jackson, a states' rights advocate himself, issued his own proclamation reiterating Marshall's affirmation that the government was of the people, not of the states. Although Jackson was ready to send troops to South Carolina, the confrontation was avoided by a lowering of the tariffs and South Carolina's repeal of the Nullification Act.

States' rights doctrines continued to be pervasive in American history—from the refusal of Ohio, Massachusetts, and Wisconsin to comply with the Fugitive Slave Act in 1850, to the secession of the South in the Civil War, to protests against Franklin D. Roosevelt's New Deal, to attempts in the South to resist integration, to President Reagan's assertion that the federal government should be less concerned with regulation of the states. Although the issue may lie dormant for periods, it continually reappears in a new form, testing the balance of powers of state and federal government, testing the Constitution "intended to endure for ages to come, and . . . to be adapted to the various crises of human affairs."

Notes

1.   *Dartmouth College* v. *Woodward*, 4 Wheat. 518, 654 (1819).

2.   All quotes from the oral arguments are taken from transcript in the opinion, 4 Wheat. 316 (1819).

3.   This and the following quotes are from the opinion in *McCulloch* v. *Maryland*, 4 Wheat. 316 (1819).

Epilogue

Marshall's broad definition of national authority ("Let the end be legitimate, let it be within the scope of the constitution, and all means which are appropriate . . .") made possible over time the creation of a powerful central government. Now there is virtually no area of our lives not touched by the national government. In recent years, however, Ronald Reagan advocated "New Federalism," whose purpose was to return certain national programs and responsibilities to the states. The push for New Federalism encouraged the already growing initiative of the states, an example of which is described in the next selection.

2.2

In an often-quoted dissent in the case of *New State Ice Co.* v. *Liebman*, Supreme Court Justice Louis Brandeis wrote, "It is one of the happy incidents of the federal system that a single courageous state may, if its citizens choose, serve as a laboratory; and try novel social and economic experiments without risk to the rest of the country." This was not an idle expression of philosophy by Justice Brandeis—he truly believed these words. When one of his bright law clerks, at the end of a year of service in New Deal Washington, asked where he should go to work next, Brandeis said, "Return to your home state." The puzzled young lawyer could only reply, "But Mr. Justice, Fargo, North Dakota?" It was an indication of the importance Brandeis attached to work at the state level.

David Osborne describes the current-day expression of this philosophy of state activism. Note that federalism presents both advantages and problems for states trying to experiment. An advantage of the federal structure is that state innovation can be more effective because each state can tailor programs to fit its own needs. With various states trying different solutions for the same problem, a successful program may emerge.

A disadvantage of this "laboratory" process is the lack of coordination among state programs in the same area, and between state and national efforts. Sometimes a strong national role is necessary. Some problems, such as acid rain, are not confined to one state, and so cannot be solved by an individual state. Further, some states lack the financial resources to implement their plans fully.

Osborne's description of Arizona's efforts to tackle water policy under Governor Bruce Babbitt depicts one of the success stories of federalism. It also shows the consequences of Ronald Reagan's policy of New Federalism, under which the national government turned over to the states certain financial responsibilities, such as sharing in the cost of federal reclamation projects. On the one hand, a strong governor such as

Laboratories of Democracy

David Osborne

From David Osborne, *Laboratories of Democracy* (Boston: Harvard Business School Press, 1988), pp. 1–3, 111–21, 142–43. Reprinted by permission of International Creative Management, Inc. Copyright © 1988 by David Osborne.

Babbitt can transform the direction of state policy rather dramatically. On the other hand, there is often little choice: when powers are turned back to the states in order for them to share in the cost of certain projects, states are faced with putting more money into these programs or seeing them die.

BRUCE BABBITT   Democratic governor of Arizona, 1979–1987.

JACK PFISTER   General manager of Arizona's largest water and power utility.

RONALD REAGAN   President of the United States, 1981–1989; espoused New Federalism.

▶ Franklin Roosevelt once said of the New Deal, "Practically all the things we've done in the federal government are like things Al Smith did as governor of New York." There was surprising honesty in Roosevelt's remark, though he might have credited other states as well. Many of FDR's initiatives—including unemployment compensation, massive public works programs, deposit insurance, and social security—were modeled on successful state programs. The groundwork for much of the New Deal social agenda was laid in the states during the Progressive Era.*

A similar process is under way today, particularly in the economic arena. The 1980s [were] a decade of enormous innovation at the state level. For those unfamiliar with state politics—and given the media's relentless focus on Washington, that includes most Americans—the specifics are often startling. While the Reagan administration was denouncing government intervention in the marketplace, governors of both parties were embracing an unprecedented role as economic activists. Over the past decade, they have created well over 100 public investment funds, to make loans to and investments in businesses. Half the states have set up public venture capital funds; others have invested public money in the creation of private financial institutions. At least 40 states have created programs to stimulate technological innovation, which now number at least 200. Dozens of states have overhauled their public education systems. Tripartite business-labor-government boards have sprung up, often with the purpose of financing local committees dedicated to restructuring labor-management relations. A few states have even launched cooperative efforts with management and labor to revitalize regional industries.

Why this sudden burst of innovation at the state level? Just 25 years ago, state governments were widely regarded as the enemies of change, their resistance

---

* The Progressive Era, roughly the period between 1895 and 1920, was characterized by a number of reform movements that targeted such problems as political corruption, crime, poverty, and lack of social, political, and economic opportunity.

symbolized by George Wallace in the schoolhouse door.* The answer has to do with the profound and wrenching economic transition the United States has experienced over the past two decades. In the 1980s, a fundamentally new economy [was] born. With it has come a series of new problems, new opportunities, and new challenges. In the states, government has responded.

The notion that America has left the industrial era behind is now commonplace. Some call the new age the "postindustrial era," some the "information age," others the "era of human capital." But most agree that the fundamental organization of the American and international economies that prevailed for three decades after World War II has changed. The United States has evolved from an industrial economy built upon assembly-line manufacturing in large, stable firms to a rapidly changing, knowledge-intensive economy built upon technological innovation.

The most obvious symptoms of this transition are idle factories, dislocated workers, and depressed manufacturing regions. Less obvious are the problems that inhibit our ability to innovate: a poorly educated and trained work force; adversarial relations between labor and management; inadequate supplies of risk capital; and corporate institutions that lag behind their foreign competitors in the speed with which they commercialize the fruits of their research, adopt new production technologies, and exploit foreign markets.

Jimmy Carter was elected just as the public began to sense that something had gone wrong with the American economy. Like other national politicians of his day, he only dimly perceived the emerging realities of the new economy. Ronald Reagan owed his election to the deepening economic crisis, but his solution was to reach back to the free-market myths of the preindustrial era. He had the luxury to do so because he governed an enormously diverse nation, in which rapid growth along both coasts balanced the pain experienced in the industrial and agricultural heartland.

Most governors have not had that luxury. When unemployment approached 13 percent in Massachusetts, or 15 percent in Pennsylvania, or 18 percent in Michigan, governors had to respond. They could not afford to wait for the next recovery, or to evoke the nostrums of free-market theory.

The same dynamic occurred during the last great economic transformation: the birth of our industrial economy. The Progressive movement, which originated at the state and local level, grew up in response to the new problems created by rapid industrialization: the explosion of the cities, the emergence of massive corporate trusts, the growth of urban political machines, the exploitation of industrial labor. Many Progressive reforms introduced in the cities or states were gradually institutionalized at the federal level—culminating in the New Deal.

---

* In the early 1960s, Governor George Wallace fought to keep blacks out of the University of Alabama. In the spring of 1963, federal officials forced the university to desegregate after Wallace defied federal orders to admit blacks.

This reality led Supreme Court Justice Louis Brandeis to coin his famous phrase, "laboratories of democracy." One of America's leading Progressive activists during the early decades of the twentieth century, Brandeis viewed the states as laboratories in which the Progressives could experiment with new solutions to social and economic problems. Those that worked could be applied nationally; those that failed could be discarded.

Brandeis's phrase captured the peculiar, pragmatic genius of the federal system. As one approach to government—one political paradigm—wears thin, its successor is molded in the states, piece by piece. The process has little to do with ideology and everything to do with trial-and-error, seat-of-the-pants pragmatism. Part of the beauty, as Brandeis pointed out, is that new ideas can be tested on a limited scale—to see if they work, and to see if they sell—before they are imposed on the entire nation.

Today, at both the state and local levels, we are in the midst of a new progressive era. Just as the state and local Progressivism of Brandeis's day foreshadowed the New Deal, the state and local experimentation of the 1980s may foreshadow a new national agenda. Already the issues that . . . dominated state politics in the 1980s—economic competitiveness and excellence in education—are emerging as major themes in [presidential politics]. . . .

Life in Arizona is something few Americans raised east of the Mississippi would recognize. Two-thirds of all state residents were born elsewhere. Half arrived in the last fifteen years. Every fall a third of the students in the typical Phoenix school district are new. In 1986, *61* new shopping centers were completed or under way in the Phoenix metropolitan area.

In the mid-1980s, Phoenix was the nation's fastest growing city; Arizona one of its fastest growing states. At the current pace, the Phoenix area will double its population of 1.9 million—nearly half the state total—within 15 years. Every year this mushrooming metropolis—an endless expanse of one-story, suburban-style homes and shopping centers—gobbles up thousands of acres of desert in a race for the horizon. At 400 square miles, it now covers more ground than New York City.

This explosive growth has transformed a dusty, sparsely populated frontier state into a land of the modern, Sunbelt metropolis. Arizona was the last of the contiguous 48 states to join the union, in 1912. By 1940, it had only 500,000 people, spread out in small, desert towns and over vast Indian reservations. Phoenix had only 65,000 people. But World War II brought military bases and defense plants, and the postwar boom brought air conditioning and air travel. Suddenly Arizona's location and climate were advantages, rather than disadvantages. The defense contractors, aerospace companies, and electronics manufacturers poured in, bringing an army of young engineers and technicians with their wives and their children. This was the Eisenhower generation—raised during the depression, hardened by World War II, anxious for the security of a job, a home, and a future for their children. With their crew cuts and their conservatism, they transformed Arizona from a sleepy, almost southern Democratic state into a bastion of Sunbelt Republicanism.

Before the Republican takeover in the 1950s, the farmers, the mining companies, and the bankers had run the state. Copper, cotton, and cattle were king. "It used to be that there were five or six men who would sit around a luncheon table at the old Arizona Club and pretty much decide on how things were going to be," says Jack Pfister, general manager of the Salt River Project, the state's largest water and power utility. "Some legislators were said to wear a copper collar."

At first, the new suburban middle class did not change this arrangement a great deal. Real estate developers, the new millionaires on the block, joined the club. But even as the Republicans cemented their control in the 1960s, rural legislators held onto the reins of seniority—and thus power. State government was tiny, the governor a figurehead. And the new suburbanites embraced the frontier ethos in which the old Arizona had taken such pride. Ignoring the fact that without major government investments—in military bases, defense plants, and dams—Arizona would still be a rural backwater, they believed their newfound prosperity was the product of untrammeled free enterprise. Beginning in 1952, they voted Republican in every presidential election. They had little truck with Washington. In the 1950s, Arizona declined to participate in the federal Interstate Highway System; in the 1960s, it turned down medicaid. As local people still say with a hint of pride, Arizona is the last preserve of the lone gun slinger.

The combination of explosive growth and a frontier mentality created problems very different from those encountered by the other states. . . . "In the East, you have old cities, old infrastructure, and a fight for economic survival," says Republican Senator Anne Lindemann. "Here, we're trying to control the growth as best we can."

This process was not without its lessons for the rest of the nation, however. Because Arizona is a desert, with a fragile ecosystem, its rapid growth threw into sharp relief the most serious environmental problems of the postindustrial era—particularly those involving water and toxic chemicals. And because the political climate makes public resources so scarce, the struggle to cope with the social problems created by a modern economy stimulated a degree of creativity rarely seen in a conservative state.

The task of dragging Arizona into the modern era fell to Bruce Babbitt, who by the time he left office in 1987 had changed the very nature of the governorship. A lanky, scholarly type whose habitual slouch and thoughtful manner hide an enormous drive, Babbitt looks like a cross between Donald Sutherland and Tom Poston. He has sandy hair, a lined face that has begun to sag with the wear of 14 years in politics, and large, pale eyes that bulge out from behind his eyebrows when he scowls. In a small group, when he is in his natural, analytic

mode, Babbitt can be brilliant. On a dais, when he tries to sound like a politician, his body stiffens, his eyes bulge, and he does a good imitation of Don
Knotts.

Despite his weakness as a public speaker, Babbitt captivated the Arizona
electorate. He was elected in 1978 with 52 percent of the vote, re-elected four
years later, during a recession, with 62 percent. Summing up the Babbitt years,
the *Arizona Republic,* a conservative newspaper, called him the "take-charge
governor." "He is without a doubt the smartest, quickest elected official I have
ever met," an environmental activist told me, in a comment echoed by many
others. "Babbitt plays it on the precipice," added a state senator. "He is constantly pushing this state forward, and he has an uncanny ability to pull it
off." . . .

Traditionally, the governor's office in Arizona had been extremely weak. Arizona was perhaps the only state in the union in which a governor would consider the ambassadorship to Argentina a step up. State government was run by
a small group of senior legislators and their staffs, who brought out the governor for ceremonial occasions. The notion that a governor might try to set an
agenda for the state, or dare to veto a bill, never crossed most politicians' minds.

Babbitt immediately set out to change that. Six weeks into his term he vetoed
two bills on the same day—then timed his veto message for the evening news,
knocking the wind out of a planned override. The legislature reacted with
shock. "Our idea of an activist governor was one who met with us once a month
to seek our advice," said Alfredo Gutierrez. "This guy called us daily to tell us
what he wanted to do."

Babbitt vetoed 21 bills in 1979, 30 more over the next two years. His total of
114 vetoes in nine years was more than double the record set by Arizona's first
governor, who served for 13 years. "My business friends used to complain that
we had a weak governor," says Jack Pfister. "After Babbitt was in there about
two or three years, you never heard anybody complain about that again. What
he demonstrated was that it was more the individual than the structure of the
office itself."

The Environment

In his second year as governor, Babbitt tackled the one issue that dwarfs all
others in Arizona: water. In the postindustrial era, environmental protection is
no longer an obstacle to growth; it is a central ingredient of growth. As a society,
we need new institutions through which we can come together to design equi-
table solutions to difficult environmental issues. No state has provided a better
model than Arizona—because no state is more threatened by the limits of its
fragile environment.

Phoenix gets seven inches of rain a year. (Boston gets 44.) Where the metropolis ends, the desert begins. Even in the midst of plenty, luxurious homes are meticulously landscaped—with rocks, dirt, and cactus.

Phoenix and Tucson were both settled because of water. The Spaniards built a walled presidio along the lush marsh lands of the Santa Cruz River, and Tucson was born. The U.S. cavalry harvested galleta hay that grew wild along the Salt River, then planted crops in the beds of ancient irrigation canals that combed the valley. Gradually Phoenix grew up.

Except in abnormally wet months, the Salt and Santa Cruz rivers are now dry, dusty scars in Phoenix and Tucson, memories of a time when water was not so precious. Residents of Tucson have pumped so much water out of the ground that the Santa Cruz River has simply dried up. In Phoenix, the Salt River Project built a dam 32 miles east of town and siphoned every drop of water into a 1,262-mile grid of aqueducts that serves the valley. Farmers literally call in their orders, whereupon engineers send the proper amount of water down from the storage dams to the diversion dam and through the canals, where it is guided by remote control into the right irrigation ditches.

But river water could not quench Phoenix's thirst. By 1980, Arizonans were pumping almost five million acre feet of water out of the ground every year, nearly twice the amount nature was putting back in. (An acre foot is enough to cover one acre to a depth of one foot.) In central Arizona, where most of the people live, groundwater levels were dropping ten feet a year. Huge fissures—up to nine miles long and four hundred feet wide—had begun to open up in the parched ground. . . .

[In the early 1980s] the Reagan administration announced a new policy encouraging states to share in the cost of federal reclamation projects.* Without significant new money from the state, the Central Arizona Project (CAP), which would bring Colorado River water by aqueduct to Phoenix and Tucson, would be seriously delayed. Babbitt established and chaired a committee that spent ten months negotiating a cost-sharing deal in which the state wound up shouldering $371 million of the project's remaining $1 billion price tag. It was the first time a state had agreed to match federal reclamation money on this scale, and it ensured that CAP water would complete its 333-mile journey from the Colorado River to Tucson during the 1990s.

CAP provided a new supply of surface water [but did not touch] the issue of water quality. Throughout the 1980s, one toxic pollution scare had followed another. Drinking water wells had been closed in both the Tucson and Phoenix

---

* A *reclamation project* is one undertaken to restore an environmentally damaged area (such as strip-mined land, or a polluted stream) to its original pristine state.

areas. With high-tech giants Motorola and Hughes Aircraft allowing toxic chemicals to seep into the groundwater, people began to worry that by the time the state reached safe yield, the water would no longer be safe to drink.

The legislature wrestled with the issue for two years, deadlocking over which state agency should be given regulatory power over this new problem: Industry favored the Arizona Water Control Council, which it dominated; environmentalists favored the state Department of Health Services.

What finally broke the logjam was a decision by several environmental organizations to put a water quality measure on the ballot. Industry leaders understood that it might pass. Their principal ally, Senate majority leader Burton Barr, wanted to run for governor—but not as the dirty water candidate. With both sides ready to compromise, Babbitt pulled together an Ad Hoc Water Quality Committee in January 1986. It included Republicans and Democrats, industry representatives and environmentalists, and representatives of the farmers, mining companies, and cities.

As a partisan of clean water, Babbitt took a . . . forceful position. . . . When his subcommittees reported back on the difficult issues, he would listen carefully to the various arguments made by those around the table, then finally announce the position he would support. "He was really kind of the judge," says Priscilla Robinson, one of the environmental representatives. "He would say to us, 'You can't have that.' "

Babbitt relied on an implicit threat that he would veto any bill he was not satisfied with, and that the environmentalists' initiative would then appear on the ballot. "Industry people would make a case," says Robinson, "and he would smile at them in his congenial way and say, 'You've failed to convince me. Let's proceed. On to the next item.' And that was it. He controlled the process. Of course what he was saying was, 'I'd veto that.' "

The resulting bill has been widely described as the toughest water quality law in the country. It created a new Department of Environmental Quality (DEQ), prohibited all discharges of groundwater-threatening pollutants without a permit from DEQ, and strengthened the regulation of fertilizers, pesticides, and so on. It also made polluters liable for the cost of cleaning up tainted water and established a $5-million-a-year state superfund for use when the culprit could not be identified. The environmentalists' major victory, however, was a requirement that all groundwater be kept pure enough for drinking. Unless explicitly reclassified by the new department, every aquifer in the state must meet federal EPA standards for what will eventually be a list of 120 chemicals. For months the mining companies, which have polluted many aquifers, resisted this. But the environmentalists insisted. Finally, when the mining companies had won several other concessions, they gave in.

With the new Environmental Quality Act in place, Arizona completed its transformation from the state with the least environmental regulation to the state with the most. Delegations from other states—and nations—now regularly visit Arizona to look at its water management system. The most important lessons Arizona teaches, however, are to be found in the realm of politics. Bruce Babbitt proved that with the right kind of leadership, even the most intractable environmental disputes can be resolved. What it takes is a leader willing to bring the right parties to the table and capable of bringing the right pressures to bear. . . .

Epilogue

Although this selection describes a success story, New Federalism was not the large-scale success that Ronald Reagan had hoped for. For example, Reagan wanted the national and state governments to swap certain programs. In particular, he wanted financial and administrative responsibility for Aid to Families with Dependent Children and the food stamp program to be turned back to the states, in exchange for a federal takeover of Medicaid. But widespread fear that most states would not be able to handle the financial burden stalled the plans.

Arizona's efforts did not mean long-term success for Bruce Babbitt, either. He ran for the Democratic nomination for president in 1988, and although he impressed the public with his intellect and innovative thinking, he did not win many votes and had to drop out of the race after the New Hampshire primary. And we can only wonder what governors will face in the 1990s. Will they be able to continue ambitious programs in the face of growing budget and economic problems?

How to Fight Wildfires? Trust the Guy in the Green Shirt

Richard D. Manning

The American federal system has changed over time in response to a variety of factors, including the nature of the actors making decisions, the timing of those decisions, and the issues involved. States may be "laboratories of democracy," as David Osborne describes, but how do those laboratories fit into the federal structure as a whole? Or do they fit at all? In this selection, Richard Manning discusses both the problems of the old-style federalism and the potential solutions presented by the new-style federalism.

Until roughly Franklin Roosevelt's New Deal, state government and programs were seen as separate from, and subordinate to, the overarching national government. The result was like a layer cake, with neither level infringing on the other, and was called "Dual Federalism." Because of the problems of delineating and maintaining the boundaries of these levels, the Roosevelt administration began a move toward "Cooperative Federalism," which looked more like a marble cake in our visual image. Each government tried to cooperate with the other in handling problems, but the efforts were still as distinct as the marbleized color pattern in the marble cake. As Manning shows in the wildfire-fighting area, everyone had responsibility and yet no one had responsibility in a crisis. At best, actions would be uncoordinated; at worst, nothing would be done at all.

In an effort to remedy this situation, the Forest Service, "the guys in the green shirt," developed the "incident command system," in which one person from the national government took charge of the fire-fighting effort. This system may seem like a top-down, almost dictatorial management style, but it is, in fact, an example of the new "picket fence" style of federal response. All of the various levels of government responsible for dealing with an issue unite in an integrated effort to handle a problem. The united levels then divide into functional groups according to the problem being handled. As you will see from this article, a coordinated response is absolutely mandatory in such a crisis as a forest fire.

RONALD HENDRICKSON A chief firefighter for the National Forest Service.

JAMES F. MANN Head of fire fighting for the Forest Service in the northern Rockies.

DAVE PONCIN Head of the Class I federal fire-fighting team.

TED SCHWINDEN Governor of Montana, 1981–1989.

JOSEPH J. WAGENFEHR A chief firefighter for the National Forest Service.

▶ It was not a promising beginning. Early in the 1988 forest fire season, which was to become the worst on record in the Northern Rockies, a wildfire sprinted out of the timbered hills of eastern Montana and across the drought-dry plains.

When there is fire in the wild lands of the West, it is up to the U.S. Forest Service and the intergovernmental cavalry of troops it leads to ride to the rescue. Ride they did on that fire, but with a curious result. Local ranchers, incensed with Forest Service tactics, met their would-be rescuers with what Ted Schwinden, then the Democratic governor of Montana, called an "ugly confrontation." Worse, the Forest Service's firefighting organization, an alphabet soup of state and federal bureaucracies, faced a sheriff even madder than the ranchers who elected him. Joe Carey tried twice to arrest the guy directing the firefighters—to incarcerate Smokey the Bear. Understand that all this hassle swirled around an organization that bills itself as the very model of intergovernmental cooperation.

Indeed, it was not a good beginning for the organization that would face more than 1,400 fires—at least 100 of them classified as "major"—on nearly 3 million acres in Montana, Wyoming and Idaho during the summer of 1988. It was a summer of crisis in the Northern Rockies, a crisis met with the civilian equivalent of going to war. More than 15,000 people organized under the Forest Service, the Bureau of Land Management, the National Park Service, the Bureau of Indian Affairs, the Army and a conglomeration of state and local agencies worked within a single command to battle the blazes. Firefighters and engines from all 50 states, and from as far away as the Virgin Islands, became conscripts in the wild-lands war. The total tab for all this will approach half a billion dollars.

More than a lesson in firefighting, that early-season blaze, which was known as the Brewer Fire, and the recalcitrant sheriff provided a case study in how government relates to its community, in this instance, a hostile community. Yet it is precisely a strong sense of community that governs firefighting in the West. The firefighters have developed a system with enough flexibility to respond to the diversity of the physical and social environment, yet with a firm enough structure to bring a variety of agencies and skills together effectively. The system hinges on a formal management plan developed to fight fires in California and now being used to handle emergencies nationwide—and even, once, a rock concert.

In Missoula, Montana, headquarters of the Forest Service office that superintended the worst of the nation's fires last year, there is a warehouse full of parachutes, pumps and the paraphernalia of fighting forest fires. There workers are whiling away the winter sharpening thousands of Pulaskis, gizmos that look like the results of a marriage between a hoe and a pickax and serve as the single most essential tool in the trench warfare of fighting fires.

Meanwhile, in nearby offices, James F. Mann, Ronald Hendrickson and Joseph J. Wagenfehr, the Forest Service's three top firefighters in the Northern Rockies, are honing policy. As much as Pulaskis, policy fights fire. There are rules for everything, from how one hires mules and bulldozers to how one decides not to fight a fire and to let it rage across forests unchecked. There may well be some changes in the rules now, especially in the controversial provisions that let some fires burn with no effort to stop them. The core of the rules, however, likely will stay intact. That core is a framework called the "incident command system." It is this system that both observers and professional firefighters point to as the endeavor's best-honed tool.

Schwinden says the system is so successful that it has melded state and federal agencies with a seamless joint. "Things are so integrated now, you don't even know who is in charge," he says. As a measure of that, consider that the federal firefighters often, on their own initiative, attack fires on state land, then charge the states for services rendered. For that, Schwinden's administration received a bill for about $10 million—a lot of money in a state with a population of 800,000 and a general-fund budget of $780 million. Before leaving office in January, Schwinden sent the legislature a budget recommending that the bill be paid without question. "You've got to trust the guy in the green [Forest Service] shirt," he says.

The incident command system developed in the aftermath of a raging fire season in Southern California in 1978. Those fires swept hot and fast through explosively dry brush. Residential areas in the fires' paths made evacuations common. The resulting dislocations meant that even after the fast-burning fires were out, there remained major tasks in dealing with human needs. "After two or three days of those fast-moving fires, the fire may not be a problem anymore, but there is still a hell of a lot of work to be done," Wagenfehr says.

Where the old Forest Service system came up short before 1978 was that the person in charge—then called a fire boss—was responsible for putting out the blaze. Period. Other tasks, such as conducting evacuations or repairing environmental damage or even protecting homes instead of brush from fire, fell haphazardly to other agencies and people. Under the new system, the person in charge is called the incident commander. He is responsible for everything from quelling the flames to conducting town meetings to ensuring that the presence of several thousand firefighters in a small mountain town doesn't disrupt the economy.

"They are managers of situations rather than directors of tactics," Wagenfehr says. That responsibility, he explains, extends to such questions as whether firefighting teams are draining local supermarkets by buying all their hand soap, so that residents can't do down and buy some themselves.

To handle these tasks, each commander is assigned a team that stays together throughout the fire season. Each team has members in charge of specific specialties, such as managing aircraft, figuring payrolls or devising the firefighting strategy. The team's members are drawn from state, local and federal agencies and trained in advance for their jobs. Command teams fall into two categories, including regional teams that handle the lesser fires and what are called Class I teams. There are 18 of those in the nation, and they are shipped around the country to face the nation's worst wildfires. Typically, when a routine fire gets out of hand, the regional Class II command team is pulled off to make room for the hotshots. That is exactly what was happening when the sheriff and the ranchers got out of hand in that eastern Montana incident.

"The political fire was burning as hot as the Brewer Fire," says Dave Poncin, the federal firefighter from Idaho who headed the Class I team sent to take over. What stoked the political blaze was a plan by the Forest Service to light backfires, which are fires deliberately set to rob the main fire of fuel. It is a common technique, but the ranchers decided they had already seen quite enough fire. It was up to Poncin to deal with the ranchers' objections. Incident commanders are trained to handle political conflagrations.

On the scene, Poncin took some specific steps that demonstrate how the incident command system works. First, Poncin handled the angry ranchers. Figuring that their ire was fueled by tough economic times brought on by years of drought, he hired them as firefighters and listened to their counsel.

As to the sheriff, Poncin says it may not be exactly true that he ignored him—with the blessings of Schwinden—but that's not far from the mark. "We found we couldn't work with him the way we normally work with sheriffs, so we didn't," Poncin says.

Guiding Poncin's actions were a couple of principles that show up repeatedly in the system: He considered the community as a resource instead of a barrier and tapped what information it was able to offer. Above that, though, is a second factor that is vital to the operation of the system. Poncin, as a local commander, had the autonomy and latitude to act as he saw fit, including ignoring the local sheriff.

Curiously, Poncin's ad hoc politicking placated even the sheriff. "This Dave Poncin was real good in being able to talk to the people. He really knew what he was doing," Carey says. Poncin says Carey backed off from his threats of arrest and never had specified what the charge might be.

Mann, who heads the Forest Service's firefighting effort in the region, says it is that kind of autonomy for the commanders in the field that makes the system work. There is a temptation to look at the system, with its flow charts (each commander in the field answers to a multi-agency group in Missoula called the Regional Incident Command Organization), uniforms, jargon, aircraft and use of terms such as "command," and say the system only apes the military, only works because it has matched its warlike tasks to warlike methods. To some extent it does. Mann and his staff say, however, that the key to the system's success is that it is decidedly unmilitary.

In the 1940s, when someone first thought of parachuting from airplanes into forest fires, the nation's first smoke jumpers were World War II conscientious objectors. That streak remains. Mann says the chief distinction from the military is autonomy, the ability of the person in the field to call the shots, especially when it comes to tactics. Each commander is given specific policy directives that have been set in individual forest plans before fires begin. They specify areas where fires should be allowed to burn, and where valuable stands of timber and structures are located. The commander also gets a list of people and equipment he will have to do the job. Within those limits, the commander is largely free to do as he sees fit.

Hendrickson, one of Mann's chief staffers, says that the difference becomes most evident when the Forest Service links with units of the regular Army, something it frequently does. The link with state agencies and other federal agencies most often comes off without a hitch, but marriages with military brass are generally less than blissful, Hendrickson says. The military units "don't have a coordination center. They have a general. When he snaps his fingers, a hundred lieutenants go in every direction, and they've each got a little job to do, and it never comes together," Hendrickson says. The biggest difference between the Forest Service and the military is that the lieutenants in the Forest Service can and do make crucial decisions by working with one another, not through the general.

Given the autonomy built into the system, the key question then becomes control of local commanders to balance the competing needs of, at times, literally hundreds of separate fires around the region. The system does that by using a sophisticated information network to control where the money and effort go.

The firefighters are the first to admit that the autonomous system does create problems. For instance, although the highly publicized fires in Yellowstone National Park last summer [1988] were only a part of the overall picture, they drew the biggest share of both public attention and resources. That led to some local commanders at the Yellowstone fires hogging crews and equipment, Hendrickson says. "The Park Service wouldn't give us back our crews," he says. "We almost had to go out there with buses and load them up and take them away." The regional office at Missoula has the power to say what fire gets what tools.

"We finally got to the point that we said, okay, damn it, we're not going to give [Yellowstone] anything," he says. The power to deny tools is the stick, but the regional office balances that with a big carrot: It has enormous power to fill local needs, largely because it ties into a national network of interagency agreements that shifts firefighters and equipment around the country. At one point, that network came into play when a Yellowstone commander advised Wagenfehr that unless help came fast, fires would overrun historic buildings at Old

Faithful. "There were fire engines from Phoenix in Yellowstone within 48 hours," Wagenfehr says.

The Forest Service's system relies heavily on moving people and equipment around the country where they are required to avoid the need for vast firefighting crews and caches of equipment in each area. By using the network to share a common pool of equipment and firefighters, federal, state and local government can significantly trim capital expenses, Wagenfehr says.

That idea of portability also shapes the incident command system. The system is uniform nationwide, meaning a firefighter trained in the system in Alabama can be shipped to Colorado and be ready to work within a few hours. His job, jargon and tools are the same. To accomplish this, the Forest Service has set up training courses at each of 10 regional offices in the nation, not only for its own people but for state and local officials as well. Of the 1,254 people trained at the Missoula regional office in the past three years, 248 have been from either state or local government.

That cadre of converts has in turn spread the system to other emergency services, such as handling hazardous-waste spills and a manhunt near Helena, Montana, two years ago. It also has been used during floods and earthquakes in California and even in the big Mexico City earthquake, says Martin Barrows, who works for the Forest Service in San Bernardino, California.

Barrows, who helped develop the system during the past decade, says the most novel use to date has been managing crowds and security at a rock concert called the US Festival in San Bernardino. A range of agencies, including the Forest Service, California Highway Patrol, local sheriff's department and state parks officials, cooperated in that effort under a command structure organized by task, not agency. "It makes for a team effort. Everybody knows their position and assignment and knows what their responsibility is," Barrows says.

What also makes it work is that lacing all of this business together—this flexibility, cooperation and autonomy—is information, beginning with tidbits of knowledge that flow literally from the ground up.

At nearly 20 locations in Montana alone, sensors wired to small wooden dowels read the moisture content of the wood—a key factor in predicting fire behavior. The sensors beep readings to a satellite that beeps back at a computer in North Carolina, which in turn corresponds with its electronic colleague in Boise, Idaho. The Boise computer then chirps its message on to Missoula.

Meanwhile, one of the first boxes unpacked at a fire camp is a computer. Connected either by phone or satellite, the remote computers feed information back to a mainframe computer in Missoula. That allows Mann and his staff to keep an eye on progress and to make decisions about resources.

This attention to the flow of information is contagious, and Mann says firefighters have come to understand that the flow can't only be internal—that to be effective, the lines of communication must flow into the community. "It's a two-way street, not just gathering information and holding it to your breast. You need to share it back to the people you collected it from," he says.

Poncin's first step when he took command of the eastern Montana fire was to tell the ranchers what he was up to, but he also gathered ranchers' knowledge of such specifics as local topography and resources.

The practice of sharing and seeking information materializes best in the Forest Service's strategy of contracting with private companies for many of its needs, such as De Havilland aircraft to ferry smoke jumpers, caterers to feed thousands of firefighters, psychologists to counsel stressed-out firefighters and strings of mules to pack tools to remote fire camps. Wagenfehr says that having a reliable source for those needs requires nothing less than a web of information and relationships throughout the community.

That tie to the community will have to go deeper, though, because the public plays a key role in deciding fundamental policy or, more precisely, in deciding what government should and should not do. Setting the boundaries of governmental responsibility is an issue facing most leaders today, but in the case of fire policy, it comes into particularly sharp focus. There are those who maintain that some fires should not be fought, but should be allowed to burn for economic or ecological reasons.

"All fires aren't bad," Wagenfehr says. "All fires don't have to be stomped on immediately, and there oftentimes are cheaper ways to suppress those that are undesirable rather than that go-right-out-and-stomp-it-out-by-10-o'clock-the-next-day direction that we did have."

Part of what lies behind Wagenfehr's statement is just common sense. Sometimes letting a fire take its course for a couple of days will allow it to burn to a place where weather or terrain will snuff it out.

But the reasoning goes further and leads to questioning whether the cost of extinguishing some fires is too much when what are being protected are some remote stands of timber and summer homes. There are a couple of ways to ask that question, but both lead to issues touching all of government.

First, is government spending too much to quell the blazes that everyone agrees ought to be quelled? Probably. Wagenfehr says that in any emergency, the tendency is to err on the side of overkill, so Monday-morning quarterbacks are bound to find ways that corners could have been cut. "There clearly are overexpenditures during an emergency situation," says Schwinden, the former Montana governor. "But we'd be laughed out of the state, impeached or shot if we made a two-week analysis of how many bombers you want to order."

That leads to a second question, which goes beyond efficiency: Is government deciding to fight too many fires?

"The [Forest Service] controls fires in a cost-effective manner, but they don't want cost-effectiveness questions raised about whether they should control a fire. They say, 'We don't want to squander money while we're putting this fire out, but we sure as hell want to put this fire out,'" says Tom Power, chairman of the economics department at the University of Montana.

The Forest Service often does spend more money than a stand of timber is worth to protect the timber, and certainly more than a log cabin is worth to protect someone's Shangri-La. "Logic has been provided little room to operate when it comes to fire," Power says. "The community is saying, 'We will not let nature take away your home. That's the sign of a civilized people. We limit what nature is allowed to damage. We'll bear this burden even if it is 10 times greater than the cost of the property.' It's all very noble, but I think it's silly. If we want to be noble, we can go build some homes for the homeless."

Power suggests that society deal with the issue much as it dealt with people who built homes in flood plains a decade ago. "Somehow, we shifted gears enough on the flood-control thing to say that people who build their homes in the flood plain have to have their own insurance," he says. "We have made it clear to them that they are totally responsible, that the community will not come to their aid if they choose to put themselves in that situation." Today, new homes built in a designated flood plain no longer are eligible for federally subsidized flood insurance.

Still, the Forest Service, without question, assigns fires that threaten property its top priority.

This attitude is not all the work of the firefighters. Following Power's suggestion would land the firefighters in a political inferno hotter than anything they've faced in the woods. On questions of fundamental policy, government is tied to the community's attitudes, which is best illuminated with that second class of fires, those government chooses to allow to burn for ecological reasons.

This is what has come to be known as the "let-burn" policy. It was developed a decade ago and has been in use ever since, although it didn't become controversial until this year. Basically, it says that under some conditions, naturally caused fires in formally designated wilderness areas and in some national parks should be allowed to burn.

The 1988 summer of unprecedented drought and resulting wildfires has focused considerable attention on the policy, largely because some blame it for letting certain fires, especially those around Yellowstone Park, get out of hand. The policy has been roundly criticized by residents from around the park, as well as by elected officials in several Western states.

As a result of the controversy, a federal task force made up of officials from the U.S. Departments of Agriculture and Interior reviewed the policy and, in a report issued in December, found it fundamentally sound, although the panel did recommend some modifications.

While that policy has become a roaring controversy in Yellowstone Park, it has not raised much opposition in designated wilderness areas outside the park. In fact, a 247,000-acre fire in the Scapegoat Wilderness in western Montana this summer [1988] has made independent wildlife officials and ecologists ecstatic, because it created the open areas and resulting forage that wildlife needs. In the face of some opposition, the Forest Service is trying to build on that core of support to preserve a policy its scientists see as absolutely necessary. How the agency does that is instructive.

First, it tackles political issues head on. Recovery teams are dispatched even while the fire is still burning to replace damaged structures and to stop erosion, to ease what people perceive as the ill effects of fire. When an unchecked wilderness fire jumped the wilderness boundaries and destroyed ranchers' grasses, the Forest Service enlisted the state's help in gathering free hay for the ranchers.

It's still too soon to see if this effort is convincing the public and the political leaders who influence public opinion and are, in turn, influenced by it. The Forest Service is spending the winter [1989] taking its case to both Congress and the public, but behind the persuasion is a firmer message from the Forest Service that, no matter what the public thinks, fires will continue to be a fact of nature.

Simply, the public can rail all it wants to about fire, but it can't argue with nature. In nature, trees die and gradually carpet forest floors with an explosive load of dry fuels to feed forest fires. More than a half century of fire suppression in the West has allowed that fuel load to achieve critical mass. If natural fires aren't allowed to remove some of those fuels a bit at a time, then, eventually, explosively hot fires that firefighters have no hope of controlling will.

It is a message that goes beyond persuasion. The Forest Service is suggesting that the community face the fact that nature sets limits for government, and that no amount of vigorously expressed public opinion will change what those limits are. It is through an open flow of information that government and the public will come to grips with that blunt fact.

Epilogue

Although on the surface this selection appears to describe a successful example of federalism in action, one reservation must be mentioned. Manning says, "As much as Pulaskis, policy fights fire." This is clearly the case when the decisions involve where to draw the line in protecting property and what kind of financial resources to commit to the fight. But what happens in a case where there is not such unified agreement on policy or where the costs are so great that the monetary burden cannot be met by a shared governmental response? For example, can the functional, or unified picket fence, approach be successfully applied to welfare or medical aid? Reorganizing these bureaucratic structures has proved to be far more challenging than combining fire-fighting services, and may result in another re-examination of styles of federalism.

CHAPTER 3

THE PRESIDENCY

The Birth of the Modern Presidency

William E. Leuchtenburg

"The only thing we have to fear is fear itself," begins this article, quoting from Franklin D. Roosevelt's 1933 inaugural address. And in 1933 there was more than enough justification in this country for a great deal of fear. After the stock market crash of 1929, the nation plunged into the Great Depression. By 1932, 25 percent of the country's workers were unemployed, and nearly half of the nation's banks had failed. Faced with poverty and despair, the country looked to President Herbert Hoover for relief. But Hoover, the "Great Engineer," was not up to the task. Following the old rules for conducting a presidency, he sought to balance the budget, look to the states and the people themselves to deal with their problems, and ride out the negative cycle of the economy. And so, in an overwhelming mandate, in November 1932, the nation turned to the Democratic governor of New York, Franklin D. Roosevelt, for help.

William Leuchtenburg describes how Roosevelt changed both the course of American history and the office of the presidency. Compared to the do-nothing presidency of Herbert Hoover, one is struck by the speed with which Roosevelt moved to combat the Depression. After temporarily closing the nation's banks, the administration responded to the economic crisis with regulatory laws, new agencies, and an entirely different economic philosophy. As important as these specific actions were Roosevelt's speeches, which boosted confidence in the financial community and raised hope in the American people.

Roosevelt transformed the presidency by going beyond his formal responsibilities. Although in 1933 the president was not required or expected to manage the economy, Roosevelt took the initiative in an attempt to end the Depression. For instance, he used deficit spending (a willingness to spend more than the government collects in tax revenues) to help rejuvenate the economy. He also demanded far more from Congress than any president had before, pushing through fifteen major bills in the first three months. Because of Roosevelt's activism and attitude, expectations of succeeding presidents have been high: they are expected to be crisis managers, economic managers, and legislative leaders, like Roosevelt.

HUGO BLACK   Senator from Alabama who pushed for Progressive programs.

LEWIS DOUGLAS   Roosevelt's director of the budget.

HERBERT HOOVER   President of the United States, 1929–1933.

ROBERT LA FOLLETTE   Senator from Wisconsin and one of the leaders of the Progressive movement.

FRANKLIN D. ROOSEVELT   President of the United States, 1933–1945.

ROBERT WAGNER   Senator from New York who fought for labor rights.

HENRY WALLACE   Roosevelt's first secretary of agriculture.

WILLIAM WOODIN   Roosevelt's first secretary of the treasury.

▶ "First of all," declared the new President, "let me assert my firm belief that the only thing we have to fear is fear itself—nameless, unreasoning, unjustified terror. . . ." Grim, unsmiling, chin uplifted, his voice firm, almost angry, he lashed out at the bankers. "We are stricken by no plague of locusts. . . . Plenty is at our doorstep, but a generous use of it languishes in the very sight of the supply. Primarily this is because rulers of the exchange of mankind's goods have failed through their own stubbornness and their own incompetence, have admitted their failure, and have abdicated. . . . The money changers have fled from their high seats in the temple of our civilization. We may now restore that temple to the ancient truths."

The nation, Roosevelt insisted, must move "as a trained and loyal army willing to sacrifice for the good of a common discipline." He would go to Congress with a plan of action, but if Congress did not act and the emergency persisted, the President announced, "I shall not evade the clear course of duty that will then confront me. I shall ask the Congress for the one remaining instrument to meet the crisis—broad Executive power to wage a war against the emergency, as great as the power that would be given to me if we were in fact invaded by a foreign foe."

In the main part of his Inaugural Address, his program for recovery, he had little new to offer. What he did say was so vague as to be open to any interpretation; currency, he opined, should be "adequate but sound." "He is for sound currency, but lots of it," one congressman complained. Yet this was a new Roosevelt; the air of casual gaiety, of evasiveness, had vanished—the ring of his voice, the swing of his shoulders, his call for sacrifice, discipline, and action demonstrated he was a man confident in his powers as leader of the nation. In declaring there was nothing to fear but fear, Roosevelt had minted no new platitude; Hoover had said the same thing repeatedly for three years. Yet Roosevelt had nonetheless made his greatest single contribution to the politics of the 1930's: the instillation of hope and courage in the people. He made clear that the time of waiting was over, that he had the people's interests at heart, and that he would mobilize the power of the government to help them. In the next week, nearly half a million Americans wrote their new President. He had made an impression which Hoover had never been able to create—of a man who knew how to lead and had faith in the future.

Roosevelt moved swiftly to deal with the financial illness that paralyzed the nation. On his very first night in office, he directed Secretary of the Treasury William Woodin to draft an emergency banking bill, and gave him less than five days to get it ready. Woodin found the Treasury corridors prey to rumor, the bankers empty of ideas and queasy with fear of new calamities. To buy Woodin time to prepare legislation, and to protect the nation's dwindling gold reserves, Roosevelt assumed the posture of a commander in chief in wartime. On Sunday afternoon, March 5, he approved the issue of two presidential edicts—one called Congress into special session on March 9; the other, resting on the rather doubtful legal authority of the Trading with the Enemy Act of 1917, halted transactions in gold and proclaimed a national bank holiday.

The very totality of the bank holiday helped snap the tension the country had been under all winter. "Holiday" was a delightful euphemism, and the nation, responding in good spirit, devised ingenious ways to make life go on as it always had. In Michigan, Canadian money circulated; in the Southwest, Mexican pesos; the Dow Chemical Company paid its workers in coins made of Dow-metal, a magnesium alloy; the *Princetonian* printed twenty-five-cent scrip for students. In New York City, wealthy ladies invaded automats to get twenty nickels; speakeasies extended credit; Roseland Dance Hall accepted I.O.U.'s from dancers with bank books; the Hotel Commodore sent a bellhop to a nearby church to get silver from the collection plate in exchange for bills. In most of the nation, inconveniences were minor; only in Michigan, in its fourth week of a bank moratorium, was the situation becoming critical. In Detroit, movies played to near-empty theaters, and city laborers, unable to buy food with their pay checks, fainted at work.

On March 9, the special session of Congress convened in an atmosphere of wartime crisis. Shortly before 1 P.M., Roosevelt's banking message was read, while some newly elected congressmen were still trying to find their seats. The House had no copies of the bill; the Speaker recited the text from the one available draft, which bore last-minute corrections scribbled in pencil. Members found the proposal an exceptionally conservative document. Roosevelt's assault on the bankers in his inaugural address had invited speculation that he might advocate radical reforms, even nationalization of the banks. Instead, the emergency banking measure extended government assistance to private bankers to reopen their banks. The bill validated actions the President had already taken, gave him complete control over gold movements, penalized hoarding, authorized the issue of new Federal Reserve bank notes, and arranged for the reopening of banks with liquid assets and the reorganization of the rest. The bill was largely the work of bankers such as George Harrison and of Hoover's Treasury officers. Arthur Ballantine, Hoover's Under Secretary of the Treasury, continued in the same post under Roosevelt, while Ogden Mills, Hoover's Secretary of the Treasury, hovered in the background. The emergency banking bill represented Roosevelt's stamp of approval for decisions made by Hoover's fiscal advisers.

With a unanimous shout, the House passed the bill, sight unseen, after only thirty-eight minutes of debate. Speaker Rainey observed that the situation recalled the world war, when "on both sides of this Chamber the great war measures suggested by the administration were supported with practical unanimity. . . . Today we are engaged in another war, more serious even in its character and presenting greater dangers to the Republic." Representative Robert Luce of Massachusetts explained to his Republican colleagues: "The majority leaders have brought us a bill on which I myself am unable to advise my colleagues, except to say that this is a case where judgment must be waived, where argument must be silenced, where we should take matters without criticism lest we may do harm by delay." The Senate, over the objections of a small band of progressives, approved the bill unamended 73–7 at 7:30 that evening and at 8:36 that same night it received the President's signature. One congressman later complained: "The President drove the money-changers out of the Capitol on March 4th—and they were all back on the 9th."

On Sunday night, March 12, an estimated sixty million people sat around radio sets to hear the first of President Roosevelt's "fireside chats." In warmly comforting tones, the President assured the nation it was now safe to return their savings to the banks. The next morning, banks opened their doors in the twelve Federal Reserve Bank cities. Nothing so much indicated the sharp shift in public sentiment as the fact that people were now more eager to deposit cash than to withdraw it. "The people trust this admin. as they distrusted the other," observed Agnes Meyer. "This is the secret of the whole situation." Since the President had said the banks were safe, they were; Roosevelt, observed Gerald Johnson, "had given a better demonstration than Schopenhauer ever did of the world as Will and Idea." Deprived of cash for several days, people had been expected to withdraw funds to meet immediate needs, yet in every city deposits far exceeded withdrawals. The crisis was over. "Capitalism," Raymond Moley later concluded, "was saved in eight days."

On March 10, Roosevelt fired his second message at Congress. He requested sweeping powers to slice $400 million from payments to veterans and to slash the pay of federal employees another $100 million. "Too often in recent history," the President warned, "liberal governments have been wrecked on rocks of loose fiscal policy." The economy bill reflected the influence of Director of the Budget Lewis Douglas, who thought that Hoover had indulged in "wild extravagance." Convinced that the proposal echoed the demand of Wall Street for wage slashing and that it was cruel to veterans, the Democratic caucus in the House refused to support the President. One congressman protested that the bill would benefit "big powerful banking racketeers," while another called it "a slaughter of the disabled servicemen of the United States." At any other time, such appeals would have carried both chambers, but they made little headway against the power of the President in a time of crisis. Representative John Young Brown of Kentucky declared: "I had as soon start a mutiny in the face of a foreign foe as start a mutiny today against the program of the President of the United States." "When the *Congressional Record* lies on the desk of Mr. Roosevelt in the morning he will look over the roll call," warned Congressman Clifton Woodrum of Virginia, "and from that he will know whether or not the Members of his own party were willing to go along with him in his great fight to save the country." Although more than ninety Democrats broke with Roosevelt in the House, most of them heeded Woodrum's counsel. After only two days' debate, Congress passed the economy bill. Under the leadership of Franklin Roosevelt, the budget balancers had won a victory for orthodox finance that had not been possible under Hoover.

The staccato rhythm of the Hundred Days had begun: on Thursday, Congress adopted the bank bill; on Saturday, it passed the economy measure; on Monday, March 13, the President asked Congress to fulfill the Democratic pledge of an early end to prohibition. Roosevelt's victory had speeded a remarkable revolution in sentiment; even some veteran dry congressmen now voted for liquor. In February, 1933, the wets had broken a fainthearted Senate filibuster, and the lame-duck Congress, in a startling reversal of attitude, voted to repeal the Eighteenth Amendment. While the Twenty-first Amendment was making its way through the states, Roosevelt requested quick action to amend the Volstead Act by legalizing beer of 3.2 per cent alcoholic content by weight.

Roosevelt's message touched off a raucous, rollicking debate. The drys, who had succeeded in killing a beer bill only a few weeks before, rehearsed the arguments that had been so convincing for more than a decade, but to no avail. Representative John Boylan of New York protested that this was "the same old sob story you have been telling us for the last 12 years. Why, I almost know your words verbatim—the distressed mother, the wayward son, the unruly daughter, the roadhouse, and so forth, and so forth. . . ." Impatient congressmen chanted: "Vote—vote—we want beer"; within a week both houses had passed the beer bill, and added wine for good measure, although congressmen protested that 3.2 wine was not "interesting." On March 22, Roosevelt signed the bill.

As the day of liberation approached, breweries worked feverishly to meet the anticipated demand. Operating around the clock, a St. Joseph, Missouri, factory turned out ten tons of pretzels a day, but still ran two months behind. Emanuel Koveleski, president of the New York Bartenders' Union, proclaimed: "We're all set. The bartenders will be all fine, clean, upstanding young men." On April 7, 1933, beer was sold legally in America for the first time since the advent of prohibition, and the wets made the most of it. In New York, six stout brewery horses drew a bright red Busch stake wagon to the Empire State Building, where a case of beer was presented to Al Smith, "the martyr of 1928." In the beer town of St. Louis, steam whistles and sirens sounded at midnight, while Wisconsin Avenue in Milwaukee was blocked by mobs of celebrants standing atop cars and singing "Sweet Adeline." The most important ritual took place at the Rennert Hotel bar in Baltimore: H. L. Mencken downed a glass of the new beer and assured anxious connoisseurs it was a worthy brew.

Two weeks after Roosevelt took office, the country seemed a changed place. Where once there had been apathy and despondency, there was now an immense sense of movement. If the country did not know in what direction it was moving, it had great expectations; the spell of lassitude had been snapped. On the walls of Thomas A. Edison, Inc., in West Orange, New Jersey, President Charles Edison posted a notice:

> *President Roosevelt has done his part: now you do something.*
>
> *Buy something—buy anything, anywhere; paint your kitchen, send a telegram, give a party, get a car, pay a bill, rent a flat, fix your roof, get a haircut, see a show, build a house, take a trip, sing a song, get married.*
>
> *It does not matter what you do—but get going and keep going. This old world is starting to move.*

In a single fortnight, Roosevelt, wrote Walter Lippmann, had achieved a recapture of morale comparable to the "second battle of the Marne in the summer of 1916."

Yet what had Roosevelt done? He had pursued a policy more ruthlessly deflationary than anything Hoover had dared. With $4 billion tied up in closed banks, he had embarked on a retrenchment program which still further eroded purchasing power. In his circumspect treatment of the banks, in his economy message, in his beer bill, Roosevelt had summed up the program of the arch-conservative du Pont wing of the Democratic party, the very men who had fought him so bitterly in Chicago. Under the leadership of John Raskob, they had proposed to bring the budget into balance by cutting federal spending and by creating new sources of revenue from legalized sales of liquor. Now Roosevelt had done for them what they had been unable to achieve themselves.

No one knew this better than Roosevelt. "While things look superficially rosy," he wrote Colonel House, "I realize well that thus far we have actually given more of deflation than of inflation. . . . It is simply inevitable that we must inflate and though my banker friends may be horrified, I still am seeking an inflation which will not wholly be based on additional government debt." Roosevelt had originally planned a quick session of Congress which would adjourn as soon as it had dealt with the banking crisis, but it responded so well to his first proposals that he decided to hold it in session. On March 16, the President charted a new course by sending his farm message to Congress.

In framing a farm bill, Secretary of Agriculture Henry Wallace preferred the "domestic allotment" plan developed by several economists—John Black of Minnesota and Harvard, W. J. Spillman of the Department of Agriculture, and Beardsley Ruml of the Rockefeller Foundation—and advanced most persuasively by Milburn L. Wilson of Montana State College. The domestic allotment proposal aimed to deal with the crucial problem of depressed prices and mounting surpluses. Hoover's Farm Board had tried to raise prices without curbing production, only to see a half-billion dollars go down the drain with no substantial benefit to farmers. Wilson and the other advocates of the domestic allotment plan proposed to restrict acreage; levy a tax on the processors of agricultural commodities (for example, the miller who converted wheat into flour); and pay farmers who agreed to limit production benefits based on "parity," which would give the farmer the same level of purchasing power he had had before the war.

Roosevelt had his own ideas about a satisfactory farm program—he disliked dumping, wanted decentralized administration, and stipulated the plan should obtain the consent of a majority of the farmers—but, above all, he insisted that farm leaders themselves agree on the kind of bill they wanted. In this fashion, he avoided antagonizing farm spokesmen by choosing one device in preference to another, and threw the responsibility for achieving a workable solution on the farm organizations. Not a few farm leaders disputed Roosevelt's conception of the problem. Processors and old McNary-Haugenites opposed reducing acreage and favored instead a combination of marketing agreements with dumping surpluses abroad. But they were willing to bargain and so was the administration. Wallace, who wanted a farm act before planting time, proposed an omnibus bill which would embody different alternatives, and that, after a series of conferences with farm spokesmen, was what he got.

The House quickly passed the farm bill without change, but the Senate balked at speedy action. The measure shocked conservatives and drew the wrath of lobbyists for the processors—millers, packers, canners, and others—who objected to the proposed processing tax. At the same time, the radical wing of the farm movement protested that the farmer deserved nothing less than government guarantee of his "cost of production," a conception even more elusive than "parity." Tugwell shrewdly observed: "For real radicals such as Wheeler, Frazier, etc., it is not enough; for conservatives it is too much; for Jefferson Democrats it is a new control which they distrust.* For the economic

---

* Rexford Tugwell was a political scientist from Columbia University with expertise in agricultural issues, and one of Roosevelt's principal advisers in his first term. Jefferson Democrats advocated states' rights and a weak central government.

philosophy which it represents there are no defenders at all. Nevertheless, in spite of everything, it will probably become law."

As the Senate debated the farm bill, inflation sentiment grew like the green bay tree. Despite administration opposition, the Senate on April 17 came within ten votes of adopting an amendment by Senator Burton Wheeler of Montana for the free coinage of silver, and Roosevelt was informed that "well over ten" senators had voted against the Wheeler amendment, or had refrained from voting, who favored some kind of inflation. The situation in the House, where nearly half the members had signed a petition to take up a bill to issue greenbacks, was little better. Speaker Rainey confided: "I am an irreconcilable Bryan 16 to 1 man."*

On April 18, Senate leaders warned Roosevelt that a new inflationary amendment to the farm bill, sponsored by Senator Elmer Thomas of Oklahoma, could not be defeated. Recognizing that the situation would soon be out of hand, Roosevelt decided to accept the Thomas proposal if it was rewritten to give the President discretionary powers rather than making any specific course of inflationary action mandatory. In its revised form, the Thomas amendment authorized the President to bring about inflation through remonetizing silver, printing greenbacks, or altering the gold content of the dollar. That night, hearing of Roosevelt's capitulation to the soft-money men, Lewis Douglas cried: "Well, this is the end of Western civilization."

The following day, Roosevelt, confined in bed by a sore throat, announced with a smile to the 125 newspapermen gathered in his bedroom that the United States was off the gold standard. The country had, to be sure, been on a greatly modified gold basis for some weeks. The President wrote later of an encounter with Secretary Woodin on April 20: "His face was wreathed in smiles, but I looked at him and said: 'Mr. Secretary, I have some very bad news for you. I have to announce to you the serious fact that the United States has gone off the gold standard.' Mr. Woodin is a good sport. He threw up both hands, opened his eyes wide and exclaimed: 'My heavens! What, again?'" Yet Roosevelt's embargo of the export of gold represented a decisive turn—nothing less than the jettisoning of the international gold standard.

Roosevelt took the country off gold, not simply to forestall the inflationists, but because he was deeply concerned by the deflation of the first six weeks of the New Deal. By going off gold, he sought to free himself to engage in domestic price-raising ventures. The President's action horrified conservatives. Bernard Baruch insisted: "It can't be defended except as mob rule." But Roosevelt's historic decision won applause not only from farm-state senators but, unexpectedly, from the House of Morgan. Morgan himself publicly announced his ap-

---

* Rainey was a supporter of the populist reformer William Jennings Bryan, who ran unsuccessfully for president in 1896 and 1900. Bryan advocated an inflationary economy with a program of coining free silver at a rate of 16 to 1.

proval, and Russell Leffingwell wrote the President: "Your action in going off gold saved the country from complete collapse. It was vitally necessary and the most important of all helpful things you have done."*

As Congress continued to wrangle over the farm bill, rebellion once more broke out in the Corn Belt. In late April, a mob of farmers, masked in blue bandannas, dragged Judge Charles C. Bradley from his bench in LeMars, Iowa, took him to a crossroads out of town, and nearly lynched him in a vain effort to get him to promise not to sign mortgage foreclosures. A few days later, to force the hand of Congress, the Farmers' Holiday Association, led by Milo Reno and A. C. Townley, called a national farmers' strike for May 13.

On May 12, racing to nip the farm strike in the bud, Congress passed the Agricultural Adjustment Act. Since it provided for alternative systems of subsidizing farm staples, the law simply postponed the quarrel over farm policy; within a few months, it would erupt again. But for the moment farm leaders were content to count their blessings. The act gave the farmer the price supports he desired, and more besides. The Thomas amendment held out to the debt-ridden farmer the prospect of freshly printed greenbacks; the supplementary Farm Credit Act of June 16 promised to keep the sheriff and the mortgage company away from his door. Within eighteen months, the Farm Credit Administration, a merger of government farm loan agencies under the energetic Henry Morgenthau, Jr., and his deputy, William Myers of Cornell, would refinance a fifth of all farm mortgages. After more than a half century of agitation, the farmer had come into his own.

By the spring of 1933, the needs of more than fifteen million unemployed had quite overwhelmed the resources of local governments. In some counties, as many as 90 per cent of the people were on relief. Roosevelt was not indifferent to the plea of mayors and county commissioners for federal assistance, but the relief proposal closest to his heart had more special aims: the creation of a civilian forest army to put the "wild boys of the road" and the unemployed of the cities to work in the national forests. On March 14, the President asked four of his cabinet to consider the conservation corps idea, a project which united his belief in universal service for youth with his desire to improve the nation's estate. Moreover, Roosevelt thought that the character of city men would benefit from a furlough in the country. The next day, his officials reported back with a recommendation not only for tree-army legislation but for public works and federal grants to the states for relief. The President opposed massive public works spending, since he favored retrenchment and believed there were few worthwhile projects, but Secretary of Labor Frances Perkins; Harry Hopkins, who had headed his relief program in New York; and Senators Robert La

---

* Bernard Baruch was an influential financier who advised several presidents. The House of Morgan was the Wall Street banking firm of J. P. Morgan and Co., which was the subject of regulatory attention during the New Deal. Russell Leffingwell was a powerful financier in the Morgan firm.

Follette, Jr., of Wisconsin and Edward Costigan of Colorado won him over. On March 21, the President sent an unemployment relief message to Congress which embraced all three recommendations. Congress took only eight days to create the Civilian Conservation Corps. In little more than a week, the Senate whipped through a bill authorizing half a billion dollars in direct federal grants to the states for relief, and the House gave its approval three weeks later. Before the session ended, Roosevelt had achieved the third goal of his relief program—public works—in the National Industrial Recovery Act.

According to one account, Herbert Hoover, when queried a short time after he left office if there was anything he should have done while President that he had not done, replied: "Repudiate all debts." This was an almost universal sentiment in the spring of 1933. Creditors understood that if they were to avert outright repudiation, they must work out procedures to ease the burden of debt that threatened to deprive millions of all they owned. Especially critical was the plight of homeowners. In 1932, a quarter of a million families lost their homes. In the first half of 1933, more than a thousand homes were being foreclosed every day; Philadelphia averaged 1,300 sheriff's sales a month.

In June, Congress adopted the Home Owners' Loan Act amidst cries that the law bailed out real-estate interests rather than the homeowner. Without having to scale down the debt he was owed, the mortgagor could turn in defaulted mortgages for guaranteed government bonds. Yet, however much the act was tailored to the interests of financial institutions, it proved a lifesaver for thousands of Americans. When the Home Owners' Loan Corporation opened for business in Akron, a double column stretched for three blocks down Main Street by seven in the morning: when the doors opened, five hundred people pressed into the lobby. In the end, the HOLC would help refinance one out of every five mortgaged urban private dwellings in America.

As Roosevelt followed one startling recommendation for reform legislation with yet another, the progressive bloc in Congress came to the pleasant realization that all kinds of proposals that had been doomed to defeat for more than a decade now had an excellent chance of adoption. Of all the projects espoused by the Republican progressives, one in particular symbolized their frustration during the recent reign of three Republican Presidents. Led by George Norris of Nebraska, the progressives had fought year in and year out for government operation of the Muscle Shoals properties on the Tennessee River, an electric power and nitrogen development built during World War I. Twice Congress had passed a Muscle Shoals bill; twice it had been killed by Republican Presidents. Now the progressives found an ally in the new Democratic President. Even before he took office, he had toured the Tennessee Valley with Norris. "Is he really with you?" reporters asked Norris afterward. "He is more than with me, because he plans to go even farther than I did," the Senator responded.

Norris was right. He himself was mainly interested in the potential of Muscle Shoals for hydroelectric power. Southern farm interests and their congressional spokesmen were excited chiefly by the possibility of using the project to manufacture fertilizers. "I care nothing for the power," observed Alabama's Senator Hugo Black.* Still others wanted to secure flood protection and curb soil erosion. Roosevelt, with his long-standing interest in forest, land, and water, saw all of these elements as part of a whole. He proposed not merely unified development of the resources of the valley but a vast regional experiment in social planning which would affect directly the lives of the people of the valley.

On April 10, the President asked Congress to create the Tennessee Valley Authority. The TVA would build multipurpose dams which would serve as reservoirs to control floods and at the same time generate cheap, abundant hydroelectric power. Its power operations were designed to serve as a "yardstick" to measure what would be reasonable rates for a power company to charge. The Authority, which would be a public corporation with the powers of government but the flexibility of a private corporation, would manufacture fertilizer, dig a 650-mile navigation channel from Knoxville to Paducah, engage in soil conservation and reforestation, and, to the gratification of the planners, co-operate with state and local agencies in social experiments. Utility executives argued that there would be no market for the power TVA dams would produce; Representative Joe Martin of Massachusetts declared the TVA was "patterned closely after one of the soviet dreams"; and *The New York Times* commented: "Enactment of any such bill at this time would mark the 'low' of Congressional folly." But in the remarkable springtime of the Hundred Days, few heeded. The House passed the measure by a whopping margin; Norris steered it through the Senate; and, after he had first made sure that congressional conferees had approved his more ambitious conception of the project, Franklin Roosevelt signed the Tennessee Valley Authority Act on May 18.

While Roosevelt had sent an impressive number of legislative proposals to Congress, he had still done nothing directly to stimulate industrial recovery. He had, to be sure, encouraged Senator [Robert] Wagner to look into various schemes for business self-government under federal supervision, and he had requested Raymond Moley† to commission the New York financier, James Warburg, to consolidate disparate proposals for industrial co-ordination. Yet, when Warburg reported back, Roosevelt concluded that business thought had not yet crystallized to the point where legislation was feasible. By early April, the President had decided against taking any action.

On April 6, Roosevelt received a rude awakening. In December, 1932, Senator Hugo Black of Alabama had introduced a thirty-hour bill to bar from interstate commerce articles produced in plants in which employees worked more than five days a week or six hours a day. Black, influenced by the English writer G. D. H. Cole and the Americans Arthur Dahlberg and Stuart Chase, claimed that his proposal would create six million jobs. William Green, the

---

* In 1937 Roosevelt appointed Hugo Black to the Supreme Court, where he served for thirty-four years.

† Raymond Moley was one of Roosevelt's major economic advisers.

mild-mannered president of the A.F. of L., declared the Black bill struck "at the root of the problem—technological unemployment," and startled the country, and perhaps himself, by threatening a general strike in support of the thirty-hour week. On April 6, bowing to pressure from organized labor and the American Legion, the Senate upset all Roosevelt's calculations by passing the Black bill, 53–30.

The President, who believed that the Black bill was unconstitutional, that it was inflexible, and that it would retard recovery, was stung to action. He directed Moley to start the wheels turning once again on a plan for industrial mobilization. Throughout the month of April, various people, holding vague commissions, worked on separate drafts of a recovery bill. They reflected a variety of different demands. New Dealers like Tugwell, writers like Charles Beard and Stuart Chase, and senators like Wagner and La Follette stressed the need for national planning. Wagner and La Follette, together with Senator Costigan, stepped up their campaign for federal public works, with the backing of administration leaders ranging from Secretary of Labor Frances Perkins to Secretary of War George Dern. Old Bull Moosers like the labor attorney Donald Richberg, nourished on the doctrines of the New Nationalism, revived interest in theorists of the Progressive era who had speculated about concentration and control.

The most popular of all proposals arose from the plea of such business leaders as Gerard Swope of General Electric and Henry I. Harriman of the U.S. Chamber of Commerce that the government suspend the antitrust laws to permit trade associations to engage in industrywide planning.* While trade associations had adopted "codes of fair competition" in the past, they had had to do so gingerly lest they be slapped with an antitrust suit for collusion, and they had no way to coerce fractious minorities. Some businessmen sought government sanction for business agreements simply in order to fix prices to their own advantage; others, like Swope, who had worked with Jane Addams at Hull-House,[†] conceived of the scheme as a way to benefit labor as well as capital. All shared a common revulsion against the workings of a competitive, individualistic, laissez-faire economy.

In quest of a precedent for government-business co-operation, the draftsmen of the recovery bill turned to the experience with industrial mobilization in World War I. Swope himself had served in a war agency, and his plan was one of many, like William McAdoo's proposal for a "Peace Industries Board," which drew on recollections of government co-ordination of the economy during the war. Since they rejected laissez faire, yet shrank from embracing socialism, the planners drew on the experience of the War Industries Board because it offered

---

* Antitrust laws are designed to prevent collusion among businesses. A trade association represents companies within a particular industry.

[†] Jane Addams was an urban social reformer who worked to help slum dwellers obtain education, jobs, housing, and so on.

an analogue which provided a maximum of government direction with a minimum of challenge to the institutions of a profit economy.

A number of union leaders, especially men like John L. Lewis and Sidney Hillman in the sick coal and garment industries, had come to believe that only by national action could their industries be stabilized. They were willing to agree to business proposals for a suspension of the antitrust laws because they assumed the Supreme Court would not sanction a federal wages and hours law, and they reasoned that industrial codes offered high-wage businessmen badly needed protection from operators who connived to undersell them by exploiting their workers. But Senator Wagner, the most eloquent champion of the rights of labor in Congress, insisted that if business received concessions labor must have a guarantee of collective bargaining.

On May 10, out of patience with the wrangling over the industrial recovery bill, Roosevelt named a drafting committee and told the draftsmen to lock themselves in a room and not come out until they had a bill. A week later, the President was able to present Congress with an omnibus proposal that had a little for everyone. Business got government authorization to draft code agreements exempt from the antitrust laws; the planners won their demand for government licensing of business; and labor received Section 7(a), modeled on War Labor Board practices, which guaranteed the right to collective bargaining and stipulated that the codes should set minimum wages and maximum hours. In addition, the bill provided for $3.3 billion in public works.

The House, largely as a demonstration of its support for Roosevelt, passed the bill, 325–76. In the Senate it had much tougher sledding. The Black group viewed the measure as a "sellout," inflationists favored a different remedy, and conservatives objected to the labor provisions and to the immense power given the federal government. The weightiest objections came from antitrusters such as Senator Borah, who warned that the bill sanctioned cartels and that the big interests would inevitably dominate code-making. Wagner countered by challenging the progressives to find any feasible way other than the codes to outlaw sweatshops and protect labor. "I do not think we will ever have industry in order," Wagner argued, "until we have nationally planned economy, and this is the first step toward it." In the end the Senate approved the bill, but by the narrow margin of seven votes, with both conservatives like Glass and progressives like La Follette and Norris in the opposition on the crucial roll call. On June 16, when President Roosevelt signed the National Industrial Recovery Act, he observed: "Many good men voted this new charter with misgivings. I do not share these doubts. I had part in the great cooperation of 1917 and 1918 and it is my faith that we can count on our industry once more to join in our general purpose to lift this new threat. . . ."

While Roosevelt offered industrialists a partnership in the mobilization for recovery, he insisted that the financiers be disciplined. On March 29, he sent Congress his recommendation for federal regulation of securities, a proposal which added "to the ancient rule of *caveat emptor,* the further doctrine 'let the seller also beware.'" A short while before, such legislation would have been inconceivable, but the debate on the securities bill took place as the Pecora committee was carrying the popular outcry against Wall Street to a heightened pitch.*

A tribune of righteousness, Ferdinand Pecora summoned the nation's financial rulers to the bar. In the twenties, the House of Morgan had been an arcane shrine, Morgan himself a prince of the realm who dwelt somewhere in the recesses of the marble building on Broad and Wall far removed from the common throng. Now Pecora haled Morgan before the Senate committee and put to him questions it had not seemed fit to ask him before. "Pecora has the manner and the manners of a prosecuting attorney who is trying to convict a horse thief," Morgan protested to his friends. "Some of these senators remind me of sex suppressed old maids who think everybody is trying to seduce them." On the witness stand, Morgan appeared to have been resurrected from some Dickensian countinghouse—he called one of his clerks a "clark"—but as Pecora jabbed his stubby finger at him, while Morgan fondled the heavy gold chain across his paunch, he seemed less the awesome figure of Broad and Wall, more like a Main Street banker with his eye on the main chance.

The Pecora probe made possible the adoption of the Securities Act late in May, but the law itself bore the imprint of the Brandeisian faction of the New Dealers. Sharply at variance with the NRA philosophy of government-business co-operation in the interest of national planning, the measure reflected the faith of the New Freedom in regulation rather than direction, in full disclosure rather than coercion. The Securities law, modeled on the British Companies Act, gave the Federal Trade Commission power to supervise issues of new securities, required each new stock issue to be accompanied by a statement of relevant financial information, and made company directors civilly and criminally liable for misrepresentation. Drafted in part by lawyers supplied by the Brandeisian Felix Frankfurter, and shepherded through Congress by the Wilsonian liberal Sam Rayburn,[†] the law delighted progressives who believed that Wall Street wielded too much undisciplined power over the economy. On the other hand, spokesmen for co-operation with business and advocates of planning—both of whom shared an organic conception of the economy—thought the measure regressive. William O. Douglas of the Yale Law School dismissed it as a "nineteenth-century piece of legislation" which, instead of aiding national planning, sought to restore the old capitalistic order of competitive small units.

---

* At the end of the Hoover administration, the Senate Banking Committee, led by its counsel Ferdinand Pecora, launched an investigation into banking and financial practices. The committee laid the groundwork for reform under Roosevelt: the Glass-Steagall Act (a 1933 banking reform bill) and the creation of the Securities and Exchange Commission.

† *Brandeisian* refers to a belief in states' rights, a small central government, and Progressive reforms such as the regulation of big business. *Wilsonian* means much the same thing, with an emphasis on open, reformist government.

Two days after Pecora's inquiry revealed that the twenty Morgan partners had not paid a penny in income taxes in two years, the Senate passed the Glass-Steagall banking bill without a dissenting voice. The Pecora committee had urged the separation of investment from commercial banking, and this feature of the Glass-Steagall bill, highly popular with investors, had even won the support of Winthrop Aldrich, the new head of the Chase National Bank, although Wall Street hooted that Aldrich's remarks represented an assault by Rockefeller interests on the House of Morgan. Much more controversial was the proposal for federal insurance of bank deposits, a panacea advanced by Senator Arthur Vandenberg of Michigan and by Representative Henry Steagall of Alabama, the leader of the small-bank faction in the House. They were motivated in part by a recognition of the anguish of the small depositor, but also by the conviction that the safety-fund device would protect the circulating medium and would help sustain a system of small unit banks. On the basis of past experience, the insurance proposal seemed highly questionable, and not only bankers but both Senator Glass and President Roosevelt frowned on it. Yet, unlike his more conservative fiscal advisers, such as Dean Acheson, Roosevelt recognized that the demand for federal bank insurance could not be resisted. When Congress adopted the Glass-Steagall Act, it approved not only the separation of investment from commercial banking and certain reforms of the Federal Reserve System but the creation of the Federal Deposit Insurance Corporation. A stepchild of the New Deal, the federal guarantee of bank deposits turned out to be a brilliant achievement. Fewer banks suspended during the rest of the decade than in even the best single year of the twenties.

When Congress adjourned on June 16, precisely one hundred days after the special session opened, it had written into the laws of the land the most extraordinary series of reforms in the nation's history. It had committed the country to an unprecedented program of government-industry co-operation; promised to distribute stupendous sums to millions of staple farmers; accepted responsibility for the welfare of millions of unemployed; agreed to engage in farreaching experimentation in regional planning; pledged billions of dollars to save homes and farms from foreclosure; undertaken huge public works spending; guaranteed the small bank deposits of the country; and had, for the first time, established federal regulation of Wall Street. The next day, as the President sat at his desk in the White House signing several of the bills Congress had adopted, including the largest peacetime appropriation bill ever passed, he remarked: "More history is being made today than in [any] one day of our national life." Oklahoma's Senator Thomas Gore amended: "During all time."

Roosevelt had directed the entire operation like a seasoned field general. He had sent fifteen messages up to the Hill, seen fifteen historic laws through to final passage. Supremely confident, every inch the leader, he dumfounded his critics of a few months before. . . .

The nation, at last, had found a leader.

Epilogue

Roosevelt was not as responsible for the end of the Great Depression as the events of 1933 seemed to indicate. The Depression finally ended in the 1940s because of the huge federal spending brought on by World War II. During the 1930s Roosevelt had great success in passing new regulatory and welfare legislation—only to see this legislation limited or completely overturned by a conservative Supreme Court. In 1937 Roosevelt made the mistake of suggesting a change in the composition of the Court by "packing" it—adding one justice for every sitting justice over seventy years old—only to be defeated by an overwhelmingly negative public reaction and a skeptical Congress. Nonetheless, Roosevelt was in office so long that he was able to change the composition and direction of the Court through the appointment process. Only now, with the appointment of David Souter to the Court making an apparent conservative majority, is that direction likely to change again.

The public held Herbert Hoover so responsible for the Depression and the failure of the government to respond adequately to its effects that the nature of the political parties and voting changed for generations to come. The New Deal coalition that backed Roosevelt—the southern, urban, minority, and labor votes—gave the Democrats a huge working electoral majority that is only now beginning to collapse. Franklin Roosevelt has become such a mythical figure that both Republicans and Democrats quote him and claim to be acting in his tradition. Roosevelt became the standard by which we measure subsequent presidents.

Three Cases of Command

Richard E. Neustadt

Once Franklin Roosevelt changed the nature of, and the demands upon, the American presidency, a host of new questions arose about the office. How much power does a president really have? What are the best ways to use the powers that do exist? And what is the range of possible presidential action in the American system of separation of powers? Richard Neustadt's book, *Presidential Power,* from which this selection is drawn, discusses those questions. Drawing upon both his image of Roosevelt as the most successful modern American president and his own experience in the Truman administration, Neustadt writes a modern version of Machiavelli's *The Prince,* a handbook to guide presidents in the use of their powers and scholars in the analysis of those attempts. John F. Kennedy was so impressed by this book that he instructed all of his aides to read it and hired Neustadt as a White House consultant.

Neustadt's central observation is that presidents actually have very limited power to command the actions of others. Instead, he notes, "presidential power is the power to persuade." This means that presidents must use their resources to bargain with others in the hopes of persuading them to act as desired. As this selection shows, much of that ability to persuade depends on more than just the formal powers of the office. A president's own personal charisma, the element of fear on the part of those who might be opposed, and a host of other informal powers can be just as useful in achieving success. As you will see from the selection, gaining compliance with presidential policies requires a skillful use of all types of powers.

Notice also that in each of the three cases described, the president is doing exactly the opposite of something he originally wanted to do. In comparing these "difficult choices," as Neustadt calls them, think about the criticism that recent presidents tend to be too concerned with the impact of decisions on their popularity rating. Is this a fair charge? And if you think so, could it be that Franklin Roosevelt created such a high standard in people's minds of what a president can accomplish in times of crisis that such a concern for image is the natural result?

DWIGHT D. EISENHOWER   President of the United States, 1953–1961.

ORVAL FAUBUS   Governor of Arkansas, 1955–1967.

DOUGLAS MacARTHUR   Commander of allied forces in Japan and of American forces in Asia, 1945–1951.

CHARLES SAWYER   Truman's secretary of commerce, 1948–1953.

HARRY S TRUMAN   President of the United States, 1945–1953.

CHARLES E. WILSON   Head of the Office of Defense Mobilization at the beginning of the Korean War.

▶ In the early summer of 1952, before the heat of the campaign, President Truman used to contemplate the problems of the General-become-President should Eisenhower win the forthcoming election. "He'll sit here," Truman would remark (tapping his desk for emphasis), "and he'll say, 'Do this! Do that!' *And nothing will happen.* Poor Ike—it won't be a bit like the Army. He'll find it very frustrating."

Eisenhower evidently found it so. "In the face of the continuing dissidence and disunity, the President sometimes simply exploded with exasperation," wrote Robert Donovan in comment on the early months of Eisenhower's first term. "What was the use, he demanded to know, of his trying to lead the Republican Party. . . ." And this reaction was not limited to early months alone, or to his party only. "The President still feels," an Eisenhower aide remarked to me in 1958, "that when he's decided something, that *ought* to be the end of it . . . and when it bounces back undone or done wrong, he tends to react with shocked surprise."

Truman knew whereof he spoke. With "resignation" in the place of "shocked surprise" the aide's description would have fitted Truman. The former senator may have been less shocked than the former general, but he was no less subjected to that painful and repetitive experience: "Do this, do that, and nothing will happen." Long before he came to talk of Eisenhower he had put his own experience in other words: "I sit here all day trying to persuade people to do the things they ought to have sense enough to do without my persuading them. . . . That's all the powers of the President amount to."

In these words of a President, spoken on the job, one finds the essence of the problem now before us: "powers" are no guarantee of power; clerkship is no guarantee of leadership. The President of the United States has an extraordinary range of formal powers, of authority in statute law and in the Constitution. Here is testimony that despite his "powers" he does not obtain results by giving orders—or not, at any rate, merely by giving orders. He also has extraordinary

status, *ex officio,* according to the customs of our government and politics.*
Here is testimony that despite his status he does not get action without argument. Presidential *power* is the power to persuade.

This testimony seems, at first glance, to be contradicted flatly by events in the public record of Truman's own administration and of Eisenhower's. Three cases, out of many, illustrate the seeming contradiction. In 1951 Douglas MacArthur was ordered to relinquish his commands; he did as he was told. In 1952 Truman seized the nation's steel mills; they remained in government possession for some seven weeks until he ordered them released when the Supreme Court held that he exceeded his authority. And in 1957 Eisenhower ordered Federal troops to Little Rock; the mob was dispersed, and the Negro children went to school. Evidently some commands are effective; some results can be gained simply by giving orders; some actions do get taken without argument. Truman's comments seem to be belied by his own acts and those of his successor in these instances, among others.

The contradiction is superficial. It exists if Truman's words are stretched to mean that formal powers have no bearing upon influence. It disappears the moment one takes Truman to imply that mere assertion of a formal power rarely is enough. Taken in that second sense his words are actually *substantiated* by these cases of command. For the recall of MacArthur, the seizure of the steel mills, and the Federal troops at Little Rock go far to show how special are the circumstances favoring command. They also show how narrow may be its effective reach, how costly its employment. An analysis of presidential power must begin by marking out the limits upon presidential "powers." These examples tell us much about the limits.

Before I turn to what these cases show, let me review the facts in each of them. Chronologically, the MacArthur case comes first, the steel seizure second, and the Little Rock case third. For purposes of factual review it is convenient to discuss them in that order. Once the facts are stated, chronology can be ignored.

When the Korean War broke out in late June 1950 with a drive on South Korea from the North, MacArthur was in Tokyo, 600 miles away, as supreme commander for the allied occupation of Japan and as commander of American forces in the Far East, posts he had assumed five years before when he accepted Japanese surrender. To him and to his forces, necessarily, Truman first entrusted military aid for South Korea. No other forces were at hand. When the United Nations made the war its own and gave command to the United States, Truman added to MacArthur's other titles a designation as the UN field commander.

By August the General had demonstrated both that he could keep a foothold in Korea and that he, personally, might have more in mind than throwing back

---

* *Ex officio* privileges or responsibilities come by virtue of the office.

the North Korean Communists. In the first days of the war Washington had "neutralized" Formosa, ordering the Seventh Fleet to interpose itself between the Communist regime in mainland China and the Nationalist regime which held the island. MacArthur soon met Chiang Kai-shek, and public statements by the two of them implied some sort of underwriting for Chiang's cause and some sort of involvement by the Nationalists in Korea.* These statements were at variance with policy in Washington, to say nothing of its UN associates, and Truman, ultimately, had to tell MacArthur to withdraw a further statement he had sent the Veterans of Foreign Wars.

Within three weeks of this episode Washington was ready to forgive it and forget it in delight at the successes on the battlefield. On September 15 Mac-Arthur's forces landed at Inchon; thereafter, virtual victory came in a rush. A month later Truman met the General at Wake Island. They then agreed that they had no dispute about the Chinese Nationalists, and they looked forward confidently to an early end of fighting with the occupation of all North Korea.

Their confidence was not to last. In the first week of November it was shaken as the UN troops encountered Chinese Communists. In the last week of November it was shattered by a Chinese Communist attack that caught MacArthur unprepared and woefully deployed. To extricate his forces he was compelled to retreat two thirds of the way down the peninsula. Not until mid-January 1951 did Washington begin to feel assured that new lines could form, hold, and support real recovery. Meanwhile, MacArthur had announced the coming of a "new war." He had despaired of holding any part of the peninsula, and he had publicly blamed his defeat on Washington's insistence that the fighting should be confined to Korea. Immediately after Chinese intervention he began campaigning for war measures against the Chinese Communists on their home grounds.

Truman, and his advisers, and most allied governments had quite the opposite reaction to Peking's attack. Their eyes were fixed on Europe as the cold war's greatest stake. They hoped to minimize the risk of long involvement elsewhere, and especially the risk of World War III. If the original objective of the fighting, South Korea, could be salvaged without deepening those risks, they would be well content. By February General Ridgway, who commanded the ground forces in Korea, was assuring them it could be done. By March his troops were doing it. Before that month was out substantially the whole of South Korea was again in UN hands, and Ridgway's troops were reaching north toward natural defense lines past the border.

It now seemed likely that hostilities might end with restoration, roughly, of the situation as it had been at the start. To Washington and to its European allies this seemed the best of a bad bargain; to MacArthur, and to many fellow citizens at home, it seemed the worst. Rather than accept it he began a new barrage of

---

* Formosa is now called Taiwan. Chiang Kai-shek, leader of the Chinese nationalists, fled there in 1949.

public statements aimed, apparently, at pushing Washington to "win" the war. On March 7 in a statement to the press, he called for action to "provide on the highest international levels the answer to the obscurities [of] Red China's undeclared war. . . ." On March 25 he published a demand for enemy surrender, undermining a planned presidential statement that would have expressed interest in negotiated settlement. On April 5 Joseph Martin, the Minority Leader of the House of Representatives, read into the record a letter from the General which deplored the policies of his superiors, and ended with the words "There is no substitute for victory."

By April 5 Truman's decision already had been taken; five days later MacArthur was relieved. An extraordinary burst of popular emotion heralded his homecoming. Emotion faded, and so did he, during the course of Senate Hearings which poked into every corner of official policy. Meanwhile the war remained limited. In July truce talks began; two years later these produced an armistice along a line the troops had reached by June of 1951.

So much for the facts of the MacArthur case. Next is the steel seizure case. On December 31, 1951, five months after the start of truce talks in Korea, contracts between the United Steelworkers and major steel concerns expired with a stalemate in collective bargaining. At Truman's personal request the men continued work without a contract, while he referred their dispute to the Wage Stabilization Board, a body composed equally of labor, industry, and public members, which had charge of wage control and allied functions during the Korean War. Because this Wage Board still was hearing the case, the union twice postponed a strike, again at Truman's instance. Then, with the strike set for April 9, 1952, labor and public members of the Board agreed, March 20, on terms of settlement to recommend to the disputing parties. Industry members dissented. At first sight of these majority proposals the union embraced them, the companies denounced them, and in echelons above the Board officials thought them "high."

The Wage Stabilization Board was part of a complex administrative hierarchy established in the first six months of the Korean War. At the top was the Office of Defense Mobilization (ODM), headed by Charles E. (General Electric) Wilson whom Truman had entrusted with "direction," "supervision," and "control" of the entire home-front economic effort. ODM had been superimposed on everything else in the immediate aftermath of Chinese intervention. Next in line was an Economic Stabilization Agency (ESA), which had been created before Wilson's appointment. On paper, this Agency administered discretionary powers over prices and wages conferred upon the President by the Defense Production Act. In fact, those powers were administered by two subordinate units: the Office of Price Stabilization, headed by Ellis Arnall, former governor of Georgia, and the Wage Board, itself. The Office was organized like a regular line agency. The Board was run like a regulatory commission with one of its public members in the chair. The Board had statutory authority by delegation through the ESA, to *set* maximum limits on wages. It also had a direct authorization from the

White House to *recommend* solutions for nonwage issues in labor disputes. Both functions were involved in the steel case. Wage rulings by the Board were legally enforceable; its nonwage proposals were not. Theoretically, its wage ceilings were subject to revision by the Economic Stabilizer, or the Defense Mobilizer, or the President. But practically speaking, case by case, the Board's tripartite composition and quasi-judicial procedures made majority decisions irreversible on wages and not even reviewable on other issues. In comparison, the Office of Price Stabilization was an administrative unit with no more independence of its nominal superiors than it could win by bureaucratic in-fighting, and with no nonprice duties to distract it from concern for price control. One thing, however, wage and price controllers had in common: they mistrusted those above them and were cool to one another.

The Wage Board proposals of March 20 precipitated a crisis in the steel case. The industry pronounced them unacceptable. The union termed them the least it would accept. The Administration could not disavow them without wrecking the machinery for wage stabilization. A strike was just three weeks away. According to the Pentagon the possibility of enemy offensives in Korea precluded any loss of steel production. In these circumstances Wilson, as Director of Defense Mobilization, took personal charge. His answer for the crisis was a *price* concession to the companies sufficient to induce a settlement of wage and other issues before the strike deadline. After hurried consultation with the President, who was ending a vacation at Key West, Wilson sounded out the industry on price relief. Unfortunately, in an impromptu press conference he had exposed a private distaste for the Wage Board's terms of settlement. This ended union confidence in him and cast doubt on his claims to act for the Administration. Immediately after, Wilson was rebuffed by industry officials who wanted higher prices than he had in mind and made no promises to settle with the union. Immediately after that, Wilson's nominal subordinate Ellis Arnall, the Price Director, won support from Truman for a firmer stand on price controls. Concessions were to be allowed for cost increases in the normal course, but only *after* costs had been incurred. A labor-management agreement must come first. So Arnall argued. Truman sympathized. Wilson resigned on March 29.

In the remaining days before the strike the White House, now involved directly, tried to press the companies and union to a settlement without a price concession in advance. Collective bargaining was resumed and mediation was attempted. Much jockeying and many misadventures then ensued but not a settlement. Finally, to escape a shutdown of production Truman seized the industry two hours before the strike deadline. He ordered the Secretary of Commerce to administer the mills and called upon the men to work as government employees.

The union honored Truman's call; the companies accepted government control—and went to court. In ordering his seizure the President had acted without statutory sanction. Indeed, he had ignored a statute on the books, the Taft-Hartley Act, which gave him the alternative of seeking an injunction against union strike-calls for another eighty days. In these circumstances the steel companies asserted that his seizure was illegal. So they argued in the press and in Federal District Court on April 9 and after. Government attorneys answered with appeals to the necessities of national defense. They also laid claims to unlimited, "inherent" presidential powers. The President, himself, repudiated these claims. The Court, however, was infuriated by them. The fury was shared by Congressmen and editors.

On April 29 the District Judge denied Truman's authority to seize the industry. A strike began at once. Three days later the order of that Judge was stayed by an Appeals Court decision which allowed the government to put its case before the Supreme Court. The men then straggled back to work. At Truman's request, company and union leaders went into the White House to bargain with each other then and there. On May 3 while bargaining was under way, the Supreme Court took jurisdiction of the case and pending its decision ordered that there be no change in wages. White House bargaining broke down at once; all parties turned, instead, to the Court.

On June 2 a Supreme Court majority upheld the District Judge with a set of opinions so diverse as to establish nothing but the outcome. The President at once returned the mills to private hands. Again there was a strike. This time the mills remained shut down for seven weeks until collective bargaining and White House promises of price relief produced a settlement on July 24. The men gained terms a shade less favorable than the Wage Board members had proposed; the companies gained considerably more price relief than Wilson once had offered.

Such was the outcome of steel seizure. Between it and the third case there are five years and Eisenhower's two elections. The Little Rock affair began in the first months of his second term. In April 1957 a Federal Court of Appeals approved the integration plan prepared by school authorities in Little Rock, following the Supreme Court decision of 1954 that school segregation was unconstitutional. The Little Rock School Board announced that integrated schooling would begin at Central High School in September. It intensified its efforts to accustom the community to that prospect. So matters stood in August 1957, when a local citizen brought suit, successfully, in local court to halt the integration. The local court's injunction was declared void by a Federal Judge, and legally the way was cleared for integrated classes when the school reopened on September 3.

But on September 2, Orval Faubus, Governor of Arkansas, sent National Guardsmen to surround the school. These troops, at his instruction, kept all Negroes out in order to preclude the violent citizen reaction he announced might follow from their entry. Unable to carry out its integration plan, the School Board sought instruction from the Federal Judge. He ordered the Board to proceed as planned. Faubus's troops, however, barred compliance with his order. A petition to enjoin the Governor was put before the Judge September 10 with the United States Attorney General, among others, a petitioner. The next day Faubus asked Eisenhower for a conference; the President assented. He was then on vacation in Newport, Rhode Island, and a meeting was arranged there for September 14. But the meeting produced no action on either side.

On September 20, the Federal Judge enjoined the Governor from further interference with the School Board's plan. The Governor withdrew the National Guard and on the next school day, September 23, a noisy crowd broke through police lines and molested various bystanders. The Negro children who had come to school were taken home. That afternoon the President issued a proclamation to the citizens of Little Rock ordering "all persons" to cease the obstruction of justice. That night the White House and the Mayor of Little Rock held consultations. The next morning Eisenhower called the Arkansas National Guard into Federal service, thus removing it from Faubus's hands, and ordered regular Army troops to Little Rock. Order was restored and the Negro children returned to school. They remained in school, and federal troops remained on hand, through the school year until June 1958.

Thereafter, Little Rock's attempted integration entered a new phase. By school reopening in 1958, Faubus had proposed, received, and then invoked State legislation authorizing him to close the school if it were integrated. In 1959 the Federal courts struck down that legislation, and arrangements were made to open the school on roughly the same terms as in 1957. . . .

The dismissal of MacArthur, the seizure of the steel mills, the dispatch of troops to Little Rock share a common characteristic: in terms of immediate intent the President's own order brought results as though his words were tantamount to action. He said, "Do this, do that," and *it was done*. From a presidential standpoint these three orders were self-executing. To give them was to have them carried out. Literally, no orders carry themselves out; self-executed actually means executed-by-others. But self-executing does describe the practical effect as it appeared to those who gave the orders. In the order-giver's eyes command amounted to compliance.

What lay behind "self-execution" of these orders? When troops were sent to Little Rock, Eisenhower's action took the form of an executive order which "authorized and directed" the Secretary of Defense to enforce the orders of the District Court in Arkansas, utilizing "such of the armed forces of the United States . . . as necessary." To implement this order there were successive delegations of authority from the Secretary of Defense through the Secretary of the Army down to units of the 101st Airborne Division and the Arkansas National Guard, the physical executors of Eisenhower's order. In form each delegation was discretionary. In fact, according to a White House participant, "The President decided which troops to use and how fast they should get there and what they should do when they arrived. That was worked out right here and all those fellows at the Pentagon had to do was turn the crank. They knew exactly what they were to do the minute the order was signed." They knew, also, that the

President intended to address the nation justifying action *taken*. Under such circumstances, command and compliance are easy to equate.

In the MacArthur case the equation is even easier, for the circumstances were the simplest possible: Truman, as Commander-in-Chief, signed the order that relieved the General and the latter, himself, was its executor, transferring his commands to his designated successor. Misunderstanding was impossible; argument was precluded by publication of the order and by a presidential radio address explaining it.

As for seizure of the steel industry, Truman announced his action in a nationally televised address and at the same time, by executive order, he directed the Secretary of Commerce, Charles S. Sawyer, to take possession of the mills as government administrator. To carry out this order all that was initially required of Sawyer was a telegraphed notification to the managements and a delegation of authority to company executives, with a request that they stay on the job and fly the flag over the mills. Following the nation-wide announcement the Secretary scarcely could do less and the government, thereby, was in possession without his having to do more.

This brief recital is enough to show what lay behind the ready execution of these orders. At least five common factors were at work. On each occasion the President's involvement was unambiguous. So were his words. His order was widely publicized. The men who received it had control of everything needed to carry it out. And they had no apparent doubt of his authority to issue it to them. It is no accident that these five factors can be found in all three instances. These are the factors that produce self-executing orders. Lacking any one of them the chances are that mere command will not produce compliance.

To see what happens in the absence of these favorable factors let me turn to incidents in the same factual setting as the three orders just described. These three were promptly executed. Preceding them, or following them, however, were many other orders that did not get carried out. Those others serve to illustrate what happens when a favorable factor is missing.

The first factor favoring compliance with a presidential order is assurance that the President has spoken. The three self-executing orders were given by the man himself, and not only in form but very much in fact. They were *his* orders in the double sense that they both came from him and expressed a definite decision by him personally. Recipients were left no room for doubt on either score; wording, timing, and publicity took care of that. To see what can occur when this factor is absent, one need but contrast the incident precipitating the dismissal of MacArthur: his publicized demand for enemy surrender on March 24, 1951.

The General's call for enemy surrender came at a moment when the President, in consultation with allied governments, was planning a statement that would virtually invite negotiated compromise to end the war. MacArthur got on record first with threats to spread the war. The White House statement then was set aside. To Truman, this action on MacArthur's part signified two things: deliberate sabotage of presidential policy and a deliberate violation of explicit orders. On the record there is no doubt that the President was right in both respects. For the General had been told through channels, in advance, of the impending White House initiative. And he had been under orders since the previous December to make no public statements on foreign or military policy without prior clearance from the Departments of State and Defense. "By this act," Truman writes, "MacArthur left me no choice—I could no longer tolerate his insubordination."

Truman's comment implies what the record makes plain: he virtually invited this result by tolerating a long string of prior acts nearly as insubordinate. Since the Korean outbreak, as for years past, MacArthur had regularly used press statements to counter or to influence the views of his superiors. He had not previously used this means to stop their *acts*. But no penalties of consequence had been invoked for anything he had done short of that. To Truman this extension of the General's tactic was the final straw. MacArthur may have had no notion that the White House would react so strongly.

It is true that MacArthur violated an explicit order. But on its face the order seemed another form for form's sake. Dated December 6, 1950, it was addressed to all government departments and reached Tokyo routinely from the Pentagon. The order was expressed in terms more easily construed as the concoction of press attachés to hush Assistant Secretaries than as Truman's word to his Supreme Commander. In fact MacArthur *was* the target of this order; his press statements immediately after Chinese intervention were the cause of it. His conduct was of great concern to Truman personally. But how was the General to know? The order's widespread application and routine appearance were meant to spare him personal embarrassment (a fact which speaks volumes in itself). Their effect was to minimize its impact and to blur its source. Even had he recognized himself as addressee and Truman personally as sender, MacArthur may have noted that his press offensive at the start of the "new war" had drawn from Washington no more by way of a rebuke than this pale order. When stakes of policy and pride are high, convictions sharp (and political allies powerful), why should not a Supreme Commander try in March a somewhat bolder move than he had got away with in December?

A second factor making for compliance with a President's request is clarity about his meaning. If it helps to have respondents know that *he* wants what he asks, it also helps to have them know precisely what he wants. To shift the illustration, when the Governor of Arkansas met Eisenhower at Newport, a week before the troops were sent to Little Rock, there is no doubt that Faubus knew it was the President who wanted something done. But whether he was clear on what that something was remains uncertain; they met alone and the terms of their conversation left room for misunderstanding, apparent or real. According to an Eisenhower aide, "Faubus knew perfectly well what the President wanted: the order of the court complied with and the kids in school, peaceably . . . and he promised to produce. We were double-crossed, that's all." But Ashmore of the *Arkansas Gazette* records the impression that the Governor, believing he could "put off the dread day" until after his next gubernatorial campaign, "carried this illusion with him to Newport . . . and brought it home intact. . . ."

A somewhat comparable piece of business marked the steel crisis of 1952 and led to the resignation of the Mobilization Director, Wilson. At the outset of the crisis Wilson had conferred with Truman in Key West, talking at length and alone. But scarcely a week later, in exchanging letters upon Wilson's resignation, they recorded widely different notions of their Key West conversation. Wilson charged Truman with a change of tune; Truman charged Wilson with misconstruing orders. And both may have been right. For Wilson had returned from Key West with a mandate, as he saw it, to settle the dispute by price concessions if and as he could. This was a task demanding wide discretion for effective execution, and hence some open-endedness in its assignment. When a degree of ambiguity is inescapable, as in this case, it may take but a pinch of verbal imprecision or a dash of vacation atmosphere to produce misunderstanding. Both were in the recipe at Key West—and at Newport, five years later.

A third factor favoring compliance with a President's directive is publicity. Even when there is no need for ambiguity, no possibility of imprecision, no real discretionary leeway and nothing to misunderstand, compliance may depend not only on the respondent's awareness of what he is to do, but also on the awareness of others that he has been told to do it. In sending troops to Little Rock, in seizing the steel industry, in firing MacArthur, the whole country was taken into camp, informed of the President's commitment, invited to watch the response. But the circle of observers is rarely so broad. Often it may be entirely too narrow for presidential comfort. A case in point is Secretary Sawyer's interesting behavior in his first weeks as administrator of the seized steel industry.

Having seized the mills in desperation to avert production losses, the White House wanted to be rid of them as fast as possible—which meant as fast as it could gain assurance that production would continue once they were returned to private hands. This called for some settlement of the labor dispute whose lack of settlement had led to seizure in the first place. The circle could be broken only if continued government control were made so unattractive in the eyes of both disputants that they would prefer agreement with each other. To that end a tactic was devised: the Secretary of Commerce, as administrator of the mills, was to put into effect a *portion* of the union's wage demands to which the men were automatically entitled under the existing rules of wage control (a so-called cost-of-living adjustment). At the same time, he was to ask the price controllers for the amount of price relief to which the companies were automatically entitled under "pass through" provisions of existing legislation (the so-called Capehart Amendment). Secretary Sawyer then was to announce that he would do no more. Management and labor would be faced by a *fait accompli* that satisfied neither the union's wage demands nor the company's price demands but put some things beyond dispute and foreclosed better terms for the duration. With this prospect before them both sides might conclude that more was to be gained from settlement than from continued government direction. So, at least, the White House hoped.

Within a week of seizure Truman had decided to proceed along these lines. He asked that Sawyer act at once and planned to call for bargaining by companies and union with his Secretary's action in the background. The President's intent was clear. There were no ambiguities. But Sawyer did not act. The Secretary of Commerce spoke for business in the Cabinet. Officially and personally Sawyer had no liking for the seizure. He had not wanted to administer the mills, and he had taken the assignment with distaste. He was evidently unhappy at the prospect of his signature on wage orders and price requests committing the steel industry. Although he did not refuse to act, he managed to immerse himself in preparations. Presently the District Court relieved him of embarrassment (and the government of opportunity) by denying his authority to run the mills. When the Appeals Court restored his powers, Sawyer reached the point of action only after he had won agreement from the President that in the public record his department should be seen to act on the advice of others. It was nearly four weeks after seizure when Truman brought the union and the companies together to bargain in his office. The Secretary's action was set for two days hence. By then it was too late. On the opening day of the bargaining session the Supreme Court barred changes in wages.

Had the President initially publicized his plan, Sawyer would have had to execute it promptly or resign. That was his choice upon the night of seizure. But Truman did not publicize this scheme of wage adjustments. Toward the end of the four weeks his pressure on the Secretary came to be an open secret. At the start, however, it was little known and Sawyer did not face so sharp a choice. When officials are reluctant to do as they are told, publicity spurs execution. But publicity performs this service at the risk of turning private reluctance into public defiance. Sometimes that may not matter very much, or may even promise some advantage, or the President may have no option. Here it mattered greatly. Truman had just lost his Director of Defense Mobilization (and he had just fired his Attorney General for reasons unrelated to steel). He could ill afford to lose his Secretary of Commerce, particularly on an issue involving the administration of the mills which he had just placed in the Secretary's hands. Truman had an option and he took it. He gave instructions privately and tolerated slow response.

A fourth factor favoring compliance with a President's request is actual ability to carry it out. It helps to have the order-taker in possession of the necessary means. In one respect Sawyer's situation after seizure paralleled his situation on the night of seizure: he had authority enough and resources enough to carry out the President's immediate intention. All that Sawyer needed was a staff to prepare papers, a pen with which to sign them, and access to the telegraph. Those resources were at his disposal. In this respect, on both occasions, Sawyer was in very much the same position as MacArthur when his last orders arrived, or the Secretary of the Army when the word came through on Little Rock. Each had the necessary means at *his* disposal. Without the wherewithal in his own hands a presidential agent may be unable to do as he is told no matter how good his understanding or honest his intention.

An example of a man without the means is Wilson, the Mobilization Director, in the preseizure phase of the steel crisis. Whatever Truman may or may not have said to him at Key West, it is reasonably clear that the President wanted the labor dispute settled without a strike, even at some cost to price control. But the moment Wilson tried to satisfy this want, two things became clear. The companies were in a mood to demand guarantees of price relief, but not to promise settlement. And the Price Director, Ellis Arnall, was in a mood to refuse *any* price increase save what the law would automatically require *after* settlement. In effect, Arnall's stand became "play my way or fire me," and though Wilson ranked him bureaucratically, Arnall was a *presidential* appointee. Wilson actually controlled neither the companies nor the Price Director. He could not even bring much influence to bear upon them since his claims to speak for Truman had been clouded by a clumsy press remark about the Wage Board. Wilson had no recourse but to return to the President empty-handed. When Truman leaned toward Arnall, Wilson resigned. But even had the President renewed Wilson's mandate, it is not clear what he could have done.

Another illustration of the same point can be drawn from the act of seizure itself. I have described Truman's order in this instance as "self-executing" in effect, with Sawyer the executor in fact. But Sawyer had a silent partner, the United Steelworkers. The purpose of the seizure was production. Truman's order was effective upon issuance because the men honored their union's pledge that they would work if their employer were the government. Yet until just two hours before seizure was announced, the President had planned, simultaneously, to invoke the fact-finding procedure of the Taft-Hartley Act. This plan was dropped upon the urgent plea that wild-cat strikes in protest, and thus losses of production, might result. In order to assure that Sawyer's silent partner could achieve the purpose of the presidential order, Truman had to modify it in advance.

A fifth factor making for compliance with a President's request is the sense that what he wants is his by right. The steelworkers assumed, as Truman did, that he had ample constitutional authority to seize and operate the mills. An interjection of the term "Taft-Hartley" might have altered their response, but in its absence they conformed to the convention that they would not strike against their government, accepting as *legitimate* the President's claim upon them. The sense of legitimate obligation, legitimately imposed, was present in MacArthur's transfer of his own commands and in the Army's response to its Little Rock directive, no less than in the union's action after seizure. Without a sense of that sort on the part of order-takers, those orders would not have been carried out so promptly. But judging by the illustrations offered up to now the obverse does not follow. There is no assurance that orders will be executed just because they seem legitimate to their recipients. In none of the instances cited—not even in the case of Faubus at Newport—was a President's request considered *illegiti-mate* by those who *failed* to carry it out.

Perhaps legitimacy exerts a stronger influence the more distinct is its relationship to some specific grant of constitutional authority. Truman's final order to MacArthur, for example, had a clearer constitutional foundation than Eisenhower's *tête-à-tête* with Faubus, where authority was shared and therefore blurred. But Truman's earlier order to MacArthur on the clearance of public statements had precisely the same constitutional foundation as dismissal did. That earlier order had no more effect upon the General than Eisenhower had upon the Governor. Whatever its source or its relative strength, a sense of legitimacy taken alone does not assure compliance with a President's request.

When MacArthur was dismissed, when the steel mills were seized, when troops were sent to Little Rock, five factors made command appear the equal of compliance. In each of these three instances an unambiguous directive from a determined and committed President was carried out by persons who were capable of prompt response and who accepted his authority. The appearance of self-execution was produced by all these things combined. And when in other instances there was no such combination, there was also no effect of automatic execution.

How often is that combination likely to occur? How much, then, can a President rely on sheer command to get him what he wants? It takes but a glance at the examples in this chapter to suggest the answers: not very often and not very much. "Do this, do that, and nothing will happen" was the rule in incidents surrounding the dismissal of the General, and the seizure of the steel mills, and the use of Federal troops at Central High School. Viewed in their surroundings these become exceptions to the rule. So it is with presidential business generally. Under mid-century conditions self-executing orders are anything but everyday affairs. Indeed, in the whole sweep of Truman's record and of Eisenhower's, those three stand out precisely for that reason: what they represent is relatively rare.

The recall of MacArthur, the steel seizure, and the dispatch of troops to Little Rock share still another notable characteristic: in each case, the decisive order was a painful last resort, a forced response to the exhaustion of all other remedies, suggestive less of mastery than failure—the failure of attempts to gain an end by softer means.

Truman records in his memoirs that in April 1951, after reading the Pentagon file, General [George] Marshall "concluded that MacArthur should have been fired two years ago." Not everything that Marshall read is on the public record, but quite enough is there to lend substance to the view that MacArthur's dismissal was remarkably long delayed. Even if one sets aside all pre-Korean matters, ignores all questions of *professional* performance after Inchon, and scans the record only for the insubordination that provoked the firing, one finds at least two earlier cases somewhat comparable in all respects *except* the President's response. These two are MacArthur's outcry after Chinese intervention (leading to the clearance order of December 1950), and, months earlier, his public dissent from Formosa policy. The White House announcement of his recall in April 1951 could have been issued in August or December 1950, without changing a word. Yet Truman stayed his hand on those earlier occasions (though apparently dismissal crossed his mind) and tried to patch the damage, bridge the differences, without offense to anybody's dignity except his own. The record indicates that he definitely did not want to let MacArthur go. At every challenge, save the final one, before and during the Korean War, the President sought means to keep the General both contained and on the job. Whatever his reasons Truman's pursuit of this objective—at considerable risk to policy, real sacrifice of pride—seems as persistent as anything in his career. In that sense the dismissal, when it finally came, marked failure.

And so it was with Eisenhower in the Little Rock affair. There were few things he wanted *less* than federal troops enforcing the desegregation of a Southern school. Indeed he may have helped to set the stage for Faubus by observing in July of 1957:

> *I can't imagine any set of circumstances that would ever induce me to send Federal troops . . . into any area to enforce the orders of a Federal Court, because I believe that common sense of America will never require it.*
>
> *Now there may be that kind of authority resting somewhere, but certainly I am not seeking any additional authority of that kind, and I would never believe that it would be a wise thing to do in this country.*

And when, as schools reopened in September, the Governor had National Guardsmen interfere with execution of court orders, the President made a determined effort to avoid the use of force, an effort culminating in the inconclusive Newport conversation. Eisenhower agreed to meet Faubus at Newport without exacting advance guarantees. This is testimony to the President's desire for a way out other than the one he finally chose. So is the sense of "double-cross" that long persisted in the White House *after* Newport, a natural result of wanting to believe there was another way.

As for the steel seizure, the element of failure is self-evident. Truman had sought to settle the labor dispute in order to insure against a shutdown of production. When the union contract expired in December 1951, he tried to obtain settlement without a shutdown by referring the dispute to the Wage Stabilization Board. When the Board's report brought on a crisis instead, Wilson and the President took up the search for settlement. Their disagreement had to do with tactics, not the goal. After Wilson's resignation, the search continued under White House auspices right up to the day before the seizure. That drastic act was not even considered as a serious alternative until the week before, nor chosen with finality until the very day. The White House was so anxious for a settlement that Truman cancelled plans to state his case on television some days in advance of the strike deadline, lest there be an adverse effect on last-minute collective bargaining. In consequence, when seizure came, he had to combine a grave announcement with a contentious argument—hardly the choice of a President bent on seizure in the first place. But he had no such bent. Truman did not try to prepare the country for that course, because, until the last, he was intent on an alternative.

In this instance, as in the others, command became a last resort; but save in very short-run terms, it was not "last" at all. Truman did not want the steel mills; he wanted steel production and reasonably strong price controls. Those aims could only be achieved by terms of settlement between the union and the companies not inconsistent with existing control policies. The President had no power—and seizure gave him none—to gain his ends by fiat. Seizure merely staved off their abandonment and changed the *context* of his efforts to *induce* a satisfactory settlement. Initially, the new context put new inducements at the President's disposal. But seizure produced complications also, and these ultimately cost him both of his objectives. Two months' production vanished with the strike that followed judicial invalidation of his seizure. And price controls were breached beyond repair in White House efforts to conclude the strike. Yet it does not require hindsight to perceive that seizure's nature, from the start, was that of an emergency expedient, powerfully affecting possible solutions but solving nothing of itself. This would have been the case had the outcome been happier from Truman's point of view. At best, not seizure *per se,* but the added leverage it gave to his persuasion might have brought the settlement he wanted.

The same point can be made regarding Little Rock, where Eisenhower's use of troops bought time and changed the context of his appeals to the "hearts and minds" of Southerners but solved no desegregation problems, not even the local one at Central High School. As for the MacArthur case, his removal certainly resolved command relationships in the Korean War, but these were scarcely the sole concern. What was at stake was nothing less than our strategic purpose in the conduct of the war. And Truman's order did not end MacArthur's challenge to Administration policy, however much it may have changed the context of their quarrel. The General's threat to policy was ended by the Senate inquiry that followed his removal—and by the start of truce talks in Korea. Truman dug a grave, but that alone did not suffice to push MacArthur in. Without the push administered by Senate hearings it is not entirely clear whose grave it might have been.

Not only are these "last" resorts less than conclusive, but they are also costly. Even though the order is assured of execution, drastic action rarely comes at bargain rates. It can be costly to the aims in whose defense it is employed. It can be costly, also, to objectives far afield.

When he dismissed MacArthur, for example, Truman had to pay at least one price in the coin of Korean policy. The price was public exposition, at the Senate hearings, of his regime's innermost thoughts about the further conduct of hostilities. Whatever its effect on subsequent events, Peking and Moscow thus were put on notice of American intentions through the rest of Truman's term, and at home the reading public was informed that Washington saw little point in a renewed attempt to conquer North Korea. Against this background there began the long ordeal of truce negotiations. The Chinese may not have been influenced by those disclosures; Americans certainly were. Henry Kissinger, among many others, has argued with considerable justice that ". . . by stopping [offensive] military operations . . . at the very beginning of armistice negotiations . . . we removed the only Chinese incentive for a settlement; we produced the frustration of two years of inconclusive negotiations." But no one has suggested how we were to stay on the offensive after Washington officialdom had formulated for itself and then expressed in public an intense desire to have done as soon as Peking tired of hostilities. Belabored in the hearings to define a "way out" other than MacArthur's, the Administration crystallized its own responsiveness toward offers to negotiate before they were ever made. When offers came they were seized on as "vindication." Even without the whole MacArthur uproar, it would not have been easy to press the offensive as truce talks began. After Senate hearings it seems psychologically if not politically impossible.

Besides such costs as this, directly chargeable against the purpose he was trying to protect, Truman's dismissal of MacArthur involved other costs as well, charged against other policy objectives. These "indirect" costs are hard to isolate because causation is no single-track affair, but certainly they were not inconsiderable. Among others, it is possible that Truman's inability to make his case with Congress, Court, and public in the steel crisis of 1952 resulted from exhaustion of his credit, so to speak, in the MacArthur battle a year earlier. . . .

Drastic action may be costly, but it can be less expensive than continuing inaction. Truman could no longer have retained MacArthur without yielding to him the conduct of the war. Eisenhower could no longer stay his hand in Little Rock without yielding to every Southern Governor the right—even the duty—to do what Faubus did. These consequences threatened for the obvious reason that the instant challenge openly discounted the position of the Presidency and bluntly posed the question, "Who is President?" In either case, a soft response would have been tantamount to abdication, so public was the challenge in these terms. When Truman seized the steel mills, the Pentagon was warning that a new Chinese offensive, even Soviet intervention, might be coming in Korea "as soon as the mud dries." The seizure proved a very costly venture. But on the information then available, an April shutdown of the mills could have been far more costly. By hindsight it appears that a strike instead of seizure was the cheapest course available. The Chinese did not move as forcefully as had been feared. If they had done so, seizure might have proved a notable success. Truman acted without benefit of hindsight.

Self-executing orders have their uses, however inconclusive or expensive they may be. In each of these three cases, even steel, the presidential order brought assurance that a policy objective would remain in reach just as its loss seemed irretrievable. This is a real accomplishment. But necessarily it is a *transitory* accomplishment. Even the last resorts turn out to share the character of all the softer measures they replace. They turn out to be incidents in a persuasive process whereby someone lacking absolute control seeks to get something done through others who have power to resist.

Truman is quite right when he declares that presidential power is the power to persuade. Command is but a method of persuasion, not a substitute, and not a method suitable for everyday employment.

Epilogue

Each of these decisions had an impact on the power and image of the presidency. The firing of Douglas MacArthur resulted in an immediate popular outcry, but in time MacArthur faded from the public scene, and Truman, despite being so unpopular in office that he chose not to run again in 1952, has gained increasing respect in the eyes of scholars. His action here established absolutely the power of the president as commander in chief over the military.

The right of the president to seize the steel mills was taken to the Supreme Court, where Truman was judged to have transgressed the separation of powers in taking this action. Yet in the same opinion, the Court said that future actions by Truman and other presidents might well be constitutional because the inherent, or unwritten, discretionary powers of the office might allow such action in the face of congressional silence.

Finally, the Little Rock case was one in which President Eisenhower only reluctantly implemented the intention of the Supreme Court (having already failed to throw the power of the presidency behind the 1954 school desegregation case of *Brown* v. *Board of Education*). This reluctant but forceful action by Eisenhower made clear that progress toward desegregating the nation's schools would continue even if it meant that the chief executive had to back the effort with military force. Ironically, today the Little Rock public schools are mostly black because of the flight of white families from the city and the effort by those white families still living in the city to place their children in private schools.

The Ambush

Bruce Allen Murphy

Lyndon Baines Johnson was not a man who liked to owe people. But by 1965 Johnson owed Washington attorney Abe Fortas a great deal. For example, in 1948, Johnson's political career was nearly ruined when his Senate primary win was at first taken away by a federal court judge. It was Abe Fortas who successfully argued his case before Supreme Court Justice Hugo Black. And as Senate majority leader, Johnson consulted Fortas often. Johnson told aides that if he ever became president, he would put Abe Fortas on the Supreme Court. Of course, this vow seemed to be just Johnson bluster because there had been no southern president since the Civil War. And even if Johnson did become president, the availability of seats on the Court is unpredictable.

The assassination of John F. Kennedy in 1963, however, put Vice President Johnson in the Oval Office. One of his first calls after the tragedy was to Fortas, who helped set up the new administration, and the two men resumed their close advisory relationship. For Fortas, this combination of access to political power and a lucrative partnership in the law firm of Arnold, Fortas and Porter was perfect, a situation he was not interested in changing.

As you read this description of Johnson trying to change Fortas's mind, you will see "the Johnson treatment" in action. Johnson's charisma, combined with the power of the presidency, made it almost impossible for anyone, regardless of position, to resist his wishes.

ABE FORTAS Friend and adviser to President Johnson.

JOHN KENNETH GALBRAITH Harvard economist and former ambassador to India.

ARTHUR GOLDBERG Supreme Court justice appointed by President Kennedy in 1962.

LYNDON B. JOHNSON President of the United States, 1963–1969.

▶ Nobody said no to Lyndon Baines Johnson. This was especially true when he was determined to give someone something. And it was even more true when the gift he had in mind was an appointment of some kind.

From Bruce Allen Murphy, *Fortas: The Rise and Ruin of a Supreme Court Justice* (New York: William Morrow, 1988). Copyright © 1988 by Bruce Allen Murphy. Reprinted by permission of William Morrow and Company, Inc., and the author.

No less a force than James H. Rowe, Jr., had once tried to prove this axiom wrong. When Johnson was Senate majority leader in 1956, he tried to "give" the former Franklin D. Roosevelt assistant and prominent Washington lawyer a job as his assistant. But with a thriving law practice and contacts throughout the government, Rowe had no reason to look to Johnson for such help. There wasn't a single reason for him to accept the job—except for the fact that the majority leader wanted him.

"I can't leave my law practice," Rowe responded, explaining that financial considerations and the need to support his growing family, while keeping his current list of clients happy, were now paramount considerations. Still, despite these concerns, Rowe offered one day a week of help. That was Rowe's second mistake, his first having been listening to Johnson in the first place. For Johnson saw the opening, and liked to tell the story of the man who allowed his camel to warm its nose in his tent and soon found that the animal was wholly inside while the man was outside. Here, Johnson was the camel.

So the two men negotiated, and Rowe soon offered two days of help. Then he raised it to three days of help. But Johnson wanted *every* day of Rowe's attention, and nothing else would do. It was time for "the treatment." Johnson was charismatically persuasive, learning the weaknesses of his quarry and exploiting them, slowly weaving a web around him, backing him into a corner, until there was no resisting anymore. First Rowe's law partner came by to say, "You just can't do this to Lyndon Johnson." Then people Rowe saw on the street would come up and say, "Why aren't you helping Lyndon? How can you let him down?" Then his own wife made an appeal. No matter where Rowe went, no matter what business he visited, a member of Lyndon Johnson's army was there prepared to do battle.

Rowe tried to call off the blitzkrieg, telling Johnson no once more. But the senator said, "Don't worry about the clients. I'll call them." And Rowe knew that was no idle threat. But still Rowe said no.

Finally, they had one last meeting on the subject. But even a negotiator as skilled as Rowe was no match for Lyndon Johnson. As soon as Rowe gave his final no, it brought tears to the powerful majority leader's eyes. "I am going to die," he whined, reminding his visitor of his recent massive heart attack. "You are an old friend . . . [and] you don't care. . . . It's typically selfish." Seeing the flood of tears, and no doubt thinking of having to face Lady Bird at the funeral, Rowe had no choice. "Oh, goddamn it, all right." With that, the waterworks stopped, Johnson quickly straightened up, and said smartly, "All right, just remember I make the decisions, you don't." It was, Rowe had to admit, "a great performance."

It was ironic that the man who later found it impossible to persuade the American people when speaking to them on television had such a hypnotically convincing manner when speaking in person. Johnson was charismatic, and he knew it. He fully believed that given just a few moments, he could persuade anyone to do anything. It didn't matter whether that person really wanted to do it or not. Years after the Rowe incident, when Johnson used a similar technique to "convince" George Ball to leave his new partnership at Lehman Brothers to serve for six months as ambassador to the United Nations, the president's quarry said, "My negotiating posture was destroyed. . . . L.B.J. surrounded me."

However, Abe Fortas had proven that he was one of the few people capable of resisting that irresistible force. And his refusal in 1964 to take the attorney generalship nettled the president. After all of the things that Fortas had done for Johnson over the years, including his formative efforts in the reelection effort, it was inevitable that the president would try again to give him an important job in the government.

In fact, for years, Johnson had known the perfect governmental post for a man of Fortas's talents—a seat on the Supreme Court of the United States. Johnson had been thinking about this possibility nearly as long as he had aspired to become president. In the early 1950's, as Johnson's black limousine could be seen more and more frequently at the Arnold, Fortas and Porter office while he sought advice from Fortas, he began to think about where a lawyer of this caliber belonged. Johnson frequently told [White House aide] Walter Jenkins, "Abe Fortas would make a great Supreme Court justice and I would put him there if I could." Jenkins remembered how frequently Johnson would express "his great wish" that he could accomplish this goal. Johnson believed he knew no wiser man. And, more important, there was no one to whom he owed more. But realistically everyone knew that no southerner had a chance to win the presidency. Of course, no one ever expected that the office would be handed to one.

But now he was president, and when the news came to Johnson on July 14, 1965, that United Nations Ambassador Adlai Stevenson was dead, his course of action was inevitable. Soon two men who made their living negotiating out concessions would bend to Johnson's will. Both would eventually come to regret it. But in the end, both knew there was no way they could have avoided it.

When Johnson was informed that Ambassador Stevenson was dead it did not immediately occur to him that this was not just a loss for the administration, but also a chance to do something he had been waiting nearly fifteen years to do. At the time, all that he knew was that there still was a debt to be paid. Despite his millions, Johnson lacked the resources to repay one of the biggest favors of his life. For the man he owed wanted nothing, asked for nothing, and needed nothing that Johnson had to offer. Soon, though, Johnson would see a way to reward him. And, with the best of intentions, he would force Abe Fortas to take a seat on the Supreme Court.

The only problem for the moment was that such a seat was not available. But it was Harvard economist John Kenneth Galbraith who unwittingly first suggested the move that would make it possible for President Johnson to set his plan into motion. And all Galbraith was trying to do was avoid the same charismatic persuader that two others would soon face.

As Galbraith sat in a Washington Cathedral pew listening to the memorial service for Adlai Stevenson on July 16, he received a note from one of his friends:

> *Oh God, our help in ages past*
> *Our hope for years to come*
> *You are the first on Lyndon's list*
> *In our eternal home.*

To his horror Galbraith quickly concluded that they might be right. In the two days since Stevenson had died of a heart attack in London, Johnson might well have concluded that Galbraith, his former ambassador to India, was the perfect man to take the United Nations job. Who could better understand the plight of the third-world nations than an economist concerned with the poor, who had lived and worked in a poor nation? Then, too, not only was Galbraith a genuine liberal, but he was a Kennedy liberal. Wouldn't it be nice, as LBJ removed many of the JFK old guard, to prove to them with this appointment that he still saw things their way? Finally, Galbraith was a *Harvard* professor, and everyone knew that impressed Johnson, even though he did not like to admit it. Confirming Galbraith's fears was the fact that there had been a phone call to his home in Cambridge from Lyndon Johnson the previous night, which he had missed.

But there was a hitch. Galbraith did not want the job. He had a book to write, and the United Nations ambassadorship was not a job for a person of independent viewpoints (a lesson that the man who eventually took the job would soon learn). So Galbraith, in order to resist the entreaties of the "Great Persuader," concocted a foolproof plan. He would suggest another target—Supreme Court Justice Arthur Goldberg.

Galbraith remembered a conversation he had had with Justice Goldberg a few weeks before in Cambridge. He understood that the justice was unhappy with the "more deliberative pace" of the work on the court. For a man like Goldberg, who was accustomed to the fast-paced excitement of labor law negotiations, this new position made him restless. In truth, this was probably the same gripe that all new members of the Supreme Court who come to the post from something other than the relative quiet of a law school teaching position feel as they adjust to their new lifestyle. Nearly all the justices make that transition sooner or later, though, as they realize this is a lifetime appointment from which they can not only make the law, but make history. The truth of the matter here was that Goldberg was perfectly happy on the Supreme Court. Galbraith, however, decided to take the complaint "seriously." He had to—it may have been his only effective way out of an appointment to the United Nations that he did not want, but that Johnson might force him to take.

This problem was on his mind when at 2:30 that afternoon, while meeting with McGeorge Bundy on a different subject, Galbraith and his wife were summoned by the president to the Oval Office for a chat.

The conversation lasted only fifteen minutes, but it was long enough for Galbraith to take himself off of the hook and put the Supreme Court justice on it. "That Stevenson," Johnson began. "Why did he have to die right now? He was always off in his timing. Who am I going to get to take his place?" So Galbraith immediately launched into his suggestion, saying that he had been told that Goldberg "was a little bored on the Court."

While there is no evidence that LBJ had before this time considered this possibility, it did not take him long to grasp its many possibilities. Could Goldberg be persuaded to take the job? Then, after speaking on another topic, Johnson came back with "How would Arthur get along with the A-rabs?" Indeed, a Jewish ambassador to the United Nations might well have some problems. But Galbraith was not deterred and emphasized Goldberg's skills as a negotiator. It was clear from the way that Johnson kept returning to the subject that this new idea had found a home.

But who would give up a lifetime appointment to the Supreme Court, with its absolute freedom of movement and thought, for a spot in a cauldron of controversy circumscribed by the orders of the State Department and the administration? Certainly not a man of Arthur Goldberg's intelligence. Unless, that is, he met an irresistible force. And that force was Lyndon Johnson. . . .

Johnson realized that by . . . persuading Goldberg [to leave the Court] he could finally accomplish one of his dreams. He could put his old friend Abe Fortas on the United States Supreme Court. It was a moment that Johnson had been anticipating for a long time—repaying all of his friend's kindnesses with the biggest gift within his power. But there were two problems. Goldberg did not want to leave the court, and Fortas did not want to join it.

So Lyndon Johnson began his quest to get Fortas onto the Supreme Court. It would have to be planned carefully. If Fortas sensed what was going on too early, he would back off and not even Lyndon Johnson would be able to move him. So the first step was subtle, and seemingly impromptu, while also being impossible to refuse (after all, every good salesman says the way to make a hard sale is to get your quarry to keep saying yes to everything). Who could resist a seemingly innocent spur-of-the-moment invitation to dinner at the White House alone with the Johnsons?

Not surprisingly, this was not the way that Johnson later recalled these events in his memoirs. Lest people conclude that the president had been "masterminding a great shift in the top echelons of government," Johnson recalled that he had not moved on the appointment until *after* Goldberg's decision to resign from the court on the twentieth of July, *after* "conferr[ing] with many friends and advisers," and *after* studying "the list these advisers had compiled." In fact, there was no list for Johnson, and by the time Goldberg had definitely decided to leave the court, Johnson had already offered the position to Fortas—twice.

Late on the evening of July 16, Lady Bird Johnson was sitting on the Truman Balcony speaking on the phone with Abe Fortas when the president came on the line and invited the Fortases to the White House for a late dinner. As the four of them sat down at 9:45 to eat, the president casually turned the conversation to the hot topic of the day, whom he should appoint ambassador to the United Nations. Since the required skill there was one of negotiation, they discussed the best negotiators that they knew, and Johnson surprised everyone with a suggestion of the brilliant labor mediator Arthur Goldberg. When questioned as to whether Goldberg would leave his secure position on the Supreme Court for such a job, Johnson replied cagily, "He's the sort of man who would cry if he saw an old widow woman and some hungry children. He feels that quality would be useful in dealing with underdeveloped countries and poorer nations."

Johnson was full of surprises for his guests that night. He then asked, just supposing that there was a vacancy on the Supreme Court, would Fortas take it? The president's friend was "moved, quiet, [and] grateful," but he declined. While Lady Bird Johnson wanted very much to see Fortas in this lofty position, she feared that such an appointment would leave the president and her as "the loneliest people . . . in time of trouble."

In truth, little had changed since the attorney generalship offer in 1964 to convince Fortas to return to government service. If anything, there were now powerful disincentives to reconsidering that decision. The Fortases had just committed themselves to a very high mortgage to pay for their newly purchased $250,000 house in Washington's Dumbarton Oaks area. Moreover, replacing Fortas's present salary—estimated, by some, to be in the neighborhood of $200,000 annually—with the $39,500 then being paid to members of the court would not allow them to complete the planned redecoration of their house.

But Fortas later claimed to a visitor that there were many other reasons for not wanting to change his life pattern at that point, and, he added forcefully, "none of them were financial." As before, there was the challenge of continuing to build and manage one of the most powerful law firms in Washington at that moment. A dozen new attorneys had been added to the firm in the past eighteen months to handle the recent upsurge in business since the coming to power of the Johnson administration. With even more to be added shortly, the firm was suffering growing pains. In addition, one of the founding partners, Thurman Arnold, was in poor health. So there was much truth to Fortas's claim to Lady Bird Johnson that he was responsible for "stabilizing" the law firm and that it would take a couple of years to do so.

But there was more that Fortas was not telling Mrs. Johnson. And, while it would not become evident until later that summer, it may have been the most powerful reason why Fortas felt he had to refuse the prospect of an appointment to the Supreme Court. That reason had to do with the fourth participant in the dinner on the Truman Balcony on that balmy July 16 night—Carolyn Agger, his wife. While Agger stated on that occasion that "she felt that he would make a good Justice," indicating her agreement with, or at the very least her nonopposition to the selection, events later would prove that she felt very differently.

For now, however, Johnson had a more immediate problem to work on. He knew whom he wanted for the job, but now he needed to create the position. All of his persuasive powers would be needed to charm Arthur Goldberg out of his court seat.

Unbeknownst to John Kenneth Galbraith, for President Johnson's purpose, he could not have suggested a better member of the court for the appointment to the United Nations than Arthur Goldberg. Of course there would be the loss of a liberal from the court, but most of the justices were liberal, and, in the eyes of the president, so was the prospective nominee, Abe Fortas. What made Goldberg especially attractive was that he occupied the one seat—the so-called Jewish seat—that everyone could agree should go to Fortas. He would be the latest in a line of great Jewish justices dating back to the 1916 appointment of Louis D. Brandeis by Woodrow Wilson. Brandeis, Benjamin Cardozo, Felix Frankfurter, and now Goldberg had all been seen as forces for liberalism and ethnic minorities. In fact, though, the four men had differed widely on the matter of the role that the court should play in shaping the nature of the law. But for now, the public saw at least one of the seats as reserved for a member of the Jewish legal community. Of course, no one would begin to suggest that Abe Fortas was not absolutely qualified in every respect. But the fact that Fortas was Jewish would make things that much easier for the scheming president. So Johnson prepared to make his first move.

Unless Arthur Goldberg chooses to tell his side of the story, all of the precise details of his private conversations with President Johnson during this period will never be known. To one scholar inquiring about this matter, the former justice would only say, "Have you ever had your arm twisted by Lyndon Johnson?" But one thing seems sure from an examination of the materials in the Confidential Office Files of the Johnson Library in Austin, Texas. It did not happen the way that the president recounted it in his memoirs.

According to Johnson, he told Goldberg that he "had heard that he might step down from the Court and therefore might be available for another assignment." The justice is supposed to have responded that "these reports had substance." Whereupon, when offered the post of secretary of health, education, and welfare, Goldberg allegedly told the president that "the job sounded fascinating but that he had become increasingly interested in foreign affairs." So, after a night's reflection, at the president's behest, Goldberg is supposed to have told White House aide Jack Valenti "that the job he would accept was the U.N. Ambassadorship."

Lyndon Johnson was never one to let the truth stand in the way of a good story. While Goldberg had indeed talked to Valenti, in fact the president knew very well from the memos at the time that he had said just the opposite.

According to Valenti's account of their conversation, the justice was "happy on [the] Court," and was not inclined to leave. But that did not stop a determined LBJ. Like Earl Warren before him, Goldberg had to be made to understand that it was in his and the nation's interests that he leave the court at that moment.

So, three days after the Fortas dinner at the White House, the president and Goldberg chatted as they winged their way on Air Force One on Monday morning, July 19, 1965, to the funeral of Adlai Stevenson in Illinois. The two men spoke of the importance of the position in the United Nations, especially in these troubled days of the growing Vietnam War. As Goldberg later recalled, the president used a version of the argument that had been so successful in convincing Earl Warren to put aside his judicial duties temporarily. He said that only Goldberg could help solve this problem and hinted at what might happen if he did not: "[LBJ called on him] to join in the greatest adventure of man's history—the effort to bring the rule of law to govern the relations between sovereign states. It is that or doom." At that point, Goldberg later explained how little there was that he could do. "I correctly felt that our country was in very great trouble over the Vietnam issue, and that I could not put my personal predilection which was, of course, to stay on the Court—my highest ambition—before the country's interest."

Lyndon Johnson had had three days to consider his moves and he had refined his argument for the plane ride. In case Goldberg was interested in domestic affairs or in a position of greater governmental authority, the president also offered him the soon-to-be-vacated position of secretary of health, education, and welfare. The cold truth was that he didn't really care where Goldberg ended up; the president just wanted him off of the Supreme Court. He wanted that seat vacated for Abe Fortas, whether Fortas thought he wanted it or not.

Johnson knew well that the jobs of UN ambassador and HEW secretary, while worthy positions, did not seem adequate trades for a seat on the Supreme Court. Why would anyone give up a cherished lifetime post for a short-term stint in a job of arguably limited policy impact? For this reason, one of the true mysteries from this period has always been why Arthur Goldberg even considered such a prospect, much less accepted it. Even within the administration, the speculation on this matter was interesting. Some believed that Johnson had offered Goldberg the prospect of being reappointed to the court, perhaps even to the chief justiceship, when the war was over. While this might well have been mentioned, the truth was that the president held out much, much more for Goldberg to consider. He offered him the chance to make history—how would Goldberg like one day to become the first Jewish vice president of the United States?

This was Lyndon Johnson at his most persuasive. Huey Long used to talk about two kinds of owls in the woods—the hoot owl and the scrootch owl.* The hoot owl, he said, looks for food by banging into the outside of the chicken coop wall, bursting in the window, and scooping up a hen for dinner in a flurry

---

* Huey Long was a colorful and controversial U.S. senator from Louisiana in the 1930s.

of feathers and noise. The scrootch owl, though, gently sidles up next to the hen, speaks softly into her ear, and simply charms her into falling into the owl's lap. While Johnson could be both a hoot owl *and* a scrootch owl, with Goldberg on this occasion he was only the scrootch owl. Here he not only offered the reluctant justice something that already belonged to Hubert Humphrey, but he convinced him to take it. "You never know what can happen, Arthur," the president began. Then he painted a picture of a vacancy occurring some time in the future, and Goldberg not being in a position to do anything about it. "You're over there on that Court, isolated from the action," he said, "and you can't get to the Vice Presidency from the Court." So, Johnson insisted, it would be better for him to prepare by taking on a more political role. To Goldberg, the prospect seemed irresistible.

But the irony was even greater. Johnson managed to convince Goldberg that, once in the United Nations, he would be offered the chance to take his place among the prominent presidential advisers on foreign policy. This offer, too, was illusory. As Goldberg would soon discover to his dismay, the man who actually had the most foreign policy influence with the president was also the same man who would get Goldberg's seat on the court (not to mention the offer of the chief justiceship later on)—Abe Fortas.

Having already made his pitch to Goldberg and fully confident of the results, the president called Fortas from Air Force One while still on his way back from the funeral. "I am arriving, and I am going to announce your appointment to the Supreme Court," Johnson declared proudly. Fortas was stunned; this was a whole lot more serious than the hypothetical offer at dinner on the sixteenth. "God almighty, Mr. President, you can't do that," he responded. "I have got to talk to you about it." So Johnson demurred once again—but only for the time being. Did Fortas want to do this? asked [law partner] Paul Porter when the conversation had ended. "I don't," Fortas responded immediately. And the matter seemed closed. After all, there was no vacancy on the court anyway.

All of that changed, though, shortly before ten the next morning. President Johnson phoned Arthur Goldberg and made him an ex-justice by formally offering him the appointment as UN ambassador. Just thirty-six minutes later he sealed the arrangement by announcing Goldberg's new appointment to the press in the Rose Garden. And, as Johnson was never a man to waste time, one of his guests at the White House an hour later was none other than attorney Abe Fortas.

But there was one final twist to this tale of seduction. A memorandum in the Confidential Office Files of the Johnson Library indicates just how reluctant Goldberg was to leave his seat on the court. It seems that the departing justice did not even know for sure, at the time he was giving his decision to the White House, what new position he might be agreeing to take. After considering the president's offer of either the HEW or the UN post, Goldberg spoke by phone with Jack Valenti sometime that night or early the next morning. According to Valenti's notes on the conversation, the justice said that he had "understood [that the] President had focused on [the] U.N. job—and therefore [he] did not give further thought to H.E.W. . . . . If [the] President wants him in [the] U.N., he will do it. If, on [the] other hand, [the] President wants to focus also on [the] H.E.W. job, he [Goldberg] would need to talk further with [the] President on this particular assignment." Valenti could not have been clearer in his recapitulation of the conversation: "SUMMARY—No change of heart on [the] U.N. Ready to go. If Pres[ident] wants him on H.E.W., [he] needs to talk with [the] Pres[ident]." Either way, Lyndon Johnson had his man.

But there was much work to be done before the president could pat himself on the back. Before this he had had a nominee, but no vacant court seat. Now he seemingly had a court seat, but no nominee. For now. In Lyndon Johnson's world, though, some folks just took a little longer to say yes.

After Johnson had phoned with his second appointment offer on July 19, Fortas had taken out a piece of his personal stationery and poured out his heart. So moved was the president by this penned rejection that he kept it in his coat pocket and read it aloud to his entire family at the dinner table. This was Fortas, the loyal friend, at his most eloquent. Having offered his thanks for the honor, Fortas explained:

> *After painful searching, I've decided to decline—with a heart full of gratitude. Carol thinks I should accept this greatest honor that a lawyer could receive—this highest appointive post in the nation. But I want a few more years of activity. I want a few more years to try to be of service to you and the Johnson family. And I want—and feel that in justice I should take—a few more years to stabilize this law firm in the interests of the young men who have enlisted here.*

But while the president was moved by this passionate declination, he was not convinced. LBJ was determined that his old friend would go onto the Supreme Court. And so were others.

Quite understandably, the quick resignation of Arthur Goldberg from the court led to a great deal of speculation as to the name of his successor. Much of that speculation came from those men who were most affected by the move, the other sitting justices. It was Goldberg's replacement of the judicially self-restrained Felix Frankfurter in 1962 that had changed the overall philosophy of the court to a much more liberal viewpoint. Thus, that seat was still the crucial one in dictating whether the new direction would be maintained. Of course, one could expect Lyndon Johnson to *try* to appoint another liberal, but everyone knew that liberals come in all varieties and that presidents have been known to make mistakes in predicting the future actions of their nominees.

Perhaps it was that sense of uncertainty that bothered Justice John Harlan the most. For years he had fought with his brethren, seeking to make their decisions more restrained in several areas and forcing them to become more disciplined in their approach to legal questions. Since his ally on many occasions was Justice Hugo Black, the two of them were on the telephone on the evening of the twentieth discussing the disruptive events. It had been a hard day for Black, too. Goldberg had been reluctant to tell him about the move off the high court, fearing that Black, who was known to despise extrajudicial work, would disapprove. As Black tried to reassure Harlan on the phone, they turned to a discussion of the possible replacements. Like everyone else, they arrived at the name of Abe Fortas. They also decided that United States Court of Appeals Judge Thurgood Marshall was another possibility should the president decide to appoint the first black to the court.*

It seems, though, that Chief Justice Warren's sources of information were a little better than his colleagues'. By the next day he had been informed that the post had been offered to Fortas, and also that he had already refused it. Feeling comfortable with the selection, the chief decided to try to influence Fortas's decision about his future course of action. Knowing that Hugo Black was better acquainted with Fortas—after all, it was he who had heard the crucial 1948 suit by Johnson on his Senate race—Warren phoned to ask whether Black would speak with Fortas about the decision. Black was happy to do so and he immediately placed the call. But while Fortas was grateful for the news that both Warren and Black wanted him on the court, he was noncommittal as to his course of action. All he would say was that his office was meeting at that moment to discuss the matter.

Meanwhile, the justices' avowedly liberal colleague, and a man who had always had great interest in Fortas's career, William O. Douglas, was out of the mainstream of things at his summer home in Goose Prairie, Washington State. But Douglas was never out of the action. That same day he wrote to President Johnson, recommending Fortas for the position, calling him a "superb choice." After expressing the wish that Fortas be "release[d]" for the job, Douglas used his own life experience to reassure Johnson that such a selection would hardly affect the adviser's ability to continue to "serve" the president.

While the Supreme Court was getting involved in the machinations, Lady Bird Johnson used the occasion of an afternoon discussion over the future presidential library at the University of Texas to make her own appeal to Fortas about taking the court seat. Saying that her husband would have to make the appointment shortly, she wondered whether the decision not to accept the post was "irrevocable." Once more, Fortas explained his need to "stabilize" his growing law firm, and he made an even more persuasive argument to Johnson's most loyal supporter. "If the President was faced with any real troubles," he said, "I would want to be around to help him. And if I were on the Court, I could not. That was the difference between the possibility of a Court job and the Attorney General job."

Plainly, the private practice of law offered Fortas the best of both worlds, a challenging and rewarding *independent* legal career, and the frequent chance

---

* Johnson appointed Thurgood Marshall to the Supreme Court in 1967.

to be in the center of political power when needed. While the attorney general-ship would have reduced these opportunities, the seat on the court surely would have eliminated them completely. Fortas had grown too accustomed to being in the center of the action to give it up now for what appeared to be a sideline seat making law on the court while others implemented it. So he was not inclined to take up Mrs. Johnson's closing warning that he ought to get in touch with her husband soon if he had any "doubt" about his decision. . . .

While all of this was occurring, the Department of Justice was now hard at work in developing its own list of potential nominees in case Fortas really meant no. The resulting memorandum, which was delivered to the president on July 22, contained no surprises. Despite the fact that this comprehensive memorandum was offered by Attorney General [Nicholas] Katzenbach after Fortas had already twice refused the job, it is apparent that Katzenbach had no knowledge of these events. In first examining whether the tradition of the "Jew-ish Seat" should be continued, the attorney general stated that "most Jews share with me the feeling" that religion should not be the main criterion for the posi-tion. After adding that at least one Jewish justice should be appointed before 1968, Katzenbach concluded by saying, "On balance, I think if you appoint a Jew he should be so outstanding as to be selected clearly on his own merits as an individual." Then he prefaced his recommendation of such noted legal scholars as Harvard law professor Paul Freund, University of Chicago law pro-fessor Edward Levi, court of appeals judge Henry Friendly, and eight other peo-ple, with this evaluation of his top candidate: "Before making these recommen-dations I think I should say that from a completely objective viewpoint Abe Fortas has every qualification for the Court. If you did not know him he would be my first recommendation—and still is." It was the second time in two days that a prominent member of the administration had suggested to the president Paul Freund, the man who had so narrowly lost out to Byron White and Arthur Goldberg for the last two court vacancies, as a top candidate for the post. But Freund was doomed to become the bridesmaid again.

Johnson decided that a more effective technique would be to have others attempt to persuade the reluctant prime candidate. Sometime during the next few days he contacted both Justice Douglas and former justice Goldberg to see if they could influence Fortas's decision. Douglas phoned Fortas from Yakima and received what he later described as "a firm refusal." Goldberg, on the other hand, is said to have personally visited Fortas in his law office to convey his own hope that the offer would be accepted. While the response was no differ-ent from the one given by Fortas to all of the others, Goldberg was in a most unique position to assess the future outcome of these efforts. As he told his newly appointed law clerks, "The president says he's going to appoint Abe and Abe says no. The president won't even consider other names. He's going to wear him down. He'll wait until the end of time." This Goldberg knew from experience.

But Johnson's task wasn't getting any easier. During this period he had his appointments secretary, James Jones, place a call to the Fortas household one evening in order to make another effort to "wear him down." However, Carolyn Agger initially refused to put her husband on the line because, contrary to her statement at the White House dinner, she was now opposed to the court appointment. As Jones recalls the incident, "I relayed that to the president, and he talked to Abe." While this call did not result in an immediate change of heart, Johnson was now warned that a significant obstacle lay in the path of his plans.

As of the night of the twenty-sixth, there was no doubt in Fortas's mind about his decision. So he phoned Hugo Black that night to tell him that he was definitely not going onto the court. Even Drew Pearson wrote in his column that day, "In one of the few such cases in history a lawyer turned down an appointment to the U.S. Supreme Court. He is Abe Fortas. . . ." But neither of these men had gotten the president's opinion.

Tuesday, July 27, dawned bright and sunny. It had been a full week since Arthur Goldberg had decided to resign from the court. Because no definite announcement had been made as to his replacement, the White House correspondents continued to speculate on the names. Not surprisingly, given all of the backstage negotiations, Fortas's name surfaced frequently. Someone even asked Fortas about it, but his only response was that he was not interested in any government job "from President on down." Then another member of the press quizzed Press Secretary Bill Moyers on the same matter. In confirming Fortas's account, Moyers went a bit further, reminding the reporters that he, too, had not wanted a government job, and yet "I'm here."

Perhaps, thought the press corps, the president himself might be able to shed more light on this rumor. So after a 10:30 ceremony at the Rose Garden that morning announcing the appointment of John Gardner as secretary of HEW, the reporters asked Johnson whom he planned to appoint to the court. Was there any truth to these rumors about Abe Fortas? Looking straight into the eyes of the questioner, the president responded, "I have not even begun to consider that matter."

Later that day, troubled by a difficult decision about whether to send more troops to Vietnam, Johnson met for two hours in the Oval Office with his noncandidate. More than just the decision itself, the problem of how to explain and justify it to the press and the American people troubled Johnson. During this meeting, the president made one more appeal to Fortas to take the appointment to the Supreme Court. By this time Fortas had been made to understand that more was at stake than just this appointment. Perhaps the opportunity would even come for Johnson to appoint him chief justice. For his part, Fortas was pushing his own nominee for the court, Chief Justice Walter Schaefer of the Illinois Supreme Court. Schaefer was indeed very qualified, having been described in the Department of Justice memo as ranking "with the best of the State Supreme Court Justices."

But the president was not persuaded. Instead, he used a new tactic. Johnson tried to invoke the wishes of one of Fortas's key advisers by showing him the letter from Justice Douglas recommending the appointment. While this high praise from the man who had helped to guide most of the major moves in his career must have pleased Fortas, there is no evidence that it in any way affected his decision to remain in private practice. He simply wasn't going on the court, and President Johnson had to understand that fact. But Johnson, thinking that just as a politician aspires to the top job of president, so a lawyer must aspire to be on the Supreme Court, refused to take Fortas at his word. Someday, he surely believed, Abe would thank him for it.

For Johnson and his aides, July 28 was a fateful day. In a decision the country would later come to regret, Lyndon Johnson had already made the final decision to send fifty thousand more men to Vietnam. But the president knew that this would not sit well with a nation that did not fully understand the reasons for fighting in that small country in the first place. Knowing how the media worked, Johnson decided to hold a televised press conference at midday, when the viewing audience was small, and to make a move that would flood the news bureaus of the country, perhaps even deflecting a portion of the headlines away from this military decision. In so doing, he would solve the other problem that had been plaguing him for days.

Early that morning Johnson turned to his assistants Joe Califano and Bill Moyers and said, "We've got to have some other news. I'll nominate a new justice and John Chancellor to be director of the Voice of America." The Chancellor appointment was no surprise to the two men, for Johnson had made the offer eleven days ago. Well, it had been more like a draft than an offer. The NBC reporter had been giving the White House fits with his dispatches, so LBJ decided to make him the head of the VOA, which had been leaderless since early March when Henry Loomis left the post to join the Office of Education. Despite some initial reluctance in taking the post, on July 28 John Chancellor no longer would be reporting *on* the White House, he would be reporting *for* the White House.

But Johnson's orders regarding the judicial appointment came as a surprise to the aides, since they knew that Johnson had pursued only one man and he clearly wasn't interested. Moreover, after that declination the president had yet to confer fully with the Justice Department and the FBI about other potential nominees. So Califano, who had drawn the assignment of drafting the judicial nomination statement for the press conference while Moyers worked on the Chancellor announcement, had the challenge of writing about someone who did not himself know what was about to befall him. But the aides knew only too well that no one said no to Lyndon Johnson, especially when he had an appointment to make. Not only had Moyers been reluctant to serve in the government, but Califano's appointment as a presidential assistant had also been announced before he even knew what the job was going to be.

So Califano wrote about the mystery appointee:

> *A President has few responsibilities of greater importance—or greater consequence to the country's future—than the Constitutional responsibility of nominating Justices for the Supreme Court of the United States.*
>
> *I am happy today to announce that the distinguished American who was my first choice for the position now vacant on the Supreme Court has agreed to accept the call to this vital duty. I will shortly send to the Senate my nomination of _____ to be an Associate Justice of the Supreme Court.*
>
> *For many years, I have regarded _____ as one of this nation's most able, most outstanding citizens—a scholar, a profound thinker, a lawyer of superior ability, and a man of humane and deeply compassionate feelings toward his fellow man. That opinion is shared by the legal profession, by members of Congress and by leaders of business, labor and other sectors of our national life.*

While some may argue that this description covered half the members of the bar, others may say that it covered none of them.

Meanwhile, as the White House aides labored, Abe Fortas was back at his office, seated at his desk and surrounded by piles of books, painstakingly drafting a brief for a case his firm was presenting before the Supreme Court. The last thing he needed now was to be interrupted. So of course the phone buzzed, but since it was the president the work could wait. Even though the two men had spent all that time late the previous afternoon in the Oval Office, Johnson said he needed more help from Fortas. He was about to announce the increase in troops headed for Vietnam and needed Fortas's help in putting the final polish on the press statement. Could he spare the time to come over? Since it was twelve minutes before noon and the live, televised press conference was scheduled to begin in less than half an hour, there was little time to spare before the last-minute changes in the statement had to be made and placed onto the Tele-PrompTer. So, as he had done so many times before, Fortas dropped everything on Johnson's behalf.

But as Fortas got up from his desk preparing to leave, he smelled a rat. He turned to Paul Porter and mused, "Look, you don't suppose he is going to lean on me some more about this."

"Oh," replied Porter, "I think you are off the hook from what I have heard." So Porter, enjoying one of the perquisites of working with a law partner who had an inside pipeline to the White House, turned on the television knowing that an important announcement was coming in a few minutes from the president's news conference.

One hopes that Fortas enjoyed some freedom and peace during his drive over to 1600 Pennsylvania Avenue that morning. It was the last that he would have of either for a long time to come.

As soon as Fortas arrived at the White House, he went to the living quarters to do what he had been doing so well now for nearly two years—look over what the president was about to say and give his approval. It was this scene—the two men, Fortas and Johnson, laboring over the script—that Joe Califano encountered at 12:15 when he entered the Oval Office with his mystery person's judicial nomination statement. The hidden identity had now been revealed. The time had finally come when Lyndon Johnson knew it was impossible for his friend and confidant to say no once and for all.

Failing to show the other statement to Fortas, the president asked him to come down to the press conference and sit in the front row. After all, it was such an important event that Lady Bird and Lynda Bird Johnson would be there as well. As the two men walked to the elevator and began to descend, the president casually added, "I'm going to send your name to the Supreme Court." Not even Fortas's protests would be effective now. Johnson tried to minimize all of the previously stated objections by saying that he understood that it was "young lawyers at his firm who depended on him . . . and the mortgage payments on his house" that were bothering Fortas. Then the president of the United States added, "As to the rest of it, you better let me be the judge of where you can help me best." Fortas *firmly* continued to decline. "Now look, Abe," Johnson continued, "they need you on the court. You may never have the opportunity again. *Take this job!*"

But Fortas was still saying no, adding that the two men had been through all this before, when the elevator door opened. They were halfway down the hall to the East Room, where the throngs of anticipating newsmen were waiting, when Johnson bagged his man with one final, irrefutable argument: "Well you know, I'm sending all these boys to Vietnam, and they're giving their life for their country and you can do no less. If your president asks you to do something for your country, can you run out on him?"

Fortas was beaten. "I'll accompany you," he said simply. Finally, his characteristic life pattern of hesitant uncertainty at critical career turning points had done him in. He had been overwhelmed by the persuasive magic of Lyndon Johnson. And so he marched in behind the president, sat in the front row, and waited with John Chancellor for the inevitable. Years later Fortas recalled, "To the best of my knowledge, and belief, I never said yes."

There was a very solemn mood in the East Room that day as the observers sensed the grave decision that Johnson was about to announce. His opening remarks ran nine minutes longer than the expected quarter of an hour. It was

Johnson at his most eloquent. In the middle of a very moving and effective explanation of his understanding of the need to be in Vietnam, Johnson indicated the toll that this decision was taking on him. "I don't find it easy," he began, "to send the flower of our youth, our finest young men, into battle. . . . I think I know, too, how their mothers weep and their families sorrow. This is the most agonizing and most painful duty of your President." Few would disagree with this assessment. The prepared text moved the Johnson women and even some hardened reporters to tears.

Then shortly before one o'clock, seeking to take the edge off of this tense moment and the harsh news, Johnson announced the appointments of John Chancellor and Abe Fortas. In deference to his old friend's reluctance to go onto the court, the president extemporaneously added another paragraph to Califano's prepared statement: "Mr. Fortas has, as you know, told me on numerous occasions in the last 20 months that he would not be an applicant or a candidate, or would not accept any appointment to any public office. This is, I guess, as it should be, for in this instance the job has sought the man." No one but Fortas and a handful of others knew how true that was.

Despite the sad news early in the conference, Johnson was ebullient. He had finally accomplished one of his dreams. His old friend was finally going where he belonged—the Supreme Court of the United States. However, following the ceremony, all the normally cool and collected Fortas could tell reporters after being caught up in the Johnson cyclone was that he was "a little overwhelmed." Then he added in response to questions, "I had reminded the President that I was not seeking any government post, judicial or otherwise. The President was kind enough to say it was a place where I could perform superior service."

That same day the White House tried to cover for the president's king-sized credibility problem on this incident by leaking an in-depth explanation of the events, which was attributed to "highly reliable sources." After all, not only had Johnson lied the day before, but throughout the courtship of Fortas, Press Secretary Moyers and other administration officials had been discouraging the press from discussing the possibility (though the aides probably believed their stories).

According to this new account, the president had first made the offer to Fortas on July 19, conditional upon Goldberg's resignation, thus knocking the underpinnings out of Johnson's statement that as of the day before he had not "begun to consider that matter." (Such self-contradictions were typical, though. White House reporter James Deakin recalls how Johnson himself let the cat out of the bag a week later. In seeking to demonstrate how brilliant he had been in persuading Fortas to go onto the court, he searched in his coat pocket—which was always full of memos, Senate head counts, and other relevant documents—and pulled out Fortas's handwritten rejection of the court appointment, which was also dated the nineteenth. Not even for Lyndon Johnson did 19 follow 27.)

From then on the White House explanation contained more fiction than fact. "By noon yesterday [July 27]," it explained, "after long conversations with his wife and a few close friends, Mr. Fortas had all but decided to accept the offer. He called the President with his final decision this morning, several hours before Mr. Johnson's news conference. . . ."

Following the press conference, Johnson lunched with Fortas, then left the poor Supreme Court nominee to stagger back to his office in order to finish drafting his legal brief. With his shirt drenched with perspiration, Fortas went into Porter's office, "locked the door, and threw himself down on the couch." His puzzled law partner had witnessed the spectacle on the television and could only manage, "What happened?" It was not the last time Fortas would hear that question that day, and like Goldberg before him, he probably didn't really know the answer. . . .

Years later, the man who had ended up one "no" short in dealing with Lyndon Johnson tried to sum up all of these events. . . . "[Lyndon Johnson] conferred on me the greatest honor in his power; the fact that I didn't want it was my tough luck."

Epilogue

Arthur Goldberg was never able to explain adequately why he gave up his seat on the Supreme Court, and, ironically, he was no longer able to exert much influence. It was not Goldberg, the UN ambassador, but Fortas to whom Johnson turned to for advice on Vietnam. Goldberg practiced law until his death in 1990.

It should be noted that Johnson did not manage the same degree of charisma and influence in his relationships with Congress and the public. For example, each attempt by Johnson to use television to persuade the nation that his Vietnam policy was correct resulted in further loss of support.

Today liberals point to Lyndon Johnson's manipulation as the beginning of the end of their dominance of the Supreme Court. Fortas was forced to resign from the Court in 1969 over a financial ethics scandal, and President Nixon replaced him with the much more conservative Harry Blackmun. If Johnson had not forced Fortas onto the Court, presumably Goldberg would have served until recent years and would have helped expand on the Warren Court's efforts in such areas as the rights of the accused. The tide began to turn with the appointments of Warren Burger in 1969 and Blackmun in 1970.

The No-Hands Presidency

Jane Mayer and
Doyle McManus

Presidents have different management styles, and those styles create the different natures of their administrations. The selections in this chapter so far have described the urgent crisis management style of Franklin Roosevelt, the personal command style of Harry Truman, and the reluctant command style of Dwight Eisenhower. This selection by Jane Mayer and Doyle McManus portrays the far different management style used by Ronald Reagan—the "no hands," or "nine to five" presidency.

Elected by an overwhelming majority in 1980, President Reagan ushered in his own "revolution" of government policies, which were seen as an effort to reverse the direction established by Franklin Roosevelt. One aspect of this bold governmental vision was the New Federalism discussed in Selection 2.2. Reagan's ability to communicate with the people through television afforded him six years of enormous popularity, which he translated into influence over congressional policymaking. Yet, as we have already seen, the Reagan style also resulted in one of the worst presidential disasters of the last fifty years, the Iran-contra scandal. (See Selection 5.2.) How could the same presidency contain such vastly different circumstances?

Mayer and McManus focus on Reagan's passive style and on his policy of delegating many decisions to a group of aggressive, management-oriented aides. These aides appeared to be more concerned with the image of the president than with the substance of his policies. But is this always bad? We come back to the question of what characteristics make a good president. Later in the book (Selection 4.3), we will see an example of another president, Jimmy Carter, who was studiously attentive to the details of his office but who also became ineffective—both because of his inability to work with Congress and his plummeting popularity.

Mayer and McManus appear critical of Reagan's disengaged style, and certainly his failures bear critical analysis. In addition to Iran-contra, Reagan left his suc-

cessor with a burdensome budget deficit and a costly
need to rescue the savings and loan industry, which
had collapsed due to the lack of proper government
regulation. Nonetheless, before we are too critical of
the management style portrayed here, we should remember that after the failure of two detail-oriented
presidents—Richard Nixon and Jimmy Carter—this
may well have been precisely the style the public
wanted.

JAMES A. BAKER   White House chief of
staff, 1981–1985.

MICHAEL DEAVER   Deputy chief of staff;
long-time adviser to the Reagans.

EDWIN MEESE   Long-time adviser and
counsel to President Reagan; attorney
general, 1985–1988.

RONALD REAGAN   President of the United
States, 1981–1989.

DONALD REGAN   White House chief of
staff, 1985–1987.

▶ Reagan was unabashed about delegating many of the daily responsibilities
of the presidency. When he cared deeply about an issue, he was outspoken and
stubborn. His views were often strong, even radical. But his involvement in
day-to-day governance—the actual running of the country—was slight. Since
his days in Sacramento, he'd grown accustomed to letting others translate his
goals into programs, much in the same way that he'd allowed others to run the
1984 campaign. Reagan portrayed this as a deliberate "management style," explaining to *Fortune* magazine (in an interview that pleased him more than
most) that "I believe that you surround yourself with the best people you can
find, delegate authority, and don't interfere."

Others in the office had delegated where possible, but Reagan's style of governing was unlike that of any other postwar president—each of whom had, in
different ways, been strong chief executives who dominated not just the formation of policy but also its implementation. To a great extent, Reagan left the job
of implementing his ideas to others—shunning personnel issues, rarely engaging in discussions about congressional strategy, and routinely following his
subordinates' advice on media plans. Instead, he mastered the ceremonial and
symbolic functions of the office so that he could act presidential even when he
wasn't, in the traditional sense, functioning like one.

Reagan's day generally began between 7:00 and 8:00 A.M., when the White
House operator would put through a wake-up call. By nine o'clock, after a light
breakfast and a glimpse at the morning papers and television news shows, Reagan would ride the elevator downstairs from the second floor of the 132-room
residence to the State Floor. There, a cadre of Secret Service agents would es-

cort him out across the flagstone colonnade bordering the Rose Garden, past a well-disguised emergency box containing an extra pistol, and on through the armored door of the Oval Office. His chief of staff would greet him, and they would sit down for his first meeting of the day. If it was cold, the stewards would have a fire blazing; in the summertime, they would have already plumped the pillows on the wrought-iron chaises that graced the patio outside.

By the time he arrived in the Oval Office, Reagan had usually memorized most of the lines he would deliver in his public appearances that day. His nearly photographic recall—sharpened by his training as an actor—was an enormous asset. The night before, at seven, the staff would have sent an usher to the residence with a packet of the next day's instructions—whom he'd be meeting, for how long, and what he was expected to say. On carefully typed index cards, the staff composed most of his remarks, down to the greetings and banter. They wrote out stage directions as well—where to turn and when. (One such cue card was accidentally released publicly, directing Reagan to greet a member of his own cabinet and identifying him as the gentleman sitting under Coolidge's portrait.)

Reagan carried the cards with him when he came into the office in the morning, informing the staff of any changes he thought should be made. The cards were coded by size and filed by color: green for unclassified action, yellow for unclassified information, red for classified information, white for his statements. He had one size for his breast pocket, another, always folded in two, for his outside pocket. Longer remarks were typed in large print on what he called "half sheets." The president used these cards, not only for large meetings, but also for small gatherings of regulars, such as the congressional leaders, whom he usually saw weekly. Frequently he used cards to introduce members of his own cabinet, and, in one instance, he relied on them during a ceremony honoring James Brady, the press secretary wounded beside him in the 1981 assassination attempt. He also had "phone memos," which spelled out what his end of telephone conversations should be and left space for him to jot down what the interlocutor said, so that the staff could keep track. As he moved from one event to another, his staff first gave him a briefing on every move he would make. Over the years, many advisers tried to convince Reagan to dispense with his cue cards, but, conceded [Donald] Regan, for the president "they were sort of like Linus's blue blanket."

By the standards of most other presidents, Reagan's office hours weren't long. After a 9:00 A.M. meeting with his chief of staff, Reagan attended a nine-thirty national security briefing with his national security adviser, the chief of staff, and frequently the vice president. After that the schedule varied, though usually the staff tried to give the president some private time late in the morning for reading; after lunch, some aides like David Stockman learned to avoid scheduling important business because the president was prone to nodding off.

He was often finished for the day by four o'clock, and he usually took both Wednesday and Friday afternoons off. But he was organized and orderly in his habits. He spent about an hour almost every day lifting weights in the private gym—a habit developed under doctor's orders after the 1981 assassination attempt. Where other presidents grew gray in office, Reagan managed to put an inch and a half of muscle on his chest, and he loved to have visitors feel the tone of his biceps. Inside the Oval Office, though, Reagan was formal. He felt awed enough to say "I couldn't take my jacket off in this office," and aides said he never did. They also said he never left at the end of the day without first straightening his desk—a great slab of dark wood as imposing as its donor, Queen Victoria, who had it made for Rutherford B. Hayes from the timbers of the H.M.S. *Resolute.*

At the end of the day, Reagan usually returned upstairs with paperwork and spent the evening with his wife—both in their pajamas, eating supper from trays in his study, reading, studying the next day's lines, and watching television. Nancy Reagan said her husband generally fell asleep within minutes of going to bed, usually around 11:00 P.M. Just before he did, he would alert the thirty-six-person domestic staff, one of whom would then quietly turn off any remaining lights in the family quarters.

But Reagan was more complicated than liberal caricatures would suggest. He liked to joke about his image, using such lines as: "I hear hard work's never killed anyone, but I figure, why take a chance?" Yet those around him found to their surprise that he could be diligent—even compulsive—in performing the tasks they gave him. He was always immaculately dressed, and he was so punctual that he could time a statement or an appearance down to the second. His delivery and stage presence were honed by years of training. He would follow his daily schedule meticulously, drawing a line through each completed event with an arrow pointing to the next, exactly the way screen actors mark off completed scenes on a script. The president brought self-discipline and myriad skills to the White House; they simply were not the skills usually associated with the job.

Reagan's self-confidence was an important part of his appeal. In a complex world, he trusted his instincts, frequently to surprisingly successful effect. Although he occasionally worried about appearing ill informed in front of experts, he was generally relaxed about his ability to handle the job, perhaps because, as he once explained to [Michael] Deaver, he thoroughly believed that "God has a plan for me." The American public is especially intolerant of hesitation in its presidents, and Reagan simply wasn't agonized by self-doubt, as Carter had been. Nor was he needlessly concerned with controlling minor aspects of the office. Early on, Jimmy Carter's chief of staff Jack Watson had warned that by getting involved in too much, Carter was risking blame for too much. No one needed to give that lecture to Reagan. Both his strength and his weakness rested in an ability to leave the details to others.

White House communications director David Gergen had marveled at Reagan's similarity in this respect to Dwight Eisenhower, whom Reagan admired. But the Princeton historian Fred Greenstein, in his ground-breaking reassessment of the Eisenhower era, has termed Eisenhower's a "hidden-hand presidency" and has suggested that the former military commander ran his administration more forcefully than was immediately visible. By contrast, Reagan's rule bordered—far more than anyone wanted to admit—on a no-hands presidency.

A fundamental contradiction lay at the heart of the Reagan presidency: in public Reagan pursued the ideological agenda of an activist, but in the Oval Office he was just the opposite. As long as his record of achievements seemed strong, the way he ran the White House did not seem to matter to much of the press and the voting public. But many of those who worked on the inside—close enough to observe the inner workings of the presidency under these strange conditions—were privately astounded.

They found that Reagan was not just passive, he was sometimes entirely disengaged. He did not delegate in the usual sense; he did not actively manage his staff by assigning tasks and insisting on regular progress reports. Instead, he typically gave his subordinates little or no direction. Usually, he provided the broad rhetoric and left them to infer what he wanted. When it came to the fine points of governing, he allowed his staff to take the lead. "He made almost no demands and gave almost no instructions," conceded former adviser Martin Anderson. "Essentially, he just responded to whatever was brought before his attention." He seemed to have unquestioning trust in many of the small and large decisions others made for him—and when his staff could not reach a decision, he frequently made none either unless events forced him to do so. As Ed Rollins, who worked with Reagan for five years, concluded, "The job was whatever was on his desk."

Reagan's former campaign manager, John Sears, attributed this trait to Reagan's first career, as a movie actor in an age when the studios discouraged independent thinking. As such, Sears noted, Reagan had become professionally accustomed to learning his part and "following the prescribed rules—doing what they told you to do." If something went wrong on the set, Sears said, Reagan would most likely think, Hey, I'm just the star. I'm the performer. Others were supposed to worry about the rest of the show.

This complacency was evident in cabinet and staff meetings, where Reagan was a wonderful raconteur—frequently speaking as if he were still governor of California—as well as a good listener. But he rarely made substantive points. A staff member who had also served in the Ford White House said, "Ford led the discussion; Reagan followed it." When the public began to learn of Reagan's lack of involvement in meetings, aides explained it by saying the president wanted to hide his thought process in order to avoid leaks or that he was trying to spare the feelings of those with whom he disagreed. But, as Don Regan later admitted, Reagan "sent out no strong signals. It was a rare meeting in which he made a decision or issued an order."

If the president rarely played the leading role in meetings, his aides found he was even less likely to question the paperwork they sent him. Reagan obligingly read whatever he was given—all of it—at least in the early years. One aide early on was surprised to find that the president was staying up until the early hours of the morning trying to read all the materials his staff had sent him. "He read indiscriminately," the aide marveled. "If you gave him eight hundred pages, he read every word. He used no judgment." Nancy Reagan finally stepped in and explained that her husband's workload needed to be reduced. Similarly, the staff had to monitor the amount of information they sent him to prepare for press conferences. As former communications director David Gergen recalled, "If you gave him too many pages, as good as his photographic memory is, he tries so hard to remember what he read that he sometimes gets mixed up." He was particularly susceptible to whatever arguments he had heard most recently. White House spokesman Larry Speakes used to joke that "the last thing you put in is the first thing that comes out."

Unlike other presidents, Reagan seldom requested information beyond the briefings and talking points his aides gave him. He enjoyed occasional luncheons with outside experts when they were brought in, but he rarely initiated invitations. He watched what Regan later called "a lot" of television and read a number of newspapers, although he claimed, possibly for effect, that he turned first to the comics. He was quite impressionable, particularly when it came to such arch-conservative publications as *Human Events*. After Reagan had seen it, Regan later said, "the goddamnedest things would come out of him—we had to watch what he read." He took great interest in the clippings and letters people sent him in the mail. One senior aide estimated that he opened more than half of his fifteen-minute national security briefings by reading selections from them.

Despite his position and power, Reagan often appeared to be living in contented isolation. Nancy Reagan was an inveterate telephone talker, and, in addition to acting as her husband's eyes and ears, she would occasionally put him on the line. But the president rarely initiated calls unless his staff asked him to. Nor did he keep in touch in other ways with those who were reputedly his oldest friends and advisers, on or off the White House staff. Holmes Tuttle, one of the few surviving members of Reagan's original California kitchen cabinet—the informal group of millionaires who financed his early campaigns—was usually advertised as one of the president's best friends. "We've had many years of togetherness," Tuttle affirmed. Yet when pressed he admitted, "No, he doesn't ask for advice. And as for picking up the phone and calling me, no." Similarly, Reagan's closest political friend in Washington, former Nevada senator Paul Laxalt, conceded that despite having known Reagan since 1964, "campaigning together, socializing together, camping together. . . . Do we talk about personal matters? Not at all."

Even on purely physical terms, Reagan's operating style was passive. Although he had 59 rooms in which to roam in the West Wing alone, he seldom ventured far beyond the Oval Office. In part, it was a necessary fact of life after the 1981 assassination attempt. Much as Eisenhower's schedule was restricted after his heart attack in 1955, the Secret Service became a protective wall around the president after the 1981 shooting, inevitably limiting his movement. He attended cabinet and congressional meetings and delivered speeches in the rooms set aside for those activities, but one senior White House official doubted whether, beyond these ceremonial rooms, the press room, and the barber shop, he knew his way around the West Wing complex. He even seemed unsure about the location of most of his aides' offices, and he only visited his chief of staff, who worked a few yards down the hall, two or three times a year on special occasions, like birthdays.

Likewise, White House officials rarely wandered into the Oval Office except on official, prescribed business. In the second term only six officials—the chief of staff, the vice president, the national security adviser, the military aide, the White House doctor, and the president's personal aide—had walk-in privileges, meaning they could see the president without an appointment. And even those who could drop in seldom did so, in part because the president's workday wasn't all that long, and his time was filled by an unusually large number of ceremonial functions. A telling example of Reagan's isolation came out of the Iran-contra hearings, when the White House counsel's office tallied all the time the president had spent alone with his national security adviser, John Poindexter. The total—over eleven months and twenty-three days—came to eighty-one minutes.

The obvious danger was that Reagan could easily lose touch with political reality. It was always a peril of the office. As Woodrow Wilson noted, "Things get very lonely in Washington sometimes. The real voice of the great people of America sometimes sounds faint and distant in that strange city." But for Reagan, the hazard was exacerbated by his personality, which habitually screened out discord in order to paint the rosiest possible picture. One of his own children confided that "he makes things up and believes them." As a former senior White House official said, "He has this great ability to build these little worlds and then live in them."

In the first term, the single greatest safeguard against the president's losing touch was a staff structure as unusual as the president it served, an odd system that came to be known as the troika. It consisted of an uneasy triumvirate of top White House advisers—three extremely different men, with extremely different views and backgrounds—who policed not only each other but, in the process, the president too.

Chief of staff James A. Baker, a Princeton graduate, was the scion of one of Houston's most distinguished families, a former "Tory" Democrat who converted to the GOP in time to become under secretary of commerce for Gerald Ford and campaign manager for George Bush in 1980. A dealmaker in pin stripes, he was as smooth as any political operator in Washington. Unlike

Donald Regan, who would take his place,* he enjoyed the hurly-burly of politics—having made an unsuccessful run for attorney general of Texas in 1978—and counting a handful of congressmen and senators among his close friends. He never gained the trust of the president's more conservative backers for being too "pragmatic," but the alliances he forged so skillfully in Congress were the backbone of the first term's many legislative successes.

Deputy chief of staff Michael Deaver, the son of a gas station owner at the edge of the Mojave Desert, had come to know the Reagans through his administrative work for the Republican party in California. Uninterested in the substance of policy, he'd proved a master at the imperative of the eighties: producing the presidency for television. He had a sixth sense about how to play to Reagan's strengths and cover his weaknesses. And, more than any other White House hand, he understood how to deal personally with the president and his wife; legend had it that he'd once run through a glass door in his eagerness to retrieve a purse that Mrs. Reagan had left behind. Having spent all but four months of the previous nineteen years serving them, he was one of the few people who knew how to tell both of the Reagans when they were wrong and get away with it—a skill that would be lost to the White House with his departure.

Edwin Meese, the presidential counselor who would soon be attorney general, had attended Yale as an undergraduate and law school at the University of California at Berkeley; he went on to serve as deputy district attorney in California's Alameda County. Active in crushing the student demonstrations at Berkeley in the sixties, he had a fascination with law enforcement all his life. In Sacramento, he'd been Reagan's chief of staff, and in the White House he ran the Office of Policy Development. Though the office was ridiculed for its bureaucratic inefficiency and arch-conservative agenda, it nonetheless played an important role by translating Reagan's views into programs—a function largely abandoned with Meese's departure. If Baker was the political expert and Deaver the loyal retainer, Meese was the conservative conscience.

Many complained that the troika system was divisive and inefficient, since none of the three men could make a decision on his own. But in their jealousy, each helped ensure that before the president put his imprimatur on a decision, either there was a rare consensus or he heard all their views. The system was built on mutual distrust and, although no one said so, on the premise of an impressionable president vulnerable to whatever argument he heard last.

Each member of the troika thus spent much energy trying to neutralize the others. For instance, when in 1982 Meese got Reagan to back the Treasury and Justice departments' move to reestablish tax-exempt status for racially segregated schools, Deaver, recognizing the racist image it could give the administra-

---

* During Reagan's first term, Baker was chief of staff and Regan was secretary of the treasury. They switched jobs in 1985. Baker was appointed secretary of state by George Bush in 1989.

tion, went into high gear. He successfully shepherded the few blacks serving in the White House into the Oval Office to change Reagan's mind.

At times the troika worked as a protective shield around the president, preventing interlopers from getting too close to him. Baker and Deaver, for instance, often became temporary allies in the fight against CIA director William J. Casey and other "hard-liners" on foreign affairs. After each of Casey's visits to the Oval Office, Deaver would saunter in casually and ask the president, "Did Bill have anything interesting to say?" Reagan would naturally tell his loyal retainer, and if the news was alarming, Deaver would notify Baker. Together they would then marshal some expert to make a counterargument—a congressman, family member, or longtime backer—to try to turn Reagan around. One issue given special surveillance was Casey's promotion of the secret war in Nicaragua, which Deaver believed "played to Reagan's dark side" in a dangerous way.

Baker had an equally great distrust of those serving as national security adviser—a post with a long history of back door communications aimed at getting the president's support. Baker attended the 9:30 A.M. national security meetings with the president and [Robert (Bud)] McFarlane. Even though Baker and McFarlane got along well, if the president nodded appreciatively during the briefing, as was his habit, Baker, according to a senior NSC aide, made a point of tracking McFarlane down later and saying, "If you think that was a go-ahead, think again."

Baker's deputy, Richard Darman, a skilled bureaucrat who had served in four federal agencies since 1971, set up what he proudly called "an authoritarian system" to monitor the NSC and others who sent paperwork to the president. The president's Out box became Darman's In box. If the president was out of the Oval Office and received, for instance, emergency correspondence elsewhere, Darman demanded that he get a facsimile immediately. If something was sent to the Executive Residence after hours, he insisted that the White House ushers deliver a copy to him by seven-thirty the next morning. The system was rigorous, but it wasn't foolproof.

One breakdown of the system resulted in the Strategic Defense Initiative. Two of the president's old political backers, Joseph Coors and Karl Bendetsen, managed to slip the nuclear scientist Edward Teller in to see Reagan without explaining to Baker and Deaver what the meeting was about. By the time Teller was done, the president had become a fervent convert to the untested and perhaps unfeasible notion that a shield could be built against nuclear weapons. It was a utopian concept that privately struck many of Reagan's arms control advisers as crazy; some privately rolled their eyes and called it "the dream." But once Teller had reached Reagan, the dream was policy.

When it worked, however, the troika forced Reagan to be exposed to diversity. Even if he raised no questions about an issue, his battling aides would. Moreover, they frequently forced him to play an active part in policy disputes. Ordinarily, a president would naturally serve this function, but as White House aide Johnathan Miller concluded, "Reagan is like a great race horse that performs well when you have a jockey that knows how to use a whip. If you don't use the whip, he'll just loaf." The troika wielded the crop that kept both the government and the president running.

Of course, Reagan wasn't completely pliant, as his first budget director, David Stockman, learned when he asked him to raise taxes. But those who knew him best, like John Sears, discovered that "you can't argue with him on the general, but on the precise you can see a tremendous amount of malleability." This characteristic inspired a maneuver that some staff members called "the Reagan argument." Its purpose was to persuade the president to change stubbornly held views by convincing him, in the face of contradictory evidence, that a switch in policy was only a change in tactics, not principles.

In order to make "Reagan arguments," former labor secretary William Brock recalled, senior advisers kept "Reagan files"—clips documenting his earlier stands, which could be marshaled to support whatever new position was being considered. Thus, levying $14 billion in new corporate taxes, which Reagan opposed on strong philosophical grounds, could be sold to him as "closing loopholes" in the Treasury's initial 1984 tax reform plan. Government surcharges on the price of gas could be sold, not as tax increases at all, but as "user fees" for highway use. The conservative social agenda—abortion, school prayer, and the other high-risk moral issues—was not being neglected, it was being postponed, so that his top priority, the economic program, would not be compromised.

By 1984, the more able advisers were masters of the technique. They liked to think they were saving Reagan from his own excesses—and frequently they were. But in the process, they ran the risk of manipulating the facts to fit their argument, politicizing intelligence, stretching rhetoric, and deluding a president not given to performing rigorous analysis of issues.

The troika also mastered techniques for managing the president in public. From Reagan's earliest days in politics, his advisers always feared the unpredictable results of his "going live." Although his aides never told him, they had engineered his most famous 1980 primary triumph—his insistence on opening a New Hampshire debate to all the candidates, not just front-runner George Bush—partly as a damage control maneuver. It was clear by the time of the debate that Reagan would win a narrow victory if nothing went wrong. But with Reagan, as his campaign aide James Lake explained seven years later, "if he went one-on-one against George Bush, there was a fifty-fifty chance he'd screw up." So they invited the other candidates, knowing that "if there were six guys, the risk would be spread out to one in six."

In the White House, Reagan's aides continued to limit his live exposure. They dispensed with an earlier idea of having him hold frequent "mini–press conferences," invented a rule trying to ban press questions at the daily "photo opportunities," and vetoed various proposed give-and-takes with youth groups because, as White House spokesman Larry Speakes explained, "he was too loose." Of course, spontaneous exchanges were sometimes unavoidable, but when the president's comments strayed too far afield, the White House press office sometimes managed to clean up his oral meanderings before a text was released for public consumption, thus altering the historical record along the way. In an Oval Office interview with the *Wall Street Journal*, in February 1985, for instance, Reagan mentioned that he had been talking "just this morning" about the biblical Armageddon. Some fundamentalists believe that it refers to an impending nuclear war, a provocative (and to some unnerving) notion for the president to entertain. "I don't know whether you know," he said with animation, "but a great many theologians over a number of years . . . have been struck with the fact that in recent years, as in no other time in history, have most of these prophecies been coming together." When the official transcript of the interview was released, the comments about Armageddon were gone. The White House later suggested that they had been "accidentally" omitted.

Similarly, his aides went to great lengths to conceal potentially embarrassing quirks. They were secretive about such matters as the president's and his daughter Maureen's apparently sincere belief that a ghost haunted the Lincoln Bedroom (Maureen claimed it had a "red aura"), the president's assertion that he had seen a flying saucer, and his acquiescence to Mrs. Reagan's reliance on astrology to determine his schedule.

Press access to the president was more tightly controlled than ever before, but complaints from journalists stirred little sympathy, perhaps because the problem was as old as the office. The question of how open the presidency should be to the public in this most democratic of governments was contentious right from the start. When George Washington announced that he would open his doors to the general public only twice a week, one senator fumed, "For him to be seen only in public on stated times, like an eastern Lama, would be . . . offensive." Despite such grousing, the presidency has grown progressively more closed to public inspection ever since. Herbert Hoover was the last president to set aside time once a week to receive any citizen who wanted to shake his hand. After that, the public had to rely on the press to serve as its eyes and ears—and there, too, access was progressively narrowed. Franklin Roosevelt used to give two press conferences a week, Eisenhower averaged more than two a month. Kennedy turned his frequent new conferences into witty jousting matches and took some members of the press into his closest confidence, getting protection in the bargain. But Reagan was the most remote. He didn't socialize with the working press, and he only gave five news conferences during all of 1984. Although a rotating pool of reporters traveled with him on *Air Force One* during the campaign, he never once came back to talk with them, though occasionally he waved from the Secret Service compartment. David Hoffman of the *Washington Post* used to joke that "covering Reagan means having to say you never saw him."

Yet the staff devoted huge amounts of energy to controlling and shaping the little the public did see of Reagan. This, too, was only new in the degree to which it took place. Many presidents before Reagan had harnessed public relations techniques to promote the office: Theodore Roosevelt may have created the modern "photo opportunity" by staging a press trip out West simply to dramatize his interest in conservation. The Nixon White House, more than any before it, perfected the art of controlling the press in the television age both by limiting access to the president and by planning no event without imagining the headline, photo, and story that would follow it. This system tried to ensure that every story was advantageous to the White House, no matter what the facts. This practice simply reached its apogee in Reagan's time, when in contrast to the Nixon era, the system served a consummate performer.

The result, as political essayist Leon Wieseltier described it, was that for the Reagan administration, "the truth was a problem to be solved." The solution was an art form known as "spin control," which referred to the "spin" the White House public relations experts put on news to make sure it bounced the desired way. Enterprising reporters tried to detect the spin and dig out the real story. Occasionally they were successful, but not without risking revenge. Press secretary Larry Speakes gave what he called "death sentences" to those reporters he deemed too critical or otherwise uncooperative. He would threaten to "put them out of business" by making sure their phone calls went unreturned and questions unanswered, putting them routinely at a competitive disadvantage. Speakes explained proudly, "The idea was to be subtle. They thought they were being screwed, but they were never quite sure." He froze out some reporters for years, but it is debatable how much they missed. Speakes later confessed to having fabricated several presidential quotes; even before his confession stirred a controversy, he admitted that he misled the public about how disengaged the president was. "As a rule," he said, "I did not think it was lying to suggest that the president might be aware of something when he wasn't."

These strategies shaped not only the written record but the photographic one as well. The official White House staff photographers shot an estimated eight to ten thousand pictures of Reagan every month, the best of which were released to the press. Mrs. Reagan usually determined which images the public saw, particularly when they included her. She personally went through the thousands of pictures, signing "O.K. per N.R." when they could be released and tearing off the corner of each of those she deemed unflattering.

Despite these many protective layers, someone close to the Oval Office would occasionally break ranks, providing a glimpse of a place that sounded quite strange. Terry Arthur, a staff photographer who spent countless hours quietly observing and documenting the president alone and with others, said he took the job partly "to find out who was running the show." After two solid years of traveling with the president, following him through meetings and on his weekend retreats, he concluded, "I never found out." Reagan, he said, "was like a Buddha. People would say, 'He wants this' or 'He wants that,' but you'd never really see him say so. He'd be shown the decisions others had made, and would say, 'Uh-huh.'"

Alexander Haig, Reagan's first secretary of state, was equally puzzled by the president's operating style. In his White House memoirs, he wrote: "To me, the

White House was as mysterious as a ghost ship; you heard the creak of the rigging and the groan of the timbers, and sometimes even glimpsed the crew on deck. But which of the crew had the helm? . . . It was impossible to tell."

Epilogue

In general, the lesson of this selection is clear. As we analyze the presidency we should not limit ourselves solely to the study of the officeholder. We must also examine the actions of the president's aides and subordinates for a true picture of the administration, because the personal style of each president is reflected in his appointments and in the appointees' working style. In Reagan's first term of office, the "troika" system described here led to the question of "Who's in charge?" That is, which aide had the most effect on which decisions? In Reagan's second term, former Treasury Secretary Donald Regan became the sole chief of staff. The White House came to be run more like the Wall Street firm Regan once headed, with Regan himself as an aggressive chief executive officer. His extremely aggressive management style caused him to run afoul of Nancy Reagan and eventually cost him his job.

Reagan regained his personal popularity by the end of his administration, but in contrast to his disengaged management style, George Bush has tried to adopt a much more attentive, and aggressive, decision-making posture. As we will see in the next selection, however, that style inspires another set of criticisms.

3.5

No president can serve in office without being confronted by ongoing analysis of his style by journalists, scholars, and other politicians. This effort by political scientist William Schneider to analyze and classify the presidency of George Bush at the end of his first year in office is a case in point. Despite incomplete evidence on the Bush administration at the time the article was published (January 1990), this selection represents the prevailing opinion of Bush after his first year.

Following the visionary style of Ronald Reagan, George Bush established what was seen as a more reactive, bureaucratically oriented style of leadership. As a Washington insider—having served as director of the CIA, ambassador to the United Nations, and vice president under Reagan—Bush was seen as being far more familiar than Reagan with the decision-making apparatus of Washington. Thus, he was criticized for being more concerned with the process of making decisions than with the substance of the decisions themselves. This criticism was not devastating, however, since the relative inactivity of the administration (when compared to the frenetic pace of Reagan's first term of office) was accompanied by popularity ratings that hovered between 60 and 70 percent in the public opinion polls.

The advantage of the Bush style as described here is that the government tends to "stay the course," with no major policy mistakes. Bush is not troubled by the complaint that he lacks "the vision thing," as he called it, in seeking to impose his own style on the government. On the other hand, as Schneider hints in this selection, what will be the result when a process-oriented, reactive leader is confronted by large changes in foreign policy or the economy? How would you assess Bush's prospects for success, given this evaluation by Schneider? Why do you think that a "no-hands" president like Reagan is followed by a more management-oriented president like Bush? Finally, how does Bush's style compare with the styles of the other presidents discussed in this chapter?

The In-Box President

William Schneider

William Schneider, "The In-Box President," *The Atlantic*, Jan. 1990, pp. 34–43. Reprinted by permission of the author.

JAMES A. BAKER   Bush's secretary of state.

MIKHAIL GORBACHEV   President of the Soviet Union.

GEORGE BUSH   President of the United States, 1989– .

RONALD REAGAN   President of the United States, 1981–1989.

▶ George Bush was elected President in 1988 because most American voters were satisfied with the status quo. What we got is a status-quo President.

So far, the status quo has been Bush's principal source of strength. The economy has stayed pretty much on track. There has been no major foreign-policy calamity. True, 1989 was a great year for Washington scandals, but they involved either members of Congress or Reagan Administration officials.

Bush has averaged a 63 percent job-approval rating in Gallup polls. Ronald Reagan's job-approval rating for his first year in office, when he struck out in bold new directions, averaged only 57 percent. That's what you get for taking risks.

After eight years of Reagan, Americans may have had enough vision for a while. Bush has done what the voters elected him to do. He has managed the status quo. We are, by and large, a nation of happy campers, to borrow a phrase from Vice President Dan Quayle.

The down side is that President Bush is hostage to the status quo. Suppose the economy goes into a tailspin, as it did under Reagan in 1982. Suppose Bush makes a terrible blunder, as Reagan did in the Iran-contra affair. Would the voters stay the course? And just what is the course, anyway?

Reagan was not a status-quo President. "Ronald Reagan was a successful candidate and an effective President above all else because he stood for a set of ideas," one observer has maintained. "He stated them in 1980, and it turned out that he meant them; and he wrote most of them not only into public law but into the national consciousness." That assessment was offered by Senator Edward M. Kennedy last March, at Yale University.

Reagan could be remarkably open and bold, as he was in his response to Mikhail Gorbachev. He could also be terribly naive, and his grand schemes were often grand illusions—painless deficits, Star Wars, freedom fighters, his offer at the Reykjavik summit to abolish nuclear weapons. But no one ever said Reagan was fearful of change.

That is exactly what people say about George Bush. "I think this perhaps is a time for caution," President Bush said last spring, when asked to comment on the student protests in Beijing. In China, Eastern Europe, and the Soviet Union millions of people were putting their lives on the line for democracy. But all the U.S. Secretary of State had to say was, "I don't think it would be in the best interests of the United States for us to see significant instability in the People's Republic of China, just like I don't think it's in the best interests of the United States for us to see significant instability in [the USSR]." In other words, democracy is fine so long as it doesn't disturb the status quo.

Ronald Reagan was a creature of the 1960s. He was elected governor of California in 1966 in a wave of popular revulsion over racial violence (the rioting in Watts) and student protests (the Free Speech Movement at Berkeley). Reagan often saw issues as "us" versus "them." Bush, on the other hand, set out to smooth over the bitter divisions of American politics. In his inaugural address Bush lamented the fact that "a certain divisiveness" had emerged in our political life, "in which not each other's ideas are challenged but each other's motives."

Bush called on the nation to end the 1960s. "This is the age of the offered hand," the President said. "I yearn for a greater tolerance, an easygoingness about each other's attitudes and way of life." This from the man who had just run a harsh, negative campaign attacking his opponent's "values" on issues like the pledge of allegiance and furloughs for criminals.

Bush changed his image three times in one year. During the 1988 primaries he was Bush the Wimp, the man the Democrats loved to make fun of. ("Poor George, he can't help it," the Democrats' keynote convention speaker said. "He was born with a silver foot in his mouth.") He became Bush the Tough Guy in the general election, when he followed a script written by Lee Atwater, his campaign manager. Then he got elected and changed to a script by James Baker, the ultimate Washington insider. Virtually overnight he was transformed into Bush the Old Pro—cautious, reassuring, and thoroughly pragmatic.

What is missing in Bush is the hard core of conviction that one could always sense in Reagan. "I believe in unions, I believe in nonunions," Bush once said while touring a furniture factory in North Carolina. When he refused to compromise with Congress on the budget, when he defied the air-traffic controllers' strike, and when he stood by his nomination of Judge Robert Bork to the Supreme Court, Reagan made it clear that important issues of principle were at stake.*

The Bork debate was positively elevated compared with the fight over Bush's nomination of John Tower to be Secretary of Defense. Bork raised fundamental constitutional issues like original intent and the limits of judicial activism. The only principle at stake in Bush's last-ditch defense of Tower was executive privilege. Stubbornness without conviction gets a President into trouble. Jimmy Carter was at his best—the Camp David negotiations, the Panama Canal treaties—when his stubbornness was rooted in principle. Reagan was at his worst—the Iran-contra affair, the Bitburg incident—when his principles were unclear.†

Bush also seems to lack Reagan's personal security. Reagan said a lot of nutty things, but he was at ease with himself, and that was reassuring. Over time the public became convinced that he was not going to start a nuclear war or throw old people out into the snow. (Poor people were another matter.) Bush, on the

---

* See Selection 8.3, "Battle for Justice."
† In 1985 Reagan was criticized for visiting a cemetery in Bitburg, West Germany, that contained the graves of several members of Hitler's SS.

other hand, usually says sensible things, and he goes out of his way to sound reassuring ("a kinder, gentler nation"). But he is so easily rattled that he makes people nervous. Last September, when reporters confronted him with evidence that federal agents had set up a drug deal in a park across the street from the White House to provide a prop for his speech on drug policy, Bush responded angrily, "I don't understand. I mean, has somebody got some advocates here for this drug guy?"

Bush seems paralyzed by two fears—the fear of being called a wimp and the fear of creating controversy. Our greatest tragedies as President, Lyndon Johnson and Richard Nixon, were haunted by deep personal insecurities. They kept polls in their pockets and made lists of enemies. Bush seems nowhere near that level of paranoia or vindictiveness. But he has been described as "ill at ease . . . in his own skin," and that is not a good sign.

Reagan's style was to take a firm stand, rally public support, and challenge Congress to give him what he wanted. Bush's style is to make a deal. He negotiates quietly, outside the glare of publicity and with as little rancor as possible. He then announces a compromise, shifts his position to accommodate the outcome, and invites the country to applaud the spirit of bipartisanship and cooperation.

Almost every year Reagan would go to the wall on the federal budget and military aid to the contras. Bush made deals with Congress early last year on both issues. The deals had serious flaws, but at least the two sides agreed to agree. The country was spared the usual gunfight at the O.K. Corral over budget policy and contra aid. In May, Bush averted a NATO crisis by hammering out a compromise among the allies. In October he made a deal with the Democrats to raise the minimum wage but allow for a temporary training wage for teenagers.

The Bush Administration has made progress on issues that seemed hopelessly stalemated during the Reagan years—clean air, the minimum wage, the contras. This progress has deflected criticism by the Democrats. They can hardly complain about a President who wants to make a deal with them.

Bush sees the President as the great facilitator, not the great communicator. His is an unheroic politics in which everything, or almost everything, is negotiable. Reagan believed that raising the minimum wage was wrong, that Americans have an absolute right to bear arms, and that the Sandinista government is an intolerable threat to U.S. security. Bush has been willing to compromise on all these points.

There are two issues on which Bush has drawn the line, however—abortion and taxes. Like Reagan, Bush will not compromise his "principles" on these issues.* But Reagan was an ideologue; he believed what he believed, reality be damned. Bush is a pragmatist, so the conflict with reality is more of a problem

---

* In 1990 Bush did compromise on raising certain taxes.

for him. In his only prime-time television speech to the nation, Bush called for a national war on drugs, but he refused to ask Americans to make any sacrifices to pay for it. In October he vetoed a bill that would have extended Medicaid funding to poor women who are the victims of rape or incest. Reagan's stubborn fealty to principles conveyed an image of strength. Bush's willingness to compromise on everything except abortion and taxes conveys an image of calculation, religious conservatives and affluent suburbanites being the core constituencies in the GOP coalition.

The Bush Administration does bring a high standard of professionalism to government. That's not such a bad thing, considering that professionalism was often conspicuously missing during the Reagan years. Bush's appointments have fallen into two categories. His political choices, all of them controversial, have come from the right wing of the party—Quayle for Vice President, Atwater for Republican Party chairman, and John Sununu for White House chief of staff. In the realm of policy-making, however, Bush has been more cautious. He kept on a number of Reagan appointees, all of whom were regarded as moderates—Nicholas Brady in the Treasury Department, Richard Thornburgh in the Justice Department, William Webster at the CIA, and Lauro Cavazos in the Department of Education. Bush's Secretary of State, James Baker, was reviled by conservatives when he served as Reagan's chief of staff.

These people are not agenda-setters. They are problem-solvers. Like Bush himself, they offer strong qualifications and considerable experience. Moreover, they have records of accomplishment independent of their relationship with George Bush. With Bush the rule seems to be no ideological hard-liners, no Evil Empire–baiters, no economic cranks, "no Bozos." And no bold new ideas.

What all this professionalism adds up to is not exactly leadership. It is more like management. Bush's policies have been reactive. The United States responds, cautiously and reluctantly, to others' proposals. It is an in-box approach to governing. You respond to problems as they reach your desk, and you do whatever is necessary to get them off your desk.

There is a peculiar rhythm to the Bush presidency. A crisis suddenly emerges and dominates the public agenda—an oil spill in Alaska, a new Soviet proposal on arms control, a hostage quandary in the Middle East, a stolen election in Panama, a NATO conflict, a savings-and-loan problem, mass protests in China, an emergency in Poland. The press attacks the administration for weakness and indecision. Commentators accuse Bush of having no policy to deal with the situation. The administration responds that it is being prudent. Critics say it is being timid.

Suddenly the President steps in and makes a dramatic gesture. There is a burst of activity, heads get banged together, and a compromise results. The crisis ends, even though the problem may be unresolved. (Noriega is still in power,* American hostages are still in Lebanon, and the Alaskan coastline is still befouled.) The press pronounces Bush's intervention a success. The President's popularity goes up. And public attention shifts to something else. Bush has kept up with his in-box.

Bush is a master of the politics of good intentions. In his inaugural address he declared, "We have work to do" and ticked off the nation's problems—homelessness, child poverty, crime, drug addiction. He called for "a new activism, hands-on and involved, that gets the job done." But what did he intend to do? Whatever it was, it would not involve spending a lot of money. "The old solution . . . was to think that public money alone could end these problems," the new President told the nation. "But we have learned that this is not so. . . . We have more will than wallet, but will is what we need." It is hard to quarrel with Bush's assertion that money alone cannot solve our problems. But how can they be solved *without* money? Governor Mario Cuomo tried to call Bush's bluff when he wrote in September, "President Bush has done all he can with speeches. Now he has to produce resources that will deliver on his promises or concede to the nation that he is still an unconverted conservative [trying] to earn himself some cheap grace by reciting a little Democratic poetry."

U.S. diplomatic initiatives have been as limited as U.S. domestic initiatives, and for the same reason: there isn't any money. At the economic summit in Paris last July the United States had to persuade other countries to help foot the bill on critical issues like international debt relief and economic aid for Poland and Hungary.

Mindful of appearing too defensive and reactive, George Bush began his presidency by ordering a comprehensive policy review to figure out how the United States should meet Gorbachev's bold challenge. After months of effort the review concluded that the United States could no longer remain in the position of defending the status quo. The report recommended that the United States broaden the agenda instead, and offer the world something new—"the status quo plus."

Last spring, when Gorbachev said he would stop sending weapons to Nicaragua, the White House responded with annoyance. Its press spokesman, Marlin Fitzwater, dismissed the gesture as a "public-relations gambit" perpetrated by a "drugstore cowboy." When the Soviets announced that they would withdraw 500 nuclear missiles from Europe, Secretary of Defense Dick Cheney complained that they have "so many ratholes over there in Eastern Europe that 500 is a pittance." That kind of grudging, small-minded response reinforces our status-quo image. The world changes, and the United States stands still.

When President Bush announced that he would have an "interim, informal" meeting in December with Gorbachev, he explained, "I just didn't want to, in this time of dynamic change, miss something." The world is waiting for a Bush

---

* The American invasion of Panama in December 1989 did force Noriega out of power.

Doctrine that defines the American response to the Communist Reformation. The Bush Doctrine so far might be characterized as "this might not really be happening." When East Germany opened the Berlin Wall on November 9, the country longed to hear a Kennedy or a Reagan say, "We are all Berliners now." What it heard Bush say was, "We are not trying to give anybody a hard time." When Bush announced the "non-summit summit," he said, "Neither President Gorbachev nor I anticipate that substantial decisions or agreements will emerge from this December meeting." If that is the case (and at this writing it is still unclear), 1989 could go down in history as The Year of Missed Opportunities.

In September the Senate majority leader, George Mitchell, accused the administration of being so ambivalent about changes in the communist world that it often sounded "nostalgic about the Cold War." Secretary Baker's response stirred up a controversy in Washington. He said, "When the President of the United States is rocking along with a seventy-percent approval rating on his handling of foreign policy, if I were the leader of the opposition, I might have something similar to say." The Secretary appeared to acknowledge what the poll results about foreign intervention confirm—that the Bush Administration's cautious, measured approach to foreign policy is essentially politics-driven. Reaganism without risks.

Even embarrassments can be rendered harmless, as long as the President is careful to stay within the boundaries of favorable public opinion. The United States encouraged a coup in Panama, we supported a coup in Panama, and we may have even helped plan a coup in Panama. But we did not take the risk of intervening. The polls revealed that most Americans did not support the use of U.S. troops to remove General Noriega. Nothing was ventured and nothing was gained. The administration's cautious, risk-averse approach kept us out of trouble. On the other hand, the Panama issue keeps turning up in the President's in-box.

The administration is confident, however, that its strategy of prudence will pay off. A State Department official used a revealing, and distressingly shallow, metaphor to explain the Bush foreign policy to *The New York Times*. He said, "The Soviet game is chess, where you think out your strategy ten moves ahead, and Gorbachev is a chess player. Our game is baseball. You play it one inning at a time, but it's the final score that counts. Gorbachev may hit an occasional grand slam. We are going to try to win on singles."

However timid or unimaginative their policies may be, the Republicans can usually rely on one thing to save them. That is the greater incompetence of the Democrats. The Democrats have repeatedly been spooked, for instance, by President Bush's "good cop–bad cop" routine—his habit of making gestures of bipartisanship and compromise while his party operatives play dirty.

The GOP strategy is to force roll-call votes in Congress on controversial issues like flag-burning and censorship. The expectation is that in the 1990 mid-term elections Democrats who take unpopular positions on these issues can be exposed as liberals whose values are outside the mainstream of American politics. The Republicans want to do to all Democrats what Bush did to Michael Dukakis in 1988.

In 1989, however, it was the Republicans who looked vulnerable on social issues like gun control and abortion. Nevertheless, it was the Democrats who seemed more nervous about "values." They didn't want Lee Atwater to use their records as he had used Dukakis's record, for target practice.

There is one lesson the Democrats have been unable to learn from the Republicans—how to behave like an opposition party. After thirty-five years in the minority, the Republicans in Congress have finally mastered the art of keeping Democrats on the defensive. Democrats, however, persist in believing that they run the country. After all, they have a lock on Congress. As a result, Democratic congressional leaders seem to feel more comfortable acting as partners with a Republican President than they do acting as the loyal opposition.

What's more, they don't seem to understand that their basic problem in the Bush era isn't values. It's taxes. Ever since the Great Inflation and the tax revolt of the late 1970s, Republicans have used anti-tax sentiment to control the political agenda.

From the 1930s through the 1960s the spending issue enabled Democrats to maintain their political hegemony. Now the Republicans are doing precisely the same thing with taxes. The national consensus has changed, and Democrats are finding tax cuts as irresistible as Republicans used to find spending bills. The anti-tax consensus helped produce the single biggest victory of the Bush presidency to date—the September 28 vote in the House of Representatives to lower the tax rate on capital gains for two years. Democratic leaders condemned what they called "a tax giveaway to the wealthy." But they found little popular resistance to a measure that raised no one's taxes and held out the possibility of some gains for everyone. So House Democratic leaders tried to outbid the Bush Administration by offering a better deal. They tried the same thing in 1981, when Ronald Reagan proposed his original tax cut. It didn't work in 1981, and it didn't work in 1989, at least not in the House. In the Senate, Democratic leaders stalled the tax cut by preventing the issue from coming to a vote.

The catastrophic-illness plan is a good example of the shift in the public agenda from spending to taxes. The program to insure Medicare recipients against catastrophic illnesses was the only major new domestic program of the 1980s. It passed the House of Representatives by a vote of 328 to 72 in 1988. The program was held up as a model of how to finance social initiatives in the deficit era. It would be financed in part by "supplemental premiums" paid by more-affluent Medicare recipients. Everyone in government, including Ronald Reagan and George Bush, seemed to view these premiums as user fees. Those who paid the premiums would get the insurance coverage.

But the program was strangled at birth. Elderly Americans discovered that what they were really paying was a tax. Moreover, they were being taxed to pay for a benefit that most of them felt they did not need. The result was a wave of angry protest calling for repeal of the plan. Which is exactly what the House voted to do, 360 to 66, last year. Something important had changed in American politics. The elderly had always been a prime spending constituency. Suddenly a vocal minority of them started militating against taxes. Virtually no one who stood to benefit from the new program spoke out in defense of it. This was very bad news for the Democrats. How could they talk about "a new agenda for social progress" if no one was willing to pay for it?

In the long run Bush's biggest problem will come not from the opposition party—the Democrats don't know what they are—but from the challenge of holding two different constituencies together. His tough, hard-hitting, right-wing election campaign, including the selection of Quayle as his running mate, enabled him to keep Reagan's conservative coalition together. This was the Bush who said, "Read my lips: No new taxes." Reaganites were reassured. They looked at Bush and said, "He's one of us."

Bush used his transition to reassure the Washington establishment that he was really a cautious, moderate pragmatist. This was the Bush who announced to the Republican National Convention in 1988, "I don't hate government." "Good old George," the Washington power elite said to one another. "He's one of us."

Well, which is he? The establishment is bothered by the President's occasional political vulgarity—his tolerance of Atwater, the flag-burning amendment—and by his failure to engage in serious negotiations on the deficit. But it approves of the administration's high standards of professionalism. Conservatives are uneasy about the sincerity of Bush's commitment to Star Wars, the contras, and gun control. But they are encouraged by his refusal to compromise on taxes and abortion.

The balance is holding right now because things are going well for Bush. But will either the conservatives or the establishment be there when Bush gets into trouble? Conservatives have never really trusted Bush. As Anthony Dolan, the chief speechwriter for President Reagan, wrote recently in *The New York Times*, "If [Democrats] can back the President off on his pledges to conservatives on the emotional issues—taxes, contras, defense or a Supreme Court nominee—they rob him of the intensity and the depth of personal support that would make permanent his hold on conservative voters."

Nor does the establishment's good will provide much of a political base. The power elite will stick with a President only as long as his policies are successful. If things suddenly start to fall apart, the power elite will be the first to abandon him, as it did Gerald Ford and Jimmy Carter. Like Ford and Carter—other Presidents who had trouble with "the vision thing"—Bush will be judged entirely on his effectiveness.

Bush's popularity reflects a simple fact: he appears to be the right President for the times. The country is not in the mood for big ambitions right now, and

Bush isn't offering any. Bush has only one thing to worry about—the fact that times change.

Epilogue

Fascinating as this analysis of Bush is, perhaps it is too soon to classify his presidential style. For month after month, Bush watched the greatest changes in the governments of Eastern Europe and the Soviet Union in fifty years and used the cautious style portrayed here. Yet when Manuel Noriega became too much of a problem, Bush ordered a strike into Panama and removed him from power. Then, in a two-week period in the summer of 1990, Bush displayed both his cautious "image-oriented" style and his swashbuckling, crisis-management style. When Supreme Court Justice William Brennan retired, Bush selected a brilliant but almost unknown jurist, David Souter, to replace him in the hopes of avoiding a divisive confirmation fight in the Senate. Then, after Iraq's Saddam Hussein overran Kuwait, Bush engineered a comprehensive international diplomatic and legal response, and sent an American military force of more than 400,000 to the Persian Gulf. At the same time, however, the administration appeared merely to watch as the American economy threatened to slip into a recession. And, in negotiating with Congress in September and October 1990 over a new budget bill, Bush abandoned his campaign promise not to raise taxes and seemed to switch his policy positions repeatedly. The criticisms of the "In-Box President" were heard again. Only after George Bush serves a full term in office will we be able to begin to classify his presidency.

CHAPTER 4

CONGRESS

The Unbearable Lightness of Being a Congressman

Fred Barnes

If you believe that being a member of the House of Representatives is glamorous, this selection should open your eyes. Cynics tell us that the main goal of a member of Congress is to get re-elected. Accordingly, rather than spending time trying to pass meaningful legislation, members are said to be overly concerned with doing things that will ensure their re-election. They devote their time to constituent service, frequent public appearances to keep their name before voters, reconsideration of policies to please interest groups, and, most importantly, constant fund-raising for the next campaign.

This selection by Fred Barnes allows us to test this cynical proposition on one member of the House of Representatives, John Hiler, who was swept into office as part of the so-called Reagan revolution in 1980. During this election a large number of powerful liberal members of Congress, including a half-dozen influential senators, lost their jobs to conservative Republicans who rode on Reagan's coattails. One of those congressmen was John Brademas of Indiana, who had served in the House for twenty-two years, had earned a national reputation in the field of education, had risen to the third-ranking position in the House, and seemed to be invulnerable at the polls. Yet Hiler beat him. Brademas went on to take the lucrative and nationally visible presidency at New York University. Ask yourself as you read this selection whether Hiler was better off than Brademas after beating him in 1980.

There are also larger questions about Congress as a whole. Are we sending people to Washington to govern the country and pass legislation or to ensure that they stay in Washington for as long as they can successfully get re-elected? Are the paperwork, fundraising, speeches, and the like keeping members of the House from being as effective as they might be?

JOHN GAUTIER   Rep. Hiler's administrative assistant.

JOHN HILER   Republican congressman from Indiana, 1981–1991.

Fred Barnes, "The Unbearable Lightness of Being a Congressman," *The New Republic*, Feb. 15, 1988. Reprinted by permission of *The New Republic*. © 1988, The New Republic, Inc.

▶ In his first race for the House of Representatives in 1980, John P. Hiler of La Porte, Indiana, was pure Reagan revolutionary. He was 27, single, and working in his family's foundry business. Three years out of the University of Chicago Business School, where he had attended classes of supply-side economist Arthur Laffer, Hiler was inflamed with the idea of overturning a half century of government interference with the economy. He wanted to change the world.

His opponent was the third-ranking Democrat in the House, John Brademas, who had represented the 3rd Congressional District in northern Indiana for 22 years. Brademas boasted about how much he had delivered in federal programs for the district, especially for its largest city, South Bend. Hiler took the opposite tack. He advocated the Kemp-Roth tax cut, urged dramatic reductions in federal domestic spending, more deregulation, and a military buildup. For nine months in 1980, Hiler gave the same campaign speech, and he repeated the same line over and over. "I'd rather cut down on the tax money flowing from South Bend to Washington than increase the grant money flowing from Washington to South Bend." He defeated Brademas decisively, 55 percent to 45 percent.

For a year, Hiler, one of 53 Republican freshmen, seemed the epitome of a new breed of GOP House member, styled on the model of former Representative David Stockman.* He was not only eager to slash programs for the poor, but also ready to cut corporate welfare and unwilling to seek pork barrel spending for his own district. When Mayor Roger Parent of South Bend asked him in 1981 for help in obtaining a federal loan guarantee for a $150 million ethanol plant, Hiler rebuffed him. Nor did Hiler leap into action when the United Auto Workers sought his aid in persuading the Bendix Corporation, South Bend's largest employer, from moving its facilities to the Sun Belt. Capital, Hiler explained later, "should be allowed to move freely."

By early 1982 Hiler was housebroken. He was transformed into a drudge, a workaholic with little time for what he calls "macro issues" and an obsession with the parochial interests of his district. In short, Hiler became like nearly everyone else in the House. His attention turned to the small and sometimes demeaning business of politics—schmoozing, touching as many bases as humanly possible, patting backs, and staying visible in his district.

Nothing concentrates the mind of a congressman like fear of losing his job. Hiler's trouble began with a front-page story in the *Wall Street Journal* on January 7, 1982. It featured Hiler as a "Reagan robot," and unswerving follower of Reaganomics in spite of a deepening recession. The story was reprinted in the *South Bend Tribune,* causing Hiler endless trouble. Democrats used the article and Hiler's refusal to seek money for the ethanol plant against him. Campaigning during a recession was miserable. "You couldn't find a smiling face anywhere you went to campaign," Hiler says. "By one o'clock you didn't want to

---

* David Stockman is best known as Ronald Reagan's first budget director. See Selection 5.1, "The Education of David Stockman."

get out of the car." He won, 53 percent to 47 percent, but only after Dan Rather announced erroneously on CBS on election night that Hiler was the first GOP casualty.

A new, more conventional Hiler emerged. "I've learned a lot about how to handle an issue like [the ethanol plant] if it comes up in the future," he says. He opposes Urban Development Action Grants, but doesn't hesitate to plug for UDAGs for his district. He sought one to finance a parking garage in Elkhart last year [1987]. He also tried unsuccessfully to change the rules for UDAGs to make it easier for South Bend to get one to develop the abandoned Studebaker automobile plant. When the Army switched its contract for five-ton trucks from AM General in South Bend to a company in Ohio, Hiler pushed for an emergency National Guard contract for the trucks. That failed, but he got the Pentagon to move forward the production of trucks at AM General for foreign sale.

National and foreign issues are almost off Hiler's agenda now. Despite his kinship with conservative bomb throwers such as Representative Newt Gingrich of Georgia, he hasn't joined their Conservative Opportunity Society. "It just demanded a commitment of time, with my election status, I can't give," he says. Hiler won by 47 votes in 1986, and faces another tough re-election this year [1988]. He sends out a "Weekly Report" to constituents that often discusses a national issue, but his press secretary, Linda Heacox, usually writes it. The two committees he is on—Banking and Small Business—take up some economic issues that interest Hiler, but as a Republican in a Democratic Congress, his role is small. Hiler's schedule in Washington is so full of meetings with constituents and lobbyists, receptions, and trips to the House floor for votes that his administrative assistant, John Gautier, tries to set aside an hour late in the day (6 P.M. to 7 P.M., or 7 P.M. to 8 P.M.) for national issues. But that often falls through. "When you run and get elected, you think you're going to be working on very large problems of the world," says Hiler. "You get a heavy dose of reality. It turns out you work on a lot of things very close to home."

Nothing is closer to home than the manufactured housing industry, which produces prefabricated homes that cost $20,000 to $25,000. It is probably the biggest industry in his district, and Hiler spends ten percent of his time, whether in Washington or Indiana, on matters related to it. Of course, a nice chunk of his campaign contributions comes from people in the industry. Over-regulation is a ubiquitous threat, he says, and would make prefabs too expensive. "It's affordable housing," says Hiler. "Lookit, everybody can't drive a Cadillac. Somebody's got to drive Chevettes."

Protecting a local interest may not be high-minded, but it is what most House members concentrate on. Republican Frank Wolf of northern Virginia spends his time on curbing noise at National Airport and working on local highway issues. Democrat Charles Rose of North Carolina defends the tobacco program. Nonetheless, Hiler insists that working on manufactured housing issues is the most satisfying thing he's done in Congress. And he doesn't wink when he says it.

In 1987 Hiler battled threats to the industry from both the Department of Housing and Urban Development and Congress. Ironically, Hiler wants to retain federal regulation of the industry, whereas HUD wants to hand it over to the states, which might adopt tougher regulations, as part of Reagan's new federalism. But Hiler says this would confront the industry with a hodgepodge of state regulations and make national distribution unfeasible. Hiler was tireless in lobbying HUD. "I've had more individual dealings with Hiler's office or Hiler-related matters than anybody else, " says Chris Lord, a HUD liaison with Congress. Hiler's efforts worked. HUD has now all but given up trying to get rid of regulatory authority.

For Hiler, the crowning achievement of 1987 was one tiny part of the housing bill passed last December. For years there has been pressure to apply the same HUD energy standards for single-family housing to manufactured housing. No way, says Hiler. This would drive up the price, reduce sales, and threaten jobs in Elkhart, the manufactured housing center in his district. In April Hiler got the provision knocked out when the bill was marked up in the House Banking subcommittee on housing, on which he is the senior Republican.* Then Democrat Mary Rose Oakar of Ohio put it back in when the full Banking Committee took up the bill. That version passed the House. But Hiler got it watered down during a Senate-House conference. He inserted language that says HUD standards should be "cost-effective" and "ensure the lowest total of construction and operating costs." This prompted Hiler's office to release a triumphant press release in November. "Hiler Amendment Saves Jobs in Elkhart," it said.

There are exceptions—if you were on the [Iran-contra] committee, say, or Ways and Means at tax reform time—but the daily routine of House members is mindlessly hectic and stupefyingly dull. At most, only three dozen representatives out of 435 have any real power. All but a few of these are Democratic leaders or committee chairmen. There are nearly 200 subcommittees, and a lot of what they do is duplicative. Hiler wastes little time on the Small Business Committee, for example, because anything it handles will also be worked over by other committees. Much of what the House does is makework. Republican Amo Houghton of Corning, New York, was shocked at the inefficiency of the place when he arrived last year, fresh from serving as chief executive officer of Corning Glass. "You don't resolve issues here," he says. "You circle around them."

The level of mail and requests for help from constituents is intimidating. It took a quantum leap in the early 1980s. In Hiler's office the number of letters rose from 250 to 300 a week to 500 to 600. Hiler answers every one and person-

_____

* In the *markup* session, a committee or subcommittee revises the language of a bill. See Selection 4.5, "A Season of Governing."

ally signs his responses. He say he spends about five or six percent of his time on mail alone. He has four legislative assistants in Washington, all of whom work on mail. He also has an administrative assistant, a press secretary, a computer specialist, an intern, an office manager, and a receptionist. They work on mail too. If Hiler is away for four or five days, it takes him several days to catch up with the backlog of correspondence. Hiler uses the responses his aides draft as a "briefing system" on issues he might not be keeping up with. This way, says administrative assistant Gautier, "he's never stumped" when talking to constituents. In his district office in South Bend, there are six staffers who devote themselves solely to "casework," requests for help of all sorts. Recently the office celebrated its 10,000th case.

At random, Gautier picked out a typical day in Washington for Hiler—last September 15 [1987]. The night before, he'd appeared at Academy Night at a high school in his district for those interested in an appointment to a service academy. Hiler spent the night in his duplex in La Porte, then drove 30 miles to South Bend the next morning to catch a 6 A.M. plane to Washington. It arrived at 9:35 A.M., and his first appointment, markup of a minor bill in the Banking Subcommittee on Consumer Affairs and Coinage, was at 10 A.M. At 11:30 A.M. he met with manufactured housing lobbyists for the umpteenth time. At noon the House convened and he had to be on the floor for a spell. From 1 P.M. to 2 P.M. he was double-booked. He gave a 15-minute speech to the Electronic Funds Transfer Association, which was meeting for lunch in the Rayburn House Office Building, and then rushed to a session of the Republican Policy Committee.

At 2:30 P.M. representatives from the American Medical Oxygen Sales Corporation dropped by, and at 3 P.M. a fellow from the Coin Dealers Association arrived. At 4 P.M. Hiler met with the Indiana delegation to the International Council of Shopping Centers. At 4:30 P.M. he recorded a public service announcement in the House Recording Studio for the Osteoporosis Society. At 5 P.M. there was a meeting of the Society of Statesmen, a group of GOP House members. And from 6 P.M. to 8 P.M. he was double-booked again at competing receptions on Capitol Hill, one for the Mississippi Bankers Association, the other for the National Restaurant Association. "Typically he'd stop by and see if there's anyone from Indiana there, then run to the other and see," says Gautier. "If there weren't , he'd go home and see his kids." Hiler was married in 1984 and has two children, Alison, 2, and Caitlin, 1. His family lives in a house in McLean, Virginia.

When the House is in session, Hiler spends four days a week in Washington, three in his district. Last year he spent 125 nights in Indiana. This year he figures it'll be 175. Last year he was in the district, away from his wife and kids, three out of five weekends. This year it'll be five out of six. As you might guess, he spends a lot of time in airports. He makes about 40 round trips a year between Washington and Indiana. Until two years ago, he kept a car at Midway Airport in Chicago, flying there and driving two hours to the district. Now there's a direct Piedmont flight (stopping in Dayton) that leaves Washington at 7 A.M. and returns at 3:10 P.M. For a congressman, a direct flight to the district is heaven.

I spent two days with Hiler in Indiana. He covered better than 150 miles on January 13. He left La Porte and drove 50 miles to Elkhart for a high school speech at 8:55 A.M. Then he went to a TV station for a 30-minute taped interview. At noon he spoke to the Elkhart Lions Club, giving his standard address about "five facts" (such as, 70 percent of women with school-age children are working). Few congressmen are great public speakers, and Hiler is no better than average. For them, it's more important to be seen than heard.

After lunch he drove to Warsaw, Indiana, for three events. At 2:15 P.M. he presented a flag that had flown over the Capitol to a nursing home for the retarded. At 3 P.M. he conferred with Mayor Jeff Plank and promised to help him get a Commerce Department grant to study the feasibility of a sterilization plant in Warsaw. At 3:45 P.M. he met with the president of the Warsaw Chamber of Commerce about its day-care program. Then he drove to his office in South Bend, stayed 15 minutes, and drove to La Porte for an interview with reporter Todd Dickard of the *Herald Argus News* at 7 P.M. After 30 minutes for dinner (fried perch and rice), he addressed the La Porte Jaycees. He took off his gray suit coat, rolled up his sleeves, loosened his striped tie, and repeated his "five facts" speech. He wasn't through until after 10 P.M. He never had found a spare moment to read a newspaper. In Washington he reads the *Wall Street Journal* and the front page of the *Washington Post*. He hasn't time to look at the *New York Times*.

A third of Hiler's time in the district is devoted to fund-raising, says his aide Reg Wagle. That may be more than most House members, but it's not too far out of line. The average House incumbent now spends upward of $400,000 on re-election. Even entrenched incumbents often build up war chests, if only to scare off challengers. Since he's from a marginal district and narrowly survived a 77-day recount in 1986, Hiler is braced for a tough challenge from Tom Ward, the guy he beat by 47 votes. His goal is $600,000 (he spent $336,768 in 1986), enough for television advertising at the supersaturation level. "That's $50,000 a month, $12,000 a week, $2,000 a day," he says. To raise it, he was up at 5 A.M. on January 14 and at a breakfast 50 miles away at an Elkhart restaurant by 7:30 A.M.

The pigeon was Scott T. Chapman, president of a company that produces custom vans. Two Hiler allies, banker Tom Dusthimer and manufacturer Bob Deputy, had invited Chapman, and they came along to the breakfast. They chatted about business and someone told an off-color joke about Lee Iacocca before Hiler made his pitch. Hiler said he'd been too laid-back in 1986. "Our campaign was oriented toward not losing, instead of winning. I realize now we can't do that."

"You're right," said Chapman. "In business, too."

Hiler said he can't afford to let his opponents go unanswered in 1988. "You can get away with that in a lot of districts, but in this district you can't. You take no prisoners. You have to be aggressive. You have to be creative. Sometimes you have to use humor. Sometimes you have to be nasty." He said he wants to be able to hit back in television spots within 48 hours after a charge is made. Ward, his opponent, will be made "to eat everything he said in the past." His campaign has "books that thick" of research on Ward, he said, holding his thumb and finger two inches apart.

Dusthimer turned the conversation to money. Ward got $78,000 from labor unions in 1986, he said. Democrats, Deputy added, "have made it clear they're going to spend whatever it takes" to win Hiler's seat. And Hiler said the National Republican Congressional Committee has told him "to plan on Ward spending between $400,000 and $500,000."

"Jesus," said Chapman.

"When a challenger gets $400,000 or $500,000, they can throw up a lot of stuff," said Hiler.

"I understand," said Chapman. "It's the cost of doing business."

Just then, Chapman is summoned to the phone. "Have you told him a figure?" Hiler asked his allies. "Should we hit him with one now?" No, they said, we'll get to that later.

When Chapman returned, Hiler said, "I hope we can have your financial support."

"I presumed that was coming," Chapman said.

"I presumed you knew I wasn't here just because I didn't have a place to eat breakfast," said Hiler.

"Say," one of his friends said to Hiler, "what's the most you can give? Up to $2,000?"

"Yes," said Hiler.

Chapman replied, "If you're asking for the order, sure, I'll sign that order."

At four similar meetings and a lunch, Hiler raised another $4,000, maybe $6,000. He made it back to South Bend in time to catch the 3:10 P.M. plane to Washington.

On the night of January 13, Hiler and an aide got lost while looking for a Jaycees meeting. At one point, they wandered into a church during a service. The small congregation looked up and the pastor said, "Come on in." Hiler balked. "I'm sorry. I think we're in the wrong place," he said. "No, you're not in the wrong place," the pastor said. "You're in the Lord's house." Embarrassed, Hiler backed out. He hadn't been recognized.

For all the honor of being elected every other year, the job of U.S. representative isn't all that ego-satisfying. Few House members are household names in their districts. "If you're in it for public adulation," said GOP Representative Vin Weber of Minnesota, "you'd better be in the Senate." True, there's satisfaction in having people listen to your opinions on various subjects. You get a reserved parking space at National Airport. And the pay—$89,500—isn't bad. But after three or four terms, virtually any House member could double his salary as a lobbyist.

A new study of Congress by the Center for Responsive Politics found House members to be frustrated and dissatisfied. Too much busywork and fund-raising, they complained, and too little personal time. Representatives who went to Jamaica in January to be lectured by Sovietologists worried that if they returned with tans they might be criticized for languishing on the beach. Hiler can scarcely find time to read a book. He likes to read on plane rides, but on a recent trip his briefcase was stocked with reports and studies. There were such page-turners as "Glass-Steagall Act: Current Issues Affecting Bank Underwriting, Dealing & Brokerage Activities" and "International Competition in Services" and "Mandate for Change: Restructuring the Banking Industry."

The House is a nice steppingstone. Presidents John Kennedy, Lyndon Johnson, and Richard Nixon started their political careers there. Eight House members won Senate seats in 1986. Some are so desperate they'll leap at anything. Republican Ed Bethune of Arkansas left in 1984 to run an unwinnable race for the Senate. Democrat Bill Boner of Tennessee quit last year to run for mayor of Nashville. He won. Hiler flirted last year with the idea of seeking the lieutenant governorship, the best statewide job he'd have a shot at. His path to the Senate is blocked. Indiana has two relatively young Republican senators, Richard Lugar and Dan Quayle.*

Hiler's wife, Catherine, says she's "amazed" they got married in the first place. The year they met, 1981, "37 of 52 weekends, he was gone." Their life, she says, "isn't normal. One of the things that helps is I worked on the Hill." She was minority counsel for the House Government Operations Committee, then executive director of the Federal Mine Safety Review Commission. She quit in 1984 to campaign for her husband, and was deputy director of the White House Conference on Small Business in 1985 and 1986. Now she rears the two children.

"In a sense, I have my own life," she says. "I have total responsibility for the children." Her daily routine lasts from 7 A.M. to 8 P.M., when the kids go to sleep. "When Jack comes home, he has to fit in. . . . At times, I do wonder if it's worth it. That happens when Jack's gone a few weekends in a row."

Their social life is negligible. Even when she goes back to La Porte with him, they have little time together. "Sometimes he can fit an hour in a day to see the kids," she says. At political functions, she has to stay clear of relatives. "I'm not there to talk to my family, nor is Jack." What makes the life palatable for Cather-

---

* When Dan Quayle became George Bush's vice president in 1989, Republican Dan Coats was appointed to replace him in the Senate.

ine Hiler is her belief "that it matters for him to be there. I do believe it. I do believe it."

So does Hiler. He still lives off the exhilarating days in 1981 when deep budget and tax cuts passed the House. He can describe in detail the June day when the reconciliation bill narrowly cleared the House. "You watched the votes going up [on the tally board]. Winning by three votes, you felt you'd made a difference."

By 1985 Hiler was getting depressed. Conservatives were winning few votes in the House. He thought about quitting, but never came close. The study by the Center for Responsive Politics found that, despite their complaints, few House members want to leave. "You grow up believing members of Congress are people held in high regard," says Weber. "It's hard for people to imagine when they get that job that it isn't what it's cracked up to be. So they hold on to it." . . .

Epilogue

Would a Democratic representative's time in office be more influential or more glamorous than Hiler's? Surprisingly, with the exception of a very few of the most visible and powerful members, the answer is a resounding no. What does it indicate about the prospects for political leadership when the best leaders might find a more pleasant life and reap greater rewards in the private sector?

It must be noted that life in the Senate is not much better. For example, although their term in office is six years, some senators feel they have to raise $20 million for their re-election campaigns, instead of the $600,000 that Hiler was seeking. And although well over 95 percent of congressional incumbents are re-elected in a given election year, both House and Senate members know they are always just one election away from oblivion. In 1990 Senator Bill Bradley of New Jersey outspent his Republican opponent by a twelve-to-one margin and had a huge lead in the polls two weeks before the election. Nevertheless, because Bradley failed to take seriously voter unhappiness with Democratic governor James Florio's $2.8 billion tax increase, he squeaked by with a margin of only 55,180 votes out of 1.9 million cast. The effect of this close election on Senator Bradley's presidential ambitions cannot yet be gauged, but it certainly will not help.

In 1990 John Hiler was not lucky enough to squeak by. In the 1988 congressional race, he had won re-election by a comfortable 54 to 46 percent margin. In 1990, however, Democrat Tim Roemer attacked Hiler's alleged willingness to curry favor with the business community and banking industry. In particular, Hiler was hurt by his position on the House Banking Committee and by his support for deregulation of the savings and loan industry. Because of this support, voters apparently held him partially responsible for the savings and loan crisis. Hiler, one of only a handful of members of Congress not to be re-elected, lost to Roemer by 2,809 votes out of nearly 160,000 cast.

4.2

The Speaker of the House can be a president's best friend or his worst enemy. This compelling account by D. B. Hardeman and Donald Bacon of the early relationship between John F. Kennedy and Sam Rayburn, who was generally regarded as the greatest Speaker of the House in history, illustrates the former. (The next selection, on Tip O'Neill and Jimmy Carter, will show the other side of the coin.)

The key to getting legislation passed by Congress is knowing how to overcome the obstacles built into the law-making process. Throughout the many stages involved in the legislation process, there are members of Congress, committees, and committee chairs capable of derailing the effort. (For more on this process, see Selection 4.5.) It is well within the discretion of the Speaker of the House, however, to overcome those obstacles and speed a bill on its way to passage. In the early 1960s, President Kennedy was faced with committee chairs who were members of his own party in name only. These men were conservative southern Democrats who had ascended to the chairmanships of key committees because of their long years in office. One of these chairs, Judge Howard Smith of the Rules Committee, posed an obstacle to the new president. Whenever his committee seemed destined to send liberal legislation to the full House, Smith's favorite technique was to "go fishin'"—putting the bill in his pocket, driving across the river to his Virginia farm (which did not have a phone), releasing his hunting dogs to keep visitors away—and holding on to the bill to keep it from passing out of the committee. Knowing Smith's methods, Rayburn saw that something had to be done.

As you marvel at the description of Sam Rayburn's power in this selection, realize as well what a high personal price he paid for his loyalty to President Kennedy. A Democrat from highly conservative Bonham, Texas, Rayburn was more philosophically in tune with representatives like Howard Smith than with the liberal Kennedy. Moreover, Rayburn was a disappointed suitor: his name had been mentioned as a potential running mate for Kennedy, but the vice-presidency went in-

"The Worst Fight of My Life"

D. B. Hardeman and Donald C. Bacon

stead to his protégé, Senator Lyndon Johnson. Finally, Rayburn had close personal friendships with men like Smith, who took his service in the House very seriously, while the Speaker knew all too well how little effort Kennedy had put into his own service in Congress. But politics, as they say, makes strange bedfellows, and there were few stranger than the tall, young, wealthy, charismatic liberal from Boston and the short, bald, unpretentious Speaker from Texas.

WILLIAM COLMER   Southern conservative; member of the House Rules Committee.

CHARLIE HALLECK   House Republican leader.

JOHN F. KENNEDY   President of the United States, 1961–1963.

SAM RAYBURN   Speaker of the House for the 17 years that Democrats had the majority between 1940 and 1961.

HOWARD SMITH   Virginia Democrat; chair of the House Rules Committee.

▶ On New Year's Eve in 1960, Sam Rayburn cut short his holiday at his home in Bonham and flew back to Washington for what he knew would be a tumultuous year. . . .

The Speaker looked to [the next] year with both eagerness and dread—eagerness, because a new Democratic administration was coming to power, led by young Jack Kennedy, the brash Bostonian for whom Rayburn had developed an extravagant admiration; dread, because he knew he must launch a bitter, merciless fight against some fellow Democrats, a fight he had postponed for years but could avoid no longer. Rayburn strongly felt that young Kennedy's program had to be enacted to carry out Democratic campaign pledges to the nation. The new President's most threatening obstacle lay in the House, where the Republican–conservative Democratic coalition had stymied progressive legislation for more than twenty years. To break the coalition's power, Rayburn knew that he had to strike at its heart—the Committee on Rules. If Kennedy's program could not get past the Rules Committee, his administration would be a failure from the start. The old man had made his decision. He would join the battle with the conservatives. He would try to break their stranglehold over legislation. The battle would be excruciating, the outcome uncertain. Flying to Washington that bright December Saturday, Rayburn was heading, at age 79, into what he would later describe as "the worst fight of my life."

Control of the Committee on Rules, the principal scheduling and policy committee of the House, was the most powerful weapon in the hands of the coalition. The committee was created in the late 1800s as an instrument of the House leadership to ensure the orderly flow of legislation to the floor. When the "leadership"—consisting of the Speaker, majority leader, majority whip, and chairmen of major committees, with the Speaker having the final decisive voice—decided to put a certain bill before the House, the committee determined the length of debate, type of amendments to be permitted, and other procedural questions. The committee was designed to help, not obstruct, the leadership.

Sometimes the leadership used the committee to bottle up bills on which it did not want a vote. This important function served largely to protect the House against pressures from the executive and from politically potent lobbying groups. The committee's refusal to "grant a rule" on a bill usually was its death sentence. There were other procedural devices, such as discharge petitions and Calendar Wednesday,* that could force a House vote on a bill, but they were complicated and seldom successful. The Rules Committee had, in effect, life-or-death power over most important legislation.

When the coalition was born in the late 1930s, the committee's role began to change. Conservatives sought and won places on the committee. Two southern Democrats, re-elected by their constituencies term after term, moved steadily up the committee's seniority ladder and minimized the Democratic leadership's opportunities to fill vacancies. The Republicans routinely appointed conservatives to the committee as a matter of party policy. Insidiously, the conservatives took control of the committee and dominated its actions. Instead of confining itself to procedural matters, the committee began to exercise its judgment on the contents of bills before it. Bills disliked by the coalition were simply pigeonholed. In other cases, the committee, before allowing the bill to go to the House floor for a vote, forced revision to reflect the extremely conservative views of the coalition.

Although Rayburn viewed the coalition as an outrageous usurpation of power, he lived with it because, to that point, he had usually been able to get essential bills to the floor through personal persuasion. But in August 1960, the Rules Committee Chair, Judge Howard Smith, and his supporters served notice that the days of gentlemanly personal cooperation with Rayburn were over. The coalition grew increasingly confident of its power and ignored the wishes of the Democratic leadership, which had the responsibility for directing the work of the House.

An impasse had been building for more than a year—ever since Charlie Halleck overthrew Joe Martin as House Republican leader and the party's extreme conservative wing began exercising strict control over minority affairs. Two moderate Republicans left the committee; Halleck filled the vacancies with conservatives Homer H. Budge of Idaho and B. Carroll Reece of Tennessee. Chairman Smith and his alter ego on the committee, William Colmer, Democrat of Mississippi, now had four extreme right-wing Republicans with whom they

---

* A discharge petition requires the signatures of a majority of the full House to send legislation that is stuck in any committee to the floor of the House for a vote. Calendar Wednesday refers to the fact that every Wednesday the list of committees is read alphabetically. At this time, a member can call for a two-hour debate and a vote on any bill, with no amendments.

voted on nearly every issue. The twelve-member committee was deadlocked: six Democrats would stand with Rayburn, two Democrats and four Republicans were sure to oppose him. To get a controversial bill through the committee required seven votes. The coalition now had virtually complete power to say what bills the House could consider and under what terms such bills could be debated. Rayburn's hands were tied.

In 1960, the situation became intolerable. Congress recessed for the national conventions, then reconvened in August. The session was important to Senators Kennedy and Johnson, the Democratic nominees, who hoped to push through a program on which to take their candidacies to the country. An increase in the minimum wage, federal aid to education, and an expanded housing program were the heart of their proposals. All three measures were chloroformed by the Committee on Rules. The session had been a fiasco for the Democrats. Smith, Colmer, and four Republican committee members had scuttled the Kennedy-Johnson program. Rayburn and the House Democratic leadership were humiliated; Kennedy and Johnson were embarrassed; moderate and liberal Democrats were furious; Republicans were jubilant. During the 1960 campaign, Smith, Senator Harry Byrd, and the Democratic Byrd machine sat glumly silent while Richard Nixon carried their state of Virginia; Bill Colmer bolted the Democratic party to vote for the independent "States' Rights" ticket.

Rayburn was elated by the election of Kennedy and Johnson, but he knew their victory spelled personal trouble for him. The coalition would do its best to wreck the Kennedy program, and he was determined not to let that happen. . . .

The Democratic party's future was involved. Kennedy and Johnson had promised the voters a progressive program, most of which was anathema to the coalition. If the coalition was not checked, Rayburn knew much of that program would die in the committee without the House itself ever having a chance to vote on it. Kennedy would be labeled a "do-nothing" President. Remembering the razor-thin margin by which the young President had been elected, Rayburn decided Kennedy's re-election chances would be slim indeed.

Moreover, Rayburn deeply felt that American security demanded that the nation once more get moving. There had been too much drifting during the eight Republican years, he felt, and a nation retains leadership not by drifting but by action. A Kennedy administration incapable of action would be dangerous to the national welfare.

Rayburn's own prestige was deeply involved. Continued success of the Rules Committee in obstructing his leadership in the House had led to a rising tide of complaint by some representatives and political writers that he was too old for the job, that he was losing his grip. The Speaker snorted at such criticism, but he knew it was increasing. Basically, however, Rayburn saw the fight as a matter of political principle. "The issue is very simple," he said. "Shall the elected leadership of the House run its affairs, or shall the chairman of one committee run them?" In the back of his mind, he nurtured another compelling reason for wanting to break the committee's power. He was approaching the inevitable day when his tenure as Speaker would end. His fierce pride in the institution of the Speakership instilled in him a burning determination to turn over to his successor a more powerful, more prestigious office than he had inherited. Once he said: "When the House revolted against Speaker Cannon in 1910, they cut the Speaker's powers too much. Ever since I have been Speaker, I have been trying to get some of that power back for the office."

Coalition members knew they were in trouble. Judge Smith, opposing any change in his committee, asserted he was "ready for a fight." Soon after the 1960 elections, Smith and Colmer met with House GOP Leader Charlie Halleck of Indiana to chart a strategy. Halleck promised full support; he would oppose any tampering with the committee. During November and December, attention focused on Rayburn, who was in Bonham, relaxing and keeping his silence but doing plenty of thinking. It was one of the trickiest problems of his long career. He must not only break the committee's power, but must do it as painlessly as possible to avoid permanently alienating southern Democrats, whose votes Kennedy—and Rayburn—would need later on.

President-Elect Kennedy, meeting with Rayburn and other congressional leaders in Palm Beach, agreed with his conclusions. Still furious over the embarrassment Smith and company had handed him the previous August, Kennedy concluded that unless the Rules Committee bottleneck was broken, "our whole program would be emasculated." Rayburn urged the new President to stay out of the fight. It was a House affair, and Kennedy's active involvement could do more harm than good, he argued. Besides, the Speaker explained, it was his prestige on the line. Kennedy agreed to remain in the background, providing moral support—and maybe a post office or judgeship here and there—to help Rayburn's cause. Ultimately, however, the President could not remain aloof from a battle upon whose outcome so much rested. Kennedy telephoned several members, although, according to Rayburn's later assessment, "he didn't change a vote."

Rayburn had a plan. Reaching Washington on New Year's Eve afternoon, he drove straight to the Capitol. There, after explaining his intentions to his closest Democratic allies, he telephoned Howard Smith and asked him to drop by the Speaker's Rooms for a chat. A few minutes later, Smith shuffled in and dropped his lanky frame into one of the huge black chairs that flanked the Speaker's desk. Quietly Rayburn told his adversary that the Kennedy program had a right to be considered by the House and that he intended to see that the members got that opportunity. The Rules Committee had to be reshuffled, Rayburn said, adding his hope that the change could be made without hard feelings. The easiest way was for Smith himself to propose that the committee be enlarged from twelve to fifteen members. If Smith made the proposal, a fight would be avoided. The addition of three members—two Democrats and one Republican—would let Rayburn name two Democrats friendly to the Kennedy program and the House leadership. The Kennedy-Rayburn forces would have an eight-to-seven margin on the committee.

Smith flatly rejected the offer, which was no surprise. But that was part of Rayburn's strategy—he wanted to be able to say that Smith had been given a chance to avoid open confrontation and had refused it. They shook hands and Smith departed. The die was cast. The fiercest battle for control in the House since the revolt against Speaker Joe Cannon fifty-one years before was now a certainty.

The two opponents were dramatic figures. Between them Sam Rayburn and Howard Smith had seventy-eight years of congressional service. The Speaker had served with eight of the nation's thirty-four Presidents; the Judge with five. "The two wily old congressional giants have much in common," noted *Time* magazine:

> *Sam Rayburn and Howard Smith both have the patina of age—Rayburn is 79, Smith 78—and the special dignity that accrues to old men who have long exercised power in causes greater than their own ambitions. Both are gruff on the surface, kind underneath. They were country boys, raised on farms, and they still, whenever they can get out of Washington, instinctively head for rustic serenity—the Rayburn cattle ranch near Bonham, Texas, or the Smith dairy farm near Broad Run, Va. They grew up, pinched by poverty, in a South still seething with Civil War hatreds and sunk in economic misery.*[1]

But, *Time* observed,

> *the most striking difference, the Great Divide of personality, is a matter of the temperature of the heart. Smith is a bit frosty; displays of emotion make him visibly uncomfortable. Sam Rayburn, in contrast, is a sentimentalist, a man of strong and easily stirred feelings, who unashamedly weeps in public when moved. Men who were there still choke up when they recall Rayburn's anguished speech in the House on the death of his old friend Alben Barkley, the speech that ended, "God comfort his loved ones. God comfort me."*

On January 2, Rayburn played his first ace. He told a group of liberal Democratic congressmen of Smith's refusal to sponsor enlargement of the Rules Committee. Now there was only one real choice left, Rayburn declared. He would drop the idea of enlarging the committee and, instead, seek the removal of Colmer on the grounds that he had bolted the Democratic party in November. A moderate Democrat could then be appointed to the panel. When Rayburn's plan became known, tempers flared among southern Democrats. John Bell Williams of Mississippi threatened that if the Speaker persisted in trying to purge Colmer, southern Democrats might vote with Republicans to elect a Republican Speaker instead of Rayburn. Moderate Democrats from southern and border states heard the news with anguish. They recoiled from the prospect of having to oppose the Speaker as well as the new Democratic President at the outset of his administration. On the other hand, many knew they would be subjected to excruciating pressure from powerful political and economic forces back home to resist any change in the committee. For many, it was the most painful dilemma of their political careers. "If I cross the Speaker, I'm ruined here," one said ruefully, "and if I vote with him, I can't get re-elected."

Rayburn and his lieutenants went to work, talking, pleading, cajoling members to support them. Smith and his supporters applied pressure from the other side. Tension mounted. Many members were emotionally upset, some visibly angry, others frightened. Some hedged their bets—pledging support to both Rayburn and Smith. Alabama Democrat Frank ("Everything is made for love") Boykin, an affable character who had difficulty saying no to anybody, switched sides at least six times. Whoever got to him last, got his pledge of support. Finally, Rayburn told his lieutenants to leave the anguished Alabamian alone. He ultimately voted with most other southerners—against Rayburn.

Meanwhile, Kennedy announced five key bills in his program—an expanded housing program, increased minimum wage, medical care for the aged under the Social Security system, relief for depressed areas, and federal aid to education. Dreading a showdown, Smith went to see the Speaker. He offered a guarantee that all five bills would be cleared by his committee if Rayburn would drop the plan to purge Colmer. "S__t, Howard, Kennedy may have forty bills in his program before he's through," Rayburn snorted. There would be no deal.

The purge plan, theoretically, would involve only Democrats. House rules specify that the entire House must approve all committee assignments, but by unbroken custom neither party ever interfered with the other's assignments. Rumors circulated that Halleck was planning to let Republicans vote with southern Democrats to keep Colmer on the Rules Committee. Rayburn bristled with anger: "Two can play at that game. If they start messing in our party affairs, we can do the same on Republican nominations to committees—and we have a majority." Halleck backed off.

Would-be peacemakers appeared. Moderate southerners pleaded for a compromise "so we won't have to choose between Howard and Sam." Crafty 77-year-old Carl Vinson of Georgia, hard-fisted chairman of the Committee on Armed Services, who had served longer in the House than anyone except Rayburn, was a Rayburn supporter. Vinson, who held the confidence of southern Democrats, teamed up with Francis E. "Tad" Walter, veteran Pennsylvania conservative and chairman of the Committee on Un-American Activities, a man popular with conservative southerners. Together they sought to avert a bitter confrontation.

Vinson and Walter shuttled back and forth between factions, conferring with Rayburn, with Smith, with Democrats from southern and border states. They found strong sentiment for compromise among moderate southerners, who saw the purging of Colmer as a threat to the seniority system that had served southern interests for so long. And they believed Rayburn was being unreasonable—or at least inconsistent. He had not sought to purge Harlem Congressman Adam Clayton Powell when he supported Eisenhower for President in 1956. He had not sought the removal of others who were convicted of crimes. The removal of Colmer from the seniority ranks would so anger the South, the moderates warned, that all southerners would turn against the new administration and its legislative program. Vinson and Walter sought a compromise formula. On January 10, they informed the Speaker that if he would drop his plan to purge Colmer, they could round up enough southern Democrats to put over the original plan to enlarge the committee by three members—but they warned that Smith would fight this to the finish.

Rayburn from the beginning had been aware of the arguments against purging Colmer. He had used Colmer as bait to attract what moderate southern support he could for the committee enlargement plan. The tactical maneuver had worked—many representatives had decided that enlargement was the lesser of two evils, and the one they could more easily justify to their home constituencies. Acting on the recommendation of Vinson, Walter, and John McCormack, who despite the vast ideological gulf between them was a close friend of Colmer's, the Speaker announced he was dropping the purge plan. Instead, he would throw his full weight behind the proposal to enlarge the committee by adding two Democrats and one Republican. The House, he predicted hopefully, would accept this as a "painless way to solve the problem. . . . the way to embarrass nobody if they don't want to be embarrassed."

Rayburn was in more trouble than he had foreseen. Some southern members who had promised to support enlargement of the committee if he abandoned his plan to purge Colmer now reversed themselves. Also, the decision to try to enlarge the committee broadened the battlefield. Only Democrats would have voted on purging Colmer, and Rayburn had a clear majority in his own party. But enlargement required a change in House rules, meaning that Republicans as well as Democrats would have to vote.

Republicans were certain to support Smith overwhelmingly in resisting any change in the committee. To win, Rayburn had to have some Republican votes, perhaps as many as thirty. They would be hard to come by. No Republicans relished the prospect of antagonizing their leader, Charlie Halleck, and the senior Republicans, led by Clarence Brown of Ohio, who were all fiercely opposed to tampering with the committee. A few progressive Republicans favored the change. Ex-Speaker Joe Martin wanted to help, but his influence among House Republicans had waned almost to insignificance.

Rayburn knew he would have to throw in his whole stack. Through many years, House Democrats had incurred IOUs to him. He had helped dozens of them enact their pet bills. Scores had gotten choice committee assignments because he helped them. Others had received his invaluable political help when they faced re-election troubles. He had raised campaign funds and made speeches for them in their districts, throwing his enormous prestige behind their candidacies. Now he needed their help. In the Speaker's Lobby, on the House floor, he stopped one member after another to ask: "Are you going with me?" Others he called to his office to ask the same question. He worked tirelessly, constantly. Rayburn lieutenant Frank Thompson of New Jersey kept a master list of supporters, which he updated daily with fresh reports brought to him by other Rayburn suppporters and by liberal lobbyists active in the fight. When lieutenants reported that a member was "shimmying," as Rayburn put it, the Speaker phoned him "to stiffen his backbone." Newly elected members, still lacking committee assignments, were summoned; defiance of Rayburn was not a wise way to start a House career.

Northern and western Democrats were solid in support of the Speaker. His trouble lay with the southern and border state members. He used every stratagem he could think of. Organized labor turned the heat on congressmen obligated to it. The National Education Association, pushing federal aid to education, mobilized teachers and school officials to back Rayburn. Civil rights organizations were active, except for the National Association for the Advancement of Colored People, which feared that the fight would become a race issue. But such organizations, unfortunately for Rayburn, packed little political punch in the South.

At his first press conference as President, Kennedy made it clear where he stood. "It is no secret that I would strongly believe that the members of the House should have an opportunity to vote . . . on the programs which we will present, not merely members of the Rules Committee. But the responsibility rests with members. I merely give my view as an interested citizen." Privately, Kennedy ordered Vice-President Johnson and his Cabinet to bring as much behind-the-scenes pressure for the enlargement as they could.

Smith had his own powerful allies. The southern press, with a few exceptions, conducted a noisy campaign against the Rayburn plan, insisting it was a scheme to force new civil rights legislation on the South. That was a phony issue. The coalition had dissolved in both 1957 and 1959 when the only two civil rights bills passed since Reconstruction days came before the committee. Republicans dared not oppose such legislation, coalition or no coalition. Other influential groups supporting Smith included the National Association of Manufacturers, U.S. Chamber of Commerce, American Farm Bureau Federation, and American Medical Association. House members were inundated with letters, telegrams, and phone calls generated by those groups angrily demanding their support of Smith.

On January 17, the House Democratic Caucus by voice vote formally endorsed Rayburn's proposal. Smith agreed at the meeting to bring the resolution to the floor. On January 19, the House Republican Policy Committee unanimously rejected the enlargement plan. Four days later, the Republican Conference voted overwhelmingly in caucus to oppose the plan. A few maverick Republicans were kicking over the traces, but they were under heavy pressure to stay with their party. "Charlie Halleck says he's not putting any pressure on the Republicans," said Rayburn. "I have to believe him—but somebody sure as hell is."

In fact, Halleck was making life miserable for Republicans who were not firmly committed to Smith. Angrily, Halleck stalked members of his party thought to be wavering. *Time* correspondent Neil MacNeil recalled Halleck's encounter with one such member—Glen Cunningham of Nebraska: "Halleck grabbed him on the House floor, both hands on Cunningham's coat, and literally shook him as he spat out arguments against 'packing' the Rules Committee. Cunningham wrenched himself free of Halleck's grasp and staggered away from him. 'That bastard!' Cunningham muttered."

On January 24, the day before the vote was scheduled before the House, the *New York Times* reported: "Opponents of the plan apparently have been gaining strength. . . . Speaker Rayburn appeared less confident today." Inevitably, rumors began to fly—Rayburn is in trouble . . . he's too old . . . he's losing control. Columnist Doris Fleeson wrote that Rayburn's only hope was for Kennedy to throw the full weight of the White House behind the embattled Speaker.

As the day of reckoning neared, the old Speaker grew increasingly nervous. He checked and rechecked his lists of supporters and began pondering ways he might later punish Democrats who deserted him. "Have you decided to go with me?" he would ask of those whose names were listed as doubtful. When he learned that one of his supporters, Tom Steed of Oklahoma, had scheduled a speaking engagement at home on the day of the vote, Rayburn was furious. "If you'll cancel it and stay here, I'll come to your district and make two of the damnedest speeches for you that you ever heard." Steed agreed to stay. He phoned former Governor and U.S. Senator Earle Clements of Kentucky. Could Clements help line up support in the Kentucky delegation? Clements said he would try. Despite his earlier determination to keep the White House on the sidelines, he decided to pay a call on Larry O'Brien, the President's chief lobbyist. "Do you know what to do?" he asked O'Brien. "I do," O'Brien replied. Before the fight ended, presidential assistant Ted Sorensen later recalled, the White House had "used all the influence a new administration could muster— patronage, sentiment, campaign commitments and federal actions of all kinds."

Lyndon Johnson, meanwhile, cruised the Capitol corridors like a one-man enforcer. More than one hapless congressman found himself pinned against a wall, staring into the accusing eyes of the Vice-President. "If Sam Rayburn is hurt, his blood will be on your hands," he told Texas Congressman Joe Kilgore. When a delegation of supporters appealed to the Speaker to seek a compromise with Smith, the old man exploded:

"Hell, no. We're going to vote. I've met with Howard three times and he won't give an inch. The only way to avoid a vote is for me to abdicate and I won't do it. If they lick me, that's that. For the next three months, I'll have those who vote against me come to my office,

and there'll be more ass-kicking than they ever dreamed possible.
We'll use discharge petitions and Calendar Wednesday and whatever
else we can find to get bills to the floor, and we'll just stay here until
we get a vote on Kennedy's program.

Rayburn knew that the vote would be extremely close. One count showed him winning by two or three votes—if nobody reneged on a promise of support. But much could go wrong. The risk of losing was too great. He wanted more time. With a few days' delay, his lieutenants could continue their quest for a sure majority. Also, the House would be given an opportunity to hear the new President deliver his State of the Union address. A mind or two might be changed. With the showdown just hours away, Rayburn abruptly announced a five-day postponement. Smith forces, sensing mounting uncertainty in the Rayburn camp, were gleeful.

On January 27, Carl Vinson and Tad Walter approached Rayburn with a new plan. With Rayburn's concurrence, they would offer Smith a deal: if Smith would agree to report out any bill that Kennedy wanted, the fight to enlarge the committee would be dropped. Rayburn, now more uncertain than ever about his chances, agreed. But when they took the deal to Smith, they found him sullen and unbending. "I've got the votes," he said. That evening, the Speaker told his staff: "We don't have the votes. I'm not as worried about my prestige taking a licking as you and some of my friends are. I'm one politician who cannot be hurt—I've already had mine. But Kennedy is going to remember this. He is that kind of Irishman." With a shrug of his shoulders, he added: "We're going to vote next Tuesday. If we lose, we lose."

On January 30, the eve of the vote, Bill Arbogast of the Associated Press checked with the Republicans, Judge Smith, and the Rayburn forces. His tally: for, 216; against, 218. Rayburn lieutenant Dick Bolling did his own count and came up with an identical 216 votes for Rayburn. A sure majority of the 435 House members would be 218, but there would be absentees. "When eagles are flying, it's time for us sparrows to take cover," John Holton, Rayburn's administrative assistant, joked to the staff. The "eagles" indeed were flying—Speaker Rayburn, Judge Smith, Charlie Halleck, Majority Leader John McCormack, Carl Vinson, Clarence Brown, labor lobbyists, and reporters scurried back and forth to last-minute conferences. Hundreds of phone calls were made. Little huddles of nervous men and women filled Capitol hallways. The tension was painful. Shortly after noon the issue would be decided. The outcome was still in the balance.

At 11:55 A.M., reporters crowded into Rayburn's front office for his daily pre-session press conference. The Speaker, his face showing strain, was in rare good humor. He felt relief in knowing that, whatever the outcome, the fight would soon be over. Leaning back in his tall chair, his hands clasped, he predicted, "We have the votes if all of them honor their promises."

The demand for gallery tickets had been frantic. One of the largest crowds, perhaps the largest, in the history of the House filled the Chamber. Spectators jammed all gallery steps and stood against the walls. Hundreds of others, unable to get in, thronged the corridors, struggling to press through the double swinging doors. On the floor, every seat was occupied; standing room along the sides of the Chamber was filled. The press galleries likewise were packed.

Exactly at noon, Rayburn briskly walked up the steps of the Speaker's rostrum as he had hundreds of times before. At the sight of the embattled old man, with his deep-lined face, his gleaming bald head, his square shoulders held far back, the House exploded in a roar of applause. This was a violation of custom for which longtime congressional observers could recall no precedent. Rayburn gaveled for order. H. R. Gross of Iowa, the tiny Republican gadfly, demanded a quorum call. Of 435 members, 427 were present. Among the 8 absentees was Republican ex-Speaker Joe Martin, out of the country. Rayburn sorely needed Republican votes and could have used Martin's support, which he had been promised early.

When Smith rose to speak, the House rustled. A wave of applause from Republicans and southern Democrats greeted the old Judge as he ambled, stoop-shouldered, down the aisle. Bob Donovan of the *New York Herald Tribune* was struck by Smith's drab appearance. "Wraithlike and gray—gray, bushy eyebrows, thin gray hair combed back, gray complexion, gray suit, blue-gray necktie," Donovan wrote. "He is stooped. Whatever spark he has he conceals under a drab exterior. His whole appearance is misleadingly meek."

Quietly complaining that he had only eight minutes to speak, Smith made his thrust. "A lot of people around here these days talk about this being a matter of a quarrel between the Speaker and myself. . . . I have no quarrel with the Speaker. . . . If there is any quarrel between the Speaker and myself it is all on his side." There was a roar of laughter from the tense, harried representatives. Rayburn threw his head back with a laugh.

Smith pledged, "I'll cooperate with the Democratic leadership of the House of Representatives just as long and just as far as my conscience will permit me to do." Another roar of laughter went up from Rayburn supporters. Clearly, Judge Smith's cooperation with Kennedy's New Frontier would not last long, nor go very far. Sharply stung, Smith lashed back: "Some of these gentlemen who are laughing maybe do not understand what a conscience is." Quietly, earnestly, Smith pleaded with the House to postpone action. "If this matter were left dormant on the calendar, it would remain there for two years and if this committee did something that the House thought it should not do, then you would have cause to complain and could call it up any day," he said, concluding his appeal. Republicans and southern Democrats cheered as the old battler slowly walked back to his seat.

Republican leader Halleck, labeled by the press a "gut-fighter," was the final speaker against the resolution. He came out swinging. "I have an avalanche of mail, most of it handwritten, from people opposed to this resolution. . . . They are concerned about rash and reckless platform promises repeated in the campaign. . . . They are afraid the floodgates will be let down and we will be overwhelmed with bad legislation," he shouted. Republicans clapped lustily. When Halleck finished, the House stirred uneasily. The great clock showed nine minutes of debate remaining.

Democrats and Republicans alike burst into a roar of cheers and applause—short, compact Sam Rayburn was slowly descending the steps of his rostrum to speak. Some Smith supporters were silent; the Virginian leaned far back in his chair, his expressionless face turned toward the ceiling.

"Whether you vote with me today or not," Rayburn began gently, "I want to say that I appreciate your uniform kindness and courtesy that has been displayed toward me." Then he got down to business. "This issue, in my mind, is a simple one," he said. "We have elected to the Presidency a new leader. He is going to have a program that he thinks will be in the interest of and for the benefit of the American people. We are neither in good shape domestically or in the foreign field. . . . He wants to do something about that. . . . I think this House should be allowed on great measures to work its will, and it cannot work its will if the Committee on Rules is so constituted as not to allow the House to pass on those things."

Rayburn's deep voice took on an angry tone as he went on the attack. Holding up a sheet of paper, he rumbled, "I have a letter here, that if I were easily insulted, it would rather do so to me." Judge Smith cocked his head. "The gentleman from Virginia sent out a letter and in that letter he used the words 'stack' and 'pack' four times," Rayburn went on. He angrily slammed his fist on the lectern; it rang through the House like a pistol shot. "The gentleman from Virginia nor any other member can accuse me of packing any committee for or against anything," he shouted. Smith's eyebrows arched in curiosity. "Back in 1933," Rayburn recalled, "'our side' packed the Committee on Rules with the gentleman from Virginia. Then in 1939 the gentleman from Mississippi [Colmer] came to me and said he very much desired to be on the Committee on Rules. I told him I thought it would be a mistake . . . for various reasons. But he insisted, and then we packed the committee with Mr. Colmer." House members and spectators roared with laughter. The wily Speaker had drawn blood.

Gravely, Rayburn dropped his voice. "Let us move this program. Let us be sure we can move it. And the only way that we can be sure . . . in my opinion, my beloved colleagues, is to adopt this resolution today." Finished, he turned abruptly from the lectern. Again the House chamber rang with cheers and applause as the old man slowly mounted the rostrum. Smith and his supporters sat glumly silent. Rayburn, rapping his gavel, declared, "The Clerk will call the roll."

An eerie silence settled over the House. The moment of truth had arrived. Weeks of anguish, worry, and pressure were at an end. Members scrambled for tally sheets, spreading them awkwardly on their laps to record the tense vote. "Abbitt, Abernethy, Adair, Addabbo, Addonizio . . ." the reading clerk's voice split the silence. The first three answered "no," the next two, "aye"; the running tally seesawed. Rayburn three votes ahead, now two, now one. The score was tied. Judge Smith ahead one, two, four. Each shift increased the unbearable tension. Some congressmen used their fingers to signal to gallery spectators the course of the battle. Two fingers up, now three, back to two, down to one, now all even, now one finger turned down—"We're behind by one . . ."

Only the reading clerk's call and that of the answering representatives broke the church-like silence. "Members, who generally gossip and roam about during roll calls, were fixed in their seats," wrote the *Herald Tribune*'s Bob Donovan. "The galleries were frozen." When the clerk reached Wright of Texas—with only twelve more names to be called—Rayburn was ahead by one vote, 212-211. There was a late spurt of pro-Rayburn votes as the clerk neared the bottom of the list. When the first roll call ended, Rayburn led by five votes, 214-209. The names of the eleven members who had failed to answer the first time would be called again. They could change the result. The chamber rumbled into conversation. Rayburn gaveled for order. The reading clerk called the names of the eleven. Only six answered: three for Rayburn, three for Smith.

The tally clerk handed his card to Rayburn. "On this vote, there being 217 ayes and 212 noes, the resolution is adopted," he announced serenely. Pandemonium swept the House. Members on the winning side slapped each other on the back, shook hands, shouted to friends in the gallery. Some losers looked glum. Judge Smith, expressionless, shuffled out of the Chamber, where reporters waited to ask why he had lost. "We didn't have enough votes," he said. He took out an unlighted cigar, chewed on it, looked tired. "It's all baloney," he said, walking away.

Rayburn left the Chamber smiling, brushing past members and reporters who trailed behind, offering him congratulations. A television reporter urged him to tell the American people about his victory. The Speaker waved him aside. "They'll know about it," he said. As he disappeared into his office, someone asked: "How do you feel?" Rayburn's eyes twinkled. "I feel all right. That's about as good as a man can feel. I always feel good when I win."

Notes

1. "The Congress," *Time,* Feb. 10, 1961, pp. 11–12. Copyright 1961 Time Warner Inc. Reprinted by permission.

Epilogue

Ironically, after this epic battle between two conservative southern Democrats over legislative power, the fate of President Kennedy's program rested in the hands of another conservative Democrat. The congressman who held the swing vote on the Rules Committee after the addition of the three new members was Democrat Homer Thornberry of Austin, Texas. A close friend of Lyndon Johnson's, Thornberry had taken over Johnson's House seat when he went to the Senate in 1948. And now, although he was a southern conservative, in vote after vote on such issues as civil rights, Thornberry provided the one-vote margin necessary for Kennedy's legislative agenda to proceed. Later, Johnson rewarded Thornberry with a seat on the U.S. Court of Appeals.

Although Kennedy was not in office long enough to reap the full rewards of this battle, his successor, Lyndon Johnson, used Rayburn's mastery over the Rules Committee to maximum effectiveness in creating and passing his Great Society legislative program.

The Carter Years

Thomas P.
O'Neill, Jr.

Our examination of the relationship between the president and the Speaker of the House continues with this selection from the autobiography of former Speaker Thomas P. ("Tip") O'Neill concerning the passage of some energy legislation under President Jimmy Carter. In this instance we have a liberal congressman from Boston dealing with a more conservative, populist president. In many respects, O'Neill was similar to Rayburn in his ability to fashion compromise among warring factions and to galvanize his Democratic congressional colleagues when necessary. But, as you will see in this selection, O'Neill's political skills did not play as prominent a role in the Carter administration as Rayburn's had under Kennedy. The explanation for this difference lies in the way that Carter campaigned for his office and operated his presidency following his election.

Jimmy Carter ran for the presidency promising the voters that as an "outsider"—a former governor of Georgia—who had not been tainted by long years of service in Washington, he would bring a new perspective to the office, one that was more in line with the wishes of the ordinary citizen. Once elected, despite having a valuable insider—his vice president, former Senator Walter Mondale—to advise him on relationships with Congress, Carter chose to rely on his legislative liaison from Georgia, Jack Watson. As you will see from this selection, many of O'Neill's complaints arose from the fact that Watson and Carter did not know the prevailing Washington rules and so treated Congress much as they had treated the Georgia legislature.

This insensitivity toward Congress worked to Carter's great disadvantage because by this time the Speaker had much more power than in the days of Sam Rayburn. We have seen that Rayburn relied on his finely honed ability to count votes in a legislative battle, on his knowledge of when to fight and when to back off, and on his personal charisma to shepherd legislation successfully through Congress. O'Neill, however, benefited from several changes in the power of the office that granted him more direct control over the Rules Committee.

JIMMY CARTER   President of the United States, 1977–1981.

THOMAS P. O'NEILL   Speaker of the House, 1977–1987.

▶ Ultimately, a president is judged by the legislation he initiates, and this is where Carter's political problems came home to roost. The first legislative item on his agenda—and by far the most important—was energy. But if the president's energy program was going to be passed by the House, it would be up to me to make it happen.

Over the years, there have always been those who said that Tip O'Neill wasn't much of a legislator. I guess it depends on how you define that term. There have been countless brilliant lawmakers in Congress, but the details of legislation have never been my strong suit, which is why I've always left them to other people.

My own skills had more to do with powers of persuasion and with getting things done. While other members drew up the laws, I was like a shepherd who knew how to move legislation forward and get it passed. While I couldn't always cite chapter and verse, I always knew what a bill meant, what it stood for, and which members were most likely to support it.

The energy problem had been with us since 1973, when the oil embargo following the Arab-Israeli war threw us into a panic. Four years later, we had done nothing to solve this problem, which was steadily growing worse. At the time of the embargo, for example, we were importing one-third of our oil. In 1977, when Carter came in, we were importing *half* our oil—approximately nine million barrels a day. It was amazing, but we were the only developed nation without an energy policy.

It was clear to the president that our available supplies of gas and oil would not last forever. It was also clear that it was dangerous for us to be so reliant on foreign sources of energy—as we learned all too well during the subsequent crisis with Iran. Fortunately, the solution was equally clear: we had to find ways to conserve more energy, generate more domestic production, and discover alternative sources of new energy.

The extent of our problem was driven home to me by, of all people, the shah of Iran. He was a cocky little guy who marched into my office in 1977 wearing all his medals. Right away, he started chastising me—and the entire country: "What right do you people have to be so selfish? You're only six percent of the world's population, but you use thirty-five percent of the world's energy. You're the ones who are driving up the price of oil. Right now, my country exports four million barrels a day. But next year I'm going to cut it to three million, and then down to two, and then to one. You'll have to learn to get along with less."

He never got the chance, of course, as he was overthrown by his own people. But as much as I disliked the guy, he was right about energy: we *were* being wasteful and irresponsible. The president was well aware of this, and he took extraordinary measures to rally the nation behind him.

On February 2, 1977, less than a month after he was inaugurated, Jimmy Carter gave his first speech about energy. To drive the message home, he wore a cardigan sweater and spoke from the White House library, in front of a fireplace. (I'll always remember the scene: there was only one log burning in that fireplace, which to a New Englander is a preposterous sight.)

That night, the president spoke about the importance of energy conservation. The words of his speech were terrific, but Jimmy Carter was never very effective as a communicator. People were amused by the sight of their president in a sweater, but it wasn't enough to get them to change their behavior. If Ronald Reagan in his prime had given that same speech, thermostats all over the country would have been turned down on the spot.

The president tried again in his address to the nation on April 18, when he referred to the energy crisis as "the moral equivalent of war," and "the greatest challenge our country will face in our lifetime."

After the speech, I went up to congratulate him. "That was a fine address, Mr. President," I said. "Now here's a list of members you should call to keep the pressure on, because we'll need their votes."

"No," he replied, "I described the problem to the American people in a rational way. I'm sure they'll realize that I'm right."

I could have slugged him. Did he still think he was dealing with the Georgia legislature?

"Look," I said, trying to control my frustration. "This is politics we're talking about here, not physics. We need you to push this bill through."

"It's *not* politics," he replied. "Not to me. It's simply the right thing, the rational thing. It's what needs to be done."

He was right in theory but wrong in practice. It was true that his energy plan was a rational response to a real crisis. But the president just didn't understand how to motivate Congress. The textbooks all say that Congress reflects the will of the people, and, over time, that's true. But it doesn't happen overnight. Sometimes the people are slow to catch on, and Congress has to take the lead.

The way the president goes to Congress is not always by going to the people. It's also by communicating directly with the members.

The energy package that was sent over by the Carter White House was so enormous and complex that I took one look at it and groaned. What the president and his staff failed to understand was that their legislation would be taken up by as many as *seventeen* different committees and subcommittees of the House, and that each of these committees included members who opposed certain parts of the package. I shuddered to think what would be left of the bill when it was all over—assuming we managed to get any of it through.

Forget it, I thought, as I leafed through the five volumes of legislation, each one the size of a telephone directory. This bill was going to pit one region of the country against another. A representative from Maine or New Hampshire would certainly see things very differently than his colleagues from Texas, Oklahoma, or Louisiana would.

And that was just the tip of the iceberg. The automakers would resist any efforts to force them to turn out more fuel-efficient cars, although consumer groups were insisting on it. The environmentalists wanted strict controls on pollution, while the coal producers and the utilities were screaming that we had already gone too far in that direction. The conservatives would hate the prospect of increased regulation and new taxes on energy, while the liberals would be angry that the bill didn't go further.

Everyone knows the old saying that politics is the art of the possible, but this one looked hopeless to me. And under the existing structure of congressional committees, there really *was* no way.

Unless, of course, we changed the existing structure.

When it was all over, the press and many of my colleagues called it a master stroke. To me, it was survival. I *had* to get that bill through—and quickly, so that Congress could move ahead on other fronts.

The only way to score on this play was to make an end run around the existing committees of jurisdiction, and the only way to do *that* was to create a whole new committee just for this bill. I checked with Bill Brown, the House parliamentarian, who said that although it was a little unorthodox, there was no reason it couldn't be done.

I went to John Rhodes, the Republican leader in the House, and told him I wanted to set up an ad hoc Committee on Energy. He understood perfectly that we couldn't proceed in the usual way, with the legislation going to different committees and being reported as individual bills. Not only would it take forever, but it would be nitpicked to death.

On the other hand, the relevant House committees and their chairmen would be furious if we simply ignored them. So we worked out a compromise—that the new committee would not be empowered to initiate legislation. Instead, we took the bill, divided it up, and sent it to the respective committees of jurisdiction, including Interstate and Foreign Commerce, Ways and Means, and the Subcommittee on Energy and Power. The package would then come back to the ad hoc committee, which had the right to suggest amendments.

Just about every member in the House wanted to be on the new Energy Committee, and no wonder. Here was a chance to protect the economy of your area and to be a hero back home. Besides, in 1977 energy was a hot issue and people were eager to jump on the bandwagon.

But who should be appointed? Naturally, I included the chairmen and a few key members from the standing committees which dealt with energy. But, as always, there were other considerations as well. Walter Flowers from Alabama came to me and asked to be on the committee. "I'm from a conservative area," he reminded me, "but I give you a vote whenever I can. Don't I deserve to be part of this?" He did. I also included several of the more talented younger members, who had no intention of waiting ten or twenty years before becoming involved in major issues.

We also needed the good will of members who were not on the committee, but who would be voting on the package if and when it reached the floor. I was especially concerned about Joe Waggonner of Louisiana. He was one of the leading conservative Democrats in the House, and I knew he'd be a tough adversary. But if I put him on the committee, he'd have to play ball. I did—and so did he.

To chair the new Committee on Energy, I chose Lud Ashley of Ohio, who had been in the House almost as long as I had. Lud had been an occasional participant at John McCormack's breakfast table, where I was always impressed by his intelligence.* He was one of many members whose abilities were often overlooked because he didn't happen to sit on one of the major committees. As a result, he never had the chance to show his stuff.

But Lud had an excellent reputation among his colleagues. And because he knew nothing about energy, and didn't owe any favors, he could come in as an impartial outsider. His talent was like a light hidden under a bushel, and when it came to the surface, it shone brilliantly. Lud Ashley did a great job.

In addition to organizing the entire operation with the able assistance of Ari Weiss, my brilliant young legislative aide, Lud served as the liaison among the various committees that dealt with energy matters. But his most important achievement was that he avoided creating any dislike of him as an individual. There are always institutional jealousies in the Congress, and if I had given Lud's job to one of the other chairmen, or even to a member of one of the committees that were involved, the whole thing might have dissolved in an ocean of rancor and bitterness. Lud was able to create a real team, united toward a common goal and remarkably free of bickering.

As soon as I named the team, I called in all the Democrats. "You've got to move fast," I told them, "and I'll be biting your ass to make sure you keep going. Remember, I selected you people from over a hundred and fifty applicants. My reputation, our party's reputation, and the reputation of the Congress are all tied up with this legislation. You've got to get it out.

---

* John McCormack, who succeeded Sam Rayburn, was Speaker from 1962 to 1971.

"Now I realize that each of you is opposed to some part of this bill. And I appreciate how much you're concerned about its effect on your own region. Believe me, nobody understands that better than I do. But this is an emergency, and you've got to think in terms of the national interest."

As the package moved forward, President Carter kept coming up with new ideas. We'd get part of the bill taken care of, and then he'd issue another recommendation. Carter was a great idea man, but he didn't always appreciate the difficult process of moving a bill through the House. Even with the new structure, it was a mighty struggle.

The final vote came on August 5, 1977, less than four months after the process had begun, when the president's energy package passed the House by a vote of 244 to 177. The bill succeeded for a number of reasons, but one key element was that I had managed to put the right people together to work it all out.

Unfortunately, the energy bill ran into big problems in the Senate, where two of the most influential Democrats, Russell Long of Louisiana and Henry Jackson of Washington, had strong differences of opinion, not only with the White House, but also with each other. It took more than a year before it was finally passed by the Senate, where it was watered down considerably, thanks to aggressive lobbying on the part of the auto and oil industries. The president wasn't too pleased about the bill he finally got, but as I told him more than once, he was damn lucky to have one at all. . . .

Epilogue

Jimmy Carter's dealings with Congress were among the least successful of those of recent presidents. He simply wasn't willing to play insider politics, to give a little to get a little. After Carter, Tip O'Neill had to face the radically different, conservative policies of the Reagan administration, and he spent much time fighting against Reagan's programs. His efforts were complicated by the reluctance of his liberal colleagues to oppose the highly popular Reagan and the willingness of a great number of conservative southern Democrats to support Reagan's budget-cutting philosophy. However, by the time O'Neill retired from office, the Democrats in Congress had rallied around him to defeat some key Reagan legislation and pass liberal policies of their own.

Speaker Jim Wright: Playing with the Rules

John M. Barry

Now that we have explored the Speaker's position through the perspectives of both the enormous power of the office and his relationship with the president, it is time to see what the office has become today. In 1987 reporter John Barry was given extraordinary access to observe the actions of newly elected Speaker James Wright of Texas. This excerpt from a book describing Wright's two and a half years as Speaker focuses on his efforts to pass a controversial budget bill in 1987. The nature of the arm-twisting and the inventive use of congressional rules to achieve the Speaker's ends may surprise you, but they are not unusual for such difficult legislative battles.

You will gain much more from this selection if you keep in mind the examples of Sam Rayburn and Tip O'Neill from Selections 4.2 and 4.3. Jim Wright, a long-time student of Congress, wanted desperately to become the greatest Speaker in history. Some would say, however, that Wright equated *greatest* with *most powerful.* Notice as you read this account the lack of willingness by Wright and his aides to compromise on the principles of the bill or even to consult widely with uncertain representatives who might be willing to convert to his side. By inventively using the rules, Wright does nothing that could not have been done by earlier Speakers, but in being so willing to accomplish his goals by sheer force, he leaves a spirit of combativeness rather than forgiveness in the minds of opposing or wavering members who are certain to face him on future votes.

The selection begins in the middle of year-end wrangling over a reconciliation bill, a bill that matches the amount Congress has authorized to spend with the amount available to be spent. The 1987 reconciliation bill (also called the Guaranteed Deficit Reduction Act) was the cause of fierce political fighting because the recently passed Gramm-Rudman-Hollings Act compelled the federal government to reduce its budget deficit. Proposed by liberal and moderate Democrats, this reconciliation bill contained controversial meas-

From John M. Barry, *The Ambition and the Power* (New York: Viking, 1989). Copyright © 1989 by John M. Barry. Reprinted by permission of the publisher, Viking Penguin, a division of Penguin Books USA, Inc.

ures on taxes and welfare spending cuts that the White House, House Republicans, and many conservative Democrats objected to. The vote described in this excerpt is over a rule that would determine the terms of the debate and the nature of the bill's amendments. Passage of a rule is a huge hurdle in winning passage of the bill itself.

Members of the House fought so hard because this bill would do nothing less than help determine the direction of government spending for the next year—it would decide how the government would raise revenues and how much money would be raised, and where spending would be cut. The struggle was also intense because this was a partisan fight, and Democratic leaders considered voting on the rule and bill to be a test of party loyalty. Speaker Wright knew he had to prove his leadership, calling it "the most important fight of the year."

JIM CHAPMAN   Democrat from Texas; protégé of Wright.

TONY COELHO   House majority whip; Democrat from California.

THOMAS FOLEY   House majority leader; Democrat from Washington.

NEWT GINGRICH   Partisan Republican from Georgia.

BILL GRAY   Chair of House Budget Committee; Democrat from Pennsylvania.

TRENT LOTT   House minority whip; Republican from Mississippi; now U.S. senator.

JOHN MACK   Aide to Jim Wright.

BUDDY MacKAY   Moderate Democrat from Florida.

ROBERT MICHEL   House minority leader; Republican from Illinois.

DAN ROSTENKOWSKI   Chair of House Ways and Means Committee; Democrat from Illinois.

MARTY RUSSO   Democrat from Illinois; member of Ways and Means Committee; protégé of Rostenkowski.

CHARLIE STENHOLM   Conservative Texas Democrat; led Democratic opposition to the bill.

JIM WRIGHT   Speaker of the House, 1987–1989.

▶ The vote on the rule would come at noon. The task force broke up at eleven. Members flooded the floor for a quorum call at eleven-thirty; both sides' organizations worked the members hard. GOP whip* Trent Lott complained in a floor speech, "In this case [the rule] contains ten amendments, nine of which

---

* House and Senate whips are elected by members of each party to provide party leaders with accurate vote counts, to poll members on various issues, and to keep party members in line on important votes.

you will never get to vote on separately. That's because they are automatically adopted if you accept this rule. This is what is called a self-executing rule. . . . The amendments strike all of the Education and Labor and Ways and Means welfare provisions and then insert a whole, new 148-page compromise which no one on the Rules Committee had seen when we reported this rule. . . . The only thing in this rule that is allowed separate consideration is the Republican substitute. All the Democratic amendments are self-executing, but we have to make our amendments the old-fashioned way, by earning them with separate debates and votes."

But if Democrats were exercising power, Republicans were playing politics. GOP members were unwilling to desert their political mantra of no taxes, wearing buttons that said "Kill taxes." [Robert] Michel had yielded to their sentiment. The GOP substitute did not include his own proposal for $8 billion in taxes; instead it called for a spending freeze.

That sounded good in floor speeches, and allowed Republicans to claim purity in their opposition to taxes. But spending cuts were easier to talk about than make. The deficit had to be cut at least $23 billion. The GOP proposal cut the deficit only $15 billion and left an $8-billion hole where Michel's tax plan would have been. Despite the market crash, despite the outside demands for at the very least cutting the deficit by $23 billion, given a choice between calling for taxes and falling short of the target, Republicans chose to fall short—*35 percent short*. They didn't come close.

All year partisanship had fed on itself, frustrated each side, driven each side apart. *We have just enough votes to be irresponsible*, Jerry Lewis, a member of the GOP leadership, had ruefully observed. Faced with the irresponsibility of the minority, the majority grew contemptuous of it, more determined to govern in spite of it, and more arbitrary; faced with the increasing arbitrariness of the majority, the minority grew more irresponsible, and more destructive of the institution.

While the debate proceeded, members worked the floor. [John] Dingell talked to Buddy Roemer in one part of the chamber while [Charlie] Stenholm hung back. When Dingell moved away, Stenholm moved in.* Then Stenholm with Leath. Then Stenholm with another member, and another, Stenholm ally Tim Penny with his list of names, working Roemer, shaking his hand—they got him!—[Charles] Rangel and [Tony] Coelho looking over their list. Of all the House, less than a dozen would decide the issue, all of them Democrats. Two members and [Thomas] Foley's aide George Kundanis talked to Les AuCoin. Wright talked to AuCoin. Got him!

Now Wright stood in the well of the House, the pit of the amphitheater. The chamber was full as he closed debate: "This bill contains $12 billion in real revenues. I do not think I have heard anybody say they are not real. It also commands some $11 billion in additional deficit reduction through savings. You can

---

* Dingell was a whip pushing for the bill; Stenholm was leading the opposition.

quarrel whether all of that is absolutely real, but most of it is. This bill is not perfect, but it is a start. It is something. It is deeds instead of words. . . . We can say, oh, I would have voted for it if they packaged it a little differently, or if only they had scheduled it on some other day. We can hypothecate any number of theoretical choices. Those are not the choices that we have."

As he spoke, shouts of "VOOOTTTE!" rang out in the hall. "VOOOTTTE!" The time for talking was over. "VVVOOOTTTE!"

Wright continued. "We have been marching up this hill all year, knowing we had to face this choice sooner or later. . . . That Constitution which we have been at pains to honor this year very plainly and unequivocally says that all revenue measures must originate in the House." *VVVVOOOOTTTTE!* "If we perform our duty today, we can bring something real to the bargaining table with the President and with the Senate. . . . If you are serious about deficit reduction, this is your chance. Vote aye on the resolution, aye on the rule, aye on the bill."

The vote on the rule started. The leadership fell behind almost immediately by ten votes, then fifteen. The quick spurt came from opponents who consciously tried to create a surge of momentum on their side; in close votes, with members undecided to the last, such psychological ploys sometimes influence one vote, two votes. That could make the difference. Slowly the Democratic leadership climbed back up, down twelve, down eight, down four, down two. But the mood of the House was running against them. The leadership fell back. No Republicans voted with them. Thirty-five Democrats voted no. Thirty-seven. Forty. *Forty-one!* A loud cheer went up from Republicans! *Forty-one Democrats, combined with all the Republicans, meant an absolute majority.* Then forty-three, forty-four, forty-five. Democrats who had promised to support the leadership if their votes would make the difference had started voting no. Ultimately, forty-eight Democrats voted no.

The final result: 203 in favor, 217 opposed.

On the biggest vote of the year Wright had been beaten! The Democratic juggernaut had been stopped!

The chamber was strangely still and Michel rose and addressed the chair. "Mr. Speaker, under somewhat otherwise normal conditions, noting our unanimous vote on this side, we would be elated with this victory. Mr. Speaker, we do not look upon it that way. . . . It has been my feeling that men of goodwill might bring their divergent thoughts together. . . . Members have attempted to express their desire to give their bipartisan negotiating team a chance. . . . I for one am grateful for the vote defeating the rule, but we are not gloating over it. . . . I would hope that it would signal our intention . . . to work together, hand in glove, in a bipartisan way to come to a final resolution."

Wright, on the floor, rose to respond. "I appreciate what my friend the gentleman from Illinois has suggested. He has been consistent, suggesting all along that we delay, and see if we can get some signal as to what the President will accept before we try to pass anything. If we do that, it puts the total initiative in the hands of the Executive Branch of government over something that the Constitution declared was the primary business of the House of Representatives. I bow to the majority. The majority quite obviously did not want this particular rule . . . [with] a welfare reform bill. . . . Therefore, the Rules Committee will meet at twelve-forty-five and we will be seeking another rule."

Lott rose. "What does this now mean? This matter cannot be brought up again today. . . . Are we going to be in session tomorrow to continue this effort?"

Foley answered him: "As I understand what the gentleman has just told me, it is most unlikely we will be given authority to proceed with a rule filed on the same day. Under those circumstances, it is my duty to inform the House that not only will there be roll calls this afternoon, but the House will come in at ten tomorrow and will stay in session until we finish the reconciliation bill."

Newt Gingrich rose, while hostile Democrats shouted, "Regular order!" *Don't let him speak.* "Regular order!" Lott yielded to him and Gingrich said, "I just want to make a point to every member of this House to watch the next few hours. The leadership brought a rule to the floor that a significant number of Democrats told them was unacceptable. . . . The country will not profit from the next three days being focused on this particular bill and a partisan fight in this particular House when the country is asking for a bipartisan effort and a bipartisan vote won today."

Democrats were furious. *Gingrich. Gingrich the most partisan member of the House complaining about partisanship. Gingrich gloating. God . . . damn . . . him.* Buddy MacKay jumped to his feet and Foley yielded to him. MacKay was burning, raging, his words a hiss: "I just wanted to say on behalf of a number of Democrats who have been trying to proceed in a bipartisan manner that the speech made by the gentleman from Georgia"—all of twenty seconds long—"is one of the most destructive things that could have happened today."

The chamber emptied. Members headed back to their offices. In the Speaker's Lobby, MacKay pushed his way through a flock of reporters and grabbed Wright's arm. "Mr. Speaker, I'm voting with you and I'm going to help you all I can."

This fight had only begun.

The leadership moved across the hallway to H-210. For Wright it was as if all the detritus had been cleared away, all the excuses, all the complications. What was left was pure action. It was what he loved.

"Okay. What did we lose by?"

"Fourteen. We need a change of eight."

Wright named one member. "He said he was with us on the rule and voted no. Get him in here. There are fifteen members who told me personally they would vote for the bill if welfare came out. Put together a meeting of all the moderates we can get, down in 201." He turned to Martin Frost, who asked what he wanted in the new rule, and ordered, "I want it clean."

Foley, Coelho, and [John] Mack each picked up one of the telephones scattered around the room. Wright went over names. They were going to win this thing dammit. They were going forward and would win it. Rostenkowski walked in: "You've got to get hold of Gus Hawkins. You're affecting his legislation."

A few minutes later, Wright returned to his personal office and called him. No, Hawkins, a black, didn't care if welfare came out of the bill now. He hadn't cared if it was in in the first place. Wright's jaw tightened. *That wasn't the information he had been getting.* Bill Gray reaffirmed what he had earlier told Mack: the Black Caucus didn't care. Later Charles Rangel, a black, said it was news to him that the Black Caucus had threatened to vote no if welfare came out.

Then Mack suggested something. A few years earlier [Speaker Tip] O'Neill had lost a rule. It had been a minor fight, and he had formally adjourned the House and then convened it again immediately. That had created, for parliamentary purposes, a new legislative day. The parliamentarian had ruled the action permissible. Then he had brought a new rule onto the floor.

Wright could do the same thing. They did not have to wait until tomorrow. They could bring the rule back this afternoon. There were two reasons to do so. First was convenience; members had made plans to be home tonight and in their districts tomorrow. Now they would have to cancel their appearances and stay in Washington. Second was politics. Overnight the GOP might gain momentum; the next day's papers would trumpet Wright's defeat. That would weaken him and their position in the budget negotiations. But if they voted today and won, the story would be his victory. The defeat would be erased and forgotten.

There was one reason not to do what Mack suggested. The rules prohibited considering a rule the same day the committee acted upon it. Adjournment, followed by convening again, would satisfy the technical parliamentary requirement but would clearly violate the spirit of the rules.

Did Wright want to go forward?

It was a defining moment. Everything, all year, had pointed to this bill. But that was policy. Honorable men could disagree on policy. Wright prided himself on fairness, talked of his love for the institution and his responsibility to protect and represent it. *Procedure was honor codified.* Wright wanted this bill passed. This was his responsibility too. The Constitution required that tax bills begin in the House. To do anything else, even to enter these budget talks, without a bill was to compromise the integrity of the House. *Or was it just ego? Just willfulness? Just wanting to win?* Wright was determined to act. He was caught up in his passions and his nature. *Damn everything else.*

They would do what Mack suggested.

Everything for the rest of the 100th Congress, for as long as Jim Wright would remain Speaker of the House, would flow from Wright's decision.

The decision was not totally arbitrary. If Republicans agreed, for the sake of scheduling convenience, there was no problem. Foley went to check with

Michel. Their conversation was brief. Foley later said, "If Michel had objected, we might have reconsidered. He didn't. He just sort of grunted."

Now Wright sat in his office making calls, looking for votes. . . .

[E]verything else was moving on schedule—the phone calls, the meetings, the strategy. In H-201 twenty moderates waited for him. They had all voted no. He briefed them: "This is where we are. We're getting a rule that takes welfare out. The loss was a bad signal for the market. Before we leave tonight we're going to try to reverse it." He explained that they would formally adjourn, then immediately reconvene, creating a parliamentary fiction of a second legislative day. That would allow them all to have Friday free to return to their districts as planned. In the back of the room a member shook his head in admiration and muttered, "Who digs these things up for him?"

Then they moved on. MacKay said, "Mr. Speaker, we've had a very agonizing week. I was one of those who signed a 'Dear Colleague' urging a no vote. But you might be right as well as I. I see this not as a partisan shot but as an opening in a bipartisan debate. I'm with you."

Other members echoed him. They got to their feet, clustered around Coelho, told him yes or no. Most were yes.

Half an hour later, in the same room, liberals, Ways and Means members, and blacks came in. Wright explained the situation. George Miller, who like his housemate [Marty] Russo had given Wright such a hard time on the budget agreement—except unlike Russo he had never agreed to that budget—complained about the extra $3 billion Appropriations had given to defense spending which would be voted on the following week. Wright offered to give him an amendment to strike it.

"Mr. Speaker," he said, "I don't say this as a threat. I'm not going to let you down. But I don't want an amendment. It would lose. I want you to cut the $3 billion."

"I can't give you that commitment right now. But maybe you have a point."

Then [Dan] Rostenkowski spoke angrily. "The trouble is with the group that was in here before—the whip count. Twenty gave us commitments but ten lied to us."

Already there were hard feelings in the Caucus. They would get harder, and more people would lie. . . .

It was twenty minutes to three. Foley took the floor and moved that "pursuant to clause four of rule sixteen, that when the House adjourns today it adjourn to meet at three-fifteen today."

Rumbling spread across the floor, waves of hostility coming from Republicans. What kind of new outrage was this? Lott rose angrily and demanded a roll-call vote on the motion. The vote was a question of procedural control of the House; Democrats voted yes, Republicans no. Even Stenholm voted with his party, and Foley's motion carried 243–166.

Ed Madigan, the chief deputy GOP whip from Illinois, his words masking his rage, asked, "Do I understand the purpose of our having two legislative days in one calendar day is so that the House avoids the necessity of having a two-thirds majority to be able to consider this? . . . So what we are doing is just to further diminish whatever role the minority is entitled to play in the deliberations of the assembly, is that correct?"

Foley tried to calm the Republicans, saying it was strictly a convenience to allow members to keep appointments in the district for Friday. But there *was* no calming the Republicans. This was a power play, a raw power play, and they knew it. The floor hissed and sizzled with emotion, wrapped within the tight formal constraints of decorum.

Conservative Republican Robert Walker said, "I wonder if the gentleman understands why we would be a little upset. . . . I would say to the gentleman from Washington, I mean we are being terribly abused and this is an outrage in the way the House is being conducted." Democrats on the floor interrupted with sarcastic groans. "Well, you can all moan but I will tell you this is a terrible injustice. For a party that says it stands for fairness and justice you all are abandoning any pretenses of it on the floor today."

Foley repeated, "This is nothing more than an attempt to complete the legislative program without the necessity of an unscheduled Friday session."

William Dannemeyer, another conservative Republican, said, "Genesis tells us that the Lord created the world in seven days. We are now witnessing the creation of an eighth day. I just ask the gentleman, does he have a name for this new creation?"

"Yes," replied Foley. "It is called the Guaranteed Deficit Reduction Act."

The House adjourned at 3:05.

At three-fifteen it reconvened, with all the accoutrements of a new session including a new prayer by the chaplain, and the announcement by Wright with which he opened every session, that "the chair has examined the journal of the last day's proceedings and announces to the House his approval thereof."

Angry Republicans demanded a vote on approving the journal. This was no device to bring members to the floor; this was raw anger. Walker rose again. "Parliamentary inquiry, Mr. Speaker? We are about to cast a vote. Is the journal available for inspection by the members?"

"The journal is indeed available," Wright said evenly.

"Yes," snorted a Democrat. "In shorthand."

The vote was party line again. As soon as the floor had emptied after the vote, a Republican moved to adjourn. Members returned to vote once again. But, inexorably, the Democratic machine marched forward. At four-forty-five in the afternoon, the House approved the second rule, once again on a party-line vote, once again voting on control of the House, once again even Stenholm voting with his party.

Now it was on to the issue at hand. The tax bill. At least things had reduced themselves to the simplest point. *You wanted a tax bill? Here it is. Now pass it.*

The pay-raise issue was growing, spreading. It may have been a phony issue—it would be eliminated in next week's appropriations bill—but it was a big issue. Hometown newspapers were calling members' offices. Walker was on the floor bringing it up, bringing it up: there had been an automatic cost-of-living raise in January, in February the $12,000 raise, now this cost-of-living raise of $2,700: "If the members believe that deficit reduction means raising our own salaries, then vote for this bill. . . . It is plain to the voters that you will have voted to raise their taxes so that you could raise your pay."

It had looked easy, looked assured, with MacKay's help and other moderates. And the members assumed Wright had the votes. But no one knew for sure. Several of the moderates who had told Wright they were with him told Coelho, "I don't want you all to misunderstand—I'm with you on the rule, not the bill."

The debate went forward on the floor while Wright, in his ceremonial office, worked the phone, worked one member after another. "Who the hell am I calling?" he asked at one point an instant before saying, "Hey, how are you?" while an aide wrote down the name and shoved it in front of him. It was an Oklahoma member. Wright told him his colleagues in two adjoining districts were now voting yes, protecting him, and asked, "Do you have any specific personal problem?" But the man had made a campaign pledge to vote against taxes; no favor Wright could do could outweigh that.

Wright got a report that Bill Richardson of New Mexico wanted something personal, all right: to chair the platform committee at the Democratic National Convention. Wright, the convention chairman, would have much to say about appointments but fumed, "I'm not giving that away. A fellow has to understand you don't vote against something like this and get that."

Another man in the room suggested, "You don't have to promise. Just tell him Paul Kirk* will see him next week. You don't have to say it. Have Mack say it. A staffer. That's no commitment."

Wright shook his head no. He wouldn't mislead him like that. But he could go at it another way: "Tell him you heard a member say that that SOB can't ask for something like that if he votes no here."

The leadership tried a new ploy: asking members who were going to vote no to not vote at all. It might be an easier sell than a yes vote, and members could protect themselves by pointing to a no vote on the first rule. But it was also the most delicate of all requests. The whole purpose of a member of Congress is to vote, to represent his constituents. Asking members not to was like asking them to violate their most solemn personal and institutional responsibility. Wright didn't want to ask that. But members got asked that.

---

* Kirk was chair of the Democratic National Committee.

On the floor, the debate moved forward. Off the floor there was a reception for the Minnesota Twins, who had just won the World Series. Days earlier Wright had said he would attend. Now he had other priorities. So did Stenholm, who haunted the chamber throughout the afternoon, with dogged, dogged persistence wearing colleagues down, showing them information on fact sheets, making one argument after another. Republicans could not whip Democrats, nor could Democrats whip Republicans. But Stenholm could whip Democrats. He was doing it.

At 7:05 in the evening, the time allotted to debate ran out. It was time to vote on Michel's substitute. Democrats defeated it 229–182, while Wright went from member to member, checking most closely with those who had told him they would not let the bill lose—they would vote with him if they had to. He pulled Jim Chapman aside, the man who had won the special election in Texas two years earlier largely because of Wright's personal involvement, the man whom Wright had taken care of since, naming him to Steering and Policy as the representative of the freshman class even though he had served in Congress for eighteen months before that class's election. Wright had helped him repeatedly, had just a few weeks earlier blocked an airport bill handled by another ally, Norm Mineta, from the floor until Chapman's personal concerns were taken care of. What Chapman was in the House, he owed to Wright. Chapman assured him that his would not be the vote to beat the bill.

Then came the vote on final passage. Wright took the chair. "The question is on the passage of the bill." he announced.

The first vote was by voice and pro forma—no one would accept its result—yet both sides shouted loudly.

"In the opinion of the chair," Wright announced, "the ayes have it."

"Mr. Speaker! On that I demand the yeas and nays!"

As with every roll-call vote, the panels behind the press gallery, above and behind the Speaker's Rostrum, receded and the wall became a gigantic tote board, with each member's name lit up; a red light beside it would indicate a no vote, green yes. On either side of the chamber a clock began counting from fifteen minutes down to zero while also noting the vote totals. The leadership clustered around the computer terminals—each side had two, one in the front of the chamber, one in the rear—on the floor which would show vote breakdowns by party, region, state, by almost any way of dividing the membership. Already almost the entire membership was in the chamber, eager to finish business and leave for the weekend. Quickly the count rose, and remained close throughout. The Republicans started ahead, Democrats pulled even at 158 each, then fell behind 158–162, then pulled ahead 172–168. Wright seemed in control. Nick Rahall from West Virginia, who disliked what the bill did to coal—eliminating tariffs on certain imported coal, something Rostenkowski stuck in to make Floridians Sam Gibbons and Claude Pepper happy—was surrounded by Coelho, Mary Rose Oakar, Jim Scheuer, and others, and three members literally had their arm on him. *All right, goddammit.* He voted yes. George Hochbrueckner wanted to get on the Committee on Science and Technology; he voted yes. So did Paul Kanjorski; he voted yes. Roy Rowland, the only physician in the House, wanted to get on Energy and Commerce where he could deal with health issues; he voted yes. Tim Valentine wanted to get on Armed Services; he voted yes. All of them had had discussions earlier with Coelho: no promises—a committee assignment wasn't Coelho's to give—but enough. (A week later Steering and Policy created temporary assignments on Science and Technology for Kanjorski and Hochbrueckner; the other committee seats had to wait for the next Congress.)

Coelho squeezed. He had been responsible for naming Tim Penny an at-large whip. Now Coelho told Penny he might have to reconsider Penny's role in the whip organization if he voted no. But Penny was a prince too. He voted no. Buddy MacKay, a close friend of Penny who supported Wright now, thought it was a stupid threat: "What do you need this whip thing for? To put on your résumé? They need us, we don't need them."

Suddenly a red light went up by Chapman's name. *Chapman had voted no.* Members surrounded him now—what was going on? What was wrong? Wright talked to him. Nothing was wrong, Chapman said, it was just that it looked like they wouldn't need his vote after all, things were looking pretty good, so he had voted no. If they needed him, he'd switch. But Chapman had made himself high-profile. Half a dozen other members—Hochbrueckner, Roy Dyson, Wes Watkins, had said the same thing, but they would simply vote late if needed, not attract attention by switching.

Meanwhile, George Miller and Pete Stark, two California liberals, walked into the men's room off the Speaker's Lobby. . . . Stark chaired a Ways and Means subcommittee. Members of committees, certainly Ways and Means subcommittee chairmen, supported their committee's product.

Miller was tense, volatile, an emotional man. He had ridden over in the subway thinking he would vote yes. But that $3 billion in extra defense spending gnawed at him. That afternoon he had told Wright, "I'm not going to let you down." But he remembered back when he and Russo had balked at signing the budget conference agreement and Wright had said unless Reagan signed a tax bill raising $19 billion, defense would get not one penny more. Maybe Wright hadn't meant it literally, but Miller and Russo had taken it literally, had taken it as a deal—even though Miller never signed the budget. Well, now defense had $3 billion more, and taxes would at most be $12 billion. Gray had given his word too. Suddenly Miller thought, *What am I? A horse's ass?* Wright was making a fool of him. He stiffened. Rage flooded through him. Wrought up, tense, almost in tears, he walked onto the floor, shoved his voting card into the slot, and punched the button for no.

Across the chamber, John Mack saw him come in, looked up at the board, saw the red light next to his name. "*George!*" Mack shouted.

Miller waved his arm in dismissal and disgust and stormed out. Mack shouted, "Mr. Foley! Miller just voted no!" Foley ran after him, racing against the elevator, racing to catch Miller before the elevator arrived, caught him, and said, "We're going to lose this thing."

"Tom, I'm just so goddamn mad, just stay away from me."

Foley was taken aback. "I just thought your vote was a mistake."

"I can't help you."

The elevator came. Maybe Coelho would have confronted him, demanded that he explain, gotten him back into the chamber where colleagues would have surrounded him. Or maybe Miller would have shoved him away. Foley watched him step onto the elevator. A moment later, Mack looked up at Stark's name. *Stark had voted no.*

On the other side of the chamber, Russo came in. He blamed the defeat of the rule on Wright himself, on Wright's comment in the task force that he would get a second rule if the first one lost. He was furious over the defense spending too. From Chicago and on Ways and Means, he had almost a father-and-son relationship with Rostenkowski. This was Rostenkowski's bill. Russo walked in, voted, walked out, and went straight to the airport. It was seven-thirty now. There was an eight o'clock flight to Chicago. He could make it easily. A Wright ally checked the board—*Russo voted no*—then ran up to Rostenkowski and jammed his finger into Rostenkowski's chest. "Your man f___d us!" he shouted. "Your man!"

Rostenkowski, dumbfounded, looked up at the red light by Russo's name.

Brian Donnelly rushed to the rostrum and told Wright, "If you're going to win this thing, you better get out of the chair and down on the floor."

Wright hurried down, hurried over to Rostenkowski. The leadership had computer printouts of votes, knew who had said yes but hadn't voted yes. But the printouts told you who but they didn't say where. There were 435 members of the House, and almost all of them were now swirling, wondering—or hiding. *Try to find someone on the floor who doesn't want to be found.* Wright started looking for those who had said they'd help if needed. His votes were in the back row. From the other side of the chamber Bob Michel saw the commotion, looked up at the board and saw Russo's vote, and thought, *We're going to win this thing.*

The clock counting down the remaining time stood at 0:00. Where the hell was Chapman? The vote stood 201 for the bill, 202 opposed, then 201 to 204.

The time on the clock didn't matter really. The rules said a minimum of fifteen minutes was required, but the vote stayed open at the discretion of the Speaker. The vote could stay open forever. If it was a tie, the Speaker could vote. *Where was Chapman?* Now it was 202 to 204, 203 to 204, as those members who had promised not to let Wright lose voted yes; 204 to 204. *Thank God! The Speaker could save the bill!* But suddenly the other side came up with two votes: 204 to

206. Then it was 205 to 206, 205 to 206, 205 to 206. *Where the hell was Chapman? Was he on the floor? Why wasn't he on the floor?*

"Chapman's in the cloakroom!"

Coelho ran in after him. At first he could not find him. The two cloakrooms, one Democratic, one Republican, fold around the outside of the chamber. Along one wall was a line of telephone booths; in the corner, in the middle of the cloakroom, was a hot-dog stand. Chapman was in neither area. Then Coelho looked around the corner. In the far end, on a couch, in an area where the overhead light bulb had been removed so it was darker than the rest of the room so members could lie on a couch and sleep, was Chapman. Coelho said they needed him. Chapman shook his head. He wasn't coming out.

Outside in the chamber the vote remained 205 to 206. The Republicans were exuberant, the chamber raucous. Abruptly a shout rang out from the GOP: "Make it in order!" It quickly became a refrain. "ORDER!" "MAKE IT IN ORDER!" *Make the vote final.* But a leadership aide ran up to the chair and told Wright that Russo had made a mistake, was on his way back from the airport, hold the vote for Russo. [Dave] Bonior, as if to confirm it, held up one finger and shouted, "ONE MORE!" It was a routine announcement, telling the chair to hold the vote open for someone hurrying from his office across the street. Bonior was playing for time. Jim Moody echoed, "ONE MORE!"

Coelho and Chapman argued, then Coelho came out and found Mack. "He's not coming out!" Coelho hissed. "He gave the commitment to the Speaker, not to me. You go in after him."

The chorus of Republicans in the chamber grew louder and louder. Wright announced, his voice absolutely calm, "We are proceeding under regular order. The chair has been advised that there are members on the way who desire to vote. The chair will accommodate their wishes."

The floor fell into a strange hush, a wild stillness. Trent Lott now ran across the chamber, up the aisle on the Democratic side, out into the corridor, stood outside and looked into the night, down the great stairway that leads to the plaza, then returned and shouted to the chamber at large, not to the chair, "There is no one out there, no one in sight!"

Make it in order! Make it in order! MAKE IT IN ORDER!

The clock ticked. Wright started to speak. Mike Lowry ran to the front of the chamber, playing for time. "Mr. Speaker, how am I recorded?"

Bonior echoed him. "Mr. Speaker, how am I recorded?" Then Martin Frost. Then Bill Ford.

The parliamentarian advised Wright that, ever since the electronic voting system began, such requests were considered dilatory. Mack was in the cloakroom, leaning on Chapman, leaning on him, leaning on him, not with threats but with *You owe it to him. You can't let this happen to him. Everything he's done for you, you've got to do this for him.* Wright announced, "The chair will announce that there is no procedure for members to ask how they are recorded.

Wright had acted within the rules. At eight-twenty-five the House adjourned. . . .

At one o'clock in the morning, now Friday, Rostenkowski was on the phone to Miller, raging at him not for the vote—every member's entitled to vote how he wants—but for the lack of warning. If he had told someone they could have planned for it. "You don't want to wake up out of a sound sleep with him on the other end of the phone," Miller later said. "He was livid."

Then Rostenkowski called Russo in Chicago, and raged at him. Russo loved the House, really loved it, loved working with his colleagues, loved being part of the leadership. Now where would he be? What kind of future did he have in the House? What had he done to himself? At two-thirty in the morning, upset, distraught, maybe he had had one or two, he called Coelho.

There was another phone call too. Early Saturday morning George Miller lay asleep at home in California. The phone rang and his wife woke him. It was the Speaker. Wright was calling to say he would take out the extra $3 billion in defense spending. Of Miller's vote Wright said only, "It's all behind us. Let's work together."

Miller thanked him and hung up, more puzzled than ever about the kind of man Wright was. *After what I did to him, he's doing this for me?* It didn't make sense. It didn't make any sense. Suddenly he thought that Wright was a larger man than he had believed, a larger man than he had shown.

Perhaps Wright had had to do it. On Friday several members representing the Democratic Study Group asked him to take it out. Perhaps Wright was manipulating Miller, getting mileage out of what he would do anyway. Or was he? Why call Miller, who had just hurt him so badly? *Why?* There was a mystery to Wright. Miller sat in bed, thinking, laughing, *No one's scoped Wright out yet. He's wild. Ha! Wild! And, yes, maybe he could be a great Speaker.*

Epilogue

After negotiations among the House, Senate, and White House, in December 1987 Congress came to a two-year budget agreement that raised taxes, cut welfare spending, and contained many provisions that Jim Wright had fought for. Wright largely won this battle, but he lost the proverbial war: In 1989 he became the first Speaker to resign under pressure, over charges of financial misconduct. The 1987 budget battle was the beginning of Wright's fall, for his partisanship and his willingness to steamroll the opposition poisoned his relations with the Republicans. Led by Newt Gingrich, the Republicans attacked Wright freely over the ethics allegations, and congressional Democrats were reluctant to come to Wright's defense. Moreover, Wright's majority whip, Tony Coehlo, was also forced to resign in 1989 after separate charges of violating congressional ethics. This feeding

frenzy finally died down after the Democrats tried to charge Gingrich with financial misconduct concerning a book he wrote; Gingrich, however, survived the
criticism and in March 1989 was named minority whip.

After Wright's resignation, majority leader Tom Foley of Washington was installed as Speaker. Now there is occasional criticism of his work as being too conciliatory to the Republicans and too media oriented. Does this mean he will likely
be more or less successful than Wright in the long run?

4.5

A Season of Governing

Richard F. Fenno, Jr.

"Who's Dan Quayle?" everyone asked in 1988 when George Bush chose his running mate. Political scientist Richard Fenno was fortunate already to be studying this young and relatively unknown Indiana senator. This selection is an excerpt from Fenno's account of the freshman senator in 1982, his second year in office, when he was trying to pass the Job Training Partnership Act (S 2036). The bill was intended to replace the Comprehensive Employment and Training Act (CETA), which was about to expire. This selection describes both the experiences of a novice senator learning his way around and the dynamics of the committee/subcommittee process.

In many respects, this selection is the other side of the coin described in Selection 4.1. Quayle was, like Hiler, swept into office by the Reagan electoral revolution of 1980. He, also, was a newcomer faced with the challenge of learning a very difficult job. But unlike Hiler, Quayle was in the majority party in the Senate. (The Republicans had a majority in the Senate from 1981 to 1987.) And his position served as a springboard to the vice-presidency. But as you read this piece, consider whether life was appreciably better for Quayle than it was for Hiler. You will see that to accomplish his goals, Quayle had to compromise his position, curry favor with more powerful members of his own party, worry about the actions and intentions of the White House, and hope for a little luck. Even with the apparent advantages of having his own party control the Senate and the White House, Quayle decided that final passage could be achieved only if he united with a prominent liberal, Ted Kennedy.

This selection also helps us to understand how Congress works. There was a time when the main source of power resided in the substantive committees to which all legislation must be referred. As a result of congressional reforms in the 1970s, however, the power in the Senate now lies in the smaller subcommittees. This means that the chances of getting a bill passed as originally worded depend on a handful of legislators in the subcommittees. This is where we see Quayle working on his job-training bill. His work in the markup stage of the subcommittee, the stage in which the bill is revised, shows that he had to be more concerned with the process of getting the bill passed than with the actual wording of the legislation. By changing the wording of the bill, and accepting or rejecting various amendment proposals, Quayle was able to increase his allies and thus increase the chances for victory. Before becoming law, however, the bill had to pass the full Senate, the House, and be signed by the president. Even if that happened, would the changes in the bill's wording lessen its chance for effectiveness?

As the selection begins, the bill has just been passed out of the subcommittee to the full committee by a 7–0 vote. And control of the bill has moved from subcommittee chair Dan Quayle to Labor Committee Chair Orrin Hatch.

ALBERT ANGRISANI   Assistant secretary of labor.

JAMES BAKER   White House chief of staff.

KENNETH DUBERSTEIN   Reagan's congressional liaison chief.

RAYMOND DONOVAN   Secretary of labor.

ROBERT GUTTMAN   Staff director of the Subcommittee on Employment and Productivity.

ORRIN HATCH   Republican senator from Utah; chair of the Labor and Human Resources Committee.

EDWARD M. KENNEDY   Democratic senator from Massachusetts; ranking minority member on the Labor and Human Resources Committee.

DAN QUAYLE   Republican senator from Indiana; chair of the Subcommittee on Employment and Productivity.

RONALD REAGAN   President of the United States, 1981–1989.

DAVID STOCKMAN   Reagan's budget director, 1981–1985.

▶ Subcommittee passage of S 2036 changed the negotiating context for Dan Quayle. He had gained policy momentum; but he had lost procedural control. Formal leverage had passed to the full committee chairman. And the chairman proposed to use it to bring administration views into play. One of [Orrin] Hatch's aides described the situation.

Now the ball was in Hatch's court. The administration still opposed the bill. Hatch told Quayle, "If you don't get together with the administration, I'll sit on the bill forever." The administration was pleased to hear him talk this way. But at the same time, he was on the phone to

Ed Meese telling him the administration was going to have to give a
little. He was basically sympathetic to Quayle's position, but there was
no way he was going to hold that markup until they worked out an
agreement. He kept a low profile. He was trying to get the warring
factions together, to get them around the table . . . [to get] a "Treaty
of Jobs."

Just as Quayle had manipulated Hatch in the subcommittee setting, Hatch was manipulating Quayle in the full committee setting.

"I don't know where we are on the jobs bill," said Quayle nearly three weeks after markup. "I don't know whether Hatch will call a [full committee] markup. . . . I talked with him last night. He said, 'We've got to have the administration.' I said, 'You'll never get the administration until you actually have a bill.'" He was typically optimistic about his ability to get a bill.

Oh, there's no problem at all in committee. I may lose [John] East
[R-N.C.] and [Gordon] Humphrey [R-N.H.]. But all the others are for it.
. . . I had no idea it would take so long and be so tedious and petty
when I started. But we'll get a jobs bill.

While his committee chairman temporized, however, the impatient subcommittee chairman remained, as one observer put it, "in orbit."

Hatch's desire for some kind of "treaty" was certainly on target. When the markup ended, the subcommittee chairman and the Labor Department were, indeed, at war. The secretary and the assistant secretary had flatly and formally opposed S 2036. But the subcommittee had ridden roughshod over their objections in passing the bill. The losers immediately began talking veto. Quayle's view was that,

The Labor Department ruined things with their press release just be-
fore markup saying what they would and would not accept. That was
stupid. They took everything off the table. The people down there are
not very smart about dealing with the Hill. . . . I've given up dealing
with the Department of Labor. The Department of Labor is impossible
to deal with.

The Hatch staffers saw two sides to the situation. "The administration thought Quayle was impetuous and presumptuous," said one. "Quayle felt the administration had had its chance to get aboard and had refused." In any case it was a standoff. As a subcommittee staffer put it the day after markup, "Now each side will make the other sweat and we'll see who blinks."

In view of the administration's hostility to S 2036, the Quayle-Kennedy bill, I asked the Indiana senator if he had any regrets about his alliance with the senator from Massachusetts. There were none. "If I had gone it alone," he said,

my bill would have been treated by Hatch and by the administration
as just another bill. They would have considered their own bills and

some time or other, maybe, they would have considered my bill. In order to elevate it the way I wanted to, I needed a bipartisan bill. In order to avoid bitterness and rancor and name calling in getting the bill out of committee, I needed a bipartisan bill. In order to be able to deal with the House effectively, I had to be bipartisan. So I think it was the right thing to do. But I've gotten into a lot of trouble over it. It's a jungle out there.

He conceded that a different Democrat might have made for a smoother path.

The Reagan administration, of course, doesn't like Kennedy. . . . Well, he's been around here a long time and he occupies some very important positions. In my case, he is the ranking member of the committee. If someone else was in that position, things might have been easier. After all, [Raymond] Donovan thinks Kennedy wants to put him in jail. Hypothetically, if Eagleton [Tom Eagleton, D-Mo.,] had been the ranking member, I would have the benefits of bipartisanship without the drawbacks. Kennedy has made it more difficult. There's no doubt about that. But I've enjoyed working with him. He's a lot better than his image. And he's given up a lot. You heard him say in markup that the bill isn't what he would want. It isn't. It's a real compromise.

For the time being, he would have to attend to his relations with the administration. But he did not intend to abandon his bipartisan strategy in the process.

The political standoff with the administration lasted three weeks. During that period neither Dan Quayle nor his staff heard from or dealt with the Labor Department. Bob Guttman and his counterpart on the Hatch staff, Kris Iverson, cooperated to keep track of the substantive disagreements between S 2036 and the administration and to present options to their principals.

Here, too, the subcommittee markup had changed the context. . . .

[Now] the focus of the subcommittee chairman's strategy shifted from the Labor Department to the higher echelons of the administration. "If there is no bill, there will be an extension of CETA," said an aide the day after markup. "The president knows he'll never get as good a bill as this one two years from now. So our bill is the only game in town for him. We're hoping he sees it that way." To that point, however, there was no evidence of any presidential involvement in the matter. Nor was there any evidence that anyone in the White House had yet grasped the situation from the president's perspective. But the Quayle people believed that, from the presidential perspective, subcommittee passage of S 2036 had raised public expectations sufficiently to rule out the status quo as a viable option. The president, they believed, would want—perhaps need—a bill.

"I can't imagine they'd veto," said Quayle. "[S 2036] would give people some-thing to run on," he explained, thinking ahead to Republican chances in the fall elections.

It would help with the rich/poor thing; the bill helps do something about the poor. It would help with unemployment; the bill helps people without jobs. It will help with the whole compassion argument. It's a natural. You'd think the people down there would see it. But they don't—the bastards.

The problem, Quayle thought, was that the top-level White House people had not yet focused on the situation. "I've stopped dealing with the Depart-ment of Labor. I haven't had any communication with them since the markup. I will only deal with the White House. . . . But I can't tell where I am with the White House. It's not a high priority with them. . . . They aren't paying atten-tion."

On May 11, two and a half weeks after the markup, something happened to change that situation. President Reagan called Senator Quayle personally about another bill, to ask him to withdraw a proposed amendment regarding the MX missile. Quayle agreed. And he seized the opportunity to do what he had been unable to do several weeks earlier—talk to the president about his job training bill. "I told him that I thought we were spending too much money on things like MX, but that I wouldn't do anything to harm his negotiations," Quayle re-counted a day later.

Then I said, "While I've got you here, there's something coming up I want to alert you to"—and I told him about the jobs bill. I told him it had passed the committee 7–0. I told him all the money went to the PICs [private industry councils], with 51 percent [membership of] busi-ness. I told him the governors would have more say than before. I told him that we had an absolute prohibition against public service jobs. I told him that 90 percent of the money went for training. He said, "If what you say is true, that sounds like something we should support." I told him that if we didn't get a jobs bill, we'd get CETA. He said he didn't want that and that he'd speak to some people about it. I didn't push him. I just wanted to tell him about it. We'll see what happens.

When it was all over Quayle looked backed on the chance conversation and said,

I don't know what would have happened if Reagan hadn't called me about the MX missile that day. That's when I asked him, "What about the job training program? We've got a good program." He said, "I'm for that, and I'll look into it." Right after that, things started to move. The administration started to change.

Two days after the call, Quayle was invited to the White House by the president's top political person, Chief of Staff James Baker, for a high-level negotiation on the jobs bill.

White House intervention changed the context of negotiation again. It moved the entire negotiation to a new level within the administration and brought new players into the picture. Quayle gained important new allies. The political people, Chief of Staff Baker and Congressional Liaison Chief Kenneth Duberstein, also wanted a bill and they began exerting pressure in that direction. But new opponents emerged as well. Resistance came, now, from Budget Director [David] Stockman and Counsel to the President Edwin Meese. "The administration is of two minds," said a Hatch staffer. "The budget people want to pick up money wherever they can; and they would be very happy to save $3.5 billion. But the political people want a program to show that the president isn't against the disadvantaged."

The Labor Department had ceased to be an independent force—both because of White House intervention and because Labor Secretary Donovan had become embroiled in an increasingly damaging dispute with the Judiciary Committee over his conduct as a private contractor. Shortly before the White House meeting, in fact, Orrin Hatch had called for Donovan's resignation because of it. Their relationship had become enveloped in bitterness. Hatch no longer could do business with Donovan. He could do business with Assistant Secretary [Albert] Angrisani. But Angrisani, who had insisted on dealing only with Hatch and not Quayle, had become dependent for his instructions on the White House. He remained a dogged but crippled combatant.

The White House meeting on the morning of May 13 was attended by Quayle, Hatch, Baker, Stockman, Duberstein, Donovan, Angrisani, and Pam Turner, a Duberstein assistant. "It turned out that the principals were Stockman and myself," said Quayle later,

> I had the most trouble with Stockman—my friend! He was adamantly opposed to a summer youth program, and he did not like the idea of spending money on supportive services. Jim Baker wanted a bill. He's very different from Meese. When I talked to Meese, he wanted to know just what was in the bill. He was interested in its purity and didn't want any bill that wasn't pure. Baker wanted to get together to work out an agreement. That's the way you run the government. You don't run it on ideology. You don't get anywhere if you are hung up on purity.

A Quayle staffer added that the meeting had produced "some movement."

> The legislative people in the White House made it clear they wanted a new jobs bill. . . . Baker told the Labor Department to "move toward" a bill. Donovan and Angrisani had to be given some support. After all, they have been running around saying the bill ought to be vetoed.

It was agreed that the two senators and their staffs would meet that same afternoon with Angrisani and Turner to reach agreement on such amendments to S 2036 as would be necessary to produce administration support.

After this follow-up meeting, the Quayle and Hatch people believed they had an agreement with Angrisani on the payments issue. "Supportive services" to trainees and program administration would be increased and capped at 30 percent of the available funds. The list of likely supportive services would be changed from "health care, transportation, temporary shelter, child care, financial counseling, and necessary cash assistance payments to individuals to enable them to participate in training" to "in-kind provision, cash assistance or loans for transportation, child care, meals, financial counseling or other *reasonable* expenses required for participation in the training program." [Emphasis added.] "Wages, allowances, and stipends" would be prohibited, but with an explicit exception made for a summer youth program.

Accordingly, that evening, the Quayle enterprise began preparing for full committee markup. "Stockman was the one who was tough on this," said Quayle. "I'm going to call him and tell him not to throw a monkey wrench into it." He added, "And I've got to get [Robert] Stafford's proxy. I've talked to him about it once already." "I think we've got an agreement," echoed Guttman. "We'll have to see how it goes down with the Democrats. I think if Dan gets in touch with Kennedy right now, that will help." He was anticipating only two votes in markup—one on the summer youth program, one on the 70/30 agreement.

But Assistant Secretary of Labor Angrisani had a different interpretation of the agreement. He drafted a set of amendments that included an absolute prohibition on wages and contained no mention of a summer youth program. He prepared a letter for Secretary Donovan stating that the administration would support S 2036 if all its amendments were approved, and that the administration would "withhold its support" if its amendments were not passed. In the letter, Donovan also said that the summer youth proposal was being "reviewed . . . outside the provisions of this letter."

The letter—with "withhold" changed to "reconsider"—went to each of the executive branch participants in the White House meeting and to Meese. Angrisani added his comment: "These documents fulfill the offer made by the Administration to Senators Hatch and Quayle. To date they have not officially communicated their acceptance or rejection of these Amendments." As a courtesy to Hatch, Angrisani sent Iverson a copy of these communications. As a snub to Quayle, he made Guttman go down to the Labor Department to get copies. When he read the documents, Guttman concluded that "Angrisani has reneged. . . . He won't budge until he has unambiguous instructions from the White House. Until he does, he will just keep going back to the department's original position. That's what he's done. Why he made a deal on Thursday, I don't know."

The Labor Department's continuing inability to bargain confirmed the wisdom of Quayle's decision not to deal with it. So he produced his version of the agreement and sent the relevant amendments to Chief of Staff Baker at the White House, with copies to the other participants. Its cover letter set forth the political realities as the subcommittee chairman saw them.

> *I believe these amendments can pass in the Committee, but only if there is public assurance that the Administration will support the bill with these amendments included.*
>
> *The amendments include a prohibition of wages, allowances and stipends but with an exception for a tightly drawn summer youth program. Support for a summer youth program in the Committee is sufficiently strong that we cannot report a bill that does not authorize such a program. The key question therefore is whether you can support a wage prohibition with the summer youth exception.*

With the conflicting Angrisani interpretation-plus-amendments and the Quayle interpretation-plus-amendments sitting on his desk, Baker did nothing.

Several days after Quayle's letter to Baker, a top subcommittee staffer expressed concern about the effect of delay on the chances for committee approval. He was particularly worried about swing voter Lowell Weicker. "At the time we offered our amendments, we thought we could sell them to the committee," he said.

> *I had talked to people close to Weicker and had gotten the idea that he would go for our package. He wants a summer program to campaign on this summer. But we needed quick and enthusiastic support for it by the administration. Baker hasn't answered the letter. The Kennedy people have lobbied Weicker. . . . Timing is everything. The time for taking him aside, explaining it, and asking for his vote may have passed.*

Chairman Hatch apparently shared these concerns about timing. He had scheduled a full committee markup for May 26. On May 24 Stockman asked for a postponement of "just one more day while we work things out."

At this point the impatient subcommittee chairman once again became a prime force for action. As he described it, "We weren't getting anywhere with Angrisani. They wanted us to delay the markup again. Hatch wanted to delay it. I said to him, 'No, we can't do that again. We've got to go ahead.'" Hatch agreed. He refused Stockman's request. By this time, the Quayle people believed that, because of his bitter feud with Secretary Donovan, Orrin Hatch's relationship with the Labor Department had soured and that his actions had to be interpreted in that light. He too, they believed, had become impatient with the department. "The Donovan blowup is a lot more important than all the amendments," said a Quayle staffer.

The markup deadline put pressure on all parties. Quayle applied added pressure to ensure a successful markup. He may not have realized how important the outcome would be to his career. But more than any participant he wanted a bill. He also knew that more than anyone else's the bill he got would be his. He knew he needed administration support for that bill. He believed that such a bill was very much in the president's interest, too. He pressed this line of argument with the White House on May 25.

> *I said to myself, "I don't have to deal with Angrisani." So I called Jim Baker. And I said to him, "You've got to do something if you want a bill. The Labor Department is killing it. It's your president who will be hurt. We are going to hold a markup tomorrow. Can't we do something?" Baker said that the Labor Department was their administrator, that they couldn't go around them. But he said the decision would be made in the White House. He said they would pretend to deal with the Labor Department, while really making the decision themselves. I called him in the morning. At 2:30 we had a meeting.*

"Hatch was not happy when Dan called and said they were going [to the White House] to meet with Donovan," laughed a staffer. "But Dan said, 'I'll protect you.'" More as allies, now, than as competitors, they went to negotiate for a jobs bill—Hatch to draw the lines, Quayle to fight the battle.

The participants in the second White House meeting were Baker, Quayle, Hatch, Donovan, Stockman, Duberstein, Turner, and Assistant Secretary of Labor for Congressional Relations Don Shasteen. Once again, in Quayle's words, "The principals were Stockman and myself." He recalled,

> *Donovan and Shasteen were there, but they sort of sat off to one side. That was fine with me. Donovan is very hard to bargain with. He's used to dealing with those guys up in New Jersey. Stockman and I were the principals. Stockman agreed to a separate summer program and I agreed to try to get the wage prohibition. I said, "I don't know if I can sell it, but I'll try. If we lose that in committee, we may stop the markup, regroup, and see what we can do." Then I left for Atlanta.*

On the way to the airport from the White House, he called to report the deal to staff chief Guttman.

The essence of the deal was that the summer youth program was added to the bill "as a separate title, creating a separate and free standing program to be authorized at a level of 'such sums as may be necessary,'" that no prohibition against wages would be placed in that title, but that an absolute prohibition against wages would be applied to all other titles of the bill. The administration won its central position regarding the wage prohibition and thus maintained its stand against a job training bill that looked like "CETA revisited." The price it paid was a summer program it did not want, with wages it did not want. But it was able to separate that program from the main body of the bill. Quayle, on the other hand, got the summer program, "the sweetener" he needed, but at the expense of a programmatic separation from his training bill that he never contemplated and never wanted. He also paid the price of a total wage ban that he had heretofore resisted as the one provision that could cost him his majority in the full committee.

A "Memo of Understanding" from Duberstein to Quayle also contained a reaffirmation "of our previous agreement that 70 percent of program funding should be dedicated to training and that 30 percent of program funding shall be dedicated to administrative and support services." It also included an agreement that if the amendments incorporating these several provisions "shall tie or fail" in committee, "Hatch will recess the committee to allow further discussions."

Guttman's reaction to Quayle's phone call was one of agony and dismay—philosophically and politically. "It's the worst of both worlds," he expostulated to Quayle at the other end of the line.

> When you separate the summer program from the training and from all the quality control—no performance standards, no flexibility, no local initiative—you get a crummy program. You give up the notion of a block grant with which we started and create another categorical program. You lose the argument on the merits. A separate summer program is not meritorious. Maybe it will appeal to people for that reason. It's politically attractive and it will just get pumped up and pumped up with money. That's where your costs will go. It's an income-maintenance program, not a training program. You will lose the programmatic people . . . because programmatically it's not good. But you may attract people . . . who don't care about the program. We'll be going back to all the things we talked about.

It was the quintessential plea from the staff expert to the politician, a plea for programmatic coherence in the face of coalition-building pressures. It was, of course, the politician who most wanted the bill and who, therefore, needed to bargain for support. And as Quayle himself had put it, "You can't get anywhere if you are hung up on purity." Privately, no doubt, he and Guttman had drawn the line against the administration many times. But in the more complex world the line had proven impossible to hold. And Guttman's outburst provided a measure of how much Quayle had forsaken their blueprint in the end.

Guttman expressed political reservations as well. "You'll have a hard time selling the wage prohibition," he continued. "The Democrats have been holding their staff meetings all day telling each other to hang together on that one. You'll have trouble with Weicker and probably Stafford on it, too. . . . It's impossible to predict how it will go. You just can't tell." But, he concluded, "I'll start peddling it in the morning to each of the Democrats and we'll see if it sells to any of them." Quayle said he would call Weicker when he got to Atlanta. The conversation ended.

Guttman was visibly upset. But within a catch of his breath he turned from disappointed architect to loyal builder. "It stinks," he said. "It will take us back to the same bad old programs. They'll pump it up with money without any controls. But the real problem is: Can we get nine votes for it?" Another subcommittee staffer reacted similarly. "Talk about CETA revisited! That's just what we tried to get away from." But a few minutes later she was heard saying, "Whatever Senator Quayle is for, we are for. Whatever he wants to get through, that's what we'll try to get through." The griping was over; the enterprise turned to its new task, preparing for markup.

To conclude Quayle's own account of his activities, he made two phone calls as soon as he reached Atlanta—one to Kennedy, one to Weicker.

> I called Kennedy and had a brief conversation. He was at dinner. I told him what had happened. I said, "I hope you won't give me too much trouble tomorrow. I need this one. I hope you won't get too rambunctious. I know you are opposed [to the wage prohibition], but I need some room." He said, "You'll do all right," or something like that. I called Weicker, filled him in briefly and asked if I could come around and talk with him when I got back the next day. He said, "Sure."

With the conservatives now on board, with the administration and with moderate Senator Stafford's proxy in his pocket, Quayle's remaining Republican uncertainty lay in the attitude of Lowell Weicker—"the key, the swing vote in the committee," as Quayle put it.

The next morning, he went to Weicker's office.

> I explained the situation to him. He said, "If that's the best you can do, I'll be with you." I thought I had him, but I did not know for sure that I had him. He's not the kind of person who says, "I will support you whatever bill you come up with." So I felt comfortable going into the markup.

His success in the markup would depend less on what he did in the meeting than what he had done before that. But the markup was his biggest governing test yet. And unpredictability remained.

Observations and Reflections: Full Committee Markup

In midafternoon on May 26, the members of the Labor and Human Resources Committee and their staffs crowded into a small (fifteen by twenty-five feet) room just off the Senate floor on the West Front of the Capitol. The senators sat nose to nose around a long table; the staffers stood against the wall behind their principals. Three committee members did not come at all; three others stayed very briefly; nine remained throughout most of the one hour and twenty-five minute session. Among the nine were all seven members of the subcommittee, and they monopolized the proceedings. Thirty amendments were offered; most of them were dispatched without debate, three were debated at some length, and four drew recorded votes.

As the meeting begins, Chairman Hatch sits at the head of the table with the gavel—Quayle on one side of him, Kennedy on the other. "We have come a long way," he says. Then, "I turn to Senator Quayle who has worked so long and hard on this. I hope we can help Senator Quayle today and get this matter resolved." Quayle repeats that it has been "a rather long process," and moves to the heart of the matter.

> *Although there has been a consensus developed in the Congress, we have not had agreement from the Administration. We have worked in the past to get an agreement and have been unsuccessful. I am glad to report we do have an accommodation on the summer program with the administration which has had a change of position and of heart. . . . It has been suggested and I agree that we would put in a prohibition on the payment of wages in the training program, which will be in every title except the new title, Summer Employment. I believe this is a good compromise. . . . I hope when the time comes for debate on these amendments everyone will keep their powder dry and listen to the arguments and support them.*

Kennedy, [Howard] Metzenbaum, and [Claiborne] Pell then praise Quayle for his leadership of the legislative effort. As he has in every public forum so far, Kennedy is especially generous in his praise.

> *Senator Quayle has spent hours on this issue. He has taken his subcommittee to different parts of this country. He has solicited ideas from a number of us on this side of the aisle. He has been willing to accommodate many of the points we have made. He has worked in good faith all the way through these negotiations.*

Metzenbaum "commends" the Indiana senator "for his efforts to move forward" and calls him "sensitive to the problem." Pell "congratulates" him because "he has combined the Democratic views and the Republican views." They take cognizance of Quayle's battles with the administration, which have been, to a degree, their battles too. After all, S 2036 is not an administration bill spoonfed to the Congress. It is a home-grown bill, a congressional initiative—and a bipartisan one at that. Kennedy notes that "the toughest negotiators . . . appeared to be members of the administration." Metzenbaum observes that Quayle "is acting under some restraints, which are obvious, from the administration." The atmosphere is informal and cordial, and the stakes seem well understood.

After the easy passage of a dozen amendments—including Nickles's vocational education provision and Hawkins's loan fund—Kennedy argues for greater flexibility under the 70/30 division in the definition of "supportive services." He argues that different areas have different needs for financial aid. Quayle says he thinks the phrase "reasonable expenses" will ensure flexibility, but he says he will make a "good-faith effort to try and work out, with the people whom I have to deal with, an exception." Saying that "we've gone around quite a bit on this particular one, " Kennedy accepts Quayle's assurances.

"The next two [amendments] go together," says Quayle as he offers the amendments establishing a summer youth program and prohibiting the payment of wages in the rest of the bill. "This is the basic compromise," he begins.

> *A compromise is a compromise. It is not what I prefer. It is not everything the administration prefers, but here is what it does. For the first time, if we are able to pass these amendments, we will have the support of the administration, which I think is critical to the passage of this bill and having the president sign it. There is no doubt that if he would veto a bill, in all probability it would be sustained. Everybody at this table in good-faith effort has worked exceedingly hard to get a training and unemployment bill through. These amendments are a compromise that have been worked out with the administration because they have been, up until yesterday, in opposition to a summer employment training program and . . . in opposition to paying wages through a summer employment training program.*

Again, he stresses that "reasonable expenses," to be determined by the local Private Industry Councils, provide flexibility in aiding people who need help in getting training. And he ends his brief discussion: "Friends, this is the best I could do. I hope you will support me." He is all business. There is none of the anti-administration or Hatch-teasing friskiness that marked his debut in the subcommittee.

Metzenbaum praises Quayle ("It has not been an easy task for him."), speaks at length about the necessity of a summer program and says that, except for the wage prohibition, he will support the bill. Kennedy praises Quayle for the summer program but argues at length that the wage prohibition and "the stringent formula" for supportive services plus the 30 percent cap, puts the program "in a straightjacket" as far as the poor are concerned. The best training program, he argues, is a long-term program, and without financial support the poor will be unable to take advantage of the best training programs. It is a strong speech. Quayle refers again to the flexibility of the "reasonable expenses" provision. Kennedy says, "We've been talking to each other over a long period of time and have been unable to convince each other." At that moment there are nine senators present—seven subcommittee members, Weicker, and Jennings Randolph, D-W. Va. The summer program is approved by voice vote, but Kennedy asks for a roll-call vote on the wage prohibition.

For Quayle, it is the most important vote to be taken in the Senate on S 2036. It begins:

> SENATOR STAFFORD: Aye by proxy.
> SENATOR QUAYLE: Aye.
> SENATOR WEICKER: Aye. . . .

It is very matter of fact. There are no signals of recognition that the pivotal vote has been cast. The roll-call flows swiftly on; the wage prohibition amendment passes by a party-line 9–7 vote. On the next two 8–8 roll calls, Weicker votes with the Democrats in losing causes. But on the showdown vote he has stood with Quayle. Shortly thereafter, S 2036 is voted out of full committee by a unanimous 16–0 vote. It caps Quayle's most strenuous effort and his most significant accomplishment thus far as a United States senator. . . .

Epilogue

Quayle's efforts were successful in almost every way. The full Senate passed the final bill by a vote of 95–0, and the House passed it by 339–12 (after members of the two houses met in a conference committee to resolve differences). President Reagan signed the bill into law. There was a scramble by a number of players as everyone tried to take credit for the new measure, but Quayle was generally agreed to be the one who deserved most of the credit as the chief architect of the bill.

With the country's various economic and budgetary problems, it remains to be seen what effect the deals that were forged in the subcommittee markup stage will have on the ability of the agencies governed by this law to accomplish the goal of achieving and maintaining full employment.

CHAPTER 5

THE BUREAUCRACY

The Education of David Stockman

William Greider

Ideally, the job of a bureaucrat is not to formulate policy but to implement the decisions of policymakers. If Ronald Reagan was the pilot of the "Reagan revolution," then David Stockman, director of the Office of Management and Budget, was supposed to be the navigator. William Greider's landmark article on the workings of the Reagan administration, however, shows that the navigator may have also been the pilot. Did the bureaucrat become the policymaker?

Ronald Reagan ran for president in 1980 advocating a revolutionary economic policy. He promised not to raise taxes, to increase funds to the military, and to balance the budget, which already showed a large deficit. The obvious impossibility of doing all three at the same time led George Bush, who opposed Reagan in the 1980 Republican primaries, to say that this was "voodoo economics"—a position he changed once he was nominated for the vice-presidency.

Once elected, Reagan turned the accomplishment of these economic goals over to a team of advisers headed by David Stockman. A young former congressman, Stockman had impressed the president with his ability to understand the complexities of government spending and revenues. As head of the OMB, Stockman was given control not only over the formulation of the government's budget but also over the spending initiatives of each department and agency of the executive branch.

Since the president had ruled out tax increases to garner additional revenue, and had promised to increase military spending, enacting huge spending cuts in domestic programs provided the only hope of balancing the budget. Stockman worked closely with Republican members of Congress, such as Jack Kemp of New York, who were impressed by the certainty with which he delivered his financial projections, described the economy, and suggested programs. These politicians came to believe in Stockman and staked their own reputations on his numbers. After the budget was passed, stories appeared in the press indicating that the president did not fully understand the

From William Greider, "The Education of David Stockman," *The Atlantic Monthly,* Dec. 1981. Reprinted by permission of the author.

numbers, the cuts that had been made, or the projections upon which they were based. He too had come to rely on his financial wizard.

During this period, Stockman was meeting with William Greider of the *Washington Post* for off-the-record briefings. This selection is Greider's summary of those conversations about the budget, the state of government policymaking, and the behavior and motives of the key financial bureaucrat involved in this revolutionary program. Perhaps the selection can best be summarized by Stockman's own words, which appeared above the title on the first page of this article in its original printing: "None of us really understands what's going on with all these numbers."

JAMES BAKER   White House chief of staff.

EDWIN MEESE   White House counselor; adviser to the president.

RONALD REAGAN   President of the United States, 1981–1989.

DAVID STOCKMAN   Director of the Office of Management and Budget.

▶ The struggle began in private, with Ronald Reagan's Cabinet. By inaugural week [of 1981], Stockman's staff had assembled fifty or sixty policy papers outlining major cuts and alterations, and, aiming at the target of $40 billion, Stockman was anxious to win fast approval for them, before the new Cabinet officers were fully familiar with their departments and prepared to defend their bureaucracies. During that first week, the new Cabinet members had to sit through David Stockman's recital—one proposal after another outlining drastic reductions in their programs. Brief discussion was followed by presidential approval. "I have a little nervousness about the heavy-handedness with which I am being forced to act," Stockman conceded. "It's not that I wouldn't want to give the decision papers to the Cabinet members ahead of time so they could look at them, it's just that we're getting them done at eight o'clock in the morning and rushing them to the Cabinet room. . . . It doesn't work when you have to brace these Cabinet officers in front of the President with severe reductions in their agencies, because then they're in the position of having to argue against the group line. And the group line is cut, cut, cut. So that's a very awkward position for them, and you make them resentful very fast."

Stockman proposed to White House counselor Edwin Meese an alternative approach—a budget working group, in which each Cabinet secretary could review the proposed cuts and argue against them. As the group evolved, however, with Meese, chief of staff James Baker, Treasury Secretary Donald Regan, and policy director Martin Anderson, among others, it was stacked in Stockman's favor. "Each meeting will involve only the relevant Cabinet member and his aides with four or five strong keepers of the central agenda," Stockman explained at one point. "So on Monday, when we go into the decision on synfuels programs, it will be [Energy Secretary James B.] Edwards defending them against six guys saying that, by God, we've got to cut these back or we're not going to have a savings program that will add up."

In general, the system worked. Stockman's agency did in a few weeks what normally consumes months; the process was made easier because the normal opposition forces had no time to marshal either their arguments or their constituents and because the President was fully in tune with Stockman. After the budget working group reached a decision, it would be taken to Reagan in the form of a memorandum, on which he could register his approval by checking a little box. "Once he checks it," Stockman said, "I put that in my safe and I go ahead and I don't let it come back up again."

The check marks were given to changes in twelve major budget entitlements and scores of smaller ones. Eliminate Social Security minimum benefits. Cap the runaway costs of Medicaid. Tighten eligibility for food stamps. Merge the trade adjustment assistance for unemployed industrial workers with standard unemployment compensation and shrink it. Cut education aid by a quarter. Cut grants for the arts and humanities in half. "Zero out" CETA* and the Community Services Administration and National Consumer Cooperative Bank. And so forth. "Zero out" became a favorite phrase of Stockman's; it meant closing down a program "cold turkey," in one budget year. Stockman believed that any compromise on a program that ought to be eliminated—funding that would phase it out over several years—was merely a political ruse to keep it alive, so it might still be in existence a few years hence, when a new political climate could allow its restoration to full funding.

"I just wish that there were more hours in the day or that we didn't have to do this so fast. I have these stacks of briefing books and I've got to make decisions about specific options . . . I don't have time, trying to put this whole package together in three weeks, so you just start making snap judgments."

In the private deliberations, Stockman began to encounter more resistance from Cabinet members. He was proposing to cut $752 million from the Export-Import Bank, which provides subsidized financing for international trade—a cut of crucial symbolic importance, because of Stockman's desire for equity. Two thirds of the Ex-Im's direct loans benefit some of America's major manufacturers—Boeing, Lockheed, General Electric, Westinghouse, McDonnell Douglas, Western Electric, Combustion Engineering—and, not surprisingly, the program had a strong Republican constituency on Capitol Hill. Stockman thought the trade subsidies offended the free-market principles that all conservatives

---

* The replacement program for the Comprehensive Employment and Training Act (CETA) is discussed in Selection 4.5.

espouse—in particular, President Reagan's objective of withdrawing Washington from business decision-making. Supporters of the subsidies made a practical argument: the U.S. companies, big as they were, needed the financial subsidies to stay even against government-subsidized competition from Europe and Japan.

The counter-offensive against the cut was led by Commerce Secretary Malcolm Baldrige and U.S. Trade Representative William Brock, who argued eloquently before the budget working group for a partial restoration of Ex-Im funds. By Stockman's account, the two "fought, argued, pounded the table," and the meeting seemed headed for deadlock. "I sort of innocently asked, well, isn't there a terrible political spin on this? It's my impression that most of the money goes to a handful of big corporations, and if we are ever caught not cutting this while we're biting deeply into the social programs, we're going to have big problems." Stockman asked if anyone at the table had any relevant data. Deputy Secretary of the Treasury Tim McNamar thereupon produced a list of Ex-Im's major beneficiaries (a list that Stockman had given him before the meeting). "So then I went into this demagogic tirade about how in the world can I cut food stamps and social services and CETA jobs and EDA jobs and you're going to tell me you can't give up one penny for Boeing?"

Stockman won that argument, for the moment. But, as with all the other issues in the budget debate, the argument was only the beginning. "I've got to take something out of Boeing's hide to make this look right. . . . You can measure me on this, because I'll probably lose but I'll give it a helluva fight." . . .

The only cabinet officer Stockman did not challenge was, of course, the secretary of defense. In the frantic preparation of the Reagan budget message, delivered in broad outline to Congress on February 18, the OMB review officers did not give even their usual scrutiny to the new budget projections from Defense. Reagan had promised to increase military spending by 7 percent a year, adjusted for inflation, and this pledge translated into the biggest peacetime arms buildup in the history of the republic—$1.6 trillion over the next five years, which would more than double the Pentagon's annual budget while domestic spending was shrinking. Stockman acknowledged that OMB had taken only a cursory glance at the new defense budget, but he was confident that later on, when things settled down a bit, he could go back and analyze it more carefully.

In late February, months before the defense budget became a subject of Cabinet debate, Stockman privately predicted that Defense Secretary Caspar Weinberger, himself a budget director during the Nixon years, would be an ally when he got around to cutting back military spending. "As soon as we get past this first phase in the process, I'm really going to go after the Pentagon. The whole question is blatant inefficiency, poor deployment of manpower, contracting idiocy, and, hell, I think that Cap's going to be a pretty good mark over there. He's not a tool of the military-industrial complex. I mean, he hasn't been steeped in its excuses and rationalizations and ideology for twenty years, and

I think that he'll back off on a lot of this stuff, but you just can't challenge him head-on without your facts in line. And we're going to get our case in line and just force it through the presses."

Stockman shared the general view of the Reagan Administration that the United States needed a major build-up of its armed forces. But he also recognized that the Pentagon, as sole customer for weapons systems, subsidized the arms manufacturers in many direct ways and violated many free-market principles. "The defense budgets in the out-years won't be nearly as high as we are showing now, in my judgment. Hell, I think there's a kind of swamp of $10 to $20 to $30 billion worth of waste that can be ferreted out if you really push hard."

Long before President Reagan's speech to Congress, most of the painful details of the $41.4 billion in proposed reductions were already known to Capitol Hill and the public. In early February, preparing the political ground, Stockman started delivering his "black book" to Republican leaders and committee chairmen. He knew that once the information was circulating on the Hill, it would soon be available to the news media, and he was not at all upset by the daily storm of headlines revealing the dimensions of what lay ahead. The news conveyed, in its drama and quantity of detail, the appropriate political message: President Reagan would not be proposing business as usual. The President had in mind what Stockman saw as a "fiscal revolution."

But it was not generally understood that the new budget director had already lost a major component of his revolution—another set of proposals, which he called "Chapter II," that was not sent to Capitol Hill because the President had vetoed its most controversial elements.

Stockman had thought "Chapter II" would help him on two fronts: it would provide substantially increased revenues and thus help reduce the huge deficits of the next three years; but it would also mollify liberal critics complaining about the cuts in social welfare, because it was aimed primarily at tax expenditures (popularly known as "loopholes") benefiting oil and other business interests. "We have a gap which we couldn't fill even with all these budget cuts, too big a deficit," Stockman explained. "Chapter II comes out totally on the opposite of the equity question. That was part of my strategy to force acquiescence at the last minute into a lot of things you'd never see a Republican administration propose. I had a meeting this morning at the White House. The President wasn't involved, but all the other key senior people were. We brought a program of additional tax savings that don't touch any social programs. But they touch tax expenditures." Stockman hesitated to discuss details, for the package was politically sensitive, but it included elimination of the oil-depletion allowance; an attack on tax-exempt industrial-development bonds; user fees for owners of private airplanes and barges; a potential ceiling on home-mortgage deductions (which Stockman called a "mansion cap," since it would affect only the wealthy); some defense reductions; and other items, ten in all. Total additional savings: somewhere in the neighborhood of $20 billion. Stockman was proud of "Chapter II" and also very nervous about it, because, while liberal Democrats might applaud the closing of "loopholes" that they had attacked for years, powerful lobbies—in Congress and business—would mobilize against it.

Did President Reagan approve? "If there's a consensus on it, he's not going to buck it, probably."

Two weeks later, Stockman cheerfully explained that the President had rejected his "tax-expenditures" savings. The "Chapter II" issues had seemed crucial to Stockman when he was preparing them, but he dismissed them as inconsequential now that he had lost. "Those were more like ornaments I was thinking of on the tax side," he insisted. "I call them equity ornaments. They're not really too good. They're not essential to the economics of the thing."

The President was willing to propose user fees for aircraft, private boats, and barges, but turned down the proposal to eliminate the oil-depletion allowance. "The President has a very clear philosophy," Stockman explained. "A lot of people criticize him for being short on the details, but he knows when something's wrong. He just jumped all over my tax proposals."

Stockman dropped other proposals. Nevertheless, he was buoyant. The reactions from Capitol Hill were clamorous, as expected, but the budget director was more impressed by the silences, the stutter and hesitation of the myriad interest groups. Stockman was becoming a favorite caricature for newspaper cartoonists—the grim reaper of the Reagan Administration, the Republican Robespierre—but in his many sessions on the Hill he sensed confusion and caution on the other side.

"There are more and more guys coming around to our side," he reported. "What's happening is that the plan is so sweeping and it covers all the bases sufficiently, so that it's like a magnifying glass that reveals everybody's pores. . . . In the past, people could easily get votes for their projects or their interests by saying, well, if they would cut food stamps and CETA jobs and two or three other things, then maybe we would go along with it, but they are just picking on my program. But, now, everybody perceives that everybody's sacred cows are being cut. If that's what it takes, so be it. The parochial player will not be the norm, I think. For a while."

On Capitol Hill, ideological consistency is not a highly ranked virtue but its absence is useful grounds for scolding the opposition. David Stockman endured considerable needling when his budget appeared, revealing that many programs that he had opposed as a congressman had survived. The most glaring was the fast-breeder nuclear reactor at Clinch River, Tennessee. Why hadn't Stockman cut the nuclear subsidy that he had so long criticized? The answer was Senator Howard Baker, of Tennessee, majority leader. "I didn't have to get rolled," Stockman said, "I just got out of the way. It just wasn't worth fighting. This package will go nowhere without Baker, and Clinch River is just life or death to Baker. A very poor reason, I know."

Consistency, he knew, was an important asset in the new environment. The package of budget cuts would be swiftly picked apart if members of Congress perceived that they could save their pet programs, one by one, from the general reductions. "All those guys are looking for ways out," he said. "If they can detect an alleged pattern of preferential treatment for somebody else or discriminatory treatment between rural and urban interests or between farm interests and industrial interests, they can concoct a case for theirs."

Even by Washington standards, where overachieving young people with excessive adrenalin are commonplace, Stockman was busy. Back and forth, back and forth he went, from his vast office at the Old Executive Office Building, with its classic high ceilings and its fireplace, to the cloakrooms and hideaway offices and hearing chambers of the Capitol, to the West Wing of the White House. Usually, he carried an impossible stack of books and papers under his arm, like a harried high school student who has not been given a locker. He promised friends he would relax—take a day off, or at least sleep later than 5 A.M., when he usually arose to read policy papers before breakfast. But he did not relax easily. What was social life compared with the thrill of reshaping the federal establishment?

In the early skirmishing on Capitol Hill, Stockman actually proposed a tight control system: Senator Baker and the House Republican leader, Robert Michel, of Illinois, would be empowered to clear all budget trades on particular programs—and no one else, not even the highest White House advisers, could negotiate any deals. "If you have multiple channels for deals to be cut and retreats to be made," Stockman explained, "then it will be possible for everybody to start side-dooring me, going in to see Meese, who doesn't understand the policy background, and making the case, or [James] Baker making a deal with a subcommittee chairman." Neither the White House nor the congressional leadership liked his idea, and it was soon buried.

By March, however, Stockman could see the status quo yielding to the shock of the Reagan agenda. In dozens of meetings and hearings, public and private, Stockman perceived that it was now inappropriate for a senator or a congressman to plead for his special interests, at least in front of other members with other interests. At one caucus, a Tennessee Republican began to lecture him on the reduced financing for TVA; other Republicans scolded him. Stockman cut public-works funding for the Red River project in Louisiana, which he knew would arouse Russell Long, former chairman of the Senate Finance Committee. Long appealed personally at the White House, and Reagan stood firm.

One by one, small signals such as these began to change Stockman's estimate of the political struggle. He began to believe that the Reagan budget package, despite its scale, perhaps because of its scale, could survive in Congress. With skillful tactics by political managers, with appropriate public drama provided by the President, the relentless growth rate of the federal budget, a permanent reality of Washington for twenty years, could actually be contained.

Stockman's analysis was borne out a few weeks later, in early April, when the Senate adopted its first budget-cutting measures, 88–10, a package close enough to the administration's proposals to convince Stockman of the vulnerability of "constituency-based" politics. "That could well be a turning point in this whole process," Stockman said afterward. . . .

The President's televised address, in April [1981], was masterly and effective: the nation responded with a deluge of mail and telephone calls, and the House of Representatives accepted Reagan's version of budget reconciliation over the Democratic alternative. The final roll call on the Gramm-Latta resolution was not even close,* with sixty-three Democrats joining all House Republicans in support of the President. The stunning victory and the disorganized opposition from the Democrats confirmed for Stockman a political hunch he had first developed when he saw the outlines of Representative Jim Jones's resolution, mimicking the administration's budget-cutting.† The 1980 election results may not have been "ideological," but the members of Congress seemed to be interpreting them that way.

This new context, Stockman felt, would be invaluable for the weeks ahead, as the budget-and-tax issues moved into the more complicated and vulnerable areas of action. The generalized budget-cutting instructions voted by the House were now sent to each of the authorizing committees, most of them chaired by old-line liberal Democrats who would try to save the programs in their jurisdictions, but their ability to counterattack was clearly limited by the knowledge that President Reagan, not Speaker Tip O'Neill, controlled the floor of the House. Stockman expected the Democratic chairmen to employ all of their best legislative tricks to feign cooperation while actually undermining the Reagan budget cuts, but he was already preparing another Republican resolution, dubbed "Son of Gramm-Latta," to make sure the substantive differences were maintained—the block grants that melded social programs and turned them over to the states, the "caps" on Medicaid and other open-ended entitlement programs, the "zeroing out" of others.

In the first round, Stockman felt that he had retreated on very little. He made the trade with Representative Montgomery on VA hospitals, and his old friend Representative Gramm had restored some "phase-out" funds for EDA, the agency Stockman so much wished to abolish.‡ "He put it in there over my

---

* The Gramm-Latta resolution, named for Democrat Phil Gramm of Texas and Republican Delbert Latta of Ohio, was the Reagan administration's budget cut package.

† Democrat Jim Jones, chair of the House Budget Committee, had proposed a budget resolution that Stockman considered to be mostly political gimmick, favoring Democratic interests in social programs and defense spending rather than genuinely trying to cut the budget.

‡ The Economic Development Administration, which provides federal funds for economic recovery to states, localities, and businesses, has not been abolished.

objections," Stockman explained, "because he needed to keep three or four people happy. I said okay, but we're not bound by it." The Republican resolution also projected a lower deficit than Stockman thought was realistic, as a tactical necessity. "Gramm felt he couldn't win on the floor unless they had a lower deficit, closer to Jones's deficit, so they got it down to $31 billion by hook or by crook, mostly the latter."

Stockman was supremely confident at that point. The Reagan Administration had taken the measure of its political opposition and had created a new climate in Washington, a new agenda. Now what remained was to follow through in a systematic way that would convince the financial markets. In the middle of May, he made another prediction: the bull market on Wall Street, the one he had expected in April, would arrive by late summer or early fall.

"I think we're on the verge of the response in the financial markets. It takes one more piece of the puzzle, resolution of the tax bill. And that may happen relatively quickly, and when it does, I think you'll start a long bull market, by the end of the summer and early fall. The reinforcement that the President got politically in the legislative process will be doubled, barring some new war in the Middle East, by a perceived economic situation in which things are visibly improving. I'm much more confident now."

Stockman was wrong, of course, about the bull market. But his misinterpretation of events was more profound than that. Without recognizing it at the time, the budget director was headed into a summer in which not only financial markets but life itself seemed to be absolutely perverse. The Reagan program kept winning in public, a series of well-celebrated political victories in Congress —yet privately Stockman was losing his struggle.

Stockman was changing, in a manner that perhaps he himself did not recognize. His conversations began to reflect a new sense of fatalism, a brittle edge of uncertainty.

"There was a certain dimension of our theory that was unrealistic. . . ."

"The system has an enormous amount of inertia. . . ."

"I don't believe too much in the momentum theory any more. . . ."

"I have a new theory—there are no *real* conservatives in Congress. . . ."

The turning point, which Stockman did not grasp at the time, came in May, shortly after the first House victory. Buoyed by the momentum, the White House put forward, with inadequate political soundings, the Stockman plan for Social Security reform. Among other things, it proposed a drastic reduction in the benefits for early retirement at age sixty-two. Stockman thought this was a privilege that older citizens could comfortably yield, but 64 percent of those eligible for Social Security were now taking early retirement, and the "reform" plan set off a sudden tempest on Capitol Hill. Democrats accused Reagan of reneging on his promise to exempt Social Security from the budget cuts and accused Stockman of trying to balance his budget at the expense of Social Security recipients, which, of course, he was. "The Social Security problem is not simply one of satisfying actuaries," Stockman conceded. "It's one of satisfying the here-and-now of budget requirements." In the initial flurry of reaction, the Senate passed a unanimous resolution opposing the OMB version of how to reform Social Security, and across the nation, the elderly were alarmed enough to begin writing and calling their representatives in Congress. But Stockman seemed not to grasp the depth of his political problem; he still believed that congressional reaction would quiet down eventually and Democrats would cooperate with him.

"Three things," he explained. "First, the politicians in the White House are over-reacting. They're overly alarmed. Second, there is a serious political problem with it, but not of insurmountable dimensions. And third, basically I screwed up quite a bit on the way the damn thing was handled."

Stockman said that Republicans on Ways and Means were urging him to propose an administration reform plan as an alternative to the Democrats'; Stockman misjudged the political climate. The White House plan, put together in haste, had "a lot of technical bloopers," which made it even more vulnerable to attack, Stockman said. "I was just racing against the clock. All the office things I knew ought to be done by way of groundwork, advance preparation, and so forth just fell by the wayside. . . . Now we're taking the flak from all the rest of the Republicans because we didn't inform them."

Despite the political uproar, Stockman thought a compromise would eventually emerge, because of the pressure to "save" Social Security. This would give him at least a portion of the budget savings he needed. "I still think we'll recover a good deal of ground from this. It will permit the politicians to make it look like they're doing something *for* the beneficiary population when they are doing something *to* it which they normally wouldn't have the courage to undertake."

But there was less "courage" among politicians than Stockman assumed. Indeed, one politician who scurried away from the President's proposed cuts in Social Security was the President. Stockman wanted him to go on television again, address the nation on Social Security's impending bankruptcy, and build a popular constituency for the changes. But White House advisers did not.

"The President was very interested [in the reform package] and he believed it was the right thing to do. The problem is that the politicians are so wary of the Social Security issue per se that they want to keep him away from it, thinking they could somehow have an administration initiative that came out of the boondocks somewhere and the President wouldn't be tagged with it. Well, that was just pure naive nonsense. . . . My view was, if you had to play this thing over, you should have the President go on TV and give a twenty-minute Fireside Chat, with some nice charts. . . . You could have created a climate in which major things could be changed."

The White House rejected that idea. Ronald Reagan kept his distance from the controversy, but it would not go away. In September, Reagan did finally address the issue in a televised chat with the nation: he disowned Stockman's reform plan. Reagan said that there was a lot of "misinformation" about in the land, to the effect that the President wanted to cut Social Security. Not true, he declared, though Reagan had proposed such a cut in May. Indeed, the President not only buried the Social Security cuts he had proposed earlier but retreated on one reform measure—elimination of the minimum benefits—that Congress had already, reluctantly, approved. As though he had missed the long debate on that issue, Reagan announced that it was never his intention to deprive any-one who was in genuine need. Any legislative action toward altering Social Se-curity would be postponed until 1983, after the 1982 congressional elections, and too late to help Stockman with his stubborn deficits. In the meantime, Rea-gan accepted a temporary solution advocated by the Democrats and de-nounced by Stockman as "irresponsible"—borrowing from another federal trust fund that was in surplus, the health-care fund, to cover Social Security's problems. Everyone put the best face on it, including Stockman. The tactical retreat, they explained, was the only thing Reagan could do under the circum-stances—a smart move, given the explosive nature of the Social Security pro-test. Still, it was a retreat, and, for David Stockman, a fundamental defeat. He lost one major source of potential budget savings. The political outcome did not suggest that he would do much better when he proposed reforms for Medicare, Social Security's twin. . . .

[O]ver the next six weeks, Stockman . . . was preoccupied with controlling . . . the furious bumping-and-trading for the final budget-cutting measure, the rec-onciliation bill. The thirteen authorizing committees of the House were drawing up the legislative parts to comply with the budget instructions voted by the House in May; simultaneously, the Republican minority members of those com-mittees were drawing up their alternatives, which would become pieces of the administration's alternative—"Son of Gramm-Latta." Stockman was working closely with the Republican drafting in the House, but at the same time he was trying to keep the specific cuts and policy changes in line with the work of the Republican committee chairmen in the Senate. Stockman had a believable nightmare: if House and Senate produced drastically different versions of the final reconciliation measure, there could be a conference committee between the two chambers that would include hundreds of members and months of combat over the differences. Failure to settle quickly could sink the entire budget-cutting enterprise.

Some of the Democratic committee chairmen were playing the "Washington Monument game" (a metaphor for phony budget cuts, in which the National Park Service, ordered to save money, announces that it is closing the Washing-ton Monument). The Education and Labor Committee made deep cuts in pro-grams that it knew were politically sacred: Head Start and impact aid for local schools, and care for the elderly. The Post Office and Civil Service Committee proposed closing 5,000 post offices. Stockman could deal with those ploys—indeed, he felt they strengthened his hand—but he was weakened on other fronts. Again, he had to hold all Republicans and win several dozen of the "boll weevils"—to demonstrate that Ronald Reagan controlled the House.* It was not a matter of trading with liberal constituencies and their representatives; Stockman had to do his trading with the conservatives. "In that kind of game," he said, "everybody can ask a big price for one vote."

The final pasted-together measure would be several thousand pages of legislative action and, Stockman feared, another version of the Trojan horse—"a Trojan horse filled full of all kinds of budget-busting measures and secondary agendas."

A group of twenty northern and midwestern, more moderate Republicans, who organized themselves as "gypsy moths" as a counterweight to the "boll weevils," threatened defection. In the end, concessions were made: $350 million more for Medicaid, $400 million more for home-heating subsidies for the poor, $260 million in mass-transit operating funds, more money for Amtrak and Conrail. The administration agreed to put even more money into the nuclear-power project that Stockman loathed, the Clinch River fast-breeder reactor. It accepted a large authorization for the Export-Import Bank, and more.

Stockman tried to keep everything in line. When he agreed with House Republicans to restore $100 million or so to Amtrak, he had to go back and alert Bob Packwood, of Oregon, chairman of the Senate committee. "The Senate level which his committee tentatively voted out would have shut down a train in Oregon," Stockman said, "and he didn't relish the prospect of not being able to defend his train in the Senate and have it put back in by House Republicans."

In private, the budget director claimed that these new spending figures that Republicans had agreed upon for the various federal programs were not final but merely authorization ceilings, which could be reduced later on, when the appropriations bills for departments and agencies worked their way through the legislative process. "It doesn't mean that you've lost ground," he said blithely of his compromises, "because in the appropriations process we can still insist on $100 million (or whatever other figures appeared in the original Reagan budget) and veto the bill if it goes over. . . . On these authorizations, we can give some ground and then have another run at it."

This codicil of Stockman's was apparently not communicated to the Republicans with whom he was making deals. They presumed that the final figures negotiated with Stockman were final figures. Later on, they discovered that the budget director didn't agree. When in September the President announced a new round of reductions, $13 billion in across-the-board cuts for fiscal year 1982, the ranks of his congressional supporters accused Stockman of breaking his word. In private, some used stronger language. The new budget cuts Stockman prepared in September did, indeed, scrap many of the agreements he negotiated in June when he was collecting enough votes to pass the President's

---

* The "boll weevils" were about forty southern conservative House Democrats who often voted with the Republicans, particularly at the beginning of the Reagan administration.

reconciliation bill. In the political morality that prevails in Washington, this was regarded as dishonorable behavior, and Stockman's personal standing was damaged.

"Piranhas," Stockman called the Republican dealers. Yet he was a willing participant in one of the rankest trades—his casual promise that the Reagan Administration would not oppose revival of sugar supports, a scandalous price-support loan program killed by Congress in 1979. Sugar subsidies might not cost the government anything, but could cost consumers $2 to $5 billion. "In economic principle, it's kind of a rotten idea," he conceded. Did Ronald Reagan's White House object? "They don't care, over in the White House. They want to win."

This process of trading, vote by vote, injured Stockman in more profound ways, beyond the care or cautions of his fellow politicians. It was undermining his original moral premise—the idea that honest free-market conservatism could unshackle the government from the costly claims of interest-group politics in a way that was fair to both the weak and the strong. To reject weak claims from powerful clients—that was the intellectual credo that allowed him to hack away so confidently at wasteful social programs, believing that he was being equally tough-minded on the wasteful business subsidies. Now, as the final balance was being struck, he was forced to concede in private that the claim of equity in shrinking the government was significantly compromised if not obliterated.

The final reconciliation measure authorized budget reductions of $35.1 billion, about $6 billion less than the President's original proposal, though Stockman and others said the difference would be made up through shrinking "off-budget" programs, which are not included in the appropriations process. The block grants and reductions and caps that Reagan proposed were partially successful—some sixty major programs were consolidated in different block-grant categories—though Stockman lost several important reforms in the final scrambling, among them the cap on the runaway costs of Medicaid, and user fees for federal waterways. The Reagan Administration eliminated dozens of smaller activities and drastically scaled down dozens of others.

In political terms, it was a great victory. Ronald Reagan became the first President since Lyndon Johnson to demonstrate both the tactical skill and the popular strength to stare down the natural institutional opposition of Congress. Moreover, he forced Congress to slog through a series of unique and painful legislative steps—a genuine reconciliation measure—that undermined the parochial baronies of the committee chairmen. Around Washington, even among the critics who despised what he was attempting, there was general agreement that the Reagan Administration would not have succeeded, perhaps would not even have gotten started, without the extraordinary young man who had a plan. He knew what he wanted to attack and he knew Congress well enough to know how to attack.

Yet, in the glow of victory, why was David Stockman so downcast? Another young man, ambitious for his future, might have seized the moment to claim his full share of praise. Stockman did appear on the Sunday talk shows, and was interviewed by the usual columnists. But in private, he was surprisingly modest about his achievement. Two weeks after selling Congress on the biggest package of budget reductions in the history of the republic, Stockman was willing to dismiss the accomplishment as less significant than the participants realized. Why? Because he knew that much more traumatic budget decisions still confronted them. Because he knew that the budget-resolution numbers were an exaggeration. The total of $35 billion was less than it seemed, because the "cuts" were from an imaginary number—hypothetical projections from the Congressional Budget Office on where spending would go if nothing changed in policy or economic activity. Stockman knew that the CBO base was a bit unreal. Therefore, the total of "cuts" was, too.

Stockman explained: "There was less there than met the eye. Nobody has figured it out yet. Let's say that you and I walked outside and I waved a wand and said, I've just lowered the temperature from 110 to 78. Would you believe me? What this was was a cut from an artificial CBO base. That's why it looked so big. But it wasn't. It was a significant and helpful cut from what you might call the moving track of the budget of the government, but the numbers are just out of this world. The government never would have been up at those levels in the CBO base."

Stockman was proud of what had been changed—shutting down the $4 billion CETA jobs program and others, putting real caps on runaway programs such as the trade adjustment assistance for unemployed industrial workers. "Those were powerful spending programs that have been curtailed," he said, "but there was a kind of consensus emerging for that anyway, even before this administration."

All in all, Stockman gave a modest summary of what had been wrought by the budget victory: "It has really slowed down the momentum, but it hasn't stopped what you would call the excessive growth of the budget. Because the budget isn't something you reconstruct each year. The budget is a sort of rolling history of decisions. All kinds of decisions, made five, ten, fifteen years ago, are coming back to bite us unexpectedly. Therefore, in my judgment, it will take three or four or five years to subdue it. Whether anyone can maintain the political momentum to fight the beast for that long, I don't know."

Stockman, the natural optimist, was not especially optimistic. The future of fiscal conservatism, in a political community where there are "no real conservatives," no longer seemed so promising to him. He spoke in an analytical tone, a sober intellect trying to figure things out, and only marginally bitter, as he assessed what had happened to his hopes since January. In July, he was forced to conclude that, despite the appearance of a great triumph, his original agenda was fading, not flourishing.

"I don't believe too much in the momentum theory any more," he said. "I believe in institutional inertia. Two months of response can't beat fifteen years of political infrastructure. I'm talking about K Street* and all of the interest groups in this town, the community of interest groups. We sort of stunned it, but it just went underground for the winter. It will be back. . . . Can we win? A lot of it depends on events and luck. If we got some bad luck, a flareup in the Middle East, a scandal, it could all fall apart." . . .

Epilogue

The firestorm of controversy and criticism caused by this article preoccupied the Reagan administration for weeks. Republican congressional allies were angered that they had been so cold-bloodedly manipulated. Financial experts were worried that the entire plan had been based on very shaky economic projections. Reagan himself came under fire for turning so much authority over to his OMB head. Few people now believed the program would work, and, indeed, within a year the administration was back before Congress calling for even deeper spending cuts to accomplish the original aims.

It was widely predicted that Stockman would be fired, and observers were amazed when he was not. Instead he left on his own much later (only to prove that he did know some economics by signing a contract for a reported two million dollars to write his memoirs). Today the budget deficit has grown to nearly one trillion dollars, largely because of the inconsistencies of the Reagan budget policy.

---

* K Street is a Washington, D.C., street known for its many offices of lawyers, lobbyists, and consulting firms.

5.2

The study of bureaucracy involves the examination of both the functions of administrative institutions and the actions of the people within those institutions. One such administrative agency, the National Security Council (NSC), was created by Congress in 1947 to help the president formulate foreign policy. Although the major roles in the council have been played by such people as the secretary of state, the secretary of defense, the vice president, and the director of the Central Intelligence Agency, the council has also contained a staff of professional foreign policy analysts.

This agency, which was created largely to try to control Harry Truman, has become whatever a president wants it to be. Dwight Eisenhower relied heavily on the agency, and John Kennedy used the advice of both McGeorge Bundy, who was national security adviser (head of the NSC), and Secretary of State Dean Rusk in formulating his foreign policy. The lines between the NSC and the State Department, the agency officially in charge of conducting foreign policy, were blurred in the Nixon administration when National Security Adviser Henry Kissinger ran foreign policy regardless of the wishes of the secretary of state, William Rogers. For awhile, Kissinger even held both positions.

This selection, from Joseph Persico's biography of CIA head William Casey, describes how the Reagan administration ran aground in the Iran-contra scandal. In an attempt to free hostages being held in Iran, the Reagan administration sold arms to that country, even though it was an avowed enemy of the United States, and then used the profits from those arms sales to fund a counterrevolutionary group (the contras) that was trying to overthrow the communist-backed Nicaraguan government (the Sandinistas). The second part of this scheme violated the explicit wishes of Congress with respect to American foreign policy in Central America. Through the Boland Amendment, Congress had expressly prohibited the White House from financially aiding the Nicaraguan cause without congressional consent. As you will see, though, the failure of Congress to

Ollie and Uncle Bill

Joseph E. Persico

From Joseph E. Persico, *Casey: The Lives and Secrets of William J. Casey: From the OSS to the CIA* (New York: Viking Press, 1990). Copyright © 1990 by Joseph E. Persico. Reprinted by permission of Viking Penguin, a division of Penguin Books USA, Inc., and Curtis Brown, Ltd.

cover *all* of the policymaking possibilities in the legislation left a rather large loophole. Notice how Casey, the ultimate bureaucrat, realizes that the law that covers his agency, the CIA, can be circumscribed by operating through another agency, the NSC.

When the scandal broke, President Reagan claimed that he had no knowledge of the scheme. This admission meant that the president either was not telling the full truth, did not remember the full truth, or did not know fully the actions of his own bureaucracy. In trying to sort out what the president actually knew about these plans, Persico takes us inside the foreign policymaking machinery of the NSC. We see how an agency charged with analyzing and formulating foreign policy actually comes to conduct that policy, and how it does so with the express intention of defying Congress. The personal relationship between Colonel Oliver North, a staffer on Reagan's NSC, and William Casey, the director of the CIA and one of President Reagan's closest allies, helps explain how one of the worst presidential scandals in the twentieth century could occur. In the end, this is sirnply the story of a bureaucratic organization gone awry.

WILLIAM CASEY   Director of the CIA, 1981–1987.

ALAN FIERS   Head of the CIA's Central American Task Force.

ROBERT (BUD) McFARLANE   National security adviser, 1982–1985.

EDWIN MEESE   White House counselor; later attorney general.

CONSTANTINE MENGES   National Security Council deputy for Latin America.

OLIVER NORTH   National Security Council staff member, 1981–1986.

STANLEY SPORKIN   A lawyer for the CIA.

▶ He was to become one day a hero, a burning patriot to millions, a zealot, a misguided missile to others, but an undeniable American phenomenon. In the spring of 1984, however, Lieutenant Colonel Oliver L. North was known only to a small fraternity of national security specialists in State, Defense, the military, the NSC, and the CIA. . . .

North had two attributes that are rarer even than intelligence: he was indefatigable and he was ambitious. He was capable of putting in an eighteen-hour day, sleeping for three hours, and going back to work. His NSC assignments grew to encompass two of [William] Casey's hottest interests, antiterrorism and

Latin America. As a colleague on the NSC described Ollie North in action: "Some of his ideas and plans will be based on a great deal of knowledge and will be really smart things to do. Others will be based on no knowledge and will be really dumb things to do. But you won't be able to tell the difference by listening to him, because they will both sound the same."

John Horton, before his exit from the CIA, often worked with North, and spotted a talented player. "Ollie learned quickly how you get from here to there in the bureaucracy," Horton observed. "He knew how to use paper, how to call a meeting, who to bring in, who to cut out. He was a skillful bureaucratic predator."

The early weakness for embellishing the truth continued. North liked to tell how he had taken a map into the Oval Office to "the old man" and persuaded President Reagan to carry off the invasion of Grenada. North and his intimate sessions with the President became a staple of his well-told tales. But Ollie North was never, ever alone with the President.

Constantine Menges, as the NSC's deputy for Latin America, also worked with North and came away half mesmerized, half appalled. Menges once listened to North tell him in great detail about a dinner he had had the previous weekend with Jeane Kirkpatrick, then the U.N. ambassador. When Menges saw Kirkpatrick, he questioned her about it. "I've never had dinner with Oliver North," she answered.

On another occasion, Menges came into North's office while North was on the phone. North was telling the caller that Henry Kissinger was with him and that he would have to call him back because he and Kissinger were going to be busy writing a report on Central America. Menges at first thought that North was kidding. "Ya, Ollie, we haf got to finish dis discussion," Menges said in his best Kissinger imitation. But as the phone conversation went on, he could see that North was conning the caller.

Chance made North and Casey EOB [Executive Office Building] neighbors. Casey had a choice corner office that looked out over Pennsylvania Avenue and Seventeenth Street NW. The room was high-ceilinged, Victorian, and full of the feel of history. Casey loved it. There, the phones rang less than at Langley.* The visitors were fewer. He had time to think. North's office was just seconds away, down a black-and-white-tiled corridor in room 302. Along the way were the offices of the President's Foreign Intelligence Advisory Board, PFIAB (re-created at Casey's insistence after President Carter had killed it), the Intelligence Oversight Board, and a string of other NSC offices in what was called Spook Alley.

The relationship that grew between the seventy-one-year-old Casey and the forty-one-year-old North is best described by North: "Bill Casey was, for me, a man of immense proportions and a man whose advice I admired greatly. . . .

---

* CIA headquarters are in Langley, Virginia.

I know who my superiors are and I know the chain of command. And he wasn't a boss so much as he was a personal friend and an adviser, and a person with whom I could consult and get good advice."

The man Casey came to know was no intellectual. But he had worked hard at the Naval War College and had good retention of what he read. But all the knowledge he assimilated went to buttress his primal convictions rather than to enlarge his mind.

The legendary chief of the German general staff, Alfred, Graf von Schlieffen, was said to have divided his officers into four categories: Schlieffen I, bright and ambitious, an able officer, possibly dangerous politically; Schlieffen II, stupid and lazy, a harmless officer all around; Schlieffen III, bright and lazy, the best officer because he will find the easiest way to do the job and yet create no political problems; Schlieffen IV, stupid and ambitious, the most dangerous officer of all. Where North fit is an open question, except that he was clearly not II or III.

That spring [1984], the fortunes of the contras had reached a low ebb. The latest $24-million appropriation was virtually spent. The writing on the wall stood out in bold italics as Casey's handling of the mining affair shrank congressional support.* The likelihood was that the Senate would follow the House, approve the Boland Amendment, and cut off aid completely. Without support, the contras could be expected to collapse within six to ten months. The grim joke around the Agency was that the only territory the contras would then control was part of Miami.

While the press and Congress were raking Casey over the coals for going too far in Nicaragua, he was meeting secretly with the President and Bud McFarlane, now the national security adviser, to prepare for the day when the money was shut off and the CIA was legally shut out. The President's wishes were clear. As word was relayed down the line, he wanted the contras kept alive as a viable fighting force.

The pending Boland Amendment read: "None of the funds appropriated for the Central Intelligence Agency or any other department, agency, or entity of the United States involved in intelligence activities may be obligated or expended for the purpose or which would have the effect of supporting, directly or indirectly, military or paramilitary operations in Nicaragua by any nation, group, organization, movement or individual." In short, no U.S. military aid for the contras.

But in a manner that had by now become as instinctual to him as breathing, Casey read this language not for what it prohibited but for what it missed, and he saw a crack the contras could slip through. The amendment barred government agencies "involved in intelligence activities" from aiding the contras. That

---

* In late 1983 and 1984 the CIA mined Nicaraguan harbors, hoping to cripple that country's economy by blocking ships bringing oil and supplies. Casey's failure to inform Congress fully of the mining alienated the agency's traditional supporters on the Senate Intelligence Committee.

clearly meant the CIA, and State, Defense, and the FBI for that matter. But what about the NSC? The statute creating the NSC read: "The function of the council shall be to advise the President with respect to the integration of domestic, foreign and military policies relating to the national security, as to enable the military services and other departments and agencies of the government to cooperate more effectively in matters involving the national security." Nothing about "intelligence activities" there. If pushed to the wall, the administration could always get a legal opinion from Casey's next-door neighbor in the EOB, the Intelligence Oversight Board. This small, three-member body, appointed by the President, was charged with keeping intelligence agencies honest by reporting to the President any improper or illegal activities.

In all this, Casey played two roles. The first was as director of Central Intelligence. His responsibility here was to see that the CIA was never again maneuvered, as it had been in the 1970s, into questionable, even illegal, and ultimately destructive activities foisted on it by the White House. He had worked hard to rebuild the battered intelligence service that he had inherited. Nothing must reverse the gains made.

But there was another Bill Casey. This Casey was a member of the Reagan cabinet, a shaper of Reagan foreign policy, a trusted confidant of the President of the United States who was going to do all in his power to serve that man's ends. Could he play both roles? Inevitably they must collide. But he had spent his life skirting the edge of the abyss. He was nimble, agile, sure of foot. Why should it be different now?

At this point, with Boland still pending, the CIA still had legal authority to help the contras. But the point was academic, since there was virtually no money left. And Congress refused to ante up a supplemental appropriation. To wait while a blind, obstinate Congress let the contras starve was foolish. The time to act was now. But if the Boland Amendment was passed, the CIA's skirts must be kept clean. Who, then, should carry out the President's wishes to keep the contras together as a fighting force at all costs? To Casey, the choice was obvious. That spring, he told the President that the man was Oliver North. The President accepted Casey's judgment.

The chain of command, however, was to be scrupulously observed. North still worked for McFarlane, and it was McFarlane who actually handed North the assignment. As North later described his situation, "Mr. McFarlane tasked me to be the person who was the principal action officer." And McFarlane passed along to him the President's order: "Your mission is to hold the resistance together body and soul." Nothing was put in writing. No finding was made.* North nevertheless understood that he was to carry out covert operations from the NSC, in cooperation with the CIA for the time being, but without the Agency, should Boland become law.

---

* A *finding* is a formal, written, legal determination, which is signed by the president, that a covert operation of the CIA is legal and important to national security.

Thus it was that in May of 1984, North had found himself standing next to Dewey Clarridge at a base in Honduras, as Clarridge explained to the contras that this was the man who would never let them down.*

To Casey, the great human failing was lack of imagination, the inability to see the larger possibilities. All the money in the world was not in the purse of Congress. Plenty more could be found in the coffers of countries that wanted to help—indeed, that owed help to this administration. Casey started to tap alternate sources of aid for the contras. As early as March 27, Casey and McFarlane talked about making a pitch to the Israelis. Casey urged McFarlane to try other countries too. One rumor had it that Casey met secretly to put the arm on King Fahd aboard the royal Saudi yacht off the French Riviera. Not true: they met in the royal palace in Riyadh. Fahd had been receptive. Ultimately, a deal was cut whereby the Saudis provided $1 million a month to the contras.

That spring, Casey made another bid for the huge cache of Cuban arms captured in Angola by the South Africans. The chief of staff of the South African armed forces was in town, and Casey had him out to Langley for lunch. The two men had gotten along well during Casey's visit to South Africa. The South African was eager to please. His country was becoming a global pariah; and the antiapartheid pressure coming out of America was a strong contributor to South Africa's image problems. Helping the Reagan administration in Central America might, he reasoned, ease at least some of the pressure.

Casey practically salivated over the arms South Africa was willing to part with. But a CIA analyst on the South African desk spotted potential disaster. Congressman Louis Stokes of Ohio, a black, an articulate, respected man, was a member of HPSCI.† The administration was already being accused of being soft on apartheid. Imagine, on the heels of the Nicaraguan mining debacle, to have the next headlines read that the Reagan administration was in bed with the South African military!

The administration's attempts to tap third countries for aid for the contras inevitably leaked. Exactly one week after apologizing to the committees for the mining affair, Casey had been back on the griddle at the House intelligence committee. The *Washington Post* and other news media had gotten wind that lethal assistance for the contras was being sought from Israel and South Africa. Congressman Wyche Fowler, Jr., the sharp-tongued Georgia Democrat, asked Casey point-blank, "Is any element of our government approaching another element of another government to obtain aid for the contras?" Casey answered: "We have not been involved in that at all. No, not to my knowledge."

Casey did not like to lie; his preference was to control the truth by omission. But occasionally one had to lie to protect an operation. No, "lie" was a harsh

---

* Duane "Dewey" Clarridge was head of the CIA's Latin American Division and a strong Casey ally.
† The House Permanent Select Committee on Intelligence (HPSCI) is in charge of overseeing intelligence operations.

word. A lie was a deliberate falsehood told to advance one's selfish interests, possibly at the expense of an innocent party. What he had done was protect a national security secret. There was, in his mind, a clear distinction. Still, he did not enjoy it, because lies were like dry rot: exposed, they undermined support by destroying confidence. These third-country appeals were going to require some law to lean on.

And so Casey arranged with McFarlane to have third-country aid for the contras placed on the agenda for an NSPG meeting set for June 25.* Both the President and the Vice-President were present. The meeting opened with George Shultz and Cap Weinberger discussing the prospects for a negotiated peace in the region. Casey's reaction was quiet scorn. The President said the sort of thing that endeared him to Casey: "That's too farfetched to imagine, that a Communist government like that would make any reasonable deal with us." What the President preferred, he repeated, was to keep the anti-Sandinistas in the fight. Casey saw his opening and suggested that the way to do it was to get third countries to kick in.

Shultz bristled visibly. "You can't do indirectly what you can't do directly," he said. The U.S. government could only raise and spend money through congressional appropriations. They were getting into deep water. Shultz mentioned the horrible of horribles: they might be talking about "impeachable offenses." All eyes were averted from his.

They were not talking about the United States spending other countries' money, Casey argued. Let the third countries give aid to the contras directly. That, under the current finding, was legal.

Shultz was unpersuaded. "I think we need an opinion from the attorney general."

Ed Meese came to Casey's rescue. Meese recalled that the attorney general, William French Smith, had made a recent ruling on the subject. Meese understood that third-country solicitations were legal.

McFarlane recognized that they were playing with rocket fuel, and as the meeting broke up he said, "I certainly hope none of this will be made public in any way." The President agreed. "If such a story gets out, we'll all be hanging by our thumbs in front of the White House until we find out who did it." And then he spoiled the threat with his good-guy smile.

The meeting ended with neither McFarlane nor Casey mentioning one fact: both of them already had made third-country solicitations. He needed a legal leg to stand on in the future, Casey told [Stanley] Sporkin when he got back to Langley. The next day, he and Sporkin went to the Department of Justice and talked to the attorney general. William French Smith confirmed what Meese had said: it was perfectly appropriate to ask a third country to help the Nicaraguan

---

* The National Security Planning Group (NSPG) is a subgroup of the National Security Council; it became the principal formulator of foreign policy during the Reagan administration.

resistance, provided that country expected no form of repayment from the United States for its help. Good, Casey said. He would have this opinion in his back pocket the next time Congress pressed him. . . .

Ollie North had little idea how he was to run a foreign guerrilla army from two thousand miles away without any U.S. funds. And he was self-aware enough to know that he was in over his head. But he knew where he could get smart fast: he had only to walk around the corner from his room in the EOB, number 302, to Casey's corner office at 345.

McFarlane already had directed North to set up an offshore account. They needed a place, insulated from the United States, McFarlane told him, where they could park money coming in for the contras from third countries. According to North, Casey told him how to set up an operational account offshore. And as North was later to testify when the Iran-contra affair came under investigation, "All of the transactions were recorded on a ledger that Director Casey gave me for this purpose." North cleared the offshore arrangement with McFarlane and directed Adolfo Calero, the contras' political director, to set up an account in the Caribbean into which, according to North, "shortly thereafter, money began to flow."

Casey also proposed the enlistment of Major General Richard V. Secord in the contra-aid operation. Secord had been deputy assistant secretary of Defense for the Near East and South Asia. He had been the administration's point man in the successful fight for sale of the AWACS aircraft to Saudi Arabia. Later, the man had allegedly been linked to business deals with Edwin Wilson, the former CIA agent who eventually went to prison for life for illegal arms traffic with Libya's Muammar Qaddafi. After that suspicion surfaced, Secord's career stalled. In May of 1983, a bitter Dick Secord resigned from the Air Force. To Casey, Secord had been poorly used by his country.

Secord knew his way around the Pentagon; he knew his way around covert operations; he knew his way around the international arms market. Secord was, in fact, in private business now, selling arms and security devices. Should North have any qualms over the old Secord-Wilson association, Casey showed him a document, North later recalled, a determination by a judge in the U.S. District Court establishing Secord's innocence. The guy had been screwed, Casey said. He was perfectly honest. Secord was a patriotic American, and tailor-made to help North in his new assignment.

North took Casey's suggestion back to his boss, McFarlane. As North later explained, "I don't want either of my previous superiors to think that I was working for Director Casey. I know who I worked for." As far as Casey was concerned, it was just as well. Guiding this eager-beaver Marine served both Casey roles: the President's wishes regarding the contras would be carried out, and at the same time there would be no CIA fingerprints on North's contra supply operation.

Shortly thereafter, North gave Secord his first assignment. Secord was to start buying guns for the contras from the money coming into the private offshore account. They had a name for the operation. They called it the Enterprise.

On July 31, Casey took North with him on a quiet trip to a secret rendezvous in Central America, where they met with CIA station chiefs and embassy people in the region. Casey also took North to meet Panama's virtual dictator, General Manuel Noriega. Noriega, a longtime CIA asset, was well placed to help North bring arms into the region and ultimately into the hands of the contras.

North, with a life lived almost wholly in the military, held Casey's vast experience virtually in awe. Casey was a shrewd lawyer, and it was a comfort to have him available as they navigated treacherous shoals. The Enterprise was so legally fragile that, as North was to phrase it later, "I guess that Director Casey was the one who pointed out that there would come a time when there would need to be, if these activities were exposed, somebody to stand up and take the heat for it." Being the "fall guy" was one way of putting it; but that had a criminal ring. What North understood better was the Marine who throws himself on the hand grenade to save his buddies. And North understood one other thing: Casey wanted to know as little as possible of the specifics of North's activities to supply the contras. . . .

On October 12, both houses of Congress passed Public Law 98-473, which appropriated funds for the continuing operation of the government. Attached to the bill was the second Boland Amendment. The President would have no choice: since 98-473 was an omnibus spending bill, he would have to sign it, the Boland Amendment included. The United States had finally cut off all military aid to the contras. . . .

Casey had moved quickly to put the CIA into a safe post-Boland posture. He had Sporkin draft what he called a "compliance code," the rules of engagement under Boland. It read: "Field stations are to cease and desist with actions that can be construed to be providing any type of support, either direct or indirect, to the various entities with whom we dealt under the program. All future contact with those parties are, until further notice, to be *solely*, repeat *solely*, for the purpose of collecting positive and counter-intelligence information of interest to the United States."

The CIA was officially out of the war. [Alan] Fiers was to live by the compliance code. Yet Casey kept pressing him to do everything short of breaking the law to aid the contras. Stanley Sporkin offered what Fiers called "the best advice anyone ever gave me. He told me to put a lawyer on the Central American Task Force, somebody who could test everything I was doing against the law. I had this guy at my right arm as we tried to figure out what we could and couldn't do. We made up lists of dos and don'ts. The big don't if you were CIA was 'Don't cross the Nicaraguan border.'"

But the line was fine. Fiers tried to play it safe by going to the oversight committees on close calls, in effect making them a party to his decisions. On one trip to the Hill he asked, could his people give the contras intelligence that they were walking into a trap? Yes, the House committee staff advised him. Could they give the contras weapons to fight their way out? No. It seemed to Fiers a weird way to run a railroad.

What Ronald Reagan had told the NSPG was unequivocal, Boland Amendment or not: "I don't want to pull out our support for the contras for any reason. This would be an unacceptable option." And so the administration, through the NSC and North, supplanted the CIA and began to run the Nicaraguan resistance. The NSC was acting in a legal limbo, which was its advantage. Unlike the CIA, it had no legal obligation to obtain findings for conducting covert operations. It was not required to notify Congress of its activities. It did not have to defend a covert-operations budget to Congress. It escaped these controls simply because nobody expected this paper-processing outfit to be carrying out guerrilla warfare.

Epilogue

Ironically, it was the president North and Casey were trying to serve who paid the highest price for this scheme. The furor over Iran-contra tarnished Ronald Reagan irreparably. Administration defenders cited the president's authority in foreign affairs and his power to determine what actions are in the national interest. However, this position was hard to maintain when the president himself denied full knowledge of the plan. As a result, Reagan was no longer able to control Congress, as evidenced by his inability to secure the confirmation of Robert Bork for the Supreme Court. Only Reagan's personal popularity helped him leave office with some of his reputation intact. The impression of an administration out of control led to a variety of changes by the next president, George Bush, in an attempt to assert more control over foreign policymaking.

Oliver North appeared before the congressional committee investigating this scandal and became a hero to some. North's position that he was only taking orders, that he was serving his president and his country, and that he would do the same again, given the stakes in Nicaragua, played well with a nation looking for patriots and heroes. But it did not play well with Lawrence Walsh, the special prosecutor investigating the scandal. Although Walsh was able to secure convictions on various charges for both North and former National Security Adviser John Poindexter, it is unlikely that either man will serve time in jail. For his part, William Casey left this earth still a figure of mystery. Casey was struck down with a fatal illness before appearing before Congress, and so his precise role in the operation will never be known. As the ultimate warrior and spy as well as the ultimate bureaucrat, however, it is unlikely that William Casey would have given Congress very much to use against him.

5.3

No bureaucrat in American history has been more powerful—or more beyond presidential control—than FBI
director J. Edgar Hoover. He served in office longer
than any other major bureaucrat in history—forty-eight
years—and operated under eight presidents. One reason for his extensive power was his knowledge about
each presidents' opponents. Another reason was his
files on the presidents themselves.

　Appointed by Attorney General A. Mitchell Palmer in
1924, Hoover made his early reputation fighting legendary bank robbers like John Dillinger and Baby Face
Nelson (though some argue that the credit belonged to
Melvin Purvis and other Hoover lieutenants). Over time
Hoover began to fashion an image as the nation's major
protector against the communist threat. By the 1960s
he was anxious to implement his own antileftist, anti-
communist, and anti–civil rights agenda.

　By this time, Hoover had become very set in his
ways, and the FBI seemed as reactionary as its director. Not only did Hoover's agents have to toe the line,
but so did Attorney General Robert Kennedy. When, for
example, Hoover wanted to investigate the Reverend
Martin Luther King, Jr., by using wiretaps and electronic eavesdropping, the Kennedys had to acquiesce
because of information that Hoover had acquired on
President Kennedy's extramarital behavior. In this dramatic selection from Richard Gid Powers's biography
of Hoover, watch what happens when one of Hoover's
own prized lieutenants, William Sullivan, shows signs
of opposing the director.

J. Edgar Hoover's FBI

Richard Gid Powers

J. EDGAR HOOVER　Director of the FBI,
1924–1972.

WILLIAM C. SULLIVAN　Protégé of Hoover;
head of FBI's Domestic Intelligence Division.

▶ Hoover began his career providing A. Mitchell Palmer with the research, the
analysis, and the strategy for the 1919–1920 antiradical drive. In the 1960s, Hoover found *himself* relying on an ambitious, younger aide for knowledge of developments in the radical movement, plans to combat it, and analyses of his

agents' reports. This was William C. Sullivan, who had entered the Bureau in 1941 at the age of twenty-nine. From 1961, when Hoover promoted Sullivan to head the Bureau's Domestic Intelligence Division, until 1971, when he left the Bureau under fire, Sullivan was Hoover's window into radical America.

Sullivan, who as head of the Research Section of the Domestic Intelligence Division prepared the monograph that served as the plan for COINTELPRO against the Communist party in 1956, was responsible for the extension of that program to the Socialist Workers party in 1961, the Ku Klux Klan in 1964, the Black Nationalists in 1967, and, finally, in 1968, the New Left.* William Sullivan was the FBI official most responsible for the Bureau's shift after 1963 from a strategy that stressed preparations for an "internal security emergency" (primarily utilizing the Emergency Detention Act of 1950) to one that aimed at combating domestic unrest.

By the 1960s, the tight discipline Hoover maintained over his subordinates and his insistence on absolute loyalty and conformity made it unlikely that an independent thinker would reach the top ranks. In William Sullivan, however, Hoover thought he had chosen and trained a man whose judgments he could rely on, a man of integrity and intelligence who could chart the Bureau's course through the shifting currents of American radical politics. Hoover was profoundly mistaken, however, and what he took for initiative and independence in Sullivan was in reality a surpassing ability to flatter Hoover by catering to his prejudices. Near the end of his life Hoover finally admitted that "the greatest mistake I ever made was to promote Sullivan."

William C. Sullivan was not a typical FBI executive. An exception to the rule drilled into FBI personnel that an "agent never volunteers information," Sullivan was opinionated and willing to share his ideas with an unusual range of acquaintances: professors, writers, reporters, and intellectuals. He even looked different from the conventional G-man. Unlike the smooth organization men who staffed Hoover's executive conferences, Sullivan was a short Irishman who reminded one writer of a "James Cagney type with a New England accent thrown in." He had an unpredictable personality: He was personally sloppy, typed his own memos, full of errors, and picked up the nickname "Crazy Billy" from his colleagues. There were important officials who could not abide him, including Tolson and DeLoach, but many others would not stand for a word against him even after he left the Bureau—among them Courtney Evans and John Mohr.

Like Hoover, Sullivan had a talent for turning laws and programs to purposes unforeseen by their creators. As Hoover had made use of the deportation statutes to cripple American radicalism, Sullivan adapted the techniques developed against Nazi and Soviet agents during World War II and the early cold war and

---

* COINTELPRO (Counter-Intelligence Program) was an FBI plan to destroy the American Communist party (CPUSA) and its members through a disinformation program that included a variety of "dirty tricks."

used them to fight domestic radicals. While coordinating COINTELPRO–CPUSA in Washington, Sullivan became the greatest expert on communism the Bureau ever produced—except for Hoover himself, of course. The Bureau's blanket surveillance of the Party put Sullivan in a position to analyze every meeting, every phone call, every conversation of the Party leadership. He probably knew more about American communism than the Communists themselves.

Hoover seems to have seen a younger version of himself in Sullivan. He encouraged Sullivan to develop anti-Communist tactics so innovative as to recall Hoover's own creative period, four decades earlier. Like the young Hoover, Sullivan understood the value of research and looked for novel ways to use the fruits of that research against his enemies. Sullivan was willing to get out of his office and talk to independent scholars and Communist intellectuals. He built up contacts among academicians, and during the early sixties even gave a series of lectures at the Harvard Graduate School of Business Administration. He collected a personal library of 3,000 volumes on communism, which he lent to his colleagues. In all this he was almost unique; the only other man in the FBI who had ever investigated Communist thought and history so thoroughly had been Hoover himself.

In no other subordinate did Hoover ever tolerate Sullivan's sort of independence. Sullivan seemed to cast a spell over Hoover; some FBI colleagues saw a father-son bond between them. One small indication was Hoover's use of a familiar form of address with Sullivan. Hoover's practice was to call his agents "Mister." When they reached the executive level he dropped the "Mister" and called them by their last name. But Tolson he called Clyde; Louis Nichols was Nick. After Nichols left the Bureau in 1959, the only man Hoover ever again called by a nickname or first name was Bill Sullivan.

On August 23, 1963, at the height of his investigation of the Martin Luther King–Stanley Levison–Jack O'Dell relationship,* Sullivan gave Hoover a sixty-seven-page brief on the Communist party's efforts to infiltrate the civil rights movement. Sullivan's report concluded, "There has been an obvious failure of the Communist Party of the United States to appreciably infiltrate, influence, or control large numbers of American Negroes in this country." The report did contain the careful qualification that "time alone will tell" whether future efforts by the Party to exploit blacks would be as unsuccessful as those in the past. Nevertheless, Sullivan's meaning was plainly that Communist infiltration of the civil rights movement need be of no further concern to the Bureau or the country.

---

* Stanley Levison was a New York attorney who was one of Martin Luther King's closest advisers, and Jack O'Dell was hired by Levison for the New York office of the Southern Christian Leadership Conference. Incorrectly believing both men to be members of or at least sympathizers with the American Communist party, Hoover relentlessly investigated a possible connection between King and the party, even wiretapping King's offices, home, and hotel rooms.

Hoover was baffled. Sullivan's latest memo not only contradicted the steady stream of reports he had been sending the director about the Communist influence on Martin Luther King, Jr., but everything the Bureau had been saying about communism and civil rights for decades. Hoover fired the report back to Sullivan with the handwritten comment that "this memo reminds me vividly of those I received when Castro took over Cuba. You contended then that Castro and his cohorts were not communists and not influenced by communists. Time alone proved you wrong. I for one can't ignore the memos re [deletion, presumably Levison and O'Dell] as having only an infinitesimal effect on the efforts to exploit the American Negro by the Communists."

Hoover's rejection of his memo threw Sullivan into a state of panic. His own account of this controversy is self-serving and has to be weighed carefully; Sullivan told his story after he left the Bureau in 1971 and had broken with Hoover. There is no reason, though, to doubt his statement that the August 23 report precipitated a crisis: "This [memorandum] set me at odds with Hoover. . . . A few months went by before he would speak to me. Everything was conducted by exchange of written communications. It was evident that we had to change our ways or we would all be out on the street."

In the weeks immediately following Sullivan's August 23 memo, whenever Domestic Intelligence sent Hoover a report on King and Levison (or, for that matter, any report on Communist activities), Hoover would ridicule it with comments like "just infinitesimal!" (on a report on Communist plans for taking part in the August 28 March on Washington) or "I assume CP functionary claims are all frivolous" (on a report on Communist plans to hold follow-up rallies after the march to advance "the cause of socialism in the United States"). Sullivan was caught in a trap of his own making: He had programmed his division to produce an unending flow of reports on Communist activities that hardly made sense in light of his August 23 brief. Conversely, the August 23 brief was refuted by the division's own reports on continuing Communist machinations.

According to Sullivan, the men of the Domestic Intelligence Division were in an uproar. They thought they would all be transferred out of Washington; selling their homes and uprooting their families would ruin them financially. They wanted another memo written to the director to "get us out of this trouble we were in."

Instead of holding to what he felt was an accurate assessment of the declining fortunes of the American Communists, Sullivan wrote a memo to Hoover on August 30 that retracted everything he had said on August 23, and tried to smooth the dispute with flattery:

The director is correct. We were completely wrong about believing the evidence was not sufficient to determine some years ago that Fidel Castro was not a communist or under communist influence. On investigating and writing about communism and the American

*Negro, we had better remember this and profit by the lesson it should
teach us.*

*Personally, I believe in the light of King's powerful demagogic
speech yesterday [the "I have a dream" speech] he stands head and
shoulders above all other Negro leaders put together when it comes to
influencing great masses of Negroes. We must mark him now, if we
have not done so before, as the most dangerous Negro of the future in
this nation from the standpoint of communism, the Negro, and national security.*

*It may be unrealistic to limit ourselves as we have been doing to
legalistic proofs or definitely conclusive evidence that would stand up
in testimony in court or before Congressional Committees that the
Communist Party, USA, does wield substantial influence over Negroes
which one day could become decisive.*

*We greatly regret that the memorandum did not measure up to
what the director has a right to expect from our analysis.*

On September 16, 1963, Sullivan followed this memo with a recommendation
of "increased coverage of communist influence on the Negro." He now proposed something new: "We are stressing the urgent need for imaginative and
aggressive tactics to be utilized through our Counterintelligence Program—
these designed to neutralize or disrupt the Party's activities in the Negro field."
Stripped of terms of art, Sullivan was proposing unleashing the COINTELPRO
techniques on Martin Luther King, Jr.

Hoover reacted to this dizzying shift by challenging Sullivan once more to
back up the August 23 report. He rejected Sullivan's latest reversal of position
and his recommendation of intensified efforts against the Party:

*No, I can't understand how you can so agilely switch your thinking
and evaluation. Just a few weeks ago you contended that the Communist influence in the racial movement was ineffective and infinitesimal. This—notwithstanding many memos of specific instances of infiltration. Now you want to load down the Field with more coverage
in spite of your recent memo depreciating CP influence in racial
movement. I don't intend to waste time and money until you can
make up your minds what the situation really is.*

After he left the Bureau, Sullivan tried to justify his vacillations by arguing
that he was acting under duress when he altered his convictions and "engage[d]
in a lot of nonsense." He argued that Hoover's objections to his memos were
not sincere, that Hoover was deviously maneuvering his subordinates into providing him with the conclusions he wanted. Hoover, Sullivan later held, was
challenging him to "come back and say, 'Mr. Hoover, you are right, we are
wrong. There is communist infiltration of the American Negro. We think we
should go ahead and carry on an intensified program against it.' He knew,

when he wrote this, he knew precisely what kind of reply he was going to get." . . .

Rather than trying to maneuver Sullivan into furnishing him with dishonest evaluations of Communist influence in the civil rights movement, as Sullivan claimed, Hoover seems to have been trying to discover the actual situation. Throughout his career, Hoover had always made sure he had the facts on his side when he sallied forth into political controversy. The Bureau's position had always been that the Communists were continually attempting, but failing, to gain influence over American blacks; that position had provided the context within which Hoover had interpreted connections between civil rights and communism whenever they were discovered. But at this critical moment in the history of the civil rights movement, when it was essential that he be acquainted with the truth, Hoover was let down by Sullivan, who readily admitted later that he knew he was being dishonest: "Here again we had to engage in a lot of non-sense which we ourselves really did not believe in. We either had to do this or we would be finished." But Hoover's whole career shows that he was a serious person. He did not want nonsense; he wanted the facts.

After he retracted his August 23 memorandum, Sullivan tried to prove the sincerity of his latest set of convictions. He became the moving force behind the Bureau's aggressive campaign to discredit King within the government, to disrupt and neutralize his movement, and to destroy him professionally and personally. For the rest of his FBI career, Sullivan seemed to try to redeem himself for his brief show of independence by becoming ever more extreme in his attacks against protesters and dissenters.

Sullivan's dishonesty, of course, does not excuse Hoover. He had created a system in which, finally, advancement came to opportunists who had learned persuasive ways of giving back to Hoover his own prejudices and opinions disguised as independent, objective, corroborative thinking.

On October 15, 1963, the Intelligence Division gave Hoover a fuller statement of its revised position on Communist influence in the civil rights movement. This was a monograph by Sullivan called "Communism and the Negro Movement—a Current Analysis." In an effort to distance himself from his August 23 memo, Sullivan was so extreme in his treatment of Martin Luther King that Sullivan's superior, Assistant to the Director Alan Belmont, characterized the October 15 memo as a "personal attack" on the civil rights leader that he predicted would "startle" Robert Kennedy "in view of his past association with King." Nevertheless, Belmont said, "we will be carrying out our responsibility by disseminating [it] outside the Bureau." Hoover approved its distribution, writing in the margin, "We must do our duty" and "I am glad you recognize at last there is such influence." The October 15 report did, in fact, anger Robert Kennedy, especially when he heard that the Pentagon was using it to justify its own opposition to civil rights. He ordered Hoover to retrieve all copies.

That attempted smear of King was just one of many in the brutal assault on King that Sullivan (with Hoover's approval) would direct until King's death in

1968. The King affair revealed the extent to which Hoover's iron discipline had turned the Bureau into an echo chamber resounding with his passions and phobias. The assistants on whom he depended for information about the world fed him reports designed to anticipate and reinforce his increasingly rigid fixations and obsessions. This was partly because Hoover was increasingly loath to accept information that challenged his priorities and the policy of his Bureau. It was also partly the result of the structure of the Bureau. Everything depended on Hoover, and his subordinates were too intimidated to correct his misconceptions; and for that, Hoover had only himself to blame.

Sullivan's abasing himself before Hoover was not unusual within the Bureau: It was the norm. Agents seemed to be both proud and embarrassed about stories that showed how completely Hoover dominated them. The system of discipline that Hoover had developed in the 1920s to protect himself from the errors of his agents now was proving incapable of producing agents who could protect him from his own mistakes.

The tall tales agents told about life in the Bureau largely revolved around their absolute subjugation to Hoover's whims. One classic story had Hoover announce that an agent had been killed in a gunfight. Actually, he was only wounded, but since the director could never be wrong, his buddies drew straws to see who would go to the hospital to finish him off. Another legend claimed that Hoover's driver once got into an accident while turning left. Forever after, the rule for his chauffeur was, "No left turns!" Because Hoover used the margins of memos for his comments, he became irritated whenever the typist failed to leave enough room. Once, when the margins got too narrow, he scrawled "Watch the borders!" His puzzled lieutenants put the Bureau offices near Mexico and Canada on alert. Hoover was supposed to have objected to the appearance of a new agent and whispered to an assistant director, "One of them is a pinhead. Get rid of him." The aide checked the hats of the group and, to be safe, fired the owners of the three smallest.

A pair of young agents who entered the Bureau in 1960 gave remarkably consistent descriptions of an organization in absolute thrall to the arbitrary will of one man. As part of their training, new agents were indoctrinated in an idealized legend of Hoover's life, and how "he built this Bureau from the ground up." A lecturer told the trainees that "the Director chose the path of sacrifice, and electing to forgo private wealth and what to lesser men are the pleasures of life, he dedicated himself instead to the creation of the organization we are proud to serve today. Against all odds, our Director stuck doggedly to his purpose; today he remains the guiding light of the F.B.I.—in spite of liberal-leftist moves for his ouster." Despite the fact that "our Director has served thirteen attorney generals, has assisted seven presidents . . . he still works longer hours than any of us, every day of the year . . . yes, boys, J. Edgar Hoover is an inspiration to us all. Indeed, it has been said, and truly—'the sunshine of his presence lights our lives.'"

The culmination of the new agents' indoctrination was a meeting with Hoover, and there were days of rehearsals for the great moment. "Everything you say and do must be positive," the recruits were told. "If you look away from the Director's face like you just did with me you'll be fired! Just like that. If there's a quiver in your voice or you wipe your mouth or pick at your nose . . . the Director doesn't miss things like that. They're signs of weakness! Another thing—don't let me catch you standing around in the corridors with your hands in your pockets"—the instructor stuttered—"d-deviates do that. P-playing with themselves. You know. . . ."

As part of their military-style preparation for meeting Hoover, the recruits studied his height (5′ 9″), and his weight—which varied between 168 and 200 (190 in 1961). They were given three "approved" greetings: "Good morning, Mister Hoover," "Pleased to meet you," or "How do you do?" Deviations from these formulas, said the instructors, might be dangerous, but these three "have been tested hundreds of times and nothing ever happened."

They were told not to scuff their feet on the carpet, and not to look down, because "occasionally, our Director enjoys standing on a little box when he greets people in his office. Of course, it's just a small one, only six inches high. Pretend you never even notice it! Not long ago we had a new agent who for some reason just couldn't keep his eyes off it. He was fired." They had to carry handkerchiefs, because the director was supposed not to like moist handshakes.

A trainee would remember his introduction to Hoover the rest of his life. "The face was impossible, like papier-mâché, and much older than any of the photographs revealed, but there was strength in those hard eyes and in his hand as we exchanged a firm Bureau handshake that would have made our administrator proud."

In January 1962, a disgruntled ex-agent, Jack Levine, sent a thirty-eight-page memo to Herbert J. Miller, the assistant attorney general in charge of the Criminal Division of the Justice Department, complaining about Hoover's management of the Bureau. Levine's complaints ranged over topics like anti-Semitism, racial prejudice, and right-wing proselytizing, but almost all concerned Hoover's unlimited power over the lives and careers of agents.

Like other agents, Levine recounted many of the folktales that illustrated the power of Hoover's prejudices in the administration of the Bureau. There were stories about a supervisor fired because he had hired a clerk with pimples, another criticized for buying *Playboy* "because the Director looks upon those who read such magazines as moral degenerates." Levine himself was advised to resign because a whiskey bottle was found in an apartment where he was rooming. These "unreasonable perfectionist attitudes of the Bureau and the futility in protesting or offering constructive criticism," he said, made agents afraid to bring problems to the attention of headquarters, so headquarters was denied the information needed to administer the FBI intelligently.

One reason for the demoralization of the Bureau, Levine thought, was Hoover's practice of enforcing regulations by means of disciplinary transfers. Levine pointed out the severe economic consequences for the agents of this policy, which may have been an important factor in turning the Bureau into an organization of yes-men. When Hoover established his system of discipline, agents rented their homes or lived in rooming houses or hotels. In the years after World War II, however, America had become a nation of homeowners, and agents owned homes, too. Now an administrative transfer—orders to report immediately to a post that was likely to be on the other side of the continent—was a catastrophe that could cost an agent thousands of dollars from a forced sale. Agents were willing to do almost anything to avoid the director's wrath if it meant that kind of punishment.

Levine also thought that the strict rules and regulations had become so onerous, and the demands for performance so great, that the only recourse for many agents was to evade rules, falsify records, and otherwise compromise their integrity. The result was moral rot pervading the Bureau, caused, ironically, by the very system Hoover had installed to prevent dishonest and unprofessional behavior. Levine offered as an extreme example the system of "voluntary" overtime combined with demands that the Bureau show an improvement in this area each year. At the time Levine wrote, the quota had reached the incredible average of three and a half hours per day per agent. Widespread cheating was necessary to achieve this, and since everyone was doing it, administrative chaos resulted, which allowed many to evade all supervision. Levine also reported that pressure for convictions led to unreported use of illegal microphone surveillance, wiretaps, and mail openings.

William C. Sullivan's decision to swallow his principles and misrepresent his convictions about the danger of communism in America in 1963 had drastic consequences for American society. The ease with which he abandoned his convictions on that critical matter may have been conditioned by countless smaller compromises he had had to make over the years to survive in Hoover's FBI. Hoover's system of leadership was turning his men into liars, and so, eventually, he had to rely on liars for advice.

Epilogue

This selection should put to rest the notion that bureaucracies simply implement governmental decisions in a nonpolitical way. In September 1971, Hoover engineered a situation in which he could force a bitter William Sullivan to retire from the agency in disgrace. The following month, President Nixon decided that it was time to remove Hoover himself, ostensibly because of sagging departmental morale, but also because Hoover was not acquiescing to the Nixon administration's own illegal activities. But the president could not bring himself to finish the deed, and only Hoover's death in May 1972 finally removed him from office.

Since then, Congress and the president have taken steps to ensure that no director becomes that powerful again. Whereas once every American knew the name of the director of the FBI, now few even know that there still is a director. The agency itself has lost a lot of its glamour and image of invincibility in the fight against crime, although it is probably no less effective now than it was under Hoover. Still, without Hoover's efforts during the early years of the FBI, one wonders whether the agency would have become what it is today.

5.4

In his farewell address to the nation, outgoing President Dwight D. Eisenhower, a former five-star general, warned against the development of the "military-industrial complex." The military, private contractors, and Congress, he argued, would conspire to increase spending for weapons, to the financial and political detriment of the American people. The interaction Eisenhower was describing is now known as the "iron triangle," sometimes called a "subgovernment." Government policy may be set by the White House and Congress, but its implementation is actually undertaken by the unique bureaucratic relationship among the congressional committees, executive agencies, and interest groups concerned with the various policy areas. In this selection, Hedrick Smith describes the efforts of one congressman, Denny Smith, to unravel and defeat the defense industry iron triangle.

It matters little to the members of the armed services congressional committees, the defense industries, and the Pentagon which weapons are built—only that they are built. It matters little whether these weapons actually work, because others can be built should they fail. Many members of Congress fight hard for military contracts for the army bases and defense industries in their home district. This is the process of "going native," by which members of the bureaucracy and the government take on the characteristics and interests of the very groups they are supposed to be governing. Obviously, this is not the optimum way for government to operate.

Hedrick Smith argues that opposing this bureaucratic relationship is another triangle, the "dissident triangle," which consists of internal critics within the Pentagon (who leak information), the individual defense department critics in Congress, and the press. Still, the task of derailing the powerful defense iron triangle is not an easy one. Even with superb inside information on the Divad gun, and the expertise to understand that data, notice how difficult it is for Representative Smith to defeat the Pentagon. And think about how

The Power Game

Hedrick Smith

many Pentagon decisions there are compared to the number of critics like Denny Smith.

DENNY SMITH   Republican congressman from Oregon.

CASPAR WEINBERGER   Secretary of Defense, 1981–1987.

▶ When I first met Denny Smith, a clean-cut Republican conservative from Oregon, he struck me as a very unlikely Pentagon gadfly. He greeted me one evening in his office, in shirt-sleeves and unbuttoned vest, looking like a hard-working FBI agent. He is an air force veteran of 180 combat missions in Vietnam in an F-4 Phantom jet. He conjures up images of *The Right Stuff,* a Republican John Glenn, a Boy Scout in politics. Denny Smith lacks Glenn's winning smile, but he projects earnestness and sincerity. He has the close-cropped good looks and coat-and-tie decorum of an airline pilot or a businessman, both of which he has been. He is not a typical Pentagon baiter.

His political credentials match the personal impression. Denny Smith arrived in Congress in 1982; he had no political experience, but his voting quickly established him on the Republican right. The American Conservative Union, an anti-big-government lobby, gave him a one-hundred-percent rating in his first two years in Congress. In short, Denny Smith appeared to be a regular, not a maverick. He was a perfect guy to play ball with the administration—only he was not picked for the team. Even as a veteran, he was not put on the main committees dealing with defense.

For those familiar with the Washington power game, two clues about Denny Smith—besides Boy Scout innocence and integrity—foreshadowed his maverick role. First, he came from one of those rare congressional districts which has *no* military base and *no* major defense contractor. "Oregon ranks forty-ninth out of fifty states in defense spending," he told me. Lacking vested Pentagon interests, Denny Smith had the luxury of being able to challenge the Pentagon without fear of serious retribution back home. This was the main reason Smith was left off the defense committees. He fit an old pattern; generally the Pentagon's most dogged critics have come from states with little Pentagon business: Proxmire and Aspin from Wisconsin; Grassley from Iowa; in the 1970s, Iowa's Democratic senators Dick Clark and John Culver.

Second, Denny Smith had unusually good entrée to the Pentagon; he had a channel to the anchor leg of the dissident triangle: middle-level military officers and defense civilians dismayed and outraged at what they honestly saw as the waste, rigidity, and cover-ups of the Pentagon hierarchy and military contractors. No sooner had Denny Smith, then in his mid-forties, arrived in Washington than he contacted old military buddies, now well-connected colonels. "They became my kitchen cabinet," he said, fifteen or twenty strong, telling him about hidden failures of weapons systems on which billions were being spent. Over time, Smith built a network of moles in the Pentagon, who armed him with under-the-table documents.

"It's surprising how many people down in the ranks don't buy the line of the top brass of the Pentagon," Smith told me. "You wouldn't believe how many of them will come in here in civilian clothes on their day off and tell you that they don't want their names bandied about, but there's something wrong with such-and-such program."

By now, the pattern is well established. Some whistle-blowers have come out of the closet and deal directly with the press and Congress. Notoriety protects them. The foremost figures in this "Pentagon underground" are:

— A. Ernest Fitzgerald, who nearly twenty years ago exposed $2 billion cost overruns on the C-5A transport plane, then was fired by the Air Force and went to court to be reinstated;

— Franklin C. Spinney, a systems analyst who made the cover of *Time* in 1983 with his criticism of the Pentagon's endemic underestimating of weapons costs;

— John Boyd, an Air Force colonel who has challenged the "gold-plating" of modern weapons with excessive costly gadgetry that constantly breaks down;

— Colonel Jim Burton, another Air Force colonel, forced into retirement in 1986 after he took a tough stance on tests of the Army's Bradley Fighting Vehicle; and

— Tom Amilie, former technical director of the Navy's Special Weapons Laboratory at China Lake, California, who joined Fitzgerald as a cost fighter.

Most Pentagon dissidents, however, prefer anonymity. These people find a Denny Smith, or they pass their material to intermediaries such as Dina Rasor, a thirty-one-year-old former news assistant for ABC News who now runs the Project on Military Procurement. The project became a major channel for the dissident triangle, gathering and disseminating inside information—usually documents—on Pentagon weapons. It is passed along by as many as one hundred Pentagon sources, Rasor said to me, "from the airman on the flight line who sees a spare part he thinks is too much, clear up to people who are working very closely with the secretary of Defense."

Denny Smith's feuds with the army and navy over multibillion-dollar weapons systems are case studies of how the dissident triangle works. They offer insight into the inner politics of the Pentagon: the bunker mentality at the top, the cover-ups of weapons failures, the stubborn inertia, and the ingenious game of the middle echelons to expose, even undercut, their own top brass. These examples are all the more striking because Denny Smith was no Democrat out to score partisan points against a Republican-run Pentagon; nor was he a liberal ideologically opposed to big military budgets. He was largely reacting as a citizen-politician, innocent about the ways of Washington, at first upset and later angered.

His first tangle came with the Navy: In June 1983, he became suspicious of Pentagon claims that the new super-high-tech, guided-missile Aegis cruiser, the *Ticonderoga,* had hit thirteen out of thirteen target planes in a simulated test attack.

From combat experience, Denny Smith was convinced that no defender could have such perfect results in realistic tests. He asked the Navy to see the test report. He also asked his own mole network about the tests. Denny Smith was embarking on a familiar path, for Congress usually tackles the Pentagon's weapons policy with two major questions: 1. Does the weapon work? and 2. Does it cost too much? The deeper questions of whether it is really needed and how it fits into an overall strategy are rarely addressed in earnest. Few members of Congress have a sure enough grasp to handle those questions. What's more, questions like that could open a Pandora's box, a free-for-all debate on national strategy that most military commanders, congressmen, and policymakers want to avoid.

The Pentagon moles provided shocking confirmation of the Oregon congressman's suspicions about the cruiser's tests. Later, a press article reported that the *Ticonderoga* had hit only five of twenty-one targets, and Smith indicated that was pretty accurate. The Navy stonewalled for five months on Smith's request to see the test report. It was a typical bureaucratic reflex: Keep an iron grip on all information so that policy cannot be effectively challenged.

"The reason the Pentagon doesn't like testing is that testing may interrupt the money flow to its programs," an Air Force colonel explained to me. "That's the strategy in the Pentagon: Don't interrupt the money flow."

Denny Smith's bout with the Navy was a vintage example of the clashing political cultures of Congress and the bureaucracy, typical of their power games. The congressman was trying to open up the policy debate; the Navy was keeping it shut tight. If Smith had been on the Armed Services or Appropriations committees, his vote on military programs would have given him leverage with the Pentagon. But as a freshman who was not on those committees, Smith had no political clout with the Navy. He had to appeal for help from more senior congressmen.

Finally, in December 1983, the Navy sent a six-man delegation to appease and silence Smith by offering him a quick, temporary peek at the voluminous technical report on the *Ticonderoga's* test results. But they had underestimated their man. Glancing through the report, Smith immediately spotted that page A-29 was missing. From his own secretly obtained copy, Smith knew that *that page* contained the test report.

"Where's page A-29?" the congressman demanded.

Naval faces blanched white as naval uniforms. "Oh, isn't it there?" a Navy captain said, simulating innocence.

"Well, I don't find it here," Smith insisted.

A civilian engineer with the Navy cadre offered Smith his copy. "Here it is, right here in mine," he said, and Smith took permanent possession of the damning test report.

"Gosh, it must have been the Xerox," one of the Navy men said. Later, Denny Smith told me he felt the vital page had been purposefully omitted "because the rest of the report is about as dull as toilet paper."

Armed with the damning data, Smith called on the Navy to hold more tests of the Aegis cruiser. Fellow Republicans suggested he was out to "get" the military. Trent Lott, the House Republican whip, asked Smith if he knew that killing the Navy's Aegis cruiser program could affect sixteen thousand jobs at Ingalls Shipyard in Lott's home state of Mississippi.

"Hey, listen Trent, we're not trying to cancel the program," Smith replied. "What we're trying to do is get the Navy to be honest, number one, and, number two, if there are flaws in that ship, let's fix them."

The stakes were enormous because the Navy planned twenty-six Aegis guided-missile cruisers at $1.25 billion apiece, and sixty destroyers, with similar technology, costing $1 billion each.

"I decided to go after them to prove that the ship could survive," Smith explained. "If we were going to spend $90 billion on this huge armada of radar ships to go out there and try to protect the fleet, let's be sure they work. The MX missile program is known by everybody in the country; it's about a $20 billion program. It's peanuts alongside of this thing."

Grudgingly, the Navy called the *Ticonderoga* home from the Mediterranean for further testing, in April 1984. This time, the Navy reported ten out of eleven hits, but the mole network passed word that the tests were too easy because there had been no low-level attackers and no saturation attacks by several planes at one time. Once again, Smith asked the Navy for the test report but never got it. The moles shifted him to another target.

Divad: The Gun with Nine Lives

In the Aegis cruiser episode, Denny Smith had been a green congressman who did not know how to gain political leverage through the press and allies in Congress. But by the time he went after the Army's Divad antiaircraft gun, Smith had political allies. He had become one of four cochairmen of the Military Reform Caucus, a bipartisan group of more than fifty senators and House members, ranging from Senator Gary Hart on the Democratic left to Representative Newt Gingrich on the Republican right. This group was pressing questions about military strategy, not to oppose defense but to make it more efficient. Linked to the caucus, Denny Smith's voice had more weight.

Divad, moreover, was a more vulnerable target. By mid-1984, it was deep in trouble, plagued by technical snafus, facing some high-level opposition within the Pentagon, and wounded by news leaks of rigged tests and embarrassing failures. Still, the Army top brass clung to it, and [Caspar] Weinberger sided with the Army.

Divad (short for division air defense) had been conceived in the mid-1970s to provide antiaircraft protection for Army tank divisions against Soviet fighters and helicopters. By most estimates, more modern air protection was needed. But Denny Smith, as an old fighter pilot, thought an expensive high-tech gun such as Divad was unnecessary and ill conceived. Flyers, he told me, have greater fear of traditional antiaircraft batteries, which are harder to evade.

With all its gear and ammunition, Divad cost upward of $6.3 million per gun, more than three times the cost of the M-1 tank it was supposed to protect. The Army ultimately intended spending $4.5 billion for 618 Divads. To speed up Divad's development, the Army combined several proven components: the chassis of an M-48 tank, two Swedish forty-millimeter cannons, radar adapted from the F-16 jet fighter, plus a one-million-dollar computer and other fancy electronics. But the real speed-up, and one major cause of Divad's problems, was the Army's policy of building and producing Divad *while* it was being tested, rather than testing it first.

Some strange decisions were made along the way. In a shoot-off competition between Ford Aerospace and General Dynamics in November 1980, Ford Aerospace scored worse but got the contract. General Dynamics hit nineteen targets and Ford only nine. The Army later said that Ford had a lot of near-misses which were counted. High Pentagon civilians on Weinberger's staff such as David Chu, director of Program Analysis and Evaluation, and Lawrence Korb, assistant secretary of Defense for Manpower, Installations and Logistics, opposed Divad. They warned that future Soviet helicopters would be able to stand outside Divad's best theoretical range of four thousand meters and fire at American tanks. Chu's staff also pointed out that Divad's reaction time was too slow, and its odds of killing Soviet planes only one-half to one-third of what the Army claimed. Nonetheless, Frank Carlucci, who was Weinberger's deputy at the time, signed a $1.5 billion contract in May 1982 to buy 276 Divads.

Any new weapon has kinks, but Divad's were comic omens: In one check-out test in February 1982, top American and British Army brass went to Fort Bliss, Texas, to see Divad perform. Suddenly, Divad's turret swerved away from a target drone back toward the reviewing stand. The brass all ducked for cover. The gun did not fire at them, but it spent the rest of the day missing targets and lobbing shells into the weeds. Then in January 1984, the first full-fledged production model that Ford was proudly preparing to turn over to the Army made an embarrassing test debut: The radar-guided, computer-operated fire-control system focused on a false target—a rotating latrine fan in a nearby building—which the computer singled out as the closest threatening target.

This produced guffaws within the Army. One hand-drawn Army cartoon showed two GIs, one pointing to the sky and saying, "The Soviets have come up with a new way to foil the Divad." It pictured a Soviet helicopter towing an airborne outhouse to distract Divad.

The incident showed that Divad's radar was still having great difficulty distinguishing the right targets from "ground clutter" (other objects on the terrain). Senator Warren Rudman of New Hampshire, another Divad critic, said this problem highlighted a defect in the gun's basic design. The designers had used a radar system built for jet fighters and for operating against the clutter-free background of the sky, not on the ground. From the outset, Rudman told me, the Army set unrealistic requirements for Divad, dooming it to failure. Nonetheless, the Army stubbornly pressed on, partly out of need, partly out of pride, mostly out of bureaucratic momentum.

"The Divad is a classic example of how the military system keeps alive a weapons program that doesn't make any sense," Denny Smith remarked. "Once the system buys onto the program, there's almost no way you can stop the program. If you try to, you're either unpatriotic, you don't understand the situation, or you're out for publicity. They try to go after you. You can almost tell when they have a bad system because they get so defensive and come after you."

Even so, Congress was growing wary of Divad. More awkward disclosures got into the news. Divad flunked cold-weather tests in early 1984. It had to be heated for six hours with the field equivalent of a hair dryer before it was ready to fire. In another test, the Army had to attach four large metal reflectors to an old target helicopter to help Divad's radar find the target. By late 1984, Ford Aerospace was months behind its production schedule, and Congress had barred further purchase until Divad passed realistic operational field tests. Congressional pressures forced Weinberger to take a personal interest.

In the spring of 1985, the Army ran a massive monthlong mock battle in the California desert with tanks, Bradley fighting vehicles, and Divads opposing A-10 and F-4 fighter planes and AH-64 Apache helicopters. The finale was the "live fire" tests at White Sands, New Mexico, in May 1985.

Afterward, the Army brass jubilantly proclaimed that Divad had hit and destroyed its targets. Jack Krings, civilian head of the Pentagon's new Office of Operational Tests and Evaluation, telephoned Denny Smith. "Boy, really impressive," Krings said. "Blew those mothers right out of the air." Army Secretary John Marsh, Undersecretary James Ambrose, and General John A. Wickam, Jr., the Army chief of staff, all recommended that Weinberger move ahead with Divad. Ambrose, a former Ford Aerospace vice president who had helped launch the Divad program while still at Ford, told me he felt Divad was a big leap forward, a ten- to twenty-percent improvement on existing antiaircraft weapons.

But the Dissident Triangle had a very different story: It informed Congressman Smith that the mock battle showed Divad's range was inadequate, and the live fire tests were unrealistic; the Army's claims of success were misleading. What Denny Smith learned, he told me later, was that the target fighter planes were patsies. They were flown right past the Divad guns "at a suicide elevation of four hundred to five hundred feet, flying straight and level at 420 knots with no jinking [pilot talk for no evasive maneuvers]. The helicopters were flown up to a higher elevation than any sane person would ever do in a combat zone. What they set up was a shooting gallery and, even then, there were *no* direct hits—*none!*"

If so, I asked, how could the Army be claiming success?

Moles at the test site had tipped off Smith to shenanigans on the firing range. For proof, he went after videotapes. The Army happily supplied tapes showing Divad firing and target drones exploding. "You could see that they had been destroyed almost immediately, and you thought maybe the guns had done that," Smith told me later. "The picture would be on the airplane. It would show maybe a couple of sparks. And then almost immediately, they'd blow up, looking like they'd been hit. But we knew better. We'd been told. The range-safety officer destroyed every one of the drones from the ground. None of them were destroyed by hits from the guns."

Others were less categorical than Smith. Two Pentagon skeptics told me that gunbursts showed a few Divad kills but asserted that on the large majority, the range-safety officer had been unusually quick to detonate safety charges on the target planes. Safety measures are routine, but Denny Smith and Lieutenant Colonel Tom Carter, a top Pentagon test analyst and a Vietnam veteran with 408 air missions, told me the safety officer used a fast trigger to make it look as though Divad had scored hits.

"We felt they were certainly flawed tests if they destroyed the drones that quickly," Smith told me. "Why didn't they let them go on for twenty more seconds?" Smith fired off protest letters to top Pentagon officials. The Army brass fought back, defending its weapon.

Smith's blast that Divad had not made "a single direct hit" touched off a firestorm in the media. The Early Bird gave hot running coverage to the charges of the maverick network for Weinberger's ride-to-work reading.* The Schattschneider dynamic was at work: Television networks and news weeklies became seized with Divad.† The videotapes of the live fire tests, and Smith's charges about how the targets were destroyed, gave the whiff of scandal and rigged tests to Divad.

Inside the Pentagon, the final test evaluations were being drafted for Weinberger in mid-August. One of them, done in the Office of Developmental Testing and Evaluation by Colonel Tom Carter, was a blistering and fatal indictment

---

* "Early Bird" is the nickname for the *Current News*, a sixteen-page daily digest of news about the Pentagon from major newspapers, wire services, and television networks.
† Political scientist E. E. Schattschneider's theory is that there are two groups who must be observed in a conflict: the participants and the onlookers who are drawn to the scene. Schattschneider believes that the behavior of the audience, which can include the news media, influences the outcome of the conflict.

of Divad. "My worst suspicions were confirmed," Carter later told me. "The Divad gun couldn't detect and track and engage and shoot down enemy aircraft, unless the enemy's aircraft were using unrealistic tactics which no pilot—Russian or American—in his right mind will fly. The weapon failed miserably to perform."

What happened to Carter's official report was an amusing wrinkle of the Dissident Triangle operations—not leaking, but flooding. My sources told me that the original draft of the second report, prepared by Jack Krings, director of the Office of Operational (as opposed to "Developmental") Testing and Analysis, was nowhere near as harsh as Carter's. On August 22, nine copies of Carter's no-nonsense report were circulated to top Pentagon officials. The next day, the top Pentagon echelon tried to squelch it. Orders were given to retrieve every copy, but it was too late. Instead of nine copies, thirteen copies came back.

"That's what we call the flood strategy," one Pentagon gadfly told me with a grin. "Never leak anything yourself, but make plenty of copies. Flood the building. God will take care of the rest. As soon as Krings's people saw those thirteen copies, they knew they had a P.R. disaster on their hands, because the test results had gotten out of the building."

It was Friday afternoon, and Weinberger had already headed for a weekend in Maine. Krings's office spent the weekend redrafting its report to toughen it, more in line with Carter's.

The "flooder" was right. On August 22, Denny Smith wrote Weinberger a letter to say that he had "obtained and reviewed" the test reports on the Divad which "verify the same criticisms of the weapons flaws leveled over and over again since the inception of the program." He urged Weinberger to cancel the program, and on Monday, from his home in Oregon, Smith telephoned Weinberger to underscore the fact that he had the damaging report in his possession. "I hope you've seen that report, Mr. Secretary, and I just urge you to read that before you make your decision," he said with an implicit threat to go public if Weinberger did not act on the negative report.

The next day, Weinberger announced that he was canceling Divad because "operational tests have demonstrated that the system's performance does not effectively meet the growing military threat." What Divad would offer over existing weapons, he said, was "not worth the additional cost." He identified its main problems as "the lack of range and the lack of reliability. . . . The system didn't work well enough."

At that point, the Pentagon had sunk $1.8 billion into the program. Weinberger's decision to kill Divad marked a rare victory for the dissident triangle—one case in hundreds. I have heard many tales of other weapons systems having serious flaws, but they roll on. A few get stopped in the research-and-testing phase. Senator Warren Rudman, a combat infantry captain in the Korean War, fought three years to block production funds for the Viper, a defective anti-tank weapon with skyrocketing costs. He finally won before production was started.

But it is almost unheard of for the Pentagon to kill a weapon, such as Divad, once it is in production. Only pressure from the Dissident Triangle did that, by forcing the issue into the open and then hawking Weinberger relentlessly.

The Iron Triangle at Work

Far more powerful than the Dissident Triangle is the Iron Triangle—the symbiotic partnership of military services, defense contractors, and members of Congress from states and districts where military spending is heavy and visible.

President Eisenhower called it the military-industrial complex. Others have called it an incestuous family network, where political, economic, and bureaucratic interests mesh and where cozy relations are nurtured not only by mutual back scratching, but also by a flow of corporate executives criss-crossing between high Pentagon jobs and the defense industry and a steady stream of retiring colonels, admirals, and generals moving right into jobs with Pentagon contractors. In 1983, for example, 13,682 Pentagon civilians and officers cashed in on their Pentagon connections by taking jobs in the defense industry.

To those two legs of the Iron Triangle, add the congressional defense committees. For Pentagon procurement is driven by what Anthony Battista, for years an influential senior staffer for the House Armed Services Committee, calls the "unholy alliance between congressional pork barrel and Pentagon wish lists."

In fairness, the Iron Triangle is not unique to the Defense Department. That paradigm operates for virtually every department in the executive branch, for every major interest group, for every major region of the country. The Iron Triangle is a powerful force in the nation's farm policy, forging links between the Agriculture Department, farm organizations and farm-state senators and congressmen, usually concentrated on the agriculture committees of Congress. Basically, they unite to protect farm interests against competing demands for urban development or industrial bailouts. Ditto for the Labor Department, the Department of Health and Human Services, and so on. Rocky Mountain politicians gravitate toward the interior committees to watch over water and land use. Coastal representatives, like salmon instinctively swimming upstream to spawn, head for the maritime and fisheries committees. All form their own iron triangles—iron, because the partners want an unbreakable lock on the policies most vital to them and they want to shut out outsiders. The object of the Iron Triangle is a closed power game, just as the object of the Dissident Triangle is to open up the power game.

What gives the Pentagon's Iron Triangle extraordinary importance is its great influence on national security policy and the enormous sums of money at stake. In the five-year period from late 1981 into 1986, military spending was close to

$1.3 trillion. With domestic programs largely held in check, the Pentagon budget was the one whopping federal cornucopia left for private contractors, the best remaining source of patronage for Congress. A local chunk of some big defense contract dwarfs any other government grant a congressman can deliver. The Pentagon budget is the last really big barrel of pork; its sheer volume feeds economic appetites.

"The military services want more money than they can afford, and the Pentagon wants more money than the country can afford," a longtime prodefense Senate committee staffer observed to me. "The senator or House member wants more for his district than the budget can afford. Each party is motivated by greed. The interests of the service and the contractors is to start new programs and not to worry about efficiency. Contractors like to stretch out production of weapons because they can employ more people for more years. And congressmen like to stretch out programs in their districts for the same reason and because Congress hates to take the responsibility for killing any weapons system."

One reason Divad survived so long was the protection of its own iron triangle. In 1983, when a wildcat effort was made on the House floor to kill Divad, its five most vociferous defenders had political and economic links to Divad:

— Robert Badham, a California Republican and a member of the House Armed Services Committee from the district where Divad was assembled;

— Marjorie Holt, another Republican on the Armed Services Committee from a Maryland district where Westinghouse Electric built Divad's radar;

— Bill Nichols, an Alabama Democrat from Anniston, where Divad's chassis was made;

— Ronald Coleman, a Texas Democrat whose district held the Army base where Divad was conceived, fostered and tested; and

— Samuel Stratton, a New York Democrat and chairman of the Armed Services Subcommittee on Procurement, who had a working relationship with the Army and saw his political role as buying weapons systems.

"The way the game is played now is one word: *jobs*," asserted New Hampshire Senator Warren Rudman, an evangelical skinflint. By jobs, Rudman meant jobs for the contractor and jobs back home for which senators and congressmen could claim credit—but also the careers of the third leg of the Iron Triangle: the layers of Army brass from the Divad program officers up to General John Wickham, then Army chief of staff, who felt their careers were riding on its success.

"The Army's strategy is to keep you going and keep you going and delay you, until they are so far into you in terms of money that you can't afford to abandon the weapons program," Rudman complained. "They'll admit to you that the weapon may not work as well as it was supposed to, but they'll say it works pretty well. I don't think people in the Army thought the Divad was such a good weapon; it's just that too many careers were involved. The Army was committed to it because the top brass felt naked without a new air defense gun."

"Somebody's career is made by keeping a program alive—in the contractors, in the military and in Congress, too," was the way Denny Smith put it. "It's not just the Army. The Navy designs a weapon and if it doesn't work, their attitude is get the ship hull in the water and then we'll fix it later." A three-star Army general agreed. "Divad survived so long because it remained at the level of program managers and staff officers overseeing the program," the general told me. "These majors and lieutenant colonels thought only of their program, and they drove the generals over the brink." Actually, it is a vicious circle: The generals ordered weapons built, and the lieutenant colonels felt compelled to deliver weapons, *not* bad news. Their optimistic reports kept the generals locked into programs such as Divad, for the incentives of the defense game are to build, spend, and appropriate, *not* to oppose, question, or delay.

On the industrial side, the hierarchy at Ford Aerospace and its subcontractors fought tenaciously for jobs and profits from Divad. One Ford Aerospace vice president, James Ambrose, became undersecretary of the Army, and though he claimed to have stayed on the sidelines, several Pentagon officials told me Ambrose fought hard to save Divad. Plenty of others had a personal stake in the program. Early in the competition for Divad, Ford Aerospace hired four recently retired three-star Army generals. Gregg Easterbrook of *The Atlantic,* who has written several detailed articles on Divad, asserted that having these revolving-door links helped Ford beat out General Dynamics. Ford denied any "improprieties or illegalities."

But revolving-door connections do keep programs going and reduce critical questioning. They breed a coziness within the iron triangle that often costs taxpayers money, diminishes real competition, and sometimes perpetuates defective weapons.

In Congress, too, powerful members gain reputations as protectors of certain weapons and contractors. For years, Senator Henry Jackson was known as "the senator from Boeing" because he so openly pushed the interests of Boeing Aircraft, the biggest military contractor in his home state of Washington. Senator Barry Goldwater of Arizona, a retired major general in the Air Force Reserve who loved to fly jet fighters, watched over pet air force programs. Senator John Tower of Texas teamed up with another powerful Texan, George Mahon, to keep LTV's A-7 attack bomber in production at Fort Worth long after the Navy tired of the plane. The most legendary military pork barreler was L. Mendel Rivers; he landed so many bases and contracts for Charleston, South Carolina, during his thirty years in the House that Carl Vinson, another wily practitioner, once teased him: "Mendel, you put anything else down there in your district, and it's gonna sink."

Now, after the dispersal of power in Congress in the mid-1970s, such concentrated largesse in the district of a committee chairman is virtually impossible. More players have power, and all want their slices of Pentagon bacon. The Iron Triangle game has been expanded: The Navy, for example, has shipyards and bases on all coasts, insuring allies among senators intent on protecting thousands of jobs at home: John Warner of Virginia, John Stennis of Mississippi, William Cohen of Maine, Chris Dodd of Connecticut, John Chaffee of Rhode Island, Pete Wilson of California. Warner, a former Navy secretary, is perhaps the Navy's most ardent advocate. His state houses the Atlantic Fleet headquarters at Norfolk and the shipyard that builds aircraft carriers at Newport News.

Charles Bennett, a veteran Florida congressman and chairman of the House Armed Services Seapower Subcommittee, minces no words about how his politics are influenced by the Navy base just outside Jacksonville. "The Navy brings $1 billion to my home district every year," he told me. "That's a big deal. It's the biggest thing we've got commercially. They've got some forty-odd ships there and they're going to get more. Anybody from Jacksonville would want to get onto the Armed Services Committee to protect that."

The committee structure of Congress anchors the Iron Triangle. That is true as well for the Agriculture Department, Interior Department, Labor, and so on. For decades, the Armed Services committees in both houses, along with the appropriations subcommittees that oversee military spending, have been the Pentagon's staunchest partisans. These committees are more promilitary than Congress as a whole, though in recent years they have been infiltrated by a few Pentagon critics. But most members are there for logrolling. Generally, they approach the defense budget, not as a whole but piecemeal, weapon system by weapon system. The committee chairman often operates like a ward politician, parceling out goodies to the members. After the big money is doled out, a defense appropriations subcommittee aide told me: "If you've got something you want in your district, you can say, 'Put this in,' and no one will argue. Most of them are below $10 million, but sometimes more. If you get over $100 million, people will raise questions."

Political doves join the scramble, too. Senator Alan Cranston, a big advocate of arms control and the nuclear freeze, supports the B-1 bomber whose prime contractor is based in California. Senator Carl Levin of Michigan, another Pentagon critic, has added money to Army requests for the M-1 tank which is manufactured in Michigan. Senator Edward Kennedy and House Speaker Tip O'Neill have backed the F-18 fighter and other projects because Massachusetts gets large subcontracts. Mervyn Dymally, a liberal Democratic member of the Black Caucus, normally given to low-cost housing and programs for the poor, has voted for the MX missile because defense plants around his Los Angeles district mean jobs to his constituents. Dick Bolling of Missouri told me of Harry Truman's warning to him: "Dick, the one thing I'll tell you, never try to get a military installation in your district. It'll ruin you."

In sum, the first law of the Pentagon's Iron Triangle is that "the district commands over ideology," says Gordon Adams, director for the Center on Budget and Policy Priorities, a private group that opposes high defense spending. In Speaker O'Neill's memorable aphorism, All politics is local—most emphatically in military procurement. "If your congressional district has dominant economic interests, you go with the people who work at those companies," Adams asserts. "People forget these guys in Congress are elected from a very small piece of geography every two years, and they can't afford to buck all the economic interests of their district."

Few members of Congress epitomized this basic job protecting role more dramatically than the late Joseph Addabbo, a shrewd veteran with a little brush mustache and a wispy tuft on his bald pate. From 1960 until his death in 1986, Addabbo represented an Archie Bunker district in Queens, New York. As chairman of the House Appropriations Defense Subcommittee, Addabbo was a maverick in the Iron Triangle—a liberal Democrat, an advocate of arms control, and a tough-minded Pentagon critic. He led the 1982 fight against the MX missile; earlier he had opposed the B-1 bomber. As subcommittee chairman, he helped whack $50 billion off President Reagan's Pentagon budgets. Nonetheless, he fought and finagled for two military contractors within commuting distance of his Long Island district, Grumman and Fairchild Industries. He badgered the Navy to homeport a battleship on Staten Island to help New York City. And he used his leverage to get other military deals for New York State.

As Grumman's protector, Addabbo was a motive force in getting the Navy to increase its buy of F-14 fighters from 425 to 700. When the Navy wanted to stop production of Grumman's A-6 attack bomber in 1978, Addabbo just kept pushing funds into the appropriations bills. He went to his deathbed opposing Air Force efforts to kill Fairchild's T-46 trainer.

But Addabbo's battle for Fairchild's A-10 was a case study in protecting pork for the home folks. The A-10 is a slow two-engine fighter used for close air support of ground troops, a mission that bores Air Force jet fighter jockeys. In 1983, the Air Force stopped asking for money for the A-10, but Addabbo put money in. In 1984, John Tower, then Senate Armed Services Committee chairman, did the Pentagon's bidding and cut all funds for the A-10—violating a logrolling taboo. For a second rule of the Iron Triangle is that members of key committees do not shoot down each others' favorite projects. Addabbo retaliated by squeezing one of Tower's homestate projects: production of the Harm missile by Texas Instruments. Because the missile was needed, Addabbo did not kill it; he put in a requirement that the Pentagon buy it from two sources, taking some business away from Texas Instruments. So Tower backed off.

When I asked Addabbo about the inconsistency between his general anti-Pentagon stance and his protection of Long Island defense plants, he shrugged. "I fought for the A-10 and the A-6 because there was nothing around like them, and you needed them," he asserted. "So why not build them in your own area, the same as everyone else does."

Contract Spreading Gets Weapons Built

The third basic rule of the Iron Triangle is for defense contractors and military services to make sure that enough regions get a piece of the pie so that a weapons program develops wide political support. All the services need new technology, and so they have a constant flow of projects at various stages of development. The standard technique is to get a project started by having the prime contractor give a low initial cost estimate to make it seem affordable and wait to add fancy electronics and other gadgets much later through engineering "change orders," which jack up the price and the profits. Anyone who has been through building or remodeling a house knows the problem.

"This is called the buy-in game," an experienced Senate defense staff specialist confided. "In conjunction with the contractors, the services give very rosy estimates of what the weapon will cost *per copy,* so Congress will buy in. Their estimates are based on the largest buy and the most efficient production rate—which never materializes." Once the Pentagon leaders and Congress are on board, costs rise, creating the "bow-wave" effect. Like waves on the bow of the ship, the costs start small, grow gradually as the project picks up speed, then swell for several years during the peak production phase, reach a crest, and subside. That initial commitment—first to research and then to development of a new system—is vital. It rarely bears much relationship to the ultimate cost. The key is to get the program going and keep it alive. Then if the subcontracts are well spread out politically, the weapon system has a secure future in the politics of procurement.

No case better illustrates the politics of contract spreading than Rockwell International's formidable campaign for the B-1 bomber. Joseph Addabbo told me that at Nellis Air Force Base in Nevada in 1983, he had seen a Rockwell display that illustrated the political strings Rockwell had tied to the B-1. It was a blown-up photo of the needle-nosed bomber with colored strings coming out of various components—the fuselage, wings, engine, tail section, cockpit, landing gear, and so on—to the states and districts where the parts were made.

"The whole country was covered with these strings," Addabbo said. "Other contractors had done this thing, spreading the subcontracts, but the B-1 was the first time we really saw it in large numbers. This was the biggest of that type of operation by far. People would come to me and say, 'Joe, I'm not for it, but it's one of the biggest employers in my district. I've got to go with them.'"

Thomas Downey, a Long Island Democrat, told me that when he arrived in Congress in 1975 and landed on the Armed Services Committee, Rockwell International was lobbying aggressively to keep the program going. "Rockwell would show you the B-1 program and bring out that it had forty-eight states of the Union covered—to prevent what they called [political] 'turbulence'—that was their great term. Translated, *turbulence* meant canceling the contract," Downey told me.

"They thought I was crazy the first few times Rockwell briefed me," he went on. "I was one of the leading advocates to kill the B-1. One guy from Airborne Instruments Labs in my district, which makes the electronic countermeasures for the B-1, said to me: 'This is the third biggest contract we have, congressman. Except for the engine and the airframe, it's the third biggest. It's $2 billion just in the first few years.' I said, 'I know. I just think the plane's a bad idea.' Rockwell had it all worked up in a briefing kit. Defense had a map, showing where the subcontracts were. They said forty-eight states. Conscious decision on their part from day one."

Air Force and Rockwell officials claim the contract spreading happened naturally—that the B-1 is such a complex, modern system of weaponry and electronics that it naturally tapped a vast and diverse network of parts suppliers all over the country. Practically no one in Congress takes that claim at face value; virtually everyone regards B-1 contract spreading as deliberate. In the mid-1970s Rockwell paid Chase Econometrics $110,000 for a study to help show each senator and representative the impact of the project in his area. Over seven years, Rockwell figured the $30 billion B-1 program meant 192,000 jobs for a total of 5,200 subcontractors and nearby businesses "due to the economic cascade effect." Its lobbyists worked hundreds of members of Congress, one by one, with specific information about the subcontractors, jobs, and money involved in their districts.

Bill Gray, the House Budget Committee chairman, told me one computer printout showed subcontractors in more than 400 of the 435 congressional districts, a phenomenal political spread. This big a project activates industrial unions as well as corporate management, especially in key states such as California, Ohio, and Massachusetts. Rockwell also had stockholders and employees writing members of Congress—on company time, which meant at least partly at taxpayers' expense.

"That is one of the ways they sell these things to Congress," protested Representative John Seiberling, an Ohio Democrat. "That is another scandal—that we are allowing this engine of spending taxpayers' money for defense programs to be used to propagandize and manipulate the Congress."

Seiberling showed me a letter from J. W. Rane, Jr., of Rockwell's B-1 Division in June 1973 asserting that Seiberling's fourteenth district of Ohio had "a potential of approximately $60 million new business" from development of the B-1 prototype, mainly to Goodyear Aerospace, for brakes and wheels. But Seiberling was skeptical. His staff calculated that the subcontracts were so small that his district would pay out more in taxes to underwrite the B-1 than it would earn from the B-1. Seiberling argued that was typical for most congressional districts, but he was no match for Rockwell.

The company's enormous lobbying effort was so potent that Congress nearly overrode President Carter's decision in 1977 against B-1 production. Strong congressional support did keep alive research and development for testing four prototype bombers. Rockwell did an uncanny job of keeping together its skilled work force for a quick start-up of B-1 production, banking on a Republican president in 1981. Reagan aides told me of financial contributions to Reagan's campaign by Rockwell company executives, and the company's lobbying of the Reagan forces during the 1980 campaign, gaining entrée through Michael Deaver, Reagan's public relations adviser. When Reagan entered the White House, the B-1 was one of the first military projects revived, a hallmark of Reagan defense policy—and of Rockwell's success at the Iron Triangle game.

The B-1 has become a model for other contractors. It has been imitated by the Reagan administration itself with the rapid spread of contracts for its strategic defense initiative (SDI), not only in this country but in Western Europe and possibly Japan and Israel. By 1986, Reagan's strategic defense program had research contracts in forty-two of the fifty states, covering seventeen of the nineteen states represented on the Senate Armed Services Committee and twenty of the twenty-six on the Appropriations Committee. Paul Warnke, a former Carter administration arms control adviser, suggested that Reagan's Star Wars proposal was being converted "from stardust and moonbeams to that great pork barrel in the sky." Moreover, the initial alarm of West European governments about the SDI program abated as Weinberger worked out agreements for the British, Germans, Japanese, and Israelis, among others, to bid for the project's research contracts.

"This is the internationalization of the military-industrial complex that Eisenhower talked about," Gary Hart commented ruefully. "What you've got with Star Wars is a unique phenomenon where they're building not just a national constituency, but an international constituency."

What left the program's long-term future in doubt was congressional resistance to going beyond the research phase. For the critical point in building political support for any big weapons system, Gordon Adams observed, comes with moving from research into development and production and with the selection of a prime contractor, which, like Rockwell, leads the political campaign. Research involves relatively small teams of white-collar scientists and engineers, but production involves tens of thousands of blue-collar workers. That massive job constituency gives a weapon system almost irresistible momentum.

In *The Defense Game,* a book drawing on his nineteen years experience as a defense specialist for the Office of Management and Budget through six presidential administrations, Richard Stubbings bluntly summarized the workings of the Iron Triangle:

> *At stake in our defense program is not only our national security, but also large opportunities for personal and economic success. Congressmen favor programs and facilities in their states and districts regardless of efficiency. Industry officials seek to boost their sales and profits, ofttimes at the expense of the government and the taxpayer. Military officers seek promotion and advancement under accepted standards of performance which often conflict with hard-nosed business prac-*

*tices. And the service hierarchies see close working relations with the
other services as not in their interest. Thus, not only is the defense
budget the vehicle by which our nation plans how to fight the battles
of tomorrow, but it is also a battleground itself, where politicians, corporations, and military officers seek to serve their personal and parochial interests.*

Epilogue

Imagine that you are a soldier involved in a firefight in the Middle East. When your
faulty weapon does not work, will it be any consolation to you or your family that
the governmental bureaucratic system did not work properly? The job of the bureaucracy was to build a weapon that would work and be cost-efficient. Yet you
can see from this selection that there is no incentive to any of the players in the
iron triangle to do anything but protect their own individual interests.

With the Cold War apparently over, many people expected massive cutbacks
in defense spending. The Persian Gulf crisis, however, has provided defense industry interests with a golden opportunity to preserve their spending prerogatives. When that crisis ends, it will be interesting to see whether the defense industry iron triangle or the dissident triangle becomes dominant.

CHAPTER 6

THE SUPREME COURT AND CIVIL LIBERTIES

The Case of the Missing Commissions

John A. Garraty

Schoolchildren are taught that George Washington was the "father of our country," but a case can be made that Chief Justice John Marshall was the "father of the national government." Take a look at Article III of the Constitution, which deals with the federal court system, and see if you can ascertain how much power is given to the Supreme Court. Interestingly, the answer is not there. As John Garraty describes in this selection, the Supreme Court's power derives from the efforts of Marshall in the case of *Marbury* v. *Madison.* By establishing the concept of judicial review—making the Supreme Court the final interpreter of the Constitution—Marshall gave the Court the power to say no to the president, the Congress, and the state governments. Marshall accomplished this task knowing that one mistake would have allowed his political enemies to destroy the Court's power. As you read this selection, pay attention to how Marshall performed this legal magic act. In addition, ask yourself whether Marshall, as the secretary of state responsible for Marbury not getting his commission from the government in the first place, should have been involved in deciding this case.

It is important to understand that although the framers did not include the concept of judicial review in the Constitution, it had been discussed. James Madison and others considered creating a "council of revision," a committee of Supreme Court justices and members of the executive branch that would have had the power to declare acts of the state legislatures unconstitutional. In the end, however, this committee was not created. In *The Federalist,* No. 78, the devoutly nationalistic Alexander Hamilton argued that the Supreme Court should have final power of interpretation of the Constitution. His argument consisted of the following philosophical syllogism: the Supreme Court interprets law, the Constitution is law, and so the Supreme Court interprets the Constitution. John Marshall, an astute politician as well as a legal scholar, used this argument to maximum advantage in the *Marbury* case. Without this case, the development of the Supreme Court, American government, and American history would have been very different indeed.

JOHN ADAMS   President from 1797 to March 1801.

THOMAS JEFFERSON   Became president in March 1801.

CHARLES LEE   Attorney for Marbury.

LEVI LINCOLN   Attorney general under Jefferson.

JAMES MADISON   Secretary of state under Jefferson.

WILLIAM MARBURY   Adams appointee for justice of the peace.

JOHN MARSHALL   Secretary of state under Adams; appointed chief justice of the United States by Adams in early 1801.

▶ It was the evening of March 3, 1801, his last day in office, and President John Adams was in a black and bitter mood. Assailed by his enemies, betrayed by some of his most trusted friends, he and his Federalist party had gone down to defeat the previous November before the forces of Thomas Jefferson. His world seemed to have crumbled about his doughty shoulders.

Conservatives of Adams's persuasion were convinced that Thomas Jefferson was a dangerous radical. He would, they thought, in the name of individual liberty and states' rights import the worst excesses of the French Revolution, undermine the very foundations of American society, and bring the proud edifice of the national government, so laboriously erected under Washington and Adams, tumbling to the ground. Jefferson was a "visionary," Chief Justice Oliver Ellsworth had said. With him as President, "there would be no national energy." Secretary of State John Marshall, an ardent believer in a powerful central government, feared that Jefferson would "sap the fundamental principles of government." Others went so far as to call Jefferson a "howling atheist."

Adams himself was not quite so disturbed as some, but he was deeply troubled. "What course is it we steer?" he had written to an old friend after the election. "To what harbor are we bound?" Now on the morrow Jefferson was to be inaugurated, and Adams was so disgruntled that he was unwilling to remain for the ceremonies, the first to be held in the new capital on the Potomac. At the moment, however, John Adams was still President of the United States, and not about to abandon what he called "all virtuous exertion" in the pursuit of his duty. Sitting at his desk in the damp, drafty, still unfinished sandstone "palace" soon to be known as the White House, he was writing his name on official papers in his large, quavering hand.

The documents he was signing were mostly commissions appointing various staunch Federalists to positions in the national judiciary, but the President did not consider his actions routine. On the contrary: he believed he was saving the Republic itself. Jefferson was to be President and his Democratic Republicans would control Congress, but the courts, thank goodness, would be beyond his control. As soon as the extent of Jefferson's triumph was known, Adams had determined to make the judiciary a stronghold of Federalism. Responding enthusiastically to his request, the lame-duck Congress had established sixteen new circuit judgeships (and a host of marshals, attorneys, and clerks as well). It had also given the President authority to create as many justices of the peace for the new District of Columbia as he saw fit, and—to postpone the evil day when Jefferson would be able to put one of his sympathizers on the Supreme Court—it provided that when the next vacancy occurred it should not be filled, thus reducing the Court from six justices to five.

In this same period between the election and Jefferson's inauguration, Chief Justice Ellsworth, who was old and feeble, had resigned, and Adams had replaced him with Secretary of State Marshall. John Marshall was primarily a soldier and politician; he knew relatively little of the law. But he had a powerful mind, and, as Adams reflected, his "reading of the science" was "fresh in his head." He was also but forty-five years of age, and vigorous. A more forceful opponent of Jeffersonian principles would have been hard to find.

Marshall had been confirmed by the Senate on January 27, and without resigning as secretary of state he had begun at once to help Adams strengthen the judicial branch of the government. Perforce they had worked rapidly, for time was short. The new courts were authorized by Congress on February 13; within two weeks Adams had submitted a full slate of officials for confirmation by the Senate. The new justices of the peace for the District of Columbia were authorized on February 27; within three days Adams had submitted for confirmation the names of no less than forty-two justices for that sparsely populated region. The Federalist Senate had done its part nobly too, pushing through the necessary confirmations with dispatch. Now, in the lamplight of his last night in Washington, John Adams was affixing his signature to the commissions appointing these "midnight justices" to office.

Working with his customary diligence, Adams completed his work by nine o'clock, and went off to bed for the last time as President of the United States, presumably with a clear conscience. The papers were carried to the State Department, where Secretary Marshall was to affix to each the Great Seal of the United States and see to it that the documents were then dispatched to the new appointees. But Marshall, a Virginian with something of the easygoing carelessness about detail that is said to be characteristic of Southerners, failed to complete this routine task. All the important new circuit judgeships were taken care of, and most of the other appointments as well. But in the bustle of last-minute arrangements, the commissions of the new District of Columbia justices of the peace went astray. As a result of this slipup, and entirely without anyone's having planned it, a fundamental principle of the Constitution—affecting the lives of countless millions of future Americans—was to be forever established. Because *Secretary of State* Marshall made his last mistake, *Chief*

Justice Marshall was soon to make the first—and in some respects the greatest—of his decisions.

It is still not entirely clear what happened to the missing commissions on the night of March 3. To help with the rush of work, Adams had borrowed two State Department clerks, Jacob Wagner and Daniel Brent. Among his other tasks that fateful night, Brent prepared a list of the forty-two new justices and gave it to another clerk, who "filled up" the appropriate blank commissions. As fast as batches of these were made ready, Brent took them to Adams's office, where he turned them over to William Smith Shaw, the President's private secretary. After Adams had signed them, Brent brought them back to the State Department, where Marshall was supposed to attach the Great Seal. Evidently Marshall did seal these documents, but he did not trouble to make sure that they were delivered to the appointees. As he later said: "I did not send out the commissions because I apprehended such . . . to be completed when signed & sealed." He admitted that he would have sent them out in any case "but for the extreme hurry of the time & the absence of Mr. Wagner who had been called on by the President to act as his private secretary."

March 4 dawned and Jefferson, who does not seem to have digested the significance of Adams's partisan appointments at this time, prepared to take the oath of office and deliver his brilliant inaugural address. His mood, as the speech indicated, was friendly and conciliatory. He even asked Chief Justice Marshall, who administered the inaugural oath, to stay on briefly as secretary of state while the new administration was getting established.

That morning it would still have been possible to deliver the commissions. As a matter of fact, a few actually were delivered, although quite by chance. Marshall's brother James (whom Adams had just made circuit judge for the District of Columbia) was disturbed by rumors that there was going to be a riot in Alexandria in connection with the inaugural festivities. Feeling the need of some justices of the peace in case trouble developed, he went to the State Department and picked up a batch of the commissions. He signed a receipt for them, but "finding that he could not conveniently carry the whole," he returned several, crossing out the names of these from the receipt. Among the ones returned were those appointing William Harper and Robert Townshend Hooe. By failing to deliver these commissions, Judge James M. Marshall unknowingly enabled Harper and Hooe, obscure men, to win for themselves a small claim to legal immortality.

The new President was eager to mollify the Federalists, but when he realized the extent to which they had packed the judiciary with his "most ardent political enemies," he was indignant. Adams's behavior, he said at the time, was an "outrage on decency," and some years later, when passions had cooled a little, he wrote sorrowfully: "I can say with truth that one act of Mr. Adams' life, and only one, ever gave me a moment's personal displeasure. I did consider his last appointments to office as personally unkind." When he discovered the J.P. commissions in the State Department, he decided at once not to allow them to be delivered.

James Madison, the new secretary of state, was not yet in Washington. So Jefferson called in his attorney general, a Massachusetts lawyer named Levi Lincoln, whom he had designated acting secretary. Giving Lincoln a new list of justices of the peace, he told him to put them "into a general commission" and notify the men of their selection.

In truth, Jefferson acted with remarkable forbearance. He reduced the number of justices to thirty, fifteen each for Washington and Alexandria counties. But only seven of his appointees were new men; the rest he chose from among the forty-two names originally submitted by Adams. (One of Jefferson's choices was Thomas Corcoran, father of W. W. Corcoran, the banker and philanthropist who founded the Corcoran Gallery of Art.) Lincoln prepared the general commissions, one for each county, and notified the appointees. Then, almost certainly, he destroyed the original commissions signed by Adams.

For some time thereafter Jefferson did very little about the way Adams had packed the judiciary. Indeed, despite his famous remark that officeholders seldom die and never resign, he dismissed relatively few persons from the government service. For example, the State Department clerks, Wagner and Brent, were permitted to keep their jobs. The new President learned quickly how hard it was to institute basic changes in a going organization. "The great machine of society" could not easily be moved, he admitted, adding that it was impossible "to advance the notions of a whole people suddenly to ideal right." Soon some of his more impatient supporters, like John Randolph of Roanoke, were grumbling about the President's moderation.

But Jefferson was merely biding his time. Within a month of the inauguration he conferred with Madison at Monticello and made the basic decision to try to abolish the new system of circuit courts. Aside from removing the newly appointed marshals and attorneys, who served at the pleasure of the chief executive, little could be done until the new Congress met in December. Then, however, he struck. In his annual message he urged the "contemplation" by Congress of the Judiciary Act of 1801. To direct the lawmakers' thinking, he submitted a statistical report showing how few cases the federal courts had been called upon to deal with since 1789. In January, 1802, a repeal bill was introduced; after long debate it passed early in March, thus abolishing the jobs of the new circuit judges.

Some of the deposed jurists petitioned Congress for "relief," but their plea was coldly rejected. Since these men had been appointed for life, the Federalists claimed that the Repeal Act was unconstitutional, but to prevent the Supreme Court from quickly so declaring, Congress passed another bill abolishing the June term of the Court and setting the second Monday of February, 1803, for its next session. By that time, the Jeffersonians reasoned, the old system would be dead beyond resurrection.

This assault on the courts thoroughly alarmed the conservative Federalists; to them the foundations of stable government seemed threatened if the "independence" of the judiciary could be thus destroyed. No one was more disturbed than the new chief justice, John Marshall, nor was anyone better equipped by temperament and intellect to resist it. Headstrong but shrewd, contemptuous of detail and of abstractions but a powerful logician, he detested Jefferson, to whom he was distantly related, and the President fully returned his dislike.

In the developing conflict Marshall operated at a disadvantage that a modern chief justice would not have to face. The Supreme Court had none of the prestige and little of the accepted authority it now possesses. Few cases had come before it, and none of much importance. A prominent newspaper of the day referred to the chief justiceship, with considerable truth, as a "sinecure." Before appointing Marshall, Adams had offered the chief justiceship to John Jay, the first man to hold the post. Jay had resigned from the Court in 1795 to become governor of New York. He refused reappointment, saying the Court lacked "energy, weight, and dignity." One of the reasons Marshall had accepted the post was his belief that it would afford him ample leisure for writing the biography of his hero, George Washington. Indeed, in the grandiose plans for the new capital, no thought had been given to housing the Supreme Court, so that when Marshall took office in 1801 the judges had to meet in the office of the clerk of the Senate, a small room on the first floor of what is now the North Wing of the Capitol.

Nevertheless, Marshall struck out at every opportunity against the power and authority of the new President. But the opportunities were few. In one case, he refused to allow a presidential message to be read into the record on the ground that this would bring the President into the Court in violation of the principle of separation of powers. In another, he ruled that Jefferson's action in a ship seizure case was illegal. But these were matters of small importance. When he tried to move more boldly, his colleagues would not sustain him. He was ready to declare the Judicial Repeal Act unconstitutional, but none of the deposed circuit court judges would bring a case to court. Marshall also tried to persuade his associates that it was unconstitutional for Supreme Court justices to ride the circuit, as they must again do since the lower courts had been abolished. But although they agreed with his legal reasoning, they refused to go along because, they said, years of acquiescence in the practice lent sanction to the law requiring it. Thus frustrated, Marshall was eager for any chance to attack his enemy, and when a case that was to be known as *Marbury* v. *Madison* came before the Court in December 1801, he took it up with gusto.

William Marbury, a forty-one-year-old Washingtonian, was one of the justices of the peace for the District of Columbia whose commissions Jefferson had held up. Originally from Annapolis, he had moved to Washington to work as an aide to the first secretary of the navy, Benjamin Stoddert. It was probably his service to this staunch Federalist that earned him the appointment by Adams. Together with one Dennis Ramsay and Messrs. Harper and Hooe, whose commissions James Marshall had *almost* delivered, Marbury was asking the Court to issue an order (a writ of mandamus) requiring Secretary of State Madison to hand over their "missing" commissions.* Marshall willingly assumed jurisdiction and issued a rule calling upon Madison to show cause at the next term of the Supreme Court why such a writ should not be drawn. Clearly here was an opportunity to get at the President through one of his chief agents, to assert the authority of the Court over the executive branch of the government.

This small controversy quickly became a matter of great moment both to the administration and to Marshall. The decision to do away with the June term of the Court was made in part to give Madison more time before having to deal with Marshall's order. The abolition of the circuit courts and the postponement of the next Supreme Court session to February 1803 made Marshall even more determined to use the Marbury case to attack Jefferson. Of course, Marshall was embarrassingly involved in this case, since his carelessness was the cause of its very existence. He ought to have disqualified himself, but his fighting spirit was aroused, and he was in no mood to back out.

On the other hand, the Jeffersonians, eager to block any judicial investigation of executive affairs, used every conceivable mode of obstruction to prevent the case from being decided. Madison ignored Marshall's order. When Marbury and Ramsay called on the secretary to inquire whether their commissions had been duly signed (Hooe and Harper could count on the testimony of James Marshall to prove that theirs had been attended to), he gave them no satisfactory answer. When they asked to *see* the documents, Madison referred them to the clerk, Jacob Wagner. He, in turn, would only say that the commissions were not then in the State Department files.

Unless the plaintiffs could prove that Adams had appointed them their case would collapse. Frustrated at the State Department, they turned to the Senate for help. A friendly senator introduced a motion calling upon the secretary of the Senate to produce the record of the action in an executive session on their nominations. But the motion was defeated after an angry debate on January 31, 1803. Thus tempers were hot when the Court finally met on February 9 to deal with the case.

In addition to Marshall, only Justices Bushrod Washington and Samuel Chase were on the bench, and the chief justice dominated the proceedings. The almost childishly obstructive tactics of the administration witnesses were no match for his fair but forthright management of the hearing. The plaintiffs' lawyer was Charles Lee, an able advocate and brother of "Light-Horse Harry" Lee; he had served as attorney general under both Washington and Adams. He was a close

---

* A court issues a *writ of mandamus* to order a lower court, an official, or a government body to do something specific.

friend of Marshall, and his dislike of Jefferson had been magnified by the repeal of the Judiciary Act of 1801, for he was another of the circuit court judges whose "midnight" appointments repeal had canceled.

Lee's task was to prove that the commissions had been completed by Adams and Marshall, and to demonstrate that the Court had authority to compel Madison to issue them. He summoned Wagner and Brent, and when they objected to being sworn in because "they were clerks in the Department of State, and not bound to disclose any facts relating to the business or transactions in the office," he argued that in addition to their "confidential" duties as agents of the President, the secretary and his deputies had duties "of a public nature" delegated to them by Congress. They must testify about these public matters, just as, in a suit involving property, a clerk in the land office could be compelled to state whether or not a particular land patent was on file.

Marshall agreed and ordered the clerks to testify. They then disclosed many of the details of what had gone on in the President's "palace" and in the State Department on the evening of March 3, 1801. But they claimed to be unsure of the fate of the particular commissions of the plaintiffs.

Next Lee called Attorney General Levi Lincoln. He too objected strenuously to testifying. He demanded that Lee submit his questions in writing so that he might consider carefully his obligations both to the Court and to the President before making up his mind. He also suggested that it might be necessary for him to exercise his constitutional right (under the Fifth Amendment) to refuse to give evidence that might "criminate" him. Lee then wrote out four questions. After studying them, Lincoln asked to be excused from answering, but the justices ruled against him. Still hesitant, the attorney general asked for time to consider his position further, and Marshall agreed to an overnight adjournment.

The next day, the tenth of February, Lincoln offered to answer all of Lee's questions but the last: What had he done with the commissions? He had seen "a considerable number of commissions" signed and sealed, but could not remember—he claimed—whether the plaintiffs' were among them. He did not know if Madison had ever seen these documents, but was certain that *he* had not given them to the secretary. On the basis of this last statement, Marshall ruled that the embarrassing question as to what Lincoln had done with the commissions was irrelevant; he excused Lincoln from answering it.

Despite these reluctant witnesses, Lee was able to show conclusively through affidavits submitted by another clerk and by James Marshall that the commissions had been signed and sealed. In his closing argument he stressed the significance of the case as a test of the principle of judicial independence. "The emoluments or the dignity of the office," he said, "are no objects with the applicants." This was undoubtedly true; the positions were unimportant and two years of the five-year terms had already expired. As Jefferson later pointed out, the controversy itself had become "a moot case" by 1803. But Marshall saw it as a last-ditch fight against an administration campaign to make lackeys of all federal judges, while Jefferson looked at it as an attempt by the Federalist-dominated judiciary to usurp the power of the executive.

In this controversy over principle, Marshall and the Federalists were of necessity the aggressors. The administration boycotted the hearings. After Lee's summation, no government spokesman came forward to argue the other side, Attorney General Lincoln coldly announcing that he "had received no instructions to appear." With his control over Congress, Jefferson was content to wait for Marshall to act. If he overreached himself, the chief justice could be impeached. If he backed down, the already trifling prestige of his court would be further reduced.

Marshall had acted throughout with characteristic boldness; quite possibly it was he who had persuaded the four aggrieved justices of the peace to press their suit in the first place. But now his combative temperament seemed to have driven him too far. As he considered the Marbury case after the close of the hearings, he must have realized this himself, for he was indeed in a fearful predicament. However sound his logic and just his cause, he was on dangerous ground. Both political partisanship and his sense of justice prompted him to issue the writ sought by Marbury and his fellows, but what effect would the mandamus produce? Madison almost certainly would ignore it and Jefferson would back him up. No power but public opinion could make the Executive Department obey an order of the Court. Since Jefferson was riding the crest of a wave of popularity, to issue the writ would be an act of futile defiance; it might even trigger impeachment proceedings against Marshall that, if successful, would destroy him and reduce the Court to servility.

Yet what was the alternative? To find against the petitioners would be to abandon principle and surrender abjectly to Jefferson. This a man of Marshall's character simply could not consider. Either horn of the dilemma threatened disaster; that it was disaster of his own making could only make the chief justice's discomfiture the more complete.

But at some point between the close of the hearings on February 11 and the announcement of his decision on the twenty-fourth, Marshall found a way out. It was an inspired solution, surely the cleverest of his long career. It provided a perfect escape from the dilemma, which probably explains why he was able to persuade the associate justices to agree to it despite the fact that it was based on questionable legal logic. The issue, Marshall saw, involved a conflict between the Court and the President, the problem being how to check the President without exposing the Court to his might. Marshall's solution was to state vigorously the justice of the plaintiffs' cause and to condemn the action of the Executive, but to deny the Court's power to provide the plaintiffs with relief.

Marbury and his associates were legally entitled to their commissions, Marshall announced. In withholding them Madison was acting "in plain violation" of the law of the land. But the Supreme Court could not issue a writ of mandamus because the provision of the Judiciary Act of 1789 authorizing the Court to issue such writs was unconstitutional. In other words, Congress did not have the legal right to give that power to the Court!

So far as it concerned the Judiciary Act, modern commentators agree that Marshall's decision was based on a very weak argument. The Act of 1789 stated (section 13) that the Supreme Court could issue the writ to "persons holding office under the authority of the United States." This law had been framed by experts thoroughly familiar with the Constitution, including William Paterson, who now sat by Marshall's side on the Supreme Bench. The justices had issued the writ in earlier cases without questioning section 13 for a moment. But Marshall now claimed that the Court could not issue a mandamus except in cases that came to it *on appeal* from a lower court, since, under the Constitution, the Court was specifically granted original jurisdiction only over "cases affecting ambassadors, other public ministers and consuls, and those in which a state shall be a party." The Marbury case had *originated* in the Supreme Court; since it did not involve a diplomat or a state, any law that gave the Court the right to decide it was unauthorized.

This was shaky reasoning because the Constitution does not say the Court may exercise original jurisdiction *only* in such cases. But Marshall was on solid ground when he went on to argue that "the constitution controls any legislative act repugnant to it," which he called "one of the fundamental principles of our society." The Constitution is "the *supreme* law of the land," he emphasized. Since it is "the duty of the judicial department to say what the law is," the Supreme Court must overturn any law of Congress that violates the Constitution. "A law repugnant to the constitution," he concluded, "is void." By this reasoning section 13 of the Act of 1789 simply ceased to exist and without it the Court could not issue the writ of mandamus. By thus denying himself authority, Marshall found the means to flay his enemies without exposing himself to their wrath.

Although this was the first time the Court had declared an act of Congress unconstitutional, its right to do so had not been seriously challenged by most authorities. Even Jefferson accepted the principle, claiming only that the executive as well as the judiciary could decide questions of constitutionality. Jefferson was furious over what he called the "twistifications" of Marshall's gratuitous opinion in *Marbury* v. *Madison,* but his anger was directed at the chief justice's stinging criticisms of his behavior, not at the constitutional doctrine Marshall had enunciated.

Even in 1803, the idea of judicial review had had a long history in America. The concept of natural law (the belief that certain principles of right and justice transcend the laws of mere men) was thoroughly established in American thinking. It is seen, for example, in Jefferson's statement in the Declaration of Independence that men "are endowed by their Creator" with "unalienable" rights. Although not a direct precedent for Marshall's decision, the colonial practice of "disallowance," whereby laws had been ruled void on the ground that local legislatures had exceeded their powers in passing them, illustrates the belief that there is a limit to legislative power and that courts may determine when it has been overstepped.

More specifically, Lord Coke had declared early in the seventeenth century that "the common law will controul acts of Parliament."* One of the chief legal apologists of the American Revolution, James Otis, had drawn upon this argument a century and a half later in his famous denunciation of the Writs of Assistance.† In the 1780s courts in New Jersey, New York, Rhode Island, and North Carolina had exercised judicial review over the acts of state legislatures. The debates at the Constitutional Convention and some of the *Federalist Papers* (especially No. 78) indicated that most of the Founding Fathers accepted the idea of judicial review as already established. The Supreme Court, in fact, had considered the constitutionality of an act of Congress before—when it upheld a federal tax law in 1796—and it had encountered little questioning of its right to do so. All these precedents, when taken together with the fact that the section of the Act of 1789 nullified by Marshall's decision was of minor importance, explain why no one paid much attention to this part of the decision.

Thus the "case of the missing commissions" passed into history, seemingly a fracas of slight significance. When it was over, Marbury and his frustrated colleagues disappeared into the obscurity whence they had arisen. In the partisan struggle for power between Marshall and Jefferson, the incident was of secondary importance. The real showdown came later in the impeachment proceedings against Justice Chase and the treason trial of Aaron Burr. In the long run, Marshall won his fight to preserve the independence and integrity of the federal judiciary, but generally speaking, the Courts have not been able to exert much influence over the appointive and dismissal powers of the President. Even the enunciation of the Court's power to void acts of Congress wrought no immediate change in American life. Indeed, more than half a century passed before another federal law was overturned.

Nevertheless, this squabble over some small political plums was of vital importance. For with the expansion of the federal government into new areas of activity in more recent times, the power of the Supreme Court to nullify acts of Congress has been repeatedly employed, with profound effects upon our social, economic, and political life. At various times income tax, child labor, wage and hours laws, and many other types of legislation have been thrown out by the Court, and always, in the last analysis, its right to do so has depended upon the decision John Marshall made to escape from a dilemma of his own making. The irony is that in 1803 no one—not even the great chief justice himself—realized how tremendously significant the case of the missing commissions would one day become.

---

* Lord Coke was an English jurist.
† See the introduction to Selection 6.4 for a discussion of the writs of assistance.

Epilogue

As Garraty makes clear, because of the absence of other members of the Court, if Marshall had decided not to participate in the case, it could not have been decided at all. Then the right to decide questions of constitutionality would have reverted to the Jefferson administration.

After establishing the right of the Court to use judicial review, in case after case Marshall led a unanimous Court in fashioning a powerful national government. In one case, *McCulloch* v. *Maryland,* involving the power of the national government to create a national bank, Marshall established both the supremacy of national over state laws and the power of Congress under Article I, Section 8 of the Constitution to do anything "necessary and proper" to carry out its laws. Marshall's charisma allowed him to maintain a unanimous Court even when the backgrounds of his colleagues (such as Justice Joseph Story, who was a member of the Jeffersonian Republican party) should have led them to different conclusions. Marshall was clearly one of our greatest chief justices, but, as we will see in the next selection, he was not without a peer.

Arrival of the Superchief

Richard Kluger

When Chief Justice Fred Vinson died in 1953, in the middle of the Supreme Court's consideration of the *Brown* v. *Board of Education* (1954) school desegregation case, the volatile and atheistic Justice Felix Frankfurter was moved to say that he was now convinced there was a God in heaven. Frankfurter was concerned about *Brown* because it was one of five appeals accepted by the Court on the question of whether segregated public schools were constitutional. According to *Plessy* v. *Ferguson* (1896), segregated public facilities were acceptable as long as they were "separate but equal." By the 1950s, however, the courts were becoming aware that separate facilities were never really equal. Frankfurter believed that the southern loyalties of the Kentuckian Vinson would have prevented the Court from handling the issue of desegregation directly and effectively. Shortly, the Court had a new leader, Earl Warren, and an implicit mandate to reconsider the national legal policy on this deeply divisive issue.

The way that the most talented chief justice since John Marshall came to his new post was unusual, to say the least. At the 1952 Republican convention, Earl Warren, then governor of California, threw his votes from that state to Dwight Eisenhower, ensuring that Eisenhower and not Warren's sworn enemy, Richard Nixon, would get the nomination. In return, Eisenhower promised Warren the first vacancy on the Supreme Court. When Vinson died, Warren expected to be named chief justice. Attorney General–elect Herbert Brownell tried to back out of the deal, saying that the promise had been for an associate justice opening, but Warren would not budge. Ironically, out of this very political deal, and Warren's deeply political background, which included the governorship and a stint as a district attorney, came one of the Supreme Court's most devoted, nonpolitical judges, a man dedicated to protecting the rights of the oppressed and the accused.

As you read this selection by Richard Kluger, realize that, like John Marshall, Warren's consummate political skill helped to make him a great chief justice. The Supreme Court at that time was dominated by highly talented, egotistical, and combative jurists largely appointed by Roosevelt and Truman. One of the justices, Robert Jackson, was battling with his colleagues over his differing legal philosophy and his term as prosecutor at the Nuremberg trials. Justice Felix Frankfurter was involved in disputes with Justices Hugo Black and William O. Douglas stemming from his loss of the liberal leadership on the Court. And Justice Stanley Reed was not willing to turn his back on his southern origins when voting on the issue of race in schools. Furthermore, there was little evidence that the nation, especially the South, was ready for a revolutionary change in the desegregation policies set by the Court in *Plessy* v. *Ferguson.* Out of this judicial and political minefield, however, Earl Warren was able to find a revolutionary approach to the issue—and to do so in unanimous fashion. This accomplishment is one of the greatest moments in Supreme Court history.

FELIX FRANKFURTER   Appointed to the Court by Franklin Roosevelt in 1939.

ROBERT JACKSON   Appointed to the Court by Roosevelt in 1941.

EARL POLLOCK   One of Warren's law clerks in 1954.

STANLEY REED   Conservative Southern Democratic jurist appointed to the Court by Roosevelt in 1938.

EARL WARREN   Chief justice of the United States, 1953–1969.

▶ Earl Warren was confirmed as Chief Justice on March 1, 1954. No Senator voted against him. . . .

By the time the Senate gave him its blessing five months after he had come to the Court, the new Chief Justice had won the admiration of his brethren for traits of character if not breathtaking legal acumen. "It must have been enormously difficult to come from the life he had late been leading to the cloistered atmosphere of the Court," remarks Earl Pollock, one of his clerks that first term, "and he was the first to say that he was no legal scholar, but he was a very endearing, very complex, and very human man. I liked him very much."

His colleagues on the bench seemed to like him for the way he had applied himself to the job. For one thing, he was a good listener in a city of talkers. For another, he had become, since the *Brown* reargument,* a lucid interrogator during the Court's oral sessions. "Before you sit down," he would say to the advocate before him, "I would like to hear you on—" and then specify often enough precisely the terrain the lawyer had hoped to avoid. And, according to James Reston in the *New York Times* of March 4, 1954, word had seeped out to the press that the Chief's conduct of the Court's conferences displayed a number of traits that were greatly welcomed: "an ability to concentrate on the concrete; a capacity to do his homework; a sensible, friendly manner, wholly devoid of pretense, and a self-command and natural dignity so useful in presiding over the court."

His initial voting record, moreover, did not place Warren at either end of the Court and hardly qualified him as a devoted civil-libertarian. Early in his first term, he joined a narrow five-to-four majority in *Irvine* v. *California,* in which the Court upheld a gambling prosecution based on evidence obtained from a microphone planted in the bedroom of the defendant. [Robert] Jackson's opinion, while condemning the police action, found no ground for reversing the conviction, but he was joined by Warren, who had been a California law-enforcement officer for twenty-two years, in suggesting that the Justice Department investigate the case to see if the police had not violated the civil-rights statutes. [Hugo] Black, [William O.] Douglas, [Felix] Frankfurter, and [Harold H.] Burton dissented. In a yet more startling and unlibertarian vote later in the term, Warren was part of a six-man majority in *Barsky* v. *Board of Regents,* in which the Court declined to overrule New York medical authorities who had suspended a prominent physician's license to practice because he refused to produce the records of a group called the Joint Anti-Fascist Refugee Committee, subpoenaed by the House Un-American Activities Committee, which suspected it of fellow-traveling.† Only Black, Douglas, and Frankfurter dissented from this late spasm in the finally ebbing Red witch-hunt. Justice Jackson in particular must have been comforted by having the Chief with him in both cases.

Some time between late February and late March, the Court voted at one of its Saturday conferences on the school-segregation cases. The date is in doubt because the Justices had agreed that the case was of such magnitude that no word ought to leak out before the decision was announced. As a result, no record of the vote seems to have been written down in any of the docket books that each Justice maintained. The tally sheet in Burton's docket book records no vote beyond the one to take the cases in June of 1952. One of Tom Clark's clerks recalls that his tally book, which had a built-in lock on it as did all the

---

* The original arguments for *Brown* took place in December 1952. When the Court could not come to a decision, it held rearguments on five questions in October 1953. The final decision was announced on May 17, 1954, two and a half months after Warren was confirmed.

† *Fellow-traveling* referred to suspicion that a person or organization sympathized with, or was linked to, the Communist party.

Justices' books, was generally available to his clerks who wished to look through it and see the disposition of the Court on any given case. But there was no tally sheet on *Brown* in Tom Clark's docket book that term, the clerk recalls.

Warren himself gave conflicting information on the date of the vote. On direct inquiry by the author, the retired Chief Justice replied on June 16, 1971: "I don't think we took a vote on it till the end of February—and then I took my time writing the opinion." And in response to a written query, he wrote on November 20, 1973, that "the formal vote in the *Brown* case was taken around the middle of February 1954." The slight discrepancy suggests that neither he nor any other official of the Court recorded the precise date—a departure from custom. (His lack of precision may also have meant, of course, that he had not bothered to check his records for the date.) But there is added evidence that there was no written record: in the May 1974 issue of *Ebony,* staff writer Jack Slater reported that in an interview for an article marking the twentieth anniversary of the *Brown* decision, Warren said: ". . . Eventually there were so many briefs that we decided to depart from the usual procedure and consider the case as it developed. And so, week by week, we discussed it, from the middle of November to the latter part of March, when we took a vote. There was no divisiveness and no arguing."

Late March seems the more likely moment for the vote. In February, he still had not been confirmed by the Senate, and while such a consideration might have been irrelevant to him, Earl Warren was a man dedicated to the formal procedures of democracy, and it is likely that he greatly preferred to confront his eminent fellow judges, convoked to decide a case of surpassing magnitude and grave national importance, only after having been fully and properly invested with the authority of his high office. The vote was apparently eight to strike down segregation and one, [Stanley] Reed, to uphold it. But it was far from certain still whether Jackson was going to file a separate concurrence or whether Frankfurter might or whether the two of them might agree on one; their thoughts on the cases were certainly close enough, to judge by their uncirculated memos. Warren, of course, wished to avoid concurring opinions; the fewer voices with which the Court spoke, the better. And he did not give up his hope that Stanley Reed, in the end, would abandon his dissenting position. The Chief assigned himself the all-important task of writing the majority opinion.

Before Warren put pencil to paper, it is almost certain, the Justices had agreed on the basic compromise formula for deciding the case. The Court would rule segregated schools unconstitutional before the close of the 1953 Term, but it would hold the cases over for reargument the following term in order to get the detailed views of the litigants on the most fitting way for the constitutional decision to be implemented. There would be no decree, then, at the current term. That would give the South nearly a year to condition itself to the Court's edict.

But on the basic issue itself, the Court had voted to declare Jim Crow an outlaw.* Beyond that, speculated Alexander Bickel, who remained on close terms with Justice Frankfurter and would write at length on the Court in books and magazines during the next two decades: "There is little doubt in my mind that at whatever conference the decision was taken in 1954, Justices Frankfurter, Black and Jackson left the room with a mutual understanding of the general form that the eventual decree of the Court would take—that it would provide for gradual enforcement and not forthwith as was the usual practice." Warren himself later offered a less revealing summation of the Court's consensus by the time he sat down to write: "There was no particular disagreement about the course of settling only the constitutional question then or that the question of implementation could well stand additional argument."

On March 30, fate intruded anew on the Court's deliberations. Justice Jackson, who had seemed in good spirits and robust health to that moment, was felled by a serious heart attack. He was hospitalized, with the immediate prospect that he would not return to the Court before the end of the term.

Whether the Chief Justice was aware that the stricken Justice had composed a draft for a concurring opinion, an opinion that Warren did not want written, is not known. . . . Jackson's illness, at any rate, seemed to reduce the likelihood that he would be inclined to make the effort to turn out a persuasive concurrence. The Court might, of course, have chosen to hold over its major cases until Jackson was fully recuperated, but a decision in the segregation cases had already been put off for quite some time; besides, the full Court had already voted on *Brown*. At the April 3 conference, the Justices therefore decided to hear out the rest of the calendar without Jackson and hold over for reargument cases of special importance and those in which the Court was evenly split. Warren then went to work on the draft of the *Brown* opinion.

By mid-April, he had something to show Earl Pollock, the clerk who probably worked most closely with him on the opinion. It was a delicate task but one that Warren must have relished. "If there were three things of great value and stimulation to him," recalls Pollock, who later became a prominent Chicago attorney, "they were (1) equality, (2) education, and (3) young people." The writing process itself went smoothly. "The opinion never greatly changed after the first draft," Warren disclosed. "The speed with which it was prepared was almost breathtaking," adds Pollock. "I think his feeling was: let's get it done and out, now that we have a solid Court."

Pollock's account seems corroborated by the chronology traceable in surviving documents. Warren apparently did not circulate his draft of the opinions—

---

* Jim Crow laws, which spread in the South after the Civil War, allowed segregation in buses, public restrooms, hospitals, theaters, parks, and other public areas.

one covering the state segregation cases, the other the District of Columbia case*—until Friday, May 7, the date of a memo he dispatched to members of the Court. The attached drafts, the Chief wrote, were offered as "a basis for discussion of the segregation cases" and "were prepared on the theory that the opinions should be short, readable by the lay public, non-rhetorical, unemotional and, above all, non-accusatory." His aspirations were those of a statesman, not a poet.

The drafts of the Warren opinions were carried by the Chief himself to those Justices who were in their chambers when the proofs came up from the print shop. Earl Pollock brought Hugo Black his copy while the Justice was playing tennis at his home in Alexandria and carried Sherman Minton's to his rarely seen apartment. No copies were allowed to float around Washington unaccounted for.

The Chief did not have long to wait for the returns to come in. Burton's response was probably among the most immediate and most enthusiastic: he told his diary on May 8 that he had read the Chief's drafts and written him "my enthusiastic approval—with a few minor suggestions. He has done, I believe, a magnificent job that may win a unanimous Court. . . ." Black, Douglas, Minton, and Clark, it is likely, had only minor suggestions to make and, to one degree or another, shared Burton's pleased response. It was with the three remaining members of the Court that Warren could have anticipated problems: any of them might still choose to write his own opinion.

But Felix Frankfurter had, from the beginning, been working for a unified Court. Nothing could have been worse, for the Court or the nation itself, than a flurry of conflicting opinions that would confuse and anger the American people. And nothing could have been better than a unanimous, low-key, but utterly resolute opinion. So long as the Chief was willing to fashion his opinion in a frank, carefully modulated way, Frankfurter had intended to go along. And all the signs were that if the Chief's opinion had not filled Frankfurter's minimum requirements, he would have discussed the problems with Warren fully and the latter would have given him every consideration. Relations between the two men at that time were "superb," in the opinion of Frank E. A. Sander, one of Frankfurter's clerks that term. That judgment would seem to be confirmed indisputably by a letter Frankfurter wrote to Jackson in the hospital on April 15; in passing, Frankfurter mentioned that on the previous day he had had "another experience with the Chief, confirming all the others." The matter had to do with a long-neglected piece of Court business unrelated to any of the cases before the Justices. "E.W. was properly outraged over the indifference," Frankfurter told Jackson, "and showed the understanding that comes from caring for the

---

* *Brown* was one of five school segregation cases—four state cases and one in the District of Columbia—considered by the Court at the same time.

real responsibility that that problem implies. What a pleasure to do business with him."

Rumors survive that Frankfurter drafted a dissenting opinion in *Brown* or perhaps a concurrence, but none of his clerks ever saw it if he did. The only documentary evidence that he was even considering a concurrence is the short, undated memo discovered in his papers. . . . But he was habitually composing such memos against the day when he would decide whether he would write in any given case before the Court. He may not have made up his mind to go along with the Chief's *Brown* opinion until after visiting Jackson at the hospital on Monday, May 10, but since Frankfurter had received his copy of the draft only a few days earlier, he can scarcely be characterized as having been a holdout.

Warren personally delivered his draft opinions to Jackson's hospital room and left them for the ailing Justice to study. "I think he was greatly relieved by the Chief's opinion," says Barrett Prettyman, who was with Jackson at the time.

Jackson gave his trusted clerk [Prettyman] his copy of the draft and asked him to read it. "I went out in the hall and went over it," Prettyman recounts. "When I came back in, he asked me what I thought of it. I said that I wished that it had more law in it but I didn't find anything glaringly unacceptable in it. The genius of the Warren opinion"—and Prettyman makes clear that he does not rate Warren's performance on the Court generally in the genius category—"was that it was so simple and unobtrusive. He had come from political life and had a keen sense of what you could say in this opinion without getting everybody's back up. His opinion took the sting off the decision, it wasn't accusatory, and it didn't pretend that the Fourteenth Amendment was more helpful than the history suggested—he didn't equivocate on that point."*

All those features made Warren's opinion attractive to Jackson, who would probably have preferred a more gracefully executed piece of writing for so important an occasion but was willing to settle for one whose principal virtue seemed to be its temperate tone. Jackson did work up two suggested insertions in the opinion and offered them orally to the Chief Justice when he returned to the hospital later that same day. One of the proposed additions Warren declined to accept because he felt it could be interpreted as being directed toward segregation in general, not only in public education, and as Prettyman puts it, "He wanted the decision to be narrowly circumscribed." But the Chief did accept a one-sentence insertion from Jackson, noting the professional success of Negroes in many fields of endeavor—a far cry from their compulsory benighted state at the time the Fourteenth Amendment was under debate. Jackson, more-

---

* The Fourteenth Amendment (adopted in 1868) protects liberties under the due process clause and guarantees that they be enforced equally for all citizens under the equal protection clause. In *Brown*, the Court asked both parties to analyze whether the framers of the amendment intended for its language to extend to the abolition of segregation in public schools.

over, was still in a weakened state from his heart condition and would have been likely to activate his concurrence memorandum only if Warren's opinion had seemed to him a piece of irresponsible butchery.

Having decided to join in the Chief's opinion, Jackson was absolutely determined that the Court should give it solid backing. Even if he were not fully recuperated, he would try to make it to the courtroom on the day the Chief was ready to read the opinion.

On May 12, Burton wrote in his diary: ". . . The Chief Justice also read to me his latest revision (slight) of his drafts in the *Segregation* cases. It looks like a unanimous opinion. A major accomplishment for his leadership. . . ." The entry invites the inference that the Chief had by then won over the Court's would-be dissenter, Stanley Reed.

To his brethren, Reed was anything but a petulant loner. On the contrary, he was an amiable, even-tempered colleague, and the rest of the Justices recognized that his position in the segregation cases stemmed from a deeply held conviction that the nation had been taking big strides in race relations and that the Court's decision to outlaw separate schools threatened to impede that march, if not halt it altogether. There was never a breakdown in the dialogue between Reed and the Chief Justice, who, in addition to all their other contacts during the Court's regular business, lunched together along with the genial Burton at least twenty times between the December conference at which the cases were first discussed and the middle of May. At the end, Warren put it to him directly, according to Reed's clerk, George Mickum, who was on hand at one of the Chief Justice's final interviews with the Kentuckian.

"He said, 'Stan, you're all by yourself in this now,'" Mickum recalls. "'You've got to decide whether it's really the best thing for the country.' He was not particularly eloquent and certainly not bombastic. Throughout, the Chief Justice was quite low-key and very sensitive to the problems that the decision would present to the South. He empathized with Justice Reed's concern. But he was quite firm on the Court's need for unanimity on a matter of this sensitivity."

After the Chief Justice had left, Reed asked Mickum, who had been raised in a community with segregated schools, how he felt about the Justice's going along with the rest of the Court. Mickum, a man not notably more convinced of the natural equality of the Negro than Reed himself was, suggested that the demands of conscience seemed to require his going beyond the knowable facts in the case and asking himself, as Warren had, what was best for America. "I think he was really troubled by the possible consequences of his position," Mickum adds. "Because he was a Southerner, even a lone dissent by him would give a lot of people a lot of grist for making trouble. For the good of the country, he put aside his own basis for dissent." The only condition he extracted from Warren for going along, Mickum believes, was a pledge that the Court implementation decree would allow segregation to be dismantled gradually instead of being wrenched apart.

The Warren opinion was "finally approved" at the May 15 conference, Burton noted in his diary. The man from California had won the support of every member of the Court.

Not long before the Court's decision in *Brown* was announced, Warren told *Ebony* magazine twenty years later, he had decided to spend a few days visiting Civil War monuments in Virginia. He went by automobile with a black chauffeur.

At the end of the first day, the Chief Justice's car pulled up at a hotel, where he had made arrangements to spend the night. Warren simply assumed that his chauffeur would stay somewhere else, presumably at a less expensive place. When the Chief Justice came out of his hotel the next morning to resume his tour, he soon figured out that the chauffeur had spent the night in the car. He asked the black man why.

"Well, Mr. Chief Justice," the chauffeur began, "I just couldn't find a place— couldn't find a place to . . ."

Warren was stricken by his own thoughtlessness in bringing an employee of his to a town where lodgings were not available to the man solely because of his color. "I was embarrassed, I was ashamed," Warren recalled. "We turned back immediately. . . ."

Epilogue

At the end of his presidency, Dwight Eisenhower looked at the liberal views espoused by Earl Warren and his Court and pronounced Warren's appointment the "biggest damfool mistake" he had made in the White House. One of the Court's decisions that Eisenhower implemented only reluctantly was *Brown,* which declared unconstitutional the concept of "separate but equal" for public schools. The Court said that separate facilities would never be equal and ordered desegregation. (Selection 3.2, "Three Cases of Command," describes Eisenhower's decision to send federal troops to desegregate Little Rock's Central High School in compliance with *Brown.*) The Supreme Court held more hearings to determine how implementation of *Brown* would take place, and in 1955, *Brown* v. *Board of Education II* ordered that desegregation occur "with all deliberate speed." This contradictory phrase is the reason that, almost forty years later, we are still debating how far and how fast to proceed in accomplishing the lofty goals of *Brown* v. *Board of Education.*

Felix Frankfurter retired in 1962 (he was replaced by Arthur Goldberg), and the Warren Court went on to revolutionize legal doctrine in many areas, including defendants' rights, freedom of speech and religion, and equal protection. It is important to note that the unanimity of the Court on the issue of race broke down only when Earl Warren was replaced by Warren Burger and the coalitions on the Court were changed by the appointments of Richard Nixon.

6.3

When Clarence Earl Gideon, an indigent, was charged with breaking into a Florida pool hall in 1961, he asked the judge to appoint an attorney for his defense because he did not have money to hire one himself. The judge refused, pointing out that Florida law called for appointed counsel only for a capital offense. Such a restriction had been supported by the Supreme Court's decision in *Betts* v. *Brady* (1942), which declared that the due process clause of the Fourteenth Amendment (no one shall be deprived of "life, liberty, or property, without due process of law") did not require counsel to be provided in all criminal trials. The Supreme Court was reluctant to compromise states' rights by supervising the criminal justice systems of all the states. The Court, therefore, insisted on "special circumstances" —such as low mental capacity or illiteracy—before forcing a state to provide counsel. Gideon fit into none of the Court's special categories. He did not receive an appointed attorney, and after putting up his own defense he was convicted of the robbery.

But Gideon did not take his conviction passively. After going over law texts in the prison library, he submitted a handwritten petition to the Supreme Court. (The Court allows certain people to proceed *in forma pauperis*, "in the manner of a pauper"—to be exempt from usual procedures and costs if they are unable to afford them.) Gideon's petition argued that the Constitution entitles criminal defendants to counsel.

Gideon's appointed lawyer for the Supreme Court hearing, Abe Fortas, understood why the judges took the case. Although the *Betts* decision had limited the effect of the Fourteenth Amendment, in the twenty years since that case, the Court had greatly expanded the category of "special circumstances" necessary to require the states to appoint counsel. In 1963 the Court appeared ready to overrule *Betts* and invoke the Sixth Amendment's guarantee of counsel for all criminal cases. Fortas, in fact, suspected that he would win the case and hoped to broaden the impact of the decision by getting a unanimous opinion, despite Justice John

Oral Argument

Anthony Lewis

"Oral Argument" from Anthony Lewis, *Gideon's Trumpet* (New York: Vintage Books, 1964). Copyright © 1964 by Anthony Lewis. Reprinted by permission of Vintage Books, a division of Random House, Inc.

Marshall Harlan's concern with states' rights. Indeed, *Gideon* v. *Wainwright* (1963) became a landmark case for defendants' rights. As we join the story, oral arguments are about to begin.

ABE FORTAS   Appointed counsel for Gideon in *Gideon* v. *Wainwright;* appointed to the Supreme Court in 1965.

CLARENCE EARL GIDEON   Petitioner in landmark case for defendants' rights.

JOHN MARSHALL HARLAN   Associate justice of the Supreme Court; concerned with states' rights.

BRUCE JACOB   Florida assistant attorney general.

GEORGE MENTZ   Alabama assistant attorney general; "friend of the court" for Florida in *Gideon.*

J. LEE RANKIN   Former solicitor general; "friend of the court" in support of Gideon.

▶ Only a small part of the process of decision in the Supreme Court is exposed to public view, and of that portion by far the most interesting and the most revealing is oral argument. Even the citizen wholly unfamiliar with the Court can gain some sense of the institution by sitting in the back of the chamber and listening to an argument. The exhaustive probing of a single set of facts shows, if it is done well, how our adversary system of justice can make truth emerge from conflict. It shows also how close the questions are that the Supreme Court must answer; characteristically, the listener finds himself persuaded by the last voice he has heard. The comments from the bench—sometimes funny, sometimes quite blunt—bring out the personalities of the justices and remind us that the Court is a collection of strong-minded individuals, much less institutionalized than the typical agency of the Executive Branch.

Oral argument is more important in the Court's decisional process than many lawyers realize. Too often they seem to regard it as a ceremonial affair, serving only to put a gloss on the contentions so carefully made in their briefs [written arguments]. But the Court does not feel that way. The justices who have spoken on the subject—and many have—say that oral argument performs a distinct function, in some ways more influential than that of the briefs. A good argument, Justice [John Marshall] Harlan said, "may in many cases make the difference between winning and losing, no matter how good the briefs are."

There are two reasons for this. One is that a brief cannot answer back when a justice reading it expresses doubt about some line of reasoning. Oral argument presents a great opportunity to answer the doubts and questions raised from the bench, to mollify one's critics and arm one's friends. This opportunity is the greater because of the Supreme Court tradition that oral argument is not an exhibition of high school oratory but an exchange between counsel and Court. The rules state that the Court "looks with disfavor on any oral argument that is read from a prepared text"; it is a time for *argument,* not declamation.

Justice [Felix] Frankfurter once said that the Court saw itself not as "a dozing audience for the reading of soliloquies, but as a questioning body, utilizing oral argument as a means for exposing the difficulties of a case with a view to meeting them." And so there are likely to be a great many questions from the bench. Unfortunately, some lawyers—not excluding well-known names of the Wall Street firms—seem to resent them, seeing questions as an intrusion on their well-ordered schemes of argument rather than as invitations to persuade. Justice [Robert] Jackson, who was one of the great oral advocates of his day before he went on the bench, said in his wonderfully astringent style that he felt "there should be some comfort derived from any question from the bench. It is clear proof that the inquiring justice is not asleep. If the question is relevant, it denotes he is grappling with your contention, even though he has not grasped it. It gives you opportunity to inflate his ego by letting him think he has discovered an idea for himself."

The second reason for the importance of oral argument is the place it has in the timetable of the decisional process. The justices customarily take a tentative vote, at their Friday conference, on all the cases argued that week. The argument is likely to be fresh in their minds. Most members of the Court, Justice Jackson said, "form at least a tentative conclusion from it in a large percentage of the cases." Moreover, a lawyer who at argument succeeds in arousing a strongly favorable interest on the part of even one justice thereby obtains for his cause a spokesman in the privacy of the conference room.

Given the significance of argument, its potential is realized far too infrequently. Many, probably most, arguments in the Supreme Court are dreary affairs. Counsel are often ill-at-ease, ill-prepared or—worse yet—overconfident. One of the worst sins is to brush off questions or answer them less than candidly. (On the other hand, Justice [Oliver Wendell] Holmes once complimented a lawyer on his candor and then, as the gentleman was preening himself, remarked: "You know, candor is one of the most effective instruments in deception.") Another mistake is to take the lofty approach, arguing only large abstractions; such tactics inevitably produce glazed expressions on the bench. The justices seem more interested when a lawyer sticks to homely, factual arguments.

Often in their questions the members of the Court try to find out what the case means in human terms, as if in their ivory tower they were lonesome for the real world. Justice Jackson had a slightly different explanation for the Court's fascination with the facts at arguments. "The purpose of a hearing is that the Court may learn what it does not know," he said, "and it knows least about the facts. It may sound paradoxical, but most contentions of law are won or lost on the facts. They often incline a judge to one side or the other."

It is said, correctly, that no oral presentation, however effective, is likely to be able to change the deep-rooted philosophical positions that a justice inevitably comes to hold after some years on the bench. But there are ways of getting around those entrenchments, of suggesting narrow grounds (which the Court almost always prefers) for a decision in favor of one's client. There are also ways of alienating votes that should be favorable. Probably more cases are lost than won by argument. . . .

The argument [in the *Gideon* case] presented no novel challenge to Abe Fortas, a man of experience and reputation in the Supreme Court. But to Bruce Jacob, who had never even seen the courtroom before, the prospect was unnerving. He flew to Washington on Saturday, January 12th, two days before the Clerk's Office had indicated the case would be reached. The flight was bumpy, doing nothing to improve Jacob's already queasy stomach. He spent the weekend in the hotel trying to anticipate questions he might be asked, worrying over his argument outline, worrying in general. Early on Monday morning he had another minor concern to dispose of: to arrange his admission to the Supreme Court bar. Anyone is eligible after three years in the bar of his state's highest court. Membership qualifies one to file briefs and argue in the Supreme Court. Jacob barely met the three-year requirement, but under the usual practice he would have been admitted *pro hac vice,* for this one occasion only, to make his argument. . . .

As he entered the Supreme Court building that Monday morning and then for the first time watched the justices at work, Bruce Jacob experienced the confusing change of emotions that any sensitive person feels in that curious place. For the Court is a place of contrasts, of paradoxes. It is grandiose and intimate, ritualistic and informal, austere and human—at the same time the most aloof and the most approachable of all the institutions of government.

Grandiose is the word for the physical setting. The W.P.A. Guide to Washington called the Supreme Court building a "great marble temple" which "by its august scale and mighty splendor seems to bear little relation to the functional purposes of government." Shortly before the justices moved into the building in 1935 from their old chamber across the street in the Capitol, Justice [Harlan F.] Stone wrote his sons: "The place is almost bombastically pretentious, and thus it seems to me wholly inappropriate for a quiet group of old boys such as the Supreme Court." He told his friends that the justices would be "nine black beetles in the Temple of Karnak."

The visitor who climbs the marble steps and passes through the marble columns of the huge pseudo-classical façade finds himself in a cold, lofty hall, again all marble. Great bronze gates exclude him from the area of the building where the justices work in private—their offices, library and conference room. In the courtroom, which is always open to the public, the atmosphere of austere pomp is continued: there are more columns, an enormously high ceiling, red velvet hangings, friezes carved high on the walls. The ritual opening of each day's session adds to the feeling of awe. The Court Crier to the right of the bench smashes his gavel down sharply on a wooden block, everyone rises and the justices file in through the red draperies behind the bench and stand at their places as the Crier intones the traditional opening: "The honorable, the Chief Justice and the Associate Justices of the Supreme Court of the United States.

Oyez, oyez, oyez. All persons having business before the honorable, the Supreme Court of the United States, are admonished to draw near and give their attention, for the Court is now sitting. God save the United States and this honorable Court."

But then, when an argument begins, all the trappings and ceremony seem to fade, and the scene takes on an extraordinary intimacy. In the most informal way, altogether without pomp, Court and counsel converse. It is conversation—as direct, unpretentious and focused discussion as can be found anywhere in Washington.

"It was nothing like I expected," Bruce Jacob said later. "It was so informal—I just couldn't believe it. Usually judges are so sober-looking; they don't laugh. Not that they're inhuman, but they're nothing like Supreme Court justices. I just got the impression that these men had a real good time, talking to each other and asking questions."

The case of *Gideon* v. *Cochran* was not reached that day.* Chief Deputy Cullinan always has counsel in Court earlier than necessary, so that there is no chance of a case ending early and no other being ready for the justices. There is no exact time for each case to start; the Court simply sits for argument from 10 A.M. to 2:30 P.M. (with 12 to 12:30 out for lunch), Monday through Thursday, and when one case is finished the next is called. Because this was a Monday, arguments were delayed for the reading of opinions. Then, at noon, there was a special interruption because the justices had to be at the Capitol to hear President Kennedy read his State of the Union message. Later that afternoon and the next morning, counsel in the Gideon case sat and listened with at least half an ear to the argument of an important antitrust case by two able advocates, Solicitor General Archibald Cox and Gerhard A. Gesell of Washington. They concluded at 11:06 Tuesday morning.

Chief Justice Warren, as is the custom, called the next case by reading aloud its full title: Number 155, Clarence Earl Gideon, petitioner, versus H. G. Cochran, Jr., director, Division of Corrections, State of Florida. From his desk at the left of the bench the Clerk of the Court, John F. Davis, said "Counsel are present," and the lawyers in the Gideon case moved forward to two long tables just below the bench.

The justices are seated in an order fixed by tradition. At the far right (as seen by the spectators) was the newest member of the Court, Arthur J. Goldberg of Illinois, fifty-four years old, the gray-haired labor lawyer who had made such a dynamic Secretary of Labor before President Kennedy appointed him to the bench. At the far left was the other Kennedy appointee, Byron R. White of Colorado, forty-five, physically powerful but scholarly in appearance, as befits an All-American football hero who was also a Rhodes Scholar. Next to Justice

---

* At the time of the oral argument, the case was known as *Gideon* v. *Cochran* because H. G. Cochran was director of the Florida Division of Corrections. Before the Court's decision, Louie L. Wainwright became director, and the case became *Gideon* v. *Wainwright*.

Goldberg was Potter Stewart of Ohio, forty-seven but still collegiate in his good looks, whom President Eisenhower made a Court of Appeals judge and then raised to the Supreme Court in 1958. Second from the left was the smallish, brisk figure of William J. Brennan, Jr., fifty-six, a New Jersey Supreme Court justice who was a surprise Eisenhower appointee (because he was a Democrat) in 1956; he is the only Roman Catholic on the Court. On the right, again was John Marshall Harlan, sixty-three, a Wall Street lawyer picked by Eisenhower for the Court of Appeals and advanced to the Supreme Court in 1955, looking perhaps more like a judge than anyone else, appropriately enough for the grandson and namesake of an earlier Supreme Court justice. Third from the left was Tom C. Clark, also sixty-three, a friendly Texan, former Attorney General, the only Truman appointee (1949) still on the Court. To the right of the Chief Justice was William O. Douglas, sixty-four, a ruddy-faced outdoorsman from the state of Washington, a law-school professor and New Deal official appointed by Franklin Roosevelt in 1939. On the other side of the Chief was Hugo L. Black, seventy-six years old but still a tough competitor at tennis, hawk-nosed, with the soft sound of rural Alabama in his voice, a Senator when Roosevelt put him on the Court in 1937. Finally, at the center sat Earl Warren, seventy-one, a county law officer for twenty years, attorney general of California for four, an immensely popular governor for ten, Republican candidate for Vice-President in 1948; a huge, white-haired figure, named Chief Justice by Eisenhower in 1953.

The lawyer arguing a case stands at a small rostrum between the two counsel tables, facing the Chief Justice. The party that lost in the lower court goes first, and so the argument in *Gideon* v. *Cochran* was begun by Abe Fortas. As he stood, the Chief Justice gave him the customary greeting, "Mr. Fortas," and he made the customary opening: "Mr. Chief Justice, may it please the Court. . . ."

This case presents "a narrow question," Fortas said—the right to counsel— unencumbered by extraneous issues. The charge was a felony, not any lesser offense; Gideon's indigence was conceded; he had unquestionably made a timely request for counsel, and the demand was for a lawyer at his trial, not at any earlier and hence more doubtful point in the criminal proceeding.

Fortas began reciting the facts. In his deep, deliberate, somewhat mournful voice, occasionally removing his horn-rimmed glasses and gesturing with them for emphasis, he told the justices about the morning Clarence Earl Gideon was supposed to have broken into the Bay Harbor Poolroom and stolen "some wine, perhaps some cigarettes and an unstated amount of money." Fortas described Gideon's active participation in his own trial, his attempts to cross-examine and address the jury. Then, on this brief foundation of the facts, he began to build his legal argument.

"This record does not indicate that Clarence Earl Gideon was a person of low intelligence," Fortas said, "or that the judge was unfair to him. But to me this case shows the basic difficulty with Betts versus Brady. It shows that no man, however intelligent, can conduct his own defense adequately."

At this point Justice Harlan intervened. He was the Court's most convinced believer in the value of state independence, and Fortas had anticipated the greatest difficulty in persuading him to overrule *Betts*.

"That's not the point, is it, Mr. Fortas?" Justice Harlan asked. "*Betts* didn't go on the assumption that a man can do as well without an attorney as he can with one, did it? Everyone knows that isn't so."

In fact, it could be fairly argued that Justice [Owen J.] Roberts, in *Betts,* had gone on exactly that assumption. He certainly had said that that particular trial was so simple that there would have been little for a lawyer to do. But Fortas, instead of challenging Justice Harlan's proposition, accepted it for the implicit concession it was and used it to drive on to his point about federalism.

"I entirely agree, Mr. Justice Harlan, with the point you are making: Namely, that of course a man cannot have a fair trial without a lawyer, but *Betts* held that this consideration was outweighed by the demands of federalism. . . .

"My purpose was to show that this case is not Tweedledum and Tweedledee with one tried by counsel. I believe this case dramatically illustrates that you cannot have a fair trial without counsel. Under our adversary system of justice, how can our civilized nation pretend that there is a fair trial without the counsel for the prosecution doing all he can within the limits of decency, and the counsel for the defense doing his best within the same limits, and from that clash will emerge the truth? . . . I think there is a tendency to forget what happens to these poor, miserable, indigent people—in these strange and awesome circumstances. Sometimes in this Court there is a tendency to forget what happens downstairs. . . . I was reminded the other night, as I was pondering this case, of Clarence Darrow when he was prosecuted for trying to fix a jury. The first thing he realized was that he needed a lawyer—he, one of the country's great criminal lawyers. . . .

"And so the real basis of Betts against Brady must be the understanding sensitivity of this Court to the pull of federalism."

This last statement of Fortas's seemed, for some not readily understandable reason, to anger Justice Harlan. This usually gentle man visibly reddened, leaned forward and said very sharply, "Really, Mr. Fortas, 'understanding sensitivity' seems to me a most unfortunate term to describe one of the fundamental principles of our constitutional system."

"Mr. Justice Harlan," Fortas replied without a flicker of emotion, "I believe in federalism. It is a fundamental principle for which I personally have the highest regard and concern, and which I feel must be reconciled with the result I advocate. But I believe that Betts against Brady does not incorporate a proper regard for federalism. It requires a case-by-case supervision by this Court of state criminal proceedings, and that cannot be wholesome. . . . Intervention should be in the least abrasive, the least corrosive way possible."

That was the argument that Fortas considered central to his case. He had expected to make it later in his presentation, after more of a build-up, but Justice Harlan's question had given him the opportunity to make the point dramatically; as a skillful advocate he had abandoned his earlier outline and made the thrust at once. Whether the answer satisfied Justice Harlan was a question only the justice could answer, but he did lean back and appear somewhat happier.

Fortas traced the history of the right to counsel in the Supreme Court, beginning with the Scottsboro case, *Powell* v. *Alabama,* in 1932. He described the *Betts* doctrine and the subsequent cases in which the Court had or had not found the special circumstances requiring counsel.

"I have read all the cases now," he said, "state and federal, and it is a fascinating inquiry. As I read the opinions of this Court, I hope I may be forgiven for saying that my heart was full of compassion for the judges having to review those records and look for 'special circumstances.'"

Justice Stewart: "When was the last time we did not find special circumstances? I think there have been none in my four and one-half terms on the Court."

Fortas: "I think it was Quicksall and Michigan, in 1950. . . . Of course this [the special-circumstances approach] is wrong. How can a judge, when a man is arraigned, look at him and say there are special circumstances? Does the judge say, 'You look stupid,' or 'Your case involves complicated facts'? It is administratively unworkable."

Justice Harlan: "The states are recognizing that."

Fortas took up that point and outlined the situation in the states . . . : thirty-seven states now provided counsel for the poor in all felony trials, eight others frequently did so as a matter of practice, five made no regular provision for counsel except in capital cases. But he did not agree with any implication in Justice Harlan's question that the movement by the states to act themselves argued against a step forward now by the Supreme Court. He noted the brief *amicus curiae* for twenty-three states in favor of overruling *Betts* and said he was "proud of this document as an American."* Then he argued that the growing acceptance of the right to counsel made a reinterpretation of the Constitution easier.

"I believe we can confidently say that overruling Betts versus Brady at this time would be in accord with the opinion of those entitled to an opinion. That is not always true of great constitutional questions. . . . We may be comforted in this constitutional moment by the fact that what we are doing is a deliberate change after twenty years of experience—a change that has the overwhelming support of the bench, the bar and even of the states."

Justice Goldberg raised the problem of the limits on what Fortas was asking. At what stage of a criminal case must a lawyer be supplied? In what kinds of cases?

"Do we have to pass on that?" Justice Clark interjected.

---

* An *amicus curiae* ("friend of the court") brief is filed, with the permission of a court, by an individual or group that is not a party in the litigation but that has an interest in the decision. Sometimes a friend of the court is allowed to testify.

"No, sir, not at this time," Fortas said. But he went on to give his own opinion anyway: A lawyer should be provided at least from the first arraignment of the prisoner before a magistrate, through his trial and appeal; and the right should apply in all save "petty offenses."

Justice Stewart thought the definition of "petty offenses" might produce difficulties, might be "more of this *ad hoc* judging you're trying to get away from. . . . What about traffic violations?" Fortas said he personally saw no difficulty in providing lawyers even for traffic offenders who wanted them. He knew that sounded strange, but it would work. Only an occasional odd-ball would ask, and it would be easy to say to him: "Yes, sir, go right down the hall to that door, that's the public defender's office, they'll see you."

It was noon by this time, and the Court rose for lunch. Afterwards Fortas hoped to say just a few words more, then reserve about ten minutes of his time for a rebuttal, as the opening counsel is allowed to do. But he was still being questioned when the marshal of the Court, sitting to the right of the bench, threw the switch for the small white light on the lectern that indicates counsel has only five minutes left. And the questions continued.

Justice Stewart asked whether he was right in his impression that Fortas was not arguing the old proposition that the Fourteenth Amendment had incorporated the Sixth Amendment as such. Fortas agreed—he was not. But the answer that pleases one justice may arouse another, and this one aroused the member of the Court who had been arguing for a generation that the Fourteenth Amendment incorporated the entire original Bill of Rights—Justice Black. He asked in a puzzled way why Fortas was laying aside that argument.

"Mr. Justice Black," Fortas replied, "I like that argument that you have made so eloquently. But I cannot as an advocate make that argument because this Court has rejected it so many times. I hope you never cease making it."

Justice Black joined in the general laughter.

"You are saying," Justice Brennan said helpfully to Fortas, "that the right to counsel is assured by the Fourteenth Amendment whether by absorption, incorporation or whatever."

"Mr. Justice," said Fortas, "you seem to know me well."

At that the red light on the lectern went on, meaning that Fortas's hour was up. But as he sat down, the Chief Justice gave him an additional five minutes for rebuttal, adding the same to Jacob's time on the other side.

Next came [J. Lee] Rankin's appearance as a friend of the court. As he had when he was Solicitor General, he spoke softly, in homely phrases, and with an air of deep sincerity.

"Judges have a special responsibility here," Rankin began, "and so do lawyers. It just isn't true that laymen know these rules of law (the sophisticated concepts of criminal law). That's what's wrong with *Betts*. It is time—long past time—that our profession stood up and said: 'We know a man cannot get a fair trial when he represents himself.' It is enough of a fiction to claim that an ordinary lawyer can present a case as well as the prosecutor with all his experience in court. But when you take a layman and put him at odds, you can't have a fair trial except by accident."

Thus Rankin, appropriately for his role, was focusing less on Gideon the individual and more on the broad problem from the viewpoint of the legal profession. Justice Harlan accused him of making too "sweeping generalizations" about the impossibility of fair trial without counsel. Rankin agreed that it was not absolutely impossible to be tried fairly without a lawyer's help, but he said *Betts* had the generalization backward—it assumed that only in the special case did a man need a lawyer, while the truth was that it was the rare case where one did not need counsel.

Justice Goldberg: "If it's a generalization (the need for counsel), isn't there substantial support for it in the Constitution? The framers of the Sixth Amendment thought there should always be counsel." [That was, historically, a doubtful proposition.]

Rankin: "That's what I think."

Justice Stewart: "Isn't that generalization the assumption behind the legal profession? Florida wouldn't let Gideon, a non-lawyer, go into court and represent anyone else."

Rankin ended by dismissing as unproved prediction the charge that overruling *Betts* would empty the jails. He said the Court should apply the new doctrine assuring counsel retrospectively, to past as well as future cases. Justice Harlan asked whether the Court could constitutionally limit a decision to future operation. Rankin said he was doubtful.

At 1:10 in the afternoon Bruce Jacob's turn came. Looking extremely young and earnest, he began by giving a little more description of Gideon—his age (fifty-two), color (white) and previous felony convictions (four). Then he complained about the inclusion of the trial transcript in the printed record.

Justice Harlan: "Why do you bother about that?"

Jacob: "Okay, I won't press it."

Justice White: "You are not questioning our jurisdiction in this case?"

Jacob: "No, your Honor."

From then on, Jacob was deluged by questions. There was scarcely a consecutive five-minute period when he could talk without interruption. Considering his unfamiliarity with the process and the unpopularity of his cause, he showed commendable stamina.

Justice Black: "Why isn't it *[Betts]* as much interference with the states as an absolute rule? One of my reactions to *Betts* was the uncertainty in which it leaves the states."

Jacob: "I don't think *Betts* is that unclear."

Justice Black: "How do you know what the 'special circumstances' are?"

Jacob: "Each time this Court decides a case, we know another special circumstance."

Justice Brennan: "In recent years—in four cases I think—we have reversed cases from your state every time."

Jacob: "We prefer case-by-case adjudication. . . . It may not be precise, but we prefer it that way because it gives the state some freedom in devising its own rules of criminal procedure."

Jacob: "History argues against the drawing of inflexible lines, and this Court has never laid down any fixed rules on the right to counsel."

Justice Brennan: "What about Powell against Alabama? Doesn't that lay down a rule for capital cases?"

Jacob: "That was decided on the circumstances. . . ."

Justice Harlan: "Perhaps so, but subsequent cases have made clear that there is a fixed rule for capital cases. There is no point in your arguing that."

Justice Black: "What historical support have you found for the distinction between capital and non-capital cases?"

Jacob: "Your honor, I can't think of any."

Justice Black: "I can't either. That's why I asked."

Justice Stewart: "There is nothing in the language of the Fourteenth Amendment, certainly, to make the distinction. It speaks of life, liberty or property."

Jacob: "There is a practical distinction between capital and non-capital cases if you want to draw the line somewhere. Everyone is fearful of being put to death. . . ."

Justice Black: "Maybe they're fearful of spending years in the penitentiary, too."

Jacob: "By imposing an inflexible rule, we feel this Court would be intruding into an area historically reserved to the states. It would stifle state experimentation. For example, a state might eliminate prosecutors as well as defense counsel and leave the whole trial to the judge."

Justice Harlan: "Don't go too far now."

Justice Stewart (repeating a point he had made to Rankin): "Gideon would not be allowed to represent others in court."

Jacob: "If a defendant asked for him, I'm sure the judge wouldn't object."

Justice Black: "The local bar association might!"

Jacob: "I'm sorry, your honor, that was a stupid answer."

Jacob next talked about the consequences of overruling *Betts* v. *Brady*—grave consequences, as he saw them. The new doctrine would necessarily extend to trivial cases, and the cost of providing counsel would be "a tremendous burden on the taxpayers." The next thing one knew, indigents would also be demanding other free services—psychiatrists, expert witnesses and so forth. "In effect, this court would be requiring the states to adopt socialism, or a welfare program." Finally, Jacob emphasized the 5,093 convicts now in Florida prisons who were tried without counsel and might now be eligible for release if *Betts* were overruled. "If the Court does reverse, we implore it to find some way not to make it retroactive. We have followed *Betts* in good faith. . . ."

Chief Justice Warren wanted to know whether some of those 5,093 Florida convicts were illiterate. His point was plain—and deadly. An illiterate defendant was entitled to counsel even under *Betts* v. *Brady,* since illiteracy qualified as a special circumstance, so the chances were that any illiterates among those 5,093 tried without counsel had been deprived of their constitutional rights. Because they lacked Clarence Earl Gideon's determination, or luck, they had not won redress in the courts.

"I have no way of knowing," Jacob said to the Chief Justice.

"No, but what do you think?" the Chief Justice pressed. "Do you think most of them are literate or illiterate?"

"I don't know, but I am sure some of them are illiterate."

Jacob concluded without using his extra five minutes, and then George Mentz of Alabama took over. He was an older man, gray-haired, more experienced than Jacob and much more at ease. He was questioned just as frequently, but the questions seemed to give him less pain. He answered in a charming Southern voice, making graceful concessions.

"I candidly admit," he began, "that it would be desirable for the states to furnish counsel in all criminal cases. But we say the states should have the right to make that decision themselves."

Justice Harlan: "Supposing *Betts* is not overruled. How many years is it going to take Alabama to pass a law like New York and the other states?"

Mentz: "I don't know, but there is a growing feeling in the trial courts that something should be done."

Mentz: "Our judges are conscientious in protecting indigent defendants."

Justice Stewart: "We can assume all of that with you, but a judge's job is to be a judge. This way he would be an advocate for one of the litigants."

Justice Goldberg: "What about the vital matter of the final address to the jury? Surely a judge can't take over that job of advocacy."

Mentz: "That is true. . . . But prosecutors are more lenient with unrepresented defendants. . . ."

Justice Stewart: "Isn't that a matter of trial strategy? It might backfire if the prosecutor were tough and the jury saw the defendant there helpless."

Mentz: "Well, yes, sir."

Justice Stewart: "All you're saying is that the absence of counsel impedes the adversary system of justice."

Mentz: "I didn't mean to go that far."

Justice Stewart: "I'm sure you didn't."

Mentz: "In actuality, indigents without lawyers probably get off easier. The average Alabama lawyer is not equipped to deal with the career prosecutor. An articulate defendant may get his story across to the jury better."

Justice Black: "That's not very complimentary to our profession."

Mentz (good-humoredly): "No, sir."

Justice Douglas: "Maybe if laymen are as effective as you say, we should get the Sixth Amendment repealed."

Mentz: "Mr. Justice, I didn't mean to go that far. I meant only that laymen are not at so great a disadvantage—"

Justice Douglas: "—as some appellate judges think."

Justice Harlan: "Supposing you had a choice—as you see it, representing the state—of maintaining *Betts* on the books and then having a succession of cases come to this Court every one of which was reversed by finding special circumstances, so that everyone would know we were only paying lip service to *Betts,* or of overruling it."

Mentz: "We'd rather see them decided case by case."

Justice Harlan: "Even though you know how all of them will come out."

Mentz: "'Hope springs eternal.'" [Laughter in the courtroom.]

Then Fortas got up for his rebuttal. He said a word about *Mapp* v. *Ohio,* the case in which—two years before—the Supreme Court had reinterpreted the Constitution to bar the use of illegally seized evidence in state trials. "To paraphrase Mr. Justice Clark's opinion there, time has set its face against Betts and Brady." He noted also Justice Clark's opinion in the second overseas court-martial cases, saying they removed any basis for a constitutional distinction between crimes subject to the death penalty and others.

"I think Betts and Brady was wrong when it was decided," Fortas said in his peroration. "I think time has made that clear. And I think time has now made it possible for the correct rule, the civilized rule, the rule of American constitutionalism, the rule of due process to be stated by this Court with limited disturbance to the states."

Justice Harlan had one more question. Had Mr. Fortas, in his research, found any errors in Justice [Owen J.] Roberts' exposition of the history of the right to counsel in his opinion in *Betts* v. *Brady?* Clearly Justice Harlan would find it much easier to overrule *Betts* if that decision could be shown to have been based on erroneous historical premises. But Fortas had no comfort to offer there. He replied: "We would have some differences, perhaps, but I don't say that the historical technique of constitutional interpretation will reach my result."

In order to overrule *Betts,* then, Justice Harlan would have to look at the same problem that had faced Justice Roberts in 1942 and say that a different answer was required in 1963. As a believer in *stare decisis* he would not find that easy to do, and yet he seemed to want to turn away from *Betts* v. *Brady.** The last word in the argument was Justice Harlan's, and it showed the struggle going on inside him. "What one is left with," he said, "is getting one's hands on something that has happened in the last twenty years. . . ."

---

* *Stare decisis* is Latin for "let the decision stand"; Justice Harlan believed in judicial decision making according to precedent.

Epilogue

Fortas's arguments were so persuasive that the Court handed down a unanimous decision to extend the right to appointed counsel to all defendants accused of felonies (which can result in a lengthy jail sentence and/or fine). Since *Gideon,* the Court has extended the right to an attorney to defendants in other types of cases and in other pre- and post-trial situations. *Gideon* also led to the expansion of state public defender programs and to the establishment of federal legal services programs.

Gideon himself returned to Florida to stand trial once again, refused the offer of counsel by Fortas and retained a local defense attorney, and was found innocent. Years later, Arthur Goldberg was walking on the streets of Washington when a disheveled panhandler approached him with his hand out. Thinking that the man wanted money, Goldberg reached into his pocket for a dollar bill. Instead, the man said, "No, Mr. Justice, I don't want your money. I just want to shake your hand. My name is Clarence Earl Gideon, and I want to thank you for what you did for me and so many others."

6.4

The framers of the Constitution were gravely concerned with the issue of privacy. In Britain, government documents called writs of assistance gave investigators free rein to ransack people's homes or offices looking for any evidence of crime or treason against the Crown. To prevent that from occurring in the United States, the Fourth Amendment was written; it requires that government investigators not make "unreasonable searches and seizures," and that, ideally, before making a search they obtain a search warrant describing the place to be searched and the thing to be seized. In this way, the privacy of the individual is preserved, as is the right of the government to investigate in an effort to control crime.

The right of privacy discussed in this selection has a different twist. Here it takes the form of personal autonomy—the right to live one's life and use one's body as one pleases. Where, if at all, is that protection granted in the Constitution? This was the question facing Estelle Griswold (*Griswold* v. *Connecticut*) and Norma McCorvey (*Roe* v. *Wade*) in challenging the Connecticut anticontraception and Texas antiabortion laws. It was also the challenge faced by William O. Douglas and Harry Blackmun when writing the opinions in these cases. As you will see in this selection by Fred Friendly and Martha Elliott, in both cases the justices were unable to point to any particular provision of the Constitution or Bill of Rights that guaranteed these rights.

In *Griswold,* Justice Douglas looked to what he called the "penumbras" of several different amendments. (A penumbra is a partial shadow, such as that created in an eclipse.) By this he meant that although privacy is not mentioned specifically in the language of any amendment, it is implied in the "shadows" between several amendments. And in *Roe,* Justice Blackmun expanded the privacy right to include a woman's choice to terminate a pregnancy. Because the right to privacy is not explicit in the Constitution, the two decisions are difficult to defend for any other reason than

Umpiring "Harmless, Empty Shadows": The Right of Privacy

Fred W. Friendly and Martha J. H. Elliott

"Umpiring 'Harmless, Empty Shadows'" from Fred W. Friendly and Martha J. H. Elliott, *The Constitution: That Delicate Balance* (New York: Random House, 1984), pp. 189–208. Copyright © 1984 by Random House, Inc. Reprinted by permission of Random House, Inc.

the fact that one may agree with them. When you are finished with this selection, you will understand why *Griswold* and *Roe* are among the most controversial Supreme Court decisions.

HARRY A. BLACKMUN   Supreme Court justice since 1970 who wrote the majority opinion in *Roe* v. *Wade*.

CHARLES LEE BUXTON   Medical director of a birth-control clinic; Estelle Griswold's codefendant.

WILLIAM O. DOUGLAS   Supreme Court justice (1939–1975) who wrote the majority opinion in *Griswold*.

ESTELLE T. GRISWOLD   Executive director of Connecticut Planned Parenthood.

NORMA McCORVEY   "Jane Roe" in *Roe* v. *Wade*.

CATHERINE RORABACK   An attorney for Griswold and Buxton.

SARAH WEDDINGTON   Attorney for McCorvey.

What are these people—doctor and patients—to do? Flout the law and go to prison? Violate the law surreptitiously and hope they will not get caught? . . . It is not a choice they need have under . . . our constitutional system.

Justice William O. Douglas,
dissenting in *Poe* v. *Ullman*

▶ It was a put-up job, a test case in which the players knew exactly what roles they were to play and were willing to take the risk to fight for what they believed in. For Estelle T. Griswold, executive director of the Connecticut Planned Parenthood League, it was an overt act of civil disobedience. When, on November 1, 1961, she opened the doors of a birth control clinic at 79 Trumbull Street in New Haven, she was begging to be arrested. It would not take long for the police to comply. Mrs. Griswold and her codefendant, Dr. Charles Lee Buxton, medical director of the clinic, would soon be arrested and convicted.

Although Justice Felix Frankfurter once observed that "the safeguards of liberty have frequently been forged in controversies involving not very nice people," Mrs. Griswold and Dr. Buxton prove there are exceptions to that generalization. Griswold was a well-educated Connecticut matron, slight, handsome, and cultured. She has been described as "a Connecticut Yankee who scrounged around for furniture for the clinic and scrubbed its floors." Catherine Roraback, one of the attorneys who would represent the pair, remembers Griswold as a "very dynamic woman, and I mean woman, with a capital W. . . . She felt very strongly that there should be birth control service for women in Connecticut. And she was quite willing to push it as far as she could." She fought the battle for birth control despite the fact that she had not been able to have children of her own.

Griswold's dedication came from her grasp of the problems of world over-population. She had worked in Europe after World War II helping to relocate displaced people. After touring some of the countries where she had placed people, she later reflected:

> *I saw poor, hungry people in the slums of Favola in Rio de Janeiro, in the La Perla area of Puerto Rico and Algiers.*
>
> *You think of people as civilized. . . . each human being living in comfort and wealth feels he is a dignified individual. A look at the slums of the world, at the chaos of a war-scorched earth, and you realize that life at the point of survival, where food, water and shelter are unobtainable is close to reversion to an animal order. Survival is first; civilization is second.*

It was this perspective which led Griswold to join Connecticut's Planned Parenthood League in 1954 and to become its executive director a few years later.

Whereas Griswold was global in her view, her codefendant, Dr. Buxton, was more concerned for the poor women of Connecticut who could not afford private doctors. Roraback remembers Buxton constantly reminding her that "the problem is that women who have private doctors can get all the information they want and get prescriptions [for birth control]. . . . The real problem in Connecticut is that poor women who do not have private doctors cannot get that kind of care." White-haired and bespectacled, the 60-year-old physician was described as "a gentle crusader" who shunned publicity. A Princeton undergraduate and a Columbia Medical School graduate, Buxton was the head of Yale's obstetrics and gynecology department. Although research oriented, he always had time for patients and spent hours trying to set up classes for teenagers in "human physiology"—sex education.

The lifelong dedication of those two people would lead to a case that would have revolutionary effect on the rights of Americans. When it was over, the United States Supreme Court would not only declare Connecticut's ancient anti–birth-control law unconstitutional, as Griswold and Buxton had hoped, but would also add a new gloss to the Constitution, the right of privacy. That right was not specifically written into any of the provisions of the Bill of Rights, but a majority of the Court would find "penumbras" and combinations of explicit rights that they felt guaranteed a natural or fundamental right of privacy. This new reading of the Constitution would have emanations and repercussions that would lead to a whole body of case law on civil liberties.

From Comstock to Trumbull Street

Anthony Comstock and Margaret Sanger had one thing in common, birth control legislation. Comstock devoted himself to getting it passed; Sanger devoted herself to getting it repealed. Comstock, a "lifelong crusader for God, Country, motherhood [in wedlock] and clean living," was special legislative agent for the Y.M.C.A.'s Committee for the Suppression of Vice. Through his lobbying efforts, the Congress passed on March 3, 1873 (the eve of Ulysses S. Grant's inauguration) the Comstock Act, which barred a long list of "obscene" and "immoral" materials from the United States mails.[1] Among the banned items were "every article, instrument, substance, drug, medicine, or thing which is advertised or described in a manner calculated to lead another to use or apply it for preventing conception or producing abortion."

In 1879, six years later, Connecticut, Comstock's home state, followed suit and enacted its own legislation. The Connecticut law went even further than the federal legislation: it banned the "use" of any birth control device. It is interesting to note that Comstock had never intended for the legislation to limit what doctors could prescribe to patients, which is exactly what the Connecticut law was interpreted to mean.

In 1912 Margaret Sanger was a nurse in New York City when she heard a doctor warn Sadie Sachs, a poor working mother, that one more pregnancy would kill her. Under the New York State law, as in many other states at the time, the only birth control the physician could prescribe was to recommend to Sadie that her husband "sleep on the roof." Not long after, Sanger attended Sadie at her deathbed following a botched abortion. That event turned Sanger into a crusader. She became devoted to ending the injustice inflicted on lower-class women, who could not afford proper medical help and "whose miseries were as vast as the sky." Sanger traveled throughout the country and became the mother of the nation's birth control movement as she tried to undo all the "wrong" that had been done by earlier crusaders such as Comstock. An ardent feminist and Marxist, who saw all anti–birth-control legislation as a capitalist plot "which compels a woman to serve as a sex implement for man's use," Sanger founded the Planned Parenthood Federation of America. She also opened the first birth control clinic in New York, for which act she was jailed in 1916.

Sanger was instrumental in starting Connecticut's birth control movement. In 1921 she traveled from New York to nearby Connecticut to state her case before the state legislature in Hartford, shouting her familiar cry of "Feminists, come out from under the cover of morbid respectability and let's get a look at you." Three prominent Connecticut women—Mrs. Katharine Houghton Hepburn, Mrs. Katharine Beech Day, and Mrs. Josephine Bennett—didn't have to be convinced. They formed her welcoming committee, as well as the core of what would become the Connecticut Birth Control League (later the Connecticut Planned Parenthood League).

The legislature lent a deaf ear to Sanger, but her trip had sparked a deep-seated commitment in the Hartford trio of Hepburn, Day, and Bennett. The three had been active in the suffrage movement, and as Hepburn's daughter explains, "This was the next logical step. Mother felt the first thing that women had to have was the vote and then some control over their reproductive processes. . . . It was a process of female empowerment." On February 11, 1923, they organized the first public meeting on birth control to be held in the state. To their surprise and delight, the turnout was so large that the gallery of the Parsons Theater in Hartford had to be opened.

The group grew larger and more active, perhaps in part because many women realized that Connecticut was the only state in the nation that placed an absolute ban on the *use* of birth control. Each year they lobbied for repeal of Connecticut's rigid law, and each year the effort was unfruitful. Occasionally the Connecticut House of Representatives, which largely consisted of Protestants from rural areas, would pass a repeal; however, the Senate, in which Connecticut's urban, Catholic population was better represented, invariably voted the measure down.

None of these defeats stopped the determined advocates of the birth control movement. By the 1930s, Hepburn had become so involved in the fight that she was sometimes referred to in newspapers as the "Anti-Stork Chief." Her family laughs at the label. "Mother wasn't anti-stork, or anti-baby. She had six children of her own,"[2] says Marian Hepburn Grant, her daughter. "She used to argue against a very nice lady who was the mother of three children. And mother would say, 'I have six children and I use birth control. If I didn't, I would have 25 children. . . . You have to be sympathetic to the ones of us who are more fertile.'"

Hepburn traveled around Connecticut and the rest of the country, making speeches for birth control. A powerful speaker, whose voice could reach the back row of any assemblage, Hepburn successfully countered the arguments of her debating opponents. In one debate, arguing against the position that birth control interfered with nature, she stated:

> [Birth control] is unnatural only in the way every other bit of our civilization is unnatural—the lighting of this room, the riding in automobiles and airplanes instead of walking barefoot.
>
> The use of the human brain is natural, be it ever so hard to make some people do it. Birth Control is the use of human intelligence that God gave us to control the forces of nature.

During another debate, she countered her opponent: "To say that God wills children to be born into the world who have no chance to grow up to be normal, healthy human beings is an insult to God."

In arguing against the Connecticut law, Hepburn emphasized its unfairness. Upper-class women could get birth control information from their private doctors, but the very people who needed it most—those who were poor or on relief—could not. That was the unequal justice of the Connecticut law. No legal authorities dared interfere with private physicians offering advice to affluent women; in fact, there were only a few instances where drugstores were raided for dispensing birth control prescriptions. Yet the poor were without help.

The Connecticut Birth Control League decided to do something concrete about this injustice. In 1935 it opened up the first birth control clinic in Hartford, just a few blocks from the state legislature. Within the next four years, clinics were established in Stamford, Danbury, Westport, New Britain, Greenwich, Norwalk, Bridgeport, and Waterbury. At these clinics patients were seen only if they were married and already had at least one child.

The Waterbury clinic was one of the last to open but the first to be closed. Just six months after it began operation, on June 12, 1939, police raided the clinic, located in Chase Memorial Dispensary, and arrested doctors Roger B. Nelson and William A. Goodrich and nurse Clara L. McTernan. As evidence, the officers confiscated all the clinic's contraceptive supplies. The Waterbury raid may have been triggered by the pressure from a Jesuit priest, who admonished his congregation for permitting the law of God to be violated and who accused State Attorney William B. Fitzgerald of shirking his duty to uphold the law.

Although a trial date was set for the three Waterbury staffers, their lawyer, J. Warren Upson, filed a demurrer—a pleading which acknowledges that the facts are true but argues that the defendants are not guilty because the law was unconstitutional. Upson argued that the Connecticut law was an "unconstitutional interference with the individual liberty of the citizens of Connecticut." He stipulated:

> It is respectfully submitted that the decision as to whether or not a married couple shall have children is a decision peculiarly their own and that it is a natural right which is inherent in citizens of the State of Connecticut and has been preserved to them through the centuries. If the people of Connecticut have any natural rights whatsoever, one of them certainly is the right to decide whether or not they shall have children, and to this natural right, the right to use contraceptive devices is a natural concomitant. With the powers of the State ever encroaching upon the rights of its citizens, it is surely time for the Courts to fix a point beyond which the State cannot go.

What is important about Upson's argument is that it was the first statement of a natural right associated with marriage and childbearing. Although he did not specifically mention a right to privacy, his position would be echoed in the decision in Estelle Griswold's case 26 years later.

In a move that surprised almost everyone, Judge Wynne sustained the demurrer in *State* v. *Nelson,* not on the grounds of a natural right, but on the grounds of a doctor's right to prescribe medicine. After noting that the state's objective "of morality and chastity" is "laudable," he asked, "Is a doctor to be prosecuted as a criminal for doing something that is sound and right in the best tenets and traditions of a high calling dedicated and devoted to health?" He answered his question in the negative and concluded that the "statute is defective on the broad constitutional grounds."

The state of Connecticut appealed the ruling, and three of the five judges on the State Supreme Court of Errors rejected Judge Wynne's ruling. To them the question of birth control was "to be addressed to the General Assembly rather than to the Court." Citing a previous Massachusetts case in which the United States Supreme Court had found no constitutional problem with an anti–birth-control statute, the Connecticut court decided that the law was constitutional.

The decision was unappealable because the Connecticut high court had merely overturned Wynne's sustaining of the demurrer and ordered a trial. The state later withdrew the charges and the three defendants were never prosecuted, leaving *State* v. *Nelson* on the books. That meant that when another case came before the Connecticut courts the controlling decision would be the Connecticut Supreme Court's decision that the birth-control law was constitutional.

In the meantime, the other clinics shut down. Planned Parenthood groups were relegated to their annual fight before the Connecticut legislature and to "border runs," in which poor women were transported to clinics in New York and Rhode Island where dispensing birth control was now permitted.

Then, in the late 1950s, the birth control advocates began to look for another legal route. The law firm they hired to come up with a strategy decided that what they needed were women whose lives would be threatened by a pregnancy. Attorney Catherine Roraback explains the climate in Connecticut in the late 1950s: "It was felt quite literally that the best we would probably accomplish in any form of litigation was an exception . . . written into the law that a doctor could prescribe contraceptives for a patient . . . where pregnancy would be a life-threatening situation."

Eventually two women showed up at the Yale offices of Dr. Buxton, a dedicated member of Connecticut Planned Parenthood, who wanted the law changed. One, 26 years old, had had three congenitally abnormal children who had died shortly after birth. Dr. Buxton felt that another pregnancy would be disturbing to her physical and mental health. To the courts, she would be known as Jane Poe. The case of the second woman, known as Jane Doe, was even stronger. Twenty-five years old, she had come near death after her last pregnancy. She had remained unconscious for two weeks and was left with partial paralysis and impaired speech. Dr. Buxton felt another pregnancy would kill her. Both women trusted Dr. Buxton completely and were willing to challenge the law.

The two cases were joined along with a separate complaint by Dr. Buxton arguing that the Connecticut law deprived him of his Fourteenth Amendment due process rights. As expected, citing the *Nelson* precedent, the Connecticut courts ruled against them.

Roraback handled the case up through the Connecticut courts, but when the time came to argue it before the Supreme Court, Planned Parenthood began looking for another lawyer. As Roraback comments, "It was not considered that a woman could argue the case in front of the Supreme Court, so you had to find a man." The man they found was Fowler Harper, a law professor at Yale who specialized in the First Amendment; he based his argument on the doctor's First Amendment freedom of expression—to candidly advise his patients.

But the United States Supreme Court ultimately dismissed the case on the grounds that it did not present a real controversy. Justice Felix Frankfurter called it a dead letter issue and wrote that the high court "cannot be umpire to debates concerning harmless, empty shadows."[3] He reasoned that the "fear of enforcement" was "chimerical," or imaginary, because the provisions of the law had gone unenforced for so many years.

Justice William O. Douglas blasted his brethren with a fiery dissent, pointing out that owners of Connecticut drugstores selling contraceptives had been prosecuted and that for several years no public or private birth control clinic had dared operate in the state. He wrote:

> What are these people—doctor and patients—to do? Flout the law and go to prison? Violate the law surreptitiously and hope they will not get caught? By today's decision we leave them no other alternatives. It is not the choice they need have under . . . our constitutional system. It is not the choice worthy of a civilized society. A sick wife, a concerned husband, a conscientious doctor seek a dignified, discreet, orderly answer to the critical problem confronting them. We should not turn them away and make them flout the law and get arrested to have their constitutional rights determined. . . . They are entitled to an answer to their predicament here and now.[4]

In a concurring opinion, Justice William Brennan, a Roman Catholic, pointed out the crux of the legal problem in Connecticut and, in doing so, virtually invited the next Supreme Court case. "The true controversy in this case," he concluded, "is over the opening of birth-control clinics on a large scale; it is that which the State has prevented in the past, not the use of contraceptives by isolated and individual married couples." He wrote that the constitutional questions could be decided "when, if ever, that real controversy flares up again."[5]

Estelle Griswold and Lee Buxton were about to give the Court that chance; they were about to turn those "empty shadows" into a real controversy. On the same day that the Court announced the decision against Poe and Doe—June 20, 1961—Planned Parenthood announced that it would soon be opening a clinic on Trumbull Street in New Haven.

The Arrest

Four-and-a-half months later, Justice Brennan's "flare up" was about to ignite. One man from West Haven who was more than willing to add fuel to that fire was James G. Morris, a night manager of a car rental agency near the building in which the clinic was to open. A devout Roman Catholic, Morris believed that "a Planned Parenthood Center is like a house of prostitution. . . . It is against

the natural law which says marital relations are for procreation and not entertainment. It is against the state law. I think the state law is a good law and it
should be enforced." After he heard that the center was about to open, Morris
wrote a letter to the county prosecutor and called the state police and the New
Haven mayor. When nothing happened, he went to the local media. Whether
the police and prosecutor would have done anything about the clinic without
Morris's complaint is unclear, but his vocal assault did bring the controversy
into the public view. As one Planned Parenthood official bragged, Morris "fell
right into our laps."

Just three days after the clinic opened, detectives John Blazi and Harold Berg
were knocking on the second-floor door of the Trumbull Street building. Estelle
Griswold had an almost "Doctor Livingstone, I presume" greeting for the officers. She knew exactly who the two men were and what they wanted; just three
years earlier, she had presented Blazi with an award on behalf of the New Haven Human Relations Council.

"It was one of the easiest types of investigations you could get involved in,"
Detective Berg remembers. Mrs. Griswold and Dr. Buxton gave the detectives
a guided tour of the clinic, pointing out the condoms and vaginal foam they
were dispensing. "It wasn't one of those investigations where you had to dig
out the information. . . . It was sort of 'Here it is; Here we are; Take us in; We
want to test this.'"

While the "raid" was going on, several patients were receiving counsel about
contraception. When they realized what was going on, one woman said, "We're
going on a sit down strike until we get what we came for." But the investigation
was amicable and, having all the information they needed, the detectives left
without making any arrests or confiscating any files.

Morris was outraged that everyone hadn't been arrested right off the bat. He
kept up his tirade as the local press over the next few days repeatedly asked
the question, "Will the state uphold the law?" New Haven Circuit Court Prosecutor Julius Maretz and Sixth Circuit Court Judge J. Robert Lacey soon answered
that question when they issued a warrant for the arrest of Griswold and Buxton.
A deal was worked out whereby the two defendants appeared voluntarily at the
police court on November 10 and were booked and charged under the law that
made the use of any contraceptives illegal and under another provision of the
Connecticut code which made it a crime to aid and abet anyone in the commission of a crime. Griswold and Buxton, who were not handcuffed or finger-
printed, were released on $100 bail each.

Planned Parenthood voluntarily closed the clinic. During the few days it had
been open, 42 women had been examined and given contraceptives. More than
75 others had set up appointments. This, according to Morris, "did an awful lot
of damage."

Prior to the arrests, Roraback, who was once again involved and was concerned about the privacy of the patients, had struck a deal with the prosecutor.
"We made an agreement that if he would agree not to just go and grab all the

clinic's records," Planned Parenthood would provide him with the records of a few consenting patients. Roraback found three women who were willing to risk arrest: Joan B. Forsberg, the wife of a minister, later to become one herself; Marie Tindall, executive director of the Dixwell Community House, which served low-income families; and Rosemary Ann Stevens, a graduate student in the Yale School of Public Health.

Forsberg, who had participated in "border runs" for the league, had come to the clinic in its first days and obtained a prescription for birth control pills. As she left, she ran into Griswold and offered her help in any way. A couple of days later, she was, as a result of the agreement with the prosecutor, being asked to turn state's evidence against the center. Forsberg was perfectly willing. However, when the police officer interviewed her, he took the birth control pills as evidence. She immediately called Griswold and said, "Now, I don't mind going to jail for this case, but getting pregnant would be something else." Griswold got Forsberg another prescription.

Giving Life to Dead Words

The trial was set for November 24. Roraback had waived her clients' right to a jury trial because she feared that a jury might be sympathetic; she wanted to make sure that there was a conviction. On the opening day she filed a demurrer based on the First and Fourteenth Amendment rights of freedom of expression of the doctors and social workers in the clinic. But Judge Lacey rejected the plea. When the trial was resumed on January 2, it went swiftly, with the three women testifying against Griswold and Buxton and two obstetricians testifying for them. It didn't take Lacey long to conclude that "the evidence was clear" and that the two defendants were guilty. They were each fined $100.

"This time," Griswold said after the trial, "I don't see how Mr. Justice Frankfurter can call the law dead words." (Curiously enough, by the time that the Supreme Court heard the case, March 1965, Justice Frankfurter had retired in ill health and had been replaced by Byron White.)

Attorneys Roraback and Harper immediately began the long process of appeal; not surprisingly, the Connecticut courts upheld the convictions. As the lawyers prepared their briefs for the Supreme Court, they relied on the First and Fourteenth Amendments. They argued that the Connecticut statute deprived doctors, such as Buxton, and clinic operators, such as Griswold, of the right to life, liberty, and property without due process of law. In addition, they said, under the due process clause, laws cannot be "arbitrary and capricious"; they must have a reasonable relationship to the legislative purpose. The purpose of this law was for "public morality" and to discourage extramarital relations. Prohibiting the use of birth control by married couples, in Roraback and Harper's view, was not directly tied to public morality and was therefore arbitrary, capricious, and unconstitutional. It also violated a doctor's and counselor's First Amendment right of free speech—their right to counsel their patients.

While the legal strategy was being worked out, Harper called Roraback, pointing out a *New York University Law Review* article on the Ninth and Tenth Amendments and the right of privacy. "I said," Roraback remembers, "I really didn't think it was relevant. . . . But Fowler said, 'I think we ought to have it in there.'" So they included in the brief a section which argued that the Connecticut law was an unwarranted invasion of privacy.

> *In our constitutional system, the principle of safeguarding the private sector of the citizen's life has always been a vital element. The Constitution nowhere refers to a right of privacy in express terms. But various provisions of the Constitution embody separate aspects of it. And the demands of modern life require that the composite of these specific protections be accorded the status of a recognized constitutional right.*

Planned Parenthood was arguing that although there was no *specific* mention of privacy in the Constitution, there *ought* to be. Furthermore, it argued that one could look at the First Amendment (freedom of expression and association), the Third Amendment (no quartering of soldiers in times of peace), the Fourth Amendment (no unreasonable search and seizure), and the Ninth Amendment ("the enumeration in the Constitution, of certain rights, shall not be construed to deny or disparage others retained by the people")—together with the "liberty" guaranteed by the Fourteenth Amendment—and come up with a right of privacy.

The privacy issue came to play a larger role in the legal strategy, to be emphasized over the argument based on the First Amendment. Part of the reason may be that when Fowler Harper died in 1963, Professor Thomas I. Emerson of Yale helped finish the briefs and then argued the case before the Supreme Court. As Emerson recalls, "Fowler Harper was more sanguine about the progress under the First Amendment than I was." He said he did not think the Court would decide the case on a doctor's right to give medical advice. He adds, "[What is involved] really is a right to keep the government out of a certain zone of activity, particularly dealing with sexual matters and intimacy of the home."

Roraback stresses that the idea was not to "establish a right of privacy" but to "knock out the Connecticut birth control statute. . . . It was a bad statute." In working through litigation strategy, she explains, "you have a very concrete case with people and concerns, and what you're trying to do is to accomplish an immediate goal for those people. . . . You're not thinking of the long-term strategy of trying to establish the right of people to live their lives."

The brief for the state of Connecticut argued that the "decision of the General Assembly of Connecticut that the use of contraceptives should be banned is a proper exercise of the police power of the state." In other words, it was one of those decisions properly left to the state, not to a court. The state also argued that the law did not infringe upon Buxton's right to practice medicine, because the practice of medicine is the "treatment, cure, and/or prevention of disease" and the women who testified were in perfect health. In the state's view, Planned Parenthood was not practicing medicine; it was dispensing contraceptives. Reasoning along these same lines, the state said that Buxton and Griswold's free speech had not been violated, because dispensing birth control was not speech but action.

As to the privacy issue, the state flatly denied that anyone's privacy had been violated, inasmuch as the three women who testified had done so voluntarily.

The Court Decides

On June 7, 1965, Justice William O. Douglas, who had written the angry dissent in *Poe,* had the privilege of turning his minority opinion into a majority when the Court, in a 7-to-2 vote, decided that the Connecticut law was unconstitutional.

Beginning with the disclaimer that the Supreme Court does "not sit as a super-legislature," Douglas went on to say that the marital relations of husband and wife were basic rights, not mentioned in the Constitution but nevertheless protected by it. Accepting the Planned Parenthood arguments, Douglas pointed to specific amendments that imply a right to privacy. He said that the "First Amendment has a penumbra where privacy is protected from governmental intrusion."[6] He reasoned that other sections of the Bill of Rights "have penumbras, formed by emanations from those guarantees that help give them life and substance. . . . Various guarantees create zones of privacy. . . . The present case . . . concerns a relationship lying within the zone of privacy created by several fundamental constitutional guarantees."[7]

It is important to note that the zone of privacy was only mentioned in terms of *married* people. As Douglas concluded:

> We deal with a right of privacy older than the Bill of Rights—older than our political parties, older than our school system. Marriage is a coming together for better or worse, hopefully enduring, and intimate to the degree of being sacred. It is an association that promotes a way of life, not causes; a harmony in living, not political faiths; a bilateral loyalty, not commercial or social projects. Yet it is an association for as noble a purpose as any involved in our prior decisions.[8]

Justice [Arthur] Goldberg wrote a concurring opinion in which he was joined by Chief Justice [Earl] Warren and Justice [William J.] Brennan. He began by asserting that he rejected the idea that the Fourteenth Amendment incorporates the Bill of Rights but believed that the "concept of liberty" protects certain fundamental rights, which are not restricted to the rights spelled out in the Bill of

Rights. To Goldberg, marital privacy, though not mentioned in the Constitution, was one of those fundamental rights. He based his judgment on the fact that "the language and history of the Ninth Amendment reveal that the Framers of the Constitution believed that there are additional fundamental rights, protected from governmental infringement, which exist alongside those fundamental rights specifically mentioned in the first eight constitutional amendments."

Justice Goldberg noted that the Court, in a long series of cases, had insisted that where fundamental liberties are at stake, the state must have a compelling reason for abridging those liberties. In his view the Connecticut justification of discouraging extramarital relations did not meet that test.

Justice [John Marshall] Harlan also wrote a separate concurrence, in which he relied on the due process clause of the Fourteenth Amendment. He said that the question was whether the law "violates basic values 'implicit in the concept of ordered liberty.'" Differing from Douglas, Harlan added that the decision need not depend on "radiations" from the Bill of Rights. "The Due Process Clause of the Fourteenth Amendment stands, in my opinion, on its own bottom."

Although he agreed with the majority, Justice [Byron] White also wrote his own concurring opinion, in which he relied on earlier decisions of the court which "affirm that there is a 'realm of family life which the state cannot enter' without substantial justification. . . . Surely the right invoked in this case, to be free of regulation of the intimacies of the marriage relationship" came within that realm. He said that the rationale of discouraging illicit sexual relations was not sufficient state justification for the "sweeping scope of the statute," and concluded that the statute "deprives [married] persons of liberty without due process of law."

Justices [Potter] Stewart and [Hugo] Black were the lone dissenters in the case. Each wrote a separate dissenting opinion in which the other joined. Justice Black admitted that the "law is every bit as offensive to me as it is to my Brethren," but reasoned that its "evil qualities" did not make it "unconstitutional." He continued: "I like my privacy as well as the next one, but I am nevertheless compelled to admit that government has a right to invade it unless prohibited by some specific constitutional provision." He said that it was not up to judges to decide what laws are unwise or unnecessary; that was the job of the legislatures.

Black chided his colleagues for reverting to the "substantive due process" rationale which had been used by the Court to strike down economic legislation in the late nineteenth and early twentieth century. . . . "That formula . . . is no less dangerous when used to enforce this Court's view about personal rights than those about economic rights." Thus, finding no constitutional justification to do otherwise, Black said he would uphold the law.

Justice Stewart began by declaring the Connecticut statute "an uncommonly silly law," but added that the Court was not asked whether the law was "unwise, or even asinine. We are asked to hold that it violates the United States Constitution." He said he could find no general rights of privacy in the Bill of Rights or in any other part of the Constitution. "[T]o say that the Ninth Amendment," he wrote "has anything to do with this case is to turn somersaults with history." He concluded that it was the Court's duty to "subordinate our own personal views, our own ideas of what legislation is wise and what is not." If the people of Connecticut thought the law unwise, they should persuade the legislature "to take this law off the books."

Two days later, the *New York Times* published an editorial rebuke to Justices Black and Stewart:

> *A reasonable and convincing argument can be made—and was made by the dissenters—that this infringement on personal freedom represented in the laws of Connecticut and many other states should have been corrected by the legislatures. But the fact is that it was not corrected. To what forum but the Supreme Court could the people then repair, after years of frustration, for relief from bigotry and enslavement?*

Three months later, on September 20, 1965, Estelle Griswold and Lee Buxton reopened their birth control clinic in New Haven.

Griswold's Legacy: Jane Roe

The decision in *Griswold* meant much more than the reopening of the clinic. . . . It established a right of privacy for married couples. Seven years later, in *Eisenstadt* v. *Baird,* the Court extended that right to single persons. William Baird was a 40-year-old former medical student who traveled around the Northeast giving birth control advice to the poor. He was convicted in Massachusetts for displaying contraceptives at a lecture at Boston University and for giving a female student some vaginal foam. His case reached the Supreme Court in 1972, and Justice Brennan wrote the opinion for the majority:

> *The marital couple is not an independent entity with a mind and heart of its own, but an association of two individuals each with separate intellectual and emotional makeup. If the right of privacy means anything, it is the right of the* individual, *married or single, to be free from unwarranted governmental intrusion into matters so fundamentally affecting a person as the decision whether to bear or beget a child.*

But *Griswold's* major impact came the following year in *Roe* v. *Wade.* Norma McCorvey was a 25-year-old unmarried woman who had no intention of changing the Constitution; all she wanted was a legal abortion in Texas. In August 1969, McCorvey had been working in a small town in Georgia as a ticket seller for a freak-animal side show in a traveling circus. She describes herself as "an army brat" with only a ninth-grade education who was down on her luck and trying to make ends meet. She tells the graphic story of how one night on her way back to her motel room, three men and two women attacked and raped her, leaving her lying on a country road. She finally made it back to her motel room and collapsed, but she says she was afraid to report the attack to the police. "I just thought, this is it. I'm going home back to Texas. I pawned a portable radio and an electric shaver to buy a ticket. I had no money even to eat. I walked to the bus station. . . . I finally got back to Texas and called a friend who nursed me back to the point where I could get a job."

But a short time after McCorvey got back, she began feeling ill. Since she had had a child by a previous marriage, she suspected that she was pregnant and confirmed her suspicion with a visit to a clinic. She then went to the doctor who had delivered her daughter and said she wanted to have an abortion. "He said that it was against the law in Texas and that I'd have to go to New York or California or carry the baby to term." McCorvey remembers she was outraged. She said she would have the baby "but I won't keep it. I would hate it." She told the doctor she would give the baby up for adoption.

Her doctor gave her the name of an attorney who handled adoptions, but when she went to see him he asked her a number of insinuating questions about the rape. McCorvey walked out of his office. She then decided to look for a doctor who would perform an abortion; she finally found one who told her the price was $650. When she told him she didn't have that much money, he said he couldn't help her.

"I don't know if I was really touchy at the time, but it seemed that everybody I went to for help didn't have the time. . . . I felt that life had dealt me a dirty deal. I wasn't getting any aces," she now puts it. About that time, her luck changed; she met an attorney named Linda Coffee. Coffee sent her to another lawyer, Henry McCloskey, Jr., who specialized in arranging adoptions. Coffee also introduced her to Sarah Weddington, a 25-year-old graduate of the University of Texas Law School, who wanted to help McCorvey fight the Texas abortion law.

McCorvey, Coffee, and Weddington first met together at Columbo's Pizza on Mockingbird Lane in Dallas. After a few beers, Weddington turned to McCorvey and said, "Well don't you think it's aggravating that you cannot have total control of your body?" McCorvey answered, "Yea, I think it's damn rude." According to McCorvey, Weddington then said, "Let's take it to the Supreme Court." "And I said, 'Why don't we?' Little did I know that she was terribly serious. I never realized. When she said Supreme Court, the only supreme court I'd ever heard of was the Federal Building in Dallas. I thought, well, she's going to go up there and argue with those people."

McCorvey says that in that first and in several subsequent conversations, Weddington questioned her closely to make sure that she was willing to go all the way with a suit. "I said, 'Damn right. It's time women should have the right to do whatever they want with their bodies.'" McCorvey only had one stipulation: she wanted to be anonymous. She now explains, "My child was very young at the time, and I didn't want her to be subject to public ridicule. I did not want my name to be exploited all over the newspapers." She also didn't want her family to know. (Her mother was a Roman Catholic and her father a Jehovah's Witness, but she says it wasn't their religious affiliations that made her want anonymity. She just knew that they would never understand.) As a result, for the purposes of the lawsuit, she was known as Jane Roe. For more than a decade no one but her lawyers knew that Jane Roe was Norma McCorvey.

Weddington and Coffee (who later dropped out of the suit) first filed a complaint against Dallas District Attorney Henry Wade, whose job it was to enforce the abortion laws. The suit specifically named McCorvey (as Roe) but was also a class action suit for all other women—past, present, and future—in the state of Texas seeking an abortion. Norma McCorvey's complaint charged that the Texas law violated a woman's right to decide whether or not to bear children and invaded the right of privacy (protected by the First, Fourth, Fifth, Ninth, and Fourteenth Amendments) in the doctor-patient relationship. For the next few months, while the case was making its way through the courts, McCorvey "went underground," staying in "flophouses for hippies" and with friends. From time to time she would contact Weddington to find out what was happening with the case.

The gestation period of a baby is shorter than that of a constitutional issue. In June 1970 McCorvey gave birth to a daughter. She explains that the hospital made a mistake and initially brought the baby to her. Another nurse then came in and took the baby away from her. "I just got out of that bed like you wouldn't believe, and I grabbed her and I said 'Hey, wait a minute, that's my kid.'" McCorvey says she was then sedated and never saw the child again. Perhaps it was this experience which made her question the suit at one point. "I got to thinking, is it true what people are saying that abortion is killing babies? Is it true? Then I thought about all these poor children who I had personally seen parked in front of just dives—hungry, dirty, neglected, and abused. Their families were inside boozing it up. Why should these children be subject to this kind of abuse? If these people don't want these children why do they have them? And I thought I did the right thing. Because there for a long time I had my doubts. . . . If it hadn't been for Sarah's support, I don't know where I would have been."

Since McCorvey never went to any of the court proceedings, she only knew of the case through Weddington and the newspapers. Finally one day, Weddington came to her to explain that she was going to Washington to argue the case before the Supreme Court. "I said, 'What's there to argue about? It happened.' And she explained to me in minute detail exactly how it would happen and I said, 'God, the Supreme Court of the United States. My God, all those people are so important. They don't have time to listen to some little old Texas girl who got in trouble.' And she said, 'You are not understanding what I'm telling you. I have a good feeling that we're going to win this case.'"

Oral Arguments

On December 13, 1971, Sarah Weddington, only four years out of law school, made her first appearance before the Supreme Court. The Texas abortion law was defended by Jay Floyd, an assistant attorney general.

Weddington told the Court that "pregnancy to a woman can completely disrupt her life." She pointed out that in the state of Texas many schools and colleges required a woman to quit if she was pregnant; women were often forced to leave their jobs in the early part of their pregnancies, and the state provided no unemployment compensation or welfare for them. She asserted:

> *So, a pregnancy to a woman is perhaps one of the most determinative aspects of her life. It disrupts her education. It disrupts her employment. And it often disrupts her family life. And we feel that, because of the impact on women, this certainly—in as far as there are any rights which are fundamental—is a matter which is of such fundamental and basic concern to the woman involved that she should be allowed to make the choice as to whether to continue or terminate her pregnancy.*

As to the rights of the unborn child, Weddington said, "The Constitution, as I read it . . . attaches protection to the person at the time of birth. These persons born are citizens. . . . The Constitution, as I see it, gives protection to people after birth."

Jay Floyd argued that the case was moot (no longer a controversy) because Roe was no longer pregnant. She had had the child. However, one of the justices reminded him that it was a class-action suit: "Surely, you would—I suppose we could almost take judicial notice of the fact that there are, at any given time, unmarried pregnant females in the State of Texas."

Floyd then moved on to the crux of the case. He asserted that "there is life from the moment of impregnation." Countering Weddington's argument that women should have control of their bodies, Floyd said, "As far as freedom over one's body is concerned, this is not absolute." He cited as examples laws that prohibit the use of illicit drugs, indecent exposure, and adultery.

In his summation Floyd said, "We think these matters are matters of policy which can be properly addressed by the State legislature. We think that considerations should be given to the unborn, and in some instances, a consideration should be given to the father, if he would be objective to abortion."

Because of the heightened emotions surrounding this case (48 *amicus curiae* briefs were filed), the Court called for reargument in October 1972. One significant issue for the Court was the purpose of the 1854 Texas statute prohibiting abortion. During the second oral argument, Weddington contended that the Texas statute—like the anti-abortion laws of many other states—had been enacted to protect women from crude and life-threatening back-street abortions. During the nineteenth century, an abortion meant death for at least 50 percent of the women who underwent them. The position of the abortion rights advocates was that the anti-abortion statutes were *not* passed to protect the fetus. One fact that supported this contention was that it was not a crime in Texas for a woman to perform an abortion on herself. In addition, doctors prosecuted for performing abortions were only charged with murder if the *woman* died. Weddington's briefs and arguments pointed out that since the 1850s abortion had become safer even than childbearing. Thus the purpose of the Texas statute was no longer valid. Weddington said:

> *We are not here to advocate abortion. We do not ask the Court to rule that abortion is good, or desirable in any particular situation. We are here to advocate that the decision as to whether or not a particular woman will continue to carry or will terminate her pregnancy is a decision that should be made by that individual; that, in fact, she has a constitutional right to make that decision for herself; and that the State has shown no [compelling] interest in interfering with that decision.*

For the state of Texas Assistant Attorney General Robert C. Flowers asserted again that a fetus was a person from the moment of conception. Flowers said, "If we declare, as the appellees in this case have asked the Court to declare, that an embryo or a fetus is a mass of protoplasm similar to a tumor, then of course the State has no compelling interest whatsoever." However, Flowers argued that the unborn child was a person and was therefore entitled to constitutional protection: the state had a compelling interest to protect that life.

Underlying these two divergent views was the Fourteenth Amendment, which defined a citizen as a person *born* in the United States. So the Supreme Court would have to decide whether an unborn fetus was a person, entitled to constitutional protection, and whether the state of Texas could legislate to protect it.

The Court Decides

The Supreme Court's decision in *Roe* came down on January 22, 1973, the same day that former President Lyndon Johnson died. Writing for the 7-to-2 majority, Justice Harry Blackmun ruled first on the mootness issue: the case was not moot. "[T]he normal 266-day human gestation period is so short that the pregnancy will come to term before the usual appellate process is complete. If that termination makes a case moot, pregnancy litigation seldom will survive much beyond the trial state, and appellate review will be effectively denied."[9] Blackmun then ruled that the Texas statute "sweeps too broadly" and was unconstitutional. The Court had decided that "the word 'person' as used in the Fourteenth Amendment, does not include the unborn." Although there was no mention of "penumbras" of amendments, the Court did root its decision in the right of privacy established in *Griswold*:

> *The Constitution does not explicitly mention any right of privacy. In a line of decisions, however . . . the Court has recognized that a right of personal privacy, or a guarantee of certain areas or zones of privacy, does exist under the Constitution. . . . This right of privacy, whether it be founded in the Fourteenth Amendment's concept of personal liberty and restrictions upon state action, as we feel it is, or . . . in the Ninth Amendment's reservation of rights to the people, is broad enough to encompass a woman's decision whether or not to terminate her pregnancy.*[10]

However, Blackmun said the right of privacy was not absolute and added a restriction: "[T]his right is not unqualified and must be considered against important state interests in regulation."[11] Thus all abortions are not legal. The Court came up with a formula based on a division of pregnancy into trimesters. In the first three months of pregnancy, the right of privacy prevails and the abortion decision is up to the woman and her doctor. However, in the second trimester states could regulate abortions in ways related to maternal health. In other words, they could require that abortions be performed under certain conditions. During the last stage of pregnancy, when the fetus was viable (could live on its own outside the mother's womb), state laws could prohibit abortion—except under circumstances in which the life or health of the mother was in danger.

Norma McCorvey first heard of the Court's decision when her roommate pointed it out in the newspaper. She had never told her friend of her involvement in the case. But when McCorvey began crying, her roommate looked at the paper and said, "Don't tell me you knew LBJ?" McCorvey said, "No, I'm Jane Roe." Two days later Sarah Weddington called. She said, "How does it make you feel to know that women are going to be able to go to a clinic and get a legal abortion?" McCorvey answered, "It makes me feel like I'm on the top of Mount Everest."

Reaction to the decision was intense. There was jubilation among women's rights and birth-control organizations. Catholic organizations assailed the decision. John Cardinal Krol of Philadelphia called the decision "an unspeakable tragedy for this nation."

How far this right of privacy may extend has not yet been determined by the Court. There was a time when the Court refused to rule on the birth control issue because it was not considered a real controversy and a time when the Court would not have interfered with a state's right to ban abortions. So far the

Supreme Court has not tackled other issues associated with the right of privacy—such as the right to die.* Does privacy mean that the state cannot interfere with a doctor and a family's decision to turn off a respirator? Whose privacy is involved when a severely deformed infant is kept alive by extraordinary or so-called heroic medicine? the baby's? the parents'? Should the state have an interest in preserving that life? What about suicide? So far these excruciating questions have not been considered by the high court. Perhaps they are not yet "ripe" for judicial decision. Whatever a future Court may decide, modern technology and "medical miracles" will undoubtedly make its deliberations over the right to live and the right to die even more agonizing.

Notes

1. Congress does not have direct power to ban such materials but can regulate interstate commerce and the federal mails.

2. One of her six children, Katharine, would become a famous actress.

3. *Poe* v. *Ullman*, 367 U.S. 497, 508 (1961).

4. Ibid., p. 513 (Douglas, J., dissenting).

5. Ibid., p. 509.

6. *Griswold* v. *Connecticut*, 381 U.S. 479, 482–483 (1965).

7. Ibid., pp. 484–485.

8. Ibid., p. 486.

9. *Roe* v. *Wade*, 410 U.S. 113, 125 (1973).

10. Ibid., pp. 158, 152–153.

11. Ibid., p. 154.

---

* In June 1990 the Supreme Court handed down a very limited ruling on this question in the case of *Cruzan* v. *Director, Missouri Department of Public Health*. The Court upheld the Missouri Supreme Court's ruling that the tubes feeding Nancy Cruzan, who was in an irreversible coma after a car accident, could be removed only if "clear and convincing evidence" existed that the patient herself would have wanted this. (In December 1990 another hearing in Missouri found that such evidence did exist. A judge allowed the tubes to be removed, and Cruzan died several days later.)

Epilogue

Conservatives hope that President Bush's appointment of David Souter to the Supreme Court will lead to the overturning of *Roe* and *Griswold*. There is no question that the future of these decisions is in doubt. In 1986 the Court ruled in *Bowers* v. *Hardwick* that the right to privacy does *not* extend to the protection of persons of the same sex engaged in the act of sodomy. Many see the specter of the police entering the bedroom to enforce state laws of any kind as unpalatable. But because the Court has ruled that single people of the same sex do not have a right to privacy in the bedroom, it is possible that the Court will at some point reexamine the assertion in *Griswold* of the fundamental right to privacy for married people. As a demonstration of the degree of controversy regarding privacy, it is noteworthy that retired Justice Lewis Powell, who cast the deciding vote in the *Bowers* case (ruling for the state and against the rights of individuals), recently admitted that the losing party "may have had the better of the arguments."

On the issue of abortion, in recent years the Court has upheld governmental limits on both public funding for, and access to, the procedure. For instance, in 1989 the Court refused in a Missouri case (*Webster* v. *Reproductive Health Services*) to overturn *Roe* completely, but did expand the powers of state governments to regulate abortion rights. In the last few years the Court has also limited the general right to privacy in other areas such as police searches and drug testing.

The direction of the Court in the immediate future will depend partly on the judgment of Justice Souter, and partly on the willingness of any of the present members of the Court to change their previous decisions in reaction to his votes. Should the Court decide to eliminate the right of privacy or abortion, it may spur groups to seek amendments to the Constitution to restore rights of personal autonomy. Without a doubt, this entire area will continue to be one of the major constitutional battlegrounds in the coming years.

The Hill Case

Leonard Garment

Imagine that you unwittingly become involved in a major news story. What rights do you have? This was the problem faced by the Hills, a quiet family from a Philadelphia suburb. After becoming the victims of a hostage situation in the early 1950s, they were forced to relive the tragedy through a Broadway play and an article in *Life* magazine. The legal issue was to what degree people involuntarily thrust into the limelight are protected from libel (written defamation of character). Should freedom of the press be limited in such circumstances?

The problem facing failed presidential candidate Richard Nixon, who in the mid-1960s was attempting one of his many political comebacks by taking the Hills' Supreme Court appeal, was that the current libel law did not help the Hills. In *New York Times* v. *Sullivan* (1964), the Supreme Court had ruled that public officials, which it later expanded to "public figures," have little protection. Showing that its priority was freedom of the press, the Court ruled in *Sullivan* that when printing stories about such figures, newspapers do not have to prove that they have been completely accurate, only that they did not print the story with "actual malice" or "with knowledge that it was false or with reckless disregard of whether [the story] was false or not." In other words, if there was at least minimal effort to check a story's accuracy and if there was no apparent ill will by the reporter or editor, then there was no libel.

But *Time, Inc.* v. *Hill* (1967) came to the Court at the height of the Warren Court, which often went to extraordinary lengths to protect the rights of individuals. There were two sets of rights in conflict here—the Hills' right to privacy and *Life* magazine's right to publish what it pleased. The question became which party the Court was more eager to protect.

In addition to discussing the evolution of libel law, this selection provides a glimpse of how the interaction of personalities on the Court shapes the law. Unknown to Nixon at the time, the relationship between Justices Hugo Black and Abe Fortas apparently affected the

Leonard Garment, "The Hill Case," *The New Yorker*, Apr. 17, 1989. Reprinted by permission. © 1989 Leonard Garment.

decision in *Hill.* Black was unhappy with the newly appointed Fortas because of Fortas's interpretation of the Constitution and his growing personal influence on the Court. Black himself had become much more conservative in recent years. How might freedom-of-the-press and privacy law have developed differently if the two men had been getting along better?

The author, Leonard Garment, who worked with Nixon on the *Hill* case, later worked on Nixon's 1968 presidential campaign and joined his White House staff in 1970.

HUGO BLACK   Moderate liberal (but increasingly conservative) Supreme Court justice, 1937–1971.

ABE FORTAS   Activist liberal Supreme Court justice, 1965–1969.

JAMES AND ELIZABETH HILL   Crime victims who became parties in a First Amendment case.

HAROLD MEDINA   Counsel for Time, Inc.

RICHARD M. NIXON   Former vice president who would be elected president in 1968; counsel for the Hills.

▶ It is said that Richard Nixon, after his defeat in the 1962 California gubernatorial election, was persuaded (I think it more likely he decided on his own) to go East to establish a new venue for his contingent careers in law and politics. Elmer Bobst, chairman of the Warner-Lambert Pharmaceutical Company and a paterfamilias to the Nixons, brought him together with Warner-Lambert's law firm of Mudge, Stern, Baldwin & Todd. After all the shuffling, the firm emerged with the name Nixon, Mudge, Rose, Guthrie & Alexander. I had been with that firm since my graduation from Brooklyn Law School, in 1949, and by 1963, when Nixon joined the firm, I was more or less its chief of litigation.

As a matter of self-interest and personal curiosity, I took it upon myself to help Nixon adjust to the jargon and the style of a Wall Street law firm. Although I was not a Republican, I was not much of a Democrat, either, so the task of fitting the firm and its new senior partner together did not involve any great ideological deformation for me. And, while I was interested in politics as a form of litigation and in Nixon as a part of history, my main objective was to involve Nixon with legal work that was suitable to his talents and his public standing.

Working with the other senior members of the firm, Nixon was quickly successful in attracting and handling corporate clients. Finding the right piece of litigation for him to "go public" with took a little more time. The opportunity came when a case I had tried to a successful conclusion before a New York State court jury in 1962 went to the United States Supreme Court. The New York jury had decided that Time, Inc., had violated the privacy of our clients, the Hill family. Time, Inc., had appealed.

The decision of the Supreme Court to hear the case established that public issues of large consequence were involved. It also offered an attractive political twist: Richard Nixon, who had apparently passed from the political scene, arguing for the right of privacy against one of the nation's largest publishers. I suggested to Nixon that he argue the appeal, the clients joined in the request, and Nixon agreed to do so.

Nixon believed that he ran a large risk, because some of his old ideological enemies now sat on the Court and would have their knives out for him. But he also saw that his emergence as a skilled Supreme Court advocate could form a valuable part of people's perception of him as a "new Nixon." Moreover, the Hills were sympathetic clients—a normal middle-class mother and father who valued their privacy and their children's. In arguing their case, Nixon would have the best possible forum in which to express his deeply held feelings about press abuses of privacy. He would be seen as a disciplined advocate respectful of constitutional principles, not as the bitter politician who after losing the California gubernatorial race had lashed out at the press in his famous "last press conference."

So the stage was set for Nixon to make his debut before the Supreme Court.

On September 9, 1952, three convicts escaped from the federal penitentiary, in Lewisburg, Pennsylvania, and, a few days later, after stealing an automobile, shotguns, ammunition, and money, invaded the home of James and Elizabeth Hill, in the Philadelphia suburb of Whitemarsh. Hill, his wife, and their three daughters, aged eleven, fifteen, and seventeen, and twin sons, aged four, were held hostage for nineteen hours. Except, of course, for the general restraint, the convicts behaved in a decent, even gentlemanly, manner toward the terrified captives, and left without doing harm to the family. Ten days after the event, the convicts were apprehended on the Upper West Side of Manhattan. Two of them and a detective were killed in a gun battle, and the third was captured alive.

The immediate aftermath saw a great deal of public and press interest, particularly while the convicts were still at large, and also some open speculation that there had been acts of sexual violence involving Mrs. Hill and her teen-age daughters. The Hills tried to keep publicity to a minimum, emphasizing the absence of violence and otherwise declining all comment.

That November, the Hills moved to Connecticut, and they subsequently took pains to shield the family from reminders of the bizarre episode. They rejected all requests for magazine interviews and all offers of payment for their collaboration in telling the story of the incident. "For the best interests of our children," Mr. Hill wrote in answer to one such request, "we have felt that it was best to avoid any course of action that might remind them of our experience in September 1952. Following this policy we have refused all radio, television, magazine, newspaper, etc. offers connected with that experience." Gradually, public curiosity died away.

More than two years later, in the February 28, 1955, issue of *Life,* a review of a new Broadway drama, "The Desperate Hours," described the play as a "re-enacted" account of the ordeal of the Hill family. Neither the word "fictionalized" nor any word suggesting fictionalization appeared in the piece. The review was part of what *Life* called a "True Crime" story, and it was accompanied by photographs of the Hills' former home, in Whitemarsh. Members of the cast of the play, which was then having a pre-New York tryout in Philadelphia, were transported by *Life* to what it called the "actual" house and were photographed there in episodes from the play. Some of the large photographs depicted a series of vivid scenes of violence—scenes of a kind that the Hills had repeatedly said had not occurred during the actual incident.

Because of the *Life* story, the incident once again became a central part of the Hills' life. The original curiosity and speculative questioning flared up, with increased vigor, in their new community. A few days after the article appeared, Mr. Hill called upon a Harvard classmate, Randolph H. Guthrie—who was my senior law partner—and asked him to take legal action. The case was assigned to me for investigation and trial. Our first step, of course, was simply to ask *Life* to print a retraction of the story. *Life* refused. We filed suit.

Extensive pretrial discovery took place. It revealed that the *Life* article and the ensuing reemergence of the Hill family into the public eye were essentially the result of a coincidence: the pre-Broadway tryout of "The Desperate Hours" was in Philadelphia, and thus near a spot—the former Hill home—where a superficially similar incident had occurred. A chance remark about this coincidence in a brief corridor conversation between *Life*'s entertainment editor, Tom Prideaux, and a colleague stimulated the idea of a review with an unusual "news" angle—something that to *Life,* as a photo-news magazine, was of particular interest. The idea was described by one of *Life*'s editorial people as a "good gimmick." The trial evidence, however, showed that the relationship between the Hill incident and "The Desperate Hours" was extremely thin. The theme of the play had been drawn in a general way from a large number of hostage cases, of which the Hill incident was only one, and the plot was fundamentally different from the actual Hill case. . . .

A central theme of the novel and play is the subjection of the father and daughter to the will of the convicts. They are forced to leave the house to help the convicts with their criminal plans to the extent of being virtual accessories in a plot to murder the deputy sheriff. As his family is abused, his son attacked, his daughter threatened, his home turned into a shambles of verbal filth and horror, the father is driven to the point of almost committing murder. A final act of imagination and daring by the father forces the convicts out of the house and saves the family. The gang leader, in a state of shock and under the delusion that he and his brother are once again teen-agers defying their hated father, runs from the house, brandishing an empty gun, and is shot down on the front porch by the deputy sheriff. As the play ends, the father stands on a stairway as the other members of the family return, one by one, to what the play's script describes as the "havoc" that was their home.

Obviously, as [author] Joseph Hayes testified at the trial, "The Desperate Hours" was not in any sense the story or a reenactment of the Hills' experience. The principal elements of "The Desperate Hours," and the elements that made it a sensational and commercially successful melodrama, are bloody violence, drunkenness, profanity, sex, and heroism. These are precisely the elements that were absent from the Hills' actual experience. The Hills' calm acceptance of their difficult and frightening situation and the surprisingly civil behavior of the convicts were the antithesis of the drama of terror and violence which Hayes created and which became "The Desperate Hours"—so much so that the civility in the Hill incident was the focus of *Time* magazine's original news account of the actual episode, which bore the title "House Party."

Hayes had made these facts clear in a news article that appeared in the *Times* in January, 1955. "Instead of researching any of the specific 'cases'" of hostage-taking, he wrote, "I found it best to let my imagination play with the idea." *Life's* writers and editors read this article and other, similar pieces that Hayes had written elsewhere, at the time the Hill feature was in preparation.

Pretrial discovery also revealed that *Life's* editors had decided that *Life's* "True Crime" format required a highly explicit connection between the Hill incident and the play under review in order for the article to make sense. Accordingly, a series of drafts of the article's text showed a gradual tightening of the relationship. In the first draft, the connection was a generalized one. Then *Life's* editorial process transformed it. The final, published version categorically described "The Desperate Hours" as a re-creation of the Hill incident. "Americans all over the country" who "read about the desperate ordeal of the James Hill family," said *Life* boldly, "can see the story reenacted in Hayes' Broadway play based on the book."

The core of *Life's* response to the Hills' claims was that, notwithstanding disputes concerning its accuracy, the article was protected by the First Amendment. To this the Hills responded that deliberate falsities (*Life's* saying that there was a close factual link between the play and the Hill incident, and the portrayal of the Hills in a false light) constituted the article's main assertions. They argued that in spite of the realistic format the article was not news but fabrication. The falsities were a wrongful and actionable invasion of the Hills' privacy for purposes of commercial exploitation rather than a constitutionally protected report or comment on newsworthy matters.

After a two-week trial in 1962, the jury found in favor of Mr. and Mrs. Hill and made a large award of damages. (At the insistence of the Hills, no claim was made on behalf of the five Hill children, so that they would not be exposed to the litigation.) The decision establishing the liability of Time, Inc., was affirmed by a 4–1 vote in the New York State Appellate Division and then a 5–2 vote in the New York State Court of Appeals.

Richard Nixon's preparation of his Supreme Court argument in the Hill case began in 1965, shortly after the Court granted Time, Inc.'s, application for an appeal. Just the previous year, in the landmark case of *New York Times Co.* v. *Sullivan,* the Supreme Court had decided that a public official suing for libel was obliged to prove that the offending material was published with knowledge of falsity or with reckless disregard of the truth.

Sullivan grew out of the civil-rights struggle of the early nineteen-sixties and the deadly hatred it engendered in many Southern whites for Northern liberalism and its agents. Sullivan himself, an elected city commissioner of Montgomery, Alabama, whose duties included supervision of the police department, brought suit in the Alabama state courts charging that he had been libelled by a full-page advertisement in the *Times* which depicted, in dramatic terms, alleged violations of the rights of local black citizens by the Montgomery police. The advertisement had been placed by the Committee to Defend Martin Luther King and the Struggle for Freedom in the South, a militant civil-rights organization.

The advertisement was vouched for by a responsible person and signed by many well-known figures, and it seemed accurate on its face. The *Times* therefore published it without making a separate check on its accuracy. Nowhere in the ad was any charge made against Sullivan by name. Yet the Alabama Supreme Court held that the impersonal statements in the ad were libellous per se—that is, without any need for the plaintiff to prove he had suffered damage—and upheld a then-huge jury verdict for the plaintiff of five hundred thousand dollars.

The Supreme Court reversed the decision on broad constitutional grounds, saying that the challenged advertisement was well within the zone protected by the First Amendment and that political speech of this sort must be protected even if it contains errors, or else political debate cannot be truly free. Therefore, the Court said in *Sullivan,* a public official cannot collect libel damages for falsehoods relating to his official conduct "unless he proves that the statement was made with 'actual malice'—that is, with knowledge that it was false or with reckless disregard of whether it was false or not."

In the wake of *Sullivan,* fresh aspects of First Amendment law were being debated in the courts. The *Hill* case involved a first look by the Supreme Court at competing claims of individual privacy and institutional press freedom in the post-*Sullivan* world.

The legal stakes were substantial, and for Nixon, who was preparing to seek the 1968 Presidential nomination, the political and personal stakes were just as high. He could not afford to stumble before his old political adversaries or be seen as simply continuing his war against the press by new means, in a new forum. The only possible answer to these concerns was, as Nixon saw it, meticulous preparation, and I consequently had the opportunity during 1965 and 1966 to see how Nixon prepared himself for a professional "crisis" such as periodically marked his public career.

He began by reading and virtually committing to memory not only the trial record and the state-court decisions in the *Hill* case but copious quantities of additional background material, including federal and state case law, lawreview articles, and philosophical writings on libel and privacy. . . . The famous Nixon yellow pads accumulated, filled with summaries, questions, and preliminary lines of oral argument. As his grasp of the issues tightened, requests came to me for memoranda on fine points that needed elaboration. He scribbled endlessly on drafts and galleys of Supreme Court briefs. As the day of argument approached, there were almost continuous "skull sessions"—question-andanswer sessions with his law-firm colleagues which simulated a court argument. He worked particularly hard at grinding his points down to their essentials, using trial exhibits—especially blowups of photographs and drafts of the offending text—to give his argument its maximum impact. His preparation was almost obsessive; he left nothing to chance. His behavior was not only a matter of professional pride but a sign of his determination not to let his recent defeats drive him from the political arena. . . .

Nixon's process of preparation continued until the morning of April 27, 1966, when I anxiously summoned him from the lawyers' lounge in the Supreme Court just before the Court was scheduled to convene. He was still flipping through his yellow pads. When I tried to move him along, he laid a restraining hand on me and said, "Never rush into a public place." We strode slowly to our counsel seats, as if to the strains of "Hail to the Chief"; of course, only he heard them.

At precisely ten o'clock, the nine Justices appeared silently from the redvelvet-draped background, moved to the bench, and took their seats quickly. Chief Justice [Earl] Warren called the first case, an antitrust case in which the government was trying to force the Pabst Brewing Company, of Milwaukee, Wisconsin, to give up another beer company it had acquired some years before. Then, shortly after noon, he called the appeal in *Time, Inc.* v. *Hill.*

Arguing for Time, Inc., Harold Medina, of Cravath, Swaine & Moore, focussed his oral argument on two main points. First, the *Life* article's "falsity" was of an incidental and innocent nature. The article, he said, was basically an accurate depiction of the connection between the Hill family's captivity and the story of "The Desperate Hours." It was therefore constitutionally protected as comment on news. Medina's oral argument dealt principally with this issue, and thus with the similarities between the Hill incident and the play.

Medina also argued that the New York privacy statute involved in the case was overbroad on its face, because it penalized publication even of newsworthy material if the publication was primarily "for the purposes of trade." This argument was drawn from an obiter dictum—an observation by a judge that is not a necessary part of the court's decision—from a single judge, Benjamin Rabin, in a lower-court concurring opinion. Judge Rabin's statement was murky but could be read as suggesting that even truthful and newsworthy material might be actionable if it was intended solely for commercial purposes. If this was the case, Medina argued, the New York statute would be unconstitutional.

Nixon's oral argument emphasized the point that Judge Rabin's lone statement was only an incidental remark, not an integral part of court reasoning in the case. The law of New York, Nixon argued, had been settled otherwise by sixty years of decisions stating that a truthful news account was constitutionally protected. Nixon's main effort, apart from this argument, was to demonstrate that the method by which the text and photographs of the *Life* article had evolved proved that the magazine had created a fictionalized description of "The Desperate Hours" as a "reenacted" account of the Hill incident—in other words, a deliberate fabrication and an admitted "gimmick," designed to justify the use of the former Hill home as the "True Crime" site of a photo-news review of the play. This, in Nixon's submission, satisfied the constitutional test for liability, including the then only two-year-old formulation in *New York Times Co.* v. *Sullivan,* even though the original trial of the Hill case had taken place before Sullivan was decided and therefore had not met the Sullivan arguments head-on.

The atmosphere of the Court during the argument provided surprises and intimations. Both lawyers quickly displayed a comprehensive grasp of High Court forensics. Medina, as senior litigation partner at Cravath, had been around the track many times; the surprise was Nixon. In this, his first argument in an appellate court, he sounded like a polished professional of the bar—his footing confident, his language lawyerlike, his organization of material sure and clear. He had true "bottom," responding to dozens of tough questions, and the Court clearly relished the performance. John MacKenzie, who was then covering the Court for the Washington *Post,* wrote that in Nixon's presentation the Court and spectators "heard one of the better oral arguments of the year." At their luncheon after the argument, the Justices . . . expressed surprise that Nixon had done so well. . . . [A]mong comments circulating around Washington at the time was that of Justice Abe Fortas, who said that Nixon made "one of the best arguments that he had heard since he had been on the Court," and that, with work, he could be "one of the great advocates of our times."

The questioning and comments in the Court were ambiguous and tentative, yet furnished some interesting clues. The Chief Justice and Justice Fortas were almost outspokenly on Nixon's side. Chief Justice Warren asked the question that enabled Nixon to address what we thought was the central issue of the case:

Mr. Chief Justice Warren: Suppose that *Life* magazine, instead of doing this the way it did, said that this play of Mr. Hayes' is *reminiscent* [italics added] of the Hill incident. . . . Would you say . . . *Life* could do that without violating your law?

MR. NIXON: Mr. Chief Justice, cruel as it might be . . . I believe that would not
be a violation under New York law.

Justice Potter Stewart also seemed favorable, though with considerably less
force. Justice [Hugo] Black, in keeping with his long-standing position that any
restraint on press freedom, including libel and privacy claims, was unconstitutional, was clearly negative, indicating as much in a persistent line of questioning about whether New York State's privacy statute put impermissible limits
on freedom of speech. Justice [William] Douglas, who shared Black's absolute
view of First Amendment press protection, was silent. Justice Byron White was
openly troubled by Medina's argument on statutory overbreadth and by other
technical issues, and wondered aloud whether the New York law might be read
as unconstitutionally permitting a suit based on a truthful and newsworthy publication if it was shown to be for purely commercial purposes. The preliminary
disposition of Justices John Harlan and Tom Clark was unclear. Justice [William]
Brennan's comments were neutral and brief.

Nixon and I came away from the argument feeling that we had scratched out
a narrow majority. A sufficient number of Justices seemed to feel that the case
involved a real wrong by the *Life* editorial staff and that significant harm had
been done to nonpublic people who prized their privacy. The forceful statements by Warren and Fortas were particularly surprising and encouraging.
Nixon later commented that these two were political men and so knew first-
hand how fierce and lacerating the press could be when it fastened on a target.
They would know that for private persons unwanted and false public exposure
could be, in Nixon's words, "as traumatic as a physical blow." . . .

Arriving at work at about ten the next morning, I found on my desk a five-page,
single-spaced memorandum addressed to me from Nixon. This document is the
most instructive example of Richard Nixon's tenacity and work habits that I've
read in all the time I've known him, including the Presidential and post-
Presidential years. It was prepared shortly after we had parted at the airport.
Upon arriving at his Fifth Avenue apartment, overlooking Central Park and a
few floors below the apartment of Nelson Rockefeller, Nixon had dictated a
tape of detailed self-critical comments on his own argument and an assessment
of points, suggested by the Court's questioning, that he would now handle differently, and the tape had been transcribed by Nixon's secretary, Rose Mary
Woods, early the following morning. . . .

Nixon's memo concluded with an analysis of the constitutional underpinnings of the right of privacy. Nixon found and predicted the problems inherent
in the Supreme Court's free-floating rationale for a general right of privacy, as
it was stated in *Griswold* v. *Connecticut* (1965), the case invalidating a state ban
on the prescription or use of contraceptives. In the course of striking down the
Connecticut law, Justice Douglas, writing for the majority, created what had not
existed before in constitutional jurisprudence—a constitutional right of privacy

more general than anything specifically mentioned in the Bill of Rights. This right of privacy, said Justice Douglas, could not be found in any single constitutional amendment, but could be derived from the "penumbras" and "emanations," as he put it, that surrounded the separate clauses. . . .*

Some of *Griswold*'s effect on the privacy debate, though, was clear soon after the decision. During the *Hill* arguments before the Supreme Court, Medina, evidently not wanting to be thought an enemy of privacy, remarked, "Now, it just so happens there is this right of privacy. Whether you find it in the Fourth, Fifth, Ninth, or Fourteenth, I don't know. We recognize it and are for it." Whichever right of privacy Medina was talking about, it was certainly not the privacy right in the New York State statute at issue in the *Hill* case.

Nixon wrote in his midnight memo:

> ***The Constitutional Nature of the Privacy Right:***   *I think what would have been most helpful to the Court in writing the opinion would have been a brief statement clearing up Medina's fuzzy reference to a right of privacy being a constitutional right emanating from the Fourth, Fifth, Ninth and other Amendments (in other words, using the* Griswold *analogy). This kind of analysis, if followed to its conclusion, is both inaccurate and potentially dangerous from a constitutional standpoint. In* Griswold, *it was essential to find that there was a "constitutional right to privacy in marriage" since the issue there was the power of the* state *to impair that right. Unless it had been found that the right of privacy in marriage had constitutional status, the Connecticut statute could not have been declared unconstitutional.*
>
> *Here the question is not the power of the state to infringe on a right but the power of the state to recognize and implement a right.*

The memo revealed two things that were on Nixon's mind. . . . First, he believed he had missed opportunities to highlight factual arguments that would have helped place the *Hill* case farther outside the zone of constitutional protection defined in *Sullivan*. More important, he regretted his failure to give fuller and more precise expression to his intuition that Justice Douglas's weak reasoning in *Griswold* was going to get the Court into deep and dangerous constitutional waters.

His objective in the argument he wished he had made would have been to point out that the Court already had a serious problem in its future because of the privacy right created by *Griswold* and should not compound it by treading still further on state libel and privacy laws. He knew that by making this argument he would demote the concept of privacy from the high status that *Griswold* had given it—an ironic task for James Hill's lawyer. He thought, though,

---

* See the introduction to Selection 6.4 for an explanation of penumbras.

that if he had laid greater stress on this point the Court might have been more hesitant to impair the vitality of the New York State privacy law governing the *Hill* case.

May and most of June passed without word from the Court. On June 20th, the last day of the term, we had disappointing news: An order had come down restoring the case to the docket for reargument in the fall and specifying the questions to be addressed, most of them dealing with the coverage of the New York statute, the effect of the Rabin concurring opinion, and the definition of "fictionalization" as it related to First Amendment requirements. These questions reflected the doubts voiced by Justice White during the oral argument.

Reargument on October 18 and 19, 1966, was another smooth, professional performance by Medina and Nixon, but the atmosphere was now less dramatic, more routine. Nixon had interrupted his cross-country campaigning for Republican candidates in the 1966 midterm elections—a crucial phase of his burgeoning Presidential effort—and had set aside three weeks to focus intensively on the altered array of arguments. I felt that Nixon was even better and more relaxed this time. The Court was active in its questions. But the attitudes and the apparent lineup of opinion had clearly changed—and from our point of view, as it turned out, for the worse.

Justice White was now firmly fixed on his concern about the constitutional problems on the face of the New York statute; Justice Brennan's questions were shaped within Sullivan-case contours; and Justice Black engaged Nixon in a fierce ten-minute colloquy in which neither yielded an inch of ground:

MR. NIXON: The article ["Fiction out of Fact," by Joseph Hayes] is significant . . . as to the question of whether "The Desperate Hours," the article on "The Desperate Hours" in *Time* magazine and the book and the play were reenactments of the Hill incident. . . .

MR. JUSTICE BLACK: . . . it showed where he got his inspiration?

MR. NIXON: The question, Mr. Justice Black, is not a question of inspiration. The question is whether the *Life* article is false or true in stating that the Hill incident was a reenactment, not only in terms of the one word but—

MR. JUSTICE BLACK: That word "reenactment"—you could use many other words. If it would have said "reminiscent," it would have been all right?

MR. NIXON: I would beg to qualify that by stating that in answer to the Chief Justice's question on "reminiscent"—his question was quite explicit, his question was in the event that they had used the word "reminiscent" and then had described the Hill incident as it occurred, would there have been liability, and my answer was no. But that is not what happened here. . . .

It has been our argument and our contention throughout this case that "The Desperate Hours"—the heart of "The Desperate Hours"—is a story of violence and bloodshed; that the heart of the Hill incident was the fact that it was one that was distinguished by a lack of violence and bloodshed. And here we have it in the author's own words. . . .

The point that we are making in this case is that the *Life* article is false, false in stating by picture, by every editorial device—with no qualification whatever—that the Hill incident was reenacted in "The Desperate Hours"; that "The Desperate Hours" family is the Hill family; that the violence that occurred in "The Desperate Hours"—the father beating the son; the violence in respect to the murder of the trashman; the participation, for example, of the father in a plot—unwillingly, of course—for the purpose of murdering the deputy sheriff; the wounding of a boyfriend—as a matter of fact, there was no boyfriend. All of these incidents, all of them that were in "The Desperate Hours" and made it the hit that it was, did not occur to the Hills.

MR. JUSTICE BLACK: That was a blending of fiction with fact.

MR. NIXON: It was stating fiction *was* [italics added] fact. It was more than that; it was fictionalizing the Hills. It was using the Hills as commercial props for the purpose of selling more magazines. It was creating a story, rather than reporting a story. And that is the heart of the tort under the New York law. If it had stated—and Mr. Chief Justice Warren very precisely hit this point in his question, if it had stated that this was reminiscent of this item, and then had described the Hill incident as it occurred, then *Life* magazine would not have been liable. But I should also point out, *Life* magazine would not have had a story.

MR. JUSTICE BLACK: Why wouldn't it?

MR. NIXON: Why, it wouldn't have had the story because it wouldn't have been newsworthy.

MR. JUSTICE BLACK: They could certainly have referred to other things in this play?

MR. NIXON: Let us go, then, to why? Why *Life* magazine—when I refer to "*Life* magazine," I am referring, of course, to an institution, twenty-four senior editors, forty-one other managing editors, and two hundred and eight—

MR. JUSTICE BLACK: You don't think they are all liable?

MR. NIXON: But what I am suggesting is, I am referring to any one of the individuals who may have worked on the article; but in this particular instance, *Life* magazine, as far as checking on this item, did not do so. And they did not do so because *Life* magazine knew what the truth was. The reason—

MR. JUSTICE BLACK: Maybe they didn't do so because any reasonable person would have thought; as I read this record—

MR. NIXON: Yes, sir.

MR. JUSTICE BLACK: From what this man said, the author, that he did found it on the Hill incident. Any reasonable man would have reached that conclusion, particularly when they took him down to the house and made the pictures.

MR. NIXON: And reasonable men can disagree. I would say that any reasonable man reading the Hayes article, "Fiction out of Fact," which Prideaux did, and which stated specifically that "The Desperate Hours" was different from any hostage incident, then that certainly put him on notice that "The Desperate Hours" was not a reenactment. And certainly it would indicate that the editors of *Life* should check to see whether or not editorially they should strike out the

words "somewhat fictionalized," or they should strike out the words "this is the
Hills' former home"; whether or not they should change the article to be "The
Story of the Hills" rather than the story of the play. In other words, the head
being "True Crime" rather than "The Desperate Hours."

Understand, this is editorial changing and altering the facts substantially for
the purpose of making the article, and I quote from *Life*'s own editorial staff,
"more newsy."

It was [described by *Life*] as a gimmick, an editorial gimmick. And the question is: Are private persons, involuntarily drawn into the vortex of a public issue, as counsel for the appellant has indicated—are private persons by this
Court to be allowed, in effect, to be used as gimmicks for commercial purposes
in a falsified situation in which, I would suggest here, an editorial organization,
the largest in the world, with more resources to question the facts than any
other, used them in a fictionalized situation?

MR. JUSTICE BLACK: The commercial purpose you refer to is selling magazines? . . . Selling magazines for profit?

MR. NIXON: Magazines are sold for profit.

MR. JUSTICE BLACK: Is there anything wrong with that?

MR. NIXON: Not at all.

Justice Black finally desisted, but he was obviously beyond persuasion. As
the questions and comments by the Court proceeded, it seemed clear that only
the Chief Justice and Justice Fortas were holding fast to their sympathies for the
Hills' claim.

The decision of the Supreme Court came down on January 9, 1967, reversing
the New York State Court of Appeals and remanding the case for further proceedings in New York in accordance with the Court's opinion. The vote was
5–4, with five Justices writing separate opinions.

Justice Brennan wrote the opinion for the majority, holding that the trial
court's charge did not instruct the jury with constitutional clarity under the now
operative rule of *New York Times Co.* v. *Sullivan,* which, like Supreme Court
decisions in civil matters generally, applied to all cases not yet finally decided
and which required a finding that the publication was made with legal malice—that is, with knowledge of falsity or with reckless indifference to truth or
falsity. Justices Black and Douglas, in a concurring opinion, repeated their "absolute" First Amendment view that knowing or reckless falsity on the part of the
press was constitutionally protected. Justices White and Stewart formed the rest
of the majority. Justice Harlan dissented, asserting his belief that a lesser standard than legal malice—namely, negligence—was an adequate constitutional
basis for state protection of private individuals from invasions of privacy and
from libel.

The principal dissent was written by Justice Fortas, joined by the Chief Justice
and Justice Clark. The dissent argued that the trial court's charge, while not a

"textbook model," nevertheless satisfied the standard of *New York Times Co.* v. *Sullivan.*

When I learned of the decision, through a telephone call from the Clerk of the Court, I called Nixon, at his apartment. He listened, asked one or two questions about the authorship of the opinions, and then said, "I always knew I wouldn't be permitted to win a big appeal against the press. Now, Len, get this absolutely clear: I never want to hear about the *Hill* case again." Without a pause, he turned to some business involving the 1968 campaign.

Ever since hearing in June of 1966 that we would have to reargue the *Hill* case, Nixon had suspected that for some reason a major change had occurred in the Court's basic predisposition. I shared Nixon's view, and after the decision I was convinced that something inexplicable had indeed happened between the original argument and the reargument. Over time, though, I gradually overcame my puzzlement and disappointment, and accepted the result as yet another proof that the distant and magisterial action of the Supreme Court may not always satisfy the losing counsel as working fairly in a particular case. I did not totally discount the possibility that Nixon had been correct in fearing that this was an ideological battle his opponents simply would not let him win.

And that was that for the *Hill* case for twenty years. During those years, I had the lukewarm comfort of seeing libel law turn around in *Gertz* v. *Robert Welch, Inc.* (1974), in which the Supreme Court—in an opinion by a Nixon appointee, Justice Lewis Powell—held that the rule in *New York Times Co.* v. *Sullivan* was applicable to public officials and public figures but not to private individuals. Ironically, the ultimate effect of *Hill* had been to sensitize the legal community to the arguments that private, as opposed to public, persons could make in such cases. The distinction had grown more sharply focussed in law-review articles and case commentary in the years between *Hill* and *Gertz.*

In *Gertz*, Justice Powell put it clearly: "States should retain substantial latitude in their efforts to enforce a legal remedy for defamatory falsehood injurious to the reputation of a private individual." He was equally clear about the rationale: "The communications media are entitled to act on the assumption that public officials and public figures have voluntarily exposed themselves to increased risk of injury from defamatory falsehood concerning them. No such assumption is justified with respect to a private individual. . . . He has relinquished no part of his interest in the protection of his own good name, and consequently he has a more compelling call on the courts for redress of injury inflicted by defamatory falsehood. Thus, private individuals are not only more vulnerable to injury than public officials and public figures; they are also more deserving of recovery." Under *Gertz*, the Hill family would have won in the Supreme Court.

Then, in 1985, came Professor [Bernard] Schwartz's "The Unpublished Opinions of the Warren Court," with its behind-the-scenes internal memoranda and draft opinions of the Supreme Court after the first argument of the *Hill* case. And when the Anthony Lewis review of the book was published in the *Times* Nixon broke his vow, asking me to read the Schwartz book and see what had happened in "that case."

At the first private conference of the Supreme Court on April 29, 1966, two days after the original oral argument, the vote was 6–3 to affirm the judgment for the Hills. All the Justices but Black, Douglas, and White agreed with Chief Justice Warren's position that there was no First Amendment problem, because the *Life* article was a "fictionalization of these people's experience and false." The Chief Justice assigned the drafting of the Court's opinion in the *Hill* case to Justice Fortas, and Fortas wrote a sixteen-page document that made its points in language that verged on excoriation—imprudently so, it turned out. . . .

In his draft opinion for the Court in the *Hill* case, Justice Fortas said, "The facts of this case are unavoidably distressing. Needless, heedless, wanton and deliberate injury of the sort inflicted by *Life*'s picture story is not an essential instrument of responsible journalism. . . . The prerogatives of the press—essential to our liberty—do not preclude reasonable care and avoidance of casual infliction of injury. . . . They do not confer a license for pointless assault." Next, he condemned the *Life* article as "a fictionalized version of the Hill incident, deliberately or heedlessly distorted beyond semblance of reality." Finally, he wrote a passionate defense of privacy, a defense which, according to Professor Schwartz, was "as broad a statement of that right as any ever made by a member of the highest court."

Even as a newcomer to the Court, joining it in 1965, Abe Fortas was a strong, confident figure. . . . [T]he *Times* law reporter Fred Graham called the freshman Justice "a promising member of 'the club'" and a man who was fast becoming "a power on the Supreme Court"; *Newsweek* called him "rookie of the year"; and *U.S. News & World Report* predicted that he could be "counted among those who will set the tone and style of the Court in the future."

One member of the Court, Hugo Black, violently disagreed. Black, who had worn the liberal mantle on the Court since his appointment by Roosevelt, in 1937, disliked everything about Fortas, and saw him . . . as a "pretender to the throne of leadership" on the Court. Black therefore welcomed the broad scope and the intensity of the Fortas draft opinion in *Hill*. These weaknesses presented an opportunity to cut Fortas down to size; but for this task Black needed time. During the circulation of draft opinions, Fortas, because of comments by his colleagues, found it necessary to make changes tempering the language of his first draft opinion for the Court and seeking to answer, in particular, Justice White's challenge to the constitutionality of the New York statute. By adroit maneuvering, Justice Black took advantage of these changes. In . . . a "petulant" note to Justice Fortas, he insisted that because of Fortas's alterations he needed extra time—more than the current term allowed—to rewrite the response he was preparing. Black's hostility, together with White's more specific doubts, persuaded Fortas, as the author of the majority opinion, to agree to reargument, and it was scheduled for the fall term. Meanwhile, Black continued his campaign against Justice Fortas and his draft opinion. To his Court colleagues he said that Fortas's was "the worst First Amendment opinion he had seen in a dozen years." He added . . . that "it would take him all summer to write his dissent," which "would be the greatest dissent of his life."

Justice Black's product, an internal memorandum sixteen pages long, was distributed to the Court the day before reargument; it was a blockbuster denunciation of Justice Fortas and his position. It was, as promised, one of the most forceful statements ever made by Black of his judicial philosophy. He attacked the general idea of the "weighing" approach, which when applied to First Amendment issues dictates that in each case the worth to society of freedom of expression must be weighed against the worth of the individual rights and values threatened by a particular use of that freedom. Then he attacked the weighing approach as applied to the right of privacy in particular, and castigated Justice Fortas's opinion in terms like these: "After mature reflection I am unable to recall any prior case in this Court that offers a greater threat to freedom of speech and press than this one does, either in the tone and temper of the Court's opinion or in its resulting holding and judgment."

An example of Justice Black's ferocity of argument was a contention that Fortas was urging a "general, unconditional, unequivocal 'right to privacy' or 'to be let alone,'" under which, Black argued, "burglars, rapists, robbers, murderers and other law violators would be completely immune from all governmental investigations, arrests, trials and punishments."

Timed for the eve of reargument, Black's intense lobbying and his pre-reargument memorandum had the intended effect. The Court's questioning moved in a direction charted by him and by Justice White. In the first post-reargument vote, on October 21st, the Court switched from 6–3 for affirmance to 7–2 for reversal, with only the Chief Justice still strongly supporting Fortas. Before the case was finally decided, Justices Harlan and Clark returned to the Fortas side, producing a tie vote of 4–4, and that was resolved, finally, by Justice Stewart's vote to reverse. This deciding fifth vote to reverse was obtained by Brennan's addition of a paragraph expressly leaving open the rules to apply in libel actions by private individuals. Stewart had earlier expressed concern for the reputation and feelings of private individuals in a concurring opinion in *Rosenblatt* v. *Baer* (1966). He wrote to Brennan the day after he read this addition, saying he was now glad to join in Brennan's opinion.

The irony of this struggle is that after all the speculation about how the Court would respond to Richard Nixon, the personal animus that determined the course of the *Hill* case was not antagonism toward Nixon by any member of the Court. The two Justices who had always detested Nixon's politics—Warren and Fortas—were unshakable defenders of his position in the *Hill* case. The central clash in *Hill* was actually between Hugo Black and Abe Fortas.

. . . Justice Black's intense antipathy to Fortas was rather mysterious. It was apparent almost from the day Fortas joined the Court and intensified sharply from that point forward. In Fortas, Black surely saw a philosophical heir to his ancient adversary Felix Frankfurter, the proponent of the doctrine of balancing competing constitutional interests—a philosophy that was deeply offensive to the absolutist soul of Hugo Black. What is clear is that in the *Hill* case Abe Fortas's old-style liberal, pluralist notion of press freedom as a value to be weighed against other values gave way to Black's idea of press rights, which was much larger and more uncompromising in its claims. In time, the Court would come around to Fortas's view.

The *Hill* case left me with a permanent collection of what-ifs.

Would the great expansion of press protection in the *Sullivan* case have occurred if it hadn't been for the chilling nature of the restraint imposed by the Southern court and jury that decided the case against that symbol of northern liberalism, the *Times,* as the civil-rights revolution moved thousands of blacks and their supporters into the streets and the courts?

Might the *Hill* decision have been affirmed if *Time's* appeal to the Supreme Court had not followed so quickly on the heels of *Sullivan* and the surrounding pro-press enthusiasm of the public and the courts?

Would the *Hill* case have engendered an earlier and more constructive exploration of appropriate distinctions between the protection of private and public figures from press comment, as Justice Harlan suggested, if the case had not been distorted by a bitter personal vendetta by one Justice toward another?

What might have happened if Watergate had not apotheosized the investigative journalist and made the idea of restraint, self-imposed or court-imposed, anathema to dominant journalistic opinion? . . .

Chief Justice Warren, Justice Fortas, and Justice Harlan, in their response to the *Hill* facts, intuitively anticipated just such developments as have occurred. They saw the case as one of nontechnical justice—two ordinary American parents touched by near-tragedy and trying to shield themselves and their five young children from the cheapening effects of unwanted and distorted publicity. These Justices did not think that protecting the Hills entailed any new categorical press restraint or that it required any great jurisdictional analysis. Justice Harlan, in particular, emphasized not only the constitutional difference between public and private persons but the "severe risk of irremediable harm" that such publicity could bring upon "individuals involuntarily exposed to it and powerless to protect themselves against it." And, indeed, at the trial there had been testimony that the *Life* article had caused Mrs. Hill lasting emotional injury. Two eminent psychiatrists had explained the causal dynamics of the trauma inflicted on her. Both said she had come through the original hostage incident well but had fallen apart when the *Life* article brought back her memories transformed into her worst nightmares and presented them to the world as reality. Both said she was and would for an indefinite time remain a psychological tinderbox. In August, 1971, Mrs. Hill took her life. . . .

The combination of *Sullivan* and *Hill* with the superheated environment of the late nineteen-sixties and early seventies had large political consequences.

There were journalists who came to believe that the First Amendment's writ ran without limit; many citizens thought otherwise. The resentment engendered by what was viewed as the arrogance of the press may have played a role in forming, through these years, the country's increasingly conservative disposition. It may be that, just as *Hill* had the ironic effect of bringing about more attention to private persons' rights against the press, the generation of journalists formed by the events of the late nineteen-sixties and early seventies had a part, albeit unwittingly, in the election of Richard Nixon, Ronald Reagan, and George Bush. And, partisan considerations aside, the press now finds itself in a hostile environment that threatens the liberty Hugo Black thought he was securing. It is time to start finding our way back.

Epilogue

This tension between the right of privacy and freedom of the press persists. Over time an increasingly conservative Court has narrowed the class of people who are considered "public figures" and has forced the media to meet a tougher standard when they are sued.

Certain tactics of the press will continue to raise these issues. For example, the journalistic investigation of Supreme Court nominee Robert Bork included publication of a list of his video rentals. Hugo Black and William O. Douglas would have argued simply that the Constitution addresses this in the First Amendment: "Congress shall make no law . . . abridging the freedom . . . of the press." "No law" meant exactly that. (Remarkably, Black felt this strongly even though, after his appointment to the Supreme Court, his career had almost been destroyed by a journalist who wrote a story revealing that Black had been a member of the Ku Klux Klan.) In the end, the extent of judicial supervision of the press may be determined by the willingness of the media to restrain and regulate themselves in reaction to a Supreme Court and general public less inclined to support freedom of the press.

CHAPTER 7

V. Lawrence '90

PARTIES AND
CAMPAIGNS

GOP Chairman Lee Atwater: Playing Hardball

Eric Alterman

When people thought about the inner workings of the major political parties, the image that used to pop into their minds was the traditional "smoke-filled room." According to this cliché, leaders of the party, usually envisioned as fat, balding, cigar-smoking men who eat, drink, and sleep politics, made the behind-the-scenes decisions that shaped the issues, candidates, and outcomes of the elections. However, a new era in politics was launched in 1972. Reforms in the Democratic and Republican parties opened up the nomination process, and it became necessary to reach out to a wider audience and influence a larger voting constituency. This fact was clearly illustrated when a brilliant young idealist, Gary Hart, masterminded Democrat George McGovern's nomination in 1972 with a grassroots campaign based on networks of committed voters. Then, in 1976, another effective young strategist, Hamilton Jordan, revolutionized the nomination process by guiding a relatively unknown Democratic governor, Jimmy Carter of Georgia, to a presidential nomination over a number of better-known Democratic candidates.

Eric Alterman's portrait of former Republican party chairman Lee Atwater, a member of the latest generation of these brilliant, committed, highly partisan, and extremely talented campaign strategists, provides a revealing description of the man, his party, the present occupant of the White House, and the state of American politics today. The two sides of Atwater—his populist, hometown, blues-loving side and his hardball, dedicated, politically oriented side—are explored in this selection in a way that explains how he was able to tap into the very soul of the American voting public. Governed by unfailing political instincts, Atwater was able to shape both the nature of the issues in the campaign and the appearance of the candidate himself, enabling the minority Republican party to dominate the presidential election.

Atwater made effective use of a strategy that has become very controversial: "negative campaigning," which used to be called "mudslinging." He encouraged the candidate to go for the opponent's jugular by launching whatever charges might be dug up, whether they were true or not, figuring that the average voter will tend to believe the charges without further investigation and vote accordingly. (See Selection 7.3 for more on how Atwater was able to shape the negatively oriented 1988 presidential campaign of George Bush.)

LEE ATWATER   Chair of the Republican party, 1989–1990.

GEORGE BUSH   President of the United States, 1989– .

MICHAEL DUKAKIS   Democratic nominee for president in 1988.

JACK KEMP   Former Republican congressman and candidate for president; Bush's secretary of housing and urban development.

▶ It's 2 A.M. on a sultry Saturday in Columbia, S.C. Does the Republican Party know where its chairman is?

Harvey Lee Atwater, hometown boy, is on stage at Bullwinkle's, a smoky dive with two pool tables, dollar beers and the raunchy, long-haired Mojo Blues band shaking the rafters.

The overflow crowd is packed against the wall, forcing overdressed Republican gentry to rub elbows with the Bullwinkle regulars. Atwater has changed out of his blue blazer and tie into a "Late Night" T-shirt that David Letterman gave him. His guitar was a gift from Ron Wood of the Rolling Stones—a souvenir of Atwater's gala blues celebration at a Presidential inaugural ball.

Drinking beer straight from the pitcher, sweat pouring down his face, Atwater apologizes for going home so early, but the St. Patrick's Day Parade is just seven hours away and he is the grand marshal. His final number is a repeat of his opener: Eddie Taylor's "Bad Boy." "I'm bad, I'm bad," cries the man who masterminded George Bush's 1988 Presidential campaign, "I'm the worst you ever had."

A Republican national chairman like no other before him, Lee Atwater is undoubtedly the most controversial and successful political operative in America. Nominated by President Bush for the top G.O.P. post just eight days after the election, Atwater is, at 38, the first professional campaign consultant to head either political party. Known as a hardball specialist and a virtuoso in the art of negative campaigning, he has demonstrated a singular ability for hammering away at sensitive social issues that drive a wedge between traditional Democratic constituencies.

Atwater's appointment has energized the Republicans and galvanized the opposition. One group of incumbent Democratic senators recently organized a seminar on political campaigns "in the age of Atwater." In the contest for chairman of the Democratic National Committee, former Congressman Michael

Barnes advertised himself as the "ex-Marine who is taking on Lee Atwater." In early March, more than 3,000 students at Howard University, the nation's premier black school, occupied Howard's administration building and demanded Atwater's removal from the school's board of trustees.

Spending an extended period of time in his company, one begins to wonder whether there are, in fact, two Lee Atwaters occupying the same body. The first Lee Atwater is every inch a political operative. A visionary, ruthless strategist, Atwater has risen to the top of a cutthroat business by working harder, doing more research, incorporating more sources and, when necessary, cutting more throats than the competition. This Lee Atwater reportedly walked into Bush campaign headquarters last summer [1988] and announced that the time had come "to scrape the bark off" Gov. Michael S. Dukakis.

The second Lee Atwater is a true-blue American archetype: a fun-loving, hell-raising Dixie party animal. "Animal House" was not a movie for Lee Atwater; it was autobiography. Atwater was known in his own fraternity as the guy who stayed up singing and dancing until dawn and then "woke up the day shift with a flip-top at 6." Though he's now a married man with two daughters and no longer drinks much, he's still the kind of guy who will jump up to grab a pretty woman in a restaurant and sit her down at his table because a guest has noticed her looks.

Walking around the St. Patrick's Day fair with Lee Atwater in 1989 is a little like cruising the Grand Concourse in the Bronx with Joe DiMaggio in 1941. Everyone in Columbia, it seems, went to school with Atwater, worked on a campaign with him or stayed up late to watch him play guitar on television. Atwater hugs the guys and kisses the women—often by way of introduction.

It is the combination of the two Atwaters that so understandably concerns the Democrats. Here is a man, after all, who privately visits soul-music legend James Brown in a South Carolina state prison on his way to see Chief of Staff John H. Sununu at the White House; a party functionary who turns down the offer of a part in a Chuck Norris film because flying to the Philippines would take too much time away from his day job. Imagine, if you will, a guitar-wielding political synthesis of Huck Finn and Machiavelli. Now try to imagine winning an election against him.

"The real problem with Lee Atwater," says Patricia Schroeder, the Democratic Congresswoman from Colorado, "is that his tactics are contagious." Indeed, the question Democrats around the country are asking themselves is, "Can you beat Lee Atwater unless you join him?"

In April 1985, Vice President Bush invited all his siblings and children to Camp David, Md., for a weekend retreat. The purpose of the gathering was to give the Bush family a chance to meet "the new squad" on his Presidential campaign team. Seated around a table, in sweaters and slacks, Atwater and White House pollster Robert M. Teeter each described their strategy for the election. Bush

had chosen Atwater, then just 34, as his campaign manager over Atwater's former White House boss, Ed Rollins.

Bush was impressed with the plan that Atwater and Teeter had conceived for
the election. But the family—a crucial component in any George Bush campaign—had concerns about Atwater's loyalty. George Bush Jr. was worried because two of Atwater's business partners were working for Jack F. Kemp. The
Bush children, moreover, shared a distrust of Atwater's entire profession. "I
have been in these political campaigns long enough to see the self-serving nature of the game," notes Jeb Bush. Consultants "tend to treat their candidates
like red meat," adds Marvin.

Atwater did his best to assuage the family's concerns, but he continued to
feel uneasy about their lack of trust. It wasn't long before he hit on an idea.
To prove his own loyalty and increase his leverage with the family, he invited—
demanded, actually—that George Jr. join him full time in the campaign. "It was
a twofer," he recalls. Not only would it end their questions of loyalty, but Atwater got the services of a staff member who could organize the family at a
moment's notice. "He turned out to be the most political and the most loyal to
my father," Jeb Bush now says. "Atwater could go to hell tomorrow and I'd be
a supporter. He has proved himself with our family."

Unlike most campaign consultants, Atwater rarely fashions political appeals
around computer-generated demographic studies. Although he is literate in the
technical aspects of campaign work, he relies much more heavily upon his own
intuitive grasp of American political culture. How else explain Atwater's confidence in the summer of 1988, when Dukakis led Bush by more than 17 points
in national opinion polls? "We were all ready to fall apart," remembers his chief
of staff, Mary Matalin, "but Lee held us together with pep talks, history lessons
and weird statistics." Atwater sensed at the time that most voters were not yet
ready to focus on the election. Just to make certain, however, he flew to Los
Angeles and spent a day at the beach confirming his hypothesis.

In order to understand Atwater's almost psychic connection to middle-
American political culture, one must return to the roots of his childhood.
Atwater grew up in what he calls "the middle of the middle class," in the Forest
Acres section of Columbia. It was a place, in the 1950's and 1960's, where the
white middle-class American dream of the good life, with good schools, safe
streets and plenty of space for a boy to make mischief, came true with a vengeance. Atwater's parents—his mother is a teacher and his father a retired insurance adjuster—owned a trim, one-story home near a series of breathtaking
lakes. Today when Lee comes home to visit, he sleeps in his old bedroom, now
decorated with a blow-up of the 31-year-old organizer flanked by Ronald
Reagan and Strom Thurmond.

Unlike most Washington politicos, Atwater remains just as comfortable with
people out of his nonpolitical past as he is with pollsters and media men. At a
St. Patrick's Day cocktail party in suburban Columbia, old friends from high

school and college come up one by one to regale a "Yankee reporter" with stories of Atwater outrages gone by. Most of these involve some combination of guitars, girls and beer. His 11th-grade English teacher, Robert C. Ellenburg, remembers the day when Atwater was due to give a book report. After winning a two-hour extension on his deadline, the young man proceeded to walk to the front of the class and speak for 10 minutes on the literary merit of the Columbia telephone directory. "He said it jumped around too much from character to character without sustaining any of them," Ellenburg fondly recalls. "He predicted it would have to be revised next year."

Atwater also managed to impress A. C. Flora High School with his genius for politics. In his first campaign consultancy, he engineered the election strategy of his friend David Yon, promising students free beer in the cafeteria, no grades lower than B's and unlimited cuts. Yon won, but the principal annulled the vote.

Atwater's grades reflected the time he spent playing the blues and chasing girls. (His own mother, a Spanish teacher, once gave him a D−.) He ended up at nearby Newberry College—a "pretty laid-back environment" when Atwater entered in 1969, according to Ridge Edwards, a history professor of Atwater's, with none of the political upheavals prevalent at many other college campuses.

Atwater and his fraternity brothers used to rent black-and-white pornographic movies and charge 50 cents admission. "You can bet nobody asked for their damn money back on those flicks," he volunteers, sitting with his wife and parents in the family living room. "We weren't like the guys who took your money and then showed a bunch of people horsing around in leotards."

Had Toddy Atwater not arranged for her son to spend the summer after his sophomore year working as an intern in the office of South Carolina Senator Strom Thurmond, he might still be traveling the roadhouse blues circuit today. That summer, however, Atwater experienced an intellectual awakening and the beginnings of a lifelong passion for political warfare. "I decided that summer it was time to get serious," he recalls.

Thurmond remembers a bright young boy of extraordinary energy and charm who, in seven years, progressed from college intern to political director of Thurmond's re-election campaign. Atwater remembers listening to a man who embodied for him the virtues of Southern conservatism: economic libertarianism, a strong military, and opposition to Federal interference. Both men insist that the historical identification of Thurmond with segregation is unfair; the issue, then as now, Thurmond insists, was "states' rights."

When Atwater returned for his junior year, his energies had found a new focus. He soon began to combine fraternity socializing with political organizing and was rewarded in 1973 with an appointment as national director of College Republicans. The party's chairman at the time was George Bush.

Lee Atwater did not invent the campaign consultancy business, but he may be the person most responsible for the way it's practiced today. Campaign consultants have replaced the old party bosses as the ultimate wielders of power within the American political system.

Atwater's tactics have become legendary. South Carolina politicos still talk about his first major campaign victory, in Strom Thurmond's 1978 re-election battle with Charles (Pug) Ravenel, then the rising young star of Charleston politics. Thurmond's commercials made relentless reference to a comment reported in a tiny weekly newspaper called *Manhattan East,* in which Ravenel was alleged to have told a Park Avenue fund-raiser that he would be a "third senator from New York." Ravenel denies ever making any such remark, but hardly a single South Carolinian who went to the polls that year was unaware of it. Despite predictions of a tight race, Thurmond won handily.

In a 1980 Congressional race, a Democratic legislator named Tom Turnipseed accused Atwater of masterminding a series of anonymous phone calls alerting voters to Turnipseed's membership in the N.A.A.C.P. and planting questions with a reporter about Turnipseed's electroshock therapy experience as a teenager. Atwater said he would not respond to allegations made by someone who had been "hooked up to jumper cables." Today Atwater says he "feels terrible" about what he said and wishes that "journalists would stop bringing it up."

But of all the things of which he has been accused, he says, the one that makes him the maddest concerns the charge of anti-Semitism in the 1978 Congressional victory by the current Governor of South Carolina, Carroll A. Campbell Jr., over Max Heller, the former Mayor of Greenville and a Jewish refugee from Austria who had fled the Nazis.

Atwater's accusers claim that as an informal adviser to Campbell, he passed secret polling information to Don Sprouse, a third-party candidate, who then used the information to undermine Heller's campaign. Political analyst Alan Baron has revealed that Campbell's pollster in 1978, Arthur J. Finkelstein, of Irvington, N.Y., told him that his data showed South Carolina voters would reject "a foreign-born Jew who did not believe in Jesus Christ as the savior." Marvin Chernoff, a Democratic consultant in Columbia, claims that Atwater specifically told him of passing Finkelstein's secret poll to Sprouse.

Atwater denies all of it. Finkelstein and all of the Campbell campaign staffers contacted also deny the accusations. But Campbell's campaign manager has since admitted to a late-night meeting with Sprouse representatives in a Greenville parking lot before the election, and the Finkelstein poll released by Campbell did ask voters to compare how they would feel about a race between a "Jewish immigrant" and a "native South Carolinian."

The difference between Lee Atwater and the rest of us," observes Charles R. Black, Atwater's former business partner and Jack Kemp's 1988 campaign manager, is that "Lee is simply more relentless." That relentlessness is evident in the 12 to 15 hours Atwater puts in each day. After being driven to his office by a

Republican National Committee-supplied Lincoln Town Car, Atwater meets with senior staff every morning at 7. The meeting is followed by a steady stream of staff talks, recruitment calls, press briefings, campaign strategy discussions with members of Congress and, more often than not, evening speaking engagements and fund-raising appearances. A typical Atwater week is likely to include five public appearances, at least two flights to local Republican gatherings around the country and no fewer than four telephone calls from President Bush. In addition, Atwater talks with White House Chief of Staff John Sununu virtually every day.

Ed Rogers, Sununu's deputy and an Atwater protégé, says Atwater "knows the field" better than anyone who has ever sat in the party head's chair. Jack Kemp, the Administration's Secretary of Housing and Urban Development, concurs. Atwater's "mechanical abilities, his nuts-and-bolts political sense," are his greatest strength, says Kemp.

In fact, most Atwater campaigns are strategically simple. Almost never is his candidate outflanked on the right in a Republican primary. Almost always, his victories depend heavily upon previously "populist" voters. Populist voters, in the Atwater playbook, "are always the swing voters." They are "middle-middle class" families earning between $25,000 and $35,000 annually. In the South, they are white Protestants; in the North, they are often ethnic Catholics. It is on right-wing populist cultural turf—the so-called "values" issues of gun control, school prayer, national defense, taxes and welfare reform—that most Atwater campaigns are fought. The key, according to Atwater, is fashioning an "Us"— the voter—against "Them"—the arrogant liberal elitists—appeal.

Atwater's impressive performance in the 1980 Reagan campaign led to his appointment as a deputy political director in the first Reagan White House. He worked there for four years before leaving to merge the consulting firm he had founded with that of Black, Manafort and Stone, one of the top Republican political consulting firms—while writing a still-unfinished doctoral thesis at the University of South Carolina in his spare time. Then, in mid-December 1984, came the call from George Bush.

The Atwater strategic plan called for Bush to paint his opponent as a captive of the far-left wing of the Democratic party: soft on crime and national defense and out of step with the American "mainstream" on social issues. Atwater was elated by the Democrats' choice of a Northeastern "liberal" Governor without a populist chromosome in his body. In a feat that nearly defies comprehension, Atwater managed to position George Herbert Walker Bush of Andover and Yale and his multimillionaire running mate, J. Danforth Quayle, as champions of Southern populist values. Dukakis seemed incapable of understanding, much less blunting the attack. Instead of discussing the budget deficit, the Iran-contra scandal or the end of the Cold War, the two candidates argued over who was tougher on the Russians, who was more enamored of the Pledge of Allegiance and who was more likely to keep criminals locked up.

The success of Atwater's campaign strategy was undeniable, but it came under heavy fire. By far the most troubling tactic was his creation of the so-called "Willie Horton" or "prison furlough" issue. Horton, a black man convicted of murder, raped a white woman while on a weekend furlough from a Massachusetts state prison.

Atwater served notice on two occasions that the Horton furlough would be a central "wedge" issue for the Republicans. "If I can make Willie Horton a household name," he reportedly predicted to a group of Republican activists early in June, "we'll win the election." Today Atwater cannot recall making the remark. To a Republican unity gathering in Atlanta he reportedly observed, "there's a story about a fellow named Willie Horton who, for all I know, may end up being Dukakis's running mate."

Atwater does not remember the second comment either, though both were widely quoted in the press. But he insists that "if I did say it that way, the juxtaposition was inadvertent" and says he wishes, in retrospect, the campaign had found a white person. The issue, in his eyes, was not race but crime. He says he personally forbade the use of any pictures of Horton and sent a letter to Bush campaign groups around the country asking them to cease all Horton-related advertising.

Sitting on the porch of his parents' house, Atwater grows angry at the suggestion that he may have exploited racism in the campaign. His blue eyes sharpen and the thick Carolina drawl loses any trace of its former geniality. The question confirms his worst fears. "As a white Southerner," he asserts, "I have always known I had to go the extra mile to avoid being tagged a racist by liberal Northerners. If anybody from the white South says or does anything, it's always racially motivated. I defy you to find any other campaign I have done where race has become the issue." (In a calmer moment, he adds a pragmatic argument: "Race, politically, is a loser.")

Atwater may have a point. His life-long devotion to rhythm-and-blues bespeaks a man who has always shown a strong affinity for black musical culture as well as for the musicians who embodied it. But is it the whole story? Going back over Atwater's entire career, Charles T. Ferillo, a Columbia Democratic consultant, argues that "Atwater and his ilk have developed a whole set of campaign techniques that perfected these back-handed appeals" to white racists. "Indirect appeals to race are a problem," concedes Earl Black, a professor of political science at the University of South Carolina and academic adviser to Atwater—"and Lee's image is very close to the line."

David Duke is a former Ku Klux Klan Grand Wizard and Nazi sympathizer who embarrassed Atwater and the national Republican party by winning election to the Louisiana State Legislature last February as a registered Republican. Atwater engineered a censure of Duke by the Republican National Committee and called him a "charlatan" and an "opportunist." Duke says he is confused by the treatment he has received from his party's chairman and continues to insist that he is "just as Republican as Lee Atwater."

Atwater's Duke headache was still fresh in the minds of the nation's pundits when the protests at Howard University broke out. Atwater was named to the university's board and looked forward to the opportunity to prove himself a friend to the black community and help the school raise funds. But students demanding Atwater's resignation interrupted an anniversary ceremony and, a few days later, occupied the administration building.

The student-run newspaper, *The Hilltop,* blamed Atwater for concocting "the most racist strategy in a national Presidential campaign in the 20th century." The student leadership of the protest also made much of the creeping force of "Atwaterism," which, in the words of Howard University Student Association President Garfield L. Swaby is a tactic designed to "scare white people about black people." Atwater did eventually resign, but only, he says, to prevent an outbreak of violence.

Neither national embarrassment could have come at a worse time for Atwater. Black support for Republican candidates usually hovers between 8 percent and 10 percent in national elections. Atwater's first speech as chairman of the Republican National Committee last January centered on a "minority outreach" program based on his belief that while the Democrats had "taken minority Americans for granted," the Republicans were now ready to "take them for real."

The outreach program is perhaps the most important component of Atwater's goal to force Republican gains at the Presidential level down to the states and build a majority party by the year 2000. But ultimate success, Jack Kemp observes, will depend on "George Bush and the rest of us trying to keep the recovery going and make the effort to raise the economic tide in the ghetto and the barrio."

Neither Duke's election nor the Howard student protests were helpful to Republican outreach efforts, but inside the Washington Beltway, Atwater-watchers were already scrutinizing his speeches for evidence of an ulterior political motive.

Theory number one, advanced by Democratic consultant Greg Schneiders, suggests that by feigning an effort to secure the minority vote, Atwater is really adopting the "make them think you're going to attack their base approach." The ultimate aim of such a strategy is to force the national Democratic party to shore up its base with black voters, particularly the black Democratic leader Jesse Jackson, and thereby further alienate white conservatives.

The more popular interpretation is only slightly less cynical. In the opinion of the conservative analyst Kevin Phillips, Atwater's strategy is aimed at upper-middle-class suburban voters who agree with Republican economics but don't feel comfortable voting for a party that has a reputation for apathy—or worse—toward blacks. A Republican minority outreach program, even if it doesn't accomplish much, will help assuage their consciences.

If nothing else, the Atwater minority outreach program highlights the opportunities offered the Republicans by increasingly bitter divisions among the various racial and ethnic constituencies that form the backbone of the Democratic party. The proof of Republican sincerity, as Kemp likes to say, will be in the pudding. But in the meantime, Atwater swears that, Howard or no Howard, he is in the minority recruitment business for the long haul.

Nursing a late-evening iced tea in the Arlington, Va., barbecued-rib pit of which he is part owner, Atwater muses on the long-term impact of his recent spate of bad publicity. "I got severely rebuked," he admits, "but I didn't quit. . . . We're going after the Democratic lifeblood, and they know I'm serious. They're gonna try and knock me on my ass every week about it. Maybe they'll be successful, but they're not going to win it without a fight."

Epilogue

Lee Atwater would not get the chance to continue to shape the future of the Republican party; in March 1991 he died of a brain tumor. In a *Life* magazine article published in early 1991, a repentant Atwater apologized to Michael Dukakis for the negativity of the 1988 Bush campaign and for his own inflammatory statements about the Democratic candidate.

Some analysts feel that the decline in electoral strength at every level of the Republican party in the 1990 elections may have been partially the result of the loss of Atwater's vision, energy, and strategic decision making. It will be interesting to observe both the attempt of the next Republican party chair to fill Atwater's shoes and the effort of the Democratic party to respond to Atwater's legacy. George Bush's secretary of agriculture, Clayton Yeutter, has been chosen to head the Republican party. The next selection profiles the man who will lead the Democrats.

Ron Brown's Party Line

Robert Kuttner

There was a time when being the chair of the Democratic party required that one be the ultimate Washington insider. The party chair and local party bosses would deliberate in secret to pick a candidate for the presidency who would not only be successful in the election but pliable to their wishes after it. During the eras of Franklin D. Roosevelt and Harry Truman, chairmen such as James Farley and Robert Hannegan spent much of their time dividing up the jobs and perquisites of the party according to how much their followers had done for the various candidates. Now, as you will see from this selection by Robert Kuttner, the role of party chairs has changed significantly. The times are different, the issues are different, the party is different—and the party leadership must respond to those changes.

The current chairman of the Democratic party, Ron Brown, fills a number of different roles. He is a fundraiser, an image nurturer, an organization builder, an adviser to officeholders, and, of course, a field general whose goal is to have Democrats win elections around the nation. These tasks, and the modern emphasis on the media, require that the old cigar-chomping, beer-bellied party boss be replaced by a slick, visually appealing, and highly intelligent individual who is comfortable in front of both the camera and party groups of any size. Instead of running private meetings, the modern party chair must be comfortable mounting a grass-roots campaign. As you will see, in becoming the first black chairman of the party, Ron Brown has become a symbol of what the Democratic party would like to be.

Balancing all of these roles is a difficult task for a man linked to charismatic but controversial former presidential candidate Jesse Jackson. Brown's job is also made difficult by his close attachment to Senator Ted Kennedy at a time when the party is questioning its liberal roots. But, as Kuttner makes clear, Ron Brown is able to use his considerable personal charisma and professional resources to manage this delicate balancing act.

RON BROWN   Chair of the Democratic
party since 1989.

JESSE JACKSON   Candidate for the
Democratic presidential nomination in 1984
and 1988.

▶ It is Thursday morning, Nov. 9 [1989], two days after an election night sweeter
than any in recent Democratic memory, and the party chairman, Ron Brown,
is beaming out at a crowd of well-wishers and reporters assembled in the Mansfield Room of the Capitol. Gathered around the chairman and the Democratic
leaders of Congress are L. Douglas Wilder, elected Virginia's, and the nation's,
first black Governor; David N. Dinkins, elected New York City's first black
Mayor, and four of the freshmen Congressmen who have won special elections
during Brown's tenure. The mood is celebratory as Senator George J. Mitchell
of Maine, the majority leader, begins to speak: "Several months ago, I read an
article asking 'Where Are the Democrats?' Well, ladies and gentlemen, here they
are!"

For Democrats, for blacks and for liberals, the 1989 election was, in Brown's
own election-night words, "a slam dunk." Not only did the wins in Virginia,
New York City and elsewhere make it a satisfying moment for the prophets of
multiracial coalition—the party also had the satisfaction of taking a frankly liberal stand on a controversial issue, abortion, and finding that a majority of voters liked the party's position and appreciated its willingness to lead. Moreover,
all the party's successful candidates for mayor and governor, even the fairly
moderate Wilder, had called for activist government in the traditional Democratic mold—government that would take an active role in strengthening Americans' economic prospects while staying out of their personal lives.

For Ronald Harmon Brown, the election was something of a personal vindication. A year ago, with the Democrats reeling from their third successive landslide Presidential defeat and another blowout in the once-solid South, the last
thing many party strategists wanted was an unabashedly liberal chairman with
longtime associations to Senator Edward M. Kennedy—let alone a black man,
let alone one whose most recent credit was convention manager of the Jesse
Jackson campaign.

But Brown went on to win the chairmanship handily. It was the opposite of
affirmative action—an older, Jackie Robinson sort of breakthrough, in which
the most effective contender broke the color line by simply outplaying the opposition. To the surprise of many in the party, Brown managed to win the early
support not only of liberals like [New York governor] Mario Cuomo and Ted
Kennedy, but also of moderates like Senator Bill Bradley and former Arizona
Gov. Bruce Babbitt, a founder of the Democratic Leadership Council, the
party's center-right coalition.

Some party moderates saw in Brown a "Nixon-to-China" effect: a more mainstream black chairman, with a long history of working inside the system to bro-

ker incremental progress, might be the perfect antidote to Jackson. And many of the party's Jewish leaders saw Brown as someone who could repair the damage done to black-Jewish relations by the strains of the Jackson Presidential campaign.

"He is such a very different guy from Jesse Jackson," observed North Carolina Congressman David Price, another moderate stalwart who backed Brown for party chairman. "He doesn't have the same inner demons. He doesn't have that bottomless thirst for respect." But if Brown was able to become chairman partly because he was so different from Jackson, it was nonetheless the very power of the Jackson campaign as a symbol of blacks coming of age within the party that led to the emergence of a Ron Brown.

Brown combines in his own résumé the contradictions of a party which includes among its ranks poor black voters enamored of Jesse Jackson—whose convention strategy Brown ran—and elite Washington law firms like Patton, Boggs & Blow, where Brown had become the first black partner. As a successful black man who moves comfortably in both worlds, Brown quite literally personifies the strains within a coalition party that must rouse the enthusiasm of its "base" of working class, poor and minority voters while reaching out to reclaim the broad middle class. If he can reconcile these contradictions, perhaps the Democratic party can, too.

The party's recent Presidential nominees did neither. Dazzled by the electoral success of Ronald Reagan, they pulled their punches, leaving the voters who form the party's traditional base unroused and the "swing voters"—the so-called "Reagan Democrats"—unconvinced. Afraid to run on ideology, the Democrats ran as technicians; and they were beaten by better technicians who were clearer about their own ideology and thus better able to manipulate powerful symbols. For more than a decade, the national Democratic party has been outspent, out-organized, and out-strategized by the Republicans, while its electoral base has eroded.

For many party moderates and conservatives, the erosion of Democratic strength during the 1980's was the liberals' fault. This has been a familiar refrain for two decades—ever since the split over Vietnam cost Hubert H. Humphrey the White House in 1968, and paved the way for George S. McGovern, four years later, to throw the party open to grass roots activists, cultural radicals, pacifists—and ignominious defeat.

According to this view, the Democratic Party has been too liberal for most voters, particularly white male voters, and especially during Presidential campaigns. And Brown seemed part of the same liberal cabal—the A.F.L.-C.I.O., Ted Kennedy and organized minorities—that has kept Democrats out of the White House; the Jackson connection only compounded the damage.

It was this sort of reasoning that led to the Democratic Leadership Council, the center-right caucus of elected officials that was founded after the debacle of the 1984 Walter Mondale campaign for the express purpose of wresting control of the Democratic Party from the likes of Ron Brown. In a recent policy paper, the political scientists William Galston and Elaine Ciulla Kamarck criticize the "liberal fundamentalism" of recent years and advise the party to identify more with "middle-class values—individual responsibility, hard work, equal opportunity—rather than the language of compensation."

For his part, Brown has bent over backwards to reassure the party moderates, delivering his maiden address as chairman at the annual D.L.C. conference in Philadelphia last March. There was Brown, preaching the mainstream gospel to the D.L.C. choir, declaring that "there is no one tougher than Democrats when it comes to protecting our children against drugs, our cities against crime," and calling for "a new ethic which links rights with responsibilities in the context of fiscal prudence." A predictable ovation followed.

But in the bars and corridors, there was skepticism. "It couldn't have been a more gracious speech," said one prominent party fund-raiser. "But he still needs some dramatic gesture to show that he's broken from Teddy and Jesse." The word was that the party's money men were hanging back until they saw more.

During the months that followed, they saw the party, under Brown's leadership, build an effective machine and—the most convincing argument of all—win elections. And he did it as an unrepentant progressive, demonstrating that, with effective candidates, good organization and, above all, a unified party, liberals can win elections too.

October found a smiling Ron Brown presiding over the party's 11th annual gala, resplendent in a custom-tailored black tuxedo. The dinner pulled in more than $2.3 million, a record. Among the 1,700 guests assembled at Washington's ornate National Building Museum were a record 150 Congressmen, as well as most of the skeptical high rollers. Florida developer Bill Crotty, a prominent party fund-raiser who at first was wary of Brown, was in for $3,000. "Ron has gone out of his way to reach out to people who felt maybe they weren't welcome," said Crotty. Maryland party chairman Nathan Landow, another influential fund-raiser who initially had backed another candidate, was back as well.

It is, of course, ironic that the litmus test for the chairman of the party of the common American should be his ability to appease millionaires; this remains one of the party's contradictions. And to the extent that the difficulty is Brown's race, appeasement has its natural limits. Brown's predecessor, Paul E. Kirk Jr., also an ally of Kennedy and the A.F.L.-C.I.O., also dampened criticism by moving to appease the political center. But Brown cannot compromise by becoming a shade or two more Caucasian.

Despite the mainstreaming of Ron Brown, a man who was never really outside the mainstream, in the unreconstructed white South where many rural voters elect Democrats out of habit rather than ideological conviction, Brown's tenure produces anxiety. "Some people call themselves Democrats because in many rural counties there was no Republican Party and the local establishment always controlled the Democratic Party," says David Dunn, an Alabama native who is Brown's friend and law partner. "An event like Ron Brown's election forces a reckoning."

In Florida, where the Governor, the Secretary of State and two Congressmen are all former Democrats, Republican officials have skillfully exploited Brown's past Kennedy and Jackson connections, and his color, to accelerate the wave of party defections. In four Florida counties, there have been numerous conversions of sheriffs, clerks of the court and county commissioners to the Republican Party. "A year ago, damn few county commissioners could name the chairman of the D.N.C.," a key Florida Democrat says ruefully. "They sure know who he is now."

The inevitable contrast between Brown and Republican National Chairman Lee Atwater highlights the dilemma. It is Atwater who revels in his down-home image, and Brown who acts the part of blueblood Washington lawyer, sporting monogrammed shirts and cufflinks, quietly elegant suits and stylish suspenders. Atwater is the one who plays rhythm and blues. It worries some Democrats that a conservative Republican gets to play the populist, while their own man is both too much a part of the resented Washington power elite—and too irrevocably a symbol of minority rights.

Ron Brown grew up in Harlem, where his father was manager of the famous Theresa Hotel on 125th Street, a center of the Harlem Renaissance. He played basketball on a makeshift court on the hotel roof and watched the soapbox orators haranguing the crowds outside. Brown was an only child, doted on by his college-educated parents and by the notables who frequented the Theresa. His father, Bill Brown, who died in September 1988, was one of the first black officials in Franklin D. Roosevelt's Federal Housing and Home Finance Agency. "I learned my politics from my Dad," says Brown. At the Democratic Convention in July 1988, Brown arranged honored guest credentials for his father, and seated him in the VIP box next to Rosa Parks of the Montgomery bus boycott.

His parents sent him out of Harlem, first to the Hunter College day school, then to the Walden School and the Rhodes school on Manhattan's West Side. At Middlebury College, he was rushed by several fraternities; he eventually chose Sigma Phi Epsilon. But its charter had a whites-only clause, and after Brown rejected a proposed compromise which offered him house privileges but not full membership, his fraternity brothers went ahead and included Brown as a brother; the fraternity was disaffiliated from the national organization.

Yet like many pioneer blacks attending elite northern colleges during the 1960's, Brown was not a creature of "the movement." He was a pre-med student, switching to political science only after an unfortunate encounter with organic chemistry. He graduated in 1962, and after a brief time in law school, joined the Army. As a 21-year-old second lieutenant in Germany, Brown had some 60 German civilians reporting to him, most of whom were twice his age. "I looked like I was about 12," he recalls. In a second tour, in Korea, Captain

Brown was commandant of an elite training school that indoctrinated Korean soldiers in the American way of life.

By the time he returned home to the turbulence of the late 1960's, Brown had enjoyed ample success as a black in a white world; and though he was innocent of militant politics, he remained very much a son of Harlem. Driving south with his bride, Alma, en route to Fort Eustis, Va., he encountered segregated restaurants. Back home in New York, Brown chose to pursue his political ideals as a social worker in the tenements of the Lower East Side, while completing his law degree at St. John's University at night. In 1967, he joined the National Urban League, and quickly rose to become director of its Washington office, earning wide respect as a lobbyist.

Though he had had white friends since early childhood, the real "crossover" point for him came in 1979, when he moved to Ted Kennedy's staff. Brown recalls that on his first trip with the Senator, Kennedy took him to New Hampshire, which had almost no black voters. "It was a small but very significant thing," Brown recalls. "Like many blacks who came out of civil rights work, I wanted some assurance that I was not being hired just to run 'the black desk.'"

In August 1980, Kennedy offered Brown the job of chief counsel of the Senate Judiciary Committee. But three months later, the Democrats lost control of the Senate, and Brown found himself with the far less influential post of chief counsel to the Democratic minority. He moved back to Kennedy's office as staff director and general counsel, and the following July left to join Patton, Boggs & Blow.

Because Brown had always been very much on the mainstream side of the civil rights movement and party politics, many Democrats were surprised in April 1988, when he agreed to become Jesse Jackson's convention manager. Earlier, Brown had declined Jackson's offer to manage his Presidential campaign. But after Jackson's stunning win in the Michigan caucuses, Brown attended a Jackson campaign meeting at Georgetown's Pisces club. Placing his hand on Brown's shoulder, Jackson spoke of the historic moment and how it was "time to bring in the first team."

"I was deeply moved," says Brown. But, characteristically, he spent a week telephoning party leaders to discuss the pros and cons before signing on. "Everybody said not just 'Do it,'" recalls a Kennedy aide, "they begged him to do it." When Jackson announced his convention leadership team, including Brown as convention manager, it was signal that the candidate wanted to play as a regular, not a spoiler.

Brown's political history contrasts with Jesse Jackson's in almost every respect. Yet, like most black political leaders, who eventually repaired to Jackson's banner with complex feelings of bemused affection, exasperation, pride and inevitability, Brown saw in Jackson the first national figure in two decades who was rallying black hopes, pushing the issues of poverty and racism back onto center stage, and genuinely trying to address racially charged social dilemmas in nonracial terms.

"When I joined the Jackson campaign," he says, Jackson "had made tremendous strides in broadening his base and in making people feel more comfortable with him. He'd accomplished something for blacks and for progressive politics. I didn't want him to blow it. He wanted to be viewed as a constructive force in the Democratic Party. My job was to make everybody a winner."

As the campaign progressed, Brown deftly negotiated his way through a series of near-disasters, the most memorable of which was the failure of Presidential candidate Michael Dukakis to notify Jackson that he'd selected Lloyd Bentsen as his running mate. "When Ron called me to say that Jesse had gotten the news from a reporter," says former Dukakis campaign manager Susan Estrich, "he was steaming. But his position was, 'We've got a problem. How do we fix it? How do we limit the damage?' A lot of other people would have let it fester."

As it turned out, the 1988 Democratic convention ended in a love feast in which the Jackson children became the symbol of America's hopes, Dukakis treated Jackson with just the right blend of distance and respect, and Jackson, as the cliché went, "behaved himself." Whatever the other causes of the subsequent Dukakis fade, open convention disarray was not among them. If this was quickly forgotten by the public, it stuck in the memory of party insiders, many of whom gave substantial credit to Ron Brown.

Brown cannot overcome all of the Democrats' ideological and sectoral divisions, any more than he can change his complexion. But he hopes to quiet his critics by proving he can deliver the nitty gritty stuff of effective politics—and above all, that he can win elections. He is determined to fuse the 50 state parties, the two Congressional fund-raising committees, and the Democratic National Committee into a coordinated campaign organization that will help the Democrats spell out a more coherent message and deploy more effective tactics.

"What the party does over here and over there should be strategically connected," Brown says. "The voter registration, the redistricting, the state party building and the campaigns—everything should be connected to winning elections."

After becoming chairman in February, Brown moved quickly to send D.N.C. money and staff into two special Congressional by-elections in Alabama and Indiana; he also managed the unprecedented feat of persuading party organizations in neighboring states to donate money and troops. Democrats won both. The Alabama win was reassuring, because the state party chairman, John Baker, had been one of Brown's most outspoken opponents and a Republican win there would have confirmed fears that Brown was scaring off white voters. The upset victory in Indiana was especially sweet, capturing as it did a Republican district once represented by Vice President Dan Quayle. In a third special election, in heavily Republican Wyoming, the Democrats lost a close race.

More recently, the Democrats narrowly lost the Miami seat once held by Claude Pepper, to a Cuban-born Republican in a district that had become heavily Hispanic and conservative. But they held former House Speaker Jim Wright's Fort Worth seat in yet another close race, and won a stunning upset to take back a Mississippi seat that the Republicans had held since 1973.

In these races, and especially in the Virginia contest that brought Douglas Wilder to office, local party leaders have praised the Democratic National Committee for not only bringing resources to the table—staff, money, polling and get-out-the-vote expertise—but also insisting that local candidates pool their own resources and run coordinated campaigns.

In Virginia, where in 1985 the Democratic field was notable for its intramural squabbles, Brown withheld party money until the various campaigns agreed to collaborate. It was the sort of exercise in "knocking heads together" that a Democratic President might have performed. "There is a tremendous vacuum in national Democratic politics when we are out of power," says Brown. "The national party ought to play a large part in filling that vacuum."

The Brown regime has had its gaffes, though they have been few. Last April, the chairman found himself attending a poorly staffed "Black Summit" in New Orleans where, after having been assured that no black radicals were involved, he was appalled to find Louis Farrakhan on the program. He gave his speech, and got out of town before Farrakhan arrived. In September, Brown gave a wide-ranging keynote address to a conference on the 1992 Presidential election, noting among other things that Democrats, in attacking the Bush Administration for making grandiose commitments without the resources to pay for them, ought not to make new taxes the centerpiece of their alternative.

"The first Democrat who comes along and loudly proclaims his preference for immediate taxation to raise the money for a real war on drugs," he said, "is plastered all over the evening news. You can hear America sigh: 'The tax-and-spend Democrats; there they go again.'"

At the time, the observation had the ring of a mild cautionary note to beware falling into the media stereotypes. But Brown's admonition was seized on by reporters and ended up on the front page of *The New York Times,* under the headline: "Party Chief Faults Democrats for Asking Drug War Taxes." The episode served to remind Brown that he lives in a fish bowl—a fact that he sometimes forgets.

In the end, the affair did not seem to hurt his relationship with Congressional leaders. He worked closely with majority leader Mitchell on persuading Democratic legislators to hold the line against the Bush Administration's proposal to cut the capital gains tax. Late in October, Brown was surprised to receive a call from three moderate Democratic Senators who had previously been supporters of capital gains reductions. Now, they wanted the party chairman's advice. Brown urged them to back the popular Mitchell, for the sake of party unity. To Mitchell's surprise and delight, they did, and the capital gains cut, which only shortly before had looked like a sure winner for the Republicans, was blocked.

The 1989 election is sure to bolster Democratic self-confidence. Public opinion has unmistakably swung back to activist government. In George Mitchell and Speaker of the House Thomas S. Foley, the party has an attractive pair of Congressional leaders. Meanwhile, past party schisms are being overtaken by events. Jesse Jackson may well take himself out of the 1992 Presidential race to run for Mayor of Washington.* The winding down of the cold war has cooled the most emotional left-right issue, one that has tended to favor Republicans. (Nobody in either party seriously advocates a defense buildup now.)

Both parties are campaigning on traditionally Democratic territory, talking about improving education, housing, job training, child care, and health insurance. Even the emotionally charged abortion issue, to everyone's surprise, broke in the Democrats' favor. With every local and state election that moderate Democrats win with the help of the national party, the moderate critique seems not so much wrong as somewhat beside the point; the D.L.C. people can declare victory and go home.

Amid all the good news, however, one paradox remains, embodied in the party's chairman. Ron Brown is about as Establishment a figure as white America could ever hope for in a political leader. But as a black man, he remains a living symbol of a party heritage that is a source of pride to some in the Democratic coalition, and pain to others. The task of overcoming the imagery of the Democrats as the party that is soft on traditional values is not so hard to accomplish; overcoming racial division without sacrificing racial justice will not be so easy. For the problem runs far deeper than the Democratic Party.

The great strength of the Democratic Party, Ron Brown likes to say, is the great strength of America—its diversity. But the great weakness of both is racial enmity. It is the triumph and trauma of the modern Democratic Party to have launched the second era of reconstruction. That achievement left immense scars. Bitterness lingers among many white Southern Democrats, and some of their Northern cousins as well. For the Democrats, irrevocably, are the party of social change and minority opportunity and the party that inflicted school integration on unwilling white communities. That history remains etched in the memory of those who lived through it, while among younger voters there is only faint memory of Democrats as the lunch-bucket liberals.

"You can't run away from this issue; you have to work through it," says Arkansas Gov. Bill Clinton. "When we do, we'll be a much stronger party." By stressing economic development and education, and appealing to Democrats who call themselves moderates as well as liberals, Clinton has managed to build

---

* In 1990, Jackson ran instead for, and won, the "shadow" Senate seat from Washington.

a new-style Democratic majority in Arkansas that is genuinely bi-racial and mildly populist. But in those states and counties where the Democratic Party still elects local officials based largely on inertia, the erosion of Democratic power is likely to continue until the party develops a philosophy of affirmative government that voters of both races might enthusiastically support.

"The party has to be rebuilt anyway," says Bruce Babbitt of Arizona, the key party moderate whose surprise declaration of support helped defuse an incipient stop-Brown movement in the contest for party chairman a year ago. "We have to take these risks because all the alternatives are worse. The idea of turning our backs on racial justice is unthinkable. At that point, you lose the reason for being a Democrat. Ron Brown is a man of immense reason and charm and sensitivity. We ought to showcase him. Rather than tiptoe around the problem, we should make clear that in Ron Brown we have an exemplar of what America can be."

Epilogue

Bruce Babbitt closes this piece by saying that the Democratic party should showcase Ron Brown. But the challenge for the party will be whether it can go beyond such symbolism toward actually changing its substantive policy directions. Doing so might solidify the Democratic party coalition, according to some analysts, but the fear of other strategists is that it also might cause certain elements of the party to split off (such as the conservative Democrats who voted for Ronald Reagan). Of course, Brown's first challenges will be finding the right candidate to run against George Bush, and trying to guide that candidate through the campaign minefield without dividing the party. The next selection details how George Bush's campaign team accomplished this trick in 1988.

The Remaking of George Bush

Peter Goldman,
Tom Matthews,
and the *Newsweek*
Special Election
Team

This fascinating selection by the reportorial staff of *Newsweek* magazine on the 1988 presidential election raises some challenging questions. Why did George Bush win the election so handily after being so far behind when the campaign started? Was it a function of the changing nature of party support in our electoral system? Was it a matter of a better-run campaign? Was it the nature of the candidate himself, including his ability to adjust to the demands of the voters and the times? Or, should the piece be retitled "How Dukakis Lost"? This selection suggests that all of these explanations may be correct.

As you read this excerpt, reflect on its relationship to other selections. First, notice how the campaign staff, under Lee Atwater, used the type of hardball tactics described in Selection 7.1. Part of that effort required various high-tech processes, which will be described further in Selection 7.4. This style of campaigning is far more elaborate than the campaign strategy Larry O'Brien employed for John Kennedy's candidacy in West Virginia (see Section 9.1) or the selling of Richard Nixon by Roger Ailes and others (see Selection 9.2). Now, through the use of elaborate and constant polling, and the focus groups described so well in this piece, campaign teams can tap into the innermost demands and fears of the voters while positioning their candidates perfectly to take advantage of that information.

Most of all, however, we should reflect on what the voters want and what they get from the presidential campaign process. After the "no hands" presidency of Ronald Reagan (see Selection 3.4), symbolized by the Iran-contra scandal (see Selection 5.2), were there any real issues in the 1988 campaign other than how closely the candidates would adhere to the Reagan philosophy while simultaneously veering away from his management style? Although Dukakis ran on a platform of competence in government, it was Bush who more competently ran his campaign staff and thus won the election.

From *The Quest for the Presidency 1988*, by Peter Goldman, Tom Matthews, and the *Newsweek* Special Election Team (New York: Simon & Schuster, 1989). Copyright © 1989 by Newsweek, Inc. Reprinted by permission of Simon & Schuster, Inc.

ROGER AILES   Media consultant for Bush's 1988 presidential campaign.

LEE ATWATER   Campaign manager for Bush.

JAMES BAKER   Resigned as Reagan's secretary of the treasury to run the Bush campaign in its latter stages.

GEORGE BUSH   Republican nominee for president in 1988.

MICHAEL DUKAKIS   Democratic nominee for president in 1988.

CRAIG FULLER   Assistant to Vice President Bush.

JESSE JACKSON   Candidate for the 1988 Democratic presidential nomination.

JIM PINKERTON   Bush's research director.

STU SPENCER   Adviser and friend to President Reagan.

JOHN SUNUNU   Governor of New Hampshire; adviser to the Bush campaign.

ROBERT TEETER   Pollster for the Bush campaign.

▶ It was a sunwashed spring Friday in Southern California, a day made for dreaming, but in the shadows in the backseat of his silver Cadillac, George Bush was in an oddly elegiac mode—the manner of a man composing his own political obituary. He wasn't about to let his self-doubt show in public—no way. His nomination was safely in hand, his speeches everywhere were upbeat, and his political reflexes, while still mechanical, appeared to be in working order. He was in midsoliloquy on the subject of his sagging fortunes when he spied a couple of workmen on a street corner, gawking at his motorcade. Gotta get a little eye contact here, he told himself, the candidate as salesman preparing to make a call; you make the eye contact, you get the vote. "Hi, boys," he called out to the workmen with a cheery wave, and when they stared blankly back at him, he seemed not to mind.

What weighed on him instead were the numbers he kept reading, the polls showing him far back of Mike Dukakis and slipping farther. He tried to shrug it all off as something he called "generic overlay," the natural disposition of the voters toward someone new, different and Democratic, at a point when the real line between him and the governor hadn't yet been drawn. Drawing it was his job, he mused, and if he did it well he would win. If not—well, he had learned to live with the consequences. Iowa had taught him that, he said; it hurt having his best friends write him off for dead, but it had made him tougher, less fragile, less uptight. He had discovered, looking inward, that it would not be the worst thing in the world to be gainfully unemployed, free at last to say, "Sorry, I don't want to do the head table." He had sorted it all out philosophically, he told a friend in the car. He had conditioned his psyche to the possibility that he might lose.

The Invisible Man

That Bush could be preparing himself for defeat in the rosy afterglow of victory was a reflection of the gloom endemic in his campaign—a want of faith, at bottom, in the candidate himself. Bush had only just proven himself in combat, wrapping up the race earlier and more decisively than anyone in the history of nomination-by-primary. He had, moreover, been dealt the strongest hand an incumbent might have wished for: the dollar was strong, the Dow was steadying, the economic-misery index was low, and peace was breaking out everywhere from Angola to Afghanistan.

And yet some of his own inner-circle strategists were quoting odds as high as 60–40 that a rank unknown named Dukakis was going to beat the vice president, decisively, in the fall. Their reasons, stripped of the elegant demographic analyses and the raw intramural backbiting, usually came back to George Bush. They liked and admired Bush the man, for the most part, but, as professional managers, they did not really believe in him as a candidate. They were, in fact, moving toward a consensus that he could not win on his own low-watt incandescence and would prevail only by making Mike Dukakis look worse.

His campaign had been adrift since Illinois, a man-of-war cut loose from its moorings with no more battles to be fought; it was as if his success had come too early, John Sununu thought, and no one seemed to know what to do next. Dukakis was dominating the news, putting his clockwork victory of the week on the board against his obliging sparring partner, Jesse Jackson, while Bush roamed the secondary media markets he would not be able to cover in the fall. His backwater itinerary, sensible on paper, played badly in practice and in the press. His name all but disappeared from the headlines except when some fresh bit of bad news attached to it, a new twist in the Noriega scandal or a further dip in the polls. Otherwise, it was as if he and his candidacy had sailed off the edge of the earth.

The nearest thing to a game plan for early spring came out of the internals in Bob Teeter's polling, a vein of public concern about America's competitive slide in commerce and technology. The response was to cart the candidate around from photo op to photo op in high-tech settings—all those f____g chipmakers, [Bush campaign press secretary] Pete Teeley complained, and no red meat. One day, the aspiring leader of the free world found himself at a conference table at Procter & Gamble, being briefed on how superabsorbent polymers had revolutionized the look, fit and efficaciousness of the contemporary diaper. At another stop, at a research center near Fresno, he inspected a state-of-the-art display of irrigation equipment while his Secret Service guards gazed out over the surrounding farm fields, watching, so far as anyone could tell, for the attack of the killer carrots.

His people seemed baffled for a time as to what was happening—why Bush's polls were tumbling when the objective circumstances seemed so favorable to his cause. The simplest argument was that people wanted change for its own sake—that, as Nixon liked to say, paraphrasing de Tocqueville, Americans have always felt a certain restlessness in prosperity and that the in party was likely to pay the dues. Prosperity, indeed, had been crowded back to the business pages after more than five years of sustained economic growth, no matter how hard Bush tried to focus attention on it; there was so much good news that he couldn't leverage it anymore.

"The economy is in great shape," Lee Atwater grumbled over breakfast one day with his fallen adversary, David Keene. "Why aren't we getting any credit for it?"

"Winston Churchill won the war," Keene reminded him, tersely and accurately, "and they threw his ass out."

But when other explanations were exhausted, the biopsies within the campaign kept coming back to Bush himself—to his own stumble-prone deficiencies as a candidate and to his stubborn refusal to disengage himself from his patron, the president. A message might have helped, but as Stu Spencer, a latecomer to his strategy councils, worried aloud, he still didn't have one, after seven years of hoping and three more in active pursuit of the prize. In a largely issueless environment, Spencer thought, the comfort level between the people and the candidate could be decisive, and it wasn't there for the vice president. It was hard for people to get comfortable with a man who seemed so palpably uncomfortable with himself; it seemed to Spencer that Bush, in his middle sixties, still didn't know who he was or where he wanted to go.

His public profile, as a consequence, remained a montage of his vices rather than his virtues; his negatives, against an otherwise blank backdrop, were all the definition he had. The most enduring had to do with his perceived softness, and even his friend Jim Baker worried about the sheer intractability of the problem. Baker had come up against a similar threshold question managing Jerry Ford in 1976, except that with Ford the issue was whether he was *smart* enough to be president; with Bush, it was whether he was *strong* enough. The answer in both cases was yes, Baker believed, but smarts were easier to prove in politics than strength, and a way would have to be found, most likely in hand-to-hand combat with Dukakis. For Bush to win, Dukakis would have to be made to lose.

There was the further matter of Bush's iron handhold on the president's coattails, even when his loyalty had manifestly become dangerous to his health. The separation problem had been seen by his men as a drag on his campaign from the beginning, and with Reagan's fabled luck having suddenly given way to a series of scandals—Iran-Contra, Noriega, Ed Meese—Bush found himself entangled by his own free will in a form of guilt by association.*

But it was hard for Bush's own people to budge him from his set-in-concrete solidarity with the president. He was as peevish as ever about being managed—handled, as he put it, like a piece of meat—and they found themselves en-

---

* Panamanian leader Manuel Noriega had been indicted on drug-trafficking charges, and questions were being raised about Bush's dealings with him when Bush was director of the CIA in the mid-1970s. Reagan's attorney general, Edwin Meese, was accused of conflict of interest in several ways with respect to his business affairs. After an intensive investigation, none of the charges were proven, and eventually Meese resigned from the office.

listing surrogates among his key supporters to bear their message for them. He was even persuaded, in April, to receive Richard Nixon, a rendezvous he had hitherto found as welcome as an invitation to a leper colony.

His reluctance had not escaped the former president's notice, and the air was further cooled by a published remark of Nixon's, after Iowa, that Bush did not appear to be up to winning the presidency. His attitude, as intimates knew, had not really changed, about Bush or his prospects, and did not during the course of their evening together; in a privately circulated memo three months later, Nixon would once again express his "grave misgivings" about Bush's prospects in an election that ought on paper to have been his by a landslide. But the two men reached an understanding of sorts over drinks alone in the study, and afterward, at table with the Bushes and Lee Atwater, Nixon offered some home thoughts on the battle ahead.

His advice ranged widely from the geopolitics of autumn—zero in on Ohio, he said—to the choice of a running mate. He did not push his case for [Robert] Dole directly, thinking it presumptuous to do so, but his specifications seemed tailored to fit the senator. Forget about looking for someone you thought would help you electorally, Nixon said; he had made that mistake choosing Henry Cabot Lodge in 1960. He thought Bush should shop instead for someone experienced, someone, he said, who was up to big-league pitching. Dukakis, in Nixon's view, needed to be painted as a typical Massachusetts liberal and a dewy-eyed dove besides, and Bush was too much the gentleman to do it, too visibly ill-at-ease on the attack. He needed someone strong on the ticket to do it for him, the way Nixon himself had taken on Adlai Stevenson for Eisenhower.

But his bottom-line counsel, drawn again from his own experience, was to step out of Reagan's shadow. "I lost the 1960 election because I was never viewed as my own man," he said. He had wanted, for example, to come out for more defense spending, but Ike had opposed it, and Nixon had had to sit silently by while Kennedy made off with the issue. "You've got to make news," he told Bush, and his loyalty to Reagan was not the way to do it. It was instead, in Nixon's critique, a recipe for invisibility.

More messengers were brought in to underscore the point in a series of meetings with Bush. One such group, a random mix of party leaders from the South, the East and the Midwest, sat down with the vice president one May morning in Washington to urge him to do something to shake loose of Reagan and jump-start his campaign. They had been primed by Atwater, Teeter and [Deputy Campaign Manager] Rich Bond over dinner the night before at Joe & Mo's restaurant, a haunt much favored by the die-makers of presidential politics, and when they sat down with the vice president their message had been honed to a sharp edge. Bush was, as one of them put it, digging himself as deep a hole as Jerry Ford had been in twelve years earlier, thirty points behind Jimmy Carter in August. If he didn't do something, and soon, the race would be over.

"I don't agree with you," Bush said. His tone was arctic. He didn't like criticism, and he didn't like doom-crying.

He was no happier at the specifics laid before him, mainly that he disengage from the administration on the Meese mess and on an attempted plea bargain with General Noriega in his Florida drug case. The former particularly troubled one of his guests, a onetime United States attorney from the Midwest.

You can't be associated with it, he told Bush. It's not *you*.

Bush preferred a stealth approach to the case, something quiet and discreet as against loud and vulgar. "Look," he said, "I could go out there today and say Ed Meese ought to go. But what purpose is that going to serve?"

The view in the room was that it might just resurrect his campaign, but the air was turning contentious to no useful end, and the meeting broke up after an hour.

"This is a pretty strong dose of medicine for this early in the morning," Bush said, seeing his guests out empty-handed.

He seemed to have a particularly hard time stepping up to the question of Meese's periodic toe-dancing at the outer edges of the ethical code. The independent prosecutor on the case let it be known early that he didn't mean to recommend criminal charges, but Meese had clearly been reckless of appearances in his off-duty business dealings, and his continuation in office was becoming a major embarrassment to Reagan *and* Bush—the embodiment of what the other side had taken to calling the Sleaze Factor in the Reagan government.

Bush was well aware of the problem, but the president's public support for his old friend Ed left him nearly speechless. For weeks, his strongest words on the subject were that Meese wouldn't be attorney general in *his* administration, a promise so empty as to be just as well left unsaid. His recalcitrance became a kind of litmus test of his courage, for his own people no less than for the press. Maybe Bush would *never* be his own man, some of his handlers brooded over drinks in the late hours one night after work. Maybe he *wasn't* tough enough to be president.

The chief worrier, as it happened, was Jim Baker, then still a gray eminence in the campaign. Baker knew Bush too well and liked him too much to question his intestinal fortitude, but he saw the Meese case as George's millstone. Either he could drag its crippling weight through the rest of the campaign or he could demonstrate his strength convincingly by casting it off.

"It's a freebie to separate yourself from Ed Meese," he told Bush. The attorney general was practically friendless in the government and the press, and not even Reagan would be offended if his vice president broke ranks just this once.

But Bush resisted, and for a troubled passage Baker was in suspense as to the outcome. If George didn't separate himself from Reagan on so easy an issue, he worried to colleagues in the campaign, he would never be able to separate himself on anything.

A window of opportunity finally opened when Baker persuaded Bush to go ask Reagan for leave to speak up; the president, Baker argued, was politically grown-up enough to understand Bush's begging to differ. The sitting was finally arranged, in June, and Reagan was as empathic as Baker had predicted he would be. Meese would be leaving before the election anyway, and if Bush felt he needed to get out from under the problem sooner rather than later, well, Reagan would not stand in his way.

As it worked out, Bush had procrastinated one beat too long. A scenario had been stitched up for him, delicate in weave and design; the White House would alert him in advance when the prosecutor's report on the affair was to be made public, whereupon Bush would sorrowfully tell the world that it was time for Meese to go. The single essential piece of the picture, one of the plotters remarked, was that he be the first to say so. In fact he was the second; it was Meese himself who scooped him, early in July, resigning on his own motion, and Bush was one more voice, dimly heard in the background, saying that Ed had done the right thing. "It's history, baby," a ringleader in the cabal exulted, but a faint tint of disappointment colored the celebration, a sense of opportunity lost.

The Zero-Sum Game

A campaign fallen on hard times is never wanting for advice, and Bush got plenty, much of it the moral equivalent of asking him to empty his closets of his J. Press haberdashery and restock them from Banana Republic. His rich-boy image clung to him, so stubbornly that one adviser suggested that he do a speech actually *declaring* himself to be culturally disadvantaged. His compound in Kennebunkport was a particular symbol of his affluent remove from the rest of America, and his regular retreats there became a point of contention in the campaign, [Craig] Fuller arguing that they were restorative for the candidate, Atwater fretting over the patrician look of the thing.

Bush cut off the internal debate; he didn't need a lot of advice from image-makers, he said, on where the hell he was going to go for a weekend. But outsiders kept dragging the Kennebunkport Question back into play. One day in July, some of the Bush command gathered in Atwater's office and put together a conference call to some of the viziers of Texas Republican politics. The nominal subject was [Dukakis's running mate] Lloyd Bentsen, but the state's earthenware governor, William P. Clements, came back again and again to the visuals of Bush as summer person on the coast of Maine.

"Close that goddam house in Kenne*buck*port up," he huffed, his precision gone the way of his patience.

"Governor," Bob Mosbacher answered from the borders of his own frustration, "we've told the vice president that, and we'll continue to tell him that."

The more urgent message, in their view, was that he had to turn things around in the only way left to him, by the systematic dismemberment of Mike Dukakis. The venue for selling this line to the candidate, by wry irony, was Kennebunkport in June. Dukakis by then was beating Bush by eighteen points in Robert Teeter's polls, with no bottom in sight, and Wirthlin's numbers, privately communicated to his friends at Bush Inc., showed him running behind Mikhail Gorbachev in public esteem. The press and the political industry had already begun consigning him to an early grave when he convened a series of meetings in the quiet of his summer place to plan his resuscitation.

His people only lately had been divided along the usual lines, the hawks on Fifteenth Street arguing for a strategy of attack, the doves in the OVP [Office of the Vice President] and in Bush's circle of friends countering that they ought to save their bullets for the fall campaign. The unlikely model for the hawks was 1948, when another uncharismatic vice president, named Harry Truman, had run a conscious scare campaign against Thomas E. Dewey and had won against all odds. The analogy had first been put forward by Bush's research director, Jim Pinkerton, a bright, gangly conservative of thirty who had bailed out of Hollywood for politics after two unsold screenplays. Like Bush, he wrote in a prescient early memo, Truman had been maligned and underrated early in his campaign, but he had succeeded in making it sound dangerous to vote Republican, and Pinkerton recommended lifting some variant on his basic message: Don't let them take it away.

But the walk-soft wing then ascendant at Bush Inc. was, or appeared to be, under the spell of Jerry Ford's extraordinary catch-up run against Jimmy Carter in 1976. Even so canny a campaigner as Baker, who had managed Ford, seemed to a friend to have come away with this mental image that you could make up twenty-eight points starting on August 20 if you had to; he had at times to be reminded that the last point or two had been a bridge too far and that Ford had lost the election.

As the meetings in Maine drew near, there were hardly any doves left—none, that is, except Bush himself. The forming consensus was that the vice president had to come out of the August convention no worse than ten to twelve points down to stay in reaching distance, and even then he might not catch Dukakis before mid- to late October. If they just sat still, they would find themselves twenty-five points down, a mountain too steep to climb.

The parallels with Ford were forgotten. The analogy to Truman was inviting. The time-for-a-change factor was working against Bush, as it had been against Truman, and nothing positive seemed to help, not even that golden oldie called peace and prosperity; it was, Stu Spencer guessed, as if the people in their contentment were ready to let the other guy, the little technocrat from Massachusetts, come in and fine-tune what Reagan had wrought. Bush's personal appeal in poll after poll was strongest among brand-name Republican voters, people who would cast ballots for Conan the Barbarian if he were the party's nominee. He was staggering under the weight of his forty-plus negative ratings, a level his own man Atwater had always considered fatal. He had to go bare-knuckle against Dukakis, in the settling view of his command group. If they let Dukakis get away with his Massachusetts Miracle stuff unchallenged, [Roger] Ailes argued, he would win. Ailes was confident that they could cut into Bush's negatives, but it was a lot easier to raise the other guy's. They had to make the fall campaign a zero-sum game, Bush pumping himself up by tearing Dukakis down.

The last convert to the scorched-earth strategy was Bush himself. He seemed to his men to understand intellectually what he had to do, but politics, for him, had always been a grubby business, distasteful in direct relation to its degree of incivility. Dukakis was a decent man, an able man, he mused in his car one day; he was just coming at things from a different direction, and once people saw how different, the governor wasn't gonna get a free ride anymore. What Bush seemed loath to do was rush into the ring and start swinging. His usual response to the hawks, on the attack strategy as on the separation problem, was that it was too early to be pushing panic buttons. The traditional Labor Day start-up would be soon enough; it was as if he held out some secret hope that if he waited long enough the need to get down and dirty would go away.

His people had to persuade him otherwise. Late in April, Bob Teeter sat down at his home in Ann Arbor with *his* polltaker, Fred Steeper, to start thinking beyond the primaries to the fall campaign. The news in their numbers was unsettling: people were doing well enough economically, but there was an incongruous restlessness out there, Steeper thought, a sense that things were going wrong and that it was time for a change. No one issue drove them; it was instead a worry list of seven or eight things—the environment, the deficit, the homeless—and if Dukakis managed to put them all together, he could win.

He *was* winning, at that point, and the men on Fifteenth Street knew what needed to be done. They had to do what Ailes would call a paint job on Mike Dukakis. The question was how to get Gentleman George fighting mad, and by the time they arrived in Kennebunkport they had the answer.

The Paramus Tapes

The night before the retreat was to begin, five senior hands peeled away from the Bush tour in New Jersey, drove to an office building on Route 17 near the Paramus Park shopping mall, and took seats behind a one-way mirror looking out into a small conference room. On the far side of the glass, a dozen or so residents of the area—all white, all Catholic, all middle-class, all Reagan Democrats leaning to Dukakis—had filed in from a buffet dinner and settled into upholstered chairs around a big, round conference table. A microphone dangled from the ceiling. A camera, out of sight, recorded them on videotape. A moderator was urging them to speak freely; there were no "right" or "wrong" answers. They were that new fountainhead of wisdom in politics, a focus group, and, while they didn't know it at the time, they were about to tell George Bush what to do next.

It was only spring, but the meter was running, and the prospect was bleak. Atwater believed, and would tell Bush straight out a couple of weeks later, that he had no better than a 30 percent chance of winning. The Kennebunkport meetings, in Atwater's view, would be decisive; like the others, he meant to use the retreat to push the vice president into a tougher, more combative mode. The Democratic convention, he reckoned, would be an automatic ten points for Dukakis, blowing his lead out from seventeen points to twenty-seven or twenty-eight. Bush would be in Ford country, so far behind that he could run a perfect campaign and still not catch up.

The focus group in Paramus, along with others like it there and in similar Middletown settings across the country, confirmed to them that they were on the right track. The first lesson was that no one knew either man. The second was that they liked what little they had heard about Dukakis more than what they had seen of Bush. Their impression of the governor was furry but favorable; they found him appealing for his immigrant roots, his plain lifestyle, his seemingly moderate politics, and his look of inner strength—a quality they found wanting in the vice president. It didn't seem to work to tell them that Massachusetts was a hotbed of liberalism, or that a Dukakis administration would be unduly influenced by Jesse Jackson; all that Bush's men got on the latter charge were blank stares.

Bush's image, by contrast, was blank. The good news was that the sample group didn't *dis*like him or believe the business about his being a wimp. The bad news was that they knew nothing at all about him except for the fact that he was vice president; the single person in the room aware that he *had* a past thought, incorrectly, that he had once been a senator. He had neither pedigree nor profile. The words that attached to him were "wishy-washy," even "evasive"; he seemed reluctant, people said, to take a forceful position on anything.

So there were two men to define, and the focus group in Paramus became the taste-testing kitchen. "If you learned the following things about Dukakis," the moderator said, "would it change your mind about him?"

The men behind the mirror leaned forward; it was the point of the exercise. For weeks, Jim Pinkerton had been closeted in his cubicle on Fifteenth Street assembling a dossier of unflattering newspaper cuttings and Nexis files on Dukakis. The euphemism in politics for work like his was "opposition research," which sounded sanitary, almost academic. A more apt analogy might have been dum-dum bullets, and the moderator began firing them. Dukakis had vetoed a bill mandating the Pledge of Allegiance in public schools. He was against the death penalty, even for kingpins in the drug trade. He opposed prayer in the schools. He had stood up for his state's generous program of weekend passes for convicts, even murderers serving life sentences without hope of parole.

No one shot in the volley seemed to draw much blood, but the cumulative effect was dramatic. A palpable unquiet fell over the table. "I didn't realize all these things when I said I was for Dukakis," one woman said. Close to half the people in the room switched to Bush.

Sheltered by the mirror, the vice president's men exchanged glances. Ailes, thinking strategically, was impatient; he regarded focus groups as hand jobs, a new profit center for polltakers, and he had seen enough in the first fifty minutes to confirm what he already knew needed to be done. Atwater, thinking tactically, was ecstatic. They had the means to bring Bush around.

He started the courtship with Bob Teeter the next day, sitting with him at rallies, sharing rides in motorcades, slipping into the chair beside him at a family-style dinner in Kennebunkport that evening. Teeter and Fuller had been slow coming around to the power of negative thinking; until lately, they had thought Atwater a sort of Southern-fried Chicken Little, running around using scare words like "free fall" to describe Bush's situation. But Fuller had seen the Paramus focus group and had got the message. That left Teeter, and while he too was in the picture Atwater devoted the day to stiffening his spine. If Atwater could sell Teeter on the need to move to a war footing, Nick Brady would go along, and once Brady was aboard, Bush would probably follow.

The Kennebunkport meetings became an exercise in persuasion, a united G-6 instructing the vice president that, as Atwater put it, the fat lady had already sung for the Democrats;* Dukakis was going to be the nominee, a knight in undented armor, and Bush's abstemious argument that it was too early to start shooting would no longer do. At one session before the fireplace in the family living room, Teeter walked him through the numbers. They were grim, and Fuller reduced them to more graphic terms, sketching a rude chart on the back of a briefing paper. The message in the widening distance between Bush's trend line and Dukakis's was unmistakable: they were in serious danger of losing.

Bush was still hesitant. Teeter got out tapes of two focus groups conducted in Paramus—the one Bush's men had seen and another held the same day.

"I think you should take a look at these," Teeter said.

They regathered the next morning on the back deck of the Bush home, looking out over the rocky Atlantic coastline. The sky was a cloudless spring blue. The buoys marking lobster traps bobbed on the surface of the water. Every twenty minutes or so, a tour boat would chug by with a cargo of sightseers waving at the vice president and his campaign command.

The men on the deck were oblivious to the view. Bush had sat up alone watching the Paramus tapes, and was stunned by what he had seen; some of the participants had actually thought Dukakis was more conservative than he.

"They don't know this guy's record," he said. "They don't know enough about him."

The screening had had its desired effect. Bush still needed more jollying, still wanted assurance that he wouldn't have to get personal or use the hot attack rhetoric known in the trade as red language. But his resistance to the basic strategy melted like butter on a warm biscuit. He never quite said yes. He rarely did, confronting a tough political call. His manner instead was deferential, acquiescing in a decision as if he had no other choice; his virginity, or at least his deniability, was thus preserved. He watched the consensus for action take form

---

* G-6 refers to the "Group of Six," Bush's six key campaign advisers—Roger Ailes, Lee Atwater, Nicholas Brady, Craig Fuller, Robert Mosbacher, and Robert Teeter.

around him, passively, more observer than participant. Well, he said finally, you guys are the boss. You all do what you think.

The next day, Atwater flew back to Washington, more hopeful than he had felt for weeks. There was nothing left for him to accomplish in Kennebunkport; the rest of the retreat would be taken up with public-policy discussions—all kinds of eggheads, he thought, talking all kinds of stuff a Bush administration should do once in office. That wasn't Atwater's thing, and he had made quickly for the exit. It's kind of ironical, he thought on the plane down to Washington and his war room on Fifteenth Street. They'll be spending six days up there talking about all these high-blown issues, when it took us six minutes to figure out the only issues we're really going to need.

With Bush's return to the wars, his soul-searching ended, and a season of Dukakis-bashing began. Its first objective, made plain by the Paramus tapes, was to spoil Dukakis's image as a dead-centrist efficiency expert, a perception nourished through the primary season by his Tuesday-night fights with the Reverend Jackson. He had to be driven leftward, Stu Spencer thought, preparing, during the summer, to enlist in the campaign. Spencer had been a bridging figure between the old politics and the new, a salty street fighter who had brought the language and the instincts of the clubhouse to the media age at its dawning in California. His own ideology was elastic, his two all-time favorite clients having been Nelson A. Rockefeller* and Ronald Reagan; political belief was a tool for him, not a cause as it seemed to be for some of the kids just coming into the game. His view of his mission was matter-of-fact, almost surgical. Dukakis hadn't had to take any real heat yet, he thought. They had to rattle him, and the way to do it was to bludgeon him with left hooks.

George & Ted & Dan & Willie

The calculated gamble in the strategy was putting Bush out front in the assault. The normal rule in politics is to keep the candidate on the high road and leave the pit-bull campaigning to his ads and his surrogates. But the Bush campaign had come out of California broke, with no more money to spend on advertising until the fall campaign; they would therefore have to rely on what handlers call "free," or sometimes "earned," media—stories in newspapers and magazines and pictures on TV. There was the further necessity of convincing an unpersuaded electorate that Bush cared enough about something—*anything*—to fight for it. He would have to get over his qualms and do the bashing himself; if he was in fact to become the avatar of Harry Truman, a polite give-'em-heck campaign of the sort he had been waging since New Hampshire wouldn't do.

---

* Rockefeller was a moderate Republican who served as governor of New York and as vice president under Gerald Ford.

To catch the notice of the boys and girls on the bus, he first had to court them. He was in this like a suitor coming back to an old flame he had once jilted. The national press had been held in a kind of traveling quarantine through much of the spring; only unthreatening local reporters were granted interviews, while the eminences of the Big Media brooded ominously in hotel lobbies and lounges. A key decision of the Kennebunkport retreat was to be cozier with them. Bush had resisted similar suggestions in the past, given his chariness of the press. But this time he acquiesced, and Walker's Point was soon aswarm with reporters eating burgers, pitching horseshoes and taking speedboat rides with the vice president of the United States; it was not hard for a man of his social graces to convey that their company was all he wanted, not their hearts and minds.

The new message was staticky at first. The intent of the paint job was to picture Dukakis as a liberal at odds with the most basic American values. But Bush's early attack speeches were occasionally marred by his tendency to land his left hooks on his own chin; the sound of a Yale man accusing his rival of shopping for foreign-policy ideas at "Harvard Yard's boutique" provoked more amusement than applause.

The dissonance of a campaign run by six colonels without a general added to the noise on the line. It was understood that the G-6 was waiting for the absent seventh man, Jim Baker, to take his place at the head of the table. But he was delaying his arrival as long as he gracefully could, and in his absence the cost in coherence could be almost comically plain. There was, for example, the time in June when Teeter and Fuller booked Bush for an interview on ABC-TV's *Nightline* without troubling to notify Ailes in advance. Operation Paint Job had, by unlucky coincidence, begun only that afternoon in Houston, with a sharp script by Peggy Noonan and a strong performance by Bush himself.* The message needed to be clutter-free, and Ailes was furious on being told, just twenty-four hours before airtime, about the late date with Ted Koppel on network TV.

"Are you s____g me?" he roared. "Who dinged me on this?"

The answer was his own colleagues on Fifteenth Street, and when Ailes next confronted them his anger was at a rolling boil. "I only understand friendship or scorched earth," he said, his tone revealing which was his mood of the day. He had a contractual right to be at any senior staff meeting, as he reminded them, and, while he hadn't technically been excluded from the session that settled on the *Nightline* booking, he hadn't been told that they were contemplating throwing Bush into a cage with Koppel on national TV.

"Are you guys nuts?" he bellowed. "You people are crazy. You'd take more time than this to prepare him if he were going to address the PTA."

Fuller explained apologetically that they had treated the interview as a question of scheduling, which was on his watch, and not one of media, which was

---

* See Selection 9.4 by Peggy Noonan on presidential speechwriting.

on Ailes's. Ailes was not appeased. If that was the way they were going to treat him, he said, stalking out of the room, he had better things to do with his time.

Atwater followed him back to his office and sat with him for fifteen minutes or so, trying to calm him. "You're right," he said. "We f____d this one up."

Bush himself seemed bewildered at the booking, coming as it did at the end of a red-eyed, three-time-zone day; too tired to rehearse, he went jogging, took some steam, dragged Ailes off to a joint in the Memorial district for barbecue and a beer, and headed for the studio with a full belly and a numb mind.

"What in the hell are we doing this for?" he asked Ailes.

"Sir," Ailes said, "I'm not sure."

The show was the Dan Rather interview in parodic instant replay, history repeating itself as farce, and the Houston speech was drowned out by the laughter. Koppel, like Rather, had prepared an ambush for the vice president, arming himself with stiletto-tipped questions on both the Iran-Contra and Noriega affairs. This time, Bush walked into it unprepared.

His answers wandered lamely through the briar patch of scandal, which was bad enough. Worse still, he seemed confused as to who exactly was asking the questions at the other end of the live-feed line from Koppel's set in Washington. He had apparently scrambled Koppel with Rather and had called him "Dan" three times when Ailes, in desperation, held up a sign reading TED in his line of sight. It didn't work. "Ted" came out "Dan" yet again. Koppel, obviously miffed, finally reminded Bush who he was, and the vice president wound up apologizing on the air for what must, he said, have been a Freudian slip.

But the attack strategy fell into coherent form in the days and weeks that followed, and Bush's men began assembling a supporting cast around him, the victims and the villains of Dukakis's crypto-liberalism. Their search was made easier by the fact that Dukakis, unlike Bush, had a long, open public record and a train of enemies ready to quote it chapter and verse. There was, for one thing, his affiliation with the American Civil Liberties Union; the governor himself had handed them that one, announcing that he was a "card-carrying member" of the organization. There were those schoolchildren in Massachusetts, denied the daily comfort of saluting the flag. That tip came from Andy Card, a former White House staffer who had been a Massachusetts state legislator at the time; he had joined a majority, some singing "God Bless America," in voting to pass the measure over Dukakis's legalistically framed veto.

And there was, downstage center, Willie Horton, a black convict who had stabbed a white man and raped a white woman in Maryland while on furlough from a life sentence for murder in Massachusetts. Jim Pinkerton—Pink, to his corps of fresh-faced young Duke-busters on Fifteenth Street—had been poring over their findings one day in April when an exchange between Dukakis and [Senator Albert] Gore caught his eye. Gore had made an issue of the Massachusetts furlough program. Most states had one, and so did the Federal government, but, as Gore noted, only Massachusetts permitted "weekend passes" for murderers doing life without parole; eleven, he said, had fled, and two had killed again. Dukakis, as it happened, had inherited the program from a Republican predecessor. Still, he had defended it until after the Horton scandal, and his sniffish response to Gore never really addressed the question.

A light had gone off over Pinkerton's head; it was less like a flashbulb than like a neon sign—*weekend passes for first-degree murderers*—and Willie Horton had soon been caught in its lurid glow. Andy Card had remembered the story from a newspaper in the state, *The Lawrence Eagle-Tribune*. So had John Sununu, who despised Dukakis across the distance between their neighboring states and their polar politics; he had clipped and saved it for his own atrocity file early in 1987, meaning to feed it to some Southern candidate to use against the governor in the Democratic primaries. So had Alex Castellanos, a media consultant who remembered a petition campaign against the furlough program; he would commend the Horton story to Ailes's attention later that month, "in case," he wrote, "you need to lob a small, agenda-changing battlefield nuclear weapon against Dukakis in the fall."

Pinkerton had taken his find first to Lee Atwater, who had been his mentor in politics in the Reagan White House and later at Bush's PAC [political action committee]. There would be sales resistance in other quarters on Fifteenth Street at that innocent time, the discomfort of genteel men who questioned the issue's relevance to a presidential election. Atwater had had no such qualms. His single concern had been that Pinkerton be sure of his facts; it the tale was true, Atwater had thought, it was the gold-mine issue of all time.

Its yield, moreover, was greatly magnified when *Reader's Digest* published its own fortuitously timed version of the furlough story. Both the magazine and the author of the piece, an obscure free-lancer named Robert James Bidinotto, denied any intent to do Dukakis harm. Bidinotto had first undertaken his inquest for a small and failing conservative journal in New Jersey, meaning it, he said, as a victims'-rights story and not a political piece at all. The magazine had folded before he finished, whereupon he offered it to the *Digest*. The editors there were similarly insistent that there was nothing personal or political in their decision to run it. It hardly mattered. The *Digest* bought the piece in April, when Dukakis was clearly the Democratic front-runner, and published it to its fifty million readers in mid-June, when Bush had only just begun working the Horton story into his repertoire. The headline was: GETTING AWAY WITH MURDER.

As an issue, the Horton case required delicate handling. Bush's men would insist afterward that there was no racial undertone to the story, no conscious design to inflame white fears of black crime. Their evidence was that the campaign's official advertising never showed Horton's face or alluded to his color; the story, in the official line, was a metaphor for Dukakis's peculiar values, and the race of its protagonist had nothing to do with it. But Horton's mug shot would appear in some independently produced commercials and fliers, and the men on Fifteenth Street sometimes made careless use of his story. When Atwater suggested publicly that Dukakis might just put Horton on the Democratic ticket, it was too much for Bush, even on his new regimen of nasty pills.

I don't like that stuff, he scolded Atwater, and I don't want to hear any more of it.

He would hear more of it, some in his own voice; a strategy had been born at Kennebunkport, a commitment to a campaign aimed less at the elevation of George Bush than at the destruction of Mike Dukakis. It seemed the only recourse at the time; the governor's lead was then still in or near double digits, and, as Atwater told a war council of Western party leaders in Denver in the late spring, Bush might never be ahead in the polls—not till the one that counted on Election Day. The trick was to keep from falling too far behind, and the key to that, Atwater said, his drawl slower and smokier than usual, was to start getting together your compare-and-contrasts—the portrayal of Dukakis as a bona-fide, double-dip, Frost Belt, McGovern-style liberal whose most basic values were alien to most of America.

The neglected problem, in the gloom of summer, was giving people reasons to vote for the vice president, not just against his opponent. The solution kept being postponed, so long as the search-and-destroy mission seemed to be working. Bush's downhill slide in the polls bottomed out between conventions, and there was no great impetus to rush out five-point programs for the public weal or seven-layer confections of visionary prose. The strategy of choice instead was the un-Americanization of Mike Dukakis, and the details fit on a single three-by-five note card in Lee Atwater's pocket, typed edge to edge with the governor's heresies against orthodox middle-class values:

1. High-tax, high spending. Refuses to rule out a tax hike next year. In 1974, said no new taxes, then raised them. Raised taxes in the middle of this campaign. Mass. state spending up 70 percent.
2. To the left of Carter-Mondale in opposing every defense program. Against MX, Midgetman testing. Monroe Doctrine superseded. Against all aid to contras and freedom fighters.
3. Social issues. McGovern/Kennedy/Jackson liberal:
   — prison furloughs, 85 convicted felons
   — opposes the death penalty in every case
   — "card-carrying member of the ACLU"
   — supports gun control; "disarm the state"
   — #1 pro-abortion candidate
   — vetoed Pledge of Allegiance

The card could fairly be said to embrace the basic plan of action for the Bush campaign—an accentuate-the-negative strategy aimed at elevating the vice president to the presidency over Dukakis's broken body. The result, as summer faded into fall, would be one of the meanest national campaigns since the McCarthy era—so mean, in its worst moments, as to invite the suspicion that George Bush would say nearly anything to win.

Epilogue

The enduring impressions of the 1988 presidential campaign are Dukakis's mistakes—his attempt to look "macho" by riding in a tank; his unemotional response to the opening question of the second debate, which asked what he would do if his wife, Kitty, were brutally murdered. "You just don't get it," Ted Koppel tried to tell the candidate on "Nightline" days before the election. "You are losing the race." In the end, Dukakis's inability to identify his constituency, plus the highly competent, slick, consistent campaign style of the Bush team, cost him the election.

7.4

Politicking Goes High-Tech

Steven V. Roberts

The theory of electoral politicking has not changed. The game is still simply a matter of the candidates reaching the voters, convincing them of the merits of their views, and persuading them to vote one way or the other. What has changed, of course, is the way that politicians reach the voters. In the last century and the first part of this century, voters got to know the candidates through long public debates. With the coming of the railroad, candidates took to whistle-stop campaigns in which they would step out on a train platform in each station on a long, multistate tour and give the same speech to small groups of voters. Now, in the age of television and computers, it has become possible to face huge numbers of voters directly without ever leaving a studio. Furthermore, the nature of the campaign appeal can be refined by first polling the voters to determine what concerns them most.

The negative aspects of these technological breakthroughs, however, cannot be overlooked. Extensive surveys of the potential voting public and subsequent polling analysis result in the issues and the candidate being shaped to meet the concerns of the voters, rather than the other way around. As you will see in Selection 9.2, candidates can now be packaged and sold to the voters like any other product. Furthermore, the expense of appearing on television has made it necessary to reduce campaign appeals to a very few words and dramatic visual images. This need to be brief but powerful has led to more use of negative campaigning. Mudslinging in a campaign is as old as electoral politics itself, but the verbal warfare that takes place nightly on television and in the newspapers during a campaign has risen to new heights (or, more appropriately, fallen to new depths).

In this selection, originally published two days before the November 1986 election, Steven Roberts portrays the dramatic effect of high-tech negative campaigning in the 1986 race in Missouri for a U.S. Senate seat, between Republican Christopher S. (Kit) Bond and liberal Democrat Harriett Woods.

CHRISTOPHER BOND   Republican candidate for the Missouri Senate seat in 1986.

KATIE BOYLE   Press secretary for Bond.

WARREN ERDMAN   Campaign manager for Bond.

HARRISON HICKMAN   Pollster for Woods.

PAUL MASLIN   Pollster for Woods.

JODY NEWMAN   Campaign manager for Woods.

DONALD SIPPLE   Media adviser for Bond.

ROBERT SQUIER   Media adviser for Woods.

JOE WHITE   Long-time adviser to Woods.

HARRIETT WOODS   Democratic candidate for the Missouri Senate seat in 1986.

▶ When the Senate race in Missouri entered the homestretch early last month [October 1986], campaign strategists for Republican Christopher S. (Kit) Bond began to take nightly readings of the voters' mood. As soon as they learned that the Reagan-Gorbachev meeting in Iceland had collapsed on Sunday, Oct. 12, they inserted three new questions into their polls. On Monday night, the President spoke to the nation about the meeting; by Tuesday night, Don Sipple, Mr. Bond's media adviser, sensed he was onto something big.

What he read in the polls astounded him: Missouri voters were backing the President by margins of 6 and 7 to 1. Mr. Bond was already running a television commercial that stressed his support for the Strategic Defense Initiative (the President's space-based missile shield) and attacked the arms-control policy of his Democratic opponent, Harriett Woods. Mr. Sipple decided to recast the spot to take advantage of the talks. By Wednesday morning, the consultant had sent Mr. Bond a new introduction, emphasizing that the President had been able to negotiate in Iceland from a "position of strength." By Friday, the revised commercial was on the air.

With the use of increasingly sophisticated polling methods, videotape machines and satellite technology, political consultants like Don Sipple can now monitor the public mood on an hour-by-hour, day-to-day basis, searching for a cresting emotion that might sway a bloc of marginal voters. Today's media whiz then tries to capture, and manipulate, that emotion in a new television commercial that can be put on the air overnight. "It used to take two or three weeks for information to reach the voters," says the pollster Harrison Hickman, "but now it's film at 11. Clearly, we've pushed the edge of the envelope on this stuff."

During the current battle for control of the Senate, this high-tech, high-stakes struggle by consultants and pollsters for the hearts and minds of the voting public has reached a new level of importance and visibility. When voters cast their ballots in Missouri and other states on Tuesday, they will be making choices based largely on impressions created by these media consultants. Marshall McLuhan was right: the medium is the message. In American politics today, the medium is television, and that medium is dominated by an elite of highly paid but unelected consultants. The democratic ideal, of a candidate talking directly to the voters and appealing for support, has been profoundly distorted.

These electronic contests sometimes resemble a new form of television game show—one could call them "Spot Wars"—and the cost is staggering. Kit Bond and Harriett Woods will each spend about $4 million on their campaigns, with 60 percent going toward buying television time.

The Missouri Senate race has attracted national interest for a number of reasons. Both of the contestants are tough, seasoned campaigners. Kit Bond, a 47-year-old lawyer, is a moderate conservative who won his first statewide race for auditor at age 31 and has served two terms as Governor. Harriett Woods, who is 59 and a journalist by profession, peppers her liberal stance with populist swipes at the big banks and corporations that have contributed heavily to her rival. She lost a close Senate race in 1982 to John C. Danforth, but was elected Lieutenant Governor in 1984.

Moreover, both parties feel that the larger battle for control of the Senate next year hinges on a handful of key races. And Missouri, where the retirement of Democrat Thomas F. Eagleton gives the Republicans a chance to pick up a vacant seat, is one of them.

Not surprisingly, the race attracted the top guns in the consulting business and promised to be the Super Bowl of media advisers. Mr. Bond's man, Don Sipple is a partner in the Washington firm of Bailey, Deardourff, Sipple, which has a superb track record in selling Republicans. The Woods team at the outset was led by the hottest name on the Democratic side, Robert Squier, who is also based in Washington. Top guns do not come cheap. Mr. Squier, for example, charges a $60,000 fee plus 15 percent of the "media buy," or another $350,000, in a state like Missouri.

Consultants, of course, also work in gubernatorial and House campaigns, but those races do not usually involve the sort of media warfare that dominates the major Senate contests; there is much less money available for the candidates since many national contributors are more interested in senatorial campaigns. The cost of television advertising, however, has grown so rapidly that today, Senate campaigns design most of their tactics for one of three purposes, and sometimes all three: generating free television and radio coverage, raising money to finance paid commercials, and energizing supporters to go out and raise more money.

In Missouri, one 30-second spot on the popular evening game show "Wheel of Fortune" costs about $3,000, and as the race moved into the final hectic month, both candidates were spending about $250,000 a week apiece on television alone. The financial pressures have grown so great that candidates can spend up to half their time appealing for funds, often on the phone with individual donors. "The price of running for the Senate today," says Harriett Woods, "is spending more time than you'd like to spend asking people for more money than they'd like to give."

The Woods campaign actually started organizing its fund-raising effort in March 1985. "Without money," explained Jody Newman, the campaign manager, "we couldn't be on TV, and without TV, we couldn't win."

Fund raising in any senatorial campaign takes place on both the local and national levels. Within the home state, the techniques have remained standard: breakfasts and lunches, pool parties and cocktail parties that charge anywhere from $10 to $500 a head. The pitch is generally about local issues, because the contributors are more interested in what the candidates will do for the state than in the way they will affect policy in Washington.

No Senate candidate, however, can raise enough at home these days to finance a campaign. So, while the elections are generally decided by local issues, the money used to publicize those issues must be raised in Los Angeles and Detroit, Chicago and Houston and, above all, in New York and Washington.

During their campaigns, both Kit Bond and Harriett Woods have made regular trips to New York City in search of money. While the Republican mainly worked the Wall Street crowd, the Democrat concentrated on the city's large liberal community, and Harriett Woods was continually running into other candidates in Manhattan. "We follow one another through the same art galleries and restaurants and living rooms," she said.

But no city is more important in the fund-raising game than Washington, and few Senate campaigns this year are without a new breed of Washington consultant, who does nothing but pry money out of the political action committees, or PAC's. There are now more than 4,000 PAC's, providing almost one-quarter of all contributions to Senate campaigns.

When Mrs. Woods scheduled a party for PAC representatives in September, her Washington fund-raiser, Sara G. Garland, was up at 5 A.M. for several days, addressing the invitations by hand. Ms. Garland also asked the Democratic Senators who signed the invitation to call special friends in the PAC's and urge them to buy tickets. As one veteran fund-raiser put it, "In Washington, nothing happens until the fifth phone call."

The evening garnered $130,000, enough for perhaps four days of commercials and Mrs. Woods was back again in October for a final dip into the Washington money pool. Ms. Garland also organized a series of smaller meetings between Mrs. Woods and groups of PAC's devoted to specific subjects. For example, at one breakfast meeting last July, the guest list included PAC's related to health, a major Woods concern. The hosts for the event were Representative Henry A. Waxman of California and Senator Max Baucus of Montana, senior Democrats on the committees handling health issues.

One PAC official resisted all appeals until Ms. Garland said. "This is an opportunity for you. I promise you a seat next to the Senator." The response was immediate: "I'm coming."

These days, Republicans enjoy an obvious fund-raising advantage. Ronald Reagan's farm and trade policies might not be popular in Missouri, but the President raised $450,000 for Mr. Bond at one luncheon in St. Louis. Some PAC's hedge their bets and back both candidates, but most choose sides, and the competition is fierce. For example, Mr. Bond received help from John Danforth, who, as chairman of the influential Senate Commerce Committee, has "closed a few doors for us," according to Ms. Garland. "A lot of PAC's are going to support Bond because Danforth talked to the C.E.O. or made a call to the vice president for government relations," she said.

Once their fund-raising efforts were in gear, both camps started exploring campaign themes. In the fall of 1985, Don Sipple organized "focus groups" around the state—small gatherings of about a dozen voters. "Focus groups give you a feel you can't get from any polling," said Mr. Sipple, who once served on Mr. Bond's staff in the Missouri Statehouse.

What Mr. Sipple discovered was that voters saw Mr. Bond as a "good guy, a good Governor," but not as an inspiring leader. Accordingly, Mr. Sipple reasoned, the Bond campaign should play to the candidate's strength by emphasizing the "comfort level" he had achieved with many voters.

The focus groups told Mr. Sipple that there were some "very clear differences" between the two candidates on a range of issues, particularly budget and fiscal matters, and the strategist thought he could label Mrs. Woods a "tax and spend" Democrat. The groups also indicated that Mrs. Woods was coming across as "too harsh" and "too liberal," but that information had to be handled delicately. "It was infinitely easier for us to work on the liberal thing than on the harsh thing," Mr. Sipple explained. "When you engage in attacks on personal qualities, that can be very dangerous."

Meanwhile, Mrs. Woods had hired Harrison Hickman and Paul Maslin, two poll-takers based in Washington, who took a survey for her in February. Mrs. Woods was the preference of 47 percent of those polled, as opposed to 44 percent for Mr. Bond. But that early in a campaign, political experts are more interested in what they call "internals," answers to specific questions that reveal a candidate's particular strengths and weaknesses. One of the key findings was that Mrs. Woods rated high on questions of personal character.

The poll revealed a major Bond weakness: his image as a wealthy "country-club Republican." But Messrs. Hickman and Maslin also uncovered evidence of Mr. Bond's strength. On the question of who has the "experience and qualifications a Senator needs," Mr. Bond led 2 to 1.

Bob Squier is a Washington celebrity, widely quoted in the press and seen at the best parties, a charming self-promoter with a good record in close races. In 1984, he worked for Paul Simon of Illinois, one of only two Democrats to oust an incumbent Republican Senator. Mr. Squier actively sought the Missouri assignment, because it promised to be one of the top races of the year, and Mrs. Woods and her staff were flattered by his attention. He would give them instant credibility in Washington and leverage with the PAC's. He had a seasoned organization that offered a full range of services, from debate preparation and research to a music composer and editing facility.

By contrast, Joe Slade White, who had worked for Mrs. Woods in her previous campaigns, was practically a one-man operation, with little experience in major Senate races. In explaining the choice of Bob Squier over Joe White, Jody Newman, Mrs. Woods's campaign manager, said: "What often happens in races like this is that you have a fight over the airwaves. One candidate puts on a message, and the other has to decide how to respond. At times you have to rely on experience and instinct, and you have to have the capability of getting on the air instantly."

Nonetheless, while they wanted Mr. Squier's contacts and his organization, Mrs. Woods and her close-knit core of advisers were not prepared to take his advice. Ms. Newman has devoted much of her professional life to promoting Mrs. Woods, and she approached the campaign with a simple, heartfelt premise: "If people really knew Harriett, they would vote for her." But Mr. Squier and the poll-takers had looked at the numbers. They knew their client's weaknesses as well as her strengths, and they were not ready to canonize her. During one planning meeting with the Woods staff, Bob Squier turned to Harrison Hickman and muttered, "All they have to do is pin wings on her and she'll fly to the Senate."

One key question in any Senate campaign is: Which side goes on the air first with paid commercials? The Woods team agreed to let Mr. Bond take the lead. He had more money, so the shorter the campaign, the better for Mrs. Woods. A longer campaign was also likely to tarnish Mrs. Woods's "halo effect," as Mr. Hickman put it. "She would look more and more like a politician."

Don Sipple was reading the situation in the same way, and decided to begin Mr. Bond's media campaign in May. "We wanted to draw her out," he said. "We wanted to make her spend more money than she wanted to before the primary in August."

The initial Bond spots were low-key. In one, he wandered through a field, talking to a farmer about agricultural issues, and casually mentioned that ladybugs help control aphids in a field of alfalfa. "That comment just said so much," said Mr. Sipple. "In a highly charged political environment, when the farm issue will be a political football, let's find out who knows about agriculture."

A second aim of the ads, added Mr. Sipple, was to "tighten up" his candidate's elitist image. Mr. Bond attended prep school at Deerfield, Mass., college at Princeton and law school at the University of Virginia—not exactly a man of the people. So the television spots invariably showed him in a checked sports shirt, speaking directly to ordinary voters, who nodded sympathetically. During a trip to a state fair, where Mr. Bond was going to film some commercials, the candidate doffed his lawyer's shirt and tie in the car and put on one of his made-for-television plaids—with the price tag still on it.

Don Sipple also prepared a second package of spots that focused on Missouri's troubled economy, taking care to separate Kit Bond from the Administration on such issues as trade policy. The White House offered to provide the Bond campaign with a videotape of President Reagan meeting with the Republican, but "we passed," said the consultant, "much to the consternation of the White House."

The Bond media campaign was functioning smoothly, so well in fact that a Woods poll in early June showed that the Democrat had lost 11 points and was behind, 48 to 40. More importantly, there was a marked decline in her advantage on character questions, the strongest element of her appeal. The original strategy had been to run a series of positive spots after Mr. Bond's initial wave, but the poll results forced a re-evaluation. It was time for something dramatic.

The Woods camp had received a juicy piece of information: Kit Bond sat on the board of an insurance company, Mutual Benefit Life, that held farm loans in Missouri and had foreclosed on local farmers. After a Kansas City paper ran a story on one of the families, David and Marilyn Peterson of Maysville, Mr. Squier took a film crew to their house for an interview.

During the filming, David Peterson broke into sobs while talking about his lost dairy herd. The Woods campaign, in Harrison Hickman's words, thought they had found a "silver bullet." Mr. Squier edited the material into a three-part series that ended with an attack on Kit Bond for opposing a moratorium on farm foreclosures. The consultants recommended skipping the original positive spots and coming straight out with the negative "crying farmer" spots. Mrs. Woods and her staff agreed.

The first two in the series began running in mid-June. The third spot, with Mr. Peterson's outburst and the attack on Mr. Bond, followed. That night, a group of Bond staff members gathered in Kansas City to watch the commercial. Katie Boyle, Mr. Bond's press secretary, felt as if someone had punched her.

Warren Erdman, Mr. Bond's campaign manager, immediately called Don Sipple. The two men decided to hold their fire and try to determine how the ad was affecting voters. Mr. Erdman traveled to his hometown of Higginsville and showed the commercials to a focus group. "As they watched the third spot, I watched their eyes. I wanted to see their expressions," said Mr. Erdman. When the citizens of Higginsville expressed distaste for the attack on Kit Bond, Mr. Erdman breathed easily for the first time in days.

A strategy was then formulated. Katie Boyle would express sympathy for the Petersons, but would denounce the Woods campaign for "gutter" politics. The Bond camp also encouraged critical stories in the news media about the Woods spot. With a tip from Katie Boyle, Mike Reilly, a reporter for *The Columbia Daily Tribune,* tracked down the Petersons and, after a lengthy interview with Marilyn Peterson, wrote a story quoting her as saying, "I kinda felt like we had been used" by the Woods campaign.

Miss Boyle rushed copies of the article to the Kansas City television stations and two of them used it on the air that night. Within days, the outcry against the spot had reached a crescendo around the state. It was, Bob Squier later conceded, a masterful job of using the news media.

The Woods camp was reeling. Jody Newman was on the phone with Bob Squier, saying that supporters were upset about the negative tone of the ad. The candidate herself was complaining about how she looked. Messrs. Hickman and Maslin took a quick poll and found decidedly mixed results. In the St. Louis area, Mr. Bond had actually increased his overall lead to 10 points. But many voters who said their income was dependent on agriculture liked the spots and shifted in favor of Mrs. Woods.

In a private memo accompanying the poll, Messrs. Hickman and Maslin said it would be a "tragic error" for the Woods campaign to back away from the attack. Bob Squier told Mrs. Woods and her other advisers that negative ads always cause a critical reaction at first, but are effective in the long run. "The voting public is like an organism," said Mr. Squier. "It tries to reject information that is unpleasant." In fact, the consultant had assumed that Mr. Bond would attack the commercials as dirty politics, and he had a follow-up spot ready to go, pointing out that Mr. Bond had received $26,000 for serving on the insurance company board and had failed to report the income on his Senate ethics report. (Mr. Bond later said the omission was valid because the fee went directly to his law firm.)

But Jody Newman, in a fury, told the consultants, "We've spent eight years building up Harriett Woods's image, and you've ruined it in a month." When Mr. Squier insisted that the campaign stick to the game plan, he was dismissed. (It is a sign of the times that the dumping of Bob Squier made front-page news, and Mrs. Woods complained that reporters were more interested in his status than in her speeches.)

Messrs. Hickman and Maslin, who agreed with Bob Squier, resigned a few days later. Ms. Newman hurriedly contacted the man who worked on Mrs. Woods's earlier campaigns, Joe White, at his vacation house on Long Island and asked him to replace Mr. Squier. Mr. White was in St. Louis the next day, and within a few days a new series of Woods spots were on the air.

This time, the candidate took center stage. Against a soundtrack vaguely evocative of "Chariots of Fire," a voice praised her "character and courage." Mrs. Woods was delighted with the spots. "Joe White has always made me look good," she said.

The Washington hotshots were gone and the campaign staff in St. Louis was in charge again. "In our judgment," said Ms. Newman, "Joe White would do things the way we wanted to do them."

But the "Spot Wars" were just heating up. After Joe White's first ads went on the air, Don Sipple saw an opening for a counterattack. He flew into St. Louis late one evening, and by the next morning he had produced a new spot, featuring the negative news clippings about the Woods commercial—clippings the Bond campaign had helped generate. That night it was on the air. By using the newspaper clips to make the point, and not Mr. Bond himself, Mr. Sipple got others to do the campaign's dirty work.

One of the articles quoted in Mr. Sipple's spot had called Mrs. Woods's tactics "sleazy and shallow," and Mr. White, in turn, thought he saw a target of opportunity. He put together another commercial, saying that Mr. Bond "couldn't take the truth" about his ties to the insurance company.

At that point, in mid-August, both camps lapsed into an exhausted silence. But as Labor Day approached, Joe White knew he had a big problem. Mrs. Woods was trailing Mr. Bond by 8 points in most polls. There was only one thing to do: Go negative.

Mr. White decided to attack Mr. Bond's strongest point, his reputation for sound fiscal management. Mr. Bond's own commercials boasted that, as Governor, he had taken a budget deficit and turned it into a surplus. In his commercial for Mrs. Woods, Mr. White used the first 10 seconds of the Bond spot, with its claim of financial wizardry, and froze the frame. A somber voice came on saying, "That's what Kit Bond says. What he doesn't say is the truth." The truth, the commercial concluded, was that Mr. Bond actually inherited a surplus as Governor and had to raise taxes to keep the state afloat. (The facts lie somewhere in between, and depend on the accounting method used.)

"All candidates overreact to negatives," noted Mr. White. "They tend to believe the voters will turn against them. So a negative ad throws an opponent off guard. It also gives them the problem of how to respond, and that occupies their time and resources."

The morning in early September that the spot was first televised, Kit Bond was being interviewed at a Kansas City television station, and a reporter asked for his reaction. Mr. Bond made a quick comment and privately told Katie Boyle he wanted to talk to Don Sipple. But Mr. Sipple had already called Mr. Bond at the station, leaving a number in Illinois where he was working on another campaign.

Mr. Bond was late for an appearance in St. Joseph, but once on the highway, his van pulled over at a convenience store, where two adjoining phone booths were unoccupied. On one phone, Mr. Bond called headquarters and talked to his campaign manager, Warren Erdman, who was negotiating with the Woods forces over future debates. On the other phone, his press secretary, Katie Boyle, reached Mr. Sipple in Illinois and discussed the Woods ad. At one point, as some local farmers looked on in amazement, Mr. Bond had a phone in each ear, talking to both advisers at once.

While Mr. White succeeded in initially rattling his opponents, the Bond team, after sniffing the bait, decided not to take it. Demanding that Woods withdraw her commercial would sound like a "lawyer's trick," said Mr. Sipple, and would admit that the ad had "drawn blood." Instead, Miss Boyle made a statement rebutting the charges in the commercial.

Mr. White also made seven other spots, detailing Mrs. Woods's views on such issues as drugs in the schools. Mr. White argued that since the baby-boom generation was now having kids, issues relating to children would play well. Some of the spots were only 10 seconds long, with Mrs. Woods talking directly into the camera. Because short spots are half the cost of 30-seconds ads, the campaign flooded the airwaves with them, hoping to show that Harriett Woods was knowledgeable on many subjects.

The Bond camp had been caught napping. Mrs. Woods was outspending them 2 and 3 to 1 on television time, and the attack on the Republican's fiscal record "softened up" his support with marginal voters, said Mr. Sipple. "She just kind of drowned us out." By purchasing so much air time in early September, the Woods camp hoped to influence the next round of polls. The strategy worked. The *St. Louis Globe-Democrat* showed Mrs. Woods pulling even with Mr. Bond at 40 percent apiece, with 20 percent undecided. Even before the poll was published, Ms. Garland was on the phone in Washington, using the results to encourage PAC's to contribute to Mrs. Woods. She raised $15,000 in one day.

Within days, Kit Bond was fighting back. One commercial showed ordinary voters—most of them women—attacking Mrs. Woods's "sneaky, rotten campaign tactics." Another ad said Mrs. Woods was rewriting the history of Mr. Bond's Governorship. Both commercials ran on a heavy schedule for eight days and, by the end, said Mr. Sipple, "we had pretty much stopped her move." New polls at the end of September showed Mr. Bond back in front by 7 points.

Mr. White acknowledged that Bob Squier had been right last spring in saying that Mrs. Woods could win only by undermining Mr. Bond's solid image of reliability. So for the final weeks of the campaign he produced a series of negative ads, capped by a renewed attack on the Republican's connection to the insurance industry. The point was simple: to identify Mr. Bond with "big money out-of-state bad guys." Joe White also took a gamble, producing a spot in which Mrs. Woods talked frankly about her support for a woman's right to have an abortion. The point was to stress the character issue, her concern for average people.

Don Sipple entered the final weeks with a similar strategy. Stress Mr. Bond's strength with spots that highlight his deep roots in Missouri and attack Mrs. Woods's weak points by having him identify with President Reagan's tough stance in Iceland. But that ad—by saying Mrs. Woods favored a test ban without verification—also triggered a controversy. The Democrat fired back with her own spot, accusing Mr. Bond of telling "an outright lie."

In the last 10 days of the campaign, Mr. Bond tried to capitalize on the President's post-summit popularity by appearing in a rally with him in Springfield, and running a new spot with a Presidential endorsement. At that point, Kit Bond held a 9-point lead in two polls, but the Woods camp argued that the gap was closing. In "Spot Wars," the television audience at home gets to pick the winner. . . .

Epilogue

The race did tighten a bit more in the last ten days of the campaign, but not fast enough to save Harriett Woods. Kit Bond won by a comfortable 53 percent to 47 percent margin. (Although the Republican won in Missouri, in 1986 Democrats regained control of the Senate.) Bond also outspent Woods by one million dollars. We are left to wonder if the results would have been different if Woods had stayed with Bob Squier's plans.

Senator Bond has served with distinction on the Agriculture, Nutrition and Forestry, Banking, Housing and Urban Affairs, Small Business, and Budget committees. His voting on key issues has been largely conservative: he has voted for the nomination of Robert Bork, for the death penalty for drug offenders, for funding for the "Star Wars" defense system, and for aid to the Nicaraguan contras. He is eligible for re-election in 1992.

CHAPTER 8

INTEREST GROUPS

A Sense of Urgency

Calvin Tomkins

An interest group is a group of people with common interests who work to influence public policy. How does one organize an effective interest group and keep it effective? What type of personality is required to operate in a sphere in which congressional votes and presidential signatures, both required to pass legislation, are very tough to come by? What kind of temperament does one need to take the long view of politics, knowing that a defeat in one battle means only that the fight needs to be taken up on another front? This profile of Marian Wright Edelman, head of the Children's Defense Fund, answers many of these questions. Edelman has drawn on her contact with Martin Luther King, Jr., and Robert Kennedy and on her experiences as one of a handful of black attorneys working for the NAACP Legal Defense and Educational Fund in the Deep South in the 1960s. For nearly twenty years, she has lobbied for those not able to speak for themselves—poor children.

As you read this selection, notice how long it takes to lay the groundwork both philosophically and politically for innovative legislation. (The same challenge was faced by Senator Quayle in Selection 4.5.) In many respects, Edelman is one of the people battling the results of the Reagan administration's New Federalism, which was described in Selection 2.2. When the states fail to pick up the burden of legislation for children, she is forced to go back to the national government in search of support. Notice how, once that groundwork is laid, the fight shifts to defending *her* version of the bill against the proposals of others. Finally, notice the challenges that an interest group head faces in drafting legislation in a manner that accomplishes goals, represents an acceptable compromise to potential opponents, and most importantly, keeps all of the elements of the supporting coalition together. As you will see, this last element proves to be the biggest challenge to Marian Wright Edelman.

GEORGE BUSH   Republican nominee for
president in 1988.

MICHAEL DUKAKIS   Democratic nominee
for president in 1988.

MARIAN WRIGHT EDELMAN   Head of the
Children's Defense Fund.

RICHARD NIXON   President of the United
States, 1969–1974.

RONALD REAGAN   President of the United
States, 1981–1989.

▶ . . . The Children's Defense Fund was started in 1973, when the Edelmans
were still living in Boston. A lot of ideas that had been germinating in Marian's
mind since the days of the Mississippi Head Start project came to fruition in this
new undertaking, which was designed to cut through the barriers of race and
class by focussing on the needs of children throughout the country, especially
poor children.* Her funding came from private foundations; C.D.F. has never
sought or received government funds. With help from her extensive network
of friends and admirers, both inside the government and in private life, she built
a staff and began to publish impeccably documented reports on child health,
nutrition, day care, and on other children's issues—reports that impressed more
than one information-overloaded congressman as models of their kind.

Marian was spending more than a day a week in Washington by then. Paul
Smith, C.D.F.'s chief statistician and data analyst, and one of the first people she
hired, likes to describe Marian as the ultimate outsider, someone who firmly
believes that you can influence the political system more effectively if you are
not a part of it, but in another sense she has been a Washington insider from
the time she started going up there from Mississippi to talk to legislators. There
is an easy friendliness about her—a warmth and an effervescent humor that can
disarm the most determined of her adversaries. She also has "an absolutely superb strategic and tactical sense, a real smell for how to get things done there,"
Peter Edelman says. "She understands how the system works. She's as tough
and determined as anyone can be, but always within the rules of the system."

There have been times when she gave every appearance of relishing a good
fight. It was Marian Edelman who was responsible for one of the key pieces of
evidence against George Harold Carswell, the Florida judge whom Nixon nominated to the Supreme Court in 1970. After the all-out battle that had ended with
the Senate's refusal to confirm Judge Clement F. Haynsworth, Nixon's previous
nominee, not many people thought that that body would have the stamina to
oppose Carswell. "Everybody said you couldn't do anything about it, even
though Carswell was much worse than Haynsworth, and that made me mad,"
Marian told me. "I just had a visceral reaction." She knew quite a lot about Cars-

---

* Begun in 1965 as one of Lyndon Johnson's War on Poverty programs, Head Start provides educational and health services to poor preschool children.

well, having helped to circulate a memorandum on him the year before, when Nixon elevated him from the District Court to the Fifth Circuit Court of Appeals. She knew that his rulings as a district judge had been repeatedly reversed and censured by the higher court for their blatant segregationist bias. This time, she sent one of her staff assistants down to Tallahassee to see what he could find out. The assistant came up with a copy of the legal papers changing a public golf course in Tallahassee into a private club—a transparent device to prevent blacks from playing there. The papers were signed by Carswell, as one of the incorporators. Marian and her associates produced a number of other damaging reports on Carswell's judicial record, and when Senate opposition to the nomination did get moving she played a highly active part in persuading certain influential senators to join it. Carswell's defeat came as a source of keen satisfaction to her in a very bad time.

The Nixon Administration was by no means deaf to the needs of poor people. A large increase in federal spending on food programs substantially alleviated hunger during the nineteen-seventies. Slow growth was registered in Head Start, for which the Children's Defense Fund lobbied hard in Congress each year. The conservative political climate of the Nixon years ruled out another attempt at a comprehensive child-care bill, however, and it soon became clear that the prospects for this sort of domestic legislation were not going to improve much under President Ford or President Carter. "Carter was very conservative fiscally, and it's hard to get a Democratic Congress to go against a Democratic President," Marian told me. "We tried a number of things during those years, but we had a very tough time of it. We decided to concentrate on trying to expand Head Start significantly. By that time, Head Start was being perceived in Congress as very successful, but it had never had any really big increases in funding. It was still at four hundred and twenty-five million a year when the Carter Administration came in. Over the next four years, we helped persuade Congress to move Head Start to nine hundred million. We also went after child welfare and child health improvement. We missed on child health, but Congress enacted a child-welfare bill in 1980, without a lot of help from the Administration. The Administration put its big effort into creating a separate Department of Education, and we had to spend a lot of our time fighting to keep Head Start out of it."

The Reagan revolution put an abrupt end to this period of small gains. The new Republican team made its position clear on domestic issues: twenty years of social legislation had created a welfare state, whose bureaucratic inertia had sapped the economy and increased the very problems it was meant to solve. "In the war on poverty, poverty won," the President quipped. Dismantling the welfare programs of four previous Administrations was high on the agenda of Reaganomics. Marian Edelman has described the process in a 1987 book, "Families in Peril" (Harvard), which was based on C.D.F. research:

The biggest cuts came in 1981, thanks to President Reagan's budget requests. That year Congress enacted cuts in programs for low-income families and children that totaled $10 billion . . . for 1982 and a roughly equivalent amount for each subsequent year. Among the casualties were Medicaid, Maternal and Child Health programs, family-planning services, child immunizations, Aid to Families With Dependent Children, food stamps, school lunches and breakfasts, public housing for poor people, compensatory education to enable disadvantaged youngsters to keep up in school, and day-care services to enable poor and single and teen mothers to work.

The results were immediate and brutal. In 1980, 1981, and 1982, according to C.D.F., more than a million children a year were added to the poverty rolls in this country. By 1987, the total had reached twelve and a half million children—one in five. "Mr. Reagan came in and tried to repeal or weaken everything, every single federal children's program and every program protecting the poor," Marian said recently. "It was like being caught in an avalanche. We decided that our first priority was to keep those laws on the books. In some cases, it had taken decades to get them there. Let the money go for the time being, we figured, but preserve the laws. We began to lobby very hard on the Hill. We lost a lot of money in appropriations, but the laws are still basically in place. And then, in 1984, we began to turn the corner. Poverty was increasing in the country, and there was the new phenomenon of homelessness. Congress stopped cutting in 1984, and began to give some of the money back to the poor and to children." Intensive lobbying by the Children's Defense Fund in 1984, 1986, and 1988 was a major factor in Congress's decision to expand Medicaid services to poor children. C.D.F. was able to show that increasing health services to children actually led to decreased government costs in doctor and hospital bills further down the line—an economic argument that has proved persuasive with Congress.

The Edelmans had moved back to Washington early in 1979. They bought the house in Cleveland Park, with a shady garden in back for Baptist Bar Mitzvahs and family get-togethers. Peter, who had spent the three previous years in Albany as the director of the New York State Division for Youth, was now teaching at the Georgetown University Law Center. Marian was speaking more and more widely on children's issues while continuing to direct the flow of C.D.F.'s research and advocacy. The Fund has attracted over the years a remarkably intelligent and highly motivated staff, which now numbers about ninety. While Marian is clearly the leader, the atmosphere there is collegial, informal, and very hardworking. "It's a place where self-starters do well," Sara Rosenbaum, a lawyer who is the director of programs and policy at C.D.F., says. "If people don't take hold on their own, Marian just loses confidence in them, and eventually they leave. She has no time for people who don't know what they're doing." C.D.F. has steadily widened the range of its concerns, going beyond the issues of health, family income, and early-childhood education to investigate homelessness, child abuse and child neglect (some two million two hundred thousand cases were reported in 1986), runaway youths (more than a million per year at last report), and the appalling epidemic of teen-age pregnancy. "We had always focussed more on young children," Marian told me. "But then, one day in 1983, we were putting together a book called 'Black and White Children in America,' and I saw from our own statistics that fifty-five and a half per cent of all black babies were born out of wedlock, a great many of them to teen-age girls. It just hit me over the head—that situation *insured* black child poverty for the next generation. I felt enormous guilt that I had missed seeing it until then."

Teen-age pregnancy became a high-priority issue at C.D.F. in 1983. Independent research had shown that half a million babies were born each year to teen-age girls in America, at a cost to the public (in welfare and medical payments) of a billion four hundred million dollars a year. The assumption that this was primarily a black problem turned out to be dead wrong. While the rate of teen-age pregnancy was higher among blacks than among whites, many more white than black babies were born to teen-agers each year, and the pregnancy rate for white teen-agers alone was shockingly high—more than twice the rate of pregnancy among both black and white teen-agers in Canada, France, or England. One of the two common denominators in all these cases, black and white, was poverty (the other was training in basic skills), and the all but inevitable result was a continuation of poverty. A pregnant teen-ager is more likely to drop out of school, to be unemployed, to go on welfare; less likely to get proper prenatal care (or any prenatal care at all), to provide adequately for the infant, or to function as a responsible parent. A teen-age parent earns approximately half the lifetime income of a woman who waits until the age of twenty to have her first child, according to C.D.F. In addition to calling attention to this problem in its reports and press releases, C.D.F. launched a sophisticated advertising campaign aimed at teen-agers, with posters, radio spots, and other media warnings about the long-term consequences of sex too early and sex without birth control. Its approach is pragmatic, not moralistic. The Moral Majority can put its faith in abstinence or "Christian marriage," but C.D.F. reflects Marian Edelman's belief that the world must be dealt with as it is.

About two years ago, Marian began to sense a change in the political climate. "Child care was becoming a middle-class white women's issue, for one thing," she said, "There had been this vast shift of women into the work force, and you heard more and more talk about child care. But it was not only that. In going around the country, as I do, I just found more receptivity to dealing with the truth than I'd found in all my twenty years in Washington. In spite of the illusions of many of our political leaders, the critical mass in this country seemed to me to realize that the future is really in danger, and that there are going to have to be some hard choices made. I found people listening and hearing in new ways. They actually seemed relieved to hear you say these things." It seemed to Marian that the time had come, after seventeen years, for another shot at a comprehensive child-care bill, and this became a primary C.D.F. legislative goal in 1988.

The Act for Better Child Care was developed almost entirely in the C.D.F. offices, on C Street, not far from the Capitol. "There are lots of organizations that are involved with child care, but we view ourselves as the scut workers and technicians," Marian told me. "We have the staff to do the technical, detailed work. Our child-care staff, working with the legal staff, would go out to different groups and organizations around the country and see where they were on the issue, and then come back here to work on the development process." No major snags or disagreements were encountered in the drafting process, which took nearly a year and involved discussions with a hundred and seventy different organizations or individuals—a much broader coalition than the one put together for the 1971 bill.* The result was a highly complex bill whose most prominent feature was a huge federal commitment—two and a half billion dollars the first year—to be allocated in two ways. Part of it would help low- and moderate-income families pay for child care, and the other part would go toward improving the quality of child care for all families. The provisions for establishing minimum standards of quality for all day-care programs receiving federal funds were the most difficult to write and, in Marian's view, they would be the most difficult for Congress to pass. The bill, which would be administered by states, would have allowed parents to choose among a wide range of child-care sources, but in order to receive federal funds each program, whether it was run by the school system, by the local community, by a church, or by a neighborhood woman in her own house, would have to meet the government's standards of health, safety, and quality.

Senator Christopher Dodd, a liberal Democrat from Connecticut, Senator John Chafee, a moderate Republican from Rhode Island, and Senator Alan Cranston, a liberal Democrat from California, introduced A.B.C. in the Senate on November 19, 1987. It was presented to the House on the same day by Representatives Dale Kildee, a Democrat from Michigan, and Olympia J. Snowe, a Republican from Maine. A lot of support for it had already been established in both chambers, thanks to energetic lobbying by the A.B.C. coalition. Forty-four senators supported it, and the bill had a hundred and seventy-two co-sponsors in the House. The main problem for this new bill, as for every other, was to get

---

* In 1971 Edelman worked with a coalition of teachers, welfare-rights advocates, churches, and women's groups on a child-development bill designed particularly to protect and expand Head Start. It passed both houses of Congress but was vetoed by President Nixon.

it on the calendar for consideration by the relevant congressional committees, and then to get it out of committee and onto the floor. "Conventional political wisdom says there's no chance of getting this to a vote in this session," Marian told me last May. "It's a major new piece of domestic legislation, it costs two and a half billion dollars, and we're in an election year—besides which, this is a short legislative session. On the other hand, conventional political wisdom has been wrong on just about everything this year. I'm starting to feel that the real danger, since day care has become such a hot political issue, is that we may get the wrong bill passed." She was referring to Orrin Hatch's child-care bill, which had been introduced two months before A.B.C.; this one would cost far less than A.B.C. (three hundred and seventy-five million dollars in the first year), and the money would go to the states to use in any way they saw fit, provided that it was for child care. "Hatch's is a politically cosmetic bill that talks about the private sector and has no minimum standards," Marian said.

George Bush announced his child-care plan on July 24th, shortly before the Democratic National Convention. He proposed what he called a "children's tax credit," which would give low-income parents a tax refund or credit of up to a thousand dollars a year for each child. The program, whose cost was set at two billion two hundred million dollars a year, would "put choice in the hands of parents, not in the hands of the all-powerful state," Bush said. His language was aimed at the right wing, but the proposal itself was aimed at women voters, who were showing a preference for Governor Dukakis in the polls. To Marian Edelman, it sounded like another significant acceptance of the government's role in making child care available to those who needed it. The money was clearly inadequate—proper child care costs at least three thousand dollars a year per child—and it would not touch the thousands of mothers on welfare who paid no taxes, but the proposal was a step in the right direction. Marian saw Bush's plan as a potential complement to A.B.C., not an alternative. A program that included tax credits among the range of options available to low-income parents, she felt, would provide an even stronger base for a truly comprehensive child-care system. President Reagan, who gave his blessing to Bush's tax-credit proposal, had indicated earlier that he would veto the A.B.C. bill if Congress passed it. "I'd love to give him that opportunity," Marian said when I questioned her about it. "If he wants to do that, in an election year . . . It's not impossible that we could override the veto, and what a terrific political issue that would be."

While A.B.C. was working its way through the committees—there were hearings on it in the House Education and Labor Committee in February and April, and the Senate's Labor and Human Resources Committee in March and June—a major and completely unexpected problem arose. The National Education Association, which had been part of the A.B.C. coalition from the start, had managed to insert in the draft bill some very severe restrictions on the use of A.B.C. funds by church-based day-care centers, restrictions that went beyond any existing civil-rights law: there could be no religious symbols displayed in classrooms, and religious affiliation could play no part in the acceptance of children or the recruitment of staff members. Marian Edelman was not aware of these insertions at first. They had been put in after the drafting process was supposedly completed. "I learned about them when I got a call from the Catholics saying, 'What are you *doing?*'" she said. "The N.E.A.'s provisions would have basically excluded the Catholics and some other church groups from participating in child care—and churches are the largest single provider in the country. Altogether, they provide about a third of all child-care centers. We had simply stumbled into this terrible briar patch of church-state, and a lot of us had to spend the next two months trying to work out a compromise." The compromise was finally achieved, in meetings with the Senate and House committees, after lengthy consultations with members of the A.B.C. coalition. In the amended draft, church-based centers would be forbidden to engage in "any sectarian purpose or activity," but the N.E.A.'s provisions for banning religious symbols and against religious considerations in hiring staff were dropped.

Time now was running short. As a result of the two-month delay, A.B.C. was not reported out of committee to the full Senate until July 27th, and the House received it on August 10th. Congress was devoting most of its attention to the Conventions by then, and so was the Children's Defense Fund. Delegates to both Conventions were bombarded with C.D.F. literature, and children's issues figured prominently in the rhetoric and the platforms of both parties.

The 1988 Presidential campaign was as much of a disappointment to Marian Edelman as it was to the country at large. George Bush occasionally referred to child care and child health in his efforts to project his image of a "kinder, gentler America," but Michael Dukakis, who had given a lukewarm endorsement to A.B.C. "in concept," without saying he was for the bill itself, never really committed himself on the issue or contributed to the debate on it. Marian had hoped for more from the Democratic candidate. The most shameful moment in the whole election campaign, she said later, came when Dukakis appeared at the Neshoba County Fair, in Mississippi, on August 4th, twenty-four years after the bodies of Michael Schwerner, Andrew Goodman, and James Chaney were found, and failed to refer to the murders or to mention the victims' names.

At the end of September, the National Education Association announced that it could not accept the church-state compromise that had been worked out so laboriously, and was withdrawing its support from the bill. Several other groups within the original coalition also pulled out, among them the National Congress of Parents and Teachers and the American Jewish Committee. These defections led to a flurry of political infighting on the Hill. After a certain point, Marian became convinced that the real issue for the National Education Association was not church-state at all. The N.E.A., which represents nearly two million public-school teachers, is a very powerful interest group. C.D.F. had done battle with it a decade earlier, when the N.E.A. lobbied to have Head Start put under the newly created Department of Education. "The light bulb went on in my head that this was really about funding and about control," Marian told me. "The N.E.A. people sat through the drafting process on A.B.C. for a whole year and never raised the church-state issue as a major concern. But it's clear now that the growth sector is going to be in early-childhood care—it has to be. And so the real question is: Who's going to control the money? The N.E.A. feels that if there's going to be a two-and-a-half-billion-dollar investment in early-childhood care, then why shouldn't the schools control it? In my opinion, the church-state issue was nothing more than a Trojan horse."

Nevertheless, the A.B.C. coalition had started to come unstuck over an extremely touchy political issue, thus undercutting the bill's chances in an election-year Congress. Although there appeared to be more than enough votes in both houses to pass A.B.C. if it came to the floor, the Democratic leadership managed things so that it did not. Senator Robert C. Byrd, the Majority Leader, decided to attach A.B.C. to a legislative package that included two other bills, one providing for parental leaves of absence from work when the mother gave birth or a child was seriously ill, the other having to do with measures to forbid child pornography. This packaging greatly complicated matters and added new opposition forces. The Chamber of Commerce was against the parental-leave bill. Senator Robert Dole initiated a filibuster against the package. A motion of cloture was brought to cut off debate, and, to nearly everyone's surprise, a number of Republicans voted with the Democrats for cloture. ("They were very smart," Marian said afterward. "The Republicans didn't want to be blamed for killing A.B.C.") A second cloture vote, to cut off debate on amendments, narrowly failed, however, and at that point the leadership decided to pull the bill from the floor.

Marian took the setback philosophically. "It is still a good thing to have done," she told me. "It is now on the front burner with the new Administration, and a lot of things have already been settled. There were four main hurdles in getting any new child-care bill. The first was the federal role, and that is no longer an issue. The second was whether you could expect a significant investment, and once Mr. Bush had come in with his two-billion-two-hundred-million-dollar proposal we were over that one. The third issue was church-state, which was not anticipated, but now at least we know it's there. The last issue is whether or not there will be federal standards, which is a very big issue and one I feel very strongly about. But it's nice to have two hurdles instead of four." (Since she said that, the National Education Association and virtually all other parties to the A.B.C. coalition have agreed to new compromise provisions regarding church-state, and Senator Hatch, after intricate negotiations with Senator Dodd, has joined the team and become A.B.C.'s chief Republican co-sponsor. This greatly enhances the bill's prospects in the legislative battles that lie ahead.)

"One of the gaps in our approach was that we did not spend enough time with the business community, and now we're remedying that," Marian went on to say. "I'm hiring someone full time to work with the Chamber of Commerce and the National Association of Manufacturers, among other business groups. The business community is not our enemy on the bill—it's coming to understand that there is a bottom-line relationship between child care, on the one hand, and absenteeism and stress and worker productivity, on the other. American Express, for example, is now sponsoring a public-education campaign on child care. Campbell Soup and a lot of other companies have decided it's a business issue. The Committee for Economic Development recently issued a very important report: it recognized that children are a shrinking proportion of our population as it ages, and that unless preventive investment in early childhood is made a national policy our future work force will be disproportionately poor, unhealthy, untrained, and uneducated, and we will not be able to be competitive in the global arena. As the C.E.D. report pointed out, this country can't continue to compete when a fifth of our kids live in poverty and a third grow up in ignorance. Investing in them is not a national luxury or a national choice; it's a national necessity. If the foundation of your house is crumbling, you don't say you can't afford to fix it, while you're building astronomically expensive fences to protect it from outside enemies. The issue is not are we going to pay—it's are we going to pay now, up front, or are we going to pay a whole lot more later. Anyway, A.B.C. has been reintroduced in the new session. A lot of things are changing, a lot of new elements are appearing, and the new mishmash may very well lead to a broader, better bill than the one we had. We'll have a tax credit. We want Head Start to serve all of the eligible kids, instead of the eighteen per cent it serves now. We'll have a different set of compromises, and a lot of new pieces coming together."

The sense of urgency is never absent from her thinking. Children are dying of poverty every day in this country, she says. They die in accidents that occur when no adult is watching over them; they die at birth, because of insufficient or nonexistent prenatal health care; they die of malnutrition, or drugs, or preventable diseases—but the root cause is poverty. The latest National Center for Health Statistics report on teen-age pregnancy is very disturbing: it shows that the rate of births to young black women (under fifteen) has been going up since 1983. "This indicates a greater degree of hopelessness," Marian says. "What scares me is that today people don't have the sense that they can struggle and change things. There's more real despair now. In the sixties, in Mississippi, it just never occurred to us that we weren't going to win. We always had the feeling that there was something we could do, and that there was hope. We felt in control of our lives. My sixties were not the sixties some people remember, of violence and rude behavior. My sixties were disciplined about change, with old people and young people behaving in really responsible ways. It was a wonderful time to be alive. Martin King was an active, day-to-day presence in our lives. He's deified today, but what I remember is his talking to us about how scared he was, and telling us to keep moving. 'If you can't fly, run,' he said. 'If you can't run, walk. If you can't walk, crawl, but by all means keep moving.'"

Epilogue

This selection ends on a note of hope. Edelman's group had succeeded in making child care a major priority in Congress and appeared to be on the verge of removing the obstacles that had prevented passage of a major bill. Moreover, in the 1988 presidential campaign, both candidates made child care a priority. In fact, George Bush proposed a major child-care bill of over two billion dollars. In 1990, however, when Congress passed the Family and Medical Leave bill, which would have provided unpaid family leave to care for newborns and ill family members, President Bush vetoed the bill, saying that it would harm American economic competitiveness. Instead, he called for employers to provide such benefits voluntarily.

Thus, for Marian Edelman, it is back to work. The political process never ends; it simply pauses while the forces muster for the next battle.

8.2

The story of the creation of the Tax Reform Act of 1986 reveals the influence that interest groups have in Congress. After Ronald Reagan's overwhelming victory in the 1984 presidential election, the White House tried to reorient party politics by placing the notion of tax reform on the agenda. The goals were simple: reduce the overall tax burden of a large number of Americans and make it simpler for them to file returns. The electoral payoffs for the party that could claim responsibility for this reform would be enormous. And all that stood in the way was every single interest group in the nation that benefited from tax loopholes in the existing legislation.

The selection opens with Senator Bob Packwood, a moderate Republican from Oregon and chairman of the Senate Finance Committee, trying to ram his vision of tax reform through the Senate. Knowing that it would be difficult to craft a new bill without granting a new set of tax loopholes to powerful interest groups (which would in turn scuttle the possibility of genuine tax reform) Packwood had sat down in March 1986 with his top aide, Bill Diefenderfer, to formulate a most risky legislative strategy. Facing re-election for the Senate and aware that he would have to answer to his constituents on the promise of tax reform, Packwood had proposed a series of minimum tax levels and the repeal of a few current deductions rather than rewriting the entire income tax code. This stripped-down version of the bill could still be called tax reform and was more doable in the few months before the November election. Thus, he and Diefenderfer had formulated a plan that called for reductions in the maximum individual tax rates—ranging from 15 to 27 percent, and a maximum 33 percent tax for corporations. Packwood forged a working bloc of thirty-two senators around that proposal, the so-called 15-27-33 group, and thought he had a good chance of getting his proposal passed.

Politics Is Local

Jeffrey H. Birnbaum and Alan S. Murray

As we join the story, Senator Packwood has just achieved a miraculous unanimous victory for his bill in the Senate Finance Committee. In less than two weeks he had taken a tax reform bill that was all but dead, repackaged it, and steered it through a contentious committee. In the words of then–Majority Leader Robert Dole, the bill had gone "from immovable to unstoppable." All that remained was final Senate passage.

As former Speaker of the House Tip O'Neill once observed, however, "All politics is local." By this he meant that whatever the legislation, members of Congress care only about its effect on their own districts and most prominent constituents. Moreover, legislators anxious to get re-elected pay a lot of attention to lobbyists, who represent interest groups that give financial and political support to congressional campaigns. The game for Packwood, then, was to prevent other senators from adding individual tax loopholes that would benefit certain special interests but endanger the overall bill.

As you will see, in fact, several hurdles had to be cleared before passage. Packwood's committee had sent the legislation to the Senate floor indicating that no amendments would be permitted, thus preventing the rush for change that would destroy it. It was left to Packwood, however, as the chair of the committee, to decide (1) which proposed amendments to accept in the form of "transition rules"—amendments that are supposed to ease the burden on certain social groups and industries who would be hurt by the new bill; (2) which amendments proposed by other senators to oppose (in this case it was supposed to be all of them); and (3) which amendments to accept as part of various deals (without admitting that it was permissible to amend the bill). As you watch Packwood at work, remember that his goals are not just to get some version of the bill passed in the Senate and to position the bill for negotiation with the House in the inevitable conference committee. He also wants to pass some version of the bill that President Reagan will sign into law and to make sure that he gets his share of the glory for whatever bill becomes law.

BILL BRADLEY   Tax reform proponent; Democratic senator from New Jersey.

ROBERT DOLE   Senate majority leader; Republican from Kansas.

HOWARD METZENBAUM   Crusader against special interests; Democratic senator from Ohio.

BOB PACKWOOD   Chair of the Senate Finance Committee; Republican from Oregon.

WILLIAM ROTH   Tax reduction proponent; Republican senator from Delaware.

▶ The night after his unanimous victory, [Bob] Packwood was on a plane headed home. The senator's Republican primary was less than two weeks away, but he rested comfortably during the six-hour journey, secure in the knowledge that he had left his biggest reelection problem behind him. After weeks of dawn-to-midnight days, he had turned a huge potential liability into an important political asset. Prior to that flight, the Oregon senator had heard only complaints about tax reform in general and about his earlier bill in particular. But now that was all changed. Passenger after passenger walked up the narrow airplane aisle to congratulate him for his good work. "Thank God somebody's done it," one traveler said as he shook Packwood's outstretched hand.

On the ground, Packwood got the same reaction. The criticism that had been poured on his head for his failed effort the previous month was gone. Instead of peppering Packwood with complaints about his huge campaign hoard and his giveaways to special interests, the local news media began to praise him. Prior to the triumphant final vote, a cartoon in the *Oregonian,* the state's major newspaper, had ridiculed a devilish-looking Packwood for having "seventeen versions of tax reform." Afterward, a follow-up cartoon pictured a more benign-appearing Packwood on Bill Bradley's shoulders throwing a tax-bill basketball through a hoop as the press exclaimed, "Incredible shot!" *Oregonian* editorials went so far as to concede that Packwood had "confounded the skeptics, including us" by producing a bill that would mean "real reform."

"There is special interest after special interest that is hit in this bill," Packwood gloated, pointing out that many of the injured groups "contributed to my campaign." It was a true boast. Packwood's victory was encouraging proof that moneyed interests could not always buy their way to success in Congress.

For the first time, polls unearthed a budding interest in tax reform among the populace. A *Wall Street Journal*–NBC poll showed a significant rise in public optimism about the effects of reform. Although the public still worried about losing favorite deductions, 47 percent of those asked in June 1986—after the Finance Committee had finished its work—said they thought the legislation would help them personally, up from 39 percent in November 1985, during the Ways and Means markup.* The House bill actually provided the average tax-payer with a bigger tax cut than the Finance Committee package, but it was the strong allure of lower rates that apparently won over public sentiment.

Despite the swelling support, however, the battle for tax reform was far from over. The bill's next hurdle, the Senate floor, had always promised to be one of its toughest challenges. Although the Senate operates with a veneer of gentle-manly decorum, it is often an unruly place. Its members were privately referred to as the "animals" by Majority Leader [Robert] Dole, whose tough task it was to keep them under control. Tax bills, in particular, had traditionally caused near-chaos in the Senate, as the senators struggled to win special favors for their constituents. The whole idea of tax reform was an affront to their way of operat-ing; it threatened to take away many of the goodies that they had tucked away in the income-tax code for the benefit of the folks back home. Holding together the fragile tax-reform package on the floor would not be easy. As Bradley put it: "Sometimes the Senate's a little like jazz. You can't predict what's going to happen."

The founding fathers intended the Senate to be the great deliberative body of the legislature. Statesmen like Daniel Webster, John Calhoun, and Stephen Douglas made their mark there. The grand oratory of those nineteenth-century senators had become rare by the time of the tax debate in 1986, but long-winded rhetoric had not. Modern-day senators were the sort of people, one Senate aide observed, who could give a speech in the shower. Unlike House members, who had to walk to a microphone before speaking, each senator had a microphone at his or her own desk and could rise at any moment to join in the debate. For anyone who watched the Senate, the sight was a familiar one: A senator would rise, button his jacket as if by reflex, raise his chin, and then begin. The speeches could go on for hours. The light at the top of the Capitol dome would often be seen shining late into the night, signifying that the Senate was still in session.

Unlike the House, the Senate has few rules to limit debate, or to restrict amendments. Senators may filibuster a bill—talk endlessly to prevent a vote from happening. They may delay a bill by offering amendment after amend-ment. Former Majority Leader Mike Mansfield once observed that a single obsti-nate senator "can tie up the Senate for days, and if he allies himself with a few other senators, he can tie up the Senate for weeks."

In such an unrestricted environment, tax bills were open season. During the 1981 tax bill, the senators debated for 102 hours and adopted eighty-one amendments. During the 1982 tax bill they debated for thirty-four hours and adopted forty-nine amendments. And they debated the 1984 tax bill for 111 hours, adopting eighty-six amendments. Offering a big tax-overhaul bill on the

---

*See Selection 4.5, "A Season of Governing," for a discussion of markup.

Senate floor was like tossing a piece of bread to a flock of seagulls: Everyone wanted a bite.

Although the course through the Senate would be perilous, the tax-reform bill had several important forces working in its favor.

First of all, the 20–0 Finance Committee vote had convinced highly paid business lobbyists that the tax bill now had unstoppable momentum. Their first response to the vote was shellshock. "Terror and disbelief is the reaction," said Wayne Thevenot, president of the National Realty Committee, an association of big real estate developers. "At least our people have nice, big buildings of their own to jump from." But most business lobbyists quickly concluded that it was pointless to keep fighting the bill. The Senate Finance Committee had been their last chance, and they had lost. As DuPont Chairman Richard Heckert put it: "At some point, you stop lying in the street and kicking and screaming, because nobody gives a damn anyway."

With tax reform clearly on its way to passage, the most savvy lobbyists decided it was time to jump on board. Packwood's bill, for most of them, was the lesser of two evils. It raised corporate taxes by $100 billion, while the House bill raised corporate taxes by $140 billion. That gave corporate lobbyists $40 billion worth of reasons to support Packwood's plan. Overnight, almost every business group in town became ardent supporters of the Finance Committee proposal. Even [lobbyist] Charls Walker, who had fought tax reform at every turn, now saw the futility of opposing the entire effort, and voiced support. "The Packwood tax plan deserves early passage," he said.

The most virulent opponents of the effort became born-again reformers. During the Ways and Means debate in November 1985, the Chamber of Commerce of the U.S.A. said the House tax bill "would be disastrous for the American economy, American business, and the American worker." But the Finance Committee bill, it said a half-year later, would "on balance have a positive effect on long-term economic growth and job creation." Likewise, the National Association of Manufacturers, which thought the House bill would "pose extremely high risks for the economy," urged the Senate to pass the Finance Committee bill—without alteration.

The high-sounding rhetoric masked the real reason for supporting the bill— it was the lobbyists' last chance to save themselves and at least some of their favorite tax breaks. Every interest group in Washington wanted to show support for the measure in hopes of currying favor with Packwood and his committee. The Senate bill, they knew, would not be the final bill. The ultimate fight would come later, after Senate passage, when representatives of the Ways and Means Committee and the Finance Committee sat down together to reconcile the two bills in a House-Senate conference. Many corporate interest groups already had made an enemy of [House Ways and Means Committee Chair Dan] Rostenkowski by fighting his bill in the House. They still had a chance, they thought, to make amends with Packwood and win some concessions in the final negotiating.

Another factor that helped the cause of reform was the fact that the bill would be one of the first major Senate debates broadcast on television. The House had been on the air for years, but the stodgy Senate had resisted until the summer of 1986. The Senate was an exclusive club, with customs and practices that senators feared might seem odd to the outside world. Television was viewed as an undignified intrusion, especially by old-timers like Senator [Russell] Long. But even the U.S. Senate could not block progress forever, and it finally agreed to a trial run. As the debate on tax reform approached, senators hired media consultants to spruce up their wardrobes (red ties and blue shirts were preferred) and to coif and dye their hair. Packwood even checked the camera locations to see what spot on the semicircular floor would afford him the most flattering angle. (As it turned out, the place he chose was the wrong one. It was too close to the brown leather couches in the rear of the chamber where staffers always sat; as Packwood spoke, a constant stream of scurrying aides could be seen over his shoulder.) Thanks in part to the prying eye of television, members were leery of appearing to obstruct reform. They feared that their usual long harangues might look unseemly to the public. Few wanted to risk appearing in full color on the evening news as a defender of "special interests."

The prospects for reform also got a boost from the new Gramm-Rudman budget law that had been enacted a year earlier. Under the law, amendments that increased the budget deficit could be blocked by an objection from any member of the Senate. For technical reasons, that portion of the budget law was not in place in the early summer of 1986 when the tax debate began, but the spirit of Gramm-Rudman prevailed, and the senators were under pressure to keep all amendments revenue neutral. That meant senators wishing to restore a tax break would also have to propose a way to pay for that break. It was a new discipline for the senators. A similar rule had helped the bill win approval during the final day's proceedings in the Finance Committee, and it was sure to help the measure on the Senate floor as well. Often, the Senate could tie itself in knots over the most minor tax legislation, but with this new requirement of revenue neutrality, the chances of approving major amendments diminished significantly.

To help propel the bill through the Senate, Packwood began organizing his rapidly growing band of supporters. Once again, he turned to Bill Bradley for help. Thus far in the tax-reform debate, Bradley had nudged his brainchild along mostly by giving credit to others: first to the president, then to Rostenkowski, and then to Packwood during the second and ultimately successful phase of the Finance Committee markup. "There's plenty of credit to go around," he was fond of saying. As a basketball player, Bradley said, "I always got as big a kick out of giving an assist as making a basket." Now it was time for Bradley to go to the hoop himself. He became a key coalition builder among

Democrats on the Senate floor. With typical energy, Bradley reached out—one at a time—to his fellow Democrats to recruit them to join a block of tax-reform backers.

Bradley also worked to convince Packwood to adopt an important strategy: to build a coalition to oppose *all* amendments. Packwood had initially thought his block of supporters should be sworn only to oppose amendments that were paid for by raising rates, but Bradley urged a tougher stand. He reasoned that any exception to a solid front against all changes to the bill would lead to the disintegration of the entire pro-reform coalition. An amendment that saved one tax break, he argued, might be paid for by eliminating a break that was important to other members of the group, causing dangerous schisms. The bill was fragile, and keeping it from falling apart was going to be a delicate task. As a show of good faith, Bradley even abandoned his own plans for an amendment to kill the oil drillers' tax-shelter loophole.

Packwood believed amendments would probably be inevitable on such a major bill; nevertheless, he bought Bradley's recommendation. The two men began rounding up other senators who were willing to pledge to fight every amendment. [Treasury Secretary James] Baker and [Deputy Treasury Secretary Richard] Darman also persuaded the president to back the no-amendment strategy. By the end of May, just three weeks after the Finance Committee reported its bill to the Senate floor, Packwood and Bradley had convinced thirty-two of the Senate's one hundred members to stand with them.

To help keep that block of senators together, and to gather even more votes, Packwood and Bradley sought to tap the growing support among lobbyists. Bradley had begun this process in early 1986, working closely with many of the same groups that had supported the Rostenkowski bill. He kept in contact with the CEO Tax Group and the Tax Reform Action Coalition—business groups that wanted a lower corporate rate—as well as "good government" groups, such as Common Cause and Citizens for Tax Justice, and also various anti-poverty groups. These groups became the nucleus for a far larger coalition patched together by Packwood and one of his top Finance Committee aides, Mary McAuliffe. The 15-27-33 coalition—which took its forgettable name from the all-important individual and corporate rates in the plan—grew rapidly. By the end of May, less than a month after the committee had approved its bill, the 15-27-33 coalition had expanded to well over six hundred companies and organizations, including some of the most vocal opponents of the House bill. For example, the Independent Petroleum Association of America and the General Contractors of America were members in good standing, and for good reason: Tax breaks precious to both groups were retained in the Finance Committee bill, but were curtailed by the House.

The pro-reform coalition was extremely diverse. It ranged from Amway Corporation to the Children's Defense Fund, from Church Women United to the Irish Distillers Group, from Philip Morris to the Consumer Federation of

America. There were eleven groups whose name began with the word *na-tional,* including the National Council of LaRaza, the National Puerto Rican Coalition, the National Black Child Development Institute and the National Co-alition of American Nuns. Another five began with the word *American,* includ-ing the American Association of University Women and the American Frozen Food Institute. The coalition even included the Sisters of the Humility of Mary. Only a few months earlier, Senator [William] Armstrong of Colorado had said of tax reform, "Nobody wants it." Now, the list of members of the 15-27-33 coali-tion made it look like everyone wanted it.

In late May, a week before the start of the Senate floor debate, Dole an-nounced that senators who sought to make major changes in the bill would simply be "out of luck." Tax reform had a good head of steam, and looked like it could chug right through the Senate. "In all the years I've been here," said Senator Paul Laxalt, Republican of Nevada, "I've never seen such unanimity on a piece of legislation. Most senators sense this is almost historic."

Still, tax overhaul had been burdened with problems and setbacks all along its way, and Bradley, for one, was taking nothing for granted. "You don't start worrying about the next season if you are heading to Boston to play the Celtics in the Eastern Final," the former New York Knick said. "You've got to get through the [Senate] floor. . . . Frankly, I'm very pleased that the bill is where it is, but it's still got a long way to go. And it's not over 'til it's over. Until the bill is finished, entrenched opposition always has a counteroffensive."

Faced with such strong support for the broad outlines of the Senate bill, many senators began shifting their attention to the smaller issues. The Finance Com-mittee bill was a massive document with hundreds of provisions. The amounts of money involved were so immense that provisions costing less than $100 million were referred to derisively by tax writers as "zero point one." Those costing less than $5 million were denoted simply by an asterisk. But the spare change of tax writers was a holy fortune to anyone else, and as the Senate floor debate approached, the scramble among senators and lobbyists to get some of that change became intense. Speaker [Thomas P.] O'Neill was fond of reminding his colleagues that "all politics is local." The grab for tax-bill favors was proof of that adage. Forgetting about the overarching significance of the tax-reform bill, senators worked hard to win special tax relief for certain friends back home.

The common practice for a Finance Committee chairman is to come to the floor with a kind of slush fund under his control for the purpose of dispensing transition rules. In past years, transition rules were included in the bill for the benefit of specific constituents, but were drafted in ways that would also aid others who were similarly situated. The tax-reform rules, however, were fre-quently written like rifle shots to benefit only the constituent companies or indi-viduals—and no one else. That meant that two companies or people with ex-actly the same tax situation could well be treated very differently under the bill.

The mere volume of these special handouts in the Senate alone also was unique at a staggering total of $5.5 billion. Still it was not enough. Every time Packwood ventured onto the Senate floor, his colleagues stuffed pieces of paper into his jacket pocket, with additional requests for transition rules.

All told, the Finance Committee bill granted generous transition rules to 174 beneficiaries. Many of them were corporations, such as Avon Products, General Motors, RCA, Pan American World Airways, MCI Communications, General Mills, and Control Data. Others were cities and municipal facilities such as the New Orleans Superdome and the University of Delaware. There also were some oddball winners, such as five biomedical researchers in Rochester, New York, and the estate of James H. W. Thompson, a wealthy silk merchant who mysteriously disappeared in Malaysia in 1967.

In addition to the transition rules, there were other narrow tax-law changes designed to benefit a few lucky taxpayers. Page Wodell was one of the biggest winners. A provision buried in the Finance Committee bill would save Wodell about $5 million. He had lost a bid in tax court to escape that much in tax on his grandmother's estate. Unwilling to call it quits, Wodell turned to his Yale University classmate, Senator [John] Chafee, who added the amendment to the Finance Committee bill. "It was just plain unfair," the Republican tax writer said of his schoolmate's problems.

The *Houston Chronicle* was also a winner. The Texas newspaper was owned by a tax-free foundation and was threatened by the 1969 law that prohibited such foundations from running large businesses. For seventeen years, the newspaper had been trying to get around the law. Texas Senator [Lloyd] Bentsen, a man who well understood the value of good relations with the press, was always happy to help. He had tried repeatedly to sponsor amendments exempting the *Chronicle* from the 1969 law, but his amendments had always been dropped. When the tax-reform bill came along in 1986, he decided to try his old chestnut again. "What would a tax bill be without the *Houston Chronicle* amendment?" joked John Salmon, the Ways and Means Committee's former chief counsel.

Then there was the "Marriott amendment," a name designed to convey the provision's importance to the hotel industry. Sponsored by Dole, who was a popular and well-compensated speaker at convention banquets, the amendment stated that "business meals provided as an integral part of certain convention programs would be fully deductible in 1987 and 1988." That meant that extravagant dinners at meetings in Las Vegas and Hawaii would be fully subsidized by taxpayers, while a salesman's working lunch would be limited to 80 percent.

Dole also secured an exception to protect the tax benefits for a giant renovation project in a blighted area in downtown Manhattan on behalf of the junior senator from New York, Alfonse D'Amato. On his own behalf, Dole won a special rule for the redevelopment of another downtown Manhattan—in his home state of Kansas.

Not all special-interest breaks were as easy to decipher as these. A time-worn tradition of transition rules was to camouflage their beneficiaries in indirect language. For example, General Motors was not named directly in the transition-rules sections of the bill. It was described as "an automobile manufacturer that was incorporated in Delaware on October 13, 1916." A rapid-transit line to Dulles International Airport was called "a mass-commuting facility that provides access to an international airport." A drilling project by an Alabama firm called Sonat was listed as "a binding contract entered into on October 20, 1984, for the purchase of six semi-submersible drilling units." And a tax break designed to attract outside investors to finance citrus farmers who suffered freeze damage was described this way:

> *The rules governing expensing of costs of replanting groves, orchards or vineyards destroyed by freezing or other natural disasters would be extended to replanting on land other than the land on which the plants were destroyed and to businesses having new owners who materially participate in the business so long as the new owners hold less than 50 percent interest.*

Transition rules and other specialized relief were an inescapable part of every congressional tax bill; most senators dipped into this pork barrel without hesitation. One senator, however—Democrat Howard Metzenbaum of Ohio—took it upon himself to crusade against the most unsavory of these favors. A self-made millionaire who earned his fortune in the parking-lot business, Metzenbaum had developed a reputation during a decade in the Senate as the liberal master of obstruction. He was the self-appointed guardian of the "general interest," and tax-bill provisions that benefited narrow business interests were among his favorite targets. He regularly fought the ones that he and his able aide, David Starr, deemed the most egregious. Dole liked to refer to the gadfly senator as the "Commissioner." On more than one occasion, Dole, when he was Finance Committee chairman, used the obstreperous Metzenbaum to winnow away tax subsidies that he had granted in his committee or on the floor, but he secretly wished to discard. "When you prepare an amendment or a bill, subconsciously you're thinking about Howard Metzenbaum," Senator [David] Pryor said. "Will it pass the Metzenbaum test?"

On the floor, the white-haired Ohioan unveiled a long list of what he considered the most disgraceful transition rules. For a bill that carried the title "reform," the list was startling. Senators had slipped in one provision after another benefiting small constituent groups and home-state employers. Senator [David] Boren had included an exemption from a multimillion-dollar pension-fund withdrawal penalty for Phillips Petroleum, which was a major employer in his home state of Oklahoma. Senator Long had sponsored an exemption from tax for a fund set up by Manville Corporation for victims of poisoning from one of its main products, asbestos. Senator Armstrong had championed a rule that allowed a small group of investors to save an estimated $1 million each by retaining special capital-gains treatment for their stake in a Colorado coal company.

Metzenbaum even took aim at a tax break for Bermuda that was traced to Packwood himself. Under existing law, convention trips to certain countries were deductible, but only if those countries gave the United States their banks' records for use in tax audits of American citizens. Bermuda had consistently refused to hand over such information. Nevertheless, the Finance Committee tax bill extended to Bermuda the special convention benefit. The Finance Committee staff claimed that the provision was inserted in the bill at the request of the White House because of "foreign-policy considerations." No doubt Packwood and his wife were fully briefed on the situation in July 1985, when they were flown to Bermuda in a government plane for a weekend of what a White House spokesman called "sensitive and important discussions."

Despite his crusading rhetoric, even the Commissioner did not walk away from the fray with unsoiled hands. Metzenbaum personally advocated transition rules for North Star Steel of Youngstown, the Cleveland Dome stadium, and convention centers in Columbus and Akron. In addition, he excluded from his published list of heinous transition rules the largest transition rule of the bunch, and surely the most controversial—the steel rule.

The steel provision was championed by Senator [John] Heinz at the urging of Packwood's aide, [Bill] Diefenderfer, a native Pennsylvanian. It provided to steel companies a $500 million refund of their unused investment tax credits. Steel companies at the time were suffering losses and therefore paid no tax, so their credits were worthless. The refund provision promised them ready cash in exchange for the extra tax breaks. Metzenbaum's home state of Ohio was filled with troubled steel mills; he steered clear of attacking that one.

The insertion of such a large transition rule raised the ire of several senators from states that were not big steel producers. Pryor was so angry that he wrote a letter of protest to Packwood. The steel break "looks bad, smells bad, and is bad," he said. Chafee called it "a major change in tax law that went beyond what I'd call a transition rule." Still, Packwood defended it and beat back what amounted to a halfhearted effort by Pryor to take it out. By holding tight to the provision, Packwood made some steel-state and steel-company friends for tax overhaul.

The Finance Committee was far from alone in hiding special giveaways in its tax bill. The Ways and Means reform bill, as well, was chock full of transition rules. Its most colorful example was sponsored by Representative J. J. Pickle, Democrat of Texas, and was dubbed the "turkey-buzzard amendment." Tucked away in the voluminous Ways and Means measure, the provision was worth $800,000 to Hill Country Life of Texas, an insurance company in Pickle's Austin district. The firm's emblem was a turkey buzzard and its motto seemed to fit transition-rule politics: "Keep turning over rocks and you'll eventually find some grubs."

"Grubs" such as the turkey-buzzard amendment sullied the noble intentions of tax reform, but these little tax favors kept the tax bill moving through Congress. The Treasury Department wisely turned its head when it came to the dirty business of negotiating transition rules. Even the most committed congressional reformers realized that these relatively small provisions were a necessary price to pay. If ten or fifteen billion dollars in temporary transition rules would enable Congress to close several hundred billions of dollars' worth of permanent tax loopholes, then they were willing to go along. Metzenbaum would continue his crusade, but with little success. The transition rules were a necessary evil; they would help assure passage of the bill.

The Senate debate began on June 4. It was a beautiful early summer day, before the stifling humidity of midsummer had set in. The first senators to speak made largely laudatory comments about the bill and its chances for rapid approval. Packwood called it "an opportunity that will not come this way again in a generation. It's not often this brass ring will swing by." But the rhetoric masked the serious challenges to the bill that lay ahead.

The most pressing problem involved IRAs [Individual Retirement Accounts]. Under existing law, workers could salt away as much as $2,000 in these retirement accounts each year and deduct the amount of the contribution. The Finance Committee bill proposed wiping out that deduction for people who were covered by employer-provided pension plans. IRAs were used by more than twenty-five million Americans to set aside money for retirement, and the Finance Committee's proposal would affect almost three quarters of them.

William Roth of Delaware was the IRA's most vocal supporter. A co-sponsor of the Kemp-Roth tax cuts of 1981, Roth believed that the government needed to encourage savings as a way to increase the pool of capital necessary to spur investment. He contended that IRAs, which were expanded in his 1981 bill, were one of the most important savings incentives in the federal tax code.

Economists as eminent as Federal Reserve Chairman Paul Volcker disputed the contention that IRAs instigated more savings. He and others speculated that IRAs, for the most part, only caused savings to be shifted from other accounts into IRAs. "It is hard to see an impact on the overall savings rate" from IRAs, Volcker once told a congressional hearing. "In fact, the personal savings rate has gone down" during the period since 1981.

The real importance of IRAs was political. Lawmakers judged them to be the one tax shelter in reach of the middle class. In fact, more than 45 percent of all IRA deductions were taken by taxpayers with adjusted gross incomes exceeding $40,000 a year, a group which accounted for less than 11 percent of the taxpaying public. But the "middle class" in political terms was far different from the middle class in purely economic terms. While the median income of a family of four in the United States hovered around $33,000 a year, members of Congress frequently defined the "middle" to include people whose incomes were considerably higher than that—$50,000, $60,000, even $100,000 a year. It was this group, lawmakers knew, who were politically active back home and who were most likely to make campaign contributions.

So, it was with good reason that Roth and others began to preach about the need to restore the IRA deduction, even on the first day of the tax-reform debate in the Senate. "A lot of solid, middle-class people—not rich people—use IRAs as a way of providing for their retirement," Roth asserted. Senator D'Amato of New York, led a separate group that also pushed to save the IRA. The determined D'Amato called the no-amendment effort "absolutely ludicrous. . . . I didn't get elected and I don't think senators are elected to be rubber stamps." He and Senator Christopher Dodd, Democrat of Connecticut, both of whom were standing for reelection that year, made clear they would be angling soon to shoot down Packwood's IRA provision and help out the vast "middle class" back home. Of the more than thirty amendments that senators threatened to unleash, the IRA amendments stood the best chance of success and were the greatest challenge to the no-amendment strategy.

Roth, however, poorly understood the new political dynamic of tax overhaul. He chose to pay for partial retention of the IRA deduction by curtailing tax breaks that were dear to many of his colleagues. For example, his proposal trimmed the completed-contract method of accounting, which was important to military contractors, who were big employers in several states, including Missouri, Kansas, Connecticut, and Washington. To the chagrin of rust-belt senators, Roth's proposal also eliminated the $500 million transition rule for steel companies. On Tuesday, June 10, Dole prevailed on Roth not to offer his amendment. Roth, knowing he did not have the votes, agreed and promised instead to offer a nonbinding resolution that asserted the need to retain the existing IRA deduction.

Other pro-IRA senators refused to admit defeat, however. On Wednesday, June 11, D'Amato and Dodd took the floor to promote their own IRA amendment. They were much smarter about paying for their proposal than was Roth. Instead of going after other interest groups, they chose to slightly raise the rates in the corporate and individual minimum taxes. The provision left intact the top 27-percent rate for individuals and the top 33-percent rate for corporations. While the increased minimum tax would hit some capital-intensive industries such as steel and mining, the D'Amato-Dodd tack was much easier to explain to constituents: It simply raised taxes on those who were not paying their "fair share" to Uncle Sam.

Packwood was prepared. His block of thirty-two senators opposed to all amendments was solid. He needed to convince only nineteen other senators to vote against the IRA amendment in order to defeat it. President Reagan had also been pitching the no-amendment strategy every chance he got. With all that in his favor, Packwood cavalierly predicted that the D'Amato-Dodd amendment would be defeated.

The risk of failure was high. Packwood staked the success of his bill on his ability to beat back major amendments, and this was the most dangerous amendment he had to face. If it passed, the no-amendment strategy could back-fire, and senators with gripes about the bill would be emboldened to propose other big changes. "We need to defeat this amendment so we don't start an un-raveling of the bill," Dole concluded.

When the clerk of the Senate started to call the roll on a motion to "table," or kill, the IRA amendment, Packwood's boast about easy victory began to look premature. For every aye from Packwood's coalition, there was a nay from the IRA advocates. The well of the Senate, which was in front of the presiding offi-cer's chair, was quickly filled with anxious senators curious about the outcome. Packwood was more than curious. He became extremely anxious.

In desperation, Packwood sought out a trio of Republican senators with whom he knew he could work in a pinch. Senators Slade Gorton and Daniel Evans of Washington State and Phil Gramm of Texas were ripping mad over the Finance Committee's repeal of the sales-tax deduction; their states had sales taxes and no income tax at all and stood to suffer immensely from the change. The hair-thin vote on the IRA amendment, however, gave them new and unex-pected clout.

As Packwood sought their support, the sales-tax senators issued him a chal-lenge. They said they would vote to kill the IRA amendment if he guaranteed them his support for their amendment to partially reinstate the sales-tax deduc-tion. With the credibility of his no-amendment strategy on the line, and the votes mounting rapidly, Packwood made an instant decision. "OK," he said. "I'll buy it."

The three senators walked to the well, got the attention of the clerk who was recording the votes, and lent their names to the list of those who wanted to table the IRA amendment. A few minutes later, the importance of those three votes became evident. The D'Amato-Dodd proposal was tabled by a vote of 51–48. Had Gorton, Evans, and Gramm not struck a deal, Packwood would have been dealt a major defeat, and other senators would have been encouraged to take a run at changing the bill. Packwood managed to avert that disaster only by secretly selling out his own coalition.

The Senate then went on to approve Roth's IRA resolution. Dodd called the nonbinding resolution a "charade" and a "ploy" that meant "absolutely noth-ing." Senate Minority Leader Robert Byrd, Democrat of West Virginia, asserted that the resolution was designed to "make people believe that something in-deed is being done," while, in fact, "the sense of the Senate resolution doesn't accomplish anything." Dole himself had previously referred to such nonbind-ing resolutions as "get-well cards"—a nice thought with no practical effect.

The next day, June 12, the sales-tax-state senators tried to collect on Pack-wood's promise of support, but Packwood had double-crossed them. Pack-wood had not called off his no-amendment coalition and they ran into a buzz saw of opposition. The senators' plan would have allowed taxpayers the choice of deducting either their state and local sales taxes or their income taxes, and paid for that change by closing a loophole in the bill that permitted the taking of second mortgages to finance consumer purchases.

The method of payment was, again, the amendment's Achilles' heel, and the coalition members attacked it brutally. Senators ranging from Democrat Wendell Ford of the high-sales-tax state of Kentucky to Bradley of New Jersey asserted that the proposal damaged the most sacred tax break in the code—the deduction for mortgage-interest payments. That preference, as they painted it, was almost an American birthright. The mere thought of tampering with it was unpatriotic.

During this barrage, Packwood was nowhere to be found, and the trio of senators was left without any recourse. At the urging of Dole, they withdrew the amendment to avoid certain defeat. Instead, they backed yet another meaningless resolution. "To put it mildly," Gorton said, "we were not happy with Packwood."

The defeat of the sales-tax proposal added steam to the drive of the no-amendment coalition. The operation was working like a clock. Packwood appeared able to defeat any amendment at will, and his resources seemed vast. He stationed his own personal army of lobbyists, the 15-27-33 members, in the Finance Committee hearing room. They were provided with telephones, television sets tuned to the Senate floor, and coffee. Whenever Packwood or his minions detected a wavering senator, they dispatched a pack of 15-27-33 lobbyists to plead for support.

On Friday the thirteenth, Packwood unloaded these big guns in an unusual effort to *approve* an amendment. While it appeared to run counter to the no-amendment strategy, the move actually proved to be a fierce display of force to show the consequences of not adhering to the Packwood line.

The Finance Committee chairman had placed into his committee's bill a transition rule for Union Oil Company of California (Unocal) worth about $50 million. The Unocal provision was sought by Senator Pete Wilson, Republican of California, but on the Senate floor, Wilson proved to be no friend of the Packwood bill. Despite the special favor, the California lawmaker voted against Packwood on several big issues, including IRAs and sales taxes.

With the help of the Commissioner, Packwood got his revenge. Metzenbaum argued that the Unocal rule had nothing to do with "transition" at all, but was a "fresh-off-the-shelf loophole" and an example of "simple greed." Many members of the no-amendment coalition could not help but agree. The provision was a tax break designed to help offset the extra debt Unocal amassed in the previous year to fight off a takeover attempt by corporate raider T. Boone Pickens. The rule was not only an exception to the committee bill, it also was an exception to existing law. Packwood, sensing the agitation of his no-amendment allies with some of the committee's special-interest transition rules, and angered by Wilson's votes on the floor, urged coalition members to support Metzenbaum's Unocal amendment. "When we asked Packwood how we should vote" on the Unocal matter, a coalition member told *The New York Times,* "he said, 'Sock him.'" The result was a rout. Wilson's Unocal rule was dropped from the bill by a vote of 60–33. It served as a warning to other senators not to defy Chairman Packwood.

In succession, Packwood disposed of every other major issue. He defeated an effort by Republican Senator Paul Trible of Virginia, a state heavy with federal workers, to ease the Finance Committee's tax increase on federal pensions. Packwood and his coalition also slaughtered the effort by George Mitchell of Maine to cut back benefits to wealthy individuals by imposing a 35-percent top rate. So daunting was the no-amendment block that advocates of the preferential treatment of capital gains chose not to even offer their nonbinding resolution. They feared that the margin of their victory, if they could even manage one, would be so paltry that it would kill any chance for better capital-gains treatment in the all-important House-Senate conference.

The fight dragged on for more than two weeks, with the sessions at times lasting until midnight. More than one hundred hours were devoted to the debate. When there were no amendments being contested, or when Packwood and Dole were trying to resolve problems off the Senate floor, a "quorum call" would be requested to kill time. The clerk would slowly and monotonously read through the names of the one hundred senators until someone asked that the quorum call be dispensed with so that debate could resume. At other times, Packwood would recite his version of the history of the tax code and tell why tax reform was so important. During this period, Packwood constantly paced around the chamber. He did this in part to stretch his legs, which were always tight from his almost daily games of squash, but he also walked so that members would be less inclined to stop him and ask questions.

Gradually Packwood's no-amendment strategy began to show some cracks. He was making enemies of those who resented his heavy-handedness. His manner chafed some members, but Packwood's actions were even more grating on matters of substance.

On Tuesday, June 17, the day he beat the Trible amendment, Packwood caved to pressure from his coalition to *accept* an amendment that stung two of his own committee members, [Malcolm] Wallop and Bentsen. The amendment, cleverly crafted by Metzenbaum, restored the withholding tax on foreigners that the committee bill had repealed and used the $1.2 billion raised by the tax to pay for a special tax break for hard-pressed farmers and a medical-cost deduction for the elderly. The combination of taxing foreigners and helping farmers and senior citizens was irresistible to most senators. Wallop had been a loyal supporter of the tax package, and on the last night of markup he had even helped Packwood out of a jam by offering to amend the repeal provision so it would cost less revenue. But under pressure, the chairman turned his back on the steadfast Wyoming senator. He made his second exception to the no-amendment strategy and released the coalition members to pass the Metzenbaum proposal. A visibly wounded Wallop protested at length from his seat in the rear of the chamber. The more reserved Bentsen simply left the floor.

The sales-tax senators were also still fuming about Packwood's double-cross. Packwood defended himself by telling them that he had pledged only *his* vote for their amendment, not the votes of his coalition—a story that was hard to swallow. Contrite nonetheless, Packwood began to meet Gorton, Evans, and Gramm privately, often in Dole's office, to work out some sort of face-saving compromise.

At about the same time, D'Amato, the leader of the save-the-IRA drive, was beating the bushes to find support for another major amendment. He wanted to tie together several big issues that had been defeated by the coalition. He thought that lumping the most popular issues into one package would be so attractive that senators would be loathe to vote no. "I was working on an amendment that would have taken care of the IRAs and the pension problem," he said later. "There was some consideration, too, of the sales-tax problem." D'Amato and Trible were holding serious talks about how best to combine forces.

Word about D'Amato's triple-play "killer amendment" worried the members of the coalition. They feared he might well win. Frustration with the no-amendment strategy was beginning to bubble, and could come to the surface as support for the D'Amato-Trible package.

Senators were becoming increasingly resentful of Packwood and his Finance Committee for preventing them from altering this very important bill. Many members did not believe Packwood's claims that the package was so fragile that it would disintegrate if amendments were adopted. They were itching to assert their role as lawmakers, to take care of the interests of their own folks at home, and they disliked the sometimes sanctimonious way that members of the coalition advocated their no-amendment strategy.

These feelings erupted on the night of Wednesday, June 18. Senator Paul Sarbanes, Democrat of Maryland, derided Senator [John] Danforth for giving a virtual "sermon" to his colleagues on the no-amendment strategy the night before. Sarbanes even read back into the Congressional Record Danforth's offending speech:

> *If you believe that the point of taxation is to take care of every group, and I am not putting down those interest groups, but if you believe that the point is to take care of them one after another as they come through the door, vote for this amendment and then the next amendment and then the next amendment and then the next amendment and then the next amendment, because there is no end of it. Once you say yes to one group you can never say no again.*

Danforth had gone on to praise the 15-27-33 lobbyists and described their commitment in ringing terms:

We do not agree with every detail in this bill. We do not agree with some of the things you have done. We do not agree with what you have done with real estate or what you have done to the state sales taxes. We do not agree with this, that, or the other things in the bill, but the bill is right, the bill is right. For once you are doing the right thing in the Congress of the United States. This bill is right and we will stick with you.

Sarbanes was visibly disturbed by the sappy self-righteousness of this language. After all, he noted, Danforth's own special interest—Missouri-based military contractors—had been fully protected in the Finance Committee bill. Sarbanes, like Trible, represented a large number of retired federal workers, and was frustrated by the Trible amendment's failure the night before. He did not want to leave the debate with his protest unstated. "We were being put down last night because we were offering what I thought was a perfectly reasonable amendment with respect to twenty million Americans, who are going to, in effect, be subject to double taxation," he said. "Their concerns about the impact of this legislation were perfectly reasonable concerns and ought not to be dismissed as special interests."

Sarbanes was far from alone in his disaffection. As a sign of the growing protest, other senators began proposing more and more amendments in defiance of the no-amendment stance. Shortly after eleven on that same evening, Dole appeared on the floor to announce that "the number of amendments seems to grow rapidly. At eight o'clock there were twenty-some. Now we are up to fifty-some."

Tension mounted. Shortly before midnight, one of the Senate's crustiest members, Ted Stevens, Republican of Alaska, took the floor and embarked on a lengthy speech about the way the rest of the Senate was being treated by the elite Finance Committee and its chairman. Stevens attacked the surreptitiously composed transition rules. His complaints were similar to those of Metzenbaum, but his point was the complete opposite. He wanted some Alaskan transition rules in the bill. If constituents of so many other states were to be blessed with favors, he argued, why not give more special breaks to the good people of Alaska too? In a tone that amounted to a growl, Stevens began to address himself directly to Packwood:

I would like to have my friend tell me who they are. Who are these people that have these projects that we do not name in the bill? . . . When we appropriate money for a project in Louisiana, we say where it is, who owns it, and if there is going to be a contract let for it, we say who the contractee is. We are not saying this is a project that is described in this paragraph that could fit almost anything. But you all know who they are. I do not know who they are. I do now know why I cannot try to fit some of my own projects into these exemptions already in this bill. If I can, I am going to try, okay?

In Packwood's defense, Senator Alan Simpson, Republican of Wyoming and the assistant majority leader, rose to take on the cantankerous Stevens. Simpson, a tall, balding man with intelligent eyes and a ready smile, was sometimes referred to as a modern-day Abraham Lincoln: His wit was quick and dry. He had a talent for indirection and exaggeration to make a point. He had tangled before with Stevens; the two lawmakers were not friends. Stevens's complaints about the way giveaways were handled in the tax bill were simply too much for Simpson to take without reply.

"Mr. President, I am very interested in this debate, and it is very fascinating— and a little heavy," Simpson began.

I have been here seven and a half years. I have watched with total admiration as the senator from Alaska does his work in the U.S. Senate. It should leave us all absolutely envious. Because I have seen him with his extraordinary skills insert more pieces of legislation into various bills for his state than any person that I have ever met in this place. I think the people of Alaska should be proud of that; that is why they return him here, only one of the reasons.

I have seen him work hard on the Appropriations Committee. I am not on the Appropriations Committee, but I have seen pieces of legislation come from that committee which were literally larded with material that had to do with the state of Alaska.

I am not going to get into one with the senator from Alaska because he is a pretty feisty cookie; but I can tell you if they wanted a bear to represent them in Alaska, they hired a grizzly. That is Ted Stevens.

I think that is great, but I do not think you can come in here and have a debate that has to do with talking about things and costs and so on, when I have seen things come here under the direction of the senator from Alaska which were of tremendous cost—railroads, unified commands. There is no limit to the extraordinary ways—he is the envy of us all.

I have seen him produce the most novel legislation. I have seen condition upon condition come from wherever this remarkable gentleman plies his trade, project after project, waiver after waiver.

The Simpson speech was a stunning put-down, but it was not enough to stop the growing dissent against Packwood and his no-amendment strategy. The snarling and sniping continued, and as the session came to an end in the early-morning hours, the floor leaders knew they needed to act quickly to quash the rebellion. They decided, in the words of Bradley, "to cut the core out of any growing interest in a bigger amendment."

On Thursday, June 19, Packwood took the floor to say that he had worked out an amendment with the three senators from Washington and Texas to ease the effect of eliminating the sales-tax deduction. Evans and the others introduced it, and it was adopted without objection. The provision allowed taxpayers to deduct 60 percent of their sales-tax payments, but only to the extent that the payments exceeded the amount of their state-and-local income tax liability.

The convoluted provision was drafted to help only states that had raised most of their revenue from sales taxes and to cost no more than the $1.6 billion that Packwood had found to finance it, but it served its purpose. It quieted the complaints of the sales-tax senators and cut the legs out from under the D'Amato-Trible triple-threat amendment. Dole and Packwood met with D'Amato and Trible outside the chamber in front of the large wooden timepiece known as the Ohio Clock. "Packwood made it clear that he would view our amendment as a hostile act," Trible recalls. The two dissident lawmakers already knew they did not have enough votes to beat the no-amendment coalition. They also concluded that pressing the point and then losing would so anger Packwood that they would have no leverage at all in the conference. "I realized if we tried and failed," Trible said, "our chance of gaining any relief would be lost forever. The chemistry of the situation had changed. . . . Events had passed us by."

It was the final challenge for the Senate tax-reform bill; from then on, the debate was mostly a mop-up operation. The Senate faced dozens of minor amendments, most of which were accepted as "conference bait"—provisions that would be adopted on the Senate floor, only to be dropped in the later House-Senate conference. Many of these were extremely local in focus, including provisions to benefit a truck-leasing company in Des Moines, a housing project in Massachusetts, and flood victims in West Virginia. Senator Stevens persisted in plying his "extraordinary ways"; he won a special tax treatment for Alaskan Indian tribe corporations and another for the income from reindeer, which Bradley said would better have been granted at Christmastime.

In the end, on Tuesday, June 24, only rhetoric remained. Dole attempted to trace the origins of the tax overhaul to his own tax bills since 1982. Bradley said the idea went back to the origins of the U.S. Constitution. Senator Joseph Biden, Democrat of Delaware, gave much of the credit to Bradley. Packwood gave credit to almost everyone: Rostenkowski, Reagan, Long, Bradley, Dole, Metzenbaum, the entire core group, and himself. He . . . recalled saying to Diefenderfer, "Let's give real reform a try."

For the benefit of the cameras, Dole requested that the senators vote from their own seats rather than follow their usual practice of bunching up in the well. The final vote on the 1,489-page bill was 97–3, with three Democrats dissenting—Carl Levin of Michigan, John Melcher of Montana, and Paul Simon of Illinois.

"Nothing is certain in this life; the good Lord might call us home tomorrow," Russell Long said after the vote, "but if we're here on Labor Day, there'll be a bill on the president's desk."

Epilogue

Senator Packwood's task got no easier after final Senate passage. Next he had to endure a tortuous negotiation process with the equally brilliant and equally aggressive tax reform leader in the House, Democrat Dan Rostenkowski, the head of the Ways and Means Committee. The Senate and House versions of the bill differed drastically; no one could agree on which tax loopholes to retain or even which set of economic figures to use to estimate tax revenues. In the end, however, agreement was reached; among the various compromises, both the lower capital gains tax and the deductions for state sales tax were eliminated. The bill was passed with only minor changes by both houses of Congress in late September and signed by President Reagan on the White House lawn on October 22, 1986. In the words of *Wall Street Journal* editor Albert Hunt, "In the last century Bismarck observed that two things one should never watch being made are sausage and legislation. Compared to the Tax Reform Act of 1986, a sausage factory is tidy and orderly."

Battle for Justice

Ethan Bronner

The story of the defeat by the Senate of the nomination of Judge Robert Bork for the Supreme Court is a classic portrait of the confirmation process, as well as a microcosm of the nature of interest group politics. Since 1974 Bork's name had been among the two dozen that were brought up whenever a Republican president had a Supreme Court seat to fill. Events always seemed to work against him, however. In 1981, Ronald Reagan appointed Sandra Day O'Connor to the vacancy created by the retirement of Potter Stewart because of his campaign promise to put a woman on the Court. And in 1986, the much younger and more conservative Antonin Scalia was appointed when Chief Justice Warren Burger retired (and Associate Justice William Rehnquist replaced Burger as chief justice).

Bork finally got his appointment in 1987. In politics, however, timing is everything. Now he would be a conservative justice replacing the moderate Lewis Powell on what had been a balanced Court; liberals feared that Bork would tip the Court to the right. And in 1987 the Republicans did not control the Senate as they had for the two prior Reagan appointments, meaning that the Judiciary Committee was headed by the politically ambitious Democrat Joseph Biden of Delaware rather than the sympathetic Republican Strom Thurmond of South Carolina. Knowing that they had a chance to win, liberal interest groups around the nation coalesced and lobbied in a way that had not been seen since the 1960s. In the two decades that Bork's name had been mentioned as a Supreme Court hopeful, those groups had gathered more than enough material for their files on him to make the fight very interesting and very dirty.

This dramatic account of the confirmation battle by Ethan Bronner effectively captures the desperation mode adopted by the liberal interest groups to combat Bork. Notice as you read this selection how little there is on a countermovement by conservative interest groups. That is not an oversight. In fact, while all of the events portrayed in this selection were occurring, there was very little effort by conservative activists to defend Bork. Later on, these groups would claim that they had never been mobilized by the White House. Indeed, the White House staff was on vacation for the whole month of August 1987, when the liberal groups were mobilizing. Apparently, the administration did not fully appreciate the danger facing the nomination.

As you read this selection, place yourself in the Reagan White House planning a pro-Bork counterattack. Is this fight winnable? More specifically, how will you advise the candidate as he prepares to testify before the Senate?

HOWARD BAKER   White House chief of staff.

WILLIAM BALL   White House congressional liaison.

JOSEPH BIDEN   Chair of the Senate Judiciary Committee.

ROBERT BORK   Federal appeals judge for the District of Columbia; Supreme Court nominee.

ARTHUR CULVAHOUSE   White House counsel.

EDWARD KENNEDY   Member of the Senate Judiciary Committee; led Senate anti-Bork fight.

PATRICK McGUIGAN   Conservative lobbyist.

ANTHONY PODESTA   Anti-Bork lobbyist.

LEWIS POWELL   Appointed by Nixon to the Supreme Court in 1971; resigned in 1987.

RONALD REAGAN   President of the United States, 1981–1989.

PHIL SPARKS, EMILY TYNES   Media consultants for the anti-Bork forces.

▶ For Washington's liberals, it would have been hard to invent less welcome news [than Justice Lewis Powell's retirement]. As news agency teleprinters rang with bells to signal recipients of an urgent breaking story, and radio stations announced it, and Cable News Network broadcast it, the capital's telephones began buzzing. The lobbyists remembered precisely where they were when they got the news. They recalled it the way they recalled where they had been a quarter century earlier, when they heard that President John F. Kennedy had been assassinated.

Ralph G. Neas, executive director of the Leadership Conference on Civil Rights, a grouping of 180 organizations, was in his 1984 Renault just north of Georgetown, fighting muggy weather and traffic. While the news shocked him, it did not surprise him. Only a month earlier, at the annual meeting of his group, he was going over legislative priorities for the coming year. He said then that if Lewis Powell or anyone else retired from the Supreme Court, the Supreme

Court nomination would become the top priority. He had no idea how pre-scient his words were. Neas, who was to head the unprecedented lobbying campaign against a Supreme Court nomination, stepped on the gas and planned the next half dozen telephone calls. As he put it later, "Everyone real-ized immediately what was going to be at stake, and our lives would be con-sumed, obsessed by the fight over the Powell seat."

Kate Michelman, installed not long before as director of the National Abor-tion Rights Action League, was giving a speech to a group of women's rights attorneys on Maryland Street in Washington, assessing progress and concerns of the previous year. She opened a note passed to her on the dais, looked up, and announced without a trace of irony: "Our worst fears have just been real-ized."

Paul Gewirtz, a liberal constitutional scholar at Yale Law School, was at a conference of judges in Virginia. The panel included Walter Dellinger of Duke University, Gerald Gunther of Stanford, and Paul Bator of the University of Chi-cago. Gewirtz, Dellinger, and Gunther were standing around chatting idly when they got the word.

"There was this explosion, this sinking feeling that after all this uncertainty, the moment of truth had come for the Court," Gewirtz remembered. "We knew the direction of the Court was at stake. For the next three days we talked about it endlessly. Endlessly." . . .

Powell's departure meant one thing to most Court watchers: Robert H. Bork, federal appeals judge for the District of Columbia and favorite of the Reagan administration, would be nominated.

When Kate Michelman of the National Abortion Rights Action League re-turned to her office from giving a speech, she found two television network crews waiting. What would her organization do if Bork were chosen? It would mount an unprecedented campaign against his confirmation by the Senate, Mi-chelman shot back. "We have researched his background, and we know what he stands for," she said.

When Althea Simmons, chief Washington lobbyist for the National Associ-ation for the Advancement of Colored People (NAACP), heard of the Powell departure, she was in Nassau, the Bahamas, about to address the annual con-vention of Delta Sigma Theta, the black women's sorority and service organi-zation. News came via a call from her legislative aide in Washington, and her response was: "Oh, my God. That's Bork. We've got our work cut out for us. Pull our Bork files." When she went to the podium to deliver her talk, she told the audience: "Justice Powell has resigned, and Robert Bork is on his way to the Supreme Court. We've got to get to work."

But Bork himself was skeptical. When word of the Powell resignation reached the judge, Bork was in his chambers just down Capitol Hill from the Supreme Court working on an *en banc* opinion with fellow conservative judges Douglas Ginsburg, James Buckley, and Kenneth Starr. . . .

. . . Buckley mentioned the Powell resignation and said Bork looked like the nominee. Bork dismissed it. "The administration has a well-entrenched tradition of passing me over," he said.

Bork was not alone in his concern that the administration would pass him over one more time. His supporters worried, too. Patrick McGuigan, a young, fervent Oklahoman, was director of the Judicial Reform Project for the Free Congress Foundation, a grouping of conservative organizations. He was in his cramped office in a town house near the Capitol when his summer intern peeked in the door. Had McGuigan heard about Powell's resignation?

"I immediately called John Richardson, the attorney general's chief of staff," McGuigan recounted. "John, tell the attorney general and everyone else that if you guys don't do Bork this time, I'm going to slash my wrists.'"

McGuigan added that he would explain to his people that this one was worth fighting for. He then called Peter Keisler, a twenty-seven-year-old Yale Law School graduate and former Bork clerk who was working in the White House counsel's office. He repeated his desperate message. Next, McGuigan called Dan Casey, director of the American Conservative Union, and said they ought to inundate the White House and the Hill with pro-Bork telephone calls.

"That ought to be a pretty easy sell, don't you think?" asked Casey.

"I don't trust the jerks to do the right thing, do you?" countered McGuigan.

"Not really," agreed Casey.

Bork's admirers in the Justice Department had their own jitters. Their two bosses, Attorney General Edwin Meese and his top adviser, Assistant Attorney General William Bradford Reynolds, were in flight over the Atlantic. So Charles Cooper, head of the Office of Legal Counsel, called a meeting in his office with, among others, John Bolton, the department's liaison to Congress, and Terry Eastland, the department's spokesman. The aim was to plot a strategy to get Bork nominated as quickly as possible.

These were the self-described ideological foot soldiers of the Reagan Revolution. Tough, smart, and zealous in their devotion to right-wing principles, they saw Powell's resignation in epic terms. The moment of truth had arrived. Conservatives could finally regain control of the Supreme Court and the nation's moral and legal agenda. These young Reaganites had come to government service brimming with hope. For them, it *was* morning in America and they would return their nation to its roots and traditions. What they decried as a racial and gender spoils system—the efforts of previous administrations and courts to help blacks and women as groups, rather than to correct wrongs suffered only by individuals—would end. In their Justice Department, young white men would be no less deserving of government help than anyone else. Justice would be provided to *all* Americans rather than set one group against another. Americans were decent and God-fearing. No need existed to spy out racism and sexism in every corner of the land. The existing system, which occasionally offered jobs to blacks over better qualified whites, and developed elaborate schemes of equal pay for equal work to promote gender equality, and set aside percentages of government contracts for minority-controlled firms was unjust. It must go.

The work of conservative reform proved more difficult than imagined. Radical change comes hard and slowly in a stable country. Much of what the Reagan foot soldiers objected to had become institutionalized and widely accepted.

Now came the godsend. The Court, which had legitimized so much in existing liberal programs, could also put a stop to them if it had the right people up there. But the men at Justice were afraid that the newly pragmatic White House, now run by moderate Tennesseean Howard Baker, the chief of staff, would scuttle the nomination. It would push for a candidate easier to confirm in the defiant, newly Democratic-controlled Senate. Such a nomination would be a colossal waste of a unique opportunity.

Charles Cooper, a handsome Alabaman with ice blue eyes, who had clerked for [Supreme Court Justice William] Rehnquist, finally reached Reynolds on the airplane as he and Meese returned from Europe. They agreed that Bork was, without question, their choice. They would lobby for him. John Bolton got on the phone and went so far as to suggest that when Meese landed, he go by helicopter to the White House and that the selection of Bork be made that very night. This should be accompanied, he believed, by public pressure on Senator Joseph R. Biden, Jr., of Delaware, chairman of the Judiciary Committee, to hold early confirmation hearings.

Bolton and his colleagues wanted to mount a fierce pro-Bork offensive, one impossible for Baker or the Senate to counter. This time everything they cared about was on the line. As one of them said later, "If you can't get Bob Bork on the Court, you might as well shut the door and turn all the lights out."

If right-wing activists and Justice Department officials were alarmed and wary, they were justified in being so. Within the new group running Reagan's White House, not Chief of Staff Howard Baker nor Counsel Arthur B. Culvahouse nor Communications Director Thomas Griscom was a Bork devotee. They each knew Bork was a federal judge in Washington, a smart, vociferous conservative to be found on all right-wing lists for nomination to the Supreme Court. But Baker and Culvahouse, soft-spoken southern gentlemen, were themselves closer in style and outlook to Lewis Powell than to Robert Bork. They were pragmatists, accommodators, concerned more with unity and accord than with rigid principle. They rarely used harsh words. They had come to the White House only months earlier to restore order and dignity to a presidency damaged by the Iran-contra scandal. The administration had secretly sold arms to Iran in hopes of freeing American hostages held in Lebanon. Profits from the sales were sent to right-wing Nicaraguan rebels, known as contras, despite a congressional ban on such aid. The plan failed, and both Congress and a special prosecutor were investigating. In addition, the Senate had been lost to the Democrats

the previous November. The new men in the White House were not in search
of a fight. . . .

At 6:30 A.M. on Wednesday, July 1, 1987, Robert Bork left his red-brick three-
story house in the Potomac Palisades section of Washington and drove to 716
Jackson Place NW, a minute's walk from the White House. The nineteenth-
century town house was used to lodge former presidents when they came to
town. None was in residence that day. It was this house, with its pre-Victorian
furnishings, that White House Counsel Arthur B. Culvahouse had chosen as a
place to discuss with Bork his nomination to the Supreme Court.

It was 7:00 A.M., and Culvahouse, tall, blond, and open-faced, was waiting. As
the confirmation process got under way and his exposure to Bork increased,
he was to become a fan. At the moment he was not. He knew only that trouble
lay ahead.

Bork and Culvahouse climbed to the third-floor dining room, where they sat
facing each other. Culvahouse pulled out of his briefcase a handwritten list of
some twenty questions, referring to it as his "skeleton" questionnaire.

The counsel had nicknames for a couple of them, such as the Gary Hart question, named for the former Colorado senator who had withdrawn from the 1988
race for the Democratic presidential nomination because of his sexual indiscre-
tion: Had Bork ever had any extramarital affairs?

"No," Bork replied.

Now, Culvahouse said, the John Fedders question, after the former head of
the investigative branch of the Securities and Exchange Commission whose
wife had sued him for divorce: Did Bork beat his wife or children?

"No, but don't ask them," Bork offered, trying to inject humor. Culvahouse
was stone-faced.

"Look, I've led a pretty dull life," Bork added in another attempt to loosen
things up.

"That's good," Culvahouse responded coolly.

Bork did his best to answer the other questions simply.

The questioning over, Culvahouse told Bork that he could expect a call from
Chief of Staff Howard Baker in the next few hours. Brimming with expectation,
Bork went to his chambers at the federal courthouse. Just after noon Baker
called and told Bork he should meet Baker's executive assistant, John Tuck, at
Third and D streets, a discreet street corner, so as to avoid the eyes of the media.
While prominently mentioned as the leading choice for the nomination, Bork
was still under wraps. The White House wanted to keep him that way until the
press conference.

Bork went with his secretary to the appointed spot. Dressed in a blue blazer
and gray flannel slacks, he was perspiring heavily in the midday heat. He got
into Tuck's station wagon. There was no air conditioning. Tuck took a circu-
itous route, driving down Independence Avenue, past the Jefferson Memorial,
to enter the White House. But his car and passenger were seen by a reporter

for Cable News Network, who immediately went on the air to report that Bork was the nominee.

Tuck took Bork to Baker's handsome and airy office in the White House's West Wing. There he met Baker; Culvahouse; Kenneth Duberstein, the deputy chief of staff; Thomas Griscom, director of communications; and William Ball, White House liaison to Congress. All congratulated him. They accompanied him up to the Oval Office.

Although they were soldiers in arms in the conservative movement, Bork had never known Reagan well. He had not worked for Reagan in 1980 as he had for Richard Nixon and Barry Goldwater in 1968 and 1964. Reagan, of course, had named Bork to the D.C. Circuit in 1982, but they had had minimal contact before that.

"I'd like to offer you the nomination to the Supreme Court. Will you accept it?" the president said solemnly to the judge.

"I've been thinking about it for ten to twelve minutes, and I think I like the idea," Bork responded with a satisfied twinkle. He had trouble adjusting to the self-seriousness of the White House.

The president didn't get it. "Does that mean yes?"

Incredulous, Bork stiffened and gravely responded, "Yes, sir. I'd be honored, Mr. President."

From there, the two moved to the Queen Anne chairs in front of the fireplace and the White House photographers were asked in. With staff members on the couches, Bork and Reagan smiled at each other in awkward silence. In a rarity, Bork couldn't think of anything to say.

Baker explained to Bork that the president would announce his nomination to a press conference a few minutes later; Bork was to take no questions and make no remarks. It seemed strange to the nominee that he would not be allowed at least to express his gratitude publicly to the president and say how much he looked forward to the confirmation process. But as far as he could tell, the White House men were on top of the situation, and he figured they, not he, were the political professionals.

As the group entered the press conference, Sam Donaldson, the White House correspondent of ABC News, and Bill Plante, of CBS, were sitting in the front row and feigned shock at the sight of Bork. "Surprise, surprise, surprise," they offered aloud.

With Bork at his side, President Reagan announced the nomination and said of his choice: "Judge Bork, widely regarded as the most prominent and intellectually powerful advocate of judicial restraint, shares my view that judges' personal preferences and values should not be part of their constitutional interpretations."

The battle was joined.

After the announcement Bork accompanied William L. Ball III, an affable southerner with a honey-coated accent, to his West Wing office. As Bork settled into an armchair, Ball flicked on the television to the C-SPAN network, which broadcasts live the proceedings of the Senate. He wanted to see if there was any reaction yet to the nomination made less than an hour before.

There was.

Even before the picture blinked on, Ball and Bork could detect the inimitable Brahmin accent of the senior senator from Massachusetts, Edward M. Kennedy. He declared:

> *Robert Bork's America is a land in which women would be forced into back alley abortions, blacks would sit at segregated lunch counters, rogue police could break down citizens' doors in midnight raids, school children could not be taught about evolution, writers and artists could be censored at the whim of government, and the doors of the federal courts would be shut on the fingers of millions of citizens for whom the judiciary is—and is often the only—protector of the individual rights that are the heart of our democracy.*
>
> *America is a better and freer nation than Robert Bork thinks. Yet in the current delicate balance of the Supreme Court, his rigid ideology will tip the scales of justice against the kind of country America is and ought to be.*
>
> *The damage that President Reagan will do through this nomination if it is not rejected by the Senate could live on far beyond the end of his presidential term. President Reagan is still our president. But he should not be able to reach out from the muck of Irangate, reach into the muck of Watergate, and impose his reactionary vision of the Constitution on the Supreme Court and on the next generation of Americans. No justice would be better than this injustice.*

Watching the proceedings on a television was Kennedy aide Jeffrey Blattner. He admired the way the senator unwound, delivering the statement with style and force. But he realized it was a risky speech. When it was over, he said to himself, "Now we better win."

Kennedy's was an altogether startling statement. He had shamelessly twisted Bork's world view—"rogue police could break down citizens' doors in midnight raids" was an Orwellian reference to Bork's criticism of the exclusionary rule, through which judges exclude illegally obtained evidence, and Bork had never suggested he opposed the teaching of evolution—but equally startling was that Kennedy discussed Bork's world view at all. The speech was a landmark for judicial nominations. Kennedy was saying that no longer should the Senate content itself with examining a nominee's personal integrity and legal qualifications, as had been the custom—at least publicly—for half a century. From now on the Senate and the nation should examine a nominee's vision for society. In fulfilling its constitutional duty of "advice and consent" on judicial appointments, the upper house should take politics and ideology fully into account. This was part of a growing assertion of power by the Congress and an unambiguous acknowledgment of the political nature of the Supreme Court, popularly portrayed as above politics.

To Bork and Ball, Kennedy's words seemed such a departure from tradition and such a distortion of the nominee's record as to be of no consequence. They shrugged off the speech as the ravings of a desperate politician. Kennedy, they thought, had blown it.

They were dangerously wrong in their assessment. Kennedy did distort Bork's record, but his statement was not the act of a desperate man. This was a confident and seasoned politician, one who knew how to combine passion and pragmatism in the Senate. Unlike the vast majority of those who were to oppose Bork, Kennedy believed from the beginning that the nomination would be defeated and that the loss would prove decisive in judicial politics. . . .

But for Bork and his family, Kennedy's attacks on Bork were hard to understand except as *ad hominem* assaults. Once, toward the end of a long day of the Bork hearings at which Kennedy had repeatedly assailed the nominee, the senator was walking alone out of his office. Coming in the other direction was Mary Ellen Bork, accompanied by Nancy Kennedy, a White House aide. Mrs. Bork had slept poorly the previous night and was washed out from hours of sitting in the glare of television lights. She had no desire to run into Senator Kennedy. She was afraid she would burst into tears. But the senator sought her out.

"Mrs. Bork, you must be so tired. It's a very difficult time, I know. I hope you understand that it is nothing personal," Kennedy told her, shaking her hand.

Then, before she had a chance to say much of anything, the senator turned on his heels and took his leave.

She couldn't believe he had dared speak to her at all. So surprised and fatigued was she that she had no time for response. It was a moment she played back often in her mind, relishing some choice words she wished she had addressed to the Massachusetts lawmaker.

Kennedy was unaware of how offended Mrs. Bork was by his comment. He had said something similar to Bork himself at the judge's courtesy call in early July. "Nothing personal, you understand." Bork did not understand.

To Kennedy, it really was *not* personal. Little in politics was. He had led his entire life in the public eye; his life was fodder for the supermarket tabloids. He could not be within camera distance of an attractive woman without ending up on the cover of a gossip magazine. If he took everything said about him personally, he would never survive. He had always been a symbol and had learned to operate within the politics of symbolism. Heated rhetoric was part of the game of government. When the day was over, win or lose, everyone could have a drink together. He had been trained to disjoin his inner feelings from the domain of public affairs. You could sense it when you were with him. His eyes revealed nothing. The man had venetian blinds on his soul. . . .

In his fight against Bork, as in all his battles, Kennedy did not handle the issues gently. He clawed them. Uninterested in the historical and theoretical bases of Bork's views, Kennedy shredded the legal niceties, searching for the larger societal meaning of what was at stake. When law professors briefed him on Bork's theories, he would seek ways to bring the issue down to a level everyone would understand. One scholar remembered him saying, "Look, the masses are not going to rise up over the issue of congressional standing. But they will over freedom in the bedroom."

He was dogged in his dedication. In August, September, and October 1987 he held meetings with liberal lobby groups; demanded endless hours of work from his huge, dedicated staff; sent a letter to every one of the sixty-two hundred black elected officials in the country asking for their help; stroked and poked his Senate colleagues in the cloakroom, on the floor, in the dining room; gathered key witnesses for the hearings; and exploited the inchoate sense around the country that when a Kennedy commits himself this fiercely to something, it is rarely in vain. He called on hundreds of his and his brothers' former aides, the people who made up the extended Kennedy political family, and asked them for legal and political analyses, speeches, newspaper opinion pieces, and contacts.

Anthony Podesta, a talented liberal lobbyist hired by Kennedy for the Bork fight, remembered going up to the Kennedy summer compound in Hyannis Port to help the senator make phone calls. He said that he went to Cape Cod dubious about how much work Kennedy really would do, given that he only had a few weeks off from the Senate. But Kennedy kept calling and Podesta kept phoning back to Kennedy's Capitol Hill office for more phone numbers to pass on to the senator.

Kennedy called Ernest Morial, former New Orleans mayor, and Sidney Barthelemy, the current mayor. In Alabama, he spoke with Mayor Richard Arrington of Birmingham, Mayor Johnny Ford of Tuskegee, and Joseph Reed, the Alabama Democratic Conference chief. In Atlanta he spoke at length with Mayor Andrew Young, a longtime family friend. All were black southern leaders.

At one point Kennedy woke up the Reverend Joseph Lowery at the Hyatt Hotel in New Orleans before the Southern Christian Leadership Conference's annual convention. Lowery, head of the SCLC, had planned to discuss Bork at the meeting. But after hearing from Kennedy, he turned the entire day into an anti-Bork strategy session. He told the convention about Kennedy's call, and one participant remembered how it fired up the crowd. From there the issue penetrated black churches across America. Preachers would hand out pen and paper and take ten minutes from the service for anti-Bork letter writing.

From the Cape, Kennedy called every one of the thirty executive members of the AFL-CIO. When he took his yacht out for a sail, Bork was still on his mind. He sailed up to the Maine coast, where he dropped in on Burke Marshall, Yale law professor and assistant attorney general for civil rights under President Kennedy. Stopping in at Marshall's island retreat on North Haven, Kennedy asked him if he would testify against the judge. Marshall agreed. Later in September Kennedy held a conference call with forty state labor leaders around the country.

Bork's defeat was ever present on Kennedy's mind that summer. A few weeks after the nomination the car taking Kennedy to his home in McLean, Virginia, was struck by a falling tree. The senator flew forward and hit the windshield. "I thought for a moment that there would be one vote less against Bork" was his immediate comment when he realized he was unhurt.

"The question was how to convince people that this should be a priority item, not just another cause to sign your organization's name to," reflected Podesta. "Ted would get on the phone and say, 'This is the most important fight we've had in the Senate in years. We need you to mobilize, to activate your people, to make this a top priority issue.'"

The letter Kennedy sent to the thousands of black officials included people at all levels—federal, state, city council, board of education. Written mostly by Michael Frazier, the Kennedy aide whose sole responsibility was liaison to the black community, the letter said: "The most important vote this year in the United States Senate will take place on the question of President Reagan's nomination of Robert Bork to the Supreme Court. Bork has been a lifelong opponent of civil rights, and he does not deserve a lifetime seat on the Supreme Court— and so I urge you to join me in actively opposing the nomination."

The letter, dated August 12, 1987, went on to say that in his twenty-five years of public life, Bork had "worked tirelessly against justice and progress." It said: "The Bork appointment could profoundly diminish the promise of our nation for the next decade and beyond. Everything we have worked for together in the past quarter century may be jeopardized if Bork is confirmed, and if the narrowly divided Supreme Court of today shifts in the direction of Bork's extremist ideology."

Frazier said that the idea for the letter was his and that he was the keeper of the list in the office. "The Senate was going into recess, and we had to have some way to keep this thing going, not to let it die," he said. "We were determined to show that Kennedy would go to the mat on this one."

There were two advantages to fighting this kind of nomination, as opposed to working for a piece of legislation. First, it allowed groups to focus on an individual. That had drawbacks for the senators, who had to look the man in the eye and meet his family. But for members of lobbying groups around the country it allowed vague feelings and fears to be crystallized in one person who would be seen only from afar. He could be demonized, caricatured, and made to embody all they hated. Secondly, the fight was limited in time. Three months, that was the commitment, whereas legislative fights could carry on for years. Moreover, this would be win or lose. No compromises were possible; no watered-down version could emerge. The stakes were high.

Kennedy, chairman of the Senate Labor Committee and longtime friend of organized labor, was especially effective with union leaders. Worried about Alan Dixon, Democratic senator of Illinois, who seemed inclined in Bork's fa-

vor, Kennedy called up Edward Hanley, head of the hotel and restaurant workers' union. The union was based in Chicago; Hanley and Dixon were close.
Many of Hanley's members were close in temperament and attitude to team-
sters. With Hanley, Kennedy didn't talk about women and minorities. He didn't
discuss legal briefs. He made a few comments about Bork's attitude toward
business and labor. But he said essentially: Ed, we don't call often. This one
matters to us. Dixon's shaky. Give him a call.

So Dixon, a senator for whom such things made a huge difference—his nickname, Al the Pal, flowed from his unparalleled ability to cut deals and keep
constituents happy with him—would get a call from Hanley. And after prompt-
ing from Kennedy, Dixon would also hear from Chicago Mayor Harold Washington and Representative Gus Savage, among many others. Dixon voted
against Bork.

Podesta, who had once been counsel to the machinists' union, analyzed Kennedy's calls this way: "Our opponents complained a lot about the money spent
in this campaign. But given a choice between ten thousand dollars and two
phone calls from Ed Hanley, I'd much rather have the phone calls."

Kennedy called key financiers for other senators, including those of several
southern Democrats. In one case, the man reached was due to hold a fund rais-
er for Senator Lawton Chiles, Democrat of Florida, the next evening. Chiles,
who was to face what he described as ugly and unmatched pressure on this
vote, came out against Bork. Later, for unrelated reasons, he decided not to run
again for the Senate.

The message communicated by Kennedy's calls was that this fight could be
won. People knew that Ted Kennedy was no Don Quixote. If he invested his
summer in this campaign, it could probably be done. . . .

Toward the end of the week of September 14, 1987, listeners to small radio stations in Alabama heard the following news item from a man named Henry
Griggs in Washington:

[Voice of Griggs] "As Senate hearings on the nomination of Robert Bork to
the Supreme Court continue, a number of civil rights leaders raised opposition
to Bork, saying his stands on constitutional rights of minorities are critical. The
Reverend Jesse Jackson had these comments: [Voice of Jackson] 'Judge Bork is
a threat to the future of civil rights, workers' rights and women's rights. The
achievements of the last 30 years are threatened by Judge Bork not only because he disagreed with those decisions and the Civil Rights Act of '64 or the
Voting Rights Act, but he also would have the power on the Supreme Court to
overrule or undercut those decisions. He is not just conservative; he is backwards. He is activist in his intent to undercut progress.'" (End report.)

Henry Griggs was not a news reporter. He was a public relations man for the
American Federation of State, County and Municipal Employees, a huge trade
union active in liberal causes. For August and September 1987, AFSCME lent
Griggs to the anti-Bork effort full time. An important part of his job was to make

radio spots that sounded like news and to call hundreds of radio stations around the country, offering the spots without charge. The aim was to get the reports included in the regular news broadcasts.

The term for such spots is *actualities*. Usually no more than snatches of speeches, they are used by many political campaigns. But in the Bork campaign they were more than that. They were meticulously produced and aggressively promoted with a wide variety of spokesmen and differing themes.

"Actualities are free, low tech, and highly effective," Griggs commented. "The idea is to get them as close to a radio report as we can get. For a lot of small radio stations around the country, it's great. They have budget cuts and often only have one or two reporters. They don't have that much stuff, but they have lots of time to fill. The trick is not to give them anything that is half-and-half. It's got to be a full-court press for your side. It's a kind of invisible publicity. People don't realize when they hear it that the station didn't send out a reporter and that we're the ones providing it."

Aided by comprehensive guides to radio stations around the country, Griggs sorted out formats and audiences countrywide. He targeted black stations with Jesse Jackson and NAACP Executive Director Benjamin Hooks. In the Southwest he offered interviews with Antonia Hernandez of the Mexican-American Legal Defense and Educational Fund. On the West Coast he provided officials of the Sierra Club warning that Bork would be bad for environmental protection.

One Griggs job was to keep a stable of interview subjects available for stations with last-minute needs. For example, he stayed in touch with a big Pittsburgh station that carried the Pirates' baseball games. When a rainout occurred, the station had three hours to fill. Griggs, with an eye on weather reports, would quickly offer a Bork-related interview. The Griggs campaign was quite successful. Morning and evening news broadcasts on small stations accepted some three-quarters of his offerings. He made two to three per day during the hearings.

"Often the station would take only the sound bite of the interview and take my intro off, but sometimes they would play the whole package I sent them," Griggs said.

The White House had a toll-free actualities number that played snatches of President Reagan's speeches supporting Bork's confirmation and other administration goals. But the two efforts were very different. The anti-Bork forces reached out to tiny stations in Tempe, Arizona, and St. Petersburg, Florida. Those stations rarely called the White House actualities line. And the anti-Bork spots came fully packaged and produced.

Griggs's radio work was complemented by that of a colleague, James ("Skip") Prior, in television. Prior was telecommunications coordinator at AFSCME, directing what the union dubbed the Labor News Network. Run out of the basement of AFSCME's massive Washington headquarters building, the network had a first-class studio that was put to frequent use during the Bork fight.

Prior's products were called not actualities but video news releases, or VNRs. They were occasionally fully packaged interviews but often simply the chance for television stations to interview Bork opponents without having to set up the interviews in advance. The anti-Bork campaign would gather effective spokesmen in the studio and call around to small stations in targeted states, offering free direct satellite hookups. Stations nearly always took them. The local anchor would then ask the guests why they so objected to Judge Bork's nomination. The speakers would oblige with long, well-rehearsed explanations.

Actualities and video news releases were but one aspect of the media campaign. The day after Reagan nominated Bork, People for the American Way, a high-profile, well-financed liberal lobbying group, sent out "editorial memos" to twelve hundred newspaper editorial boards and individual reporters, according to Melanne Verveer, the organization's vice-president. It continued to do so several times a week, expanding the list to seventeen hundred in the course of the campaign. The organization, by far the biggest spender in the anti-Bork camp, spent $1.4 million on its campaign, including $684,000 on advertising in newspapers, television, and radio. But the key to the anti-Bork strategy was not money. All the anti-Bork groups together did not spend more than a few million dollars. And the Justice Department and White House had more potential manpower and resources at their disposal than the opposition. The key to the battle lay elsewhere.

"The idea was to frame a strategic message," said Phil Sparks, Griggs's former boss at AFSCME and one of the liberal community's savviest public relations men. "We put out a three-page memo, listing the key themes and making sure that everyone in the coalition was singing from the same sheet. We also identified the two hundred most important reporters on this issue in Washington and constantly sent them huge amounts of stuff."

Much of the media strategy was framed by a liberal consulting firm known as the Communications Consortium, which advertised its list of nearly two thousand key media people, including such gatekeepers as assignment and news editors. Emily Tynes, who worked for the group, said her guiding notion was: If you could have a headline in the *New York Times,* what would you want it to say? She said the key to good media strategy was to give a sense of ownership on an issue, to set the terms of its debate.

Over the course of the summer the nation's high brow journals—nearly all of them more liberal than conservative—aided the anti-Bork forces. Anthony Lewis, the influential liberal columnist for the *New York Times,* devoted half a dozen columns to decrying Bork's narrow view of constitutional liberty. Magazines such as the *New Yorker,* the *New York Review of Books,* and the *New Republic* printed long, thoughtful, and angry pieces linking Bork to an unprincipled activism of the right and the Reagan social agenda and condemning him in the harshest of terms. Ronald Dworkin, a left-wing constitutional scholar at New York University, had long opposed Bork, both when they were colleagues at

Yale, and later in print. He called Bork's positions "radical" and "antilegal." Renata Adler, a liberal Republican who had taken her law degree at Yale and wrote on legal issues in a highly intellectual fashion, labeled Bork's views on the Constitution "hard to read, cynical, poorly reasoned, and ideologically extreme to a degree that is unusual even on the outermost fringes of our public life." Philip Kurland, the conservative constitutional professor at the University of Chicago, attacked Bork in the *Chicago Tribune*. Kurland charged that Bork adjusted his views to political sentiment on the right at any given time to promote himself. The notable exception to this anti-Bork barrage was the *Wall Street Journal,* whose pro-Bork editorials matched in emotional timbre the most fervent anti-Bork material.

Bork's critics were steeped in the constitutional thinking of the past quarter century. To harness their rage made it much easier to label Bork as "outside the mainstream."

Apart from seeking to frame the debate, the Communications Consortium workers played the role of media monitor, seeking out trends and themes in Bork coverage during the hearings.

"Every morning someone would come in at six-thirty and do a summary of press coverage," Tynes said. "Then there would be a meeting to develop the message for that day. My job was damage control, to see how the message was playing in the targeted areas."

Tynes recalled an incident. A leader of the anti-Bork coalition had unforgivably told a reporter that support of Bork by attorney Lloyd Cutler—former counsel to President Jimmy Carter and an establishment Democrat—was a "setback." Such a remark was forbidden. Tynes had to spend a great deal of time getting everyone to tell reporters, as casually as possible, that this was not what was meant, that in fact, things couldn't be better.

Most agreed that the anti-Bork forces worked magic. When the battle was over, Bork and his advocates made much of the full-page newspaper, radio, and television advertisements. Their concerns were partly misdirected. Paid advertising around the country amounted to between one and two million dollars, not a magnificent figure in the circumstances. Of more importance was what public relations people called "free" or "earned" media—in other words, the news media.

"Never before had I felt so much like raw meat," commented Linda Greenhouse of the *New York Times,* speaking about liberal message framing. "Even while you knew it was happening, it seemed impossible to do anything about it. You couldn't avoid it. It was like Mount Rushmore in the middle of the flight path." . . .

Ironically, Sparks and Tynes, the anti-Bork media consultants, had learned their lessons from the right wing.

"In the past decade, the right learned how to get popular support for a notion and, through the use of polls and media, spread it," Sparks said. "For every dollar spent on creating an issue, they spent three on promoting it. They really had a better feel for the sense of the nation than we did."

Emily Tynes agreed. She noted that the antiabortion movement had learned from its 1960s opponents and had taken to using songs, rhetoric, and staged events to carry its cause to the people. The right also promoted issues through television and the co-opting of popular images, a standard Madison Avenue technique.

Liberals felt themselves unable to compete, and, Tynes said, the progressive movement was in a malaise during most of the Reagan era. Tynes, a black woman, had nearly given up on political activity. For her the Bork victory was "a shot in the arm, pure adrenaline. We spoke to how people were feeling."

Jackie Blumenthal helped write anti-Bork advertisements put out by People for the American Way. She felt the ads were less important as keys to stopping Bork than as a public announcement of a liberal counteroffensive.

"When Powell resigned, there was a simultaneous electric shock," she said. "We had been sitting on our hands for eight years waiting for the exact issue that would allow us to state what had been going wrong. For eight years the conservatives had been beating our brains out. Our ads broke the notion of our kowtowing to the new ethic in town. They were a sign that that period was over. We felt it was time for us to say, 'You can't set the tone anymore.'"

These ads came under frequent attack as a distortion of the judicial selection process. But Jackie Blumenthal defended them, saying they were "kindling to make this a truly political, ideological battle, not partisan, but political."

People for the American Way had been started in 1981 by Hollywood producer Norman Lear, creator of "All in the Family" and other innovative television shows. Lear liked to say that his was probably the only organization in America that began as a TV spot. Lear's notion was that the group would enter the fray for control of the national agenda through the use of media and symbols. He understood that Americans like America, that they feel good about their country. This was something the right had understood; Lear wanted the left to realize it. That was one reason for the self-consciously—almost self-parodying—patriotic name for his organization. Lear wanted to counteract the hours of far right evangelical preaching on television and what he saw as the right's ability to control the national dialogue.

People for the American Way was particularly involved in battles over textbook banning and for freedom of information. It ran newspaper advertisements over judicial nominations, such as Daniel Manion's,* and rapidly built up a budget of more than ten million dollars and a staff of about a hundred.

Focusing on the Bork nomination was a natural for the group. As Blumenthal put it, "Jerry Falwell needed an enemy to prosper. He and others used liberal-

---

* Daniel Manion was a controversial, conservative Reagan appointee to the Seventh Circuit Court of Appeals; he was confirmed by the U.S. Senate despite vehement objections from liberal senators and interest groups.

ism, the Trilateral Commission, communism. So we have done the same with figures like Bork. But the right didn't match us on this one. They showed an unbelievable failure of intelligence over Bork. They didn't know what this was about."

The advertisement that become a lightning rod for right-wing indignation was one Blumenthal helped put together for television, with Gregory Peck as narrator. It was Lear's idea to do a television commercial. Although he rarely got involved in the daily workings of People for the American Way, he had taken a special interest in the Bork nomination and contacted Peck, who had also become concerned over Bork. Jackie Blumenthal's two young sons and her deputy and the deputy's husband were the actors in the spot, put together in twenty-four hours because of Peck's schedule. The television family was shown on the steps of the Supreme Court looking up at its slogan, "Equal Justice Under Law." A gentle breeze ruffled their hair, as Peck introduced himself on the sound track and accused Bork of opposing civil rights, privacy, and much free speech protection.

"Robert Bork could have the last word on your rights as citizens, but the Senate has the last word on him," Peck said. "Please urge your senators to vote against the Bork nomination, because if Robert Bork wins a seat on the Supreme Court, it will be for life—his life and yours."

As David Kusnet, the organization's vice-president, explained it, the ad showed two positive symbols—the Court and the American family—interacting with each other. Juxtaposed on top of them was a looming Bork threatening the people and the institution. The ad won an award from *Millimeter* magazine, a trade journal for the film and broadcasting industry.

Perhaps the greatest irony of the Peck advertisement was that it was received with cynicism by the Washington press corps when People for the American Way presented it at a news conference. Few reporters wrote about it; few news programs aired it. The ad received little attention; it was aired only eighty-five times, tiny by advertising standards, and on mostly obscure stations for two weeks. Few Americans saw it, and few reacted. But on the last day of its airing White House spokesman Marlin Fitzwater attacked it, bringing it the attention it had never received. Once it was an object of controversy, it played for free over and over again on network news programs. . . .

The goal was fifty-one senators [to defeat Bork]. To get to those senators, the anti-Bork coalition had to go out to the people. If the campaign were left as an inside-Washington maneuver, Bork, himself an insider, would win.

Ricki Seidman, legal director of People for the American Way and an experienced political campaigner for liberal causes and candidates, said: "We could have all the substance in the world on our sides and go talk to senators. But to get their votes on this one, we needed to have their constituency against Bork. Rousing interest in legislation is hard enough. The Court is so removed. No one knows about it. We had to look for strategies that would serve as attention getters. People are not worried or knowledgeable about the Supreme Court but they are about the question of turning back the clock on civil rights and the Reagan agenda. We had to make clear that the Court and Bork are linked to those things."

Within a month of the nomination the public relations specialists in the coalition all agreed that polls would be central to a comprehensive, thoughtful campaign. The Boston firm of Marttila and Kiley, which had links to the Biden campaign and had done work in the past for AFSCME, was hired to carry out the poll. AFSCME offered forty thousand dollars to pay for it.

The poll, carried out in mid-August, was a watershed. It set out not only to test feelings about the nomination but also "to gauge the potential effect on voters' attitudes of many elements of Bork's record and background that have been subject to criticism in recent weeks." In other words, which issues could be best exploited? The poll reinforced the gut feelings of the anti-Bork leaders that the thrust of their message was appropriate. But it also offered important guidance on several overlooked points.

First of all, only about a third of Americans knew the Court had nine members; therefore, a campaign built on the concept of Court "balance" promised to have little impact. While balance continued as an underlying motivator and was frequently discussed with knowledgeable audiences, its prominence in coalition literature faded.

Secondly, the conservatives' belief that most Americans were unhappy with the Supreme Court, that they saw it as usurping the power of legislatures, was misguided. Only 27 percent thought that the Court was too conservative and 23 percent that it wielded too much influence on the country's affairs.

As Tom Kiley put it in his summation of the poll, "Supporters of Robert Bork, who is already positioned as a very conservative choice, cannot predicate their campaign on the existence of a public mandate for change on the Court. Quite the contrary; when it comes to the Supreme Court, most Americans are inclined to support the status quo."

Thirdly, the poll showed the American people to be more jaundiced about the judicial selection process than many inside Washington had believed. The vast majority of Americans—70 percent—believed that Reagan had chosen Bork for his political philosophy. Those polled seemed to scoff at the notion that Bork had been selected for his competence. The public saw the Court as an instrument of political power, not as the keeper of some abstract set of principles.

Fourthly, by a surprising five-to-one margin, Americans believed the Senate should carefully scrutinize a presidential nominee from all points of view, not merely his competence and personal integrity.

A fifth point noted in the coalition's analysis was that the nomination became increasingly unattractive the more Bork could be painted as someone with biases against groups or causes. It would not be enough to show that Bork was extremely conservative; he would have to harbor some kind of agenda.

In addition, there was populist resentment of officials and others, whether businessmen or academics, who sought to interfere with the freedom of individuals to conduct their lives as they wished. Bork's failure to support a constitutional guarantee of privacy—his opposition to the Supreme Court decision that struck down a law forbidding the use of contraceptives—could be deeply mined for that theme. The poll made clear that abortion should not be stressed in the headlines since it was a divisive issue. But the contraceptive case could be used as a kind of code.

Finally, Kiley warned the coalition against too much substance in its efforts to appeal to the nation: "To engage public opinion, Bork's opponents must keep their message clear, simple and direct. Again and again, we find that forays into constitutional law or judicial theory have the effect of impeding public understanding of the fundamental objections to Bork's nomination."

Nikki Heidepriem, a political message consultant hired by the anti-Bork forces, said that casting Bork as a right-wing ideologue seemed to her a bad idea because that put liberals in the bind of one day fighting off the notion that one of their nominees was a left-wing ideologue.

"Then we had the idea of simply labeling him a rigid ideologue, someone off the charts with a stifling interpretation of a living document," she said. "The key surrogate for that notion was privacy. That allowed some southern Democrats to talk about populism without our having to do it since it had bad connotations for blacks and ethnics. Privacy as an overarching concept gave us a chance to talk about control, as in choice, and integrity of the home as government becomes more intrusive. It was especially effective in the South."

And so, while fearing Bork would turn back the clock, the anti-Bork coalition actually *did* turn back the clock to beat him. It forced the debate into the domain of issues long settled, raising the specter of birth control police, poll taxes, and literacy tests. . . .

One aim of the anti-Bork coalition was to impart a sense of unstoppable momentum. The coalition made sure that reports critical of Bork were evenly spaced, coming out when little else was happening so as to create news events. Leaders also sought constantly to expand the coalition membership, adding groups every week. Ultimately some three hundred organizations joined the anti-Bork movement. They included such groups as the Association of Flight Attendants, B'nai B'rith Women, the Disability Rights Education and Defense Fund, the Jewish War Veterans of the USA, the Organization of Chinese Americans, the National Council of Senior Citizens, the Sierra Legal Defense and Education Fund, and the YWCA. Most had never considered taking a stand on a Supreme Court nomination before. But this one was cast in such dire terms, it so concentrated the struggle between those hoping to shape the country that it was nearly impossible to remain neutral on it. As columnist George Will derisively put it, "The ease with which such groups have been swept together for the first time in such a campaign reflects, in part, the common political culture of the people who run the headquarters of the compassion industry."

Opposition became especially noteworthy among women's groups. Bork had opposed the Equal Rights Amendment, the Court's 1973 abortion decision, and the application of the Fourteenth Amendment to women as a group. Hence even moderate women's organizations felt their fate and power on the line.

The National Federation of Business and Professional Women's Clubs, Inc., whose membership is nearly half Republican and active especially in the South and Midwest, made a huge commitment to the anti-Bork effort. Monica McFadden, the group's Washington lobbyist, said this was a first for the 125,000-member organization. The Bork nomination provided the group an opportunity it had sought for several years: a public policy issue that stirred the membership.

"Here were all the issues we cared about embodied in one fight," she said. "Senators know we're not nut cases. We're very moderate as a group. The average age of our members is late forties, early fifties." She added that what excited many of the members was the way the Bork battle attracted younger women to the organization, offering it a chance to reinvigorate its role and purpose in the country.

Patrick Caddell, the Democratic pollster and Biden adviser, remembered addressing a lunch of staff members of the Republican National Convention in early September. He had been asked to offer a Democrat's perspective to a discussion with Ed Rollins, former Reagan campaign chairman and political adviser. Caddell, who enjoyed nothing more than being provocative, started attacking the Bork nomination as poison for the Republicans. He said there was no better way to drive moderates and young women into the arms of the Democrats than to threaten them on issues such as privacy and equal protection for women.

"I thought I was throwing red meat at them, but the response was amazing," Caddell remembered. "Many women there agreed. One woman said to me that the nomination could be a Pandora's box for the party."

Two organizations hesitated for many weeks about whether to take a public stand on the nomination: the American Civil Liberties Union and Common Cause. Both, while liberal in orientation, prided themselves on being process- rather than result-oriented and on fighting issues in a principled, nonpartisan fashion. The fact that the Bork battle was seen as the domain of liberal Democrats made their decisions harder because it opened them to charges of politicization. That became a major issue a year later, when Republican presidential candidate George Bush used the ACLU membership of his opponent, Massachusetts Governor Michael Dukakis, as a blunt instrument with which to club him.

For the ACLU, Bork's consistent majoritarianism, his derision of the kinds of individual rights the organization championed made it almost impossible to stay out. The problem was a fifty-year-old rule forbidding the group from taking a stand on high court nominees. At an emergency meeting at the end of August the ACLU joined the opposition. It was not unexpected, but it was newsworthy and significant. Common Cause, which had made the same decision some weeks earlier, said that because Bork rejected the traditional role of the Supreme Court, that of defender of the rights of minorities, it had no choice but to oppose his confirmation.

The work against Bork went forward long before the hearings began and well away from the Senate chamber where he would officially be questioned. It took the White House by surprise. The administration expected a difficult confirmation battle. It thought, however, that the fight would occur *inside* the hearing room, as it had with Rehnquist. All the while, it was priming its candidate on his role in Watergate and on technical legal issues. The country beyond Washington was virtually ignored until too late. While liberals had discovered an issue to embody their anger and frustration of seven years and were mobilizing their troops, the administration was in a state of confusion. . . .

White House officials protested after the confirmation had failed that they had been unfairly accused of not working hard enough. Shortly before the final Senate vote Tom Gibson, then director of public affairs at the White House, drew up an extensive listing of pro-Bork activities by various sections of the White House. It was meant to be proof that they had worked hard. And they had. But a glance at the list makes clear that the bulk of the work began in mid-September, around the time of the hearings themselves. By then the anti-Bork offensive was well on its way to victory.

For example, the first lobbying telephone call to a senator by President Reagan on the Bork nomination was listed on September 30, after most senators had made up their minds. He did not call most southern Democrats. His first meeting with Republican Senate leaders took place on the day the hearings began, September 15.

Howard Baker called all the southern Democrats on July 21 and 22 but did no more personal lobbying until mid-September. In August he did sit for eight interviews and made a dozen speeches on the subject, mostly to Republican groups. Beginning in mid-September, when he was under fire, Baker gave a lot of interviews and speeches. He also personally lobbied sixty senators in September and October.

Various lower echelons in the White House produced op-ed pieces, letters to the editors, drafts of speeches, and so on for different administration officials to sign. Again, most of that work was done in late September and October.

While the White House tried to keep conservative groups from getting too publicly involved during the summer, many were doing so on their own anyway and resented the admonition.

Patrick McGuigan of the Free Congress Foundation in Washington, recalled that Culvahouse called him once and asked him to prevail upon Daniel Popeo, legal director of the Washington Legal Foundation, from speaking out for Bork's conservative views. Popeo had made a number of just the kinds of supportive

comments about Bork that worried the White House, saying Bork would overturn half a century of bad law.

McGuigan said he replied: "No way. I'm not going to call a guy who's like
a brother to me and say those things."

Culvahouse replied that the worst thing that could happen would be for conservatives to use the nomination to promote their agenda. McGuigan shot back
that no, the worst thing that could happen would be to lose the Bork war.

McGuigan meant that. Animated by a combination of religious fervor—he
was a devout Catholic—and conservative political goals, he toiled like a beast
for Bork. For McGuigan, the contest over Bork was a personal struggle. When
the battle was over, McGuigan wrote a book offering his views on what happened. In the preface he thanked his wife for her understanding, writing: "My
wife Pamela has for these many years endured hours, days and weeks of separation to support my work but never so intense a time of tension and sadness
in our life as the final weeks of Bork's struggle, when it gradually became clear
to me he would not prevail."

Conservatives were especially effective at generating mail to senators and ultimately beat the anti-Bork forces in number of letters sent. Religious fundamentalists, hopeful that Bork would contribute to overturning the abortion decision, were the most active, although some such groups stayed away,
concerned that Bork was areligious. The Public Affairs Committee of the Southern Baptist Convention urged that its 14.6 million members "prayerfully consider writing letters to their United States Senators to support the Bork nomination." The author of the resolution, Les Csorba of the First Baptist Church in
Alexandria, Virginia, said: "Judge Bork's opinions that the Constitution does not
protect pornography, that homosexual activity is not a constitutional right, that
some public recognition of the role of religion in our history should appear in
textbooks, and his respect for the Establishment Clause,* are consistent with the
sentiments of the Southern Baptist Convention."

Dr. Robert Grant, chairman of the Christian Voice, wrote to his followers:
"Robert Bork does not support the idea of a constitutional right to engage in
sodomy. He may help us stop the gay rights issue and thus help stem the spread
of AIDS. Don't wait—act now! We must return the law of our land to godly foundations while we have a chance."

Concerned Women for America, which championed traditional family values,
worked hard for Bork. The group launched a huge direct mail campaign and
ran newspaper advertisements in Pennsylvania and Alabama, homes of Senators Arlen Specter and Howell Heflin, undecided members of the Judiciary
Committee.

McGuigan's group also ran radio advertisements in Washington, D.C., to
counter a similar campaign by People for the American Way.

---

* The establishment clause of the First Amendment to the Constitution says that "Congress shall
make no law respecting an establishment of religion. . . ."

In Chicago a group called Free the Court! generated grass-roots activity for Bork. The name suggested the need to liberate the Court from "liberal special interests," according to Steven Baer, its director as well as director of the United Republican Fund of Illinois. The group had no contact with the White House other than an encouraging nod of approval from officials there when Baer called to announce its formation. He set up Senators Biden and Simon as targets since both were committee members running for president and were against Bork. Baer's group sent a couple of dozen demonstrators to many of their campaign appearances in Iowa and Illinois.

"We wanted to spook the southern senators with coverage of our anti-Biden work," Baer said later. "Our work was small-scale. We only spent twenty-five thousand dollars. But we did manage to have Biden met by pro-Bork crowds. He was visibly irritated."

Baer's group sent a plane with a banner over the Iowa State Fair during a debate, saying BIDEN AND SIMON, BORK BASHERS, LIBERAL LAPDOGS. At the Illinois fair it handed out large tickets to a Biden and Simon Puppet Show, "starring Joe 'Absolutely Open Mind' Biden and Paul '50 Ways to Leave Your Principles' Simon, produced by bootlicking, sycophantic political ambition, directed by the liberal special interests that control the Democratic presidential primary process and the activist agenda of the Supreme Court."

The work drew some local press coverage.

But more significant were the right's failings in grass-roots efforts. A sign of that failure was the poor organization of a group begun in Southern California by Bill Roberts, onetime campaign director for Reagan. Called We the People, the group vowed to raise two million dollars but never brought in more than two hundred thousand.

Just before the hearings began, McGuigan called one of his friends at the White House to complain that [conservative lobbyist Thomas] Korologos had disparaged outside groups for not doing enough to help the confirmation. McGuigan protested that he had been killing himself over this thing and that it was the White House that had done too little. The official said Korologos was complaining about the corporate establishment, which promised help and did not deliver.

McGuigan said it was most important for the White House to begin raising money for the pro-Bork campaign. "This nomination won't get by unless some bucks get plowed into television advertising pronto," he said. Then, referring to the anti-Bork ad recorded by Gregory Peck, McGuigan added, "For God's sake, the other side has Abe Lincoln in their TV spots. You need to get the president on the horn to some of his rich buddies, and the word needs to go out that this needs to happen."

"We can't do that," the official replied. "It's just not appropriate for the president to raise money for a lobbying operation." This was partly a reference to the Iran-contra scandal when money for the contras was raised privately by those connected to the administration.

"I don't care how you do it," McGuigan replied. "I don't care if it's done with winks and nudges." The official said he would see what he could do. Nothing materialized.

Another serious setback was the failure of pro-Bork forces to persuade the National Rifle Association to help them. Perhaps the most effective conservative lobby in Washington, and one of the wealthiest, the NRA stayed out of the Bork fight despite two decisions Bork had handed down as a judge in its favor. The main reason the group sat out the fight was its concern over what it saw as Bork's cramped view of the Fourth Amendment prohibition against search and seizure. NRA leaders feared Bork would seek to close loopholes in the law regarding state troopers who stop and search vehicles, confiscating unregistered firearms. Anything that might detract from the free possession of guns was perceived as a threat by the NRA. When one of the most powerful conservative groups in the country, one which had frequently poured its funds into fights over judicial nominations, felt threatened by Bork's strict interpretation of the Constitution, it was an omen.

Epilogue

The White House made the wrong choice in its advice to Bork on how to testify before the Senate (although elsewhere in the book Bronner raises doubt about whether Bork was amenable to *any* advice). Rather than remain consistent to the conservative philosophy expressed in his earlier writings and speeches, Bork gave the impression in his testimony that he was willing to consider adopting a more expansive philosophy regarding the rights of women and minorities. This led to charges by liberals that Bork was undergoing "confirmation conversion" and doubts by conservatives that he would be as certain a vote for their cause as they once believed. Bork's nomination was defeated by a combination of votes from liberal Democrats, conservative southern Democrats, and several moderate and maverick Republicans.

In the end, there was serious doubt whether any strategy would have gotten Bork confirmed. In 1986, President Reagan had campaigned in the South for a half-dozen Republican Senate candidates promising that their election would guarantee the nomination and confirmation of a conservative Supreme Court justice. All of these candidates were defeated. Southern Democrats were therefore extremely receptive to the demands of the NAACP (which had helped defeat the Republican Senate candidates) that Bork be defeated. Politically, Bork may have been in the wrong place at the wrong time.

Ironically, the liberal coalition was so tired that, after watching Reagan's next nominee, Douglas Ginsberg, self-destruct, the liberals failed to mount a credible campaign against the third nominee, the even more conservative Anthony Kennedy, who was confirmed by the Senate. Liberals may have won the Bork battle, but they almost certainly have lost the war for control of the Court.

CHAPTER 9

POLITICS AND
THE MEDIA

John F. Kennedy and the West Virginia Primary

Theodore H. White

Rarely does a writer have the talent and the opportunity to invent a new genre—but journalist Theodore H. White did just that with *The Making of the President 1960*. White, a former *Time* magazine reporter, spent time with all of the candidates on the 1960 presidential campaign trail with the intention of telling the behind-the-scenes story of how Americans choose their president. It was his good fortune to launch this effort during one of the closest and most dramatic presidential elections of the twentieth century. White's technique of election reporting has been attempted by many others in the years since (he himself followed every election thereafter until his death), but the drama of this first volume has never really been duplicated.

Most people remember the 1960 election for the debates between Vice President Richard Nixon and Massachusetts senator John F. Kennedy, the first presidential debates ever televised. Others recall that the election turned on a relative handful of votes in several states. One of them, Illinois, went to the Democrats in what is believed to have been a tribute to the inventive vote-counting techniques of the Democratic machine in Chicago under Mayor Richard Daley. None of these events would have taken place, however, without the dramatic efforts White describes in this selection about the pivotal Democratic primary in West Virginia.

From the time of Franklin D. Roosevelt until the 1960 election, the Democratic nomination went to the candidate who had the support of party bosses around the nation. In 1952, Senator Estes Kefauver's dramatic string of primary victories meant nothing: the party bosses chose Adlai Stevenson as the Democratic nominee, even though he had not run in a single primary. In 1960, it appeared that Minnesota senator Hubert Humphrey, a leader in the civil rights battles of the 1950s, would be in the same position as Stevenson. Not only was he a senior and respected senator, but his opponent, John F. Kennedy, had established an image

From Theodore H. White, *The Making of the President 1960* (New York: Atheneum Publishers, 1961). Reprinted with permission from Atheneum Publishers, an imprint of Macmillan Publishing Company. Copyright © 1961 Atheneum House, Inc. Reprinted with permission of Laurence Pollinger Limited, Authors' Agents, London.

in the Senate that reflected glamour rather than hard work. Moreover, although no one wanted to admit that prejudice against Catholics still existed in this country in 1960, it was no accident that a Catholic had never been president. In fact, the last candidate to try, Al Smith, had fared so poorly in 1928 against Herbert Hoover that the memory of his defeat was believed to be an insurmountable hurdle to Catholic candidates. As you will see, however, Kennedy's personal energy and charisma, as well as his extremely talented campaign staff, led by Lawrence O'Brien, overcame the potential negatives.

As we join the primary race, Kennedy has just finished the Wisconsin primary and now knows that he is facing a long, difficult run for the presidential nomination. He heads for West Virginia, knowing that he must make his mark in the primaries if he is to have any effect on the party bosses in the convention voting. Unfortunately, Kennedy was dealt a setback in Wisconsin: he did not win by as large a percentage of the votes as had been expected, and his 56 percent majority gave him only six of the state's ten electoral districts. It was clear that the votes had been divided largely on religious grounds. The fear of the Kennedy team was that the conservative philosophy of the Protestant-dominated state of West Virginia would be difficult to overcome. That fear was backed by preliminary voter polling (Kennedy was the first candidate to use polling data to this extent), which indicated that the Bostonian was far behind. How the Kennedy team turned this challenge into an advantage and put the religion issue behind them is a classic example of nomination politics at its best.

LOUIS HARRIS   Kennedy's pollster.

HUBERT HUMPHREY   Candidate for 1960 Democratic presidential nomination.

JOHN F. KENNEDY   Candidate for 1960 Democratic presidential nomination.

ROBERT McDONOUGH   Head of Kennedy's West Virginia organization.

LAWRENCE O'BRIEN   Kennedy's campaign director.

FRANKLIN D. ROOSEVELT, JR.   Strong Kennedy supporter.

THEODORE SORENSON   Kennedy aide and speechwriter.

▶ West Virginia had long attracted the interest of John F. Kennedy—perhaps longer than any of the other states in the union outside his own. Two years before, while running for re-election as Senator from Massachusetts, he had retained Louis Harris to make the very first probe of public opinion outside his home state—in West Virginia, in June of 1958. (The result of the poll then was 52 for Kennedy, 38 for [Richard] Nixon, balance undecided.)

A shadow organization had been set up early in 1959 in West Virginia, its local chief being Robert McDonough, a printing-plant proprietor of Clark County, a lean, taciturn but imaginative student of his home state's bizarre politics. The original Washington strategist and director had been Ted Sorensen. Slowly, through 1959, from county to county, from center to center, the Kennedy people had woven an organization called West Virginians for Kennedy—not so much to act as to be ready to act if necessary. In December of 1959, Lou Harris had reported out of West Virginia again—this time with a 70-to-30 break for Kennedy over [Hubert] Humphrey. Still there was no Kennedy decision to act in West Virginia. A small state, its primary verdict not binding on the delegates actually elected, it seemed only conditionally worth a campaign effort in a spring of frantic exertion. The condition on which it would be worth the effort was simple: that "the trap could be baited for Humphrey to enter," as one of the Kennedy early planning papers said. When in February of 1960 Humphrey did indeed "enter the trap" by filing his primary papers in Charleston, the Kennedys jubilantly followed suit and closed the trap around him.

By April of 1960, however, after the Wisconsin primary, it was uncertain whether it was Humphrey who was caught in the trap or Kennedy himself. For between February and April the political atmosphere of the country had begun to heat. The Wisconsin primary had attracted the attention of the national press and the national television networks; and the nation had become aware that a religious issue was beginning to develop in its national politics for the first time since 1928; men and women from West Virginia to Alaska were slowly learning the identity and religion of the major candidates; and the tide in West Virginia had turned against the Boston candidate. Sampling in Charleston now, three weeks before the primary voting day of May 10th, Harris discovered that the citizens of Kanawha county—which includes Charleston, the capital—had shifted vehemently in sentiment. They were now, he reported, 60 for Humphrey, 40 for Kennedy. When Kennedy headquarters inquired of their West Virginia advisers what had happened between his 70-to-30 margin of December and the short end of the present 40-to-60 split, they were told, curtly, "But no one in West Virginia knew you were a Catholic in December. Now they know."

Only two moments of discouragement seemed seriously to shake Kennedy confidence in victory in the long year of 1960. The greater was the late-August abysm, following the Convention, when the candidate was trapped in Congress' special session. But the first was the period after Wisconsin, as the Kennedy men approached West Virginia. They had been overconfident in Wisconsin; they had been misled by the press; the vote had broken on strictly religious lines. Now they faced trial in West Virginia with every survey showing against them, fighting a man who could not win at the Convention but who, if he won here, would throw the nominating decision into the back room.

As usual with the Kennedy operation, solution proceeded at two levels—one strategic and one organizational. Both are worth examination, for both were in their way classics of American politics.

The organizational solution was, of course, O'Brien's. After ten years in the service of John F. Kennedy, Lawrence F. O'Brien is certainly one of the master political operators of the new school.

What distinguishes the new school from the old school is the political approach of exclusion versus inclusion. In a tight old-fashioned machine, the root idea is to operate with as few people as possible, keeping decision and action in the hands of as few inside men as possible. In the new style, practiced by citizens' groups and new machines (Republican and Democratic alike) the central idea is to give as many people as possible a sense of participation: participation galvanizes emotions, gives the participant a live stake in the victory of the leader.

It is always easy for a glamorous candidate to arouse the bowels of people who hear him. What is much more difficult is to give these people, once aroused, the sense that they are usefully participant. In 1958, for example, John F. Kennedy in his Massachusetts Senatorial campaign had circulated nominating petitions signed by 256,000 citizens of the Bay State—some fervid, some perfunctory. At the same time the Kennedy headquarters in Boston were overwhelmed with the offer of service from some 1,800 volunteers for whom no easily useful function could be found. The O'Brien solution: to put the volunteers to work sending out letters of thanks to each of the 256,000 signers of the nomination petitions. This is what politicians consider a nearly perfect solution: it made happy the receivers of the letters of thanks and, more importantly, gave to each volunteer the illusion of service. There are still men at the bars of South Boston who boast of the letter that Jack Kennedy sent them for signing his nominating petition in 1958. All this, of course, is codified in the O'Brien Manual—a sixty-four-page black-bound book that gives the diagram of organization for every Kennedy campaign from beginning to end. It would be superfluous to summarize this book. Its burden is that every vote counts; that every citizen likes to feel he is somehow wired into the structure of power; that making a man or woman seem useful and important to himself (or herself) in the power system of American life takes advantage of one of the simplest and noblest urges of politics in the most effective way.

Heavy with gloom, O'Brien arrived in West Virginia, sleepless from Wisconsin, on the Wednesday following the Wisconsin primary. There were at that moment four weeks to go before the voting of May 10th; and the organization then available had been prepared not for an emergency but for easy victory. Bob McDonough, as Executive Chairman, had, in the weeks preceding, added only one paid full-time worker, the hulking Matt Reese, to his staff; together Reese and McDonough had found chairmen for Kennedy volunteer organizations in thirty-nine of West Virginia's fifty-five counties. These county chairmen had been informed of what was required by O'Brien two weeks earlier: subordinate district chairmen; telephone chairmen for the women's workers; primary day chairmen for rounding up cars to haul voters to the polls; two stand-by deputy chairmen available day or night for literature distribution, whether at church socials or factory gates, by dawn or by dusk. Only twenty-five of the thirty-nine county organizations had, in whole or in part, fulfilled these assigned tasks. Now, on the day after the Wisconsin primary, with the middle-European accents of Wisconsin still ringing in their ears, O'Brien and Bobby Kennedy, with no rest or vacation, arrived in West Virginia to pull the organization together for emergency action. This was crash work; neither needed to tell the other that defeat in West Virginia would all but end John F. Kennedy's chance of nomination.

A first meeting in the morning for the northern chairmen took place at the Stonewall Jackson Hotel in Clarksburg. A second meeting for the southern chairmen took place that afternoon at the Kanawha Hotel, 100 miles away, in Charleston.

Jobs to be done:

— Organization of volunteers for door-to-door distribution of the Kennedy literature.

— Rural mailings.

— Telephone campaign. (The West Virginians explained the problem of telephoning in a state where the party line still reigns, but O'Brien insisted nonetheless.)

— Receptions to be organized. (And since tea and coffee receptions were too effete for West Virginia, it was all right to call receptions an "ox roast" in the northern part of the state, a "weenie roast" in the southern part.)

— Finally, all county chairmen were told which members of the Kennedy family (plus Franklin D. Roosevelt, Jr.) would be available to tour in what areas on which day.

— Above all: work.

Five days later, on the Monday following the Wisconsin primary, area commanders had arrived. Kennedy area commanders are in themselves also worth study, for so much has been written and will be written on the use of Kennedy money to buy elections. The controversy over Kennedy money revolves largely about the money paid out in actual campaign (legitimate and aboveboard) and the money value of the services the Kennedys commanded without payment (staggeringly large). There were to be eight main headquarters of the Kennedy campaign in the emergency program for West Virginia, and to these were later added eight more subheadquarters. These, however, were to be staffed by volunteers of such talent (and of such independent means) that the money value of their talents defies definition. Even at this late date no complete listing is available of the Kennedy volunteers who invaded West Virginia for the primary; but even a partial listing of their names would bring the total to fifty people (as against Humphrey's talent total of less than ten). There were Lem Billings, a roommate of the candidate at Choate School, an advertising man; Bill Battle, a Navy comrade of the candidate, son of a former governor of Virginia; Artist Bill Walton (assigned to the bleak deprivation of McDowell County). Other volunteers included: Benjamin Smith (Harvard), former mayor of Gloucester, Massachusetts, independently wealthy; Claude Hooton, Harvard classmate; Chuck Spalding, Harvard classmate, independently wealthy; R. Sargent Shriver (Yale), brother-in-law, independently wealthy; Richard K. Donahue, Vice-chairman of the Massachusetts Democratic Committee, a corruscatingly brilliant young lawyer from Lowell, Massachusetts; Paul B. ("Red") Fay, a comrade of his PT boat days. And besides these, the total staff of Kennedy's Senatorial office (except for the strategic-intellectual arm of Sorensen-Goodwin-Feldman), plus girls, drivers, typists, press men, chauffeurs, TV men. When Kennedy is denounced for his expenditures in West Virginia, this staff is commonly cited as an illustration of extravagance; but the key men of this staff were volunteers; they could not be recruited by money and were, indeed, worth more than money. An FBI investigation later authorized by Richard M. Nixon's friend, Attorney-General William P. Rogers, could after exhaustive study turn up no evidence of wrongdoing.

Each of the eight area commanders, plus their deputies, were in West Virginia six days after the Wisconsin primary. They met on Monday evening in the Kanawha Hotel, preparatory to being dispatched to the hills.

First instruction: to inspect all the machinery outlined by the O'Brien Manual, see whether it was functioning under the local chairmen already designated, then telephone back in three days with a full report on their area.

A week after the telephone report they were to submit a written report on their area, describing its problems, potentials and needs in exact detail. One other instruction: since all of them were alien, out-of-state and Eastern men, suspect by the mountaineers, they were enjoined to pay their first call in each district upon the local county courthouse political leader—whether friendly or hostile. Whatever they were about to do, they were instructed, they should report frankly to the local political leader before doing it. This was to be no secret Papist conspiracy. The candidate—now vacationing in Montego Bay in Jamaica—could give West Virginia no more than ten days of his time (he had Nebraska, Maryland and Oregon primaries to fight simultaneously); but when he came he would rouse the people. Their job was to harness the manpower that the candidate's leadership would trumpet up.

So spoke O'Brien—tired, benign, still unruffled.

If organization could do it, he would do it. This was his trade, and in West Virginia he was performing what will remain a masterpiece in the art of the primaries. But beyond organization was the raw stuff of American politics: those things blurted out by simple people that show their emotion, their misgiving, their trust.

And there could be no doubt about the issue that bothered these people, at least no doubt from the memories of this correspondent:

— Woman on a lawn at West Hamlin, West Virginia, as the school band plays and the incomparable tulips wave in the breeze: "I'm not prejudiced. A man's religion shouldn't have anything to do with it. But a man ought to be a good Catholic if he's going to be one. And they believe in church-and-state and I don't."

— Little old lady, under a dripping umbrella in the rain at Sutton, West Virginia ("Home of the Golden Delicious Apple" says the sign): "We've never had a Catholic President and I hope we never do. Our people built this country. If they had wanted a Catholic to be President, they would have said so in the Constitution."

— Big burly man, heavy jowls, good face, limping (the limp from World War I, in which he had been hit): "I'm a Lutheran—and you know how we feel. I haven't been in New York since we came off the boat in 1919, I hear it's changed."

— A man in front of the courthouse in Putnam County, West Virginia; the man is angry because somebody on the outskirts of the crowd is making a noise: "What's that goofball blowing off for? I'm a Baptist, but I got nothing against no man's religion."

The issue, it was clear, over and beyond anything O'Brien's organizational genius could do, was religion: the differing ways men worshipped Christ in this enclave of Western civilization.

All other issues were secondary. The Kennedy tacticians had already refined several minor lines of attack on Humphrey. They had begun and continued to stress the war record of John F. Kennedy, for in West Virginia, a state of heroes and volunteers, the stark courage of the Boston candidate in the Straits of the Solomons in the Fall of 1942 found a martial echo in every hill. ("To listen to their stuff," said an irate Humphrey man, "you'd think Jack won the war all by himself.") The Kennedy men continued to hammer at Humphrey as being "front man" for a gang-up crowd of Stevenson-Symington-Johnson supporters who refused to come into the open.* They stressed their candidate's sympathy and concern for the hungry and unemployed. Humphrey, who had known hunger

---

* Adlai Stevenson, Senator Stuart Symington of Missouri, and Senator Lyndon Johnson of Texas were all considered prospects for the Democratic nomination even though none had announced his candidacy.

in boyhood, was the natural workingman's candidate—but Kennedy's shock at the suffering he saw in West Virginia was so fresh that it communicated itself with the emotion of original discovery. Kennedy, from boyhood to manhood, had never known hunger. Now, arriving in West Virginia from a brief rest in the sun in the luxury of Montego Bay, he could scarcely bring himself to believe that human beings were forced to eat and live on these cans of dry relief rations, which he fingered like artifacts of another civilization. "Imagine," he said to one of his assistants one night, "just imagine kids who never drink milk." Of all the emotional experiences of his pre-Convention campaign, Kennedy's exposure to the misery of the mining fields probably changed him most as a man; and as he gave tongue to his indignation, one could sense him winning friends.

Yet the religious issue remained, and as the days grew closer to the voting the Kennedy staff divided on how it must be handled. His native West Virginian advisers said that West Virginia was afraid of Catholics; the fear must be erased, the matter must be tackled frontally. Lou Harris, with his poll reports in hand, concurred. But most of the Kennedy Washington staff disagreed—raise no religious issue in public, they said, religion is too explosive.

It was up to the candidate alone to decide. And, starting on April 25th, his decision became clear. He would attack—he would meet the religious issue head on.

Whether out of conviction or out of tactics, no sounder Kennedy decision could have been made. Two Democratic candidates were appealing to the commonality of the Democratic Party; once the issue could be made one of tolerance or intolerance, Hubert Humphrey was hung. No one could prove to his own conscience that by voting for Humphrey he was displaying tolerance. Yet any man, indecisive in mind on the Presidency, could prove that he was at least tolerant by voting for Jack Kennedy.

The shape of the problem made it impossible for Humphrey, himself the most tolerant of men, to run in favor of tolerance. Only Kennedy could campaign on this point and still win in good taste and without unfairness. If his religion was what they held against him, Kennedy would discuss it. And by exquisite use of TV, he did indeed discuss it.

There remains with me now a recollection of what I think is the finest TV broadcast I have ever heard any political candidate make. It is also one of the few slip-ups I know in the efficient Kennedy organization, for no transcript, no tape recording, no TV tape is known to anybody who heard Kennedy address the people of West Virginia on Sunday evening, May 8th. What I write is from memory and scattered notes.

Over that week end before the West Virginia voting, Kennedy had paid a flying visit to Nebraska, where he was required to face a primary on the same day as the West Virginia primary. He had already been hammering night and day, for ten days, the issue of religion ("I refuse to believe that I was denied the right to be President on the day I was baptized"). In Nebraska, home state of Ted

Sorensen, he had asked this closest of his aides to write down the four or five questions that bothered Protestants most when they worried about Catholics. Sorensen stayed up all night pondering the problem and came up with the questions. In West Virginia the next night, Sunday, Franklin D. Roosevelt, Jr., was summoned as the interlocutor, and on the paid telecast Roosevelt now questioned the candidate on his religion.

The religious question was planted by Roosevelt, Jr., about three or four minutes after the broadcast began, and Kennedy, as I remember it, used almost ten or twelve minutes of the half-hour show to answer. Later the same phrases were to grow sterile, but at this moment Kennedy spoke from the gut. He reviewed the long war of church on state and state on church and that greatest of all constitutional decisions: to separate church from state. Then, peering into the camera and talking directly to the people of West Virginia, he proceeded, as I remember, thus:

> . . . *so when any man stands on the steps of the Capitol and takes the oath of office of President, he is swearing to support the separation of church and state; he puts one hand on the Bible and raises the other hand to God as he takes the oath. And if he breaks his oath, he is not only committing a crime against the Constitution, for which the Congress can impeach him—and should impeach him—but he is committing a sin against God.*

Here Kennedy raised his hand from an imaginary Bible, as if lifting it to God, and, repeating softly, said, "A sin against God, for he has sworn on the Bible."

Against this issue of the campaign Humphrey was powerless. Savagely the Kennedy team increased the pressure.

In every hollow, hill and city the Kennedy operational team cultivated the courthouse bosses; they had played by the rules in Wisconsin and won squarely; they would play by the rules in West Virginia and win here, too. Under O'Brien's lash, the volunteers multiplied and then multiplied again, until by primary day O'Brien could estimate that he had 9,000 volunteer primary day workers engaged in some task or other.

In the newspapers Kennedy advertisements drummed away at the record of their war hero, or flayed Humphrey as the puppet of faceless men afraid to show their courage in a West Virginia primary.

Up and down the roads roved Kennedy names, brothers and sisters all available for speeches and appearances; to the family names was added the lustrous name of Franklin D. Roosevelt, Jr. Above all, over and over again there was the handsome, open-faced candidate on the TV screen, showing himself, proving that a Catholic wears no horns. The documentary film on TV opened with a cut of a PT boat spraying a white wake through the black night, and Kennedy was a war hero; the film next showed the quiet young man holding a book in his hand in his own library receiving the Pulitzer Prize, and he was a scholar; then the young man held his golden-curled daughter of two, reading to her as she sat on his lap, and he was the young father; and always, gravely, open-eyed, with a sincerity that could not be feigned, he would explain his own devotion to the freedom of America's faiths and the separation of church and state.

With a rush, one could feel sentiment change. Harris' pollsters, now operating across the state on a day-by-day basis, would check and recheck certain streets in specific towns at weekly intervals. "You could see them switch," says Harris. "You would meet a Madame LaFarge type all dressed in black, and she would say, 'I don't care about Humphrey, but I just don't want a Catholic.' When you had one like that, you had a germ cell infecting everyone in the street. I remember going back to one particular one the Monday before the election, after the TV speech on religion, and she took me in, pulled down the blinds and said she was going to vote for Kennedy now. 'We have enough trouble in West Virginia, let alone to be called bigots, too.'"

Kanawha County, the most populous county of West Virginia, seat of Charleston, the capital, had checked out in the first poll after Wisconsin as being 64 for Humphrey, 36 for Kennedy. Two weeks before the election, the Humphrey margin had dropped to 55 to 45; the day after the Humphrey-Kennedy TV debate it had fallen to 52 to 48; on Saturday before election, the Harris sampling showed 45 to 42 for Humphrey, the rest undecided; and after the final TV week end on religion, it had switched to a narrow Kennedy lead. (On primary day itself, Kanawha County was to go 52 to 48 *for* Kennedy.)

The orchestration of this campaign infuriated Humphrey. Once the issue had been pitched as tolerance versus intolerance, there was only one way for a West Virginian to demonstrate tolerance—and that was by voting for Kennedy. Backed against the wall by the development of an issue for which there was no conceivable response either in his heart or practical politics, Humphrey fell back on the issue of money. ("There are three kinds of politics," he would say. "The politics of big business, the politics of the big bosses, and the politics of big money, and I'm against all of them. I stand for politics of the people.")

Here, indeed, one could mourn for Humphrey. Tired from his exertions in Wisconsin, tired from his efforts in the meaningless District of Columbia primary, tired from his travels (flying by commercial airliners and carrying his own bags through the air-gates), half of Humphrey's time was spent in raising money to continue, the other half barnstorming in his lonesome bus (OVER THE HUMP WITH HUMPHREY read the bus's sign). Humphrey was being clubbed into defeat in a gladiatorial contest far from home, without funds, in a contest where victory could bring him little, and defeat would erase any influence he might have in the campaign of 1960.

Already heavily in debt for his Wisconsin campaign ($17,000 of unpaid debts hung over his head as he entered West Virginia), Humphrey had exhausted every resource and friendship he knew to raise money for this new campaign. He had been deserted now by all the old labor leaders for whom he had battled so heartfully for so many years in Washington; they wanted him out after the

Wisconsin primary; they would give him no help here. And where desertion was not voluntary, the ever-efficient Kennedy organization, knowing its own fate to hang in the balance, moved to chop off the flow of support. In New York, from which so much Stevenson money had originally come to Humphrey's coffers, Governor Abraham Ribicoff, acting on Kennedy's instructions, warned all Stevensonians that if they continued to finance the hopeless campaign of Hubert Humphrey, Adlai Stevenson would not even be *considered* for Secretary of State. Where necessary, Kennedy lieutenants were even rougher; in Connecticut, Boss John Bailey informed former Connecticut Senator William Benton, publisher of the *Encyclopaedia Britannica,* that if he continued to finance Humphrey (Benton had already given Humphrey $5,000 earlier in the spring), he would never hold another elective or appointive job in Connecticut as long as he, Bailey, had any say in Connecticut politics—which is a statement equivalent to permanent political exile in the Nutmeg State.

Strangled for lack of money (Humphrey's expenditures in West Virginia were to total only $25,000—nothing, in the scale of American politics), knowing himself in debt, aware of the nature, depth and resources of this final Kennedy drive, as the final week end approached Humphrey became a figure of pathos. He needed advertising, he needed workers, above all he needed TV to show himself across the state.

I remember the final Saturday morning, shortly after it was revealed that Kennedy's TV expenditures alone across the state had mounted to $34,000. Humphrey had had but four hours' sleep that morning and was up at seven, prepared to barnstorm north from Charleston in his bus on a rainy morning; at that point one of his assistants informed him that the TV stations that had booked him for a Sunday night half hour were threatening to cancel unless they were paid that day, cash in advance, for the time.

It was one of the few times I have seen the temper of that genial man snap. "Pay it!" snarled Humphrey. "Pay it! I don't care how, don't come to me with that kind of story!" Then, realizing that his crestfallen aide was, like himself, destitute, Hubert pulled out his checkbook at the breakfast table and said, "All right, I'll pay for it myself," and scribbled a personal check of his own.

Mrs. Humphrey watched him do so, with dark, sad eyes, and one had the feeling that the check was money from the family grocery fund—or the money earmarked to pay for the wedding of their daughter who was to be married the week following the primary.

My memory tells me that the sum of that check was $750—not a particularly large sum for a statewide hookup of half an hour. But such a grocery-money check buys time only—it does not buy the production, the preparation, the care a major television manipulation of the public requires.

What happens when a man goes on cold on TV in politics with such a grocery-money investment was grotesquely shown by Humphrey's final appeal to the voters of West Virginia on that day before the election. From somewhere he had raised another $750 for another half hour of TV time, and now (like

Richard Nixon much later in the year) he was prepared to save all with a telethon. A telethon is a political gimmick in which a candidate, theoretically but not actually, throws himself open to any and all questions from any voter who cares to call the broadcasting station. A good telethon requires good staff in order to screen questions and artfully sequence them so they give the illusion of spontaneity yet feed the candidate those pretexts on which he can masterfully develop his themes. It is commonly one of the most spurious and obnoxious devices of modern political gimmicry.

What happens when such a telethon is authentic—not spurious—Humphrey demonstrated with his modest $750 investment on that Monday. For when authentic, unscreened questions are fed to the candidate the effect is comic. Except that, watching Hubert Humphrey fight his last national battle with family grocery money, the effect was more sad than comic.

The telethon opened with Humphrey sitting alone at a desk; before him was a manual telephone with switch buttons for two lines, which he was supposed to punch alternately as questioners telephoned in. The viewing audience was to hear both unscreened question and answer over the TV set.

The first question was a normal mechanical question: "What makes you think you're qualified to be President, Senator Humphrey?" So was the second question: "Can you be nominated, Mr. Humphrey?"

Then came a rasping voice over the telephone, the whining scratch of an elderly lady somewhere high in the hills, and one could see Humphrey flinch (as the viewers flinched); and the rasp said, "You git out! You git out of West Virginia, Mr. Humphrey!" Humphrey attempted to fluster a reply and the voice overrode him, "You git out, you hear! You can't stand the Republicans gitting ahead of you! Why don't you git out?"

Humphrey had barely recovered from the blast before the next call came: what would he do about small-arms licensing for people who like to hunt? Then, what would he do about social security? None of the questions were hitting anywhere near the target area of Humphrey's campaign program, and then a sweet womanly voice began to drawl on the open switch, "How about those poor little neglected children, Mr. Humphrey, I mean how can we lower taxes like you say and take care of all those little children who need more schools and more hospitals, and more everything . . ." On and on she went, sweetly, as Humphrey (his precious, costly minutes oozing by) attempted to break in and say that he, too, was for the poor little neglected children.

By now the telethon was becoming quite a family affair, and the next voice was a fine mountain voice, easy, slow, gentle with West Virginia courtesy, and it said, "Senator Humphrey, I just want you to know that I want to apologize for that lady who told you to git out. We don't feel like that down here in West Virginia, Senator Humphrey, and I'm very sorry that she said that. . . ." He would have rambled on and on, but Humphrey, desperate, expressed quick thanks and pressed the other button.

He had barely begun to answer the question when a clipped voice interrupted on the party line of the caller, "Clear the wires, please, clear the wires,
this is an emergency!" Humphrey attempted to explain that they were on the
air, they were answering questions to a TV audience. "Clear the wires, clear the
wire at once, this is an emergency," repeated the operator on the party line that
straggled down some unknown West Virginia hill on which, perhaps, someone
was trying to summon a doctor; and Humphrey, his face blank and bedazzled,
hung up, shaken, to press the button for another call (a gruff voice, with a thick
accent, asking what he and Kennedy were going to do for the coal operators,
they'd only been talking about the miners up to now, not the operators). From
that point on the telethon lost all cohesion—proving nothing except that TV is
no medium for a poor man.

West Virginia voted on May 10th, a wet, drizzly day. By eight o'clock the polls
were closed. With 100 names on some of the local ballots, all of them more
important as jobs to West Virginians than the Presidency, the count was very
slow. Shortly before nine o'clock, however, came the first flash: Old Field Precinct, Hardy County, Eastern Panhandle, a precinct acknowledging only
twenty-five Catholic registered voters, had counted: For Kennedy, 96; for Humphrey, 36.

The count dragged on. By 9:20, with ten precincts out of 2,750 in the state
having reported, the first faint trend became visible: Kennedy, 638; Humphrey,
473—a 60-to-40 break. Yet these were from northern West Virginia, the sensi-
tized civilized north. How would the candidate do in the fundamentalist,
coal-mining south? By 9:40 the count read Kennedy, 1,566 and Humphrey, 834;
and someone in the Humphrey headquarters muttered, "We're dead."

By ten o'clock the sweep was no longer spotty but statewide. Down in Logan
County, Kennedy was outrunning the local boss; in McDowell County he was
doing better than 60 to 40. Hill pocket, hill slope, industrial town, Charleston,
Parkersburg, Wheeling, suburb, white, Negro—the Kennedy tide was moving,
powerfully, irresistibly, all across the Protestant state, writing its message for
every politician in the nation to see.

There remained then only the ceremonies of burial for the Humphrey candidacy and of triumph for Kennedy.

It is no easy thing to dismantle a Presidential candidacy, and though Hubert
Humphrey had decided to yield by ten in the evening, two and a half long hours
went by as, from his room in the Ruffner Hotel, he telephoned his supporters
and contributors all across the land (in Minnesota, in Washington, in New York)
that the end had come. At one A.M. the Western Union messenger arrived at the
Kennedy headquarters with Humphrey's telegram of concession; at 1:15 Bobby
Kennedy, representing his brother, who was sheltering in Washington that evening, walked through the rainy streets of Charleston to pay a graceful thank-you
call on Humphrey at his hotel. Equally gracious, Humphrey announced that he
would be coming to the Kennedy headquarters to greet Kennedy on his night

flight in to Charleston to claim victory. Together the two walked out into the rain and turned the corner down Capitol Street toward Kennedy headquarters at the Kanawha Hotel.

On Capitol Street, Humphrey paused a moment to enter his main (and practically only) headquarters in West Virginia. A few bitter-enders remained among the litter of wadded paper coffee cups and cigarette stubs, staring blankly at the desolate posting boards where the totals had been listed. All through the hills and hollows of West Virginia, Humphrey had been accompanied by a folk singer, singing the old depression songs, fervid with the old faith of yesterday's New Deal. Now the folk singer, Jimmy Wofford, stepped out to twang his guitar for the last time. "Vote for Hubert Humphrey," he sang. "He's your man and mine."

The Senator's eyes gleamed with tears in the bright lights that television had installed to catch the surrender. It took him a moment to get his voice under control.

"I have a brief statement to make," he said. He read the words, "I am no longer a candidate for the Democratic Presidential nomination."

Jimmy Wofford tried one last serenade. "Vote for Hubert Humphrey, he's your man and mine—"

But he could not go on. He put his head down on his guitar and cried.

Senator Humphrey went over and patted him on the shoulder. "Aw, Jimmy," he said.

Bobby Kennedy, no dryer-eyed than anyone else, walked over and put his arm around the Senator. Then they all went out into the rain again and marched in a body to the Kanawha Hotel, where Kennedy would soon be arriving. It was the end of a campaign, the end of a long year of planning and hope. . . . In the morning, when Hubert Humphrey woke, the Presidential image had evaporated. Outside the Ruffner Hotel his parked bus had overnight been given a ticket for illegal parking.

Kennedy, depressed and gloomy on primary day, feeling that here in West Virginia, despite his last-minute surge, he could not hope to win, had chosen that night to hide from the public, the press, and the West Virginians who were voting. If he were to be beaten, he would receive the defeat in private, not under the scrutiny of the world. He had flown to Washington on the morning of primary day, addressed a woman's group at lunch, retreated to his Georgetown home and invited two friends for dinner with himself and his wife. The two friends brought with them a bottle of champagne, and the candidate had said, "Well, one way or another we'll crack it open this evening."

Perfectly self-possessed while every political mechanic, operator, and prognosticator worried about his reaction and his whereabouts, Kennedy calmly invited his two friends to sneak out with him to see a movie—the returns would be late in coming in, and they might as well relax. They did not return from the movie until 11:30—to find a message on the banister from their maid to please call Charleston, West Virginia, at once. A grin split Kennedy's face as he talked to his brother Bobby at the Kanawha Hotel, and then, as he put the telephone down, he burst out with a very un-Senatorial war whoop. The champagne cork popped, the guests drank; the Senator sipped, then put his glass down and prepared to leave for West Virginia. He called to assemble his plane crew; went upstairs to dress; called his father in Massachusetts; telephoned Charleston again to make sure that no reverse trend had set in, and then drove to the airport; boarding the plane, he called for a favorite drink—a bowl of hot tomato soup—and began to enjoy the evening.

By three in the morning he had been into Charleston, thanked West Virginians over TV, met Hubert Humphrey and shaken hands ("It was very nice of you to come over, Hubert"), held a press conference ("I think," he said, "we have now buried the religious issue once and for all") and was leaving again. In the lobby of the Kanawha Hotel the throng glued itself about him, and with difficulty he pushed his way to the door into the rain.

"What are you going to do now, Jack?" asked a newspaperman of the candidate.

"I have to study up on the problems of Maryland tonight," said Kennedy. "I'm campaigning there tomorrow—Friday is primary day there."

Epilogue

The West Virginia primary represented the turning point in the race for the Democratic nomination. Now that the Catholic issue had been faced squarely, the Kennedy campaign team could turn more attention to presenting the candidate as the younger, more energetic and charismatic choice, the one most likely to serve as an antidote to the current president, Republican Dwight Eisenhower. Kennedy rolled on to the nomination (picking up nearly twice as many convention votes as Senator Lyndon Johnson, who five days before the convention launched a belated effort to capture the nomination), picked Johnson as vice president to provide balance to the ticket, and squeaked by Republican candidate Richard Nixon in the general election. As you will see in the next selection, the lessons from this campaign were not lost on Nixon or the people who would manage his next campaign for the presidency in 1968.

9.2

The Selling of the President 1968

Joe McGinniss

"The medium is the message," said communications theorist Marshall McLuhan. He meant that advances in technology change not only the manner in which people communicate with each other but also the nature of the message itself. Such has been the effect of television on electoral politics. No longer do we see just the armies of volunteers described in Selection 9.1. Now those efforts are supplemented by clever advertisements sent out to faceless masses over the airwaves. The title of Joe McGinniss's book about the 1968 campaign, *The Selling of the President 1968,* tells you all you need to know both about the content of the book and the change in the nature of presidential campaigning. So does the book's cover, which shows a picture of Republican candidate Richard Nixon gracing a cigarette box, implying that the candidate was just another product to be sold to the voters.

As you will see in this selection, the means by which the Kennedy team identified and defined the issues in the 1960 West Virginia primary and throughout the campaign changed the face of electoral politics forever. If it was possible for organized volunteers to change voter perception of the candidate (as in Selection 9.1), then surely it was also possible to poll the voters first and then re-cast the candidate's views to appear to be in line with those of most voters. In short, as you will see, things have progressed from "making" a president to "selling" a president.

Richard Nixon, who overcame so many odds in his career that he titled his first memoir *Six Crises,* faced the possible end of his career once again in 1968. He had saved his nomination for vice president in 1952, in the face of charges that he had misappropriated campaign funds, with the famous Checkers speech (in which he alluded to his family dog, Checkers, in defending his integrity). Then, after narrowly losing the presidential election to John Kennedy in 1960, he was badly beaten by Edmund ("Pat") Brown for governor of California in 1962. After this stinging defeat, an angry Nixon barked at the press, "You won't have Dick Nixon to kick around anymore." But he was wrong. After turning down the job of baseball commissioner and narrowly losing a Supreme Court case concerning privacy (see Selection 6.5), Nixon earned one last shot at the presidency in 1968.

After coming off two successive political defeats, how could he win the office? The answer, as we shall see, lay in the ability of his campaign staff to fashion a new image—"the new Nixon"—and sell it to an American public tired of liberalism, the Vietnam War, and President Johnson. The victim of this strategy was Johnson's vice president, Hubert Humphrey, who was left defending a policy he no longer believed but from which he could not extricate himself. The means by which Nixon was sold to the American public became the prototype for later political campaigns.

ROGER AILES   Media consultant to Nixon.

LEONARD GARMENT   Nixon campaign aide.

EUGENE JONES   Filmmaker hired by the Nixon organization.

RICHARD NIXON   Republican nominee for president in 1968.

FRANK SHAKESPEARE   Nixon campaign aide.

HARRY TRELEAVEN   Nixon campaign aide.

BUD WILKINSON   Legendary football coach for the University of Oklahoma; adviser to the Nixon campaign.

▶ "I am not going to barricade myself into a television studio and make this an antiseptic campaign," Richard Nixon said at a press conference a few days after his nomination.

Then he went to Chicago to open his fall campaign. The whole day was built around a television show. Even when ten thousand people stood in front of his hotel and screamed for him to greet them, he stayed locked up in his room, resting for the show.

Chicago was the site of the first ten programs that Nixon would do in states ranging from Massachusetts to Texas. The idea was to have him in the middle of a group of people, answering questions live. [Frank] Shakespeare and [Harry] Treleaven had developed the idea through the primaries and now had it sharpened to a point. Each show would run one hour. It would be live to provide suspense; there would be a studio audience to cheer Nixon's answers and make it seem to home viewers that enthusiasm for his candidacy was all but uncontrollable; and there would be an effort to achieve a conversational tone that would penetrate Nixon's stuffiness and drive out the displeasure he often seemed to feel when surrounded by other human beings instead of Bureau of the Budget reports.

One of the valuable things about this idea, from a political standpoint, was that each show would be seen only by the people who lived in that particular state or region. This meant it made no difference if Nixon's statements—for they were not really answers—were exactly the same, phrase for phrase, gesture for gesture, from state to state. Only the press would be bored and the press had been written off already. So Nixon could get through the campaign with a dozen or so carefully worded responses that would cover all the problems of America in 1968.

And, to carry it one step sideways, it made no difference either if the answer varied—in nuance—from state to state. No one, unless he traveled a lot, would hear any statement but the one designed for him. So, a question about law and order might evoke one response in New England and a slightly different one in the South. Nothing big enough to make headlines, just a subtle twist of inflection, or the presence or absence of a frown or gesture as a certain phrase was spoken. This was what the new politics was to Frank Shakespeare. And he did all he could to make sure Richard Nixon's definition would be the same.

Roger Ailes, the executive producer of the Mike Douglas Show, was hired to produce the one-hour programs. Ailes was twenty-eight years old. He had started as a prop boy on the Douglas show in 1965 and was running it within three years. He was good. When he left, Douglas' ratings collapsed. But not everyone he passed on his way up remained his friend. Not even Douglas.

Richard Nixon had been a guest on the show in the fall of 1967. While waiting to go on, he fell into conversation with Roger Ailes.

"It's a shame a man has to use gimmicks like this to get elected," Nixon said.

"Television is not a gimmick," Ailes said.

Richard Nixon liked that kind of thinking. He told Len Garment to hire the man.*

Ailes had been sent to Chicago three days before Nixon opened the fall campaign. His instructions were to select a panel of questioners and design a set. But now, on the day of the program, only six hours, in fact, before it was to begin, Ailes was having problems.

"Those stupid bastards on the set designing crew put turquoise curtains in the background. Nixon wouldn't look right unless he was carrying a pocketbook." Ailes ordered the curtains removed and three plain, almost stark wooden panels to replace them. "The wood has clean, solid, masculine lines," he said.

His biggest problem was with the panel. Shakespeare, Treleaven and Garment had felt it essential to have a "balanced" group. First, this meant a Negro.

---

* Leonard Garment is the author of Selection 6.5, "The Hill Case."

One Negro. Not two. Two would be offensive to whites, perhaps to Negroes as well. Two would be trying too hard. One was necessary and safe. Fourteen percent of the population applied to a six- or seven-member panel, equaled one. Texas would be tricky, though. Do you have a Negro *and* a Mexican-American, or if not, then which?

Besides the Negro, the panel for the first show included a Jewish attorney, the president of a Polish-Hungarian group, a suburban housewife, a business-man, a representative of the white lower middle class, and, for authenticity, two newsmen: one from Chicago, one from Moline.

That was all right, Roger Ailes said. But then someone had called from New York and insisted that he add a farmer. A farmer, for Christ's sake. Roger Ailes had been born in Ohio, but even so he knew you did not want a farmer on a television show. All they did was ask complicated questions about things like parities, which nobody else understood or cared about. Including Richard Nixon. He would appoint a secretary of agriculture when he won, yes, but why did he have to talk to farmers on live television in the campaign?

Besides, the farmer brought the panel size to eight, which Ailes said was too big. It would be impossible for Nixon to establish interpersonal relationships with eight different people in one hour. And interpersonal relationships were the key to success.

"This is the trouble with all these political people horning in," Ailes said. "Fine, they all get their lousy little groups represented but we wind up with a horses__t show."

There was to be a studio audience—three hundred people—recruited by the local Republican organization. Just enough Negroes so the press could not write "all-white" stories but not enough so it would look like a ballpark. The audience, of course, would applaud every answer Richard Nixon gave, boost-ing his confidence and giving the impression to a viewer that Nixon certainly did have charisma, and whatever other qualities he wanted his President to have.

Treleaven and his assistant, Al Scott, came to the studio late in the afternoon. They were getting nervous. "Nixon's throat is scratchy," Treleaven said, "and that's making him upset." Al Scott did not like the lighting in the studio.

"The lights are too high," he said. "They'll show the bags under RN's eyes."

Then there was a crisis about whether the press should be allowed in the studio during the show. Shakespeare had given an order that they be kept out. Now they were complaining to Herb Klein, the press relations man, that if three hundred shills could be bussed in to cheer, a pool of two or three reporters could be allowed to sit in the stands.

Shakespeare still said no. No *newspapermen* were going to interfere with his TV show. Klein kept arguing, saying that if this was how it was going to start, on the very first day of the campaign, it was going to be 1960 again within a week.

Treleaven and Ailes went upstairs, to the WBBM cafeteria, and drank vending machine coffee from paper cups.

"I agree with Frank," Ailes said. "F__k 'em. It's not a press conference."

"But if you let the audience in . . ."

"Doesn't matter. The audience is part of the show. And that's the whole point. It's a television show. Our television show. And the press has no business on the set. And goddammit, Harry, the problem is that this is an electronic election. The first there's ever been. TV has the power now. Some of the guys get arrogant and rub the reporters' faces in it and then the reporters get p____d and go out of their way to rap anything they consider staged for TV. And you know damn well that's what they'd do if they saw this from the studio. You let them in with the regular audience and they see the warmup. They see Jack Rourke out there telling the audience to applaud and to mob Nixon at the end, and that's all they'd write about. You know damn well it is." Jack Rourke was Roger Ailes's assistant.

"I'm still afraid we'll create a big incident if we lock them out entirely," Treleaven said. "I'm going to call Frank and suggest he reconsider."

But Shakespeare would not. He arranged for monitors in an adjacent studio and said the press could watch from there, seeing no more, no less, than what they would see from any living room in Illinois.

It was five o'clock now; the show was to start at nine. Ray Voege, the makeup man, borrowed from the Johnny Carson Show, had arrived.

"Oh, Ray," Roger Ailes said, "with [Bud] Wilkinson, watch that perspiration problem on the top of his forehead."

"Yes, he went a little red in Portland," Ray Voege said.

"And when he's off camera, I'd give him a treated towel, just like Mr. Nixon uses."

"Right."

Ailes turned to Jack Rourke, the assistant. "Also, I'd like to have Wilkinson in the room with Nixon before the show to kibitz around, get Nixon loose."

"Okay, I'll bring him in."

Then Treleaven and Scott went back to the Sheraton Hotel for dinner. Ailes stayed in the studio to rehearse the opening with the cameramen one more time. There was nothing he could do about what Nixon would say or would not say, but he did not want anyone turning off before the hour was over because the program was dull to watch.

The set, now that it was finished, was impressive. There was a round blue-carpeted platform, six feet in diameter and eight inches high. Richard Nixon would stand on this and face the panel, which would be seated in a semi-circle around him. Bleachers for the audience ranged out behind the panel chairs. Later, Roger Ailes would think to call the whole effect, "the arena concept" and bill Nixon as "the man in the arena." He got this from a Theodore Roosevelt quote which hung, framed, from a wall of his office in Philadelphia.

It said something about how one man in the arena was worth ten, or a hundred, or a thousand carping critics.

At nine o'clock, Central Daylight Time, Richard Nixon, freshly powdered, left his dressing room, walked down a corridor deserted save for secret service, and went through a carefully guarded doorway that opened onto the rear of the set.

Harry Treleaven had selected tape from WBBM's coverage of the noontime motorcade for the opening of the show. Tape that showed Richard Nixon riding, arms outstretched, beaming, atop an open car. Hundreds of thousands of citizens, some who had come on their own, some who had been recruited by Republican organizations, cheered, waved balloons and tossed confetti in the air. One week before, at the Democratic convention, it had been Humphrey, blood, and tear gas. Today it was Nixon, the unifying hero, the man to heal all wounds. No disorder in his crowds, just dignified Republican enthusiasm, heightened a notch or two by knowledge of the inevitable comparisons between this event and those of the previous week. If the whole world had been watching then, at least a fair portion would see this on the network news. Chicago Republicans showed a warm, assured, united front. And Harry Treleaven picked only the most magical moments for the opening of his show.

Then the director hit a button and Bud Wilkinson appeared on the screen. And what a placid, composed, substantial, reassuring figure he was: introducing his close personal friend, a man whose intelligence and judgment had won the respect of the world's leaders and the admiration of millions of his countrymen, this very same man who had been seen entering Jerusalem moments ago on tape: Richard Nixon.

And the carefully cued audience (for Jack Rourke, the warmup man, had done his job well) stood to render an ovation. Richard Nixon, grinning, waving, *thrusting,* walked to the blue riser to receive the tribute.

It was warmly given. Genuine. For Nixon suddenly represented a true alternative: peace, prosperity, an end to discord, a return to the stable values that had come under such rude and unwarranted attack. Nixon was fortification, reaffirmation of much that needed to be reaffirmed. They needed him now, these Republicans, much more than they had in 1960. Then they were smug; and they did not especially like him. They toyed with him, as a small boy would poke a frog with a stick. They made him suffer needlessly, and, in the end, their apathy had dragged a nation down. Now, on this night, this first night of his campaign to restore decency and honor to American life, they wanted to let him know they cared. To let him know 1960 would not happen again.

He looked toward his wife; the two daughters; Ed Brooke, the most useful Negro he had found; Charles Percy, the organization man; and Thruston Morton, resigned if not enthusiastic. They sat in the first row together.

Then, eagerly, forcefully, strong, confident, alive, he turned toward the panel to begin.

He was alone, with not even a chair on the platform for company; ready to face, if not the nation, at least Illinois. To communicate, man to man, eye to eye, with that mass of the ordinary whose concerns he so deeply shared; whose values were so totally his own. All the subliminal effects sank in. Nixon stood alone, ringed by forces which, if not hostile, were at least—to the viewer—unpredictable.

There was a rush of sympathy; a desire—a need, even—to root. Richard Nixon was suddenly human: facing a new and dangerous situation, alone, armed only with his wits. In image terms, he had won before he began. All the old concepts had been destroyed. He had achieved a new level of communication. The stronger his statement, the stronger the surge of warmth inside the viewer. *Received impressions.* Yes, this was a man who could lead; infinitely preferable to the gray and bumbling Johnson; the inscrutable, unsuccessful [Dean] Rusk. A man who—yes, they remembered, even through the electronic haze—had stood up to Khrushchev in the kitchen. And, it was obvious now, who would stand up to Jerry Rubin in the street.*

His statements flowed like warm milk, bathed the audience, restored faith in the Founding Fathers, rekindled the memory of a vigorous Eisenhower, of ten, of fifteen years before. "*The American Revolution has been won,*" he had said in his acceptance speech at Miami, *"the American Dream has come true."*

Morris Liebman, the Jewish attorney, asked the first question: "Would you comment on the accusation which was made from time to time that your views have shifted and that they are based on expediences?"

Richard Nixon squinted and smiled. "I suppose what you are referring to is: Is there a new Nixon or is there an old Nixon? I suppose I could counter by saying: Which Humphrey shall we listen to today?"

There was great applause for this. When it faded, Richard Nixon said, "I do want to say this: There certainly is a new Nixon. I realize, too, that as a man gets older he learns something. If I haven't learned something I am not worth anything in public life.

"We live in a new world. Half the nations in the world were born since World War Two. Half the people living in the world today were born since World War Two. The problems are different and I think I have had the good sense—I trust the intelligence—to travel the world since I left the office of Vice President and to bring my views up to date to deal with the new world.

"I think my principles are consistent. I believe very deeply in the American system. I believe very deeply in what is needed to defend that system at home

---

* Dean Rusk was secretary of state under Kennedy and Johnson. "Khrushchev in the kitchen" refers to the impromptu debate between Vice President Nixon and Soviet Premier Nikita Khrushchev in the kitchen of a model home in Moscow in 1959. Jerry Rubin was one of the "Chicago Seven," who were tried for leading antiwar demonstrations during the Democratic National Convention in Chicago in 1968.

and abroad. I think I have some ideas as to how we can promote peace, ideas that are different from what they were eight years ago, not because I have changed but because the problems have changed.

"My answer is, yes, there is a new Nixon, if you are talking in terms of new ideas for the new world and the America we live in. In terms of what I believe in the American view and the American dream, I think I am just what I was eight years ago."

Applause swept the studio. Bud Wilkinson joined in.

The farmer asked a question about farming; the Polish-Hungarian delivered an address concerning the problems of the people of eastern Europe. His remarks led to no question at all, but no matter: Richard Nixon expressed concern for the plight of eastern Europeans everywhere, including northern Illinois.

Then Warner Saunders, the Negro, and a very acceptable, very polite one he seemed to be, asked, "What does law and order mean to you?"

"I am quite aware," Richard Nixon said, "of the fact that the black community, when they hear it, think of power being used in a way that is destructive to them, and yet I think we have to also remember that the black community as well as the white community has an interest in order and in law, providing that law is with justice. To me law and order must be combined with justice. Now that's what I want for America. I want the kind of law and order which deserves respect."

John McCarter, the businessman, asked about Spiro Agnew. Nixon said, "Of all the men who I considered, Spiro Agnew had the intelligence, the courage and the principle to take on the great responsibilities of a campaigner and re-sponsibilities of Vice President. And who also had the judgment so that if any-thing happened, the President of the United States could sit in that chair and make decisions that need to be made that would make the difference between war and peace and that I would have confidence in him." Then he called Agnew "a man of compassion."

McCarter came back later wanting to know if Nixon thought the Chicago po-lice had been too harsh on demonstrators in the streets.

"It would be easy," Nixon said, "to criticize Mayor [Richard] Daley and by im-plication Vice President Humphrey. But it wouldn't be right for me to lob in criticism. I am not going to get into it. It is best for political figures not to be making partisan comments from the sidelines."

The show went on like that. At the end the audience charged from the bleach-ers, as instructed. They swarmed around Richard Nixon so that the last thing the viewer at home saw was Nixon in the middle of this big crowd of people, who all thought he was great.

Treleaven plunged into the crowd. He was excited; he thought the show had been brilliant. He got to Nixon just as Nixon was bending down to autograph a cast that a girl was wearing on her leg.

"Well, you've got a leg up," Treleaven said.

Nixon stood up and grinned and moved away.

"Gee, that was sure a funny look he gave me," Treleaven said. "I wonder if he heard me. I wonder if he knew who I was."

Three days later, Roger Ailes composed a memorandum that contained the details of his reaction to the show. He sent it to Shakespeare and Garment:

After completing the first one-hour program, I though I would put a few general comments down on paper. After you have had a chance to look them over, I'd like to discuss them briefly with you so we can steadily improve the programs up to the time he becomes President. I viewed the complete tape the morning after the show.

Mr. Nixon is strong now on television and has good control of the situation.

I. The Look:

A. He looks good on his feet and shooting "in the round" gives dimension to him.

B. Standing adds to his "feel" of confidence and the viewers' "feel" of his confidence.

C. He still uses his arms a little too "predictably" and a little too often, but at this point it is better not to inhibit him.

D. He seems to be comfortable on his feet and even appears graceful and relaxed, i.e., hands on his hips or arms folded occasionally.

E. His eye contact is good with the panelists, but he should play a little more to the home audience via the head-on camera. I would like to talk to him about this.

F. We are still working on lightening up his eyes a bit, but this is not a major problem. This will be somewhat tougher in smaller studios, but don't worry, he will never look bad:

1. I may lower the front two key spots a bit.
2. I may try slightly whiter makeup on upper eyelids.
3. I may lower the riser he stands on a couple of inches.

G. The "arena" effect is excellent and he plays to all areas well. The look has "guts."

H. Color lights are hot and he has a tendency to perspire, especially along the upper lip.

1. Whenever he is going to tape a show, the studio air conditioning should be turned up full at least four hours prior to broadcast, and camera rehearsal should be limited as much as possible in this time period to keep the lights off and the heat down. If camera rehearsal is necessary, the air conditioner should be turned on sooner and the studio sealed off. Keep all studio doors (especially the large leading doors) closed.

I. An effort should be made to keep him in the sun occasionally to maintain a fairly constant level of healthy tan.

J. Generally, he has a very "Presidential" look and style—he smiles easily (and looks good doing it). He should continue to make lighter comments once in a while for pacing.

II. The Questions and Answers:

A. First, his opening remarks are good. He should, perhaps, be prepared with an optional cut in his closing remarks in case we get into time trouble getting off the air. I don't want to take a chance of missing the shots of the audience crowding around him at the end. Bud can specifically tell him exactly how much time he has to close.

B. In the panel briefing we should tell the panelists not to ask two-part questions. This slows down the overall pace of the show and makes it difficult for the viewer to remember and thus follow. Instead, the panelists should be instructed that they can continue a dialogue with Mr. Nixon—ask two questions in a row to get the answers.

C. Some of the answers are still too long and over half tended to be the same length. Nixon in Illinois Answers:

1. Approximately 3:00
2. 1:45
3. 1:30
4. 2:33—agriculture
5. 1:30—education
6. 2:37—European question, Dr. Ripa
    —Question was longer than answer.
7. 2:09—law & order
8. 3:22—Justice Earl Warren
9. 2:15—foreign aid
10. 3:00—NATO aid
11. 2:23—police in Chicago
    —(What he really said was that he had no comment.)
12. 2:30—urban renewal
13. :25—detention camps
    —(Excellent answer—He didn't know but he was honest and the audience was with him completely.)
14. :53
15. 2:45—income tax
16. 2:15—priority of spending
17. 1:47—money
18. :25—Vietnam POWs
19. :49—David & Julie
20. Wrap-up—perfect at :58.

—On one answer from Warner Saunders, he gave an unqualified "yes" and that was good. Whenever possible he should be that definite.

D. He still needs some memorable phrases to use in wrapping up certain points. I feel that I might be able to help in this area, but don't know if you want me to or if he would take suggestions from me on this. Maybe I could have a session with Price and Buchanan.

III.   Staging:

A. The microphone cord needs to be dressed and looped to the side.

B. Bud Wilkinson felt there should be more women on the panel since over half the voters are women. Maybe combine a category, i.e., woman reporter or negro woman.

C. The panel was too large at eight. Maximum should be seven, six is still preferable to give more interaction.

D. Bud should be able to interject more often with some prepared lighter or pacing questions.

E. The family should be in the audience at every show. Should I talk with them, Whitaker, or will you?

F. Political VIPs should be in the audience for every show. Nixon handles these introductions extremely well and they are good for reaction shots.

G. I am adding extenders to the zoom lens on all cameras to allow closer shooting for reactions.

IV.   General:

A. The show got off to a slow start. Perhaps the opening could be made more exciting by:

1. adding music or applause earlier.

B. The excitement of the film made the quietness of the dissolve to the studio more apparent.

C. Bud should be introduced with applause.

D. When film is not available it might be good to have [photographer] David Douglas Duncan shoot a series of interesting stills which could be put on film and synchronized to the Connie Francis record. I'd like to try this—it might give us a classy "standard" opening to use.

E. To give the director as much advantage as possible—the fewer last-minute changes, the better. In Chicago we luckily had excellent facilities and a fast crew plus plenty of rehearsal time. In the California show, because of studio priorities, our rehearsal time is cut in half.

F. I will work with the director on the art of using the reaction shot for better overall program value.

G. In general, I usually feel "down" immediately after taping a show. I was more pleased after viewing the tape than I was that night after the show.

One day Harry Treleaven came into his office with two reels of movie film under his arm.

"Come on," he said. "I think you'd like to see this." We went into the big meeting room and he gave the film to a man in the projection booth.

The film was in black and white. There was a title: *A Face of War.* It had been made in Vietnam. It was the story of three months of fighting done by a single infantry platoon. There was no music or narration. Just the faces and sounds of jungle war.

Halfway through the first reel, Len Garment and Frank Shakespeare came in. They were there for a one o'clock meeting. They took seats and began to watch the film. Neither spoke. They watched the men crawling single file through the jungle, heard the sound the leaves made as they brushed the faces of the men and heard the sound of rain and bullets and mortar shells in the night. The reel ended. The meeting was due to begin. Harry Treleaven turned to the projection booth. "Play the second reel," he said. Ruth Jones came in for the meeting and watched the film for three minutes and left. "I can't sit through that," she said.

No one else spoke. There were only the men trying to kill and trying to avoid being killed in the jungle.

Twenty minutes later, with the film still running, Art Duram said, "Don't you think we'd better start?" No one moved or gave any sign of having heard.

"It's half past one already."

Harry Treleaven sat up in his chair and looked at his watch. "All right, that's enough," he said to the man in the projection booth.

The lights came on in the room. No one spoke for a moment. Each man was still staring at where the film had been.

"That's the most powerful thing I've ever seen," Len Garment said.

"What is it?" Frank Shakespeare said.

Harry Treleaven stood and stepped toward the projection booth. "It's called *A Face of War*," he said, "and it was made by the man I want to hire to do our spot commercials."

Originally, Treleaven had wanted David Douglas Duncan, the photographer, to make commercials. Duncan was a friend of Richard Nixon's but when Treleaven took him out to lunch he said no, he would be too busy. Then Duncan mentioned Eugene Jones.

Treleaven had wanted Duncan because he had decided to make still photography the basis of Richard Nixon's sixty-second television commercial campaign. He had learned a little about stills at J. Walter Thompson when he used them for some Pan American spots. Now he thought they were the perfect thing for Nixon because Nixon himself would not have to appear.

Treleaven could use Nixon's voice to accompany the stills but his face would not be on the screen. Instead there would be pictures, and hopefully, the pictures would prevent people from paying too much attention to the words.

The words would be the same ones Nixon always used—the words of the acceptance speech. But they would all seem fresh and lively because a series of still pictures would flash on the screen while Nixon spoke. If it were done right, it would permit Treleaven to create a Nixon image that was entirely independent of the words. Nixon would say his same old tiresome things but no one would have to listen. The words would become Muzak. Something pleasant and lulling in the background. The flashing pictures would be carefully selected to create the impression that somehow Nixon represented competence, respect for tradition, serenity, faith that the American people were better than people anywhere else, and that all these problems others shouted about meant nothing in a land blessed with the tallest buildings, strongest armies, biggest factories, cutest children, and rosiest sunsets in the world. Even better: through association with the pictures, Richard Nixon could *become* these very things.

Obviously, some technical skill would be required. David Douglas Duncan said Gene Jones was the man.

Treleaven met Jones and was impressed. "He's low-key," Treleaven said. "He doesn't come at you as a know-it-all."

Gene Jones, also in his middle forties, had been taking movies of wars half his life. He did it perhaps as well as any man ever has. Besides that, he had produced the Today show on NBC for eight years and had done a documentary series on famous people called *The World of* . . . Billy Graham, Sophia Loren, anyone who had been famous and was willing to be surrounded by Jones's cameras for a month.

Jones understood perfectly what Treleaven was after. A technique through which Richard Nixon would seem to be contemporary, imaginative, involved— without having to say anything of substance. Jones had never done commercial work before but for $110,000, from which he would pay salaries to a nine-man staff, he said he would do it for Nixon.

"A hundred and ten thousand dollars," Frank Shakespeare said after seeing *A Face of War*. "That's pretty steep."

"I wouldn't know," Treleaven said. "I have nothing to compare it to."

"It's pretty steep."

"He's pretty good."

"Yes, he is."

"What do you think?"

"Oh, I have no objection. That just hit me as a very high price."

"I'd like approval to pay it right now. I want to hire him immediately."

"Fine," Frank Shakespeare said. "You've got it."

A day or two later Jones came down to Treleaven's office to discuss details such as where he should set up a studio and what areas the first set of spots should cover.

"This will not be a commercial sell," Jones said. "It will not have the feel of something a—pardon the expression—an agency would turn out. I see it as sort of a miniature *Project 20*. And I can't see anyone turning it off a television set, quite frankly."

That same day Jones rented two floors of the building at 303 East Fifty-third Street, one flight up from a nightclub called Chuck's Composite. Within three days, he had his staff at work. Buying pictures, taking pictures, taking motion pictures of still pictures that Jones himself had cropped and arranged in a sequence.

"I'm pretty excited about this," Jones said. "I think we can give it an artistic dimension."

Harry Treleaven did not get excited about anything but he was at least intrigued by this. "It will be interesting to see how he translates his approach into political usefulness," Treleaven said.

"Yes," Frank Shakespeare said, "if he can."

Gene Jones would start work at five o'clock in the morning. Laying coffee and doughnuts on his desk, he would spread a hundred or so pictures on the floor, taken from boxes into which his staff already had filed them. The boxes had labels like VIETNAM . . . DEMOCRATIC CONVENTION . . . POVERTY: HARLEM, CITY SLUMS, GHETTOS . . . FACES; HAPPY AMERICAN PEOPLE AT WORK AND LEISURE . . .

He would select a category to fit the first line of whatever script he happened to be working with that day. The script would contain the words of Richard Nixon. Often they would be exactly the words he had used in the acceptance speech, but re-recorded in a hotel room somewhere so the tone would be better suited to commercial use.

Jones would select the most appropriate of the pictures and then arrange and rearrange, as in a game of solitaire. When he had the effect he thought he wanted he would work with a stopwatch and red pencil, marking each picture on the back to indicate what sort of angle and distance the movie camera should shoot from and how long it should linger on each still.

"The secret is in juxtaposition," Jones said. "The relationships, the arrangement. After twenty-five years, the other things—the framing and the panning, are easy."

Everyone was excited about the technique and the way it could be used to make people feel that Richard Nixon belonged in the White House. The only person who was not impressed was Nixon. He was in a hotel room in San Francisco one day, recording the words for one of the early commercials. The machine was turned on before Nixon realized it and the end of his conversation was picked up.

"I'm not sure I like this kind of a . . . of a format, incidentally," Nixon said. "Ah . . . I've seen these kinds of things and I don't think they're very . . . very effective. . . ."

Still, Nixon read the words he had been told to read:

"In recent years crime in this country has grown nine times as fast as the population. At the current rate, the crimes of violence in America will double by nineteen seventy-two. We cannot accept that kind of future. We owe it to the decent and law-abiding citizens of America to take the offensive against the criminal forces that threaten their peace and security and to rebuild respect for law across this country. I pledge to you that the wave of crime is not going to be the wave of the future in America."

There was nothing new in these words. Harry Treleaven had simply paraphrased and condensed the standard law and order message Nixon had been preaching since New Hampshire. But when the words were coupled with quickly flashing colored pictures of criminals, of policemen patrolling deserted streets, of bars on storefront windows, of disorder on a college campus, of peace demonstrators being led bleeding into a police van, then the words became something more than what they actually were. It was the whole being greater than the sum of its parts.

In the afternoons, Treleaven, Garment and Shakespeare would go to Gene Jones' studio to look at the films on a little machine called a movieola. If they were approved, Jones would take them to a sound studio down the street to blend in music, but they never were approved right away. There was not one film that Garment or Shakespeare did not order changed for a "political" reason.

Anything that might offend Strom Thurmond, that might annoy the Wallace voter whom Nixon was trying so hard for; any ethnic nuance that Jones, in his preoccupation with artistic viewpoint, might have missed: these came out.

"Gene is good," Treleaven explained, "but he needs a lot of political guidance. He doesn't always seem to be aware of the point we're trying to make."

Jones didn't like the changes. "I'm not an apprentice," he said. "I'm an experienced pro and never before in my career have I had anyone stand over my shoulder telling me to change this and change that. It might sound like bulls__t, but when you pull out a shot or two it destroys the dynamism, the whole flow."

The first spot was called simply *Vietnam*. Gene Jones had been there for ninety days, under fire, watching men kill and die, and he had been wounded in the neck himself. Out of the experience had come *A Face of War*. And out of it now came E.S.J. [for Eugene S. Jones] #1, designed to help Richard Nixon become President. Created for no other purpose.

VIDEO	AUDIO
1. OPENING NETWORK DISCLAIMER: "A POLITICAL ANNOUNCEMENT."	
2. FADEUP ON FAST PACED SCENES OF HELO ASSAULT IN VIETNAM.	SFX AND UNDER
3. WOUNDED AMERICANS AND VIET-NAMESE.	R.N. Never has so much military, economic, and diplomatic power been used as ineffectively as in Vietnam.
4. MONTAGE OF FACIAL CU's OF AMERICAN SERVICEMEN AND VIET-NAMESE NATIVES WITH QUES-TIONING, ANXIOUS, PERPLEXED ATTITUDE.	And if after all of this time and all of this sacrifice and all of this support there is still no end in sight, then I say the time has come for the American people to turn to new leadership—not tied to the policies and mistakes of the past.
5. PROUD FACES OF VIETNAMESE PEASANTS ENDING IN CU OF THE WORD "LOVE" SCRAWLED ON THE HELMET OF AMERICAN G.I. AND PULL BACK TO REVEAL HIS FACE.	I pledge to you: we will have an honorable end to the war in Vietnam. MUSIC UP AND OUT.

Harry Treleaven and Len Garment and Frank Shakespeare thought this commercial was splendid.

"Wow, that's powerful," Treleaven said.

Dead soldiers and empty words. The war was not bad because of insane suffering and death. The war was bad because it was *ineffective*.

So Richard Nixon, in his commercial, talked about new leadership for the war. New leadership like Ellsworth Bunker and Henry Cabot Lodge and U. Alexis Johnson.

Vietnam was shown across the country for the first time on September 18. Jack Gould did not like this one any more than he had liked Connie Francis.*

"The advertising agency working in behalf of Richard Nixon unveiled another unattractive campaign spot announcement," he wrote. "Scenes of wounded GIs were the visual complement for Mr. Nixon's view that he is better equipped to handle the agony of the Vietnamese war. Rudimentary good taste in politics apparently is automatically ruled out when Madison Avenue gets into the act."

The fallen soldiers bothered other people in other ways. There was on the Nixon staff an "ethnic specialist" named Kevin Phillips, whose job it was to determine what specific appeals would work with specific nationalities and in specific parts of the country. He watched *Vietnam* and sent a quick and alarmed memo to Len Garment: "This has a decidedly dovish impact as a result of the visual content and it does not seem suitable for use in the South and Southwest."

His reasoning was quite simple. A picture of a wounded soldier was a reminder that the people who fight wars get hurt. This, he felt, might cause resentment among those Americans who got such a big kick out of cheering for wars from their Legion halls and barrooms half a world away. So bury the dead in silence, Kevin Phillips said, before you blow North Carolina.

Another problem arose in the Midwest: annoyance over the word "Love" written on the soldier's helmet.

"It reminds them of hippies," Harry Treleaven said. "We've gotten several calls already from congressmen complaining. They don't think it's the sort of thing soldiers should be writing on their helmets."

Len Garment ordered the picture taken out of the commercial. Gene Jones inserted another at the end; this time a soldier whose helmet was plain.

This was the first big case of "political" guidance, and for a full week the more sensitive members of the Gene Jones staff mourned the loss of their picture.

"It was such a beautiful touch," one of them said. "And we thought, what an interesting young man it must be who would write 'Love' on his helmet even as he went into combat."

Then E.S.J. Productions received a letter from the mother of the soldier. She told what a thrill it had been to see her son's picture in one of Mr. Nixon's commercials, and she asked if there were some way that she might obtain a copy of the photograph.

The letter was signed: Mrs. William Love.

Almost all the commercials ran sixty seconds. But Jones did one, called E.S.J. #3: *Look at America,* that went more than four minutes.

---

* Jack Gould was a *New York Times* reporter. The Nixon campaign had also put out a television ad featuring Connie Francis.

VIDEO	AUDIO
2. FADEUP ON FAST, DRAMATIC RIOT IN CITY, FLAMING BUILDINGS.	ELECTRONIC MUSIC UP FULL.
3. VIETNAM COMBAT.	ELECTRONIC MUSIC CONTINUES AND UNDER.
4. G.I. IN VIETNAM SLUMPS DEJECTEDLY.	<u>R.N.</u> America is in trouble today not because her people have failed, but because her leaders have failed. Let us look at America. Let us listen to America. We see Americans dying on distant battlefields abroad.
5. RIOT & FIRES.	We see Americans hating each other; fighting each other; killing each other at home. We see cities enveloped in smoke and flame.
6. FIRE ENGINES.	We hear sirens in the night.
7. PERPLEXED FACES OF AMERICANS.	As we see and hear these things, millions of Americans cry out in anguish. Did we come all the way for this?
8. MONTAGE URBAN & RURAL DECAY—(hungry in Appalachia—poor in ghetto—ill-clothed on Indian reservations. Unemployment in cities and welfare in small towns).	MUSIC UP AND UNDER.
9. MONTAGE OF AMERICANS "CREATING AND CONTRIBUTING" MOTIVATES INTO CU's OF FACES.	<u>R.N.</u> Let us listen now to another voice. It is the voice of the great majority of Americans—the non-shouters; the non-demonstrators. They are not racists or sick; they are not guilty of the crime that plagues the land. They are black and they are white—native born and foreign born—young and old.

VIDEO

AUDIO

They work in America's factories.

They run American business.

They serve in government.

They provide most of the soldiers who died to keep us free.

They give drive to the spirit of America.

They give lift to the American Dream.

They give steel to the back-bone of America.

They are good people, decent people; they work, they save, they pay their taxes, they care. Like Theodore Roosevelt, they know that this country will not be a good place for any of us to live in unless it is a good place for all of us to live in.

This, I say, is the real voice of America. And in this year 1968, this is the message it will broadcast to America and to the world.

10. STRENGTH AND CHARACTER OF AMERICANS—BUSY FACTORIES, FARMS, CROWDS & TRAFFIC, ETC.

Let's never forget that despite her faults, America is a great nation.

11. INTO MONTAGE OF SCENIC VALUES OF AMERICA FROM THE PACIFIC OCEAN TO DESERTS, TO SNOW-COVERED MOUNTAIN. BESIDE A STILL POND A MAN WAITS.

R.N.
America is great because her people are great.

With Winston Churchill, we say: "We have not journeyed all this way across the centuries, across the oceans, across the mountains, across the prairies, because we are made of sugar candy."

12. DOLLY TOWARD SUNRISE. HOLD. FADEOUT.

America is in trouble today not because her people have failed, but because her leaders have failed.

What America needs are leaders to match the greatness of her people.

MUSIC UP AND OUT.

"Run it through again, would you please, Gene?" Len Garment said. "There's something there that bothers me."

The film was rewound and played again.

"There, that's it," Garment said. "Yeah, that will have to be changed."

"What will have to be changed?" Jones said.

The film had been stopped just as Richard Nixon, reciting his litany to the "forgotten Americans," had said, "They provide most of the soldiers who died to keep us free." The picture that went with those words was a close-up of a young American soldier in Vietnam. A young Negro soldier.

Len Garment was shaking his head.

"We can't show a Negro just as RN's saying 'most of the soldiers who died to keep us free,'" he said. "That's been one of their big claims all along—that the draft is unfair to them—and this could be interpreted in a way that would make us appear to be taking their side."

"Hey, yes, good point, Len," Frank Shakespeare said. "That's a very good point."

Harry Treleaven was nodding.

Gene Jones said okay, he would put a white soldier there instead.

A couple of weeks later, when Treleaven told Gene Jones to shoot a commercial called *Black Capitalism,* he was surprised to hear that Negroes in Harlem were reluctant to pose for the pictures.

Jones had not been able to find any pictures that showed Negroes gainfully employed, so he decided to take his own. He hired his own photographer, a white man, and sent him to Harlem with instructions to take pictures of good Negroes, Negroes who worked and smiled and acted the way white folks thought they ought to. And to take these pictures in front of Negro-owned stores and factories to make the point that this is what honest labor can do for a race.

An hour after he started work, the photographer called Gene Jones and said when he had started lining Negroes up on the street to pose he had been asked by a few young men what he was doing. When he told them he was taking pictures for a Richard Nixon commercial, it was suggested to him that he remove himself and his camera from the vicinity. Fast.

Gene Jones explained to Harry Treleaven.

"Gee, isn't that strange," Treleaven said. "I can't understand an attitude like that."

Epilogue

Nixon went on to defeat Humphrey narrowly in the general election. Democrats angry with the Johnson regime came back into the fold to work for Humphrey too late in the process to pull out the election. Interestingly, it is generally believed that a series of campaign mistakes by John Mitchell, Nixon's campaign manager, in dealing with conservative George Wallace, who ran as an independent, almost led to Nixon's defeat. Enough voters were changing their minds that, had the election been held two weeks later, the outcome might have been different.

McGinniss used the same reportorial style as Theodore White but took his analysis a step further, making bold comments about the state of the electoral process. In short, he almost made the leap from observer to participant. That final leap may have been made when reporters from the *Miami Herald* followed Democratic candidate Gary Hart around in the 1988 nomination campaign, discovered his apparent relationship with Donna Rice, and by their reporting actually became part of the process by changing the race. The role of the press in future campaigns will bear watching. For now, though, we close with selections concerning the actions of those who deal with the image of the president after the election—White House reporters and presidential speechwriters.

9.3

Behind the Front Page

David S. Broder

When presidential press conferences are aired on television, the job of White House reporter always looks like such glamorous duty. The reporter sits just a few feet from the president and has a chance to ask his or her most pressing questions on national television. Yet the more you watch these events, the more you come to understand that they are not so much information-gathering occasions as staged conversations between people reading set speeches. The president avoids as many questions as he answers, always seems to call on the same reporters, and frequently clarifies his remarks after the conference. And the reporter is never fully able to follow up on any one topic in order to gain a candid or sometimes merely comprehensible answer.

The press conference is a microcosm of the often combative relationship between the White House and the media. Can this interaction be characterized as "media *relations*" or "media *management*"? This is the question that columnist David Broder of the *Washington Post* explores in this chapter from *Behind the Front Page: A Candid Look at How the News Is Made.* Specifically, Broder helps us to understand how Ronald Reagan maintained such a magnificent image in the media through most of his presidency. When Reagan was labeled the "Teflon president" because no criticism stuck to him, was it a compliment to his media liaison team or a criticism of a passive press corps?

This question reveals the symbiotic relationship between the media and the White House. Without the media, the president would have difficulty getting any message out to the public. Without the president, the press has no news from the White House. Each side, then, has a job to do but is conscious of the limits imposed by the need to maintain good relations with the other. Reporters cannot restrict themselves to relaying the White House's press releases, but in trying to uncover the "real facts," a reporter may damage his or her relationship with the president. This in turn may hurt the reporter's ability to get a phone call returned, to make an interview appointment, or to receive information off the record. From the president's standpoint, the hundreds of reporters competing for good stories, lightning-fast communications systems, and an array of issues beyond any one human being's full understanding make dealing with the press extremely challenging. And somehow, out of this game of cat-and-mouse, the public must sort out the truth or some version of the truth.

JAMES BAKER   Reagan's chief of staff in the first term.

LOU CANNON   Reporter for the *Washington Post*.

MICHAEL DEAVER   Reagan's deputy chief of staff in the first term.

RONALD REAGAN   President of the United States, 1981–1989.

DONALD REGAN   Reagan's chief of staff in the second term.

GEORGE SHULTZ   Secretary of state under Reagan.

LARRY SPEAKES   Press spokesman for Reagan.

▶ The White House may seem a strange place to start our examination of the complex but cozy relationship between journalists and public officials. Every recent President has feuded with reporters and fussed about the coverage he has received. And yet there is an intimacy between the press (especially television) and the President. This coziness is symbolized by the location of the White House briefing room and press room in the center of the West Wing working section of the building (over the abandoned indoor swimming pool). It is cozy, in another sense, too. Space is so limited that reporters work at each other's elbows. In that respect, they are like the White House staff members, who—except for the senior six or eight—have less breathing room than the average insurance office clerk. When the Reagan administration remodeled the briefing room in 1981, it installed theater seats with brass plaques on the back, reserved for the forty television, radio, newspaper, and news magazine correspondents considered the regulars. It is like having a family pew in church.

White House reporters think of themselves as an elite group. They cover the top official of the American government and are on the air and the front page more often than other reporters. They are often the best paid and most experienced reporters in their organizations, and as the careers of Tom Brokaw, Dan Rather, and Ben Bradlee all show, covering a President or knowing one is often the way to the highest rungs of television and newspaper success.

For all the intimacy and elitism, White House reporters often seem at odds with the President and his agents. Almost daily, battles erupt between reporters and presidential spokesmen, as each side attempts to do what it considers its job, and objects to the other doing its. The press complains that the President or his agents attempt to manage the news, and the President replies that prying reporters distort or trivialize or simply interfere with important decision making.

Unlike Congress, which has only limited institutional power over how it is covered, the President has political and public relations aides who can lay down rules that work to the President's advantage. They seek to maximize publicity for some of his activities and to keep others secret. They speak volubly at times and attempt to embargo information and comment at other moments. They hoard information and disclose or leak it selectively. Reporters attempt to resist all these tactics and, in doing so, often criticize the President and his agents for being manipulative. As James Deakin, the White House correspondent for the *St. Louis Post-Dispatch* from Dwight Eisenhower through Jimmy Carter, says in his book *Straight Stuff,* "They disagree. They disagree. They disagree."

Given this pattern of disagreement, it may be surprising that, in the relationship, there is a danger of too much coziness. But because of a mutual dependence, many of the forces of antagonism are overwhelmed. For all the fussing and fighting between Presidents and the press, their basic relationship is symbiotic.

Occasionally, we see a clear picture of the cooperative and collaborative relationship between the White House and the press—or, even more, television. Ever since Jacqueline Kennedy led CBS on a backstairs tour of the remodeled White House, every President and/or First Lady has provided cameras and reporters special access, at times of their own choosing and in formats they influence if not control. Richard Nixon arranged for NBC to do the prime-time special *Christmas at the White House* and for CBS to film *A Day in the Presidency,* a day, of course, chosen and arranged by the White House. Jimmy Carter enlisted the television icon Walter Cronkite as host on a call-in program on which Carter answered questions about his energy policy. Ronald Reagan reached back to the medium in which he earlier starred and began a series of weekly five-minute radio broadcasts to the nation.

But much of the interaction takes place behind the scenes and reflects the mutual needs and problems of the two sides. Michael Baruch Grossman and Martha Joynt Kumar in their 1981 book, *Portraying the President,* estimate that at least 30 percent of the White House staff effort is devoted to the public relations aspects of the presidency, and no talent is more vital to a President than being able to handle television and the press. Of the many hats he wears, one of the most important ones, though unlisted in the Constitution, is Communicator-in-Chief. Only the President can make news whenever he wishes, at any hour of the day or night. Only the President can command simultaneous live coverage on all the television networks. Only the President can gather the nation at his feet, as if it were a family, and say, "Dear friends, here is how I see things."

The President's power as Communicator-in-Chief is at least as far-reaching, in the real world, as his authority to negotiate treaties, to dispatch troops, to impose his veto on legislation. Had the Founding Fathers foreseen its emergence, my guess is that they would have thought about providing checks and balances for this presidential authority. Since they did not, the press must do much of the balancing.

So in reviewing the relationships that have developed in the White House, we can talk about two dimensions: the President's skill at getting his message across and the press's ability to obtain and to use its access to cover the presidency. [Now] we will examine how they operate under Ronald Reagan. . . .

Ronald Reagan's relationship with the press evolved through almost six years of stunningly successful news management, followed by one of the most embarrassing and politically costly blowups in the modern presidency. In the autumn of 1986, the President's credibility was severely damaged by press exposure of secret United States arms shipments to Iran, followed by the even more stunning announcement from the White House that profits from those sales had been transferred—ostensibly without Reagan's knowledge or approval—to support one of his prized projects, the effort to harass and perhaps overthrow the leftist Sandinista government in Nicaragua.

The upheaval in the administration cast into doubt Reagan's political effectiveness in his final two years as President. But even more, it demonstrated once again how the cult of secrecy in the White House—linked to a manipulative view of press relations and rooted in a disdain and distrust of journalists—can easily turn on and victimize the very politician who creates it.

In only a few weeks, a man who seemed the master of presidential public relations saw his image begin to crumble. As an actor and as a politician, Reagan learned that sustaining popularity required cultivating the press. He used his abilities as a talented raconteur and a most engaging companion. With half a dozen other reporters and columnists, I was invited to the White House for cocktails with the President in 1984 (such invitations seem to precede elections) and threw in my share of questions. Though it was all off-the-record, Reagan seemed uncomfortable, until someone asked if he had seen any good movies lately. Well, he had, and he not only told us about *Red Dawn* but about how he thought it could have been improved. I don't know whether his criticism was right, but he certainly enjoyed talking about that picture more than about the budget or the coming campaign.

Charles McDowell, the witty Washington correspondent of the *Richmond Times-Dispatch,* spent five hours as Reagan's head-table companion at the Gridiron Dinner in 1983. All during the various skits and speeches, the President was rapt, and almost everything reminded him of a story. He entertained McDowell with a stream of anecdotes about stars of the past. At the end of the evening Reagan did a surprise turn on stage, singing a satirical chorus of "Mañana," and delivered the closing speech—a graceful, funny, sentimental, and patriotic number of the kind that he seems to toss off at will.

Yet Reagan always was one of the most difficult interviews. He has not been unavailable or unresponsive. But, along with many others, I found it almost impossible to get anything from Reagan except anecdotes and verbatim sections of his standard speeches.

Most politicians' public styles—assertive, declamatory, rhetorical—differ from their private styles, which are more ruminative, questioning, analytical. With Reagan there is almost no difference. My guess is that the President never thinks of himself as being offstage, at least when reporters are around. He is always aware of notebooks and pencils and, certainly, of cameras. He is, as a good actor, constantly aware of the impression he is making. His techniques do not vary, whether the audience is one or one thousand.

Every previous President I have known could stand back from his public positions and talk about the personal, political, and philosophical considerations that led him to take those stands, as well as the forces in the political world that might cause him to have to adjust them. But with Reagan it was particularly fruitless to explore the whys and wherefores, the ambiguities and possible inconsistencies, the derivations and the implications of his positions on issues. He almost invariably ended such discussions by reiterating that he believed exactly what he had said. Nothing more, nothing less. During many interviews between 1966 and 1980 and in several White House sessions, I have closed my notebook, knowing the ever-courteous Reagan had given me exactly what I would have got from reading his most recent speech on the subject.

Speeches were terribly important to Reagan and he did most of them superbly. He made a good living as a speechmaker when his movie and television careers flagged, and speeches were his mainstay as President. The articulation of his beliefs, his goals, and certain of his policies was central to his leadership role. Reagan's reliance on speechmaking and his reluctance to kill his own act by answering questions from the press distinctively shaped the press policies of his administration.

Those policies were based on three principles: limit the direct access to the President, make news management a major priority for trusted White House aides and cabinet secretaries, and shut down the flow of information from lower levels of the administration and the bureaucracy.

Reagan has been less accessible than his predecessors. He held only thirty-nine news conferences in his first six years in office. (He also had twenty-three of what his aides call "minis," brief exchanges with reporters, usually on a limited set of issues, and two hundred and fifty-eight office interviews, many of which were limited to specific topics or feature stories.) Reagan's news conferences are somewhat more orderly than his predecessors'. Reporters are recognized by raising their hands rather than jumping to their feet. The President keeps a seating chart on the lectern and is able to call by name those he chooses. Most reporters judge the Reagan news conferences to be less informative than Carter's. Robert Pierpoint's survey for *Parade* rated him next lowest to Lyndon Johnson of the last seven presidents for "information value" but Kennedy's closest challenger in the category of "humor."

More often than not, Reagan seems to obey an injunction he has given to reporters, when evading their questions, ever since his days in Sacramento: "Don't ask me to write your leads for you." The President tries to say as little as possible in news conferences, and the tension he often displays sharply contrasts with his confident assurance when delivering a major speech.

In November 1981, after his fifth press conference, I wrote:

> *At the last two news conferences, the impression he has created has been one of a man under great strain. The comments on Capitol Hill and in embassies suggest that the tension and anxiety the President displays when answering questions about his policies are beginning to cause concern among those here and abroad who look to the White House for leadership.*
>
> *The same anxiety is being expressed by members of the White House staff, who have come to view each press conference as a hurdle that must be negotiated with care. They have adopted what my colleague Martin Schram accurately described as a "damage control" philosophy for dealing with the press conferences: scheduling them infrequently, slowing down the pace of questioning by lengthy answers, and hoping that Reagan gets out of them without hurting himself.*

He has not always been able to do so. Reagan's responses during news conferences are studded with inaccuracies, and the White House press office regularly issues "clarifications" or simple corrections. After a February 1982 news conference, former *Post* correspondent Lee Lescaze wrote that "President Reagan rewrote the history of early U.S. involvement in Vietnam yesterday," confusing the makeup of the three colonial countries, reversing the blame for the cancellation of their scheduled 1956 elections, and asserting that President Kennedy had sent in "a division of marines," when the first 550 marines were actually dispatched by President Johnson sixteen months after Kennedy's death. Lescaze also wrote that

> *Reagan opened his news conference with a joke about press reports of his misstatements and he ended with a claim that his Jan. 19 news conference had not been studded with errors. Reagan said "the score was five to one in my favor." His count, however, refers to a White House refutation of a wire-service story on misstatements, not to the errors Reagan made at his Jan. 19 news conference, where every unemployment statistic he used was incorrect.*

In the early months of the Reagan presidency, reporters assumed that stories pointing up such misinformation would damage the President's credibility.

They did not. Voters seemed to believe his errors were inadvertent, no worse than they—or the reporters—might make. In 1982 Lou Cannon quoted one political aide who described Reagan's misstatements as "part of his charm."

The gaffes have increased the tendency of his staff to shield Reagan from frequent questioning. Although he has improved somewhat, each news conference remains a major risk. In June 1986, for instance, Reagan answered a question about a Supreme Court abortion decision with a comment on an earlier decision on the tangentially related issue of family rights to refuse medical treatment for badly malformed infants; he confused a Warsaw Pact proposal to reduce armies in Central Europe with a Soviet initiative on strategic arms; and he stated his position on the SALT II treaty so awkwardly that the White House had to issue two clarifying statements and answer a host of questions the next day. Faced with this continuing problem from the beginning, senior Reagan aides decided to take over the major information and public relations responsibilities.

At times, their efforts to shield Reagan have become ridiculous. On a 1984 tour of Chesapeake Bay designed to repair Reagan's image as an environmentalist, the President was asked about a controversial appointment he had made in that field. Several White House advance men immediately ordered the television floodlights cut off, press spokesman Larry Speakes jumped in front of him, and Reagan commented, "My guardian says I can't talk."

Such maneuvers did not embarrass Michael K. Deaver, Reagan's deputy chief of staff during his first term. Deaver laid down the doctrine that the White House must set the theme and message for its own coverage. As he once told the *Post,* "The people elected the President to determine the agenda, not the media." Each Friday during the first term, Deaver and then chief of staff James A. Baker III met with the top presidential assistants to plan the next period's communications strategy. The Reagan system built on thirty years of increasingly sophisticated White House news management techniques, going back to Jim Hagerty in the Eisenhower years. The distinction was that managing the news and public opinion was explicitly recognized by the new administration as such a central part of running the presidency that it had to become a major part of the workday of senior policy aides.

With the general outline in place, the daily 8:15 A.M. senior staff meetings nail down each day's White House program, designed to define and dominate primarily that night's network news programs and secondarily the next morning's newspaper headlines. Deaver told Robert Scheer of the *Los Angeles Times* in 1984, "The whole business is now so influenced by network television . . . 100 million people across this country get all of their news from network television. So the visual is extremely important. . . . That visual is as critical as what we're saying.

"If you only get your message across in 30 or 40 seconds on the evening news," Deaver continued, "then it's important that you restate that message in as many ways as you can. . . ." Deaver understood that providing certain pictures of the President—and no others—could largely determine that night's television story. "We try to go with one particular theme," Deaver said. "We don't want to step on our own story. . . . We plot out a decent story or a theme for every day. . . . I explain it to the President and he'll tell me whether he's comfortable with it."

The technique does not please White House television correspondents. Sam Donaldson of ABC has said, with some bitterness, "They [the White House] don't need us as long as they capture our cameras." But as Deaver told Scheer, the correspondents have little choice but to go along. "They've got to get on [the air] in order to keep their jobs," Deaver said. "What good is a TV correspondent who is never on television?"

Often the correspondents attempt to free themselves from White House manipulation by biting back in their stand-ups, the brief summation-commentaries, usually shot with the TV reporter at the scene of the story. But Lesley Stahl, CBS News's White House correspondent during the first five and a half years of Reagan's presidency, learned to her chagrin how pictures can override even the most biting commentary.

During the 1984 campaign, she put together a four-and-a-half-minute piece that showed how far the White House had gone in staging events for Reagan. "It was a very tough piece," Stahl said later, "showing how they were trying to create public amnesia about some of the issues that had turned against Reagan. I was very nervous about going back to the White House the next day. But the show was no more than off the air, when a White House official called me and congratulated me on it and said he'd loved it. I said, 'How could you love it?' And he said, 'Haven't you figured it out yet? The public doesn't pay any attention to what you say. They just look at the pictures.'" Stahl said she looked at the piece again, with the sound off, and realized that what she had shown was a magnificent montage of Reagan in a series of wonderful, upbeat scenes, with flags, balloons, children, and adoring supporters—virtually an unpaid campaign commercial.

I asked whether she agreed with the White House official. "I've come to believe it," she said. Has it changed the way she does stories? "Not really," she said. "I'm still trapped, because my pieces are written to the pictures we have."

Once the story line was settled, little was left to chance. At 9:15 each morning, Speakes would brief about twenty of the White House regulars on what was going to be available for coverage that day. In the afternoon, the White House press office aides would often call around to the three networks to find out what their White House pieces would include, and then lobby to have the tone or focus shift in the direction the White House would like it to go.

Reagan aides also try to capture or steer newspaper coverage, and to do so, they violate the tradition that the President sets the pattern of press relations. In every previous administration, if the President chose to be accessible to the press, others who worked for him were accessible. If he was aloof, so were they. The President always gave the cue. Reagan has operated differently. He has limited access to himself but has allowed, even encouraged, his top aides to be responsive to the press. The effort has involved far more than the press office. Perhaps because press secretary James Brady was critically wounded in the assassination attempt on Reagan in March 1981, and Reagan's long-time spokesman, Lyn Nofziger, declined to serve as White House press secretary, his principal spokesman, Larry Speakes, did not gain the status many of his predecessors enjoyed until after Reagan was well into his second term. (Speakes left in early 1987 to enter private business and was succeeded by Marlin Fitzwater.)

During the first term, the press office was a secondary source of information because higher-ranking officials including Baker, Deaver, deputy chief of staff Richard G. Darman, budget director David A. Stockman, and all three of the national security advisers were more accessible than their predecessors had ever been. Baker consistently gave high priority to influencing press coverage of the White House and the other White House officials took their cues from him.

Until Reagan's reelection was safely in hand, Baker saw to it that no one cut off access to journalists who had criticized the President or administration policies. Throughout the first term, the Reagan White House maintained contact with people in the major news organizations that helped shape Washington and national opinion—no matter what. I tested the policy. Though my columns were often critical, there was never any retaliation. Unlike their predecessors in the Nixon administration, the Reaganites clearly believed that as long as a *Washington Post* writer was asking for their side, they were going to provide it.

The senior staff members were even more responsive to the White House correspondents for our paper and the other major news organizations. During the first term, Lou Cannon, David Hoffman, and others who worked brief shifts at the White House could almost always get their phone calls returned by the officials they needed. Cannon and his colleagues had earned the trust of those sources by their careful, conscientious (but far from uncritical) reporting of the administration. But clearly the administration's policy was to cooperate.

However, much of what these top presidential assistants said was "on background," usable by the reporters but not for direct attribution. What they said appeared most often in the *Post* and other papers as the words or thoughts of those ubiquitous, semianonymous "White House aides" or "administration officials." . . . The access to senior White House staff was so constant and their responses so full during the first term that—despite Reagan's relative isolation from the press—readers of papers like the *Post* were often better informed about presidential decision making than ever before. For insiders, for those adept at reading the code the "White House officials" used, there were few surprises.

But there were some: In late 1981 and early 1982, the senior White House staff believed almost to a man that the administration should seek tax-law amendments to close some of the loopholes and reclaim some of the revenues

Congress had grandly squandered in the orgy of tax cutting Reagan had encouraged in his first year. By talking constantly to reporters about budget deficits and revenue steps, they encouraged a public belief that Reagan was headed in that direction. The sequence of headlines in the *New York Times* tells the story: December 21: "Reagan Aides Plan to Ask Him to Back Increases in Taxes." January 7: "Reagan's Aides Back Increases in Some Taxes." January 8: "President Studies a $30 Billion Plan for Tax Increases." January 10: "Reagan Expected to Accept Tax Rise." January 12: "Reagan Weighs New Tax-Rise Plan."

The dope stories, quoting no aides by name, did not anticipate the President's reaction correctly. When aides put the proposition to him directly, he said no—and we in the press had egg on our faces.

In retrospect, it was clear that the White House aides had used the press to try to move Reagan to accept tax hikes. When they failed, they shifted to the Republicans in Congress, encouraging them to take the lead in the euphemistic "revenue enhancement." Ultimately, Reagan bowed to the legislative initiative—and to reality—and signed a major tax-hike bill.

Obviously, the Reagan White House aides used the press to accomplish an objective, but that is not wholly bad. Their backgrounding of reporters brought into public view and public discussion a policy question that faced the President and the country. Surely, it would have been better had Reagan himself raised the issue, or responded to it during a press conference or interview, but Reagan had only three news conferences during that three-month period and was asked only five questions about budget-tax policy. He responded in his usual uninformative manner.

But if those aides had not kept White House reporters occupied and informed, there would have been a louder outcry about Reagan's lack of responsiveness. So the trade-off was that reporters got more information, albeit unattributed, and Reagan got a reprieve, in part, from being accused of closing off questioning.

This arrangement had costs both to the public and to the administration, and one compensating advantage. With the backgrounding so constant and each principal policy aide aware that he could not afford to stay out of that press game, Cannon and his colleagues were able to determine the lines of division among the President's aides on major issues—where the fault lines were developing. Dozens of such stories detailed feuds among senior staff members, between them and members of the cabinet, and some even reflected those staff members' occasional frustration with the President himself. The tone is evident in the lead on a Cannon column in the spring of 1983:

> *Meeting with a core group of longtime Reagan supporters in the White House last week, deputy chief of staff Michael K. Deaver revealed the inside story of why he has been able to lose 40 pounds during the last year.*

"The secret of the Deaver Diet," he quipped, "is that you only eat on days when senior staff members are speaking to each other."

When Donald T. Regan replaced Baker at the start of Reagan's second term and Deaver left soon afterward to become a high-priced lobbyist, the pattern of White House news management changed significantly. It became much more a closed shop, at times a hostile one.

Regan, who ran America's biggest brokerage firm before coming to Washington, centralized authority and quickly eliminated any significant competing power centers. Fewer people participated in the policy discussions, so reporters had fewer available sources. The penalties for leaking increased, and Regan lectured on the subject frequently at senior staff meetings. Where Baker had been in communication with key reporters, though largely invisible to the public, Regan was less accessible while more visible. When Regan talked, it was often on the record, but interviews became scarcer. No one really replaced Deaver as an image manager, but Regan's deputy, Dennis Thomas, met at least once a week with people from the major news organizations to guide coverage.

The White House's fundamental attitude changed. Baker and Deaver always had tried to put their "spin" on the depiction of the President and his policies, but they also wanted reporters to understand the whys and wherefores of administration decisions. Regan operated much more on a need-to-know basis, shielding the policy considerations from discussion and concentrating on selling conclusions and rebutting critics. With the evident approval of the President, he closed many of the back channels of information and guidance that in the first term had helped reporters explain the actions of an inaccessible President. When National Security Adviser Robert C. McFarlane left after clashing with Regan, he was replaced by Admiral John M. Poindexter, whose particularly closemouthed approach to reporters weakened explanations of White House foreign policy.

Reagan himself became no more accessible as the second term began, so the flow of information diminished. With no more Reagan elections in the offing, the White House seemed well pleased with the change. Patrick Buchanan, a conservative polemicist who wrote many press-bashing speeches for Vice President Spiro Agnew, came back as White House communications director. Retaliatory policies, shunned before the 1984 election, became acceptable. Reporters deemed too often critical of the administration (like me) were excluded from briefings. And what had been a spluttering effort to shut down leaks became a high-powered offensive.

Bill Kovach, then Washington editor of the *New York Times* and now editor of the *Atlanta Journal and Constitution,* was quoted in a 1985 *Washington Post* story: "There has been a consistent and organized effort on the part of this administration to reduce the flow of government information. . . .There is no area of government where information is not harder to get for us here, harder to get now than it was when I was here in the Nixon and Ford years." Helen Thomas, the UPI White House correspondent, said in the same story, "A lot of events, we're absolutely blacked out, and if you don't like it, too bad. . . . The whole attitude is, 'We will tell you what we think you should know.'"

Anthony Marro, managing editor of *Newsday* and a former Washington correspondent, wrote in a 1985 issue of the *Columbia Journalism Review* that "while it is not clear that the Reagan administration is any more duplicitous than others, it unquestionably has gone well beyond other recent administrations in its attempts to bottle up information, to prevent public access to government officials and records, to threaten and intimidate the bureaucracy in order to dry up sources of information, and to prevent the press and the public from learning how their government is functioning." Marro was reacting to the first-term restrictions, including the decisions to bar reporters from the initial phases of the invasion of Grenada and to seek restrictions on the Freedom of Information Act, and an executive order (later suspended) to use polygraph tests on a wide range of government employees, including senior White House and cabinet officials, and to assert a lifetime censorship on the writings of former officials. But these moves proved to be only a mild prelude to the efforts to shut down leaks in the second term.

The offensive was predicted on December 1, 1984, less than a month after the election, when Undersecretary of Defense Fred C. Ikle said, "The laws [on unauthorized disclosure of secrets] are not adequate. We have decided to fight it on all fronts." Less than three weeks later, the *Post* reported that Secretary of Defense Caspar W. Weinberger had urged two television networks and a number of print news organizations to withhold stories about a secret military cargo on an about-to-be-launched space shuttle, even though reporters already knew it was carrying a satellite designed to hover over the Soviet Union and intercept electronic signals. Weinberger said the story was "the height of journalistic irresponsibility" and may have given "aid and comfort to the enemy." But the *Post* maintained that its story contained only information already in the public record of congressional hearings—a view later confirmed by the Air Force chief of public information. Nonetheless, the Pentagon ordered a search for the leakers.

In November 1985, Reagan signed an order authorizing polygraph testing of thousands of government employees dealing with "sensitive compartmented information," a broad classification of "secret" documents. When it became clear that the lie-detector program might apply to cabinet officers, Secretary of State George P. Shultz said publicly that he would take such a test "once," if ordered, but then resign. "The minute in this government I am told that I'm not trusted is the day I leave," he said. Reagan and Shultz then met, and the White House, suggesting that the President had never intended to put Shultz to the test, said the issue had been resolved.

In 1986, Shultz and Weinberger each fired a mid-level political appointee—both were staunch conservatives—for leaking material to the press
critical of administration policies and actions. Central Intelligence Agency director William J. Casey stirred a much larger controversy when he said he was considering asking the Justice Department to prosecute five news organizations for
publishing information about U.S. intelligence capabilities. Casey's pronounce-
ments were part of an administration effort to shut down publicity about the
damage former National Security Agency analyst Ronald W. Pelton had done
in selling the Soviet Union secrets about electronic interception techniques.
Casey enlisted Poindexter and finally President Reagan in successfully persuading the *Post* to remove some information from a story on the subject it had
planned to publish.

When Pelton came to trial, Casey and the head of the National Security
Agency publicly "cautioned" news organizations against "speculation and reporting details beyond the information actually released at trial." The White
House endorsed the warning, but when news media officials said an implied
threat to prosecute "speculation" violated the First Amendment, Casey said he
had perhaps used the wrong word. At the same time, it was learned that the
White House was considering a recommendation for a special anit-leak "strike
force" of FBI agents and the expansion of polygraph testing. But both Baker and
Regan reportedly objected to parts of that plan.

Few of the threatened actions were taken, but the impulse to crack down on
press leaks has been a powerful one throughout the Reagan years. Lou Cannon,
who has covered Reagan longer and studied him more closely than any other
reporter, tried to explain the underlying attitude late in 1983. He traced Reagan's desire to limit press access back to several sources: his distaste for the
attention his divorce drew from Hollywood gossip columnists in his days as an
actor; his association with the conservative movement and his personal belief
that most reporters opposed its ideology; and his view, as a World War II veteran, that journalists in Vietnam did not defend the American cause and viewpoint as they had in earlier wars. Still, he quoted Deaver as contending that
Reagan values "honestness and openness" in his dealings with the press. Then
Cannon wrote:

> *The basis of these relations [with the press], however, is a premise that*
> *is shared by few members of the media. It is a view that surfaced with*
> *rare bluntness at a June 30, 1982, news conference when Reagan was*
> *asked whether the American people deserved an explanation for the*
> *resignation of Secretary of State Alexander M. Haig, Jr.*
>
> *"If I thought that there was something involved in this that the*
> *American people needed to know with regard to their own welfare,*
> *then I would be frank with the American people and tell them," Rea-*
> *gan replied.*

*It was the answer of a President who believes that it is the responsi-
bility of the government and not the media to determine what the
American people should be told.*

Despite critical stories such as Cannon's, Reagan stayed above the battle—out
of reach of the press, except on rare occasions—and somehow safely removed
from the policy and personal conflicts among his senior aides for almost six
years. In a sense, the Reagan arrangement revived the Eisenhower pattern, an
effort to focus attention on the President as head of state rather than head of
government. Eisenhower put himself at greater risk than did Reagan by holding
frequent news conferences, but he often obfuscated in his answers. Reagan,
less skillful in the press conference format, stayed away from it and instead exploited his strengths as a public speaker.

The system was deeply resented by many of the reporters covering Reagan,
even those with long memories. Helen Thomas, in a round-table reprinted in
Kenneth W. Thompson's book *The White House Press on the Presidency,* remarked that

> *. . . each President has had his troubles with the press, going back to
> George Washington. We have a photograph of FDR in our press room
> which is inscribed to the White House reporters from their "devoted
> victim." "When the press stops abusing me, I'll know I'm in the wrong
> pew," said Truman. "Reading more and enjoying it less," said Ken-
> nedy. What LBJ said is unprintable. Nixon had his enemies list, and,
> once when the press walked into the Cabinet room for picture taking,
> Nixon looked up at the press and said, "It's only coincidental that
> we're talking about pollution when the press walks in." Carter always
> seemed to be saying, "Lord, forgive them, for they know not what they
> do." As for Reagan, well, it's like being in those silent movies. He
> thinks we should be seen and not heard.*

Thomas and others on the White House beat have been justifiably angered
by the extremes to which Reagan's staff has gone to hold them at bay. Referring
to the press "pens" that are constructed at every event to keep reporters at a
distance from the President, Thomas observed that "there would be no covering
of the White House if the White House didn't have a lot of rope. People will
never know how physical is such a job and how demeaning in many ways, because we never cover a President except when they put a rope around us. We're
corralled like cattle."

During the 1984 presidential campaign, White House reporters complained
about what they felt were excessive "security" precautions aimed at them. In
a rare effort, the White House Correspondents Association issued a report in
the spring of 1985 that said there is "little doubt that the rapidly escalating security restrictions imposed on the White House press corps are often inconsistent

and frequently used by the White House staff as a form of press management. Secret Service officials acknowledge that it is not unusual for them to be asked by the White House to perform press management functions that exceed their official duties." The report included a number of recommendations on credentialing, searches, and access, but the practices that were the source of complaint continued.

Democrats complained that Reagan, by avoiding exposure and exploiting state occasions, had created a "Teflon presidency." The charge disturbed many of us journalists, because it underlined our own sense of futility in dealing with Reagan. I must have written a dozen columns a year arguing that Reagan had evaded a significant share of accountability for his own administration's policies and practices, either by not bothering to inform himself of the details or by refusing to consider their implications. One column in the summer of 1986 focused on Reagan's ability to disown responsibility for the unprecedented budget deficits incurred during his years in office. It provoked a protest from a reader named Ronald Reagan, vacationing on his California ranch. In his call he was sad rather than angry, and said he was surprised I did not realize that he was not at fault—that the problem lay in Congress.

"You have no idea, Dave, how frustrating it is to work for months preparing a budget and then just have it tossed aside by those big spenders on Capitol Hill." "Well, Mr. President, I'm sure it is. But the point I was trying to make"—and I read the operative paragraph of the column—"was that you have never in five years proposed to raise enough in taxes to pay for the spending you yourself were recommending."

"Well," the President said, "certainly you know that if Congress had accepted the spending cuts I recommended, the deficits would be billions less." "Yes, Mr. President, but they would still have been far higher than you thought frightening when Democrats were in power." We waltzed each other through three or four more steps, and then he said he wanted to take a canter on his horse, and I said it was time to get back to work, and it sure had been nice . . . and once again I realized that nothing I asked or said would wean Ronald Reagan from the screenplay unreeling in his own mind—a drama in which he was fighting the Big Spenders of the Deficit Gang, all of whom were on Capitol Hill.

For almost six years, voters seemed ready to forgive Reagan any mistake, misstatement, or contradiction in policy. As late as October 1986, when Bob Woodward reported in the *Post* an elaborate administration "disinformation program" designed to unnerve Libyan leader Moammar Ghadafi by planting false stories in American newspapers suggesting that he was about to be the target of a coup or of an American air attack, readers and voters seemed remarkably indifferent.

Woodward cited a memo written the previous August by then head of Reagan's National Security Council staff, Vice Admiral John M. Poindexter, outlining a new strategy that "combines real and illusionary events—through a disinformation program—with the basic goal of making Ghadafi think that there is a high degree of internal opposition to him within Libya, that his key trusted aides are disloyal, that the U.S. is about to move against him militarily."

Ten days after Reagan approved the plan, a Poindexter aide talked to a *Wall Street Journal* reporter, and the result was a front-page story reporting that the Reagan administration was completing planning for "a new and larger bombing of Libya" after finding new evidence that Ghadafi had again "begun plotting terrorist attacks." The day it was published, White House spokesman Larry Speakes told reporters that the *Journal* report was "authoritative," and other publications, including the *Post,* and the major networks carried similar stories.

Reagan later denied that he had authorized the deception of American reporters but said he wanted Ghadafi to "go to bed every night wondering what we might do." Secretary of State George P. Shultz told reporters he knew of "no decision to have people go out and tell lies to the media," but added, "Frankly, I don't have any problems with a little psychological warfare against Ghadafi."

Bill Kovach of the *New York Times* said he was disturbed by the seeming double standard of the administration in sanctioning the Poindexter plan while directing the FBI to set up a special unit to track down leaks of government information. "The position they've taken is that if a journalist gets the truth through unofficial channels, it's a crime," Kovach said, "but if he accepts disinformation through official channels, that's just fine."

Bernard Kalb, a veteran television journalist who had become the chief State Department spokesman under Shultz, resigned from his job in protest, saying that "anything that hurts the credibility of America hurts America." But the controversy barely caused a ripple in the broad lagoon of public support for Reagan.

A month later, however, the Teflon finally cracked and the Reagan presidency's greatest crisis began. On the morning of the mid-term election, a Syrian-backed newspaper in Lebanon reported that the United States had secretly been shipping arms to Iran in an effort to get the Ayatollah Khomeini's help in freeing Americans held hostage in Lebanon.

No American reporter could claim credit for the scoop; it had been leaked by a faction in Iran opposed to the covert dealings with the Americans. But once the story was out, the American press was on it like a horde of hungry locusts, and this time all the administration's press management and damage-control operations, designed to keep the President at a safe distance from any controversy, failed to stem the tide of disclosures—or the consternation of the public. Reagan had renounced dealing with terrorists and had said the United States would not bargain for the release of hostages. He had declared an embargo on military shipments to Iran and had urged other nations to observe it. But now it turned out he had signed off on another Poindexter plan, allowing the arms shipments as an unofficial quid pro quo for Iranian help in gaining freedom for three of the U.S. hostages in Lebanon, whose televised pleas and family petitions had become a matter of personal anguish for Reagan.

Reagan made a televised speech seeking to explain the secret decision—taken over the opposition of Shultz and Secretary of Defense Caspar W. Weinberger, and withheld from Congress despite statutes requiring "timely" disclosure of arms sales and covert activities to appropriate legislative committees. When that failed, he scheduled one of his rare news conferences, and it was worse. The President repeatedly denied that he had sanctioned arms sales by a third party, Israel, even though several high administration officials had already told reporters that the Israelis shipped arms to Iran with our approval and with our assurance that we would replace their stocks from Pentagon supplies. Within an hour of the news conference's end, the White House issued a "clarification" refuting Reagan's version.

But worse was still to come: Attorney General Edwin Meese III began his investigation at the President's direction; he discovered that between $10 million and $30 million of the profits from the arms sales to Iran had been secretly diverted to support the forces fighting the Sandinista government in Nicaragua, ostensibly without the President's knowledge or approval and in apparent violation of other laws banning such aid from the United States.

This time Poindexter was allowed to resign; and a Marine Corps National Security Council aide, Lieutenant Colonel Oliver North, who was charged with managing the funds diversion, was fired. A special prosecutor was named to investigate the whole affair, and two select congressional committees began independent inquiries as demands rose for the firing of other high administration officials who had—or presumably should have—known of the secret operations. Reagan was plainly ambivalent about what had happened. He told Hugh Sidey of *Time* magazine that North was "a national hero," and that he had "bitter bile in my throat," not toward those in the White House who had deceived him or embarrassed him, but toward the press, which had publicized the plan while two hostages he apparently believed the Iranians were on the verge of delivering remained in captivity. It took Reagan a month to say "mistakes were made," and even then he maintained that the basic decision to sell arms to Iran had been correct. By then, his standing with the voters had taken the worst tumble in six years, and doubts were being raised about his ability to function effectively as President until the end of his term.

In my columns about the affair that November, I cited the significance of the shift in information policies from first-term chief of staff, James A. Baker III, to second-term chief of staff, Donald T. Regan:

Baker's view . . . was that no policy of any scope, significance or duration could be maintained unless it could enlist support of sensible people in Congress and be explained and defended to sensible people in the press and public.

Since his departure to the Treasury and the complete takeover of the White House staff by Donald T. Regan, a very different set of assumptions has operated. Regan's belief, as he has stated it, is that he is there to fulfill the wishes of a President who carried 49 states and who therefore has a mandate which overrides any objections that may be raised from any quarter. When the lodging of objections would block the initiation of the policy (as would have been the case had Congress known of the arms shipments to Iran), then this perverse logic suggests that secrecy is not only justified but obligatory.

Ten days later, after the disclosure of the illegal diversion of money to the anti-Sandinista forces, I wrote again about "the cult of secrecy which infected the White House atmosphere in the second term."

It was Reagan who avoided all news conferences during the re-election campaign and made them as scarce as Redskins tickets thereafter. It was Reagan who went on the warpath about "leaks," Reagan who raged about "unauthorized" disclosures of his policies, Reagan who pushed—against the protests of the George Shultzes and Jim Bakers—for widespread wire-tapping of government officials.

How often do Presidents have to learn the lesson that in this society the neurotic quest for secrecy undermines effective government? How can they forget so quickly that the only sustainable policy in a nation like ours is one that can be articulated and defended in open debate? What an irony and what a tragedy to see yet another President, who has warned his associates to keep their mouths shut, come before the cameras with the pitiful complaint that those same aides did not tell him what they were up to.

The unhappy fortunes of the Reagan administration at the end of 1986 marked again the costliness of obsessive secretiveness in the White House. Yet . . . it must be observed how well and for how long the manipulation of the media worked.

From the Eisenhower administration to Ronald Reagan's, the White House propaganda machine has become an increasingly effective instrument of presidential will and presidential purpose. For all the ups and downs over those thirty or so years, the President and his agents have clearly been winning the battle to control the way the most important official of our government is covered and reported most of the time. The White House has learned to keep the President from scrutiny, while projecting his voice and his views far more widely than any other politician's. It has enhanced the power of the Communicator-in-Chief as against that of other institutions of government, particularly Congress and state and local elective officials. I would not strip any of these tools from the President, for communication is central to his leadership ability, and this system of government does not function well without strong presidential leadership.

But recognizing the White House's communication power—undefined and unlimited by the written Constitution—should clearly focus our attention on how the press can provide an alternative, nonpropagandistic view of the presidency. A major part of every White House reporter's job is simply communicating what the President says and does. He and his aides expound and we report what they say. He travels and we write about where he goes. He acts on legislation, he makes appointments, he confers with other leaders. We report all of that. That is at the heart of the beat, and there is nothing either demeaning or disgraceful about serving that function.

It is, however, a confining task, and the feeling of confinement is reinforced both by the physical arrangements and the routine. In the cramped half-partitioned stalls of the West Wing press room, where the regulars have their desks and phones, any conversation or phone call can be overheard easily by a neighbor. This tends to discourage reporters from pursuing individual story leads while working in the White House press room.

But reporters are pinned down to waiting and watching for briefings, photo opportunities, appearances in the White House driveway of those who have just met with the President—the dozens of daily, often trivial but potentially newsworthy happenings. The nightly television news programs covet film of the President from that day. The television correspondents, many of whom are excellent journalists, often do nothing more than provide lead-ins to and transitions out of what the White House propagandists let the network cameramen shoot. Newspaper correspondents have a bit more freedom, but not a lot.

Clearly reporters must go beyond that "body watch" operation, if they are to be more than auxiliaries to a White House–designed public relations and communications apparatus. Political scientists Michael B. Grossman and Martha J. Kumar studied the White House press corps and noted that the "body watch" was the overriding and almost exclusive preoccupation of the television, radio, and wire service reporters assigned to the White House, as well as many of the newspaper "specials." But they also observed that the *Post,* the *Times,* and the three news weeklies have double-teamed the White House beat, so that one of their reporters (or both, if they divide the "body watch" function between them) can spend all or a part of his time developing analytic stories. . . .

For most of Reagan's tenure, we had a split-screen picture of the President—the one on radio, television, and the news wires, shaped largely by White House communications strategists, and the one in leading newspapers and news magazines, where reporting teams had the freedom to supply a substantial correction of focus.

The second path toward improved White House coverage would be improved access to the President. Ignoring the blips of the seven presidents we have covered, the trend is toward increasing insulation of the President. From Roosevelt's 998 news conferences in a bit over twelve years to Reagan's 39 news conferences in the first six years is a quantum leap backward.

Although auxiliary contacts with the ever-growing White House press staff and policy aides are certainly valuable, none of these can substitute for access to the President himself—the opportunity to gauge his mood, his cast of mind, and to hear his own formulations of the policy choices he is making. Nothing but a direct interchange between the President and reporters provides those clues. More than seventy years ago, the institutionalized format for these exchanges became the press conference. Yet the press conference still remains an orphan, left out in the cold whenever it suits a particular President's convenience. . . .

Epilogue

Reporters are fiercely jealous of their independence. Consequently, you will occasionally see reports about the White House staff's efforts at "spin control"—the attempt to shape the media's perception of a story. This effort failed during the Iran-contra scandal, partly because the media were conscious that they had been so helpful in creating and maintaining Ronald Reagan's image. But now the game has resumed with George Bush, and our challenge as citizens is to discern whether the White House is shaping a story to its own advantage or whether it is, as is sometimes claimed, trying to compensate for the biases of the press.

Broder has recently commented on another problem in the symbiotic relationship between the media and the president. Members of the media have been taking positions in the administration for a while and then going back to their positions in the media. Such was the case with Patrick Buchanan, Reagan's communications director. Then there are those administration officials (such as Jimmy Carter's State Department spokesman, Hodding Carter) who become commentators when their president leaves office. Broder worries that this hopping back and forth between politics and journalism blurs the distinction between the two to such an extent that the independence of the news-gathering and -analysis process will be harmed.

9.4

Life as a presidential speechwriter is not easy. At first glance, the chance to write the words spoken by one of the most powerful political leaders in the world would seem to have considerable appeal. But then the realities of the job sink in. First, there is the pressure of always being on call to provide exactly the right phrases for whatever emergency arises. Then there is the knowledge that no matter how carefully those phrases are crafted, someone will misinterpret them or object to them. The challenge of capturing another person's thoughts and speaking style for so many types of audiences requires a very special talent. Moreover, the speechwriter does the job knowing that the entire effort will likely be reduced by the television news to a thirty-second sound bite and by the newspapers to a few quotations.

Furthermore, every major administration official with responsibility for a particular speech's subject matter makes suggestions both before the drafting process and as draft after draft of the speech is produced. A speech is supposed to sound like the work of a single voice, but in fact it is produced by a chorus of often discordant voices. Somehow the speechwriter must serve as both bard and traffic cop.

In "Speech! Speech!" we are treated to a glimpse of the experiences of one of the finest speechwriters of this generation, Peggy Noonan, who provided many of President Reagan's most dramatic speeches. Several of the speeches composed by Noonan are now considered classics, among which is the speech Reagan delivered after the tragic explosion of the space shuttle *Challenger.*

"Speech! Speech!"

Peggy Noonan

RICHARD DARMAN   Chief assistant to James Baker in both the White House and the Treasury Department.

BEN ELLIOTT   Chief speechwriter for Reagan.

RONALD REAGAN   President of the United States, 1981–1989.

DONALD REGAN   Reagan's chief of staff, 1985–1987.

From Peggy Noonan, *What I Saw at the Revolution* (New York: Random House, 1990). Copyright © 1990 by Peggy Noonan. Reprinted by permission of Random House, Inc., and International Creative Management.

▶ A speech is a soliloquy—one man on a bare stage with a big spotlight. He will tell us who he is and what he wants and how he will get it and what it means that he wants it and what it will mean when he does or does not get it, and . . .

And he looks up at us in the balconies and clears his throat. "Ladies and gentlemen . . ." We lean forward, hungry to hear. Now it will be said, now we will hear the thing we long for.

A speech is part theater and part political declaration; it is a personal communication between a leader and his people; it is art, and all art is a paradox, being at once a thing of great power and great delicacy.

A speech is poetry: cadence, rhythm, imagery, sweep! A speech reminds us that words, like children, have the power to make dance the dullest beanbag of a heart.

Speeches are not significant because we have the technological ability to make them heard by every member of our huge nation simultaneously. Speeches are important because they are one of the great constants of our political history. For two hundred years, from "Give me liberty or give me death" to "Ask not what your country can do for you," they have been not only the way we measure public men, they have been how we tell each other who we are. For two hundred years they have been changing—making, forcing—history: Lincoln, Bryan and the cross of gold, FDR's first inaugural, Kennedy's, Martin Luther King in '63, Reagan and the Speech in '64.* They count. They more than count, they shape what happens. (An irony: You know who doesn't really know this? Political professionals. The men who do politics as a business in America are bored by speeches. They call them "the rah rah." They prefer commercials.)

Another reason speeches are important: because the biggest problem in America, the biggest problem in any modern industrialized society, is loneliness. A great speech from a leader to the people eases our isolation, breaks down the walls, includes people: It takes them inside a spinning thing and makes them part of the gravity.

All speechwriters have things they think of when they write. I think of being a child in my family at the dinner table, with seven kids and hubbub and parents distracted by worries and responsibilities. Before I would say anything at the table, before I would approach my parents, I would plan what I would say. I would map out the narrative, sharpen the details, add color, plan momentum. This way I could hold their attention. This way I became a writer.

---

* The "cross of gold" refers to a stirring speech by William Jennings Bryan at the 1896 Democratic National Convention, in which he declared that farmers were being impaled on the cross of the gold monetary standard. Martin Luther King's "I Have a Dream" speech took place in August 1963. In October 1964, Ronald Reagan gave a strong address on behalf of Republican presidential candidate Barry Goldwater; the speech laid out Reagan's conservative principles and marked his debut as a national political figure.

The American people too are distracted by worries and responsibilities and the demands of daily life, and you have to know that and respect it—and plan the narrative, sharpen the details, add color and momentum.

I work with an image: the child in the mall. When candidates for president are on the campaign trail they always go by a mall and walk through followed by a pack of minicams and reporters. They go by Colonel Sanders and have their picture taken eating a piece of chicken, they josh around with the lady in the mall information booth, they shake hands with the shoppers. But watch: Always there is a child, a ten-year old girl, perhaps, in an inexpensive, tired-looking jacket. Perhaps she is by herself, perhaps with a friend. But she stands back, afraid of the lights, and as the candidate comes she runs away. She is afraid of his fame, afraid of the way the lights make his wire-rim glasses shine, afraid of dramatic moments, dense moments. When you are a speechwriter you should think of her when you write, and of her parents. They are Americans. They are good people for whom life has not been easy. Show them respect and be honest and logical in your approach and they will understand every word you say and hear—and know—that you thought of them.

The irony of modern speeches is that as our ability to disseminate them has exploded (an American president can speak live not only to America but to Europe, to most of the world), their quality has declined.

Why? Lots of reasons, including that we as a nation no longer learn the rhythms of public utterance from Shakespeare and the Bible. When young Lincoln was sprawled in front of the fireplace reading *Julius Caesar*—"Th' abuse of greatness is, when it disjoins remorse from power"—he was, unconsciously, learning to be a poet. You say, "That was Lincoln, not the common man." But the common man was flocking to the docks to get the latest installment of Dickens off the ship from England.

The modern egalitarian impulse has made politicians leery of flaunting high rhetoric; attempts to reach, to find the right if sometimes esoteric quote or allusion seem pretentious. They don't really know what "the common man" knows anymore; they forget that we've all had at least some education and a number of us read on our own and read certain classics in junior high and high school. The guy at the gas station read *Call of the Wild* when he was fourteen, and sometimes thinks about it. Moreover, he has imagination. Politicians forget. They go in lowest common denominator—like a newscaster.

People say the problem is soundbites. But no it isn't.

A word on the history: "Soundbite" is what television producers have long called the short tape of a politician talking, which is inserted into a longer piece voiced by a reporter. Imagine a speech as a long string of licorice; the mouth-sized bite the reporter takes as it goes by is the soundbite.

The cliché is to say, "It all has to be reduced to a tidy little thirty-second soundbite." But soundbites don't go thirty seconds, they go seven seconds. Or four seconds. When I got to the White House I never met anyone who had heard of soundbites or thought of them, and the press never wrote of them. I used to tell Ben [Elliott], "What we're going to see of this speech on TV is five seconds that a producer in New York thinks is the best or most interesting moment." Then I'd tell him what they were going to pick. I knew because I used to pick them. Now people who don't understand soundbites talk about them all the time.

Soundbites in themselves are not bad. "We have nothing to fear . . ." is a soundbite. "Ask not . . ." is a soundbite. So are "You shall not crucify mankind upon a cross of gold," and "With malice toward none; With charity for all . . ."

Great speeches have always had great soundbites. The problem now is that the young technicians who put together speeches are paying attention only to the soundbite, not to the text as a whole, not realizing that all great soundbites happen by accident, which is to say, all great soundbites are yielded up inevitably, as part of the natural expression of the text. They are part of the tapestry, they aren't a little flower somebody sewed on.

They sum up a point, or make a point in language that is pithy or profound. They are what the politician is saying! They are not separate and discrete little one-liners that a bright young speechwriter just promoted out of the press office and two years out of business school slaps on.

But that is what they've become. Young speechwriters forget the speech and write the soundbite, plop down a hunk of porridge and stick on what they think is a raisin. (In the Dukakis campaign they underlined them in the text.)

The problem is not the soundbitization of rhetoric, it's the Where's-the-beef-ization. The good news: Everyone in America is catching on to the game, and it's beginning not to work anymore. A modest hope: Politicians will stop hiring communications majors to write their speeches and go to history majors, literature majors, writers—people who can translate the candidate's impulses into literature that is alive, and true.

A speech is also a statement of policy. Sometimes it is This Is What We Must Do About the Budget and sometimes it is Why We Must Go to War, but always it is about plans and their effect on people: policy. It is impossible to separate speechwriting from policy because a policy is made of words, and the speechwriter makes the words. A speechwriter is obviously not free to invent out of whole cloth, but—by articulating a policy he invents it.

An example: If an American president goes to Berlin and stands next to the Berlin Wall, it is one thing (and one kind of policy) if he says, "The American people support the German people." It's quite another if he says, "I am a Berliner." The first means, "We support you," the second means, "We really mean it, we're really here, and if we ever abandon you it will forever be a stain on our honor." [Kennedy speechwriter Theodore] Sorensen knew it, Kennedy knew it, and the crowd knew it.

In the Reagan administration there was an unending attempt to separate the words from the policy. A bureaucrat from State who was assigned to work with the NSC on the annual economic summits used to come into speechwriting and refer to himself and his colleagues as "we substantive types" and to the speech-writers as "you wordsmiths." He was saying, We do policy and you dance around with the words. We would smile back. Our smiles said, The dancer is the dance.

It was a constant struggle over speeches, a constant struggle over who was in charge and what view would prevail and which group would triumph. Each speech was a battle in a never-ending war; when the smoke cleared there was Reagan, holding the speech and saying the words as the mist curled about his feet. I would watch and think, That's not a speech it's a truce. A temporary truce.

How were speeches made in the Reagan administration? Here's an image: Think of a bunch of wonderful, clean, shining, perfectly shaped and delicious vegetables. Then think of one of those old-fashioned metal meat grinders. Imagine the beautiful vegetables being forced through the grinder and being rendered into a smooth, dull, textureless purée.

Here's another image: The speech is a fondue pot, and everyone has a fork. And I mean everyone.

This is how a speech came about:

First, the president's top advisers would agree for him to accept an invitation to speak at a certain time or a certain place. If NYU invites the president to deliver a commencement address, someone on the president's staff might note that this would be a perfect spot to unveil the administration's new urban enterprise-zone policy. The invitation is accepted.

The speech is then included on the weekly and monthly schedule of presidential appearances. The writers would get the schedule, read it, complain about the work load and lobby for various speeches. When more than one writer wanted a speech, the decision was made by the head of the speechwriting staff—Ben Elliott, who also functioned as chief speechwriter. Ben made his decisions based on merit. I say that because he gave me a lot of good speeches.

Each speech was also assigned a researcher. There were five young researchers when I got there, and they were usually assigned more speeches than they could do well. I learned to rely on the research people not for creative input—ideas, inspiration, connections one wouldn't have thought of—but for fact-checking, at which they were uniformly reliable and sometimes spectacularly diligent.

A writer usually had a week or two to work on a big speech, or a few days to write a small one. I'd ask research to gather pertinent books from the White House library and to go through Nexis and pull out whatever there was on the subject at hand. They'd also get me the president's previous speeches on that subject or in that place. Research would get precise and up-to-date information from the advance office on the who-what-when-where-why of the event. And then I'd begin, haltingly, to write.

You may be thinking, How did she know what to say? At first I didn't, but after a while I figured it out. As for point of view, the president's stand on any given issue was usually a matter of record. He'd been in politics twenty years, and his basic philosophy wasn't exactly a secret. As for new initiatives, various agencies would phone in directives. Ben would get a call from the Department of Energy, for instance, asking that we mention some new energy initiative in the speech in Boston on Sunday. Ben would pass the word to the writer and a paragraph would be inserted.

In the research phase I'd read a lot and take notes and think of phrases and snatches of thought and type them out, and then take them home and stare at them. When I was in the writing part on an important speech I never read pertinent reference books. I would read poetry and biographies, the former because the rush of words would help loosen the rocks that clogged the words in my head, the latter because biographies are about the great, and the great lead lives of struggle, and reading about their epic pain put the small discomforts of a speech in nice perspective.

I always kept Walter Jackson Bate's biography of Samuel Johnson nearby, and Stephen Vincent Benét's *John Brown's Body,* and the Bible (especially the Psalms), and Ezra Pound's *Cantos,* though I don't think I ever understood a one. It didn't matter, the anarchy of the language and the sweeping away of syntax had force.

Also, Pound helped me with the State Department. I used to be visited by people from State who wanted to help me write. I always thought of this as the descent of the Harvardheads. They all had thick, neat, straight-back hair and little bitty wire-rim glasses and wives named Sydney, and there was only one way to handle them in my view and that was to out-Sydney them. So a man from State would come in and see the books on the coffee table and the first thing he'd do is signify:

"Oh, Pound," he'd say.

"Yes," I'd breathe, with the gravity of a Radcliffe beatnik who'd just met Lenny Bruce in a basement in the Village.

"Took a gut on Pound at Yale. Of course that was before the Deconstructionists."

"Don't laugh. They might have helped." Snap snap.

"So." He seats himself on the couch, readjusts the pillows. "Beijing. How go our efforts."

With State guys you had to remember that if you dropped the right cultural references they'd realize it might not work if they patronized you, and if they couldn't patronize you they didn't have a style to fall back on to shape the meeting so they were a little less sure, which is precisely the way you wanted them.

I'd write and rewrite. I'm about a fifth-draft speechwriter. When I was new in the White House it helped me, I think, that I was changing from writing on an electric typewriter to writing on a word processor. On a word processor you have to exert so little pressure on the keys that it didn't really seem like official writing, it felt like playing on a children's typewriter. That helped free things up.

I'd also walk around and talk to people. I'd turn to someone in the mess and say, "I'm writing a speech on Nicaragua. If there was one sentence on that subject you could communicate to the American people, what would it be?" I got some interesting and helpful answers, but I can't remember any of them.

I chain-smoked when I wrote in those days. I'd be dizzy from the chemicals. I'd do anything to avoid writing, and then I'd force myself to sit down at the computer—Edna Ferber wrote in her diary, "I could not lie down to my work today," an assertion whose implications I do not choose to ponder except to say I know what she means—and I would write very badly at first, very clunkily and awkwardly. It wasn't even grammatical. When people would come by and say, "Let me see," I'd shield the screen with my hands.

The whole speechwriting department was computerized, so I'd write my first draft on a floppy disk, and my secretary would print it out. Then I'd rewrite it from there, and ask her to run it out again. Then she'd give it to me, and I'd rewrite again. Each draft would get a little better as I relaxed and got tired. I was relaxing because I wasn't desperate because: at least I had something on paper. Then, on about the fourth draft, I'd see that I'd written three or four sentences that I liked, and that would relax me further: At least there's something of worth here! That would get my shoulders down. Then I'd really barrel.

I'd read over the final product and realize that once again I'd failed, what I thought was witty was only cute, what I thought was elegant would seem so only to the ill-read, and that imagery didn't come close. I'd hand it in, having reached the deadline. I would tell Ben, "It isn't up to snuff and I'm sorry." He would say calmly that he was sure it would be fine. I would go for a long walk and rationalize my failure: I was tired, they were working me too hard, you can't get blood from a turnip or juice from a stone or whatever the hell.

I would get it back from Ben. He would not have changed it much, but he would have written little exclamation points along the margins, and sometimes on some sections he would write, "Excellent!" And I would be shocked that Ben's critical faculties had failed him. Then I would read over the speech and realize for the first time that it was actually pretty brilliant, so delicate and yet so vital, so vital and yet so tender.

My secretary would incorporate Ben's changes. Then the speech would go out into the world for review. This is where my heart was plucked from my breast and dragged along West Exec, hauled along every pebble and pothole. This was my Heartbreak Hill, my Hanoi Hilton, this was . . . the staffing process.

In staffing, a speech was sent out to all of the pertinent federal agencies and all the important members of the White House staff and the pertinent White House offices. If the speech was relatively unimportant perhaps twenty people in all would see it and comment on it. An important speech would be gone over by fifty or so. The way the system was supposed to work was that the reviewers were to suggest changes, additions, and deletions. The key word here is suggest. They were also supposed to scrutinize all factual assertions and make corrections where necessary.

In the first administration Dick Darman received, along with the speech-writer, a copy of each suggestion, and it was Dick who had the final say on which suggestions must be included and which could be ignored. I didn't always agree with Dick's decisions, but he was open to appeal. More important, I could see his logic. He also didn't mind offending people if it meant preserving a script. I doubt anyone ever pressured him into accepting a change that was frivolous or unhelpful. He didn't care who got mad.

In the second administration a young Regan aide was given control, for a time, of the staffing process. He incorporated many more suggestions than Darman, which was in the short run bureaucratically wise because it made the twenty people who wanted changes think he was smart and easy to work with, and alienated only the speechwriter. But in the long run it proved unwise because it contributed to the diminution in the grace and effectiveness of the president's rhetoric that marked the second administration. It was the first administration that was the fondue pot, it was the second that was the meat grinder.

(The aide's problem was not that he wished to be perverse. It was that he simply could not tell the difference between good writing and bad. It was said of Donald Regan that he did not know what he did not know. His aides were oblivious to what they were oblivious to.)

Speeches in the staffing process were always in danger of becoming lowest-common-denominator art. There were so many people with so many questions, so many changes. I sometimes thought it was like sending a beautiful newborn fawn out into the jagged wilderness where the grosser animals would pierce its tender flesh and render mortal wounds; but perhaps I understate.

There were at any rate two battlefields, art and policy, and sometimes they intersected.

The art problem was . . . delicate. Most of the people in the staffing process thought of themselves as writers, which is understandable because everyone is. Everyone writes letters home to Mom or keeps a diary in weight-loss class on What Food Means to Me. Not everyone plays the piano so most people don't claim to be pianists, but everyone is a writer, and if you're a writer why can't you write the president's speeches?

Complicating this is the fact that there's an odd thing about writing as an art: The critical faculty often fails. When people who can't paint try to paint they can usually step back when they're done, smile a rueful smile, and admit that painting's not their talent. But when people who can't write try to write they often can't tell they're not good. In fact, they often think they're pretty close to wonderful, and they're genuinely hurt—and often suspicious—when told otherwise.

I always wanted to handle these people with a lovely finesse, a marvelous grace. I wanted to do it the way Gerald Murphy did when he told the off-key singer, "Ah yes, and now you must rest your lovely vocal chords." But because I always felt threatened—the people most insistent about changes were always more powerful than I—I would sputter. "I'm sorry," I'd say, "but that doesn't work. It's not quite right. Well, it just doesn't. It's just not—oh look, it's just dumb, I'm sorry it's dumb but it is, it's s__t." It's a wonderful look an undersecretary gets when you tell him this. His eyebrows jump up right over his hairline, and that's only the beginning.

The policy problem was . . . well, the policy problem was the reason we were all there every day. The policy problem was government. Government is words on paper—the communiqué after the summit, the top-secret cable to the embassy, the memo to the secretary outlining a strategy, the president's speech —it's all words on paper. Government draws aggressive people who feel that if government is words on paper then they will damn well affect the words. After all, this is why they came to Washington: to change things, to make a difference.

Speechwriting naturally started rows because debates and arguments would go on for years but finally at some point policy had to be announced and articulated in speeches. By the very process of writing and declaring we were throwing down the gauntlet. The battles were not only hard-fought, they were sometimes bizarre. Once, when I was new, I was assigned a speech in which I was to write about our conservation policy. I didn't have the faintest idea what our conservation policy was. There were few pertinent speeches to go by. I spent a lot of time phoning around asking people, "What the heck am I supposed to say?" I'd get little suggestions here and there.

Then one night a bland young man came into my office and said, "The office of"—here he lowered his voice—"uhpolicydecisionoptions, here." And he placed on my desk a nice typed list of our most recent conservation plans and priorities. I was delighted, and built the speech around it.

Then I sent the speech out. Then I ducked, because the incoming mail was fierce. My phone lit up with people screaming, "Where did you get that? Who told you that? It's all wrong." In the mess a man I didn't know pressed me aggressively, and finally I told him look, a guy walked in from some office and told me this is what's supposed to be in the speech, and I believed him.

The man sat back and shook his head. "Somebody must've found out you were new." There had been internal disagreement over various conservation ideas, he said, and I had been tricked into advancing the agenda of one group. When the speech went out people thought I was taking sides, and got mad. But at least the speech forced everyone to focus, and the policy disagreement was resolved. (I never saw the man who'd come into my office with the list again, by the way. I still wonder where he was from.)

Serious policy issues were not the only thing being worked out in the speech fights. There was plenty of vanity on display, and willfulness, and even now and then the existential willies. "Here's this speech," says Mr. Harvardhead, "and the president will say it and my friends will hear it and tomorrow excerpts will be in *The New York Times* and—and I'd better jump in there and make my presence felt! Because if I don't then I haven't affected the process! And if I haven't affected the process then I haven't used my power, and if I haven't used it then maybe it's gone, because Washington's a use-it-or-lose-it town—if you don't flick the switch then nobody knows if the current's still there, and if it's not then I'm not powerful. And if I'm not powerful then who am I? I decide therefore I am! Command is my essence! If I'm not powerful I will dry up and blow away like the dead leaves of November! If I am not powerful . . . I will die!"

All the suggested changes would come in by a certain deadline. I'd take the ones I thought helped the speech and the ones Darman told me to take. Then we'd send the speech to the president for his suggestions. He'd make changes here and there and send it back to speechwriting. At that point it was supposed to be frozen. But that's not what happened. What happened was the final battle would be fought on the plane, in the limousine, on the couch in the Oval Office. The speech was never really frozen until the president had said it; it was never really frozen until they were typing, from the audiotape, for inclusion in the big books. . . .

It was a pretty morning. It was relaxed. There was no big work pressing on me. The biggest recent personal drama for me was giving up smoking. I had for years been afraid that if I couldn't smoke I couldn't write, so intertwined were they. (I told a friend who is a writer, "But I need it at the typewriter." She said, "Maybe it's a good thing to need something while you write.") I'd stopped three months before, had written nothing worthwhile since, and hoped to snap out of it.

Ben had brought his daughter, Meredith, to work. She ran from office to office, tripping gaily as some children do. She was seven years old and happy and sensitive. She looked like girlhood pictures of Grace Kelly.

I was on the phone with a friend. The TV a few feet away was, as always, on, at the moment tuned to CNN, which was covering a space shot live. The shuttle was going up. I was laughing at something the person on the other end was saying when Nancy Roberts, Ben's assistant, came rushing in.

"Something happened to the shuttle. They think it blew up."

"What?"

The TV screen is blue with a trail of white smoke. Pieces of something are falling through the sky.

"What? What happened?"

"They think it blew up!"

Meredith walked in softly. "The teacher is on it," she said. "Is the teacher all right?"

The silence on TV is broken by a newscaster who knows as much as we do. You know it's bad when they don't know more. It's clear from the broken trail of smoke and the debris falling through the air that something terrible has happened. You know from the sound and look of things that everyone is gone.

Meredith walks over and puts her hands on my armrest. She watches, fascinated. Her face says; This isn't bad, is it? I am breathing as I did when the pope was shot, and Reagan. It is like the sixties, and This is a Special Report. I do what CBS trained me to do: handle the horror by writing the show.

"Tell your father I'm writing the president's remarks."

I press a plastic button on the IBM word processor; the screen lights up, the buzz begins.

Things to cover: update on the situation—are they dead, search continues? I need a cigarette.

Dick Darman's on the line from Treasury.

Dick.

Is he going to speak? Are you writing it?

Don't know but assume so, and yes.

Good. Every grade-school child in America was watching, and older students too, did you know that?

No, but Ben's daughter was here upset.

Well, my sons were watching. The president has to speak to the children and reassure them that the world isn't ending and that there is both inherent purpose and danger in scientific exploration.

I know.

It's very important.

I got it, Dick, thanks.

Karna Small, Bud McFarlane's assistant from the NSC [National Security Council], calls.

I was with the president at the meeting with network anchors for the State of the Union, she says, and I took notes on what he said.

Oh God, thanks. Send 'em over.

"What can you say," her notes quote him, "it's a horrible thing. I can't rid myself of the thought of the sacrifice of the families of the people on board. I'm sure all of America is more than saddened. . . ."

> Q: *Do you think it was right to have a citizen on board?*
> "They're all citizens—all volunteers. That is the last frontier, the most important, the space program has been most successful. We've become so confident that this comes as such a shock. . . ."
> Q: *Who brought the news to you?*
> "We were all sitting there [Oval] preparing for your questions when the Vice President and Admiral Poindexter came in and said they had received a flash that the space shuttle had exploded—we then went to see the TV [to the study] saw the replay—it was just a very traumatic experience.
> Q: *Do you take comfort in the fact that we have not lost as many as the Soviets?*
> "We all have pride in that, but it doesn't lessen our grief."

Q: What can you say to the children to help them understand?

"Pioneers have always given their lives on the frontier. The problem is that it's more of a shock to all as we see it happening, not just hear about something miles away—but we must make it clear [to the children] that life goes on.

Q: But how do you feel about the teacher?

"I can't put out of my mind—her husband and children—the others [other astronauts] knew they were in a hazardous occupation . . . but here, your heart goes out to them."

A call from the West Wing—the president can't go on until the search is suspended, but we need the remarks as soon as possible, keep it short, five minutes. . . .

I'm done. Type it up. Three copies, quick. And tell [White House Communications Director Patrick] Buchanan we're coming.

A meeting with Buchanan and the mice. Pat reads quickly, nods. "Terrific, let's go." Dennis shakes his head. (Pat said later, "Did you see how he held it? Like a dog had relieved himself on it!") I need a cigarette.

Into a larger meeting in Mr. Regan's office, all of us plus the chief plus [Deputy Press Secretary] Larry Speakes. Speakes reads and looks at me; his face is sensuous and dumb.

"Ah don't know if you get across that the space program continues."

Mmmmm, I say, nodding. "Uh, well, actually we do have here 'We'll continue our quest in space. There will be more shuttle flights and more shuttle crews . . . Nothing ends here—our hopes and our journeys continue.'"

"Well ah read it and ahm not sure you made it clear to me."

Well I didn't have crayons. "Maybe we can ask the president to punch up that graph."

"Ah guess."

No one is pleased, but there is no time to rewrite. I am depressed. I failed when the whole country needed something and we actually could have helped. Buchanan kept saying, "This is really good," but he was always odd man out.

They got the speech to the Oval Office. The president came on the air looking . . . unsure.

"Ladies and gentlemen, I had planned to speak to you tonight to report on the State of the Union, but the events of earlier today have led me to change those plans. Today is a day for mourning and remembering.

"Nancy and I are pained to the core by the tragedy of the shuttle *Challenger.* We know we share this pain with all of the people of our country. This is truly a national loss.

"Nineteen years ago almost to the day, we lost three astronauts in a terrible accident on the ground. But we have never lost an astronaut in flight. We have never had a tragedy like this. And perhaps we have forgotten the courage it took for the crew of the shuttle. But they, the *Challenger* Seven, were aware of the dangers—and overcame them, and did their jobs brilliantly.

"We mourn seven heroes—Michael Smith, Dick Scobee, Judith Resnik, Ronald McNair, Ellison Onizuka, Gregory Jarvis, and Christa McAuliffe. We mourn their loss as a nation, together.

"To the families of the Seven: We cannot bear, as you do, the full impact of this tragedy—but we feel the loss, and we are thinking about you so very much. Your loved ones were daring and brave and they had that special grace, that special spirit that says Give me a challenge and I'll meet it with joy. They had a hunger to explore the universe and discover its truths. They wished to serve and they did—they served us all.

"And I want to say something to the schoolchildren of America who were watching the live coverage of the shuttle's takeoff. I know it's hard to understand, but sometimes painful things like this happen—it's all part of the process of exploration and discovery—it's all part of taking a chance and expanding man's horizons. The future doesn't belong to the fainthearted, it belongs to the brave. The *Challenger* crew was pulling us into the future—and we'll continue to follow them.

"I've always had great faith in and respect for our space program—and what happened today does nothing to diminish it. We don't hide our space program, and we don't keep secrets and cover things up, we do it all up front and in public. That's the way freedom is, and we wouldn't change it for a minute.

"We'll continue our quest in space. There will be more shuttle flights and more shuttle crews and, yes, more volunteers, more civilians, more teachers in space. Nothing ends here—our hopes and our journeys continue.

"I want to add that I wish I could talk to every man and woman who works for NASA or who worked on this mission and tell them: Your dedication and professionalism have moved and impressed us for decades, and we know of your anguish. We share it.

"There's a coincidence today. On this day 390 years ago the great explorer Sir Francis Drake died aboard ship off the coast of Panama. In his lifetime the great frontiers were the oceans. And a historian later said, "He lived by the sea, died on it, and was buried in it." Today we can say of the *Challenger* Crew: Their dedication was, like Drake's, complete.

"The crew of the space shuttle *Challenger* honored us by the manner in which they lived their lives. We will never forget them, nor the last time we saw them—this morning, as they prepared for their journey, and waved good-bye, and "slipped the surly bonds of earth" to "touch the face of God.""

It went almost as written. The staffing process had no time to make it bad. The worst edit, which Ben fought off—in fact it was the worst edit I received in all my time in the White House—was from a pudgy young NSC mover who told me to change the quote at the end from "touch the face of God" to "reach out and touch someone—touch the face of God." He felt this was eloquent.

He'd heard it in a commercial. I took it to Ben and said, I'll kill, I'll kill, I'll kill him if this gets through. Ben, alarmed, assured me he would explain if pressed that you don't really change a quotation from a poem in this manner.

When the president finished, he looked lost. I knew: He didn't like what he was given.

Darman called. "Perfect."

The next morning there was a deluge. Secretary Shultz called me, Admiral Poindexter, Senator Chafee. Ann Higgins sent up telegrams. A man sent words for a song, "They left us looking heavenward." Charles Jones, the manager at the White House mail section, wrote, "I have worked in the mail section for 31 years. This is the first time that I have written to a staff member. Please excuse the intrusion, but I want to congratulate you on a great speech."

"Operator One, is this Miss Noonan? Please hold for the president." They always sound so happy, as if they're giving you a gift.

"Peggy? Well, I just wanted to say thank you for your wonderful remarks yesterday."

"Oh, Mr. President, thank you."

"Well, they were just wonderful."

"Well, it was from you. They sent me notes from what you said."

"You know, the funniest thing. I did the remarks, I read them and then at the end I just had this feeling that I'd failed. I thought that I'd done badly and I hadn't done justice. And of course I was so sad about what had happened. And I got off the air and I thought, Well, not so good. But then I got these calls and telegrams. . . ."

"I heard."

"An avalanche. And I guess, you know, it did work, and I didn't know it."

"I did something that may have put you off your stride. I forgot to write God bless you, as you always say at the end. And you were on the air and maybe sensed something was missing and couldn't think exactly what."

"That little poem, that Magee. I hadn't heard that in years, but of course I knew it from years back, the war. And I think it was written on a sort of tablet or plaque outside Patti's school that I took her to when she was a young girl."

My secret: I *knew* he knew that poem. It was precisely the kind of poem he would have known, from the days when everyone knew poems and poets were famous, everyone knew Robert Frost and Carl Sandburg. It had been popular during the war. Flyers could recite it.

"Could you send me a copy? And maybe I could read the whole poem at the prayer breakfast next week."

"Good, I'm doing those remarks. Thanks for calling, and don't worry about your delivery yesterday. If you felt sad maybe that was the right way to look. It was a sad day. And you comforted everybody."

I wanted to say: You know, I didn't have a cigarette.

That afternoon I got a call from a Hollywood press agent who said, "It's funny the president used that poem in the speech, because it was read the other night from beginning to end by Claire Trevor, you remember her, at a little party for Tyrone Power, Jr. 'High Flight' was one of his father's favorite poems—in fact, the day Ty Senior came home from the war, that night Gary and Rocky Cooper had a little party for him and they invited Ronnie, the president, and Jane, who was his wife, of course. And Ty Senior recited from memory 'High Flight.' He carried it with him all through the war—he was an air-force flyer you know— and he could recite it by heart. When he died Laurence Olivier recited it over his grave. Anyway, the president reading it brought back so many memories of the old days. Would you say hi to him and remind him of Ty reading it?"

Sure, I said, and wrote a memo.

A few hours later I got a call from a gossip columnist for the *New York Post*. He'd just had a call from an agent and wanted to know if it was true the president quoted "High Flight" because Ty Power read it to him years ago and he never forgot it? And then Claire Trevor read it at a party the other night and the president heard about it?

Not really, I said, not really.

Epilogue

In the end, Peggy Noonan fell victim not to the relentless pressure of her job but to the forces of the bureaucracy around her. Inevitably, when a person gets credit for the success of the president there are those who would prefer that this not continue. According to Noonan, Chief of Staff Donald Regan blocked what would have been a major promotion for her—head of the Office of Public Liaison. Near the end of Reagan's term of office, she submitted her resignation, telling fellow administration member Pat Buchanan, "I'm out; it's not fun anymore." After all of her efforts for the administration, Noonan received a form letter thanking her, signed by the president's autograph pen.

But the story does not end here. Peggy Noonan came out of retirement to help draft Reagan's "Farewell to the Nation" speech and to help Republican candidate George Bush on one speech. Her work on Bush's acceptance speech at the Republican National Convention resulted in two phrases that are still widely quoted. Bush called for a return to volunteerism in America to solve the nation's problems, describing volunteers as "a thousand points of light." And, in talking about the demands to balance the budget by raising taxes, Bush forcefully spoke words he would later regret: "Read my lips: No new taxes." Some believe that this speech was George Bush's finest and that it was a major factor in helping him win the office.